GW01458752

The Korean War (1950-1953) was the first – and only – full-scale air war in the jet age. It was in the skies of North Korea where Soviet and American pilots came together in fierce aerial clashes. The best pilots of the opposing systems, the most powerful air forces, and the most up-to-date aircraft in the world in this period of history came together in pitched air battles. The analysis of the air war showed that the powerful United States Air Force and its allies were unable to achieve complete superiority in the air and were unable to fulfil all the tasks they'd been given. Soviet pilots and Soviet jet fighters, which were in no way inferior to their opponents and in certain respects were even superior to them, was the reason for this. The combat experience and new tactical aerial combat tactics, which were tested for the first time in the skies of Korea, have been eagerly studied and applied by modern air forces around the world today.

This book fully discusses the Soviet participation in the Korean War and presents a view of this war from the opposite side, which is still not well known in the West from the multitude of publications by Western historians. The reason for this, of course, is the fact that Soviet records pertaining to the Korean War were for a long time highly classified, since Soviet air units were fighting in the skies of North Korea "incognito", so to speak or even more so to write about this was strictly forbidden in the Soviet Union right up to its ultimate collapse. The given work is in essence the first major work in the post-Soviet era. First published in a small edition in Russian in 1998, it was republished in Russia in 2007. For the first time, the Western reader can become acquainted with the most detailed and informative work existing on the course of the air war from the Soviet side, now in English language. The work rests primarily on the recollections of veterans of this war on the so-called 'Red' side – Soviet fighter pilots, who took direct part in this war on the side of North Korea. Their stories have been supplemented with an enormous amount of archival documents, as well as the work of Western historians. The author presents a literal day-by-day chronicle of the aerial combats and combat work of Soviet fighter regiments in the period between 1950 and 1953, and dedicates this work to all the men on both sides who fought and died in the Korean air war.

Igor Ataevich Seidov was born in 1960 in the city of Ashkhabad, in today's Independent Republic of Turkmenistan. In 1983, having graduated from a specialized technical college, he went to work as an engineer for a television company in Ashkhabad, but after moving to Russia in 2001, for a television company in Maikop. At the end of the 1980s, the author became fascinated with aviation history, and in particular the participation of the Soviet Air Force and Soviet Air Defense Force in the Korean War. In 1992, he began his literary work, and has since published more than 20 articles in a variety of Russian, Ukrainian, Czech and Spanish aviation journals. In 1998 he published his first book on the Korean air war, *Krasnye d'iavoly na 38-I paralleli* [Red Devils on the 38th Parallel] with the assistance of the veteran Soviet fighter pilot A.A. German. The book came out in a second, revised edition in 2007. In 2006, the author co-authored with Iurii Sutiagin a biography of the top Soviet ace in the war Nikolai Vasil'evich Sutiagin, an edited version of which was published in English by Pen & Sword in 2009. In 2010, the Russian publisher Russkie Vitiazi published his latest work, *Sovetskie acy koreiskoi voiny* [Soviet aces of the Korean War]. Today he continues to live and work in the city of Maikop.

Stuart Britton is a freelance translator residing in Cedar Rapids, Iowa. He has been responsible for making available in the English language a growing list of historical titles by the "new wave" of Russian historians, who have access to previously classified archival records and who write more objectively about the Red Army's campaigns and battles on the Eastern Front of the Second World War. These titles include Valeriy Zamulin's award-winning book *Demolishing the Myth* (Helion, 2011), Lev Lopukhovsky's highly praised work, *The Viaz'ma Catastrophe, 1941* (Helion, 2013), and Rostislav Aliev's study of the heroic stand by the defenders of the Brest Fortress, *The Siege of Brest 1941* (Pen & Sword, 2013). In addition, Mr. Britton has translated several memoirs by Red Army veterans, such as Petr Mikhin's *Guns Against the Reich* (Pen and Sword, 2010), Joseph Pilyushin's *Red Sniper on the Eastern Front* (Pen and Sword, 2010) and Vasiliy Krysov's *Panzer Destroyer* (Pen and Sword, 2010). Upcoming titles include a biography of Marshal K.K. Rokossovsky by Boris Sokolov, to be published by Helion.

RED DEVILS OVER THE YALU

A Chronicle of Soviet Aerial Operations in the Korean War 1950-53

Igor Seidov

Translated and edited by Stuart Britton

Helion & Company

Helion & Company Limited
26 Willow Road
Solihull
West Midlands
B91 1UE
England
Tel. 0121 705 3393
Fax 0121 711 4075
Email: info@helion.co.uk
Website: www.helion.co.uk
Twitter: @helionbooks
Visit our blog http://blog.helion.co.uk/

Published by Helion & Company 2014
Designed and typeset by Aspect Book Design (www.aspectbookdesign.com)
Cover designed by Farr out Publications, Wokingham, Berkshire
Printed by Lightning Source Limited, Milton Keynes, Buckinghamshire

Text © Igor Seidov 2013. English edition translated and edited by
Stuart Britton, © Helion & Company Limited 2013.
For © of photographs see credits within the book.
Originally published as *"Krasnye d'iavoliy" v nebe Korei – Sovetskaia aviatsiia v voine 1950-1953: Khronika vozdushnih srazhenii* (Moscow: Yauza, Eksmo, 2007).

ISBN 978 1 909384 41 5

British Library Cataloguing-in-Publication Data.
A catalogue record for this book is available from the British Library.

All rights reserved. No part of this publication may be reproduced, stored in
a retrieval system,or transmitted, in any form, or by any means, electronic,
mechanical, photocopying, recording or otherwise, without the express written
consent of Helion & Company Limited.

Front cover: The image depicts the clash between the 16th FIS's 2nd Lt. Edwin
E. Aldrin flying F-86E-10-51-2778 and the MiG-15 of Sr. Lt. Lev Kolesnikov of
the 224th IAP above the Supung hydroelectrical station on 14 May 1953.
(© Sergei Vakhrushev)

For details of other military history titles published by Helion & Company
Limited contact the above address, or visit our website: http://www.helion.co.uk.

We always welcome receiving book proposals from prospective authors.

Contents

List of illustrations

List of tables

List of abbreviations

AD	Aviation Division
AP	Aviation Regiment
BAD	Bomber Aviation Division
BG	Bombardment Group
BS	Bombardment Squadron
CPV	Chinese People's Volunteer Army
FBS	Fighter-bomber Squadron
FBG	Fighter-bomber Group
FBW	Fighter-bomber Wing
FEAF	Far East Air Forces
FEG	Fighter Escort Group
FIG	Fighter-Interceptor Group
FEW	Fighter Escort Wing
FIW	Fighter Interceptor Wing
GCI	Ground Control Intercept
GIAD	Guards Fighter Aviation Division
GIAP	Guards Fighter Aviation Regiment
IAB	Fighter Aviation Brigade
IAD	Fighter Aviation Division
IAK	Fighter Aviation Corps
IAP	Fighter Aviation Regiment
KPAAF	Korean People's Army Air Force
MTAP	Torpedo Aviation Regiment
NIAP	Night Fighter Aviation Regiment
NKPA	North Korean People's Army
PARM	Mobile Aviation Repair Shop
PDRK	People's Democratic Republic of Korea
PLA	People's Liberation Army
PLAAF	People's Liberation Army Air Force
PRC	People's Republic of China
PVO	Air Defense Forces
RAAF	Royal Australian Air Force
RAF	Royal Air Force
RO	Radar Operator
ROK	Republic of Korea
RS	Reconnaissance Squadron
SAC	Strategic Air Command
ShAD	Attack Aviation Division
ShAP	Attack Aviation Regiment

SmAK	Composite Aviation Corps
SRS	Strategic Reconnaissance Squadron
TRS	Tactical Reconnaissance Squadron
TRW	Tactical Reconnaissance Wing
UAA	Unified Air Army
UchAP	Training Aviation Regiment
USAF	United States Air Force
USAFFE	United States Army Forces in the Far East
USNAF	US Navy Air Force
VA	US Navy Attack Squadron
VF	US Navy Fighter Squadron

Editor's note

For the first time, author Igor Seidov has raised the curtain that has long concealed Soviet air operations in the Korean War. Using now de-classified Soviet-era documents and interviews with Soviet pilots that flew the missions, he provides a detailed description of the 64th Fighter Aviation Corps [IAK] staging from its bases in Manchuria to contest the airspace over North Korea. Seidov offers a daily chronicle of the missions and combats conducted by the Soviet pilots, often employing first-person accounts from the pilots themselves.

Seidov does not shy away from controversy and undoubtedly some of the things he writes will raise a few hackles. As Robert F Dorr, Jon Lake and Warren Thomspon write in *Korea War Aces* (Osprey Publishing, 1995), "The ... years that have elapsed since the end of the war have allowed the traditional accounts to become entrenched, such that the version of events written by the USAF at the height of the Cold War is widely regarded as the truth."

One such long-established "truth" was the myth that the F-86 Sabre achieved an 8:1 or even great kill ratio in its favor over the MiG-15. Many of the U.S. Sabre victories came against the inexperienced Chinese and North Korean MiG pilots. Even so, since the war, the number of USAF MiG-15 claims has been steadily revised downwards, while its admitted losses of F-86s have slowly increased. Seidov offers new totals and ratios, which further challenge long-held beliefs, but he is passing along the official 64th IAK records on this matter.

To his credit, Seidov, when working with the Soviet victory claims, does attempt to cross-check many of them with American loss records, and in places, he casts doubts on the Soviet victory claims. He was ably aided in this work by Diego Fernando Zampini, who has devoted close study to American victory and loss records. At the same time, however, Seidov challenges many American victory claims, and notes that often none of the Soviet fighter regiments had any losses on a day when American pilots put in several victory claims – and this before the Chinese began flying regular missions.

This points to an issue common to all air wars since the First World War – the tendency for victory totals to be inflated. During wars, every air force wants to cast the best possible light on its men and machines to the public back home, a desire that dovetails nicely with the pilots' natural tendency to file erroneous victory claims. In the hurly-burly of aerial dogfights, pilots rarely have the luxury to observe what happens ultimately to an aircraft they have hit with machine-gun or cannon fire. Unless the pilot bails out, a wing comes off or the aircraft explodes, the stricken plane, often trailing smoke, will go into a steep, even spinning dive toward the earth. The pilot will file a victory claim, but quite often the pilot of the stricken plane is able to regain control of his aircraft and nurse it back to base. On the basis of pilots' claims, and photographic evidence in later wars, a victory will often be recorded in such cases. However, in defense of them, if an enemy airplane is put of action by combat damage, isn't this also a victory of sorts?

This process of inflating victory totals happened in the Korean War as well, and in fact, certain flight characteristics of the MiG-15 and the F-86 may have exacerbated the problem. Certain MiG-15s (and which ones couldn't be known until each was individually flight tested) exhibited flight instability at speeds close to the red line, which the Russians called a *valezhka* – the MiG would abruptly flip over and often go into a violent, sometimes fatal spin. Naturally, any pursuing, firing Sabre pilot might put in a victory claim, if he observed hits immediately prior to the MiG's plunge. But such an event was the result of the *valezhka*, not enemy fire. Meanwhile, the standard escape tactic by an F-86 Sabre pilot was to throw his jet into a steep dive, knowing that the lighter MiG-15 wouldn't be able to stay with the Sabre. Again, a Soviet pilot could sometimes misconstrue this tactic as a sign that his cannon fire had inflicted fatal damage to the Sabre. But time and again, F-86 pilots returned home, often with gaping holes in their wing surfaces, fuselage or tail fin.

To their credit, the Soviet air force command, as Seidov notes, did take steps to tighten its victory credentials, insisting wreckage of the downed UN aircraft be located and retrieved to confirm the victory. Since all the aerial combats took place over enemy territory once the lines on the ground stabilized near the 38th Parallel, the U.S. side couldn't implement such a measure, so its victory credentials inevitably remained looser. In addition, the USAF regularly attributed losses of aircraft to enemy anti-aircraft fire or even recorded them as non-combat operational losses, when Seidov shows that it was clearly an attacking MiG-15 that inflicted the fatal damage.

Thus, the reader is advised to take any victory claims in this or any other Korean air war book with a grain of salt, unless the victory can be match to a loss recorded on the opposing side. Scholars, including Igor Seidov and Diego Zampini, are busily revising the victory and loss records and this work is still ongoing, even 50 years after the war.

Seidov also casts surprising and convincing light on the extent to which US and UN fighter pilots ignored the prohibition against crossing the Yalu River. American pilots interviewed since the war have acknowledge that this happened. For example, one unidentified pilot stated, "There were a lot of airplanes shot down in Korea by guys who ... [did] not necessarily play by the rules."[1] 2nd Lieutenant William F. Schrimsher recalled one mission: "We were well north of the Yalu, which was a real no-no, but we did it on a fairly regular basis ..."[2] Now, using Soviet records and pilots' and crews' testimony, Seidov shows that American F-86s regularly circled above the mouth of the Yalu River, waiting for MiGs to take off or come in for a landing, when they would be "easy pickings". According to Soviet documents, this became a widely used tactic; Seidov shows that many of the Soviet air combat losses came in this way, and argues that the Soviet command failed to take quick steps to counter it.

Seidov strongly criticizes the Soviet system of rotating entire fighter regiments and divisions into and out of the combat theater, contrary to the US system of rotating individual pilots. As each fighter regiment left the theater, it took with it all the accumulated combat experience that was not passed on to the incoming regiments. As Seidov shows, each new fighter regiment took combat losses on its first few missions due to their inexperience. He also criticizes the political decision that was taken by the Soviet leadership to deploy Soviet Air Defense fighter regiments to Manchuria, the pilots of which had not been trained for high-speed, maneuvering fighter combat.

In this book, Seidov also discusses the advantages and disadvantages of the aircraft flown by the opposing sides in combat, the men who flew them, and the tactics they used in Korea. His discussion is balanced and thoughtful, though some of his conclusions may be surprising. All in all, *Red Devils over MiG Alley* is not the final word on the air war in Korea, but it is a substantial contribution to our understanding of it.

Stuart Britton

ENDNOTES

1   Kenneth P. Werrell, *Sabres over MiG Alley* (Annapolis: Naval Institute Press, 2005), p. 132.
2   Warren Thompson, *F-86 Sabre Aces of the 4th Fighter Wing* (Osprey Publishing, 2006), p. 76.

Translator's note

One of the greatest challenges I faced as translator of Igor Seidov's latest book on the Korean air was once again the identification and proper transliteration of the numerous North Korean and Chinese towns and villages mentioned in the text. The Cyrillic transliteration often differs markedly from the English transliteration, and the latter has also changed the spelling of many place names since the Korean War. For example, the major Soviet air base was known as Antung by the US Air Force in Korea, but today the accepted transliteration is Andong. I quickly learned that the Soviets during the Korean War used maps they had captured from the Japanese, so the Cyrillic transliterations are those of the Japanese transliterations of the way they pronounced the names of these places. You can imagine the difficulty this posed to this translator! The result, I'm afraid, is a bit of a mish-mash of different English transliterations, reflecting the underlying changing North Korean and South Korean Romanizations. However, I adopted a consistent English transliteration for each place and individual, in order to minimize confusion.

Another problem was identifying a proper transliteration for many of the Chinese and North Korean pilots mentioned in the text. A few of the Chinese pilots were celebrated aces, so identifying them was not difficult. The same couldn't be said about their wingmen and other pilots who soldiered through the war without achieving ace status. As for the North Korean air force, little is still known about it and the pilots who flew for it in the Korean War. Identifying them presented particular difficulties.

I couldn't have achieved even a satisfactory result in my transliteration of these place names and the identification of these pilots without the invaluable contribution of two men, who deserve special mention. I would like to express my deep appreciation to Joe L. Brennan, a researcher focusing on Korean War air combat, who helped me identify many of the North Korean places and North Korean pilots from the English transliteration of the Cyrillic and offered me suitable transliterations of their names. His own deep knowledge of the Korean Air War was immensely helpful to me. I would also like to mention Zhou Wei, a Chinese translator with good knowledge of English, who resides in the People's Republic of China, and who helped me identify many of the Chinese pilots mentioned in the text.

Finally, it was also sometimes difficult identifying an American, British or other UN pilot from the Cyrillic – direct transliteration does not often give the proper spelling. To identify these men, I used the invaluable Department of Defense Korean War Aircraft Loss Database, available on-line at www.dtic.mil/dpmo/korea/reports/air, and the Air Combat Information Group's Korean War Database of U.S. Air-to Air Victories during the Korean War, compiled by Diego Fernando Zampini, Saso Knez and Joe L. Brennan, which is available at www.acig.org.

Obviously, I could not have accomplished this translation without the Internet, e-mail, and the help mentioned above. Of course, I take full responsibility for any mistakes in the translation.

Introduction and acknowledgements

This book is as if a look from the other side, from the north of the 38th Parallel, since until quite recently one could learn about this war only from the other side – south of the 38th Parallel. After the end of the Korean War, a multitude of books and publications in the periodical literature appeared in the West about the air war. Much of the information about it was one-sided and for the most part not objective – they glorified their own air forces and their "best in the world" pilots, while understating their own losses and inflating their victory totals.

Reading it, you begin to wonder – can the authors themselves really believe what they are writing? After all, it is plainly embarrassing to state that only 110 aircraft were lost in air-to-air combat in the course of a three-year major air war – even to the uninformed reader, it is clear that this cannot be true. It is understandable that these were the only figures available for Western historians, since all the data on victories and losses in this war came from the bowels of the US military organization. The Western scholars simply didn't have access to any other records. It was simply not to the advantage of the US War Department to publish accurate data on their losses in the war (just as it was disadvantageous for the Soviet Ministry of Defense in its time to do the same); the prestige of their air forces among the taxpayers, who supported the "best air force in the world" with large amounts of tax dollars, would have declined. Concealing their losses in air-to-air combats with MiGs, the Fifth Air Force's staff officers in order to polish any rough edges conceived a hardly new system for understating their real losses in aerial combats: the Americans attributed a portion of those that aircraft that failed to return from missions to enemy ground fire, while damaged aircraft that did return were frequently later written off as a non-combat loss. Take for example just the data on losses of the F-86 Sabre, which has been widely praised in Western sources as the best fighter of the war: of the 224 F-86 Sabres lost according to American data, only 110 were lost due to enemy action – less than half. The remaining losses did not result from enemy action (if so, then from what?); they either "went missing", were lost in flight incidents, or were written off for other reasons. Isn't the figure for non-combat losses suspiciously high? To this it must be added that everyone in the West writes in one voice that the training of the American pilot was on the very highest level; tyros with just 30-50 hours of flight time in jets didn't serve in the war, as they did in the case of the 64th IAK [*istrebitel'nyi aviatsionnyi korpus*, or Fighter Aviation Corps]. But if that is the case, why were the non-combat losses so high? All the answers to these questions, and accurate data regarding who, when and why they didn't return from a combat mission, are in the military archives of the United States and in those of the other countries that participated in this war on the side of the UN coalition; however, to this day they have not yet been fully released to the public. It is known until recent times there were secret documents about this war even in the

United States. It is possible that they have since been de-classified, as they have been in Russia, but we don't yet know about them.

Reading and studying the foreign publications, one becomes increasingly convinced that all these works echo one another, that the very same data are transferred from one work to the next without questioning, which resulted in a one-sided view of this conflict. Using the fact that the given subject was for a long time kept totally classified in the Soviet Union, where nothing could be written about it, Western historians and journalists all these years wrote about the role of their own air forces in this war in glowing words, belittling everything connected with the participation of the Communist bloc's air force, knowing that there could be no refutation.

I wanted to look into this: Was everything just as the Western authors assert? For almost eight years, my colleagues and I gathered data on this war across the entire country of what was once known as the USSR, and interviewed those veterans of the 64th IAK that we could locate. In addition, information from personnel documents (flight books) and the personal archives of some of the veterans were compiled, and with the active assistance of Leonid Krylov, I managed to obtain archival materials on the 64th IAK from the Ministry of Defense's Central Archive, as well as from other de-classified sources. Everything we uncovered was poured into the given work on the air war in Korea.

I started with only archival records, but sprinkled the text with abundant excerpts from the tales of the Korean War pilot veterans themselves. In essence, they themselves are telling the story of how they fought in the skies of Korea; the author's only contribution was to gather all the material together, systematically go through it, eliminate any inaccuracies as far as possible, and produce an analysis of the participation of the Soviet Air Force in this war as a balance to all those works that downplayed the combat achievements of our pilots in the Korean War, 1950-1953. This is essentially the first major work that responsibly talks about the role of the Soviet Air Force in this war.

I hope that the given work will compensate for the bitterness of oblivion and injustice to the veterans of the war in Korea, who for many years have lived without any of the benefits owed to veterans of military combat operations, who have hidden their decorations and waited for a time when they would be remembered and given what is owed to them. That time has come!

The given book does not pretend to be a complete and all-encompassing work on the role of aviation in the Korean War – "blank spots" continue to exist in the histories of those countries that participated in the war in Korea. There is still no accurate and complete information about all of the PLAAF's [People's Liberation Army Air Force] units that served in the UAA [Unified Air Army], nor is there complete information about the North Korean KPAAF [Korean People's Army Air Force] throughout the war. I would like to see accurate and complete data on losses from the American side in this war (about their victories, the Americans have already said everything that could be said); here one cannot get by with aggregate data alone.

Thus I hope this book will provide a fresh impetus to new work on this subject. Much painstaking research work remains to be done!

In conclusion, I would like to thank everyone who actively assisted me in the work on this book, especially L.E. Krylov, A.V. Kotlobovsky, A.A. German, A.V. Stankov. I would particularly like to thank those veterans who took the time to answer our questions and share their stories: B.S. Abakumov, V.N. Aleksandrov, E.G. Aseev, F.G. Afanas'ev, G.N. Berelidze, Iu.B. Borisov, V.R. Bondarenko, A.Z. Bordun, N.E. Vorob'ev, I.P. Vakhrushev, A.P. Gogolev, I.A. Grechishko, G.Kh. D'iachenko, D.V. Ermakov, M.P. Zhbanov, N.M. Zameskin, S.A. Il'iashenko, A.A. Kaliuzhny, V.I. Koliadin, V.G. Kazakov, V.F. Korochkin, L.P. Kolesnikov, G.A. Lobov, V.N. Lapygin, P.S. Milaushkin, A.S. Minin, V.G. Monakhov, P.V. Minevrin, A.N. Nikolaev, G.U. Okhai, N.K. Odintsov, E.G. Pepeliaev, M.S. Ponomarev, G.M. Pivovarenko, A.I. Perekrest, L.I. Rusakov, D.A. Samoilov, M.N. Obodnikov, Iu.N. Sutiagin, V.M. Seliverstrov, V.G. Sevast'ianov, V.P. Sazhin, G.T. Fokin, S.A. Fedorets, G.I. Khar'kovsky, N.P. Chistiakov, N.K. Shelamonov, N.I. Shkodin, P.F. Shevelev, I.I. Shashva, V.I. Shoitov, L.K. Shchukin, G.G. Iukhimenko, and many, many others. Without your active assistance, this book could never have been written!

1

The beginning of the war in the skies of Korea

Before the start of combat operations, the North Korean People's Army [NKPA] was equipped with approximately 150 combat, transportation and training aircraft. Although the *Polish Military Encyclopedia* puts the numerical strength of the KPAAF at 239 aircraft, including 172 Il-10 ground attack aircraft, this figure is plainly too high.[1] Closer to the truth are the data published in the book *Istoriia vozdushnykh voin*, which gives the following figures: the KPAAF numbered 120 combat aircraft, including 40 Yak-9U and Yak-9P fighters, 70 Il-10s, and 10 Po-2 combat-trainers (this total does not include Li-2 transport aircraft).[2] The French journal *Le Fana de l'Eviatien* gives slightly higher figures for the North Korean air force before the war: a total of 162 aircraft, including 62 Il-10s, 70 Yak-9 and La-9 fighters, eight Po-2 trainers and 22 transport planes. The People's Democratic Republic of Korea [PDRK] Navy had several Soviet-manufactured MBR-2 flying boats.

According to American estimates, the KPAAF had 132 combat aircraft, including 70 Yak-3, Yak-7B, Yak-9 and La-7 fighters, plus 62 Il-10 attack aircraft. However, Soviet military advisers before the war give precise figures for the KPAAF's numerical strength and organization: the 55th AD [Aviation Division], consisting of the 56th IAP [Fighter Aviation Regiment] with 79 Yak-9s, the 57th ShAP [Attack Aviation Regiment] with 93 Il-10s, the 58th UchAP [Training Aviation Regiment] with 67 training and liaison aircraft, plus two aviation technical battalions to service the regiments, for a total of 239 aircraft and 2,829 personnel. The aircraft were concentrated on airfields located around Pyongyang. Most of the North Korean pilots and technicians had been trained between 1946 and 1950 in the Soviet Union, China, and within North Korea.

General Van Len commanded the KPAAF; his Soviet adviser was Colonel Petrachev. By the middle of 1950, one composite aviation division was officially under their command, but its complement of aircraft was much larger than the typical Soviet aviation division. All of the KPAAF's pilots had undergone training in the Soviet Union in 1949-1950.

The South Korean Air Force was small (according to American records) and had just 20 aircraft, most of which were just T-6 Texan training aircraft. To be sure, at the moment of the PDRK's invasion, several United States Air Force [USAF] C-54 and DC-4 transport aircraft were located on airbases around the Republic of Korea [ROK], which were serving the American military contingent in South Korea.

The units of the USAF, which were operating in Korea, were organizationally under the Far East Air Forces [FEAF], commanded by Lieutenant General George E. Stratemeyer. At the start of the war, FEAF had the following composition: the Fifth Air

Force, based in Japan, had the 3rd and 38th Medium Bombardment Groups [BG], the 8th Fighter-bomber Wing [FBW], the 35th Fighter Interceptor Wing [FIW], the 49th FBW, the 347th (All Weather) Fighter Group, the separate 4th (All Weather) Fighter and 6th Fighter Squadrons, the 512th Reconnaissance Squadron [RS], and the 374th Airlift Wing. The Fifth Air Force was a powerful air army consisting of more than 1,200 combat aircraft. As of 31 May 1950, this number included 42 F-82 Twin Mustang and 47 F-51 Mustang fighters, 504 F-80 Shooting Star jet fighter-bombers, 73 B-26 Invader light bombers and 27 B-29 Superfortress heavy bombers. Non-combat aircraft at its disposal included 48 reconnaissance planes of various types, 147 C-47, C-54, C-119 and other transport aircraft, as well as 282 liaison aircraft, consisting primarily of T-6 Texans and L-4 Piper Cubs. These numbers do not include the USNAF [US Navy Air Force, staging from aircraft carriers of the US Seventh Fleet, which had 118 F4U Corsair fighters, AD-1 Skyraider attack aircraft and F9F Panther jet attack aircraft. All of this air power could take off from their bases at any minute and begin combat operations on behalf of South Korea.

In addition to the Fifth Air Force in Japan, air units from other US air armies were activated for combat operations over the territory of the PDRK. The Twentieth Air Force, based on the island of Okinawa, had under its command the 51st FIW and the 31st SRS [Strategic Reconnaissance Squadron]. The Thirteenth Air Force, which was located in the Philippine Islands, included the 18th FBW and the 419th Fighter Squadron. In the Marianna Islands, there were the 19th BG, the 21st Separate Airlift Squadron, and the 514th RS.

FEAF Headquarters, which was located in Tokyo, had direct operational control over the UN air units. All the tactical aviation (fighters, fighter-bombers, light bombers, reconnaissance and transport aircraft) in the Korean theater of operations was subordinate to the Fifth Air Force. As the war progressed, formations from other US air forces, as well as from the United States itself (including from the National Guard and the Reserve) were mobilized to serve under the Fifth Air Force command. Strategic aviation (bombers and reconnaissance) came under the command of a specially-created Provisional FEAF Bomber Command. Not all of the aforementioned units and formations took part in combat operations in Korea; however, numerous aviation units, which had not previously been under FEAF, arrived in the theater of combat operations.

As for the air forces of the People's Republic of China [PRC] and the Soviet Union, which might have been able to participate in the initial stage of this conflict, actually there was not a single combat-capable aviation unit on the territory of the PRC before the Korean War. The armed forces of the PRC were not even able to repel the raids of the small Chinese Nationalist Air Force from the island of Taiwan on mainland China – the PRC had no aviation units of its own, while its anti-aircraft guns were outdated and few in numbers. Thus the PRC government appealed to the Soviet Union for assistance in creating modern and combat-ready air force and air defense units for the People's Liberation Army (PLA). For this purpose, in March 1950 the 106th Fighter Aviation Division [IAD] of the Soviet Air Defense Forces arrived in China, consisting of two fighter aviation regiments (one flying La-9 piston-engine fighters, the other MiG-15 jet fighters) and one composite aviation regiment equipped with Il-10 ground attack aircraft and Tu-2 high-speed bombers. Soviet aviation units not only trained the PLAAF pilots and technical personnel, but also flew combat missions to cover Shanghai's industrial and civilian targets against attacks by the Chinese Nationalist Air Force. This Soviet aviation division was the only Soviet air unit on PRC territory prior to the start of combat operations in Korea.

We'll note that on the Liaodong Peninsula, which was being leased to the Soviet Union by the PRC government, the Soviets had the 83rd SmAK [*smeshannyi aviatsionnyi korpus*, or composite aviation corps], commanded by Hero of the Soviet Union Lieutenant General Iu.D. Rykachev. This air corps had two fighter aviation divisions [IAD], two bomber aviation divisions [BAD], and one attack aviation division [*shturmovaia aviatsionnaia diviziia*, or ShAD]. Two Soviet naval aviation regiments were also based here, one a fighter regiment and the other a torpedo regiment. All of the units of the 83rd SmAK were equipped with piston-engine aircraft only.

In the Soviet Maritime District near the border with China and the PDRK, the powerful 54th Separate Far Eastern Air Army was based, which was in its strength fully comparable to the USAF's Fifth Air Force. However, before the start of combat operations in Korea, this Soviet air army did not have any jet aircraft.

That was the correlation of combat aviation strength of the contending sides as of 25 June 1950 – the date when the PDRK launched its invasion of South Korea. We'll now turn to a chronicle of events during the first months of the war.

THE START OF THE WAR IN THE SKIES OF KOREA

On the morning of 25 June 1950, the USAF's 374th Transport Airlift Wing took off for the Far East with the assignment to evacuate members and their families of the American military and diplomatic missions from Seoul. F-80 and F-82 fighters, stationed on bases in Japan, escorted the transport planes and patrolled over the area of evacuation.

Pilots of the KPAAF were the first to initiate combat operations that afternoon at 1315, when two Yak-9 fighters conducted an airstrike against the South Korean airfield at Seoul, while at 1700 six Yak-9 fighters delivered one of the most effective raids of first days of the war upon the bases at Kimpo and Seoul, destroying between 7 and 10 enemy aircraft at Seoul alone. On this day the North Korean pilots opened their victory score in this war: pilots of the KPAAF's 56th IAP destroyed an American C-54 transport plane of the 374th Airlift Wing on the airfield at Kimpo. For all practical purposes, the entire South Korean Air Force was destroyed in the course of the first few days of the war on the Seoul, Kimpo and Suwon airfields.

However, already on 26 June at 0145, the USAF openly initiated combat operations in Korea. F-82 fighters from the 68th (All Weather) Fighter Squadron took off from their airbase at Itazuke (Japan) in order to conduct combat missions in the Inchon area. According to their reports, on one of the first missions in the new area of operations, the Twin Mustangs of the 68th Fighter Squadron intercepted La-7 fighters (more likely these were Yak-11 combat trainers). The flight commander Lt. William G. Hudson ordered his wing man to drop his attached fuel tanks and to attack the enemy aircraft. The Korean pilots responded by opening fire from extremely long range. The Americans also scored no hits. The first combat encounter of Americans and North Koreans thus ended without results.

The first aerial combat in this war that ended with results took place on 27 June. According to the American version, five North Korean Yak-9 fighters attempted to attack American C-54 transports, which were carrying evacuees from Seoul, but they were intercepted by five F-82s; the Americans claimed three victories in the resulting combat. The USAF's first victory was attained by the crew of F-82G (No. 46-383), consisting of the pilot 1st Lieutenant William G. Hudson and his radar operator (RO) Lt. Carl Fraser, when they downed a Yak-9B in the area of Kimpo; two more were shot down by their comrades from the 68th and 339th Fighter Squadrons. The Americans acknowledged damage to one of their aircraft in this action.

On this same day, but a bit later, pilots of the 35th FBS, flying F-80C jet fighters, distinguished themselves by driving off an attack by nine Il-10 ground attack aircraft on the Kimpo Air Base. They shot down four and damaged a fifth Il-10, which was unable to return to its base. In this battle, 1st Lieutenant Robert E. Wayne, who downed two of the North Korean attackers, and Captain Raymond E. Schillereff and 1st Lieutenant Robert H. Dewald, who claimed one victory each, had success. However, the North Korean pilots still managed to attack the airbase, and destroyed one C-54 of the 374th Transport Airlift Wing as it was taking off, as well as seven American-made T-6 Texan South Korean trainer aircraft (not recognized by the Americans officially).

To this day also goes the first loss of an aircraft in this war that is officially recognized by the Americans. A transport C-54D was shot up by Yak-9 fighters over Korea and had to conduct a forced landing in Japan at Fukuoka. The plane was written-off, but there were no injuries among the crew.

On the next day, 28 June, for the first time American B-26 Invader bombers from the 3rd BW appeared above Korea, which conducted an attack upon the Munsan rail-road hub. To be sure, the attack proved costly to the Americans, since the squadron of Invaders suffered substantial losses from North Korean anti-aircraft fire: one B-26 (No.44-34238), having been damaged over the target fell into the Yellow Sea near Chin-do Island. Two more Invaders suffered serious damage: one B-26 (No.44-34478), having been badly hit by anti-aircraft fire, fell into the sea on its way back to Ashiya; the other B-26 (No.44-34379) made a forced landing at Suwon, but the crew had to burn the damaged airplane to prevent its seizure by the enemy.

After lunch, a group of B-29 bombers attacked the rail center in Seoul, as well as the bridge across the Han River. This also marked their debut in the skies of Korea.

In response to these attacks by the USAF, four KPAAF Yak-9s attacked Suwon, and at 1830 another six Yaks struck this city's airfield. The NKPA command announced that as a result of these attacks, approximately ten enemy aircraft were destroyed at the Suwon Air Base, without any losses on its own side. In addition, on this day pilots of the KPAAF repulsed an attack by four American bombers on Pyongyang and shot down one of them – the future Hero of the PDRK Lieutenant Ri Tong Tong Gyu added another victory to his total. The US Fifth Air Force command acknowledged the loss of two of its aircraft on 28 June, and damage to four more.

According to an announcement by the NKPA's high command, the KPAAF conducted more than 10 raids south of Seoul on 27 and 28 June. On 27 June, it struck a railroad bridge, a military train, the Anyang rail station, military storage depots and other enemy targets along the road between Seoul and Suwon. On 28 June, the North Koreans claim that a flight of North Korean fighters tangled with four enemy bombers in the area of Kumchon and Kyejong, which were heading for Pyongyang. As a result, one bomber was shot down and the others turned back. This same flight then attacked the Suwon Air Base and destroyed two enemy four-engine aircraft and three other enemy planes

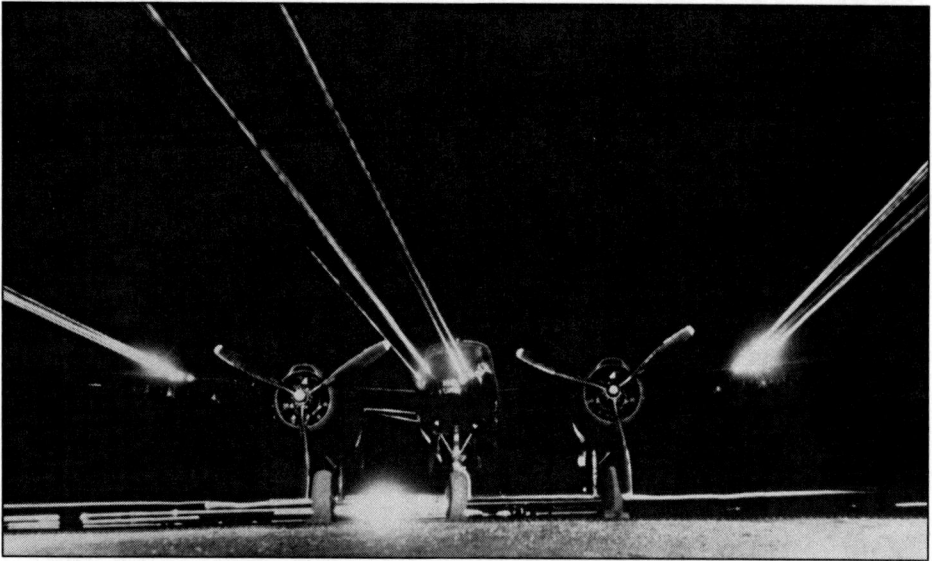

US Fifth Air Force, Korea – this USAF B-26 light bomber of the 3rd Bomb Wing has its 14 forward-firing .50 caliber machine guns tested prior to a night mission against enemy targets in North Korea. (Smithsonian National Air & Space Museum)

Airview of bombs dropped by U.S. Air Force, exploding on three parallel railroad bridges across Han River, southwest of Seoul, former capitol of Republic of Korea. Bridges were bombed early in war to delay advance of invading North Korean troops. (Smithsonian National Air & Space Museum)

on the ground. A second flight of North Korean aircraft, which also participated in this raid, shot down an enemy four-engine aircraft that was attempting to take off from this airfield. Moreover, two more enemy four-engine aircraft and three enemy light bombers were destroyed on the ground at the Suwon Air Base.[3]

On 29 June both sides exchanged attacks against airfields: the KPAAF conducted six air raids over the course of the day. In the morning, North Korean aircraft again bombed and strafed the Kimpo Air Base. An American fighter patrol hindered the attack. Shooting Stars from the 35th and 80th FBS of the 8th FBW reported downing five of the North Korean attackers. Lieutenants William Norris and Roy Marsh claimed a La-7 (most likely a misidentification of a Yak-11) and an Il-10 in this action.

In the course of the second raid of this day, now targeting Suwon, North Korean aircraft destroyed an American C-54 on the ground (which has not been acknowledged officially by the Americans), burned an F-82G (No.46-364), and inflicted serious damage against the airfield's terminal. On this same day, the 68th FS lost another F-82G, which for some unknown reason fell into the sea near Fukuoka; its pilot safely bailed out.

On this occasion, the airfield's air defenses were more successful; F-51 Mustang and F-80 Shooting Star fighters from the 8th and 35th FBS, which took off in response to an air raid alarm, shot down four North Korean ground attack planes and one North Korean fighter in aerial combat above Suwon without suffering any losses in return, while Gen. MacArthur watched from the ground. The Mustang pilots, who were making their debut in Korea, particularly distinguished themselves in this action, downing three Il-10s and one Yak-9; an F-80 pilot shot down the other North Korean Il-10.

In response to these North Korean attacks, on this same day a group of eight B-29 bombers from the 19th BG struck the Kimpo airfield, which was now in North Korean possession. According to the pilots' debriefings, the enemy suffered significant personnel losses. While returning to their base at Kadena, the B-29s came under fighter attack, as a result of which the gunners aboard the bombers claimed their first two victories in this war.

Meanwhile, at 1615, 18 B-26 bombers from the 3rd BG attacked the North Korean K-19 airfield at Haeju in the vicinity of Pyongyang, and according to American records destroyed 25 enemy aircraft on the ground. During this raid, the Invaders were jumped by a group of North Korean Yak-9s. While repulsing this attack, a machine-gunner on one of the Invaders, Staff Sergeant Nyle S. Mickly downed one of the fighters. But the Yaks also seriously damaged one of the B-26 Invaders (No.44-34277), and it fell into the sea before it could reach its base in Iwakuni (Japan). In addition, on 29 June North Korean ground attack aircraft struck the port at Inchon and sank 11 light enemy ships docked there, and also attacked the Inchon railroad station.

On the last day of June, the KPAAF launched more attacks on the Suwon Air Base and, according to an announcement by the command of the Korean People's Army, destroyed two four-engine enemy aircraft and seven fighters. The American pilots 1st Lieutenants John B. Thomas and Charles A. Wurster of the 36th FBS, flying F-80 jets, distinguished themselves by downing one Yak-9 each. The Americans acknowledged the loss of one F-80 and one C-54 on this day. In the North Korean press there was an article about the combat of two Yak-9s, flown by the pilots Ri Tong Gyu and his wingman Thae Kuk Song, against eight U.S. fighters. Noticing that four F-80s were diving on his wingman, Ri Tong Gyu rushed to his assistance, even though another four F-80s were attacking his fighter. Ri Tong Gyu saved his wingman, downing one of the Shooting

Four crew members of the 19th Bomb Group, an Okinawa-based veteran
unit of the Far East Air Forces Bomber Command, 1950.
(Smithsonian National Air & Space Museum)

Stars that had jumped Thae Kuk Song, but Ri's own Yak was damaged by an attack from
behind of another F-80, which riddled his plane's fuel tank and forced him to bail out.
Within a day he had already returned to action. After Ri's Yak went down, his wingman
Thae Kuk Song nevertheless finished off the attacking F-80. So according to this version
this combat ended with the score 2:1 in the North Koreans' favor, not the 2:0 score in
their favor that the Americans continue to claim to this very day.

The Americans do recognize the loss of one F-80C (No.49-603) from 8th FBG's
36th FBS, flown by 1st Lieutenant Edwin T. Johnson, but according to their version,
it was shot down by anti-aircraft guns 2 miles northeast of Suwon (Johnson bailed
out and was rescued). Considering that at this time the Shooting Stars were acting as
pure fighters, and not as ground attack aircraft, as well as the irrepressible desire of the
Americans to write off the majority of their losses as attributable to impersonal "ground
fire", the Korean story doesn't seem so unlikely. Moreover, the pilots of the 36th FBS
did duel with Yaks precisely in the vicinity of Suwon. This indirectly attests to the
recognition of their opponents' skill by the American pilots. It is possible to understand
the Americans; it would have been scandalous to acknowledge the loss of an up-to-date
jet fighter in a head-to-head battle against an outdated piston engine fighter flown by a
North Korean pilot.

There was one more aerial combat on this day which took place in the area of Kaesong. In it, the North Korean pilots shot down one B-26.

In connection with the advance of North Korean forces, the evacuation of the Suwon Air Base began. The American aircraft transferred to the K-10 Air Base at Chinhae, situated 11 miles east of Pusan. During the next attack by North Korean fighters, one C-54D (No.42-72468) of the 374th Troop Carrier Wing's 22nd Troop Carrier Squadron went down while climbing after takeoff and crashed and burned directly on the airbase, carrying away the lives of 23 crew members and passengers. Another C-54D of the same unit, which was also apparently damaged by the attacking fighters, crashed on the approach to Pusan. In addition on this day, two L-5 artillery spotter aircraft from the South Korean Air Force's 1st Squadron were shot down by North Korean anti-aircraft fire.

At the end of June 1950, the No. 77 Royal Australian Air Force (RAAF) Squadron arrived in Korea. It was subordinated to the USAF's Fifth Air Force.

The results of the first week of the war in the air were as follows:

a.   The actions of the KPAAF were well-prepared and well-organized, which led to its superiority in the air in the initial stage of combat operations. As a result of the planned and thoroughly prepared airstrikes against the South Korean network of airfields, almost the entire South Korean Air Force was destroyed on the ground – altogether 16 aircraft (eight L-4 Pipers, five L-5 Stinsons and three T-6 Texans). In addition, approximately 10 USAF aircraft were destroyed on the same South Korean airbases.

b.   Aerial combat was of a limited nature and conducted primarily against the USAF, which was covering the South Korean airfields, from which American diplomatic personnel were being evacuated. The USAF at this time concentrated upon driving off attacks by the North Korean Air Force on these airbases and conducted no large-scale operations against North Korea prior to 29 June, when the USAF began launching attacks against targets on the territory of the PDRK.

c.   The losses of the two sides over the first week of combat were as follows: in addition to the complete destruction of the South Korean Air Force, the USAF command acknowledged the loss of 12 aircraft on the ground and in the air, although according to the data of the opposing side, the losses of the USAF were twice as large. The losses of the KPAAF amounted to 14 aircraft: 8 Il-10 ground attack aircraft and 6 Yak-9 fighters.

The Americans officially break down their losses for various reasons over the first six days of aerial combat in June 1950 as three C-54s, five B-26s, three F-82s and one F-80. Half of these losses were due to the KPAAF. Yet the Americans officially recognize the loss of only three aircraft in aerial combat against the North Koreans. Meanwhile, according to the accounts of American pilots, the North Koreans lost 21 aircraft in aerial combat and another 25 on the ground.

THE USAF REIGNS SUPREME IN THE SKIES OF KOREA

At dawn on 3 July 1950, 16 Firefly bombers and nine Seafire fighters were launched from the British aircraft carrier HMS *Triumph* and at 0815 struck the airbase at Haeju, destroying hangars and other facilities, and returned to the *Triumph* without any losses. On the same day, the American aircraft carrier *Valley Forge* launched 16 F4U Corsairs and 12 A-1 Skyraider attack aircraft of the USNAF's VF-54 and VA-55 Squadrons. These strike aircraft were covered by eight F9F-2 Panther jet fighters from the same carrier's VF-51. Their assignment was to hit the Pyongyang Air Base.

The first to appear above the airfield were the Panthers, which pounced upon an element of Yak-9 fighters as it was taking off in response to the attack and shot both fighters down, while the second flight of Panthers attacked a hardstand where enemy aircraft were parked and set fire to one transport airplane on the ground. In a second pass over the airfield, the Panthers destroyed two more aircraft on the ground. The arriving Corsairs and Skyraiders completed the destruction of the airfield, destroying several more aircraft parked on it, three hangars, a fuel depot and almost all of the base's remaining facilities. The entire group returned to their carrier without losses. On this mission, the US Navy pilots achieved their first aerial victory: VF-51's Lt. (jg) Leonard Plog in his Panther shot down one Yak-9 over the Pyongyang Air Base.

On 4 July, aircraft of the US Navy again struck various targets in North Korea, destroying several railroad bridges and more than a dozen locomotives. This time, the fire of the North Korean anti-aircraft guns was more accurate – four VA-55 Skyraiders received damage, and one of them while making its landing on the *Valley Forge* leaped over the arresting cables at high speed and crashed into aircraft parked on the deck in front of it. One Skyraider and two Corsairs were totally demolished, and six more aircraft received heavy damage.

The KPAAF on 3 July also operated actively and continued to bomb and strafe retreating enemy troops between Seoul and Suwon and also attacked the airfield at Suwon. In aerial combat on this day, the North Korean pilots shot down one enemy aircraft.

In the first week of July 1950, the Headquarters of the US Fifth Air Force boastfully declared that they had achieved their goal, and that the Korean People's Army Air Force had been destroyed. So the surprise of the American command was all the stronger, when during an operation at Taejon (7-21 July 1950), North Korean pilots again appeared over the battlefield and inflicted substantial losses on enemy ground troops and bomber units. In this battle, the forces of the United States Army suffered their first major defeat.

On 7 July, the NKPA launched an offensive in the direction of Taejon, which ended on 20 July with the capture of the city. An unpleasant "surprise" for the American command was the active participation of the North Korean Air Force, which the American generals had already "buried". On 7 July, North Korean pilots shot down two airplanes in aerial combats, and on 9 July, they claimed two American fighters. According to the American command, over the period of fighting between 25 June and 11 July, the USAF lost 20 aircraft. This number does not include five C-54 transport aircraft and one RAAF F-51, which were all lost for unknown reasons.

Over the period between 7 July and 20 July, the North Korean fighter squadrons under the commands of Kim Ki Ok, Ri Mun Sun and Ri Tong Gyu shot down 10 enemy aircraft, including a B-29 bomber downed by a North Korean Yak-9U on 12 July. In connection with this, the Presidium of the PDRK's Supreme People's Soviet on 23 July 1950 awarded the KPAAF's 56th IAP the Guards title for its successful combat actions in the operation at Taejon, so it became the 56th GIAP [Guards Fighter Aviation Regiment].

North Korean pilots had particularly good results in combats between 12 and 17 July. For example, in one action on 12 July in the region of Chochiwon against 20 US fighters, the KPAAF's 56th IAP shot down three American planes – two B-26s and one fighter, without any losses to itself. On 13 July, two North Korean pilots, Kim Ki Ok and Ri Mun Sun attacked 10 enemy aircraft in the area of Pyongtaek and downed three of them, after which they safely returned to base. In addition on this day, a North Korean Yak-9 shot down an American L-5 artillery spotter: the crew consisting of 1st Lieutenant Bill Dusell and observer 2nd Lieutenant Don Bazzurro were adjusting artillery fire onto targets in and around Taejon. Their plane was patrolling at an altitude of 2,000 feet right behind enemy lines. Suddenly it was jumped by a North Korean Yak-9, but Dussell managed to evade the first attack by diving to extremely low altitude. On the second firing pass, the Yak pilot didn't miss and with a burst shattered a wing of the aircraft, after which Dussell lost control of it. The plane came down behind enemy lines. The American pilots were lucky. The crash had left Dussell unconscious, but alive, while Brazzurro managed to pull himself out of the wreckage despite a broken leg. With the help of a 12-year-old boy, Brazzurro made it back to UN territory and sent a patrol to evacuate Dussell.

On the following day, North Korean Yak-9s clashed with eight F-80s. Pilot Ri Tong Gyu shot down one Shooting Star, but his aircraft was also fatally struck and he had to take to the silk. His wingman Thae Kuk Song was also shot down in this battle. The KPAAF pilots had tangled with pilots of the 35th FBS. Major Vincent Cardarell and Captain Wayne Redcliff each received credit for one Yak-9.

On 5 July, a pair of Yak-9s attacked four B-26s above Taejon. According to American records, one B-26 was damaged in this action, which made a forced belly landing on the runway of the Taejon Air Base. According to an announcement by the NKPA command, there were six American B-26s in this clash, and two of them were shot down.

In connection with the sharp increase in the KPAAF's activity, the commander of the United States Army Forces in the Far East [USAFFE] General MacArthur was compelled to demand a major air offensive to suppress the KPAAF. The offensive began with the bombing of the Kimpo Air Base on 15 July. Airstrikes by the USNAF and the Royal Air Force [RAF] against the network of airbases in Korea continued for five days. On 20 July, the conclusion of this operation was announced.

Despite enemy air superiority, the North Korean pilots continued to offer resistance to the USAF. For example, on 16 July Americans launched bombing strikes against targets in and around Seoul, which were intercepted by fighters of the 56th IAP. Two American planes were shot down. Pilots of the KPAAF shot down another two American aircraft in aerial combat on 18 July, and also attacked an enemy column of 100 vehicles in the Taegu area, destroying around 60 of them.

Over four days of the operation (between 15 and 18 July), American pilots scored only one victory, when on 17 July Captain Francis Clarke of the 35th FBS downed one Yak-9 in his F-80 jet. Their luck changed on 19 July, when pilots of the USAF 8th FBG destroyed 17 enemy aircraft in aerial combat. Pilots of this Group's 36th FBS did particularly well by downing eight enemy aircraft. Pilots of the 8th FBS in their F-80s did them one better by claiming nine victories on this day. However, the NKPA command announced that on 19 July, pilots of the first Hero of the PDRK Kim Ki Ok's squadron alone shot down five American aircraft. The American command acknowledged the loss of two F-80s from the 36th FBS in combats with the Yak-9s, as well as the loss of two B-29 bombers – one of which struggled back to Kadena Air Base and crashed upon landing. The heated action continued on 20 July, when North Korean pilots downed two more enemy aircraft south of Taejon, while pilots of the 8th FBG claimed two Yak-9s.

On the whole, the KPAAF operated successfully in the Taejon operation, despite the numerical and qualitative superiority of the USAF in the air. On 17 July 1950, twelve NKPA combatants were the first in the PDRK to be awarded the high title of Hero of the People's Democratic Republic of Korea. Among their number were the North Korean aces Kim Ki Ok, Ri Tong Gyu and Ri Mun Sun, who together shot down more than 20 American aircraft. For example, Ri Tong Gyu during June-July 1950 personally downed eight American airplanes, including one B-29, while his regimental comrade Kim Ki Ok scored 10 victories over this same period, including one B-29.

AN UNEQUAL CONTEST

The NKPA's offensive operations directed toward Taegu, begun on 20 July, continued until 20 August. The NKPA was forced to conduct this offensive without the support of its own aviation, since the American airstrikes against the airfields of the PDRK, as well as aerial combat losses, forced the NKPA command to withdraw its badly damaged air units to bases near the Manchurian border for regrouping and refitting. Thus in August 1950, the KPAAF made only rare appearances in the skies of South Korea. Two more aerial combats took place before the end of July, in which American pilots shot down two North Korean aircraft. On 24 July, a pilot of the 8th FBG, Lieutenant Colonel William Samuels, shot down an Il-10, while on the next day Lieutenant Colonel L. Harold Prince of the 8th FBS claimed another victory.

In August 1950, the USAF completely ruled the skies of Korea. According to an order issued by the American command, the USAF and USNAF undertook the systematic bombing of administrative-political centers and industrial targets throughout the PDRK, hoping to spread fear among the population and to break the North Korean people's will to resist.

Already by 31 July, the chiefs of staff of the USAF had prepared a list of 53 targets on the territory of the PDRK subject to destruction. The list started with the port of Wonsan, the capital city of Pyongyang, and the cities of Hamhung and Chongjin. To assist with this objective, formations of the Strategic Air Command (SAC), equipped with B-29 and B-50 bombers, were mobilized.

At the start of the Korean War, only one bomber group was activated to support the combat operations in Korea – the 19th BG, which transferred from the island of Guam to Okinawa for this purpose. However, this proved to be insufficient, and at the beginning of July 1950 two more groups from SAC, the 98th and 307th BG, moved into the theater of operations. The two groups of B-29s (the 19th and 307th) operated from Kadena Air Base on the island of Okinawa, while the 98th BG was based at Yokota Air Base near Tokyo.

From the beginning of July and until 25 September 1950, B-29 bombers conducted around 4,000 combat sorties (3,159 according to other data) and dropped 30,000 metric tons of bombs on targets in North Korea. During these attacks, according to the American historian George Stewart, a total of four B-29s were lost, with three of them falling victim to North Korean fighters.

In addition to the SAC bombardment groups, which operated against targets deep within North Korea, American piston-engine and tactical aviation actively conducted airstrikes in support of the ground forces. In this period the American command of the Fifth Air Force initiated an operation under the code name "Interdiction", the main task of which was to isolate the NKPA, deprive it of key supplies, and fragment it into isolated units. The Americans targeted roads and railroads, bridges, ferries, fords, tunnels, supply depots, reserve positions, and both moving and stationary transportation vehicles. General MacArthur issued the order, "Stop everything that is moving. Cause everything that is motionless to move. Any male person should be viewed as a legitimate target." The primary weapon of this aerial offensive was the Fifth Air Force's fighter-bomber force, which was equipped with piston-engine F-51D Mustang and F-80 Shooting Star jet fighter-bombers.

At the start of the war in Korea, the USAF had a total of 30 F-51D Mustangs, which were located in storage in Japan. Ten of them were immediately handed over to the South Korean Air Force with the same number of pilot-instructors. The remaining 20 Mustangs were used to form the temporary 51st Squadron, which began combat operations in Korea on 15 July 1950 from the Taegu Air Base in South Korea. In addition, approximately 20 more F-51Ds were partially equipping the 35th, 36th and 8th Squadrons, though the majority of these squadrons' planes consisted of the F-80 Shooting Star. Soon the 35th and 36th Squadrons were combined to form the 8th Fighter-bomber Group, which began combat operations on 29 June 1950 from the Ashiya Air Base in Japan.

From the very start of combat, B-26 Invader light attack bombers of the 3rd BG (consisting of the 8th and 13th BS), which was based in Iwakuni, Japan, began to operate against target in the enemy's shallow rear. After winning air superiority, many units of the Fifth Air Force switched to operate against ground targets, since there quickly appeared an acute need by ground units of the U.S. and Republic of Korea [ROK] armies for direct air support on the battlefield, especially during the retreat in July 1950.

However, the force available to the Fifth Air Force at the start of Operation Interdiction was plainly inadequate. Since the B-29 groups required F-80s to escort them through enemy airspace, the 347th All-Weather Fighter Group, consisting of the 68th and 339th Squadrons, which were equipped with all-weather, piston-engine F-82G Twin Mustang fighters, was redirected to work against ground targets. Soon the 347th All-Weather Fighter Group was reinforced with another F-82 squadron – the 4th Separate Squadron. The entire group of Twin Mustangs operated from the Itazuke Air Base in Japan.

This was still not enough, though, in order to carry out MacArthur's strict order to destroy everything that was moving. On 5 July 1950, the aircraft carrier *Boxer* departed the United States, with 145 F-51 Mustangs on board.

At the end of July 1950, No. 77 Squadron of the Royal Australian Air Force [RAAF], equipped with 26 F-51D Mustangs, began to operate over the battlefields in Korea from the Pohang Air Base. Deep aerial reconnaissance was conducted by the SAC's 31st Reconnaissance Squadron, which was equipped with RB-29 and RB-50 airplanes, as well as later with the RB-45 Tornado reconnaissance jet. Reconnaissance over the battlefield and in the enemy's shallow rear was conducted by reconnaissance RF-80As of the 8th TRS [Tactical Reconnaissance Squadron] and reconnaissance RF-51s of the 45th TRS. The aerial armada of the USAF also included more than 100 F-80 jet fighter-bombers of the 8th, 51st and 18th FBG.

Of course, the numerically weak air force of the PDRK could not oppose this armada, and in August 1950 it only made sporadic appearances in the sky. Thus, on 3 August Mustangs from the 18th FBG's 67th Squadron intercepted and shot down two Yak-9s; credit for the victories went to Captains Edward Hellend and Howard Price. On 10 August, Major Arnold "Moon" Mullins of the same 67th Squadron spotted and attacked a field airstrip in his Mustang and destroyed three Yak-9 fighters on the ground. The Americans had no other encounters in the air with the enemy in the month of August.

The only successful sortie by North Korean pilots was on 22 August, when two Yak-9Us bombed the British destroyer H.M.S. *Comus* just off the eastern shore of Korea and seriously damaged it. However, the NKPA command announced that on this day, its air force had sunk two enemy ships. According to it, one group of North Korean planes sank a U.S.-built South Korean minesweeper, while two attack planes sank an American torpedo boat between the islands of Muchang and Kado near the mouth of the Yalu River. Pilots Ri Ra Sun and Yang Chae Hung delivered the fatal strikes and safely returned to base.

After re-equipping their thinned air units with new aircraft that had arrived from the USSR, the KPAAF began flying missions again, and on 1 September alone, fighters of the 56th GIAP shot down three enemy planes in aerial combat over Taegu – including one F-51 and one L-4 of the South Korean Air Force. On 9 September, defending Siniuju and Pyongyang from B-29 attacks, North Korean pilots declared that they had shot down four enemy bombers. The American acknowledged the loss of two of their B-29s from the 19th and 92nd BG.

The Americans, sensing the renewed activity of the KPAAF, immediately struck their airbases again. The USNAF and air units of the participating UN countries also played an active role in suppressing the enemy air force, as well as in supporting their own ground troops.

Prior to 1 August, the American Seventh Fleet in the area of Korea had only one aircraft carrier, the *Valley Forge*, but a second aircraft carrier, *Philippine Sea*, arrived at the beginning of August, as well as two small escort carriers, *Sicily* and *Badoeng Strait*, two days later. Already from 3 August 1950, piston-engine aircraft from these aircraft carriers began combat sorties in the Pusan area. They conducted more than 1,000 combat sorties prior to 14 September. On 15 September 1950, the Americans made an amphibious landing at Inchon on the Yellow Sea coast, and another landing at Samchok from the Sea of Japan – both in the rear of the NKPA. Already by 18 September, the invading force had seized Inchon and Kimpo. By 28 September, Seoul was firmly in their grasp, and then Suwon as well.

Caught by surprise by this powerful assault from the sea, air units of the NKPA hastily fled north, deep into the interior of North Korea. However, this didn't take place successfully everywhere: at the Kimpo Air Base, the Americans seized several intact North Korean aircraft. The North Koreans had destroyed most of their airplanes before retreating, but hadn't had time to get to get to three of them, and these became trophies for the Americans. The two Il-10s and one Yak-9T were soon disassembled and shipped back to the United States.

Even before the invasion, pilots of the 8th FBS in their F-80s had attacked one of the airfields, and Lt. Colonel Harold Prince had destroyed three Yak-9 fighters on the ground. In September 1950 there were two more aerial combats, but given their overwhelming superiority in the air, victory went to the American pilots: on 28 September 1950, 1st Lieutenant Ralph Hall of the 35th FBS, flying a Mustang, shot down one Yak-9, though it is true that pilots of the 56th GIAP also downed one F-51 from the 39th FBS in return. On 30 September, Captain Ernest Fokelberg of the 8th FBS, flying an F-80 Shooting Star, shot down two enemy aircraft.

However, despite the UN air force's evident superiority in the air, the North Korean pilots were still able to offer resistance to the enemy, even though their numbers were small. For example, on 1 September 1950, a North Korean Yak-9 shot down an L-4 observation aircraft from the South Korean Air Force's 1st Squadron. The crew of this plane, 1st Lieutenant Cheon Bong-Sik and 1st Lieutenant Sin Jeong-Hyeon, were both killed. There are also records that show that on 9 September, a B-29 bomber (No. 44-62084) of the 92nd BG's 395th BS was shot down by the KPAAF. Some of the crew was killed, while the remainder was taken prisoner by the North Koreans. Finally, on 28 September an F-51D from the 18th FBW's 39th FBS was shot down by Yak-9 fighters; its pilot, Donald L. Pitchford, was killed. Thus, the North Korean Air Force was still able to inflict rare, but painful blows to the enemy, which speaks to the fact that the KPAAF was still alive!

After the U.S. Marines' landing at Inchon, the NKPA was compelled to retreat from the southern regions of the peninsula. Then American and South Korean troops, pursuing the retreating North Korean units, invaded the territory of the PDRK. On 14 October, Wonsan was occupied. Pyongyang fell on 20 October 1950. By 24 October, separate units of the UN forces were approaching the Korean-Chinese border, and on 26 October, they captured Hungnam. After taking Pyongyang, MacArthur loudly declared that the war was over.

In September-October 1950, the KPAAF was deprived of many of its bases and was simply demoralized. It made only rare appearances in the air. For example, in the middle of October it launched several airstrikes against enemy troops in the Kimpo, Kaesong, Seoul and Inchon areas, and on 27 October bombed an enemy column in the Anju region. By the middle of October, the KPAAF had only one remaining operational airbase – the Sinuiju Air Base on the border with China, which was subjected to continuous attacks by the USAF. The KPAAF suffered heavy losses on the ground. There were no aerial battles at all in October 1950.

In October 1950, despite the courage of the North Korean pilots, the first stage of the air war in the skies of Korea ended with the complete defeat of the PDRK's air force. The destruction of the KPAAF by the USAF and USNAF in the air and on the ground at the very start of the war adversely affected the pace of the North Korean offensive. In the course of the first month of the war, the KPAAF had suffered continual attrition at the hands of American aviation in aerial combats and on airfields. According to American estimates, of the 150 combat aircraft available to the KPAAF at the start of the war, there remained only 18 by the end of August, which could undertake only sporadic, harassing attacks on Seoul. According to Soviet data, by 21 August 1950, the KPAAF had 21 combat aircraft, of which 20 were ground attack aircraft and the other a fighter. Given such a situation, it was impossible to count upon offering resistance to the USAF. In the NKPA's anti-aircraft artillery units, there were no more than 80 37mm and 85mm anti-aircraft guns, which could not cover even the most important targets, either at the front or in the rear.

The complete superiority of the enemy air force in the air deprived the NKPA of the possibility to conduct a regrouping of its forces and also severely complicated the delivery of supplies to the front.

The second stage of the air war began on 1 November 1950. Experienced pilots of the Soviet Air Force in jet MiG-15s began preparing to make their entrance into it.

THE PREPARATIONS OF THE SOVIET AIR FORCE FOR COMBAT OPERATIONS IN KOREA

In view of the collapsing NKPA and the headlong advance of the UN forces into North Korea after the Inchon landing, at the beginning of October 1950 the North Korean leader Kim Il Sung appealed to the PRC for assistance. The leadership of the Chinese Communist Party's Central Committee, headed by Mao Zedong, made the swift decision to send Chinese troops into Korea, because the combat operations were approaching the Chinese border. Indeed, its leadership had no confidence that the American forces would stop there, because political leaders in the United States had issued too many threat against the PRC.

Peng Dehuai became the commander of the so-called Chinese People's Volunteer Army (CPV). Intensive preparations of three Chinese armies for crossing the Yalu River to launch combat operations in Korea began on 4 October 1950. Simultaneously, the PRC leadership turned to the USSR for support in the form of air cover for the CPV forces on the territory of North Korea, since neither the PRC nor the PDRK had the necessary quantity of combat aircraft to carry out this combat mission. For all practical purposes, the KPAAF had been wiped out, while the People's Liberation Army Air Force [PLAAF] was still in its infancy. Moreover, neither the KPAAF nor the PLAAF had any jet aircraft or experienced flight personnel. However, on 10 October, the Soviet side informed the leadership of the Chinese Communist Party Central Committee that it was impossible at the given time to send Soviet air units to support CPV forces in Korea, as had been previously agreed upon, because it hadn't had time to prepare well for the operation.

Despite the refusal of the Soviet side to support the CPV forces from the air, the Chinese leadership nevertheless decided to introduce its forces into Korea. On 19 October 1950 at 2000, CPV armies crossed the Yalu River in three places and entered North Korean territory.

The problem at the time was that by October 1950, there were in fact several Soviet aviation divisions on Chinese territory, which were training Chinese pilots for the PLAAF. However, only one of them was equipped with jet fighters – the 151st GIAD, which consisted of three Guards aviation regiments and had arrived in China at the end of summer in 1950.

So it was the 151st GIAD with its 28th, 72nd and 139th GIAP and its airbase security battalions that became the first Soviet aviation unit to enter the war in Korea. By 11 August 1950, it had assembled on the Mukden, Liaoyang and Anshan complex of airfields, where it began to carry out the tasks of providing air cover over military and civilian sites of northeast China and the forces of the PLA's 13th Army Group, and retraining Chinese fighter pilots to fly the MiG-15 jet fighter. Before departing for Manchuria, all the Soviet markings on the MiGs had been removed, and upon their arrival in China, all the personnel were issued Chinese military uniforms.

When combat operations had started in Korea, the 5th GIAD of the Moscow District PVO [*protivo vozdushnoy oborony*, or Air Defense Forces], which was commanded by Colonel Ivan Viacheslav Belov, had been alerted. This fighter division consisted of the 28th GIAP (commanded by Colonel A. Ia. Sapozhnikov) and the 72nd GIAP (commanded by Lt. Colonel A. I. Volkov). At the beginning of July 1950, the division was reinforced with one more fighter regiment, the 139th GIAP (commanded by Lt. Colonel D. G. Zorin). The division was hastily loaded upon trains and sent in secrecy to China. When crossing the Soviet-Chinese border, the technicians and other military personnel of the 5th GIAD donned Chinese military uniforms, and upon their arrival on 10 August in Mukden (present day Shenyang), all their personal documents were taken away and replaced by new Chinese-language documents that indicated they were Chinese volunteers. The 5th GIAD also received a new designation as the 151st GIAD. After the MiG-15 jets (with the RD-45A engine) were reassembled on Mukden's North and Northwest Air Bases, the division's regiments were dispersed on the three airfields of northeast China – Mukden, Liaoyang and Anshan.

By October 1950, the pilots of this division with part of their strength were covering industrial sites in northeast China and conducting daily combat patrols, while the remaining pilots, who had experience in flight instruction, were training Chinese pilots in Mukden. The group of Soviet instructors had available for this purpose several Yak-11 trainers and four Yak-17 jet trainers. The Chinese trainees first learned to handle these before taking a seat in the MiG-15 combat jet.

Major General of Aviation I.V. Belov, the first commander of the 64th IAK.

In addition to the military advisers, who were assisting officers of the NKPA in the planning and preparation of combat operations at the front, and training cadres on PDRK territory, a significant number of Soviet air force military specialists were preparing the pilots of the North Korean aviation divisions and pilots of the PRC for combat operations against the Americans. This task was successfully carried out. In the last four months of 1950 alone, the leading flight and technical personnel of the 151st GIAD, which had been assigned as instructors, retrained 93 pilots and 357 technicians on the MiG-15bis. The services of our compatriots were duly recognized by the enemy, with which the Soviet pilots dueled in the air for approximately three years. By the end of the Korean War, China, which had not possessed any jet aircraft before the start of the war, now had an air force inferior only to those of the United States and the Soviet Union.

Regiments of the 151st GIAD, having wrapped up their instruction work (only 8-10 of the pilot-instructors remained in Mukden), were shifted closer to the border with Korea. By 1 November 1950, the division was prepared for combat operations in the skies of Korea. But the question asks itself: Why could the Soviet Air Force, which was in no way inferior to the USAF, allot only one of its aviation divisions against the entire US Fifth Air Force? Simply put, in the autumn of 1950, the Soviet Air Force could not provide adequate cover to both the industrial sites in northeast China and the CPV offensive in Korea because it lacked sufficient strength.

The broader situation in the Far East and particularly in the Soviet Maritime District was very tense – the Cold War was in full swing! Dozens of USAF and USNAF reconnaissance planes were prowling along the Soviet borders, often violating it, and there were frequent and group incursions into Soviet airspace by American aircraft. Thus, in order to guard our entire boundary in the Far East, more than one air army was necessary: the 54th Separate Air Army was covering the Maritime District, the 2nd Air Army PVO was responsible for the Khabarovsk District, the 27th Air Army was protecting the Sakhalin Islands, and so forth.

However, at the start of the Korean War, these air armies did not have a single jet aircraft. The regiments of these air armies' divisions were equipped with piston-engine aircraft of the types La-7, La-9, Yak-3, Yak-9, P-63 Kingcobra (from the American Lend-Lease program), Il-10, Tu-2, Pe-2, Il-4, A-20 Boston and others. Naturally, it would have been senseless to send these air units into the furnace of a war, where the USAF was making wide use of jet aircraft, since this likely would have meant heavy losses to our side. Indeed, the bitter lesson that the KPAAF had received from the jet aircraft of the USAF in the recent fighting spoke for itself.

In August 1950, only the 52nd Air Army's MiG-equipped 303rd IAD, which had been covering Moscow, arrived in the Maritime District. However, even it could not be sent into China, because it had received a strict order to focus on quickly retraining the units of the 54th Separate Air Army on jets and to cover the eastern borders of the USSR. The situation in this area was extremely tense: the border was troubled, experiencing constant violations and provocations from the American aircraft.

Two incidents in particular that occurred shortly before the introduction of CPV forces into Korea sorely tested the patience of the Soviet side. On 4 September 1950, not far from the Soviet naval base in Port Arthur, a Soviet A-20 reconnaissance aircraft of the Pacific Ocean Fleet's 36th MTAP [*minno-torpednyi aviatsionnyi polk*, or torpedo aviation regiment) was attacked over the Yellow Sea by 11 F4U Corsairs from VF-53 (from the carrier

Valley Forge). The Soviet aircraft was on a training flight and was attacked and shot down by US Navy fighters without any justification – all three members of the crew perished.

A little more than a month later, on 8 October 1950 in the Maritime District, deep within Soviet territory and 100 kilometers from the Soviet-Korean border, at 1617 local time, two USAF F-80 fighters that had penetrated Soviet airspace in the vicinity of Lake Khanko attacked the Soviet Sukhaia Rechka military airbase, where the Kingcobra-equipped 821st IAP was based at the time. The regiment was preparing to conduct planned training exercises in the given Maritime area. The two American jet fighter-bombers unexpectedly appeared from behind a low range of hills, and having made a climbing turn over the airfield, dove upon some loaded and fueled parked aircraft that were on standby status, and attacked them with all their onboard weapons. The attack was so unexpected that no one understood who was attacking or why. Then the regiment command made an unwise decision and refused to launch readied aircraft to intercept the intruders. The regiment commander believed that this would lead to greater losses and casualties.

As a result, the pair of F-80s without any interference, having sealed the Soviet airfield, conducted two attacks upon the parked Kingcobras before slipping away with impunity into North Korean airspace. Fortunately, there were no casualties, not even any wounded. However, eight of the 821st IAP's aircraft were damaged, but only one of them had to be written-off. The remaining seven Kingcobras were quickly made serviceable.

In connection with this incident, a vigorous protest was delivered to the American side, but the Americans only expressed regret over it. They viewed the matter as a case of misunderstanding. As they explained it, two young pilots of the USAF 49th FBG had mistakenly crossed into Soviet airspace, misperceived the Soviet airfield as a North Korean one, and attacked it.

Of course, this was all simply a diplomatic smoke screen. In reality, the incident was a deliberate provocation on the part of the United States, because the weather on this day was clear with an unlimited ceiling, and it was impossible to become disoriented. In addition, the parked aircraft were clearly marked with Soviet recognition symbols and the approach route of the F-80s indicated a well-planned operation.

The cited incidents only sharpened the already tense situation on the border with Korea, which had drawn additional Soviet ground and air units to the area (five Soviet motorized divisions were ready to be sent to Korea). In addition, the incidents nudged the Soviet leadership to take more decisive steps with respect to rendering assistance to the PDRK. A flood of Soviet weapons poured into the Far East and into China as well, including the new aviation jet equipment – MiG-15 fighters.

Already in the second half of October 1950, four jet-equipped Soviet IAD arrived in China: the 328th IAD (with the 126th IAP and the 57th and 137th GIAP, as well as the separate 180th GIAP from the 15th GIAD, which became part of the newly created 20th IAD that was strengthening Beijing's air defenses), the 17th IAD (with the 28th and 445th IAP), and the 144th IAD PVO (consisting of the 383rd and 439th IAP). Each regiment was equipped with 30-32 MiG-9, one or two Yak-17 trainers, one Yak-11 and one Po-2. The main assignment of these Soviet aviation divisions was to retrain Chinese and North Korean pilots to fly jet aircraft. The primary combat aircraft in the cited aviation divisions was the MiG-9 fighter, which was already by this time too outdated to take on the jets of the US Fifth Air Force in battle. The Soviet pilots of these newly arrived aviation divisions began training the flight personnel of our allies already in October.

In October 1950, a new Soviet IAD, which received the designation 50th IAD, began to form up on the Liaodong Peninsula. It was organized on the basis of two regiments with experienced pilots, and was armed with MiG-15 jets that had just arrived in Liaodong. Colonel A.I. Khalutin was in charge of forming the division. This division was created especially for participation in combat operations in the skies of Korea.

In addition, in October 1950 the 186th ShAD from the Zabaikal Military District's 45th Air Army was sent to China. It had been necessary to form on its basis an attack aviation division consisting of two regiments with 30 Il-10 attack aircraft in each, plus an additional separate attack regiment.

In the month of November 1950, two more Soviet aviation divisions arrived in the PRC. These were the 297th IAD with its subordinate 304th and 401st IAP (equipped with La-11s), and the 162nd BAD, on the basis of which the PLAAF 8th BAD was to be formed (consisting of the 838th and 970th BAP, each with 30 Tu-2 high-speed bombers) and sent to Mukden by 10 November. In addition, several dozen Soviet instructors arrived in China to teach in the flight schools of the PRC and the PDRK.

Finally, at the end of summer 1950, at the insistence of the North Koreans, Stalin offered a compromise to Pyongyang and sent a telegram with the following contents to Comrade Shtykov at the Soviet Embassy in North Korea:

> To Comrade SHTYKOV, for Comrade KIM IL SUNG.
> I received your telegram about the preparation of pilot cadres with a delay due to technical problems.
> According to the opinion of our military leaders, it is most expedient to solve this problem in the following manner:
> 1. Organize the preparation of 200-300 pilots from among the ranks of Korean students on the territory of MANCHURIA at the already operational flight school in YANGTZE. Soviet instructors will be sent for this supplementary contingent of trainees.
> 2. The preparation of pilots for two jet fighter regiments can be organized by one of our MiG-15 divisions, which is located in MANCHURIA. After the training of the pilots, our MiG-15 airplanes will be turned over to the North Koreans for this complement.
> As concerns the preparation of pilots for one bomber aviation regiment, it will be more convenient to train them in our Korean school in the Maritime District. The equipment, Tu-2 aircraft, will also be turned over to the bomber regiment.
> 3. We are in agreement to accept another 120 men into our Korean flight school located in the Maritime for the training of their aviation technicians and ground attack pilots.
> 4. It will be better for the Korean pilots to receive flying practice there, where they will be trained, that is to say in MANCHURIA and with us in the Maritime District.
> In the case of your agreement with these proposals, our military command will be given the corresponding orders.
>
> Fyn Si [Stalin]

Naturally, in the Soviet leadership no one could disagree with Stalin and of course all of these directives, which were spelled out in the given code message under the contrived Chinese family name of Fyn Si, were immediately accepted by the leadership and implemented straight away.

The Korean flight school, which Stalin mentioned in the coded message to Comrade Shtykov, was located near Khorol' in the Maritime District. Colonel (in reserve) Vasilii Nikolaevich Sinkevich, a former instructor of the Amavir Military Aviation School for Pilots, trained the North Korean pilots in this school. Here is what he recalls of those distant events:

> In the summer of 1950 I was an instructor at the Amavir Military Aviation School for Pilots, with the rank of senior lieutenant. Somewhere around July-August 1950 a group of 12-14 instructors was selected in the Amavir aviation school. From our training aviation regiment, I and Senior Lieutenant Valerii Ivanovich Gumenlikov wound up in this group. A captain was appointed as the group's senior in command, an Ossete by nationality, whose name, alas, I've already forgotten. We were all training specialists for the Yak-3 and Yak-9.
>
> They took us across the entire country aboard a train to the Maritime [District] at the end of summer 1950, and we set up operations around the city of Khorol'. Soon several dozen Koreans arrived, who we were supposed to train to fly Yak-3 fighters. Several training aviation squadrons were created, each with three instructors, who were also the flight commanders. The commanders of the aviation squadrons and their deputies were also from among the Soviet instructors.
>
> We trained the Koreans in the Yak-3 and dual cockpit Yak-7 fighters. Each squadron had its own airfield and operated autonomously, that is to say, without communication with the other training squadrons. All the Yak-3s were without identification markings and in the standard light green color.
>
> I was a flight commander in one of the training squadrons, and it fell to me to train four Korean cadets: Kim Shi Bom, Pak Tae Il, Kim Im Chan and Pak Dae Du. The arriving students already had some flying experience, since recently they had completed something like one of our aviation clubs. They were all young fellows, 18-19 years of age, but none of them yet had any combat experience against the Americans.
>
> Frequently the commander of the KPAAF came by the aviation school; he was a former pilot in the Japanese air force, who after the end of the Second World War flew from South Korea to North Korea and who enjoyed the enormous respect of the North Korean pilots. He came to check on the preparation of his subordinates. The weakest pilots were kicked out of the training squadron and sent to a training squadron that prepared pilots on the Po-2, and they learned to drop bombs from this airplane.
>
> In my flight, the cadet Kim Shi Bom, who was an excellent shot, particularly stood out. On one flight to practice firing at a towed target sleeve, he almost shot down my airplane, which was towing the sleeve, because he was distracted by his attack upon the target. We taught the Koreans not only piloting skills, but also their combat application. During the entire time of training, we never had a single breakdown or crash.

As a result, by the beginning of 1951 after five months of training, we had fully prepared the entire group of Korean pilots and handed them over to the KPAAF. On this occasion, a large banquet was organized in the school, after which all the Korean pilots were assembled and shipped off to China. All the Yak-3 airplanes remained at the aviation school.

After we had prepared almost an entire regiment of Korean pilots, all the instructors were sent to various flight schools in the USSR, and we were forbidden to talk about what we'd been doing in the Maritime District. After our departure, a different group of instructors from the Amavir Military Aviation School for Pilots arrived in the Maritime and took our place. I myself returned to the Amavir school, where I continued to train our cadets.

Simultaneously, young Chinese pilots, who had recently completed training in PRC aviation schools were also preparing for combat in the Korean skies with the Soviet pilots. Here's how the former commander of the PLAAF, Hero of the People's Republic of China Wang Hai, who fought in the Korean War and became an ace, describes the training of the Chinese pilots for aerial combat above Korea in his memoirs:

… For the rendering of assistance to Korea, which had become enveloped in the flames of war, and for ensuring the security of our Motherland, the Central Committee of the Chinese Communist Party and Chairman Mao Zedong in response to a request of the Korean Workers' Party and the government of the PDRK announced a policy of "War of resistance to American aggression and the rendering of assistance to the Korean people", created the Chinese People's Volunteer Army under the deputy commander of the PLA Peng Dehuai, which crossed the Yalu River and, entering into war together with the heroic Korean People's Army, delivered a blow to the American aggressors.

The people of all of China participated in the movement "We will defend the Motherland!" The young PLAAF, which declared its burning desire to take part in the war, also actively responded to the call of the Party and the State. At the time, the central government of China, experiencing an acute shortage of resources for resolving the most various tasks, expended them for the purchase of aircraft and the construction of air bases. Then all the peoples of the country began to collect money to purchase airplanes.

Because of the changes that were taking place in the global arena, the PLA shifted its efforts from preparing for the liberation of Taiwan to participation in the "War of resistance against American aggression". Urgent measures were taken in the air force as well, which accelerated the formation of new units. After the 4th SmAB was formed, on 1 October 1950 the 3rd IAB [fighter aviation brigade] was being formed in Shenyang, consisting of the 7th, 8th and 9th IAP. The 209th Separate Infantry Division and its 625th, 626th and 627th Infantry Regiments provided the bulk of the cadres of this brigade. The commandant of the 5th Aviation School Fang Ziyi was placed in command of the 3rd IAB, while the former commander of the 209th Infantry Division Gao Houliang became its political commissar.

In the last ten days of October 1950, 88 graduates of the 4th, 5th and 6th Flight Schools arrived and embarked upon intensive training. The 4th SmAB, which had arrived here from Shanghai, on 28 October, was reformed as the 4th IAB; Fang Ziyi became its commander, while the commander of the 4th SmAB's 10th Regiment Xia Boshiung temporarily took command of the 3rd IAB. The former commissar of the 4th SmAB Li Shian became the commissar of the 3rd IAB. At this time at the decision of the Central Military Council, the table of organization for an air force aviation brigade was changed from three regiments to two regiments. The 10th IAP and the 12th IAP (the former 7th IAP of the 4th IAB) joined the 3rd IAB. The 8th IAP of the 3rd IAB became the 7th IAP.

On 31 October at the instruction of Chairman Mao, the brigades were renamed as divisions, while at the same time the indication of whether it belonged to fighter aviation or bomber aviation was dropped. Accordingly, the 3rd and 4th IAB became the air force's 3rd and 4th Aviation Divisions [AD].

On 25 November, the 2nd AD was formed in Shanghai, with most of its personnel coming from the Eastern China Military District. The 11th AP, which had previously been part of the 4th SmAB, provided the basis for the new aviation division, while at the same time its identification changed to the 4th AP. From personnel of the 208th Separate Infantry Division's 624th Infantry Regiment, the second regiment of the 2nd AD was formed, which received designation as the 6th AP. Liu Shanben was appointed commander of the 2nd AD, and his commissar was Zhang Baichun.

After the formation of these units and formations, with the assistance of Soviet aviators, flying and combat training were urgently initiated. Since the 3rd AD lacked experienced pilots, I and several other former pilots of the 4th SmAB's 10th and 11th AP carried out our duties as squadron commanders and leaders of the regimental flight until the end of 1959. I was appointed commander of the 1st Aviation Squadron of the 3rd AD's 9th AP.

The command of the 3rd AD had rich combat experience. Both the commander of the division Xia Boxun and Yang Bin, who soon replaced the former in this post, as well as the political commissar Gao Houliang, were long-time veterans of the Chinese Red Army who had taken part in its Long March. The first two men during the war against Japan had been flight instructors in aviation units in the province of Xinjiang. The deputy commander of the division, Ji Tingxie, the chief of staff Wang Fuhua, the chief of the political department Luo Ping all participated in the war against Japan as members of the 8th Army. They all had long years of service, had seen much, knew a lot, and possessed high moral-political qualities and combat experience. Therefore, the units under their command, which had only been formed several months previously, displayed energy and demonstrated high combat spirits.

A strong leadership staff in the regiments had also been selected. Other than one pilot, all the others had come from the infantry. In my 9th Regiment, the commander Han Jinbiao, the commissar Wang Jikui, the deputy commander Lin Hu (he was a pilot and my classmate at the old aviation school in northeastern China), the deputy political commissar Zhou Zongchang, and the chief of staff Jiang Wenhua – all came to the air force from the infantry. They were all combat-hardened, and had command experience and leadership in battle.

In our squadron, most of the pilots came from the infantry. The commissar Xu Shunian had been serving in the 8th Army since 1938 and was the personal bodyguard of the commander Zhu De and General Wang Zhen, who later became a political worker. He'd never studied aviation, but he had experience that he'd gained in the 8th Army, knew people, and managed well with ideological work. Deputy squadron commander Zhou Fengxing, flight commander Zhang Zi (who later became squadron commander) and the pilots Jiao Jingwen, Liu Delin, Ma Baotang, Feng Quanmin, Yan Junwu, Tian She, Ma Lianyu, as well as flight commander Sun Shenlu, who arrived from the 2nd Aviation Squadron – all had passed through the school of combat in the infantry and were later sent to flight schools. They were all distinguished by their businesslike natures, high senses of responsibility, organizational skills and personal discipline. They were not afraid to sacrifice their lives, and were brave and resolute. Despite their youth, they were all mature men. I, a squadron commander, was also one of the pilots; we lived together from day to day, trained together, felt like brothers and together created a strong combat collective.

I arrived in the 9th Aviation Regiment at a time of the most intense training. The commander rose at 5 o'clock in the morning each day, in order to prepare the flights. At the very first stage, Soviet combat pilots helped us organize the training, preparing us individually according to their qualifications. They worked with us with enthusiasm, and we studied conscientiously, so that we mastered very quickly the complex of steps necessary to organize flights. Subsequently we independently conducted the planning and carrying out of flight and combat training.

The higher command gave the task to accelerate the flight training, to master the equipment and technology, and to enter combat as soon as possible. Our preparations were divided into two stages. In the first three months, we finished work on flight basics, primarily practicing take-offs, landings, flight navigation, and flying in pairs; we studied the zone of operations, rehearsed individual aerial combat techniques, and conducted mock combats with a wingman against a solitary target, high altitude flights with a wingman, and combats involving an entire flight. Then over the next two months we finished our work on combat techniques, primarily by learning to intercept in pairs and in full flights, and flying as a flight, in two flights, and in full regimental formations. We practiced dogfight techniques against individual targets, photoreconnaissance of ground targets, and conducted high-altitude practice missions in two-flight formations. Pilots who learned to master their weapons and how to squeeze every bit of their aircraft's performance characteristics in combat, despite temperatures of -20 or -30C. were promoted and became trainers themselves. Even on China's traditional spring holiday they didn't rest, but flew as usual. The ground crews also rose early each morning and turned in late, scrupulously serving and checking the aircraft and ensuring the pilot's safety. The regular personnel at every level were continually at the airfield, in collectives, directing the training, revealing and resolving problems, and ensuring a successful course of training.

Thanks to the combined efforts, the plan of training was successfully implemented; on average each pilot had 56 hours and 53 minutes of flight time, with a maximum of 73 hours and 50 minutes, and a minimum of 44 hours and 57 minutes. In a short period of time, the techniques of piloting and the combat use of the MiG-15 fighter were mastered.

On 25 April 1951, the division joined the combat roster of the PLAAF.

To Wang Hai's narrative, it is necessary to add that those Soviet pilots who prepared the Chinese pilots of the 3rd IAD for combat in the Korean sky were from the Soviet 151st GIAD, which was the first to arrive in the PRC in the middle of August 1950. The former commander of the 72nd GIAP Lieutenant Colonel Alekandr Ivanovich Volkov spoke in more detail in his memoirs about the training of the Chinese pilots:

> As the commander of the 72nd GIAP, I arrived in China as part of the 151st GIAD at the beginning of August 1950. Our Guards aviation division had been sent to China with an important assignment: to create a Chinese air force, that is to say, to retrain the Chinese pilots to fly MiG-15s, after which we were to turn over the jets and all the support facilities to them. The division was based on former Japanese airfields with asphalt runways. My 72nd GIAP was in Anshan, the 28th GIAP was in Mukden (Shenyang), while the 139th GIAP was in Liaoyang. The cited air bases were unsuitable for MiGs, so the local Chinese leadership headed by Gao Han decided to construct new concrete runways as quickly as possible, which was in fact accomplished in a remarkably short time – 28 days, plus another two weeks for bringing in the necessary building supplies by rail.
>
> Already in September we were able to begin retraining those Chinese pilots who had 30 hours of flight time in Yak-11s. A unified group of pilot-instructors was created under the command of the assistant division commander for aerial gunnery, Colonel Vladimir Borisovich Provorikhin. This group of instructors began training Chinese pilots in Yak-17U trainers and to prepare them for solo flights in MiG-15s. By the start of November 1950, the training was basically completed, and the 4th IAD of the People's Liberation Army Air Force began to form from the trained pilots at the Liaoyang airfield – the first Chinese air force division with a two-regiment table of organization to fly jets.
>
> By the middle of November, the formation of this division was finished. Fang Ziyi was appointed to command the division. He was an experienced commander with extensive combat experience in the army, who had completed our flight school in Urumqi (Xinjiang) in 1942. Most of the division's command and flight staff consisted of pilots who had arrived from Shanghai's PVO, and who'd flown our piston-engine La-9 fighters, as well as aircraft from other countries (these were the pilots of the 10th IAP). One of these men, for example, was the regiment commander, Zhao Dahai. He'd flown to the mainland in a B-26 together with several other pilots. We retrained them in MiG-15 jets together with some young pilots, who'd graduated from flight schools in Yak-11s.
>
> At this time, the 151st GIAD was used to form the basis of a new aviation corps and was split into two divisions, both consisting of two regiments. The 28th and 72nd GIAP remained in the 151st IAD, while the 139th GIAP and the new 67th IAP, which soon departed to join Qingdao's PVO, became part of the newly formed 28th IAD.
>
> I was among a group of 15 men who were appointed as advisers to the PLAAF's 4th IAD. Heroes of the Soviet Union Nikolai Stroikov and Viktor Borobkov, who became advisers to the regiment commanders of the 4th IAD, were also in this group. Lieutenant Colonel Doroshenko was the chief of staff in our group, which included 10 men who were technical or rear staff officers. On 20 November we

transferred to Liaoyang and began to hammer together and further improve the units of the division.

It must be said right here that our small group did an enormous amount of work in a very short time, in order to train our subordinates to direct and command their units and elements, as well as to perfect the piloting techniques of the fliers, both alone and in a group, and in elements, flights and the entire squadron.

Approximately in March 1951, the division command reported to the PLAAF on the division's readiness to become part of the Chinese People's Volunteers. Party meetings were held, and then a full meeting, where the decision to join the ranks of the People's Volunteers was voted upon. At this time, Marshal Zhu De visited the division together with a large delegation of members of China's People's Assembly, who observed flight operations and were personally convinced that China now had its own jet pilots.

In the second half of March 1951, we moved to the forward airfield at Andong [Antung], where I.N. Kozhedub's aviation division was already based, and began to prepare for combat operations.

As already mentioned above, by the end of 1950 the pilot-instructors of the 151st GIAD had prepared almost 100 Chinese pilots on jet equipment; these men provided the skeleton staff of the newly created Chinese 3rd and 4th IAD. Then another group of Soviet advisors from the 151st IAD were sent to these divisions in order to conduct additional training and to assist the commanders of these Chinese IAD, which in April 1951 became part of the UAA [Unified Air Army] and began combat operations in the skies of the PDRK. Simultaneously with the flight school for pilots that had been established in Khorol', another aviation specialist school was created in the city of Vozzhaevka in Amur Oblast in order to train flight navigators for the KPAAF.

SOVIET PILOTS ENTER THE FIGHTING

The entry of armies of the Chinese People's Volunteers into combat operations on 19 October 1950 slowed the offensive of the U.S. and its allies deep within North Korean territory, but by 24 October, the front lines in places were now within 60-70 kilometers of the Chinese border. In the regions of Chosan and Unsan, forward American elements even reached the Yalu River, which marked the border between North Korea and Manchuria. However, on 25 October, forces of the NKPA and CPV launched a counteroffensive, which continued until 5 November and hurled UN forces away from the Yalu by 50-60 kilometers in the direction of Anju. The Soviet pilots of one aviation division, the 151st IAD, participated in this counteroffensive. To be honest, the combat task that was given to the Guards aviation division was of a purely defensive nature: not to cover the very front lines and the attacking NKPA and CPV troops, but instead to defend critical targets in the PDRK, which were being subjected to numerous attacks by the USAF. First and foremost, the 151st IAD was to protect the strategically important bridge across the Yalu not far from Andong, as well as Andong itself, in which there were supplies and CPV units, which were using this bridge to move into North Korea. The Soviet pilots were categorically forbidden to cross the Yalu River or to fly over the Yellow Sea's Korea Bay, in order to avoid becoming prisoners. The point is that the US Seventh Fleet and their allies reigned supreme in the Yellow Sea, while dozens of enemy diversionary-espionage groups were operating in the front line zone, which would have been delighted to capture a downed Soviet pilot.

The Soviet pilots entered the fighting incognito, since officially the Soviet Union was not involved in the war in Korea. Thus the first Soviet pilots wore CPV uniforms, had no personal documents that would have revealed their identities, and moreover they were ordered to use only Korean commands when in the air. For this purpose, in the course of a week they learned a couple of dozen Korean phrases that were necessary for conducting battle. To be honest, the latter ban against speaking Russian in battle didn't last long; once in action, the Soviet pilots quickly forgot the Korean phrases and communicated in Russian, more than once saving their life in battle by doing so.

By the end of October, the 151st IAD was dispersed among three airfields – the 72nd GIAP had remained at the Mukden-North Air Base; the 28th GIAP had flown to the Anshan airfield; and the 139th GIAP was stationed at Liaoyang. In the last ten days of October, Soviet pilots in their MiGs, equipped with external fuel tanks because their airfields were distant from the area of operations, began to conduct patrols along the Chinese-Korean border without violating the border itself. Our pilots were familiarizing themselves with the area of combat operations and simultaneously protecting PRC airspace and Andong itself, because the American pilots were frequently intruding into Chinese airspace and bombing Chinese towns and villages, including Andong. However, there was still no order to cross the border and enter combat over North Korea.

However, on 1 November 1950, just such an order arrived. In connection with the distance of their airfield complex from the area of combat operations, all the combat sorties were carried out in the Andong-Siniuju area, which also happened to be close to the front lines at the time. This is where the first clashes between Soviet and American pilots took place. At the time, units of the US Fifth Air Force were actively operating in the Siniuju-Singisiu region. American F-51 attack aircraft and F-80 fighter-bombers were particularly active in the given region – and thus it was with them that the first encounters with the Soviet pilots took place.

Early on the morning of 1 November 1950, several MiG-15 flights from the 72nd and 28th GIAP took off at an order from the division command post to patrol the border with the PDRK. Equipped with external fuel tanks, the MiG pilots for the first time were given authorization to cross over the Yalu into North Korean air space and to conduct free hunts in search of US aircraft.

Pilots of the 28th GIAP were the first to encounter the enemy. In the vicinity of Naamsi-dong, six MiG-15s spotted and attacked four F-51s, but with a sharp maneuver the Mustangs evaded the attack and departed the area at tree-top level. In essence there was no combat, because the enemy declined it.

The first combat occurred after lunch at 1250, when five MiGs under the command of Hero of the Soviet Union Major N. V. Stroikov, the commander of the 1st Squadron, were patrolling the Andong area. Captain I. A. Guts's lead element spotted three F-51s. Attacking from above, they opened fire on the enemy formation. Apparently damaged, one of the Mustangs broke formation and began to flee in a dive. The remaining pair of Mustangs went into a left-hand turn, but upon leveling out they were jumped by a different pair of MiGs, and in this attack Lieutenant Fedor Chizh succeeded in downing one of the F-51s from short range. Thus the Soviet pilots opened the scoring in this war, having shot down the first USAF aircraft in the skies of North Korea. The downed F-51 was from the 35th FBG's 39th Squadron – its pilot was killed.

On this same day at 1412, four MiG-15s led by the 72nd GIAP's 2nd Squadron commander Major A.Z. Bordun took off on a combat assignment for the Andong area. Major A.Z. Bordun, Senior Lieutenant A.I. Sukhov, and Lieutenants S.F. Khomich and D. Esiunin were piloting the MiGs on this mission. Having patrolled above Andong for 25 minutes and without having encountered any enemy aircraft, the flight received the order to return to base. Lieutenant Esiunin had already been forced to return, since his MiG had no external fuel tanks and was running low on fuel.

As they were turning back, Lieutenant Khomich saw 10 F-80 jets below them, flying in column formation: four F-80s were in the lead, followed by two F-80s at an interval of 500-800 meters, with the other four F-80s bringing up the rear at the same interval. Receiving the permission to attack from the leader, Lieutenant Khomich alone attacked the leading foursome of Shooting Stars and shot down one of them from short range, before climbing steeply away. The trailing four F-80s attempted to attack him, but their formation was jumped by Bordun's element in turn. Breaking off its attack, the F-80 flight fled the area. Our pilots made no effort to pursue them, because fuel was running low. One F-80 from the 51st FBG's 16th Squadron was destroyed – its pilot went missing-in-action.

Thus in the course of the first air-to-air battle between jet fighters of the contending sides, in which three MiG-15s took on 10 F-80s, the Soviet pilots emerged victorious. For his victory, Guards Lieutenant Semen Fedorovich Khomich was awarded the Order of the Red Banner.

The pilots of the 28th GIAP were unlucky on this day, because the group that had taken off from this regiment on a combat assignment never encountered enemy aircraft, either failing to spot them or because the American aircraft had avoided battle, while the Soviet pilots were forbidden to cross the front lines. Thus the first day of their war ended successfully for the pilots of the 151st IAD. Two victories had been scored, and one more US aircraft was probably damaged, without any loss on the Soviet side. According to the latest publications in the American press, on 1 November 1950 the USAF lost two F-80s and one F-51, not including seven aircraft of other types.

The first aerial combats in the skies of Korea also exposed the first difficulties. The distance of the Soviet air bases from the area of operations reduced the time available to the Soviet pilots to search for and engage enemy targets. The first combats had accordingly been brief. There was only a limited number of external fuel tanks in the division's supply stocks (their production was centered back in the Soviet Maritime District), thus the Soviet pilots had to conduct missions in small groups, and not always with external fuel tanks.

Moreover, a psychological factor weighed upon the Soviet pilots: after all, they had never before met American pilots in battle, and didn't know their combat tactics, attitudes and skill. The fact that the Americans had been our allies during World War II dampened the fighting spirit of the pilots, especially after witnessing the first human losses.

The Soviet pilots knew about the tactical and technical characteristics of the enemy aircraft only by hearsay, while only combat itself might show how these aircraft could perform in battle. On 1 November, the Soviet pilots engaged Mustangs from the 18th and 35th FBG, which they encountered repeatedly in the subsequent November battles.

In the first week of November, the Soviet pilots conducted combat patrols over the Sinuiju-Singisiu area, covering the strategically important bridge near Sinuiju, the airfield there, and the roads over which supplies were flowing in a continuous stream to the NKPA and CPV forces. However, the enemy air force, alarmed by the first encounter with the MiG jets, sharply curtailed its activity in the area of their operations, and upon spotting approaching MiGs, evaded combat and departed. Thus until 6 November the pilots of the 151st GIAD had only several scrapes with enemy aircraft that had no results.

However on 6 November 1950, the Mustangs of the 8th and 18th FBG renewed their operations in the 151st GIAD's area of responsibility, as a result of which several aerial clashes took place with them. The pilots of the 151st GIAD on this day conducted several combat missions, but only one of them was crowned with success: after lunch, a flight of pilots from the 72nd GIAP dueled with a flight of F-51s, and Senior Lieutenant N. K. Kuznetsov in one head-on attack shot down one of the Mustangs from the 18th FBG's 39th Squadron, killing the pilot.

The next day of combat, 7 November, was more intense for the Soviet pilots. On this day, pilots of the 28th GIAP also opened their combat score. The successful pilot was the deputy regiment commander and Hero of the Soviet Union Major V.I. Koliadin. At 1406, he took off for the area of Singisiu at the head of four MiGs, and at 1435 at an altitude of 6,500 meters, having spotted up to 15 Mustangs, he opened fire on the tail-end flight. When climbing out of this firing pass, Koliadin encountered four more F-51s. He attacked and fired upon it, forcing the enemy aircraft to turn away. At 1438 Koliadin observed a new group of Mustangs, consisting of 20 planes in an echelon formation. After maneuvering into position, he dove upon the second flight of this group from above and behind and opened fire at a range of 500 meters, registering strikes upon

Hero of the Soviet Union Colonel V.I. Koliadin, commander of the 28th GIAP (a postwar photograph).

one target that sent it plummeting earthward. After this our pilots broke off the battle because they were running low on fuel and returned to base. In this action, other pilots of Koliadin's fight also fired upon the Mustangs, and the leader of the second element Captain N.G. Pronin presumably downed a second Mustang, but the regiment only credited Major Koliadin with a victory.

On this same day, pilots of Major A.I. Guts's flight from the 72nd GIAP also distinguished themselves: at 1326, Captain Guts's flight encountered four F-51 in the area of Singisiu, and in a swift action the leader of the second element Senior Lieutenant A.E. Sanin shot down one F-51, while the others were driven away from the defended target.

The American acknowledged that there was a combat between four F-51s from the 36th FBS and four MiG-15s, but declared that the Mustangs suffered no losses. Another four-plane flight of Mustangs, this one from the 12th FBS, encountered four MiGs in the area of the Yalu, and Major Ken Karson supposedly shot down one of the Mig-15s in combat. However it is reliably known that on 7 November, the pilots of the 151st GIAD not only had no losses, but also suffered no damage to their aircraft in the action. The Americans on this day also lost two F-80 Shooting Stars from the 8th FBS, which after a battle with MiGs, ran out of fuel on their way back to base, and the pilots of these two F-80s had to abandon their aircraft.

The intensity of combat and the number of aircraft involved from both sides increased with every passing day. In connection with this it was decided to augment the Soviet air presence in the area of combat operations. This required an organizational overhaul and triggered a shuffling in command.

As mentioned in Lieutenant Colonel Volkov's testimony above, it was decided to organize a separate fighter aviation corps on the basis of the 151st GIAD. At the beginning of November, the 139th GIAP was withdrawn from the 151st GIAD and contributed personnel and equipment in order to create a new aviation regiment, designated the 67th IAP; its commander became Hero of the Soviet Union Major N.F. Pasko. On 1 November 1950, in response to an order from the USSR's War Minister dated 18 October 1950, the 28th IAD was formed at the Liaoyang Air Base to take command of the 139th and 67th IAP. The former deputy commander of the 151st GIAD, twice Hero of the Soviet Union Colonel Aleksei Vasil'evich Aleliukhin, became the commander of the newly-formed 28th IAD.

On 20 November 1950, the 50th IAD, which also had two fighter regiments (the 29th and the 177th), arrived at the Anshan Air Base from Shanghai. Together with the 151st GIAD and new 28th IAD, it was made subordinate to the newly created 64th IAK [istrebitel'nyi aviatsionnyi korpus, or fighter aviation corps]. The former commander of the 151st IAD Major General Ivan Vasil'evich Belov assumed command of the corps. Colonel A.Ia. Sapozhnikov, the former commander of the 28th GIAP, took Belov's place in command of the 151st GIAD. The Guards aviation division also now had a two-regiment table of organization, consisting of the 28th GIAP, whose commander was Hero of the Soviet Union Lieutenant Colonel Viktor Ivanovich Koliadin, and the 72nd GIAP, the commander of which remained as before Lieutenant Colonel Aleksandr Ivanovich Volkov.

The forming of the new aviation grouping was completed on 27 November 1950. On that date, the 28th, 50th and 151st IAD were all unified under the command of the 64th IAK.

Remains of Boeing B-29A-50-BN Superfortress 44-61813. The aircraft was converted to the F-13A Photo Recon configuration. Severely damaged by MiGs, it crash landed at Johnson AB, Japan November9 1950. (US Air Force)

These three Soviet fighter divisions of the new 64th IAK were all equipped with MiG-15s. The three aviation divisions together numbered 844 officers, 1,153 sergeants and 1,274 soldiers. The command of the new fighter corps was set up in Mukden, while its subordinate fighter divisions were based on the airfields of the Chinese cities Mukden, Anshan and Andong. The combat task of the 64th IAK was formulated by the Soviet military command and expressed as follows: to cover the crossings over the Yalu River, the hydroelectric stations on the river and the airfields in the area of Andong, and the North Korean supply arteries as far as the line Pyongyang – Wonsan. In conjunction with the fighter defense, the anti-aircraft defense was to prevent bombing attacks by the enemy air force on targets in northeast China along the Mukden axis.

The Soviet government made careful efforts to conceal its participation in the war from the West. Therefore in the course of the fighting, Soviet combatants were usually located distant from the front lines, while the 64th IAK's fighters were restricted by the Yellow Sea coast and the no-fly line between Pyongyang and Wonsan. Soviet pilots were strictly forbidden to wander beyond this limited area. The Soviet air units and anti-aircraft defense emplacements in China and North Korea also observed camouflage and concealment measures, carrying out their combat assignments in the uniform of the Chinese People's Volunteer Army.

As we have seen, pilots of the 151st GIAD were the first to enter combat on the morning of 1 November 1950. Because of the organizational changes discussed above, the 28th IAD didn't embark upon combat operations until 5 November, and at that only with the single 139th GIAP stationed in Liaoyang. The pilots of the 67th IAP entered the fighting a little later. However, until 8 November the pilots of this division on their patrol flights only rarely encountered American planes; more often, the enemy simply avoided combat.

The day 8 November marked a significant change: the enemy began the day with active air operations, launching a series of strikes on several important targets in the PDRK with large groups of F-51 attack aircraft, covered by F-80 jets. The first to take off to repulse the attacks were eight MiG-15s, led by the commander of the 72nd IAP's 3rd Squadron Major V.P. Afonin. In the area of Andong they spotted four F-51s on a meeting course. Major Afonin immediately downed one of the F-51s in a head-on pass, while the other Mustangs scattered in different directions. As it was pulling out of the attack, Afonin's flight was attacked by eight F-80s on a head-on course, which were covering the Mustangs. Another four Shooting Stars were diving to join the fray. In the head-on pass with the eight F-80s, an external fuel tank on Senior Lieutenant A.E. Sanin's MiG was hit, but he safely made it back to Mukden in his jet.

Senior Lieutenant Kharitonov's 2nd Flight, which was flying above Afonin's flight when the action started, was also attacked by 10 F-80s, and then closed with four Shooting Stars in a head-on pass, but these brief engagements ended with no results and our pilots returned to their base.

The Americans believed that one of the departing MiG-15s had been downed and credited it to the 16th Squadron's 1st Lieutenant Russell Brown, the first official victory of USAF pilots over MiG-15 jets. However, as it turned out, 1st Lieutenant Brown had only lightly damaged A. E. Sanin's jet, and the very next day he took off on another mission in it. Thus, the Americans' "first victory" over the MiG-15 didn't in fact happen!

Major Afonin's group landed in Mukden at 0938, just as eight more MiGs of the 139th IAP's 3rd Squadron, under the command of squadron commander Captain M. Pakhomov, were taking off in Liaoyang for a combat assignment. When flying to the patrol area, Captain L.D. Shchegolov and his wingman became separated from the rest of the flight. Accelerating to close up with it again, Shchegolov spotted three F-51s that were attacking his wingman, who had moved in front of him. Shchegolov immediately moved to counter the Mustangs on a meeting course, and in the head-on pass shot down one F-51 with two bursts – the burning F-51 fell in the Andong area, which was confirmed by his wingman Senior Lieutenant P.M. Kustov and the auxiliary command post in this area.

At 1133, another flight of eight MiGs from the 28th GIAP, headed by Captain A.I. Akimov, took off on a combat mission. In the Andong area, the flight spotted one group of F-51s and fired upon it, then came across a second group of four F-51s. Attacking it, Captain Akimov shot down one of them, while the others evaded and escaped. A final group of eight MiGs from the 28th GIAP took off at 1343 and encountered six F-51s during its patrol, but the brief action ended with no results.

The pilots of the 64th IAK on 8 November had again dueled with Mustangs from the 18th FBG, and they had achieved three victories. The Americans, in addition to Brown's "victory", claimed an additional "probable": four F-51s of the 35th Squadron had tangled with four MiGs near the Yalu River, and supposedly 1st Lieutenant Harris Boys downed one of the Soviet jets. However, it is known reliably that on 8 November 1950, the 64th IAK had no losses.

The hottest days for the pilots of the 64th IAK were 9 and 10 November 1950, when through the joint efforts of the pilots from both divisions, several massed attacks against bridges across the Yalu in the areas of Andong and Singisiu were repulsed. Several dogfights developed with the participation of 50-60 aircraft from both sides. These two days of aerial combat became the most productive in terms of the number of achieved aerial victories.

At first on the morning of 9 November at 0900, seven MiGs from the 139th GIAP, under the command of the chief of the Regiment's aerial gunnery service Captain V. P. Bochkov, took off to intercept an attack by USNAF piston-engine fighter-bombers. In the area of the Andong bridge, the Soviet pilots spotted a large formation of enemy piston-engine aircraft that were attempting to destroy this strategically vital target. Corsairs and Skyraiders from the aircraft carrier *Philippine Sea*'s 11th Air Group were targeting the bridge. The attack formation included eight AD-2 from Squadron VA-115, approximately 20 F4U Corsairs from VF-113 and VF-114, which were being covered from above by two flights of eight F9F Panther jets each from VF-111 and VF-112.

It was with these American fighters and fighter-bombers that the pilots of the 139th GIAP collided above the bridge across the Yalu. In essence, this was the baptism of fire for the pilots of the 1st Squadron of this Guards regiment; in their combat ardor, they plunged into the thick of the enemy aircraft, and a wild melee erupted. The 1st Squadron commander Captain M.F. Grachev and the overall group leader Captain V.B. Bochkov themselves became caught up in the action, and in the heat of battle, failed to direct the combat or their subordinates. Thus the squadron formation disintegrated into isolated elements and solitary aircraft – each caught up in its own battle and failing to provide cover to each other. Despite these mistakes, the Soviet pilots fought bravely against superior enemy numbers, and in the swirling action, the enemy fighter-bombers were unable to release their bombs on the bridge with any accuracy. In this battle, the squadron commander Captain Grachev fought heroically on his own, and according to the testimony of other participants, personally shot down two or three American aircraft. Group commander Captain Bochkov also downed one Skyraider. After the significant losses at the hands of the MiGs, the attack aircraft began to flee the area – just when the covering Panther flights pounced on the scattered MiGs from above. One flight of four Panthers under the command of Captain W.T. Amen, the commanding officer of VF-111, managed to catch a solitary MiG in a pincer movement and shot it up from their 20mm guns at point-blank range. Thus, the first Soviet pilot-internationalist Captain Mikhail Fedorovich Grachev was killed in this battle. This was the first combat loss of the 64th IAK and simultaneously the first genuine officially confirmed victory of US pilots (and US Navy pilots) over an enemy jet in the form of a MiG-15 fighter.

The other pilots of the 139th GIAP were also attacked by the Panthers, but exploiting the MiG's superiority, they successfully countered these attacks and turned the tables on the Panthers. As a result one of them was shot down by Lieutenant N.I. Sannikov, and the remaining began to exit the battle. However during their departure, one flight of F9F-2 was unexpectedly attacked from below by Senior Lieutenant A.I. Stulov, who shot up one of the F9F-2 from point-blank range. Here is how Aleksandr Ivanovich Stulov recalls this combat almost 55 years later:

US Navy Skyraiders from the USS *Valley Forge* fire 5-inch wing rockets at North Korean communist field positions, October 24, 1950. (US Navy)

A US Navy AD-3 dive bomber pulls out of a dive after dropping a 2000 lb bomb on the Korean side of a bridge crossing the Yalu River at Sinuiju, into Manchuria. Note anti-aircraft gun emplacement on both sides of the river. November 15, 1950. (US Navy)

Then the next patrol of 9 November 1950 took place. The 1st Squadron with a complement of 8 or 10 aircraft took off at an alert signal. The squadron was being commanded by either Grachev or the regiment's new navigator Bochkov – I can't say exactly. It was 160 kilometers from the air base to Andong. The enemy air force was targeting the railroad bridge linking the territory of China with that of North Korea. For this purpose they used B-29 bombers, piston-engine Thunderbolt attack aircraft [more likely the AD-4 Skyraider], and twin fuselage aircraft named the Black Widow [more likely the F-82 Twin Mustang]. They had the top cover of Shooting Star jet fighters. I was Grachev's wingman; I can no longer name the other pilots on the mission – I've simply can't recall them after so many years. With all our aircraft, we went after the attack aircraft that were bombing the bridge, but they were at low altitudes that aren't very advantageous for jet fighters. A complete "fur ball" resulted and it was impossible to distinguish where your planes were and where the enemy planes were, or who was attacking whom. Moreover, these piston-engine aircraft were more maneuverable than ours and evaded out from under our attacks. It was impossible for us to steepen the angle of our dives, since we were right above the ground. In these conditions all of our aircraft scattered and we lost all coordination, not because we wanted this, but because of the situation that had developed. I, for example, attacked a Black Widow [again, more likely a Twin Mustang], but it spotted me before I could close within firing range and with a sharp, diving turn passed below me. Reversing, it then gave a wild burst at my aircraft. I went after a Thunderbolt [Skyraider], but it also didn't allow me to close within firing range. However, we carried out our task: we had disrupted the attack on the bridge.

When there were no longer any aircraft over the bridge, I started to climb to regain altitude and spotted four Shooting Stars in a compact formation, on a northward heading. I set out in pursuit of them, having first taking a look around me. Within 3 or 4 minutes, I had closed with them, making sure I stayed behind and below them so that they couldn't see me. Then, when I had drawn within 50 meters, I took careful aim and fired a short burst with everything I had. However, it happened that I encountered some turbulence in their slipstream just as I fired, which threw off my aim, and the burst went wide of the lead aircraft. I had been just a split second late in opening fire. The left-hand wingman broke left into a descending turn. There was nothing left for me to do than to follow him, cutting off his turn, and I fired a couple of more bursts at him. It looked like I had fatally stricken his plane, so I climbed away and took a quick look around, but the other three aircraft were nowhere in sight. I went into a shallow dive and headed back to base at high speed, because I didn't have much fuel left.

This was the first, and I would say, disorganized dogfight, which no one was directing in the air or from the ground. From my point of view, it would have been better for the first flight to attack in pairs and for the second flight to provide cover; then, when the first flight had pulled out of its attacking pass, to swap roles and to use the radio.

All of our aircraft returned to base one by one, except for Grachev's MiG. All the pilots were worried about him, but I suffered even more, because I knew him better than anyone else, both as a comrade and as a pilot. For about a week, no one knew what had happened with him. Then Captain Rudokovsky, the squadron's adjutant appeared, and delivered a small paper-wrapped bundle that weighed about 2 kilograms. It held all that remained of Grachev. The command decided to send me to Port Arthur for the burial of the remains, and gave me two sergeants to assist me. I pressed Rudokovsky to tell me everything he knew. He told me that they had located the place of our aircraft's crash, inside Chinese territory approximately 15-20 kilometers from the Korean border. He added that American jets had shot him down, and that there had been four of them. As I supposed, after the initial action against the piston-engine attack aircraft, he had relaxed and become less vigilant, which the enemy exploited, and having closed upon him from behind unnoticed, riddled his aircraft, after which his aircraft plunged to the ground.

Lieutenant Samuil Kumonaev shot down one more Panther in this scrap. It had been attacking his wingman, Senior Lieutenant M.I. Bolodin.

Thus the Soviet pilots in this action knocked down five or six US aircraft, but the regiment was credited with only two: one F9F-2 and one AD-2. Captain M.F. Grachev's supposed victories went uncounted, since he had been fighting alone, while his gun camera film burned up together with the aircraft. Therefore credit for any of his victories didn't go to the regiment, or else they were attributed to anti-aircraft gunners, who were also protecting this bridge and took part in repelling the attack. The command of the USNAF in Korea recognized the loss of only one of its F9F-2 Panthers from VF-51, the pilot of which was rescued. However, there are data that show that three Corsairs were lost at the beginning of November in combat actions, but the Americans still haven't released information about the exact dates when they were lost.

The losses of the 139th GIAP in this battle might have been even greater, since they had fought without any organization or cohesion. However, the pilots were bailed out by the combat experience that they had acquired in the Great Patriotic War and the MiG-15's superior performance.

A little later, just after 1000, six MiGs from the 72nd GIAP under the command of Major A.Z. Bordun took off for the Singisiu area. Once in the area, they spotted a single B-29 bomber being escorted by 16 F-80s. Senior Lieutenant A. Rodionov tied up the covering fighters in combat, while Bordun's element attacked the B-29 in turn. First to attack the bomber (an RB-29 reconnaissance aircraft No.44-61813 from the 91st SRS [Strategic Reconnaissance Squadron]) was the wingman Lieutenant A.M. Dymchenko, who fired at the B-29 at a range of 100 meters out to 800 meters, and then again at 400 meters. Next Major Bordun made a firing pass and opened up on the Superfortress from a range of 300-400 meters. The flashes of shells striking the B-29 were visible, which left the bombers's two left engines burning. Lieutenant Dymchenko attacked again and finished off the B-29; the bomber erupted in flames and its gunners were no longer firing at Dymchenko's MiG, and soon the burning B-29 fell into some clouds.

Senior Lieutenant Rodionov's flight also successfully engaged the two flights of covering F-80s, preventing them coming to the aid of the B-29, and presumably downed one Shooting Star. True, it wasn't credited to the regiment. We had no losses in this action.

Some time later, groups of MiGs from the 28th, 72nd and 139th GIAP took off at intervals of time to repulse an enemy raid in the Andong – Singisiu area, because the enemy attack lasted until 1453. In this period of time, several more clashes with American aircraft took place. For example, in the afternoon four MiGs of the 72nd GIAP under the command of Hero of the Soviet Union Major N.V. Stroikov took off on a mission to the Singisiu area. Over the target they encountered four F-80 Shooting Stars and engaged them in battle. In the course of the scrap, the element of Major N.V. Stroikov and Captain V.N. Kaznacheev so successfully attacked a pair of F-80s, that when the Shooting Stars maneuvered to evade the attack, they collided and fell in fragments to the ground. They were credited to the score of Stroikov and Kaznacheev. The remaining F-80s immediately departed without carrying out their assignment.

Thus, on 9 November the pilots of the 64th IAK tallied up to seven victories. Two F-80s, three F9F-2s, one AD-2 and one B-29 were downed, with only one loss in return.

According to American records, two downed MiG-15s were registered on this day: one (Captain Grachev's) was credited to Lt. Colonel Emmon of VF-111, while one more went to a gunner aboard the RB-29, Sgt. Kerry Lewin of the 91st Strategic Reconnaissance Squadron. However, it is reliably known that in the battle with the RB-29, none of the MiGs were even damaged, so on this occasion as well, the Americans were hasty in claiming a victory. On the other hand, according to American information, the RB-29 that had been damaged by Bordun and Dymchenko actually managed to struggle back to its base in Japan, where it crashed when making a forced landing, and five of its crew perished.

On 10 November 1950, at 0908 at a call from the auxiliary command post, eight MiGs under the command of Captain S.I. Korobov, the 28th GIAP's 3rd Squadron commander, sortied from the Mukden-North Air Base. Korobov was leading the attack flight, while Senior Lieutenant Pronin's covering flight was staggered to the left, about 800 meters behind and 1,500 meters above. On the approach to the assigned area, Korobov received an order from the auxiliary command post to go to the assistance of Major A.Z. Bordun's group, which was involved in a dogfight 15-20 kilometers south of Andong. Reaching the combat area at an altitude of 6,000 meters, at 0930 they spotted four groups of enemy aircraft inbound from the Yellow Sea at an altitude of 5,000 meters. The first and second groups consisted of four F-51 Mustangs each, while the third group had six F-51s. Four F-80s were covering the Mustangs. Korobov maneuvered into position and with his flight attacked the first group from above and behind at a target aspect angle of 0/4.[4] They pulled out of the attack at an angle and climbed toward the sun. In this attack, Captain S.I. Korobov shot down one F-51 and the formation broke apart. Startled, two of the other Mustangs collided in the air – one plummeted to the earth, while the other, damaged, limped away from the combat area.

As noted by the auxiliary command post's order, at 0908 six more MiGs under the command of Major A.Z. Bordun from the 72nd GIAP had left Mukden to repel an enemy air strike in the region of Andong. As Bordun's group was conducting a left-hand turn over the target area, Senior Lieutenant A.M. Dymchenko caught sight of one B-29 bomber at an altitude of 4,000 meters, and reported this over the radio. At the leader's command, the group began to close in for an attack. At this moment, a second B-29 was spotted, which having dropped its bombs, began to head toward the Yellow Sea in a right-hand turn. During the attempt to attack the first B-29, Bordun's group was jumped by two flights of four F-80 Shooting Stars each from above and behind, to the right and the left. Pulling out from under the attack in a chandelle to the left, Major Bordun attacked one of the F-80 flights from behind at a target angle of 1/4, and shot down one of the F-80s at a range of 600 meters. At this point, three more flights of F-80s, with eight fighters in each, were approaching the battle, and the first attempted to attack Dubrovin's element, but it evaded and in turn attacked eight F-80s on a meeting course, opening fire at 1,000 meters. Soon the group at Bordun's order exited the battle in a dive. The enemy made no attempt to pursue. At the authorization of the auxiliary command post, the group returned to base.

At 1026, eight more MiGs from the 139th GIAP's 2nd Squadron scrambled from the Liaoyang Air Base at an order from the 28th IAD command post to intercept another enemy attack group. Under the command of Major G.I. Khar'kovsky, at 1044 the group was approaching the Andong area at an altitude of 6,500 meters. At an order from the auxiliary command post, the group descended to 5,000 meters, and out in front of them, 16 kilometers away in an area east of Singisiu, they caught the glints of seven B-29 bombers, flying in a compact formation of a column of flights, being escorted by four F-51s. Having spotted the approaching MiGs, the bombers began a turn to the left. Leading the attack flight, Major Khar'kovsky and his wingman Lieutenant Iu.I. Akimov attacked the two trailing B-29s from below and behind, angling in from the left and the right. After the first aimed burst, the B-29 targeted by Khar'kovsky began to lag behind the rest of its formation. Khar'kovsky attacked it again from below and to the right, as a result of which the B-29 spouted flames. Burning, it fell in an area 25 kilometers northeast of Andong, which was confirmed by the auxiliary command post in Andong, other pilots in the group, and gun camera footage.

Lieutenant Akimov, who had attacked the other B-29, opened fire at it from a range of 600 meters and noticed that the tracers were passing behind the tail of the bomber. He ceased fire, shifted his MiG slightly to adjust his aim, and opened fire again. This time he saw his shells striking the center of the B-29. Before pulling out of the attack, Akimov noted fragments from the stricken B-29 falling away from the bomber. After the attack he formed up again with his leader. He began a repeat attack and caught sight of the bomber that had been attacked by Khar'kovsky falling away with its left wing on fire. After his second attack, Akimov watched his target, emitting smoke, fall away. Lieutenant Akimov received victory credit for this B-29, which was confirmed by the commander of the covering group Senior Lieutenant A.A. Zhdanovich, Major Khar'kovsky and gun camera footage.

Zhdanovich's flight attacked the remaining five B-29s from above and behind at great range, after which two of the B-29s fell back from the rest of the dwindling formation and descended into some clouds. The remaining three B-29s escaped beyond the Soviet no-fly line, so there was no pursuit. The pilots of Zhadovich's flight couldn't observe what happened to the two B-29s because of the poor visibility and the great range.

During the battle, the four F-51 escort fighters tried to get behind the leader of the second element of the attack group Senior Lieutenant Kapranov. His wingman Lieutenant I.I. Kakurin drove off the enemy attack, after which the Mustangs left the combat area. According to Kakurin's after-action report, these were F-82 Twin Mustangs, and that when repelling their attack on Kapranov, he had fatally damaged one of them, but he received no confirmation for this victory.

At 1053, with no enemy aircraft remaining in the area, Major Khar'kovsky gathered his group at a command from the auxiliary command post in Andong and returned to his home base without any losses. As a result of the fighting on 10 November, the pilots of the 64th IAK repelled several enemy attack groups, including the attack of the seven B-29s from the 307th BG on Uiju, and downed five enemy aircraft: two B-29s, two F-51s and one F-80. In the day's actions, the 64th IAK had no losses; only Lieutenant Kakurin's MiG received any damage, a bullet hole through his fuel tank, but he safely returned to base. The Americans acknowledge the loss of two Mustangs on this day and only one B-29.

On 11 November 1950, the 64th IAK had only one aerial engagement, but it was sufficiently bitter. At 1400 at a call from the Andong auxiliary command post, four MiGs led by the commander of the 28th GIAP Major Koliadin took off from the Anshan Air Base. In the area of Andong, at 1424 Koliadin's flight was attacked from above and behind by a group of 20 F-80s. In order to evade the attack, Koliadin banked sharply into a climbing left-hand turn. In doing so, the combat formation came apart, and the further combat was conducted in separate elements. Koliadin's wingman Captain Akimov drove off the attack on his leader and downed one of the F-80s, when he noticed that the wingman of the second element Senior Lieutenant M.P. Nasonov had not followed Koliadin in his climbing turn, but had continued flying straight ahead. Koliadin and the leader of the second element, the commander of the 2nd Squadron Hero of the Soviet Union Major V.D. Borovkov, having evaded the initial enemy attack, urgently ordered over the radio: "No. 23, you have enemy on your tail, break away!" Nasonov gave no indication that he heard the warning and continued a level turn to the left at an angle of about 30 degrees, but at this moment an F-80 opened fire at him from a range of 50 meters. Nasonov's MiG began to fall in a controlled, left-hand spiral. Borovkov went to the aid of his wingman Senior Lieutenant Nasonov, dropped onto the tail of the attacking F-80 element, and closing the range from 500 to 200 meters, shot down one of the Shooting Stars from behind. At this point Borovkov was jumped by a different pair of F-80s, and he was forced to cease his effort to cover his wingman. Attempting to make a crash landing at the airfield in Andong, which was still under construction, Senior Lieutenant M.P. Nasonov crashed and was killed.

The remaining three Soviet pilots separated from the enemy and successfully returned to Anshan. According to V.D. Borovkov, during this flight they had spotted an enemy forward airfield, where Mustangs were being stationed, and even conducted an attack on enemy aircraft that were taking off from the strip, in which he claimed that one or two enemy aircraft were destroyed. However, this author has not been able to locate any document that would confirm this claim. The American side acknowledged the loss of one F-80 and damage to a second F-80, both from the 49th FBG's 8th FBS.

On 12 November 1950, the pilots of the 151st GIAD essentially conducted the final aerial battles in the year 1950. The enemy again undertook several attacks on bridges across the Yalu with the forces of the USNAF's piston-engine aircraft and units of the Strategic Air Command. Eight MiGs led by Captain S.I. Korobov was the first to scramble to intercept an inbound enemy air strike. However, six of the MiGs immediately returned to base because they couldn't raise their landing gear. Captain Korobov's remaining element continued the mission and soon encountered 10 B-29s and six F-80s. Korobov attacked the bombers, but he himself was attacked by two of the escort fighters and only shook loose of them with difficulty. He then returned to base.

At 0905, the last combat of 1950 for the pilots of the 151st GIAD took place. It involved eight MiG-15s of the 28th GIAP. The leader Major V.D. Borovkov was engaging

12 F-80s in the Andong area. At the same time, between 0838 and 0948, six MiGs from the 72nd GIAP were dueling with six B-29s and 16 F-80s in the same area. In this action, Major Boldun's group scored no victories, but it did cause the enemy aircraft to turn back without completing its mission. After exiting the battle, Senior Lieutenant V.M. Dubrovin's element was directed by ground control toward a pair of piston-engine fighters. Maneuvering into attack position, they opened fired on them from a range of 800 meters, but observed no results from the firing. On this day, one South Korean T-6 failed to return from its reconnaissance flight; perhaps it had crashed as a result of an encounter with MiG-15s?

A little later, eight MiGs of the 139th GIAP's 1st Squadron, under the command of Captain B.V. Bochkov, lifted off a runway on the Liaoyang Air Base, tasked with defending Siniuju against an enemy air attack. At 0905 in the area south of Andong, at a command from the auxiliary command post they were directed to intercept a large group of enemy aircraft, consisting of 20 USNAF F9F-2 Panthers and AD-1 Skyraiders flying at an altitude of 8,000 meters in four-plane formations echeloned in altitude. The first to attack the enemy was Captain B.V. Bochkov's flight, which targeted a flight of four AD-1s. At this time, the wingman of the second element in Bochkov's flight Senior Lieutenant N.A. Kolesnichenko noticed four Panthers below them moving onto the tail of Senior Lieutenant A.I. Stuchkov's MiG; Kolesnichenko banked to the right and at a range of 250 meters attacked the enemy leader and downed him with two short bursts. The enemy's burning airplane fell in the vicinity of Andong, which was confirmed by the group's pilots, gun camera footage, and the auxiliary command post in Andong.

Captain Bochkov with his wingman Senior Lieutenant L.D. Shchegolev attacked the right-hand wingman in the formation of AD-1s and fired two bursts at him, after which the Skyraider snap rolled and plunged toward the ground. Bochkov overtook and passed the attacked enemy group at high speed, and didn't observe the fall of the stricken enemy aircraft, but other pilots confirmed that the AD-1 struck the ground.

In the course of the battle Lieutenant S. Kumonaev's engine flamed out and he landed at the Andong airfield. Due to fuel exhaustion, Lieutenant N.I. Sannikov and Lieutenant P.M. Kustov were also forced to land at Andong. On 14 November, all three pilots flew back to their base in Liaoyang. As a result of this action, only one downed enemy F9F-2 was confirmed; Captain Bochkov didn't receive credit for his probable victory over the AD-1. The Americans acknowledged the loss of both planes, but two days later, they also announced, of course, that the MiGs had nothing to do with either loss.

On 14 November 1950, the US Strategic Air Command undertook several attacks on Siniuju with B-29 bombers from the 19th and 307th BG. At 1040, eight MiGs from the 139th GIAP's 1st Squadron under the command of Major G.I. Khar'kovsky took off to intercept one enemy air raid. Guided by the auxiliary command post, our pilots soon spotted 20 B-29 bombers in a column of flights, covered by up to 20 F-80s. The enemy formations were approaching on a meeting course.

As the enemy aircraft neared Singisiu, Khar'kovsky with his flight conducted the first attack against two groups of B-29s from below and to the right. Khar'kovsky and his wingman Lieutenant Iu.I. Akimov opened fire from a range of 600-800 meters at the group leader and another B-29 trailing to the leader's left. As a result, the bomber attacked by Khar'kovsky burst into flames, dropped its left wing, and Lieutenant Akimov watched as it fell to the earth. After the first attack, the second element, consisting of

Senior Lieutenant A.I. Kapranov and I.I. Kakurin attacked a following group of B-29s. However, they observed no results from their firing pass. With a left-hand turn they pulled out the attack and headed to the assembly point.

After the first attack from below, Khar'kovsky and Akimov climbed to the left, came around, and then dove on the bombers again and attacked the third group of B-29s from below and behind. Suddenly Khar'kovsky was jumped by an F-80; catching a glimpse of the American fighter angling toward him, Khar'kovsky broke off his attack into a climbing turn toward the sun. Gaining altitude in a left-hand turn and with the sun now at his back, he made another firing pass and attacked the fourth group of B-29s from above, behind and to the right. As a result, the extreme bomber on the left of the formation caught fire and fell off sharply to the left. Lieutenant Akimov, following his leader, saw the burning, falling bomber. However, at this moment Akimov himself was attacked by an F-80, and he would have been in a very tight situation, had not six MiGs from the 67th IAP under the command of Captain V.I. Sokolov suddenly shown up and hurried to his assistance. Captain Sokolov's flight had engaged the cover fighters, and it was he who had seen Akimov's precarious situation and went to bail him out of it. He dropped onto the tail of the pursuing F-80 and shot it down, while the rescued Akimov exited the fight and returned to base. The pilots of Khar'kovsky group watched as Sokolov's victim burst into flames and spun wildly out of control toward the earth.

Archival documents of the division state that Captain V.I. Sokolov was leading the group of aircraft from the 28th IAD's 67th IAP, and he received credit for the only F-80 that was shot down in this action. However, surviving veterans who participated in this action recall that the commander of the 67th IAP's 3rd Squadron, Captain M. Pakhomov, was leading the 67th IAP's group that day. Alas, there are other such inconsistencies between the recollections of veterans and the regimental documents ...

Senior Lieutenant N.I. Podgorny of the 67th IAP's 1st Squadron achieved the final victory in this clash. He had taken off from the Liaoyang Air Base together with his wingman Senior Lieutenant S.S. Kuprik a little after Captain Pakhomov's flight. When he approached the combat area, he spotted a group of B-29s that were flying without cover. Banking sharply around, he attacked the formation of Superfortresses. With the abrupt maneuver, Senior Lieutenant Kuprik lost his leader and returned to base alone. At this time Podgorny attacked one of the "boxes" of B-29s, and from short range shot down the tail-end B-29; it fell to the earth in flames. Podgorny, pulling out of his first attack, swung back around and made another attack on the three B-29s. This time he managed only to damage one of the bombers, but his MiG also came under the fire of the bombers' gunners and took hits – one bullet struck the oxygen cylinder, causing it to explode and damage his MiG's nose cowling, blocking the pilot's forward vision. Reducing his speed, Podgorny exited the battle and with difficulty made it back to his base, where he safely landed his MiG (the plane was restored to service in three days). Senior Sergeant Richard W. Fisher, a gunner aboard one of the B-29s from the 307th BG's 371st Squadron, received credit for downing Podgorny's MiG, but as we have seen, he only damaged it and it returned safely to base.

As a result of the aerial clash on 14 November 1950, pilots of the 64th IAK shot down five and damaged several more American aircraft. Pilots of the 139th GIAP claimed three enemy aircraft, and all three B-29s were credited to Major G.I. Khar'kovsky, for which he was awarded the Order of Lenin. Pilots of the 67th IAP shot down the other two enemy planes. Two of our MiGs received damage: Senior Lieutenant N.I. Podgorny's jet and Lieutenant Iu.I. Akimov's aircraft, which received several bullet holes in it.

According to a contemporary report from the United Press agency, two B-29s were shot down by MiGs in this battle; another B-29 returned to its base, but upon landing it crashed into four other parked aircraft, because the pilot of this B-29 had been seriously wounded in the leg by a shell from a 23mm cannon. Another B-29 safely returned to base with heavy combat damage, but with several wounded crew members on board. One more B-29 (No. 1940) from the 307th BG's 372nd Squadron took serious damage from the cannons on Senior Lieutenant Podgorny's MiG, but it was able to return to its base on Okinawa and was restored to service. The American side acknowledged the loss of two B-29s on this day. American records also show the loss of one RB-80 from the 49th FBG, which was probably shot down by Captain Sokolov.

The pilots of the 64th IAK had no further encounters with enemy aircraft until 18 November 1950. However, on that date the 64th IAK's final battle of the year with the American air force took place when six MiGs of the 67th IAP's 3rd Squadron under the command of Captain M. Pakhomov tangled with a group of carrier-based F9F-2 Panther fighters from VF-111, which were escorting USNAF strike aircraft trying to break through to the Yalu bridges. In the course of the action, Captain A.I. Tarshinov's wingman Senior Lieutenant V. Bulaev became distracted by his own attack against one of the F9F-2s and abandoned his leader for 12 seconds. He downed the enemy aircraft, but while doing so a different pair of enemy aircraft attacked and shot down Captain Tarshinov's MiG, who was killed in his cockpit. Lieutenant Colonel W. Lamb and his wingman Lieutenant R.E. Parker of VF-111 were responsible for downing Tarshinov. However, the Americans themselves lost two aircraft in this battle: squadron commander Captain Mikhail Pakhomov shot down a second Panther. Most likely, however, in this battle the pilots of the 67th IAP had attacked a group of F-80 fighter-bombers from the 49th FBG, which had a top escort of fleet F9F-2 Panthers, because the Americans recognize the loss of two Shooting Stars on this day.

As a result of this, their final day of combat in the skies of Korea, the pilots of the 28th IAD shot down two American aircraft, but lost one of their own, in which deputy squadron commander Captain Arkadii Ivanovich Tarshinov was killed. Between 19 and 25 November 1950 inclusively, the pilots of the 28th IAD didn't fly a single combat sortie. Their last combat sortie occurred on 26 November 1950, when 16 MiGs of the division took off to intercept solitary enemy aircraft in the Andong area, but they never found one – likely the enemy aircraft departed the area before the MiGs arrived. The 28th IAD's pilots flew no more missions for the rest of the month. At the beginning of December 1950, in response to an order they flew to a new base in Qingdao, deep in the interior of China, where they spent some time training Chinese and North Korean pilots to fly the MiG-15, after which they returned to the Soviet Union. The 151st GIAD conducted its final combat sortie on 27 November 1950, when Captain S.I. Korobov's flight flew a reconnaissance mission and encountered no enemy aircraft. With this, the combat operations of the pilots of the 151st GIAD and 28th IAD in Korea came to an end.

On 30 November 1950, as part of the rotation of combat units in the theater of combat operations, pilots of the new 50th IAD, which had just joined the roster of the 64th IAK, conducted their first sorties to familiarize themselves with the area of combat operations. This fighter division, which was commanded by Hero of the Soviet Union

Colonel A.V. Pashkevich, had been formed on the Liaodong Peninsula in October 1950 on the basis of two Soviet aviation regiments: the 177th IAP of the PVO, commanded by Colonel V.Ia. Terent'ev, and the 29th GIAP commanded by Major D.V. Virich. Both regiments of the division were equipped with 30 MiG-15bis fighters each (instead of the establishment strength of 40 fighters). On 20 November 1950, both regiments of the 50th IAD flew from the Sanshilipu Air Base to Anshan Air Base, from where on 30 November they began to conduct combat sorties.

In December 1950, three more Soviet Air Force jet-equipped fighter divisions arrived in China from the Soviet Union: the 309th IAD (with the 49th and 162nd IAP armed with MiG-9 jet fighters and commanded by Colonel N.I. Stankevich), which was based in Gunshulin; the 65th IAD (with the 70th and 172nd IAP armed with MiG-9 jet fighters under the command of Colonel S.S. Pankratov), which was based in Guangzhou (Canton); and the 324th IAD (with the 196th IAP and 176th GIAP armed with MiG-15 fighters under the command of thrice Hero of the Soviet Union Colonel I.N. Kozhedub), which arrived in the PRC on 25 December and was stationed on the Dongfang Air Base in Sichuan Province. All three divisions began training Chinese pilots. All of these divisions were from the so-called second echelon, had not seen combat, and had engaged exclusively in training. They comprised the 64th IAK's reserve, which provided replacements of experienced flight personnel and technicians for the corps. In the event of a sharpening of the situation, the second-echelon divisions were ready to join combat as part of the 64th IAK's first echelon. The enemy was aware of this gathering strength in the 64th IAK's rear and had to reckon with it.

Thrice Hero of the Soviet Union Colonel I.N. Kozhedub (on the left), commander of the 324th IAD – Andong airfield, 1951.

As a result of the first month of combat in the Korean sky, the pilots of the four Soviet fighter regiments in the 151st GIAD and 28th IAD shot down or damaged 50 enemy aircraft. Of this total, 31 victories were officially recorded: 9 F-51s, 7 B-29s, 7 F-80s, 6 F9F-2s and two AD-1s. Nineteen additional enemy planes were damaged or recorded as "probable" victories in the November air battles: 6 B-29s, 5 AD-1s (it is possible that some of these were actually F4U Corsairs), 4 F-51s, 3 F-80s and 1 F-82. The pilots of the 139th GIAP had the highest score: 12 confirmed and 13 probable victories. In second place behind them were the pilots of the 72nd GIAP, which achieved 9 official and 5 probable victories. The pilots of the 28th GIAP officially downed 6 enemy aircraft (with one more recorded as a probable), while the pilots of the 67th IAP had 4 confirmed kills, and damaged an additional enemy aircraft. The top scoring Soviet pilot over the first month of fighting was the 139th GIAP's squadron commander, Major Grigorii Il'ich Khar'kovsky, who in two aerial combats downed four B-29 bombers, for which he was awarded the Order of Lenin.

The losses over the month of fighting for both divisions comprised a total of three MiG-15s and four pilots. The Soviet pilots Captain M.F. Grachev, M.P. Nasonov and A.I. Tarshinov were all killed in combat, while a pilot of the 72nd GIAP Senior Lieutenant I.M. Kuznetsov died in the month of August from encephalitis. All four men were buried in the Russian cemetery in Port Arthur.

Four MiG-15s of the divisions returned from missions with combat damage, but all were returned to service through the diligent work of the ground crews. Another one or two MiGs were lost due to flight accidents when training the Chinese pilots.

To this it is necessary to add that between 1 and 7 November, remnants of the North Korean air force's 56th GIAP actively operated in the area of Singisiu, flying piston-engine Yak-9 and La-9 fighters. In combat with American piston-engine fighters the North Korean pilots fared rather well, downing approximately 10 enemy aircraft in that week. For example, it is reliably known that on 5 November 1950, eight North Korean fighters under the command of Kim Tal Hyon joined battle against 20 American aircraft and shot down six of them, including five B-26 bombers and one B-29, without any losses of their own. Information about the other victories of the North Korean pilots is still not available to authors, though it is known that North Korean pilots of the 56th GIAP fought stubbornly against the American air force in the areas of Sinuiju and Singisiu on 1, 2 and 6 November. The Americans themselves state that on 5 November, three B-26s from the 452nd BG's 730th Squadron were attacked by four Yak-9s, which damaged two of the bombers. In November, pilots of the 18th FBG in their Mustangs shot down five Yak-9 fighters.

However, the most important thing is not in the numbers of victories and losses, but is the role that the Soviet air units played in this period of the war. In essence, the introduction of the Soviet fighter divisions into the fighting brought about a turning point in the course of the air war. The appearance of the MiG-15 jet fighters simply came as a shock to the United States command in Korea. They immediately recognized the superiority of the Soviet fighter over all the jets equipping the USAF and USNAF, which were operating in Korea at that time. Neither the F-80 Shooting Star nor the carrier-based F9F-2 Panther fighters could fight on equal terms with the Soviet MiGs. Only a top pilot in these aircraft might achieve a victory over a MiG, but even here the American aces were unlucky: all the Soviet pilots who fought in Korea in 1950 had World War II combat experience, and none of them were novices in mastering the jet technology.

The American command, alarmed by the rising aircraft losses in Korea, took a number of serious steps: Firstly, it sharply reduced the number of combat sorties by the USAF and USNAF to the Andong – Sinuiju area; secondly, after analyzing the November losses it was noted that the piston-engine F-51 Mustang attack aircraft, which at that time was the main USAF fighter-bomber in Korea, could no longer carry out combat missions in the area where MiGs were operating without strong fighter escort. This same conclusion was applicable to the main US Strategic Air Command bomber in Korea, the B-29. With the appearance of the MiG-15, the unpunished attacks by the Superfortresses on targets in the depth of North Korea came to an end, which was amply demonstrated by the loss of several Superfortresses in November. Even large numbers of escort fighters hadn't saved the B-29s from losses, and cases of failure to carry out a combat mission became not infrequent due to the opposition of the MiGs.

Equally disquieting were the conclusions with respect to the use of the F-80 Shooting Star and the carrier-based F9F-2 Panther jet fighters against the MiG-15s. Both these aircraft were quite inferior to the MiG-15 in a number of performance characteristics and could not fight with them on equal terms, which was confirmed by the results of combat between them that normally ended in the favor of the Soviet fighter. Thus it was decided to employ the F-80 no longer as a fighter, and to re-equip the fighter-bomber units with them, that is to say, to transfer the F-80 into the class of fighter-bombers and to replace the plainly outdated Mustangs in this role.

Our pilots over the first month of fighting carried out all the assignments that they'd been given to protect particularly important areas of northeast China and the border provinces of North Korea against air attack. The reliable aerial cover given to the railroad and road arteries, and the bridges and crossings over the Yalu River in the Andong – Sinuiju area secured the uninterrupted flow of supplies, providing everything necessary to sustain ground operations on the fronts of Korea, to the forces of the CPV and NKPA. All this taken together also permitted the troops of the CPV and NKPA to go on a major offensive on 25 November, which forced the UN forces to retreat down the peninsula and away from the North Korean – Manchurian border.

THEN ALONE IN BATTLE

At the end of November 1950, the 64th IAK had two Soviet fighter divisions – the 28th and 50th IAD – conducting combat operations at the front. However, because the 28th IAD early in December was withdrawn from the 64th IAK and departed into the Chinese interior in Shandong Province, only the 50th IAD based in Anshan with its two fighter regiments was left to take part in combat.

The pilots of the 29th GIAP were the first to begin flying combat sorties. Already on 30 November 1950, they had flown their first mission to the Andong area, but encountered no enemy aircraft.

The first encounter for the 29th GIAP's pilots occurred on 1 December 1950, after six MiG-15s from its 1st Squadron under the command of Captain P.I. Orlov took off from the Anshan Air Base at 1209 to intercept enemy aircraft in the Andong area. At 1224, the group was flying in a line abreast formation at an altitude of 7,000 meters, patrolling above the area of the auxiliary command posts in Andong. Seeing no enemy aircraft, though, at 1230 they received an order to return to base. However, 30 kilometers from

Andong, the group encountered three unescorted B-29 bombers flying in a wedge formation below them. Swinging around to the right, they attacked the bomber formation. During the clash, the bombers repeatedly pulled up, so that the belly gunners could fire on the MiGs. Captain Orlov's element attacked the lead B-29 and fired at it with short bursts, while Captain I.F. Bogatyrev's element attacked the right-hand bomber. Gunners aboard this B-29 managed to hit Senior Lieutenant G.M. Grebenkin's MiG, leaving it with three bullet holes in one wing and another one that smashed the cockpit canopy, wounding him lightly in the face from the broken glass. Bleeding, he exited the combat and returned to base. The remaining five MiGs conducted one more firing pass on the B-29s, then at 1315 also returned to base.

According to the pilots' post-mission briefing and gun camera footage, the lead B-29's two left engines were left damaged and smoking. Two engines on the right-hand B-29 were also damaged by the MiGs' fire, but no one saw either of the bombers fall. However, both damaged B-29s were credited to the regiment as downed and added to the personal scores of Captain P.I. Orlov and Senior Lieutenant G.M. Grebenkin. These were the first victories for the pilots of the 29th GIAP in Korea.

At this time, only the 29th GIAP was ready to conduct combat missions; the pilots of the 177th IAP were still learning the area of combat operations and polishing their formation flying. In addition, there weren't enough external fuel tanks for both regiments, so only the 29th GIAP was using them, and even then it had only a small reserve of them. Even with the external fuel tanks, due to the large distance of the Anshan Air Base from the targets they were to cover, it was rather difficult to carry out the assignment of intercepting enemy aircraft. Even as the MiGs of the 29th GIAP were arriving in the target area, the enemy aircraft would often be long gone. Thus on 3 December 1950, the entire complement of the 29th GIAP flew to the newly operational forward airfield at Andong, and already by the next day, the regiment's pilots were making combat sorties from their new base.

By this time, the forces of the CPV and NKPA as a result of the offensive they had launched on 25 November had thrown the UN forces back from the Yalu River. In the first days of December, the front lines were already 150-170 kilometers from the border with China, and CVP and NKPA troops were already fighting for Pyongyang, which they re-captured on 6 December 1950. Now in step with the receding front lines, the Soviet pilots were authorized to penetrate North Korean air space to a distance of 75 kilometers beyond the Yalu River, which of course expanded the area of combat operations for the pilots of the 64th IAK.

The adversary quickly reacted to the appearance of a new MiG air base and immediately dispatched a reconnaissance plane on 4 December to the Andong area to locate the place where the MiGs were now staging and to count their number. The reconnaissance aircraft appeared above Andong at the high altitude of 10,500 meters and proceeded on to the vicinity of Mukden. Four MiGs under the command of Captain L.P. Vvedensky were scrambled at 1140 to intercept it. Vvedensky's wingman for the flight was Senior Lieutenant A.K. Kurnosov; the second element consisted of Senior Lieutenant N.N. Petrov and his wingman Senior Lieutenant A.F. Andrianov. They spotted the target's contrails on its return from the direction of Mukden. It was flying steadily, showing no sign of concern, believing that no fighter could reach it at that altitude – and it hadn't seen the four MiGs approaching from below. The first to reach it was Kurnosov, who pulled up the nose of his MiG and opened fire. Plainly, his burst damaged the reconnaissance plane, because it began to lose altitude, enabling the other three MiGs to attack it. Soon, the burning reconnaissance plane was falling not far from Andong. Of its three crew members, only the pilot managed to bail out, and he was taken prisoner by the Chinese. According to gun camera footage, Senior Lieutenant A.F. Andrianov, who fired at the intruder from the closest range, received credit for the victory.

As it turned out, the "prize" of the 29th GIAP's 2nd Squadron proved to be a rare bird in the skies of Korea – a special four-engine RB-45A Tornado reconnaissance jet. In the autumn of 1950, three of these aircraft had been dispatched from the United State to Korea. During the transit flight, one of the Tornados caught fire and burned during refueling on an airbase in Hawaii; the two remaining RB-45s arrived at the American Yokota Air Base in Japan, where they joined the 91st Strategic Reconnaissance Squadron in the Far East. However, even they didn't last long in the skies of Korea: already on 4 December 1950, the second RB-45A (No. 48-015) was shot down by MiGs on only its third flight, while the last RB-45A was lost in April 1951, again from the fire of our MiGs.

A little later on the day of 4 December, at 1305, a flight of MiGs from the 29th GIAP's 1st Squadron under the command of Captain S.I. Naumenko flew off on a patrol. Fifteen minutes into the flight, our pilots discovered a pair of F-80 fighter-bombers, which were apparently returning to their base after conducting a mission. Having checked the air space around and not having seen any other enemy aircraft, Captain Naumenko decided to attack the enemy, especially because it seemed that the enemy pilots still hadn't spotted our MiGs. Captain Naumenko and his wingman Lieutenant A.S. Minin dove into the attack, and having closed with the still unsuspecting enemy, Naumenko first fired upon the enemy wingman. His shooting caused the target to burst into flames and sent it falling out of control toward the earth. Without ceasing his attack, Naumenko turned his attention to the lead F-80, the pilot of which apparently only now spotted the danger he was in. The enemy pilot pulled his aircraft into a steep climb to evade the MiGs' attack. However, the American pilot evidently didn't know that the MiG-15 easily outperformed a Shooting Star in the vertical, and this misjudgment could have cost him his life. Naumenko quickly caught the F-80 and struck the enemy aircraft with several short bursts from a range of 400 meters. The smoking F-80 rolled over and pulled into a steep dive toward friendly lines. Senior Lieutenant K.V. Rumiantsev attempted to catch it in the dive in order to finish it off, but in the dive Rumiantsev apparently exceeded the MiG's top permissible speed, causing a deformation in the MiG's tail assembly. His MiG never pulled out of its dive and plunged into the ground. That's how the regiment suffered its first combat loss: the pilot, Senior Lieutenant Konstantin Vladimirovich Rumiantsev was killed in the crash. Captain S.I. Naumenko was credited with two victories in this action. However, it is likely that the second F-80, despite its damage, safely returned to an American base in South Korea.

Meanwhile, combat operations continued. The activity of the USAF sharply increased, while the main targets for their attacks remained the same bridges across the Yalu, the Supung hydroelectric power station, the airfields in the areas of Sinuiju and Singisiu, and the numerous railroad stations, tunnels and bridges in North Korea.

On the morning of 5 December, four MiG-15s of the 2nd Squadron under the command of the 29th GIAP's navigator Major Iu.Ia. Keleinikov departed on a patrol flight. At 0828 our pilots in the area of Kaisen Station spotted two flights of F-80

Hero of the Soviet Union Major S.I.
Naumenko, a 1953 photograph.

fighter-bombers. The leader of the group of MiGs went on the attack, and taking advantage of the surprise, successfully jumped the lead flight of F-80s and shot down one of them. Then Keleinikov attempted to attack the second flight of Shooting Stars, but they were now alert to the MiGs' presence and evaded the attack by sharply reversing course. At this time, the remaining three Shooting Stars of the first flight turned the tables on the MiGs, and one of them dropped into firing position behind Major Keleinikov. However, before the enemy pilot could open fire, Keleinikov's wingman Senior Lieutenant N.N. Petrov swung in behind him and hit the Shooting Star with several shells. Streaming smoke, the Shooting Star rolled over and dove for the earth.

With this the sharp action with the Shooting Stars came to an end, because the MiGs' fuel tanks were running low and they were forced to return to base; fortunately, they successfully carried out their assignment to prevent the enemy attack on the station. The American side acknowledged the loss of only one F-80 Shooting Star from the 49th FBG.

On the next day, 6 December 1950, a group of five B-29 bombers were heading for the airfield in the vicinity of Singisiu. Six MiGs of the 1st Squadron under the command of Captain S.I. Naumenko were scrambled to intercept them. Around 1300, at an altitude of 6,000 meters, Lieutenant A.S. Minin reported to Naumenko that he had spotted the receding B-29 formation. Naumenko, failing to see the targets, ordered Minin to go on the attack and to mark the location of the enemy group, especially because Minin's MiG was the only one in the Soviet group that had no external fuel tanks. Minin, knowing the results of the first battle with the B-29 on 1 December, attacked a Superfortress from short range and set fire to two of its engines; the burning target dropped out of formation and began to fall toward the earth. Minin was then compelled to exit the battle and head to base, because his fuel was running low, while the remaining four MiGs under Naumenko's leadership inflicted further heavy damage to the B-29 formation. Two more

Superfortresses were shot down, with the victories going to Captains Naumenko and Bogatyrev.

Out of Naumenko's group, Senior Lieutenant N.N. Serikov failed to return from the mission. During the flight to intercept the enemy aircraft, his MiG had surged ahead of the rest of the group (it had a newer engine) and he had headed on alone to the Singisiu area. To this day his fate is unknown. Perhaps he had attacked the B-29 formation first and been shot down by one of the gunners, or something had happened with his aircraft.

Two hours later, somewhere around 1500, the 29th GIAP sent six MiGs out on patrol, this time from 2nd Squadron under the command of Captain V.N. Krymsky. In the area of Singisiu they spotted two F-80s, which were evidently searching for ground targets. They still hadn't detected the MiGs; taking advantage of this opportunity, Captain Krymsky closed on the Shooting Stars in a dive, fired on the wingman's aircraft and shot it down. Later on the same patrol, our group encountered another flight of F-80s and also attacked it. This time Captain Krymsky succeeded in damaging one Shooting Star, after which the remaining enemy aircraft evaded at low altitude.

The result of the clash around Singisiu on 6 December was in the favor of the Soviet pilots: officially three B-29s were downed; in addition, in the combat with the Shooting Stars, the commander of the 2nd Squadron Major V.N. Krymsky shot down one F-80 and damaged another. On our side, N.N. Serikov's MiG failed to return to base. The American side acknowledges only the loss of only one B-29, which made a forced landing on a runway at Kimpo and was subsequently written-off.

On the next day, 7 December 1950, the 29th GIAP's pilots conducted two successful combats against the enemy air force. At first in the morning, a MiG flight from the 2nd Squadron under the command of Captain L.P. Vvedensky encountered a flight of F-80s at 1145 in the Singisiu area, and in a brief battle, Captain Vvedensky damaged one enemy aircraft. Two hours later, two flights of MiGs from the Regiment's 3rd Squadron under the command of Captain I.I. Iurkevich took off for the same area. Soon they spotted an F-80 flight, which was at a higher altitude than the Soviet group, but this didn't hinder the latter from attacking the enemy. In the course of this climbing attack, Senior Lieutenant P.A. Pavlenko downed one Shooting Star, but then his MiG continued to climb at a steeper angle, before dropping into a steep dive from which it never pulled out. Apparently, as result of the abrupt vertical maneuver, the heavy stresses on his aircraft damaged the elevator flaps on Senior Lieutenant Pavlenko's MiG, leaving the pilot unable to pull out of the fatal dive. His wingman Senior Lieutenant M.V. Fedoseev avoided death by a miracle; because of the same extreme stresses on his MiG, its skin fractured in several places, but he was still able to bring his MiG out of the dive and fly it back to base. In this combat, Senior Lieutenant Fedoseev also claimed one F-80, but the American side confirms the loss of only one of its F-80C Shooting Stars (No. 49-682) on this day. The loss of Senior Lieutenant Pavel Andreevich Pavlenko was the last one in December.

In this period, the MiG-15 jet fighters presented the main threat to the American air forces in the Far East, and the losses the Americans were suffering due to the MiG confirm this. In addition, according to the official conclusion of the American historian and specialist on the Korean air war, Robert F. Fuller, the swept-wing MiG was plainly superior to the old F-80C, as well as the USNAF's new fighter, the F9F Panther, not to mention the World War II-era F-51 Mustang. This circumstance led the USAF commander-in-chief General Vanderburg to dispatch two squadrons from SAC and the US Air Defense Command to the Korean theater of operations: the 27th Fighter Escort Group [FEG], which was equipped with F-84E Thunderjets and designated to escort the American bomber formations, and the 4th Fighter-Interceptor Group [FIG], equipped with the latest jet fighter in the US arsenal, the F-86A Sabre, which was supposed to sweep the Korean skies clear of the MiG-15. The 27th FEG was at combat-readiness from 6 December 1950, while the 4th FIG was ready to enter combat operations on 15 December 1950.

However, it was still several weeks before the first encounter with these new adversaries; meanwhile the MiG's main opponent remained the inferior F-80. The day 9 December was quite intense for the pilots of the 29th GIAP, when they conducted five group combat sorties to intercept enemy aircraft. The 3rd Squadron, which flew three of the missions, was particularly busy on this day. The first to take off at 0815 were eight crews of the 3rd Squadron under the command of Captain A.I. Perekrest. In the vicinity of the Songchon railroad station they spotted a group of four F-80s, which were busy with an attack on this station. Taking advantage of the fact that the American pilots were focusing all their attention on the ground targets and not keeping track of threats in the air, our MiGs closed upon them at high speed and opened fire. The group leader Captain Perekrest's fire was the most accurate; the leader of one of the Shooting Star elements fell next to the station. The other F-80s broke off their attacks and immediately left the area.

Then in the neighborhood of 1000, Captain S.I. Naumenko's flight from the 1st Squadron had an unsuccessful clash with a flight of F-80s in the area of Singisiu; although Senior Lieutenant I.F. Grechko managed to damage one of the F-80s, the American pilots in turn nearly hit the MiG of the second element's leader, Senior Lieutenant S.I. Volodkin due to his mistakes. Fortunately, everything turned out well for our pilots in this action, and all the Soviet aircraft returned to base without any damage.

That afternoon at 1410, Captain Perekrest's flight from the 3rd Squadron again took off in search of enemy aircraft. Again in the area of Songchon Station, they spotted a flight of F-80 fighter-bombers. However, this time the Shooting Star pilots were on the alert and detected the Migs' approach in time; they avoided the attack by taking advantage of the hilly terrain. Several minutes later our pilots spotted another flight of F-80s, which was heading for the station, and successfully worked their way around onto its tail. The lead element of Captain Perekrest and his wingman Lieutenant V.R. Bondarenko managed to close within short range of the tail-end Shooting Star and simultaneously opened fire on it. The target burst into flames and plunged to the earth. The remaining enemy aircraft immediately fled the target area. Gun camera footage gave the victory over this F-80 to the wingman, Lieutenant Bondarenko. The American side this time acknowledged the loss of two of their aircraft: one F-80 from the 49th FBG's 8th FBS, which was downed by Captain A.I. Perekrest; its pilot was killed. In addition, the Americans report the loss of one of their carrier-based F9F-2B Panthers from VF-31, which crashed upon landing on its aircraft carrier. Most likely, this was the "F-80" that Senior Lieutenant I.F. Grechko damaged in combat, so it was with Panthers that the pilots of Captain Naumenko's flight had clashed, and not Shooting Stars. In the air, these two aircraft were quite similar, and our pilots often confused the Panthers with the Shooting Stars.

The stressful pace of combat operations continued on the following day 10 December. On this day pilots of the 29th GIAP were involved in two major dogfights in the same area of the long-suffering Songchon Station. First, at 0820 Captain S.I. Naumenko's flight participated in a difficult fight against superior enemy numbers in the form of a group of F-80s. In this battle, Captain Naumenko and his wingman Lieutenant A.S. Minin managed to latch onto the tail of a Shooting Star element, and from short range opened fire on them. Naumenko shot down the F-80 leader, while Lieutenant Minin damaged the wingman's Shooting Star.

However, the aerial clash that took place that afternoon at 1525, when the Americans launched a large formation of fighter-bombers against Songchon Station, proved to be fiercer. In order to intercept this large enemy group, 16 MiGs of the 29th GIAP took off simultaneously. Gaining altitude, they assembled into flights and subsequently turned toward the Songchon area. As they approached the target area, our pilots spotted several flights of F-80 fighter-bombers, totaling up to 20 Shooting Stars, which were arriving over the area of the station at the same time as our MiGs. In the lengthy and swirling action that ensued Senior Lieutenant Iu.I. Glinsky managed to shoot down one F-80. On our side, Senior Lieutenant N.N. Petrov's MiG took damage to the engine turbine, but our pilot managed to make a dead stick landing on the Andong airfield, which fortunately was not far from the combat area. The American side acknowledged the loss of one of its F-80s from the 80th FBS. Its pilot, 1st Lieutenant Bertram D. Wilkins managed to guide his stricken jet back to its base at Taegu with difficulty, but it crashed upon landing and he was killed. Wilkins' wingman also suffered combat damage to his F-80, but he was able to bring it down safely on a runway at the Taegu Air Base. These must have been the two F-80s that Captain Naumenko and his wingman Minin attacked.

On 12 December 1950, the 3rd Squadron of the 29th GIAP experienced its most successful day in the air. At 1300, four MiGs under the command of Senior Lieutenant A.I. Perekrest scrambled in response to an alert raised in an area where enemy aircraft were present. Here is how he himself describes this combat:

> Several minutes after takeoff, I spotted a group of four F-80s, which were circling above a railroad station, taking turns as they attacked the station and the trains parked on the rails from an altitude of 800–1,000 meters. We were at an altitude of around 4,000 meters, so we rapidly closed upon the enemy in our dive. We had maneuvered so as to emerge in the rear of the tail-end enemy aircraft. We still hadn't been spotted by the enemy. Closing to a range of 200-250 meters from the tail-end F-80, I took aim and opened fire with all my guns. A spurt of flame erupted from the target and it fell to earth near the station, while the remaining F-80s began to flee in the direction of the 38th Parallel.

However, only one of the Shooting Stars managed to escape, since in the very first attack Perekrest's wingman Lieutenant Bondarenko shot down another F-80. The other two F-80s snap rolled and pulled into a steep dive to evade the attack from the second pair of MiGs, but in so doing one of the Shooting Star pilots lost track of the altitude and one of the wings of his jet struck the top of a hill, leading to the aircraft's disintegration (Lieutenant Iu.P. Sotnikov was credited with a victory). Thus, in the course of one minute of combat, the small group of enemy aircraft was almost completely destroyed, without any damage to our side.

Most likely, Perekrest's formation had stumbled upon an air strike being conducted by two different American flights, one consisting of F-80s from the 51st FBG's 25th Squadron, and the other flight made up of the new F-84E Thunderjets from the 27th FBG. At first the flight of Shooting Stars came under attack, and Captain Perekrest shot down one of them (No. 49-260). Its pilot 2nd Lieutenant William R. Kimbro was killed. Then the trailing flight of F-84E Thunderjets came under attack, losing two of its aircraft from the attack of the MiGs. One of the pilots was killed, but the other was rescued. Thus on 12 December 1950 the pilots of the 29th GIAP encountered a new adversary and had drawn "first blood" from the American pilots of the 27th FBG, although our pilots mistakenly believed they were Shooting Stars. In addition, according to American records, the USAF lost another F-80C (No. 49-828) on 11 December, plus another F-80C (No. 49-651) on 13 December. Very likely these too were victims of MiG-15s from the 29th GIAP?

On this same day, 12 December 1950, pilots of the 177th IAP made its first group combat sortie from the Anshan Air Base, but it passed without any encounter with the enemy. The first combat action of the 177th IAP didn't take place until 17 December, but it ended with no results. However, even before this on 15 December an event occurred that would affect the further course of the war in the skies of Korea – the American command proudly introduced its new F-86 Sabres into the fight.

On this same day of 15 December 1950, one more encounter between MiGs and American strike aircraft took place. According to our pilots' post-mission briefings, they had engaged a group of F-84s, and Senior Lieutenant A.D. Ryzhov managed to down one of them. However, more likely our pilots had dueled with a group of F-80s and Ryzhov had only damaged his target – American records confirm damage on this day to F-80C (No. 49-823) from the 49th FBG's 8th FBS.

At 1345 on 17 December, four MiG-15s under the command of the chief of the 50th IAD's aerial gunnery service Lieutenant Colonel Ia.N. Efromeenko took off to intercept enemy aircraft in the Andong area. Once in that area, one of the pilots spotted four silvery swept-wing fighters with red noses, which he reported to the flight leader. The latter replied, "I see them; they're ours" – and continued to fly along the set route. However, suddenly the MiG flight was fired upon from above and behind, with most of the fire concentrating on Efromeenko's MiG. Shuddering from the hits, Efromeenko's jet burst into flames and its engine suddenly failed. The pilot, seeing the hopelessness of the situation, ejected from his aircraft. This was the Soviet Air Force's first ejection from a MiG-15 in combat conditions. Lieutenant Colonel Efromeenko came to earth and he soon returned to base. Efromeenko's wingmen briefly engaged the "strangers", but the latter soon withdrew, because another group of our MiGs was approaching to lend a hand in the fight.

Once on the ground, our pilots concluded that they had just encountered the new American F-86 Sabre fighter, the arrival of which in the theater of operations had recently been reported by the 64th IAK's intelligence section. They were of the unanimous opinion that this was a serious and dangerous adversary unlike any other they had encountered thus far. They would have to keep their eyes peeled for it, and they would have to adopt new tactics in order to duel successfully with the Sabres.

The first victory over a MiG-15 went to Lieutenant Colonel Bruce Hinton, the commander of the 4th FIG's 336th FIS, who downed Efremeenko's MiG 3 kilometers south of Sinuiju. Incidentally, initially only a total of 10 Sabres from the 4th FIG's entire complement were operational. During their shipment by sea to Korea, the humidity and salt spray caused several problems with the Sabres, so initially only 10 of them flew to an airfield near Seoul and began combat operations on 15 December 1950. As the other Sabres of the 4th FIG were overhauled and repaired, they flew to forward airfields around Seoul and joined in the combat operations.

In order to confuse the enemy, the noses of the first 10 Sabres were painted red, similar to the way our MiGs were decorated. Thus the swept-wings, silvery color and red noses of the Sabres easily confused the MiG group leader on 17 December 1950.

Therefore after the encounter on 17 December, ground crews removed the red paint from the noses on all the aircraft of the 29th GIAP. On 19 December, the next meeting with the new adversary occurred. At 0835, six MiGs of the 3rd Squadron, under the command of Captain I.I. Iurkevich, took off on a combat patrol. At 0845, they encountered a flight of F-86s on a meeting course in the vicinity of Singisiu. Both sides closed at high speeds in a head-on pass, but the extremely rapid rate of closure affected the aim, and no aircraft were hit on either side. After this pass, our flight split: Captain Iurkevich's element climbed away, while Captain Perekrest and his wingman Lieutenant V.R. Bondarenko hauled their MiGs around and went after the receding Sabres. Then suddenly Captain Perekrest's element was attacked from behind by a different flight of six Sabres that had approached to join the action. Captain Perekrest's element came under fire, or more precisely, the MiG of his wingman Lieutenant Bondarenko. His MiG's fuselage and left wing were riddled by 18 .50 caliber bullets, which knocked out several blades of his engine turbine, severed hydraulic lines, damaged the ailerons and rudder, and jammed the control stick; the plane was poorly responding to the controls. With difficulty our pair managed to shake off the Sabre pursuers, after which Valentin Bondarenko decided to abandon his crippled aircraft. The pilot threw aside the cockpit canopy and attempted to eject, but a buckle of his safety harness, as was discovered later, had jammed the lever arm of the catapult, preventing the arm from moving. Meanwhile, the ground was rapidly approaching. In a near panic, Bondarenko grabbed the control stick and pulled back on it with all his might. With an unbelievable effort, the pilot managed to haul the MiG out of its dive and regained partial control over the aircraft. With extreme difficulty, Bondarenko was able to fly the MiG back to his base and make a safe landing in his crippled aircraft. Thus the Sabres almost managed to add another MiG to their score in this war, but thanks to the courage and resolve of our pilot, as well as the durability of our MiG, this didn't happen!

Until the end of December 1950, the pilots of the 29th GIAP encountered Sabres in the skies of Korea nearly a dozen more times, but only on 21 December did they record their first victory over them. On a typical sortie to the Singisiu area, four MiGs of the 3rd Squadron led by its commander Captain I.I. Iurkevich unexpectedly spotted a group of eight F-86s approaching on a meeting course. This time our fighters had an altitude advantage, so Captain Iurkevich pounced upon this enemy group from out of the sun and fired a short burst from his 37mm cannon (a total of three shells) at one of the Sabres. He watched as one of the shells struck a wing root on the Sabre, and it dropped into a dive. However, just as on the previous occasions with the Sabres, our pilots were caught by an attack from a covering group of Sabres, which was trailing the main group, and Iurkevich's element came under attack. Bursts of .50 machine-gun fire struck Iurkevich's jet, but this time as well the MiG-15 withstood the Sabre's blow and safely returned to its base with 19 bullet holes in it. The regiment's ground crews soon restored Iurkevich's MiG to service.

Our pilots were only still learning about its new opponent, and on the first occasions they'd been lured by a decoy group of Sabres, failing to observe another group of Sabres flying above and behind the "bait", and they'd come under the covering group's attack. Thus in the first combats, success was on the side of the Sabre pilots, who over a course of a week were able to win all the battles with the MiGs, down one of them and seriously damage two more. To be sure, the Sabre pilots didn't get away unscathed. Before the end of December, according to an announcement from the American side, there were three instances of serious damage to Sabres in combat against the MiGs. Plainly one of them was the Sabre that Captain Iurkevich hit.

On 22 December, there was a major dogfight involving Sabres and MiGs, this one involving the pilots of the 177th IAP. In essence, this was the first serious combat for these pilots.

The first to score on this day was the 177th IAP's 1st Squadron. Early in the morning, eight MiGs under the command of Captain P.M. Mikhailov rose into the sky and headed toward the area of Andong. Suddenly Captain N.E. Vorob'ev reported to Mikhailov that he could see four F-86s below their formation. Mikhailov, still unable to see the enemy, ordered Vorob'ev to attack the group of Sabres. Vorob'ev accelerated, quickly gained a position behind the trailing Sabre element, and opened fire on the leader from short range. He observed the shells from his cannon striking the Sabre, including a couple that went right up the tailpipe, after which the target fell onto one wing and plummeted to the ground. At the same moment, Senior Lieutenant S.M. Akulenko shot down the wingman's Sabre, which crashed next to the wreckage of his leader's Sabre. The remaining two Sabres quickly fled in the direction of South Korea.

This was the version of the story, as told by Captain Vorob'ev himself, but Soviet records reveal a different story. In reality, somewhere around 0800 and on the approach to Songchon Station, Vorob'ev did indeed spot four F-86s and gave a warning to his leader. Captain Mikhailov and his flight attacked this group of Sabres, while Captain I.A. Grechishko's flight remained above to cover Mikhailov's attack. During the attack, Captain Mikhailov opened fire prematurely from long range, and naturally missed his target. But the leader of the second element Captain Vorob'ev didn't miss, because he waited until he had closed within short range of the enemy and hit the enemy aircraft with several shells, sending it out of control to the earth. However, at the last moment its pilot managed to eject safely and was taken prisoner.

In actual fact, two flights of Sabres from the 335th FIS were on this sortie. The flight commanded by Lieutenant Colonel Donald W. Nance was flying in the lead; the second flight under the command of Captain Janicek was flying some distance behind the lead flight. The MiGs attacked Lieutenant Colonel Nance's flight, and in a tight turn the Sabre of Captain Lawrence Bach was shot down by a high-deflection shot; the pilot was taken prisoner. Captain Ed Farrell's Sabre came under the attack of Senior Lieutenant Akulenko, but he by some miracle avoided getting hit and returned to his base. At that moment Captain Janicek's second flight of Sabres approached and covered the withdrawal of Lieutenant Colonel Nance's flight from a brief scrap with Captain Grechishko's flight, which ended with no results.

That afternoon, eight MiG-15s from the 177th IAP's 2nd Squadron under the command of Captain M.Ia. Fomin was unexpectedly jumped from above by 12 F-86 Sabres in the Singisiu area. In the difficult battle that ensued, according to our pilots, three Sabres were shot down by Captain M.Ia. Fomin, Senior Lieutenant V.K. Tishchenko and Lieutenant P.T. Riabov. The Americans acknowledge the loss of only one Sabre. In return, Senior Lieutenant S.A. Barsegian was killed; in addition, another of the 2nd Squadron's MiGs went down in the area of the Andong Air Base, but its pilot Lieutenant A.A. Zub ejected from his stricken aircraft. He broke both legs upon landing in his parachute and wound up in a hospital.

In fact, at 1435 a total of eight F-86s from the 4th FIG participated in the afternoon dogfight, but these were being commanded by experienced pilots, Second World War aces Lieutenant Colonels Glenn Eagleston (with 18.5 victories in that war) and the 4th Fighter Group's commander, John Meyer (with 24 victories). It was Eagleston who shot down Lieutenant Zub's MiG in this battle, while John Meyer downed Senior Lieutenant Barsegian's fighter. Lieutenant Paul E. Pugh damaged Senior Lieutenant V.F. Deinig's MiG, but the Soviet pilot was able to bring it safely back to base.

As a result of the fighting on 22 December 1950, pilots of the 177th IAP claimed five Sabres, but not all of them were observed to crash (there was confirmation on the ground regarding two downed Sabres on this date). Soviet losses on the day were two MiG-15s destroyed and one pilot killed. The Americans declared that in the combats on 22 December 1950, they had downed six MiG-15s, but it is reliably known that the losses of the 50th IAD on this day amounted to just two MiG-15s destroyed, plus another MiG-15 damaged.

As concerns the other "downed" F-86s, it is most likely that our pilots were taking the smoke that the F-86 emitted when the pilot applied the supercharger as a sign of fire on board the enemy aircraft – after all, this was the 2nd Squadron pilots' first combat experience with the new adversary and they were still ignorant of the technical details of the F-86 engines.

On 24 December 1950, according to staff documents of the 50th IAD, there were three combats against Sabres. First, pilots of the 29th GIAP encountered the F-86 when six MiGs under the command of Senior Lieutenant P.I. Orlov took off on a mission. In the area of Songchon Station, at 0850 they came across two flights of Sabres and engaged them. This time, the MiGs were at a higher altitude, and the Sabres didn't see them. Taking advantage of the surprise, Captain Naumenko's flight attacked the lead Sabre flight, and Naumenko managed to close upon one element of the Sabres and score hits on its leader; the Sabre crashed near the rail station, and its pilot, George Donald of the 336th FIS was killed in his cockpit. The combat then continued, but the Sabres were unable to gain any advantage against the courageous six MiG pilots and soon broke off the fight and returned to base.

At 1030, six more MiG-15s of the 177th IAP's 1st Squadron under the command of Captain N.E. Vorob'ev took off on a combat mission. They encountered a flight of six Sabres in the area of Songchon Station and engaged them. In the dogfight that followed, Senior Lieutenant D.K. Belikov succeeded in getting behind one of the Sabres and fired at him from a range of 600 meters. He saw hits being scored on the enemy aircraft, after which it began to fall out of control. Senior Lieutenant V.P. Kobzev's second element successfully evaded a Sabre attack with a zoom climb, then looped back around onto the tail of the Sabre flight passing below them. Closing on one of the Sabres, he struck it with several shells. After these troubles, the Sabre group exited the combat and headed back to friendly territory. Both F-86s were registered as victories for Belikov and Kobzev; however, according to American records, in this combat the two Sabres were only damaged and they made it safely back to their base.

At this same time, pilots of the 29th GIAP were having their own encounter with the enemy. Simultaneously with the pilots of the 177th IAP, eight MiGs of the 29th GIAP's 1st Squadron, commanded by Senior Lieutenant P.I. Orlov, took off and headed toward Songchon Station. A former pilot of the 29th GIAP, Aleksey Semenovich Minin, recalls the combat that ensued:

> We had taken off as a flight consisting of Orlov – Volodkin, Naumenko and me. Over Singisiu, Sabres jumped us in a high side attack from out of the sun. We didn't realize that they were enemy planes until we saw their tracers flashing past us. They looked so similar to our MiGs that at first we thought they were ours. The Sabres attacked us from above in a high-speed pass. Orlov – Volodkin evaded the attack in an abrupt climbing turn, while Naumenko shouted to me over the radio: "Brakes!" – and threw his aircraft downward. I also popped my speed brakes and followed him down. The pair of attacking Sabres flashed past overhead. Naumenko abruptly raised the nose of his MiG and fired at the passing Sabres, hitting first the leader and then the wingman's Sabre. In the meantime, I had to counter a second element of Sabres that was trying to attack us, which broke off their attack. Orlov and Volodkin had departed in a climb and had become tied up in combat with another four F-86s, which they had spotted. However, at this moment, two flights of MiGs appeared in the sky – pilots of the 177th IAP were coming to our assistance; the enemy, seeing they were outnumbered, immediately withdrew.

However, as is now clear 50 years later, in this battle the pilots of the 29th GIAP were dueling not with Sabres, but with F-84 Thunderjets from the 27th Fighter Group's 522nd Squadron. On a patrol flight, they had spotted the flight of MiGs, and taking advantage of their advantage in altitude, had attacked it. However, they had misjudged their angle of attack and they themselves had wound up under the guns of Captain Naumenko's element. In this action Captain Naumenko downed F-84E No. 49-2422, and its pilot 2nd Lieutenant Roger W. Bascom was killed. Thus on 24 December the pilots of the 50th IAD had taken revenge on the American pilots for the defeat they had suffered on 22 December.

Pilots of the 50th IAD claimed one more Sabre on 27 December; credit went to flight commander Captain Ivan Anufrievich Grechishko in the 177th IAP's 1st Squadron. Here is how he describes this combat:

> When the squadron scrambled eight aircraft in response to an alarm, from the command post they had transmitted that a rapidly-moving target had appeared on the radar screen. Later it turned out that this was a solitary element of enemy aircraft, flying at top speed, being trailed by an attack group of 10 Sabres. We wound up in an unfavorable situation, having taken the bait, and the Sabres

launched an attack from behind us. A "carousel" formed, as my flight consisting of Belikov, Kobzev and me chased a lone Sabre that had become separated from its formation. We boxed him in and soon finished him off. I recall that this plainly was a high-class F-86 pilot, since he had employed high-G turns and had thrown his aircraft into a cascade of highly aerobatic maneuvers. However, we weren't rookies, and still managed to get him.

However, in reality, Grechishko and his wingmen had watched as the enemy aircraft "started to smoke" and had headed toward friendly lines in a dive, but they didn't see it crash. Most likely, our pilots had once again seen the puff of smoke as the Sabre pilot applied the supercharger and taken it as a sign of fire on-board the F-86. To put it more simply, the Sabre pilot was hauling ass away from the MiGs, and having switched on the supercharger, he had gone into a dive to escape, which he in fact as a result managed to do. This was another case of a claim wrongly accepted as a victory, a problem on both sides which makes any comparisons of victory totals dubious.

Yet what the pilots of the regiment's 1st Squadron weren't able to do, their comrades from the 2nd Squadron pulled off. Having taken off in the wake of the 1st Squadron at 1407, six MiGs commanded by Captain M.Ia. Fomin, bypassing the Sabre barrier with which the pilots of the 177th IAP's 1st and 3rd Squadrons had become entangled, emerged over the area of Chongju Station, where several small groups of F-80s were conducting ground attacks. Splitting into elements, they attacked the Shooting Stars, which were operating at low altitude, from different directions. The lead element of Captain Fomin managed to catch one F-80 as it was pulling up after an attack against a ground target and struck first, downing it from a range of 200 meters. The regiment's navigator, Captain M.G. Andriushin, caught another Shooting Star and shot it down. Shooting Stars of the 51st FIW's 25th FIS were the ones that the pilots of the 177th IAP attacked, and Captain Fomin had downed F-80 No. 49-645; its pilot 2nd Lieutenant Harrison C. Jacobs managed to escape his stricken aircraft, but he was taken prisoner.

Pilots of the 50th IAD also enjoyed success on 28 December. On this day, there were two clashes with enemy aircraft, in which only the pilots of the 29th GIAP and the Chinese 10th IAP took part. Most successful was the action that involved eight MiG-15s from the 29th GIAP's 1st Squadron, led by Senior Lieutenant P.I. Orlov, and a flight of MiGs from the PLAAF's 10th IAP led by Captain Le Han. In the area of Songchon Station, the commander of the 1st Squadron Senior Lieutenant Orlov spotted a couple of F-80 fighter-bombers in a climb after making a ground attack, and attacked them with his wingman. The attack achieved excellent results, as Orlov downed one of the F-80s, while Senior Lieutenant S.I. Volokin destroyed the other Shooting Star. These were evidently F-80C No. 49-823 from the 49th FBG's 8th FBS (flown by 1st Lieutenant James G. Clayberg) and F-80C No. 49-605 from the 51st FIG's attached 80th FBS (flown by Donald C. Morgan); both USAF pilots were killed.

On one of the final December sorties on 30 December 1950, one flight of the 29th GIAP's 1st Squadron had a difficult fight against 16 F-86s. Their assignment had been to cover the valley of the Supung hydroelectric station. At an altitude of 3,000-5,000 meters, Captain Naumenko's flight was covering the station itself. Unexpectedly, Naumenko spotted an approaching element of F-86 elements and turned to engage them. Just then the leader of the second element Senior Lieutenant I.F. Grechko warned over the radio that they themselves were being attacked from behind. Grechko's element climbed to avoid the attack, while Naumenko's element dove for its airfield, but an attacking Sabre element caught the fleeing MiGs in the dive. The Sabre leader opened fire with all his machine guns and damaged Naumenko's aircraft. Wingman Senior Lieutenant S.M. Liubimov saved his leader by energetically banking toward the lead F-86 and opening fire from a range of 100-150 meters. The Sabre took several shell hits and went into a fatal dive. The Sabre wingman, seeing that his leader had been shot down, immediately withdrew. At this time, help arrived for Naumenko's flight in the form of a group of MiGs led by Major Iu.Ia. Keleinikov, so the remaining Sabres also exited the battle.

For his act, Senior Lieutenant S.M. Liubimov was awarded with the Order of the Red Star. This was the last productive aerial combat of the year conducted by pilots of the 50th IAD, and the last victory in 1950 scored by Soviet pilots.

Altogether in December 1950, the 29th GIAP alone had conducted 452 individual combat sorties, 26 group air battles, and downed 28 American aircraft – 16 F-80s (including one erroneously identified F9F Panther), 3 F-84s, 5 B-29s, 3 F-86s, and 1 RB-45A. Its own losses amounted to 4 MiG-15s and 3 pilots. Pilots of the 177th IAP conducted half as many sorties in December, but scored 10 victories (8 F-86s and 2 F-80s). Its own losses were two aircraft and one pilot.

Pilots of the USAF 4th FIG conducted 236 combat sorties in December, and claimed 8 MiGs. Their own losses, according to a report from the 4th Fighter Group command, were placed at three F-86s lost, and another three damaged. However, only one of the lost F-86s and all three of the damaged Sabres were attributed to MiG fire, which is a dubious assertion.

Of course, the appearance of the Sabre prompted more fighting in the skies of Korea, which in its intensity was simultaneously more bitter and stubborn. This is in fact unsurprising; after all, the 4th FIG was a distinguished unit of the USAF, and it was equipped with what was considered the best U.S. fighter of its time, the F-86 Sabre. In addition, the three squadrons of the 4th FIG (the 334th, 335th and 336th Squadrons) were all staffed with exceptionally experienced pilots, the majority of which had extensive combat experience in the Second World War and, judging from the number of planes each had downed in that war, were considered aces according to the American concept of that status.

Despite the enemy's numerical superiority in the air, and the restrictions which the Soviet pilots were under, they securely covered all the sites on the territory of northeastern China and North Korea under the 64th IAK's protection, and despite the great efforts of the USA to establish absolute superiority in the air and to destroy the PLAAF's fighter aviation (including the Soviet 64th IAK), they were unable to do so. The aggressor was no longer able to obtain that level of superiority in the air that it had enjoyed in the autumn of 1950. As a result of the CPV counteroffensive undertaken at the beginning of December 1950, by 30 December 1950 the armed forces of the UN had been expelled from North Korean territory and hurled back to the south.

A TEMPORARY LULL

After the disastrous retreat of the US Eighth Army and Republic of Korea [ROK] forces, the front lines in the winter of 1950-51 stabilized south of the 38th Parallel. During the retreat from the PDRK, the US Fifth Air Force hastily evacuated the network of air bases it had quickly developed in North Korea and concentrated its air formations in the southern half of the peninsula. On 4 January 1951, units of the CPV and NKPA re-occupied Seoul, the capital of South Korea, and also simultaneously seized the primary air bases near the capital – Kimpo and Suwon. Two days before, a portion of the units of the Fifth Air Force had flown off to bases further down the peninsula, while the rest had flown to bases in Japan. For example, all of the F-86A Sabres of the 4th FIG on 2 January 1951 flew to Johnson Air Base in Japan.

In connection with the jet aircraft's narrow operational radius, the UN air force's possibility to penetrate deeply into North Korean air space came to an end. At the same time, the PLAAF took to expanding its network of airfields and to strengthening its combat activity in the air space above the Korean Peninsula's central regions.

Silvery MiG-15s gained more control over the air space above the northwestern portion of Korea between the Yalu and Chongchon Rivers. In American aviation circles, they began to speak about the so-called "MiG Alley", which American reconnaissance planes only rarely attempted to enter.

By 8 January 1951, when the advance of the CPV and NKPA forces had been brought to a halt well inside South Korea, American combat air units restaged to the south of the Korean Peninsula, and the Fifth Air Force and the USNAF directed all their sorties against the attacking CPV and NKPA units on the territory of South Korea.

During this time the enemy practically made no appearance in the Andong-Siniuju area, which as before one Soviet fighter division, the 50th IAD, was covering. True, there was an airfield with a dirt runway in Sinuiju, from which piston-engine Yak-9 or La-9 fighters staged to take part in combat operations, but they didn't play any active role in covering the given region from the air. The only assistance that Soviet pilots received in January 1951 came from the PLAAF 10th IAP, which arrived on the airfield at Andong at the end of December 1950. At first, only one squadron, the 28th Fighter Squadron, of the Chinese fighter regiment arrived in Andong, but in January the rest of the regiment (the 29th and 30th Squadrons) moved to Andong. This Chinese air regiment had close, friendly ties with the pilots of the 29th GIAP, since it was the latter who had trained the Chinese to fly the MiG-15 in Shanghai back in the period between June and September 1950. The 10th IAP arrived in Andong with its MiG-15s, but in distinction from the regiments of the Soviet 50th IAD, the Chinese pilots flew in MiGs that were equipped with the less powerful RD-45A engine, while the Soviet pilots were already fighting in MiGs that had the newer VK-1A engines.

In the first half of January 1951, the 10th IAP conducted familiarization flights over the area of operations, rehearsed formation flying, and studied the enemy's combat tactics. During the Chinese pilots' sorties into MiG Alley, they were covered by pilots of the 50th IAD. In the first days of January 1951 (1, 3 and 7 January), pilots of the 29th GIAP conducted just several combat sorties, but never encountered any enemy in the air. The same was true with the missions flown by the 177th IAP on 3 and 6 January.

An encounter with the enemy didn't occur until 10 January 1951, when 10 MiGs from the 177th IAP's 1st Squadron under the command of Major P.M. Mikhailov, while carrying out a combat patrol to the Anju area, met a solitary reconnaissance RB-29 above the clouds. The entire squadron immediately attacked the enemy plane, element by element, and took it under fire, but the pilots of the 177th IAP had no combat experience with the given aircraft, and they opened fire on the reconnaissance plane from long-range. Only Captain N.E. Vorob'ev managed to close to within short range of the RB-29 and to fire an effective burst. Shells struck the right outboard engine and walked along the fuselage. The RB-29 caught fire and began to fall in a spiral. Five crew members of the plane quickly bailed out and were taken prisoner by the Koreans, but the airplane crashed into a hill not far from Anju, taking with it the other six members of the crew. Although Vorob'ev had better gun camera footage, the regiment leadership decided to award the victory to the squadron commander Major P.M. Mikhailov. Thus the leadership wanted to raise the morale of the 1st squadron commander, since to that point he had not been able to achieve a victory in the skies of Korea. This, incidentally, was also sometimes the practice in other regiments and divisions of the 64th IAK as well, but in the majority of cases this only acted to the detriment of the commander who was gifted with the victory. However, in this case, the awarding of the victory did raise Major Mikhailov's confidence in his abilities. In the future, Major Mikhailov would score two more victories in Korea, this time personally, for which he was awarded the Order of Lenin. The Americans conceal the truth that one of their aircraft was downed by pilots of the 177th IAP on 10 January, but there is supposition that the Soviet victory was over an aircraft of the US Air Rescue Service, SB-29 No. 44-84124, which deliberately or by error was registered as lost on 11 February 1951.

On the following days there were almost no sorties at all right up until 19 January, so there were also no encounters with enemy aircraft. True, recently it was revealed in American publications that on 18 January 1951, 1st Lt. Joseph H. Powers of the 4th FIG didn't return from a combat sortie; his Sabre was shot down, but most likely this was the work of anti-aircraft gunners, since neither the Soviet nor the Chinese pilots had any combats with the Americans on this day. Sabres had returned to Korea on 17 January; on this day, F-86As of the 335th FIS flew into Taegu and landed on the K-2 Air Base; the other two squadrons of the 4th Fighter Group remained in Japan. Pilots of the 335th FIS continued to operate from K-2 until 31 January, but lacked the operational range to reach MiG Alley, where the MiG-15s were operating. Thus there were no combats between Sabres and MiGs in January 1951. On 31 January, the 335th FIS returned to Japan.

On 19 January pilots of the 29th GIAP conducted two uneventful combat sorties. However, on 20 January the enemy became active in the Anju area, sending several dozen F-84 fighter-bombers from the 27th FEG there, covered by F-86s of the 4th FIG. In small groups they were working over military and civilian targets in the area. Pilots of the 50th IAD and Chinese 10th IAP were scrambled to intercept them.

However, only six MiGs from the 177th IAP's 2nd Squadron, under the command of Captain M. Ia. Fomin, were the lucky ones that day. In the area of Anju they spotted four F-80s over Kaesong Station and engaged them in battle. Here is how former Senior Lieutenant A.V.Simatov describes this action:

At a command from the auxiliary command post, in a complement of six [MiGs], we headed for an area where a group of enemy ground attack aircraft had been detected. Climbing 1,000 meters, we soon spotted four F-84s [sic], an element of which was attacking a target, while the other element provided cover. Sychev and Andriushin went after the covering element, while Kormilkin and I attacked the other pair of F-84s. However, just then I saw an F-84 diving toward us and reported this to my leader. When the adversary closed to within firing range, my leader made an abrupt, climbing left turn, and I followed him. The enemy flashed past below us, and then began to execute a wide-radius turn back in our direction. Warning the leader, I turned into the opponent's attack and we made a head-on pass, after which I banked sharply to the left. The adversary banked around to the right and again we attacked head-to-head. As we closed, I spotted a MiG-15 that was moving on a course perpendicular to our maneuver. I quickly alerted him (he turned out to be Captain Fomin), and with a left-hand turn he dropped in behind the enemy, attacked him from short range and shot him down. Captain Andriushin in this battle shot down another F-84. Our group had no losses.

In reality, our group in this battle first encountered four F-80s, and in the ensuing combat with them Captain M.G. Andriushin shot down 2nd Lieutenant Jack M. Brock's Shooting Star from the 49th FBG's 8th FBS, which crashed next to the station; the pilot was killed. Captain M. Ia. Fomin, however, only seriously damaged the Shooting Star of 1st Lieutenant Shuman H. Black of the 51st FIG's 25th FIS, who managed to bring his stricken aircraft back to base and make a successful belly landing, after which this Shooting Star was consigned to the boneyard. Both of these losses were written off by the Americans approximately a month later.

A large dogfight occurred in the Anju area on 21 January 1951, when approximately 30 MiG-15s flew off to intercept numerous ground attack aircraft – a group of MiGs from all three regiments of the 50th IAD was scrambled. Six MiGs of the 29th GIAP's 3rd Squadron took off at 0734 on the first combat sortie, and in the Anju area they encountered a flight of F-84s and engaged it. The pilots of Captain A.I. Perekrest's flight both fired at the Thunderjets, but on the ground it turned out that Lieutenant V.R. Bondarenko's gun camera footage contained the best evidence, and he received credit for one downed F-84. In actual fact, in this combat Captain Perekrest's pilots had attacked an F-80 from the 49th FBG, and Lieutenant Bondarenko had succeeded in damaging Major Irving W. Boswell's aircraft. The American pilot managed to reach friendly territory before abandoning his aircraft, because no fuel remained in its riddled fuel tanks.

On a later sortie at 0910, six MiGs from the 29th GIAP's 1st Squadron encountered a large group of F-84 Thunderjets in the area of Anju and attacked it. In the ensuing combat, Captain N.F. Bogatyrev and Senior Lieutenant Grechko each downed one Thunderjet. The Chinese pilots also distinguished themselves by scoring their first official victory in Korea – the group leader, squadron commander Le Han shot down one of the American jets. Six MiGs of the Chinese 28th Squadron had come to the assistance of the 29th GIAP's 1st Squadron, and Han downed 1st Lieutenant Grant Simpson's Thunderjet from the 27th FEG's 523rd Squadron with a high-side attack. At that point, the other F-84s exited the combat. Simpson never bailed out and his body was found in the wreckage of his jet. The Americans assert that the Chinese pilots also suffered losses in this dogfight, claiming one of the Chinese MiGs didn't return from the battle. The commander of the 523rd Squadron Lieutenant Colonel William Bertram was credited with the victory, the first for the pilots of the 27th FEG in the skies of Korea. However, Chinese sources do not confirm this loss and state that all of the pilots of the 28th Squadron safely returned to base.

At 1035, the 177th IAP's 3rd Squadron with a complement of nine MiGs also encountered eight F-84 Thunderjets in the Anju area and engaged them in a battle that smashed the enemy group. Four Thunderjets were shot down, one each by P.M. Mikhailov, S.M. Akulenko, I.A. Grechishko and I.V. Popov; Grechishko scored the final victory. Together with his wingman Belikov he maneuvered to attempt to latch onto the tail of an F-84 element, but was unable to do so until the F-84s started to run low on fuel, because they were flying at the limits of their operational radius. The Thunderjets attempted to escape, and Captain Grechishko pounced on the opportunity, dropping into position behind the wingman and shooting him down from short range. The enemy target fell on the coast of the harbor.

My assistant, Argentinean historian Diego Zampini, when studying recently published documents regarding the losses of the Fifth Air Force in Korea, discovered a discrepancy in the American data and suggested that in fact, the pilots of the 177th IAP had not tangled with Thunderjets in this action, but with a flight of F-80s from the 49th FBG's 8th FBS, which was escorting a reconnaissance RF-80 from the 8th Reconnaissance Squadron. In essence, this entire group was destroyed in the battle: one F-80 and the RF-80 were shot down immediately, and the reconnaissance pilot was taken prisoner. The other three Shooting Stars managed to nurse their damaged aircraft back to friendly territory, where the pilots either abandoned their aircraft or made forced landings wherever they could find a level, unobstructed area to make one.

However, the aerial battle above Singisiu on 23 January 1951 was the peak of the January battles in the skies of Korea. Angered by their recent losses, the pilots of the American 27th FEG decided to display their power, and the entire Group took off on a mission to the Andong area. Coming in from the direction of the Yellow Sea coastline, the 24 F-84 Thunderjets (some sources say there were 48) crossed into PRC airspace and headed for the Andong Air Base. Here is how A.I. Perekrest recalls their appearance over the airfield:

> After we had finished eating breakfast at 0700 and were leaving the on-duty hut, the sun was just beginning to rise above the horizon. We hadn't even managed to have a smoke after our meal, when we saw coming from the direction of the sea an entire column of F-84s flying at an altitude of approximately 400-500 meters; they were approaching in flights of four, one after the other, and there were no less than 45 of them. This was the first incident of a major violation of the PRC border that we witnessed. They were flying as if on parade, and didn't open fire on our parked MiGs at the air base. It was approximately 50-60 meters from the on-duty hut, where we were standing, to the MiGs' hardstands, so we immediately rushed to our MiGs, climbed into the cockpits, started the engines and began to take-off.

Approximately around 0710, 28 MiG-15s (eight from the Chinese 10th IAP, the other 20 from the 29th GIAP) subsequently took off. A savage air battle developed, in which approximately 80 fighters from both sides took part.

The first to take to the sky in response to an alert had been six MiGs of the 2nd Squadron led by Captain V.N. Krymsky, and they were the first to spot a group of eight Thunderjets, which were heading toward the Andong airfield, which lay directly opposite Singisiu across the Yalu River. Apparently the given enemy group was supposed to cover the actions of the approaching main strike group. Captain Krymsky's group attacked this covering group, and rather successfully so, since soon Captain G.P. Chumakov managed to shoot down one of the Thunderjets. At this moment, the main enemy group was arriving, and the air became filled with enemy aircraft. Krymsky's flight of six MiGs simply seemingly dissolved among the foe's aircraft. However, this numerical superiority for the enemy didn't last more than a minute, because that was when first six MiGs from the 1st Squadron under the command of Captain P.I. Orlov came on the scene, followed a minute later by eight MiGs from the 3rd Squadron, led by Captain I.I. Iurkevich. An enormous "carousel" of several dozen aircraft wheeled in the sky.

Several MiGs were fired upon by the Thunderjets as they were taking off and climbing for altitude; two of the MiGs, Captain Zhandarov's and Senior Lieutenant A.F. Andrianov's, were hit and forced to set back down on the runway, and never joined the battle. Andrianov's MiG took three bullets to the engine and might have been shot down, because a pair of F-84s had latched onto his fighter. However, he was rescued by Captain Glinsky's element, which attacked Andrianov's tormentors in the nick of time and downed one of them; the other evaded the attack in a steep turning climb.

Captain G.M. Grebenkin fought heroically in this battle, but he was boxed in by four F-84s and shot down; Captain Grebenkin didn't have time to eject. This was the regiment's only loss in this battle and its last loss in this war. However, the other pilots of the 29th GIAP more than paid back the enemy for its loss – they claimed eight F-84s as victories and damaged two or three more of the enemy aircraft. To be honest, only six victories, which were scored by the pilots P.I. Orlov, I.F. Bogatyrev, A.K. Kurnosov, A. Riazanov, G.P. Chumakov and A.I. Perekrest, received confirmation. The other two Thunderjets were downed by Iu.I. Glinsky and G.M. Grebenkin, but for various reasons these victories were not registered.

American pilots of the 27th FEG's 522nd and 523rd Squadrons claimed four MiG-15s, with two victories going to the score of Lieutenant J. Kratt, Jr., while Captains Allen McGuire and William Slaughter each received credit for one. The Americans claim three more MiG-15s as "probables". According to American records, eight F-80 fighter-bombers from the 8th FBG took part in this mission, and they were being covered by 24 F-84 Thunderjets from the 27th FEG. In addition, American records show that only one F-80 from the 80th FBS, the pilot of which was killed, was lost, while another F-80 of the 8th FBG was damaged. This information, knowing how sensitive the American command was about such losses and the efforts it took to conceal them, is rather dubious.

The young Chinese pilots that participated in this battle arrived as it was already winding down. They scored no victories, but lost two of their MiGs and one pilot, which tells of their lack of combat experience. Pilots of the 29th and 30th Squadrons of the PLAAF's 10th IAP, who had just arrived at the Andong Air Base, took part in this clash, and apparently they were the ones who became most of the victims of the 27th Fighter Group's pilots.

This was the final combat in the Korean skies for the pilots of the 29th GIAP. On 29 January, the regiment flew back to Anshan, where it turned over its MiGs to a different Soviet regiment that had recently arrived in China, and the flight staff then departed for some R&R on Liaodong Peninsula.

Only the pilots of the 177th IAP and the Chinese 10th IAP finished the January battles. Already the day after the battle near Andong, all three squadrons of the 177th

IAP became embroiled in a heavy battle with a large, mixed enemy group that consisted of approximately 30 F-80s and F-84s. Two American jets were downed: one F-84 fell victim to the cannons of Captain V.P. Grishechkin's MiG, while Senior Lieutenant D.K. Belikov was credited with one F-80. In this action Captain I.V. Popov's fighter received serious damage. It returned to base with 36 bullet holes in it, but the technicians quickly repaired the MiG and it was soon back in action. In addition, in this battle with the Thunderjets, Captain F.F. Argueev's MiG-15 received light damage from three .50 caliber bullets, but it also safely made it back to base. In this clash, eight F-80s from the 49th FBG's 9th FBS took part, covered by eight F-84s from the 27th FEG. The Americans do not acknowledge the loss of its Thunderjet in this battle, but report a victory over one of the MiGs by the 27th Fighter Group's Captain Allan Gilbert – apparently it was Gilbert who riddled Captain Popov's MiG in this action. However, the Americans do confirm the loss of its F-80 in this battle, the pilot of which 1st Lieutenant Ralph E. Jacobs of the 8th FBG's 80th FBS went missing-in-action.

Chinese pilots of the 10th IAP also participated in the 24 January battle, but had no victories or losses. On 26 January 1951, the 523rd Squadron pilot Lieutenant Jacob Kratt, Jr. in his F-84 downed one North Korean Yak-9 – his third victory in four days.

On 29 January, the young Chinese pilots of the 10th IAP conducted their most successful combat yet during their service in the skies of Korea. Eight Chinese MiG-15s from the 28th Squadron, led by Le Han, engaged a group of F-80 fighter-bombers and shot down two of the Shooting Stars without any losses of their own. The American command acknowledges the loss of two of its F-80s on this day, No. 49-850 and No. 49-557, which were piloted by 1st Lieutenant Arthur E. Hutchinson of the 8th FBG's 36th FBS and 2nd Lieutenant Robert E. Sternard of the 49th FBG's 7th FBS – both were killed. True, as usual the Americans attribute these losses to "technical causes", not MiG fire. This was the last aerial battle of January 1951. The adversaries didn't meet again until February.

Over the month of January 1951, the pilots of the 29th GIAP alone between 1 January and 23 January 1951 flew 172 individual combat sorties, became engaged in three group combats, and officially downed nine US aircraft. Their own losses for January amounted to one MiG destroyed and three MiGs damaged (all returned to service); one pilot, G.M. Grebenkin, was killed-in-action. The pilots of the 177th IAP conducted approximately 200 individual combat sorties and became engaged in five group air combats, in which they downed 11 US aircraft (1 SB-29, 3 F-80 and 7 F-84); three of the regiment's MiGs were damaged. The PLAAF 10th IAP during January became involved in four group air combats, in which they downed three US aircraft (two shot down, one damaged and written-off – all F-80s). Their own losses in return were two MiG-15s and one pilot.

The aerial combat of January 1951 was not as intense and heated as November and December 1950 had been, and after the outburst of action in the Anju area at the end of the month, a new lull settled even over MiG Alley, where there were only rare collisions between small groups of MiGs and aircraft of the US Fifth Air Force. At the beginning of February 1951, having turned over its aircraft, the 177th IAP also departed for the Soviet Union, but before this the regiment's pilots flew several more combat sorties and twice became involved in action, one of which had a result.

On 3 February 1951, 10 MiGs of the 177th IAP's 1st Squadron led by Major P.M. Mikhailov took off on a patrol. In the area of Singisiu approximately 40 kilometers northeast of the town, flight commander I.A. Grechishko spotted a solitary F-80 at an altitude of 2,500 meters. Grechishko's flight went into a left-hand turn of 135-140 degrees, swung around behind the F-80, and then Captain S.M. Akulenko attacked it from the right side and opened fire on it from a range of 350-400 meters. The F-80 dropped its right external fuel tank and made a 180 degree turn, when Captain N.E. Vorob'ev attacked it, firing six bursts from a range of 300 meters at the target aspect angles of 1/4 and 2/4. Soon the F-80 fell and crashed 15-20 kilometers southwest of Kusong. From N.E. Vorob'ev's recollections:

> It was an all-weather interceptor, a twin-engine F-94 Starfighter [sic.]. I attacked it from the side and scored hits from my cannons along the fuselage from the right (I saw the explosions of the shells). At this moment the F-94 crew dropped an external fuel tank, but the left-side tank wouldn't release and the plane began to descend. At this time the flight commander Grechishko shouted at me: "Vorob'ev, finish him off, go after him." So I did. Grechishko was on my right, as was the American; although his plane was stricken, he was feigning an uncontrolled fall. When the pilot pulled his aircraft out of the dive, I opened fire on him again and continued to fire until the airplane crashed to the ground. Its crew was killed.

On the gun camera footage it was plainly apparent that the aircraft had two engines, but although it resembled the silhouette of the F-94, it is hard to believe this was in fact a Starfighter, since the first F-94s didn't arrive in Korea until the end of spring 1951. Most likely it was a twin-engine combat training aircraft, the T-33A, which was part of the aircraft inventory of both the 49th FBG and the 51st FIG, since in its configuration it was quite similar to a Starfighter. In fact one such T-33A (No. 49-990) was written off by the Americans as lost in Korea on 5 February 1951. It is possible that this was the one that Captain Vorob'ev brought down on 3 February.

However, the combat didn't end with the crash of the reconnaissance plane, because it was being covered by four F-80s, which arrived on the scene too late. At first Major Mikhailov saw a solitary F-80 and attacked it from behind, and with his first attack shot it down (the adversary hadn't seen him). Then Senior Lieutenant Zakhartsev's element spotted another pair of F-80s to the left and maneuvered to attack it. Captain I.V. Popov's element climbed in order to cover the attack by Zakhartsev's element, but in the process Popov spotted another F-80, attacked it from the right and above, and shot it down. The remaining Shooting Star element shook off the pursuit by Zakhartsev's element and exited the battle. The pilots of the 177th IAP in this action returned without a single bullet hole in their MiGs. The Americans acknowledge the loss of two of their F-80s from the 25th FBS and the death of both Shooting Star pilots, but again they attribute it to anti-aircraft fire, not MiG fire, which isn't what really took place.

In the beginning of February 1951, Colonel A.V. Pashkevich's 50th IAD left the roster of the recently created 64th IAK, which the former commander of the 151st GIAD Major General I.V. Belov was now commanding. Over the period of its combat work between 27 November and 7 February 1951, the pilots carried out all of their assignments and reliably protected all of the military-industrial sites in northeastern China and North Korea that had been entrusted to them. Over this period, the division's pilots officially downed 64 enemy aircraft (including the three F-80s credited to the Chinese pilots of their 10th IAP, since this regiment had been temporarily attached to the 50th IAD). The pilots of the 29th GIAP over this period flew 632 individual combat sorties and engaged in 29 group air combats, in which 37 US aircraft were downed: 5 B-29, 1 RB-45, 16 F-80 (including an F9F Panther), 12 F-84 and 3 F-86. Ten more American aircraft were listed as probables. The 29th GIAP's own losses amounted to five MiG-15s and four pilots (Captain G.M. Grebenkin, and Senior Lieutenants P.A. Pavlenko, K.V. Rumiantsev and N.N. Serikov).

The pilots of the 177th IAP conducted approximately 400 individual combat sorties, engaged in 13 group aerial combats, and officially downed 24 American aircraft: 1 SB-29, 1 T-33, 7 F-80, 7 F-84 and 8 F-86). Three more US aircraft were listed as probables. Their own combat losses amounted to two MiG-15s, and one pilot was killed-in-action (Captain S.A. Barsegian). Finally, pilots of the Chinese 10th IAP in January 1951 flew approximately 100 individual combat sorties and became engaged in four or five group combats, in which they downed three F-80s. Their own losses amounted to two MiG-15s and one pilot.

After the departure of the 50th IAD, only the Chinese 10th IAP remained on the airfield in Andong, but it was soon replaced by the 7th IAP of the PLAAF's 3rd IAD. By this time, the 64th IAK only had the 151st GIAD ready for combat operations, but it was training Chinese pilots of the PLAAF's 4th IAD in Mukden. Nominally the 64th IAK also had the recently arrived (on 25 December 1950) 324th IAD under the command of thrice Hero of the Soviet Union Colonel I.N. Kozhedub. The 324th IAD was equipped with MiG-15s, but its fighters had the less powerful RD-45A engines. It was also training Chinese pilots at the Dunfyn Air Base – at this time, the 324th IAD was not ready for combat operations.

By February 1951, there were 10 more Soviet aviation divisions located in the PRC, which were not part of the 64th IAK. These were the 17th, 20th, 28th, 65th, 144th, 297th, 309th and 327th IAD, as well as the 186th ShAD and the 162nd BAD. They were performing the role of a shield inside China and creating a PVO defense line in the PRC interior. For example, the 328th IAD with its three regiments of MiG-9 fighters was guarding the PRC capital, Beijing. The 28th IAD, which had previously been part of the 64th IAK, had restaged to southern China to Qingdao in December 1950; the 139th GIAP began training a regiment of Chinese pilots at the Qingdao airfield, while the 67th IAP in Tianjin had begun training a regiment of North Korean pilots to fly the MiG-15. In the area of Canton, the MiG-9 equipped 65th IAD, which had been created just before its departure to China on the basis of the 309th IAD, was protecting the air borders of the PRC. Commanded by Colonel S.S. Pankratov, it had two regiments, the 70th and 172nd IAP, and it was located in China from 27 December 1950 until 30 September 1951. But most of the Soviet aviation divisions were stationed in Mukden, including the 17th IAD (with the 28th and 445th IAP in MiG-9 fighters), the 144th IAD (with the 383rd and 439th IAP in both piston-engine La-11 fighters and MiG-9s). In addition, Soviet pilots of the 297th IAD (with the 304th and 401st IAP, and their La-9 piston-engine fighters) were training Chinese pilots of the PLAAF's 9th IAD in the area of Qiqihar, China. Finally, the 186th ShAD and the 162nd BAD, flying piston-engine Il-10s and Tu-2s, were based in the Hardin region, and were also training Chinese pilots.

All the aforementioned aviation units were carrying out an important role in the creation of a modern air force for the PRC and the PDRK and preparing their pilots for combat operations in the Korean War. However, the majority of these Soviet aviation divisions were equipped with outdated MiG-9s, or MiG-15s with the RD-45A engine. Only the 151st GIAD was armed with the more powerful MiG-15bis. Thus it was decided to return this division, which by this time was commanded by Colonel A.Ia. Sapozhnikov, to combat operations in Korea.

Already on 8 February 1951, the full 28th GIAP under the command of Hero of the Soviet Union Lieutenant Colonel V.I. Koliadin flew to Andong. The 72nd GIAP remained in Anshan, where it continued to train Chinese pilots of the PLAAF's 4th AD. Six pilots of the 72nd GIAP were sent to the 28th GIAP as replacements, while the rest remained in Anshan.

Eight MiGs of the 28th GIAP's 2nd Squadron, under the command of Captain A.I. Akimov, conducted the regiment's first combat sortie. Taking off at 1527, our eight MiGs were covering four Chinese MiGs from the 7th IAP, which were making a familiarization flight over the area of combat operations. The first flight, consisting of Captain A.I. Akimov's element with his wingman Senior Lieutenant A.Ia. Alekseenko and Captain B.A. Lebedkin's element with his wingman Captain I.F. Krivakov, were flying 400 meters above the four Chinese pilots. Below them flew Captain I.I. Garkavenko's flight. During the flight, they were suddenly redirected by the auxiliary command post toward four F-80s that had appeared in the area. The Americans were flying in a compact formation and didn't see the MiGs, which Captain Akimov's first flight exploited and conducted an attack from above and behind. All four MiGs of the flight opened fire from short range, having allocated the targets among themselves. With the first attack three Shooting Stars were hit and fell burning to the earth. The pilots Captains A.I. Akimov, B.A. Lebedkin and A.Ia.Alekseenko all scored victories. Only one F-80 survived the devastating blow, but it had been damaged, since Captain I.F. Krivakov saw his shells striking the enemy aircraft. Thus with one swift attack, virtually the entire small group of F-80s had been destroyed. The decisive role in this success was played by the superb guidance to the target given by the radar operaters and the auxiliary command post, which achieved complete and fatal surprise over the adversary. The Chinese pilots didn't participate in this battle, though they still suffered a loss on their first combat patrol: having spotted the enemy aircraft, the Chinese flight leader executed an abrupt maneuver in the vertical, during which one of the young Chinese pilots De Zan Chin apparently lost control over his aircraft. His MiG fell into a spin from which it never emerged, killing the pilot in the crash. The Americans acknowledged the loss of only one of its Shooting Stars from the 8th FBG's 80th FBS, which raises great doubt in the completeness of the data.

Two days later, the pilots of the 28th GIAP had another encounter with a group of F-80s, and again victory was on the side of the Soviet pilots. At 1053, six MiGs from the 1st Squadron led by regiment commander Lieutenant Colonel Koliadin himself took off to intercept enemy aircraft. In the Anju area at an altitude of 1,500-2,000 meters, they engaged 10 Shooting Stars successfully; one "Shoot" (as our pilots nicknamed the F-80) was downed, while the remaining fighter-bombers abandoned their mission and withdrew without having attacked their target. In this action, F-80 No. 49-548 from the 8th FBG's 36th Squadron fell victim to the cannons of Captain A.T. Borodin's MiG, and its pilot was killed. After this battle, fighter-bombers of the US Fifth Air Force made no further appearance in MiG Alley for more than 10 days.

After the heavy losses suffered at the end of January – beginning of February 1951, the Fifth Air Force leadership realized that it could no longer send ground attack aircraft into MiG Alley without the cover of the 4th FIG's Sabres. Therefore the aircraft of the 8th, 49th, 18th and 35th FBG, as well as the F-84s of the 27th FEG, carefully avoided MiG Alley and restricted their operations to those areas that the MiG-15 could not reach – primarily along the 38th Parallel, where stubborn fighting between the opposing armies was on-going.

At this time, the Sabres of the 4th FIG were unable to cover the operations of the fighter-bombers, because their operational radius didn't allow them to operate actively over MiG Alley from their bases in Japan. The 334th FIS returned to its base in Taegu only on 22 February, but it didn't immediately initiate active operations. For the entire month of February 1951, the Sabres only conducted one group sortie into MiG Alley – this was the lowest measure of their combat activity in the skies of Korea over the entire war. The American air force generals watched with growing irritation as their former aerial superiority in this area slipped away from them. Beginning in the middle of February, they had started to assemble bomber formations, which with heavy fighter escort were to destroy the network of North Korean air bases in the northwest part of the country. However, because of the above problems, the American command was unable to execute this plan.

B-29 bombers undertook the first attempts to breakthrough to the area of Singisiu, where one of the North Korean air force's airfields was located, as well as to the Supung hydroelectric station. They flew in small groups and without fighter escort, for which as a result they paid a high price. The first attempt took place on 14 February. Ground radars got a fix on a target that was approaching MiG Alley. At 1025, 10 MiGs from the 3rd Squadron under the command of regiment commander Lieutenant Colonel Koliadin scrambled to intercept it. In the Anju area they spotted a group of eight B-29 bombers, flying in box formation. At an altitude of 5,000 meters, the B-29s were heading toward the Singisiu Air Base. However, before they could reach it, the bombers were intercepted by a pair of MiGs flown by regiment commander Koliadin and his wingman Senior Lieutenant V.F. Bushmelev, which had first spotted the enemy. Koliadin had time to conduct two head-on passes against the Superfortress formation, downing one of the bombers and crippling another. At this point, eight F-80 covering fighters approached the combat area, and Koliadin was forced to break off his attacks. However, he'd managed to knock this group of B-29s off course, which had already jettisoned their bomb loads before reaching the target.

At this time, the eight remaining MiGs of the regiment under the command of Major P.B. Ovsiannikov arrived on the scene. Spotting the group of B-29s, they noted it was unprotected by fighters, which had been apparently been diverted by their pursuit of the MiG element that had already attacked the B-29 formation. This simplified the task for the Soviet pilots. At an altitude of 10,000 meters, they attacked the formation by pairs off the approach. In the course of these attacks, two more B-29s were damaged, while the remaining turned back before reaching the target, after dropping what was left of their bombs.

Although only one B-29 crashed to the ground, victories were credited to Lieutenant Colonel Koliadin, Major Ovsiannikov and Captains Gordeev and Motov, all of whom had inflicted damage to the Boeings in this action, but with certainty only Lieutenant Colonel V.K. Koliadin had shot down a B-29. The American command doesn't report on the losses and damage to their B-29s in this battle.

Major P.V. Ovsiannikov, commander of the 28th GIAP's 3rd Squadron.

On 23 February, Soviet Army Day, the American command again decided to send a group of F-80s to the Anju area. At 1011, eight MiGs under the command of the 3rd Squadron commander Major P.B. Ovsiannikov took off to intercept the target, which was being tracked by ground radar. In the Anju area, our pilots spotted a pair of F-80 fighter-bombers at an altitude of 6,500 meters. The group turned to attack this enemy target and overlooked a different F-80 element that was approaching from below. The Shooting Stars attacked the rear element of MiGs and struck Captain I.I. Gordeev's MiG with machine-gun fire; Gordeev had to eject from his crippled aircraft. In doing so he received an injury and wound up in a hospital. He would take no further part in the air war over Korea. This was a rare occasion, when a Shooting Star pilot managed to turn inside his most dangerous adversary and to shoot it down. The identity of the American pilot that achieved this success is still unknown, because this victory was never formally recognized by the American command.

However, the enemy also didn't avoid a loss in this battle, since Major Ovsiannikov, taking advantage of his superiority in speed, managed to catch the lead element of F-80s and to open fire on it. A smoking "Shoot" began to depart toward friendly territory in a dive. This F-80 (No. 49-1860) from the 8th FBG, although it did manage to reach its base, crashed when attempting to land. Thus the score in this battle evened at 1:1!

The day after this action on 25 February, the pilots of the 28th GIAP had another encounter with B-29 bombers. At 1012, eight MiGs from the 3rd Squadron under the command of Major Ovsiannikov scrambled to intercept an enemy formation that had been detected by ground radar posts. In the area of Kaisen Station they spotted four inbound B-29s without any fighter escort, for which the bombers paid a price. Taking into account the errors that had been made in the previous encounter with the B-29s on 14 February, this time Major Ovsiannikov split his group up into elements, which attacked the B-29 group in turn at high speed from different directions. At the same time, our pilots withheld their fire until they had closed to within short range of the bombers, which led to excellent results of their fire. Three firing passes were made against the B-29 box, and all four enemy bombers took hits. One fell burning in the vicinity of Kaisen Station, while the other bombers, crippled and trailing smoking, turned back toward friendly lines. Major P.B. Ovsiannikov, Captain A.I. Parfenov and Senior Lieutenant V.G. Mokhanov all hit their targets. The gunners aboard the B-29s responded with intensive fire against the swarming MiGs, and one of them managed to hit Captain N.G. Pronin's MiG, damaging its tail fin, but Pronin pressed home his attack and set the offending aircraft on fire, after which he withdrew from the battle and safely landed his MiG back in Andong. The Americans acknowledged the loss of three B-29s and damage to a fourth, but didn't record these losses until 1 March 1951. These were bombers of the 98th BG; B-29 No. 44-61830 crashed in North Korea; two other B-29 bombers, No. 44-62106 and No. 44- 69812, although they managed to return to base with heavy damage, were later written off. Only B-29 No. 44-86335 was luckier than the other three – it was repaired and returned to service.

After the successful final fight with the Superfortresses on 25 February, another short pause in the fighting ensued that continued until the beginning of March. Between 8 and 25 February 1951, pilots of the 28th GIAP flew 175 individual combat sorties totaling 106 hours of flight time to repel enemy air raids against targets they were tasked to protect. In the resulting group aerial combats, they had destroyed or damaged 10 American aircraft (5 B-29, 5 F-80). In those combats, the following pilots had distinguished themselves: Koliadin (1 B-29), Akimov, Lebedkin, Alekseenko (1 F-80 each), Parfenov (1 B-29), Ovsiannikov (2 B-29 and 1 F-80), Pronin (1 B-29), Monakhov (1 B-29) and Borodin (1 F-80). Their own losses consisted of only one MiG. The infrequent clashes in February 1951 interrupted the overall quiet situation in the 64th IAK's operational area of MiG Alley, but this calm couldn't last forever. The enemy would not reconcile itself to the loss of air superiority in the given area, and having moved its land-based air force back to the airbases around Seoul that it had won back, the Americans renewed their aerial attacks against strategically important targets in North Korea. This concerned first of all the airfields that were under construction in North Korea, the strategically important bridges in the Siniuju area, over which the supplies to the CPV and NKPA flowed, as well as the dams in the Supung area, which furnished electricity to all of North Korea and northeastern China. Already on 1 March 1951, persistent air battles again flared up in the area of Singisiu.

ENDNOTES

1 *Pol'skaia voennaia entsiklopediia* [Polish Military Encyclopedia] Vol. 2, p. 89.

2 *Istoriia vozdushnykh voin* [History of air wars], 536.

3 As reported in the *Pravda* on 30 June 1950. Naturally, American records differ markedly. According to a surviving crew member, one B-26 bomber of the 8th BS crashed after the pilot lost control in rough weather; another B-26 of the 13th BS crashed on final approach back at its base at Ashiya, killing all aboard, with the underlying cause unknown. As for the "four-engine bomber" claimed by the North Korean pilots over Suwon, the Fifth Air Force's operational summary for 28 June only mentions that a C-54 transport evaded Yak fighters over the base.

4 Target aspect angle is the angle between the longitudinal axis of the target (projected rearward) and the line of sight to the interceptor measured from the tail of the target. Aspect angle is used in aerial gunnery for determining the angle of deflection for a firing solution. In Soviet parlance, a 0/4 target aspect angle indicates an attack from the target's 6 o'clock position, while a 4/4 target aspect angle denotes a head-on pass.

2

The Superfortresses throw in their cards before the Guards

The morning of 1 March 1951 began with a sortie at 1101 by eight MiG-15s under the command of Lieutenant Colonel V.I. Koliadin. In the region of Singisiu they were attacked by a flight of F-80 Shooting Stars and a flight of F-84 Thunderjets. In the ensuing dogfight, a pair of Shooting Stars latched onto the tail of Koliadin's MiG, but his wingman Senior Lieutenant V.F. Bushmelev saved the commander by not only forcing the Shooting Stars to break off their attack, he also managed to shoot down one of the attackers. In return, a different F-80 element jumped Bushmelev's MiG and damaged it. However, the damage was light, and our pilot refused to exit the battle and stayed with his commander until the entire group returned to base. It is most interesting that the Americans acknowledge the loss of two F-80s from the 51st FIG's 25th Squadron. Plainly Bushmelev in his counterattack managed to damage seriously both the Shooting Star of the leader Captain Forrest Parchem and that of his wingman, 1st Lieutenant R. Schmidt; both aircraft were written off after returning to base. However, as usual the American command believes that these two F-80s received their damage from ground fire.

However, the main events on this day took place in the afternoon, when the American command sent 18 B-29 bombers from the 98th BG to target the river crossings near Okkang-dong. "Specialists" in the struggle against the Superfortresses – the pilots of the 28th GIAP's 3rd Squadron – were called upon to repel this attack. Eight MiGs under the command of Major P.B. Ovsiannikov took off at 1246, followed three minutes later by six MiGs led by the regiment commander Lieutenant Colonel V.I. Koliadin. However, technical gremlins beset the Soviet group. The regiment commander's wingman, Senior Lieutenant V.F. Bushmelev, the hero of the preceding sortie, was forced to return to base because the external fuel tank refused to release, thereby cutting Koliadin's group to five. The first group also lost a pair of pilots, when the regiment's inspector of piloting technique Lieutenant Colonel P.P. Nikiforov discovered that he couldn't retract his landing gear, so he and his wingman Senior Lieutenant A. Bezmaternyi returned to their base at Andong. Thus, a total of 11 MiGs of the 28th GIAP took part in this combat with the Superfortresses.

When our MiGs from the first group spotted the first box of B-29s at 1254 and closed with the bomber formation, there was no close escort for the B-29s; as it later turned out, the covering F-80 fighters were late in arriving at the waypoint where they were supposed to rendezvous with the bombers. A gap appeared between the two formations which the Soviet pilots immediately exploited. Major Ovsiannikov's flight went on the attack against this box of B-29s by elements in turn, while Captain N.N. Motov's element remained above to cover the attack just in case. Major Ovsiannikov's element attacked the lead B-29 and set one of its engines on fire with its first pass; on the second firing pass, another of the B-29's engines began to burn. The MiGs' attacking passes caused the Superfortress formation to waver and fall apart. Scattering their dangerous loads, they began to withdraw helter skelter. Captain A.I. Parfenov's element hounded one solitary B-29, making two or three firing passes against it. Parfenov damaged the Superfortress, which started to smoke and departed in the direction of the sea. Parfenov was unable to finish it off, because it was forbidden to our pilots to cross the coastline.

At this time, Lieutenant Koliadin's five MiGs approached the combat area and attacked a different box of B-29s. Koliadin attacked without his wingman and set fire to an engine on one of the Superfortresses, while at the same time Captain A.I. Akimov's element attacked a different bomber. The attack of Major S.I. Korobov and his wingman Captain I.I. Garkavenko was also successful, crippling another one of the bombers.

After all our fighters returned to base, according to the pilots' post-mission briefings and the gun camera footage, it was determined that 10 B-29 bombers had received damage. However, according to the gun camera footage and confirmation from ground troops, only three pilots of the 28th GIAP were awarded victories over a B-29: V.I. Koliadin, P.B. Ovsiannikov and A.I. Parfenov. Most likely Major Ovsiannikov seriously damaged B-29 No. 44-69977, which crashed upon making a forced landing at the K-2 airfield in Taegu, while Lieutenant Colonel Koliadin's prize was B-29 No. 44-27341, which although in fact returned to base, it was written off because of the heavy damage it received from the MiG's cannons. All the remaining damaged Superfortresses were turned over for repairs and eventually returned to service.

According to the American command, in this combat a gunner aboard one of the B-29s from the 343rd BS, Staff Sergeant William H. Finnegan supposedly shot down one of the MiGs. However, this isn't true, since in this scrap none of the attacking MiGs were shot down or even damaged – all the MiGs returned to their base in Andong.

On the next day groups of F-84 Thunderjets from the 27th FEG made an appearance in the area of MiG Alley, covering the interdiction operations of Shooting Stars in the absence of the Sabres. At 1100, eight MiGs of the 2nd Squadron under the command of Captain A.I. Akimov and another element led by the regiment commander Lieutenant Colonel Koliadin took off to intercept enemy aircraft. By an order from the command post, our pilots were directed toward a small group of inbound F-84 Thunderjets, flying at an altitude of 7,000 meters. Apparently, they were intended to sweep the airspace in front of the strike group trailing behind them, which consisted of 12 F-80 fighter-bombers. Our pilots engaged in a battle that continued for nearly 30 minutes, and soon our pilots were running low on fuel. A flight of MiGs from the 3rd Squadron under the command of Major P.B. Ovsiannikov arrived to assist the first group and to cover its withdrawal from the battle. Twenty minutes later, another six MiGs from the 1st Squadron led by Captain A.T. Borodin took off from Andong to join the on-going combat.

The arrival of Major Ovsiannikov's was timely and successful. Selecting one of the F-80 flights, Major Ovsiannikov launched a high-side attack against a pair of "Shoots" and managed to hit the leader's F-80 from a range of 300 meters. At the same time, Ovsiannikov's wingman Senior Lieutenant V.G. Mokhanov opened fire on the wingman's Shooting Star. Emitting a stream of smoke, Mokhanov's target broke away and headed back to friendly lines.

In its turn, the arriving six MiGs of Captain Borodin's flight went after a flight of four F-84 Thunderjets. Major G.V. Timofeev managed to get one of the Thunderjets in his sights and watched it stagger under his fire before falling away.

According to the Argentinean historian Diego Zampini, in this action the pilots of the 28th GIAP had tangled with pilots of the 51st FIG's 25th Squadron and had seriously damaged Major K. E. Smith's F-80C No. 49-849 and 1st Lieutenant Donald Ferris's F-80C No. 49-739; both of the aircraft were written off three days later. Just as before, the American command attributed these losses to anti-aircraft fire. However, the American command doesn't confirm the loss of an F-84 on this day. Probably, it was the F-80C No. 49-864 that Timofeev shot up and was recorded as lost on 2 March 1951.

After such a serious defeat and significant losses, the enemy took a break from operations in MiG Alley, and made no appearance in it for more than a week. Bad weather coincided with this. During this time, all the squadrons of the 4th FIW restaged from Japan to forward airbases in South Korea: on 10 March, the 334th FIS flew into the rebuilt K-13 airbase in Suwon, while a bit later the Sabres of the 336th FIS also flew into Suwon from their previous base in Taegu. As a result, starting from 11 March 1951, the Sabres became a permanent presence in the daytime skies of North Korea.

On the other side of the Yalu River, back on 2 March 1951 a composite squadron of 10 MiGs from the 72nd GIAP under the command of Major A.Z. Bordun had flown from Anshan to Andong to assist the 28th GIAP. The pilots of Major Bordun's squadron flew their first combat mission under the watchful cover of six MiGs from the 28th GIAP's 3rd Squadron led by Major Ovsiannikov. In the Anju area they encountered eight F-86 Sabres, which after their lengthy absence had returned to North Korean skies. The dogfight was brief and had no results, but now it was clear that the menacing Sabres had rejoined the battle for air supremacy over MiG Alley.

On 12 March 1951, aerial clashes flared up in MiG Alley. Large groups of F-80 Shooting Stars from the 8th FBG, under the heavy cover of F-86 Sabres from the 4th FIG, attacked the Korean airbase in the vicinity of Singisiu. Guards Major Bordun's composite squadron from the 72nd GIAP received its baptism of fire in these combats. It was the first to take off in response to an air raid alert with a complement of 10 MiG-15s, including the new commander of the 72nd GIAP Lieutenant Colonel B.A. Mukhin, who decided to join the squadron on its first combat sortie. However, Guards Major Bordun was the group leader on this mission. In the wake of Major Bordun's squadron, a pair of MiGs under the command of Lieutenant Colonel V.I. Koliadin took off. The group adopted a stepped formation, with Major Bordun's attack flight flying a little below and in front of six covering MiGs under the command of Captain I.A. Guts.

Major Bordun's flight first encountered the enemy, a forward screening group consisting of 12 Sabres. The fight with the Sabres was lengthy and difficult, but on the Soviet side were the most experienced pilots of the 72nd IAP, all of whom had extensive combat service on the Eastern Front in World War II, and also combat experience in the skies of Korea. Plainly, this circumstance, as well as the skill of the Soviet pilots, tipped the scales of the encounter in our favor. Pilots of Bordun's group scored two victories: Guards Captain I.A. Guts downed one Sabre in the middle of the battle, and Guards Lieutenant Colonel B.A. Mukhin claimed the other when he spotted a solitary Sabre that had become isolated as the battle was winding down; approaching to within short range of it, he attacked it from above and behind, and watched it fall into the Yellow Sea.

Guards Lieutenant Colonel Koliadin's element entered the battle when it was at its peak and attacked a flight of F-86s he had spotted. Koliadin managed to hit one of the Sabres with several shells from his MiG's cannons, and it immediately dived away from the battle. In the course of this attack against superior enemy numbers, Koliadin's element split apart, and the pilots made their way back to base separately. As he was returning to Andong, Koliadin's solitary MiG came under the sudden attack of a pair of F-86 Sabres, which was being led by the commander of the 4th FIG Lieutenant Colonel Glenn Eagleston. According to Eagleston's recollections, on this day he and his wingman were on a "free hunt" for enemy planes in the area of the Yalu River, when they spotted a solitary MiG. Eagleston took advantage of the favorable situation and attacked the "loner", opening fire on the MiG from short range. However, a superb pilot, Hero of the Soviet Union Lieutenant Colonel V.I. Koliadin was sitting in the MiG's cockpit; at the last moment he managed to perform a split-S and dived away toward the Yalu. Although he couldn't avoid taking hits to his MiG, his swift reaction saved both his aircraft and his life. He managed to throw off his pursuers, and although he discovered one of his landing wheels wouldn't lower, he successfully made a two-point landing in his damaged MiG, bringing it home with 26 bullet holes in it, but he himself was intact and unharmed.

Glenn Eagleston was unable to finish off the damaged MiG, and watched as it reached its sanctuary across the Yalu River, which the American pilots were officially forbidden to cross. Eagleston couldn't assert with any confidence that he had downed the MiG in this action, and therefore he was not credited with a victory.

Just two hours later, Lieutenant Colonel Koliadin again took part in a combat sortie, flying as part of Major Bordun's group: at 1305, eight MiGs from the 1st Squadron took off to intercept enemy aircraft, followed shortly thereafter by the regiment commander Koliadin with his constant wingman, Senior Lieutenant V.F. Bushmelev. In the area of Singisiu, they spotted a group of F-80 fighter-bombers that were attacking the local airfield. Through combined attacks, the MiGs forced the Shooting Stars to break off their strike and head toward the sea. In the process, Koliadin managed to score hits on one Shooting Star and watched it crash to the ground, while Senior Lieutenant M.A. Divakov damaged another F-80. However, in this action the pilots of the 28th GIAP suffered heavy losses: during an attack on one and the same F-80, Senior Lieutenant Vasilii Fedorovich Bushsmelev's MiG collided with Senior Lieutenant Vladimir Pavlovich Sokov's fighter – in the collision both aircraft exploded and both pilots were killed. This was the heaviest loss sustained by the 151st GIAD during the entire time of the division's combat service. The shattered enemy fighter-bomber group headed for the sea, and our pilots turned back toward Andong.

In this battle, according to our pilots' claims, three F-86 Sabres and two F-80 fighter-bombers were downed. Several of the American aircraft were not seen to hit the ground, and their wreckage fragments were never found. Possibly, the fragments were widely scattered after some of the stricken aircraft exploded in mid-air, or their crash sites was given inaccurately by the pilots, because it was impossible to observe the fall of an enemy aircraft in the course of the fight. Of course, it is perhaps even more likely that the damaged enemy aircraft managed to escape the immediate combat area.

Whatever happened in the dogfight, the division registered five victories against the loss of two of its MiGs destroyed in the collision, and one MiG damaged. But the most important thing was that the enemy air strike was disrupted while the enemy suffered losses. According to the USAF command, no F-86 was lost on this day. The only confirmation it gives is for Lieutenant Colonel V.I. Koliadin's victory over an F-80C (No. 49-1828) from the 8th FBG's 36th FBS; its pilot, Captain Clarence Slack, was declared missing-in-action.

After a lull of several days, frequent aerial clashes again erupted in MiG Alley in the middle of March. Primarily these involved combats between MiG-15s and F-86 Sabres of the 4th FIG. The Americans were trying to lure the MiG-15s of the 151st IAD into dogfights and to seize aerial superiority in MiG Alley. For this purpose, as already mentioned the entire 4th FIG had restaged to forward South Korean airbases in Seoul, Kimpo and elsewhere. All three squadrons of the 4th FIG (the 334th, 335th and 336th Squadrons), which in its authorized number of aircraft was equivalent to that of a Soviet regiment (40-50 aircraft), started to make repeated sweeps through MiG Alley. In the latter half of March, Sabres of the 4th FIW equipped with drop tanks daily ranged through the air space of MiG Alley in groups of 4, 6 or 8 fighters, searching for MiG-15s, trying to sweep the area clear of their presence.

Right up until the end of March, the pilots of the 151st IAD almost daily became engaged in two or three dogfights against the Sabres. Not all of these actions were of an intense nature; more often they would end after two or three passes, and the adversaries would part in peace. The first victory in the clashes of the second half of March came on 16 March, when six MiGs of the 28th GIAP's 2nd Squadron under the command of Captain A.I. Akimov had a brief tussle with a group of six Sabres at an altitude of 10,000 meters. One Sabre was shot up at the point-blank range of 50 meters by a burst from all the cannons of Guards Captain N.R. Pisarenko's MiG. The Sabre burst into flames and went into a steep dive toward the ground, as was clearly visible on the gun camera footage and confirmed by the auxiliary command post. The American side acknowledges serious damage to F-86 No. 49-1093, which nevertheless managed to return safely to its base in South Korea.

On 17 March 1951, the composite squadron from the 72nd GIAP suffered its first loss. How this happened is told by a participant on this sortie, the former squadron commander Anatolii Zinov'evich Bordun:

> Four of us were scrambled in weather featuring totally overcast skies, with a layer of broken clouds at 100-150 meters and a visibility range of 2-4 kilometers. In response to an alarm, I and three other pilots flew off to cover a railroad station, where a particularly important train was parked. My wingman was Guards Captain L.M. Dymchenko; the second element consisted of Guards Captain V.M. Dubrovin and his wingman Guards Senior Lieutenant S.F. Khominich. The flight took place in very difficult meteorological conditions, so we flew in a column of elements. When we arrived in the area of the station, we spotted a flight of four F-80 Shooting Stars that were trying to attack it. We went after the enemy aircraft, and they immediately scattered and took to their heels. Dubrovin fired at one F-80 and followed the Shooting Star, which was already shedding fragments, into the clouds. A moment later, the target dropped out of the clouds and crashed into a hilltop. Dubrovin's pursuing MiG emerged from the clouds in a dive. When the pilot saw how close he was to the ground, he attempted to pull out of the dive, but lacked sufficient

altitude, and his MiG smashed into the hilltop next to the F-80. That's how an experienced pilot, a veteran of the Great Patriotic War, squadron deputy political commander V.M. Dubrovin was killed.

According to American records, 1st Lieutenant Howard J. Landry of the 8th FBG's 36th FBS was killed in this combat, who for some reason received credit for downing a MiG-15. Doubtlessly, this was Captain Dubrovin's MiG, which crashed on this mission, and the Americans evidently assumed that Landry had somehow fatally damaged Dubrovin's MiG, though this was not the case.

On 19 March at 1156, six crews from the regiment's 3rd Squadron under the command of Major P.B. Ovsiannikov took to the sky in response to an alarm. This group included two MiGs, flown by regiment commander Lieutenant Colonel V.I. Koliadin and his new wingman Senior Lieutenant A.A. Dubinin, who were providing top cover to Ovsiannikov's flight. Soon after takeoff, they spotted a flight of Sabres and engaged it. The Sabre pilots, seeing that they were outnumbered, attempted to avoid combat, but this they were unable to do. The Sabres were forced into an unequal fight, in the course of which Koliadin was able to latch onto the tail of one of the Sabres and watched his shells strike the target from a range of 600 meters, after which the remaining three F-86s departed in a dive. Lieutenant Koliadin, according to his gun camera footage, was given credit only for a probable victory. However, today it is possible to assume that in this fight, our pilots were dueling not with Sabres, but with a flight of Thunderjets from the 27th Fighter Group's 523rd Fighter Squadron, which was escorting a reconnaissance RF-80. Americans record the loss on this day of one F-84E, the pilot of which, Glenn Darden, was killed. Although the Americans attribute this loss to North Korean anti-aircraft gunners, it is more likely that Darden's Thunderjet was seriously damaged by the fire from Koliadin's MiG-15's cannons and soon crashed into the Korean ground.

On 20 March 1951 in the middle of the day, four MiGs from the 28th GIAP's 1st Squadron under the command of Major A.T. Borodin dueled with a flight of four F-86s. Here is how one participant in the dogfight Captain B.A. Sosna describes it:

It was somewhere around 1230, and we knew at this time that Americans didn't normally fly into MiG Alley, so I chose Valentin Pokryshkin as my wingman on the patrol. He was the older brother of the famous ace A.I. Pokryshkin, who had asked that I bring his brother home "on my wing" – that is to say, unharmed and intact. Then suddenly a signal flare streaked into the sky. We took off and almost right away after reaching our cruising altitude of 10,000 meters, we saw four F-86 Sabres flying toward us. Our flight consisted of the 1st Squadron commander Guards Major A.T. Borodin, the deputy squadron commander Guards Captain I.I. Garkavenko, Pokryshkin and I. Somehow I sensed that Borodin had missed the moment of attack and I jerked my MiG upwards, so that my wingman Pokryshkin wound up below me. I remained alone to take on the four Sabres, while Borodin's element was above me. I had time to transmit over the radio, "Don't let them climb! Look after 38 (Pokryshkin's call sign)!" and then engaged the four Sabres in a climbing, turning maneuver as we attempted to get on each other's tail. On the third time around in our carousel, I sheared off a wingman's Sabre, the crash of which was confirmed on the ground by the auxiliary command post (by Lieutenant Colonel Isaev Petrov). The remaining Sabres, seeing the attacking second element of MiGs, immediately exited the combat.

Considering the veteran's age and the large period of time that has passed since this episode, it is necessary to amend Boris Andreevich's story slightly and correct a few inaccuracies in it. On this sortie, Boris Andreevich's wingman was Senior Lieutenant A.A. Sakaev, while Captain Borodin's wingman was a different pilot, Senior Lieutenant M.A. Divakov. There is another inaccurate detail: our pilots engaged three F-86s. The regiment's documents also state that in this combat Sosna only damaged the enemy aircraft, and this was registered as only a probable victory. There is also some reason to doubt that F-86s were involved in this combat; more likely they were Thunderjets from the 27th FEG or F-80s from the 8th FBG's 80th FBS, since Americans confirm the loss of one of their F-84s and two F-80s on this day's combat sorties. Presumably, Captain B.A. Sosna's victim was Captain William R. Yoakley of the 80th FBS, whose aircraft (F-80 No. 49-1848) was shot down on one combat sortie – the pilot bailed out over Wonsan Harbor and was rescued by a Navy helicopter.

The enemy aerial activity in Mig Alley continued to increase, and in addition there were more frequent encounters with F-86 Sabres from the 4th FIW now flying from forward bases in Kimpo, South Korea. Thus it was quite difficult for just one Soviet fighter regiment to handle the large number of sorties to intercept enemy aircraft. Thus already in the middle of March 1951, another squadron from the 72nd GIAP, commanded by Major V.P. Afonin, arrived in Andong with its MiGs to reinforce the 28th GIAP. In effect, the 28th GIAP became a regiment with an operational strength of five squadrons, including the two attached squadrons from the 72nd GIAP.

On 22 March 1951, pilots of the 28th GIAP conducted their next dogfight with pilots of the 4th FIW: six MiGs from the 2nd Squadron under the command of Captain A.I. Akimov, which had taken off from Andong at 1305 and flown to a point above the Yalu River on the border, spotted a flight of Sabres at high altitude and started to climb to intercept it. As they were climbing, one of the Soviet pilots spotted another group of eight Sabres at 10,000 meters, and Akimov's flight was forced to make a head-on attack against this second group. After this pass, the MiGs swung around sharply and got in behind the Sabres. Captain Akimov managed to hit one of the Sabres, which immediately exited the battle. Seeing that the MiG pilots were in a pugnacious mood and that they no longer had an advantage in altitude, the Sabre pilots decided to break off the fight and departed toward the Yellow Sea. According to his gun camera footage, Captain A.I. Akimov received credit for downing one F-86 Sabre. However, the American command doesn't note the loss of an F-86 on this date. It is possible that Captain Akimov only damaged this Sabre.

On 23 March 1951, the American Fifth Air Force command decided to send groups of its B-29 bombers against targets in MiG Alley. Two groups of MiGs were scrambled to intercept them. First, six MiGs from the 28th GIAP's 1st Squadron under the command of Captain A.T. Borodin took off at 1120, followed a few minutes later by six MiGs from the 72nd GIAP's 3rd Squadron under the command of Major V.P. Afonin. However, this time the pilots of the 4th FIW didn't permit our pilots to break through to the bombers. Over the Yalu, they intercepted both MiG groups and tied them up in dogfights. As a result of the stubborn combat between 12 MiGs and 18 Sabres, Major Afonin managed to damage one of the Sabres, while in return, 1st Lieutenant William B. Yancey, Jr. of the 334th Fighter Squadron succeeded in damaging the MiG-15 flown by 1st Squadron commander Captain Borodin, though he was able to return safely to base with six bullet holes in his airplane. However, this time the pilots of the 151st IAD were prevented from carrying out their mission, and the B-29 groups delivered their payloads against targets in the area.

Altogether until the end of March 1951, the pilots of the 28th GIAP and 72nd GIAP conducted approximately another 10 aerial battles with the Sabres of the 4th FIW, in which between 16 and 31 March they shot down or damaged 6 Sabres; altogether for the month of March 1951, 10 Sabres were destroyed or damaged by the pilots of the 151st IAD. Of these, only four were confirmed as victories, while six were regarded as probable victories.

The pilots of the 4th FIW for the month of March 1951 flew 904 individual combat sorties and added three more MiGs to their score. However, the Soviet side confirms only one of these as an official victory, which was achieved on 30 March by a Canadian pilot who was flying with the 334th Fighter Squadron, Flight Lieutenant Joseph Levesque. The claims about the two other victories credited to pilots of the 4th FIW are dubious; two MiG-15s of the 28th GIAP, which were only damaged in dogfights on 12 and 23 March, wound up on the list of American victories. It also must disappoint the American side that the 151st IAD had no losses on 30 March or 31 March. The author has no information about the pilots of the Chinese 7th IAP, which after the departure of the 50th IAD was attached to the 151st IAD, and which also might have participated in these aerial combats. In the month of March 1951, the pilots of the 151st IAD suffered their only loss in dogfights with Sabres on 24 March. Here is how Major A.Z. Bordun describes what happened on this particular mission:

> We took off in a group of eight; I led one flight, while Major V.P. Afonin led the second flight. Approximately 50 kilometers south of Andong, we encountered at first 12 F-86s, and then another eight F-86 Sabres appeared. We became involved in combat with them at an altitude of 12,000 meters. In the course of the dogfight, Afonin's element went after a Sabre element in a steep climb, during which Afonin's wingman Senior Lieutenant Iu. P. Savinov's MiG fell into a spin, from which he emerged beneath the clouds at an altitude of 3,000 meters. However, here the Sabres caught him and shot him down, while Afonin was distracted by his pursuit of a Sabre and couldn't come to Savinov's aid in time. In the course of this dogfight, two Sabres put the squeeze on Afonin himself, and I bailed him out of his predicament by attacking and shooting down one of them. Soon thereafter the dogfight's participants began to run low on fuel, and both sides exited the battle.

Guards Senior Lieutenant Savinov fell together with his MiG and was killed-in-action, but according to different sources, the Sabres didn't shoot him down in this battle; rather, his plane fell into a spin and he was unable to pull out of it in time. Possibly, therefore this victory wasn't credited to 1st Lieutenant Richard S. Becker of the 4th FIW's 334th Squadron, because the American pilots couldn't see what happened to the MiG after it fell into some clouds, and therefore they didn't put in a claim for his victory.[1] However it went, this was the only loss that the pilots of the 151st IAD suffered in combats with Sabres for the entire month of March, not including the combat damage inflicted to Guards Lieutenant Colonel Koliadin's and Guards Major A.T. Borodin's MiGs by Sabres, but both of these aircraft were repaired. Guards Major A.Z. Bordun received no credit for the victory on 24 March, but a fellow participant in this aerial combat, Guards Captain A.E. Sanin, confirmed in his memoirs that a Sabre really was shot down in this combat, though it is true that he cannot recall who deserved the credit in this swirling dogfight.

Altogether over the period between 1 and 26 March 1951, according to the regiment's Political Report No. 0257 dated 28 March 1951, the pilots of the 28th GIAP alone conducted 279 individual combat sorties with a cumulative flight time of 168 hours and 8 minutes. In this time they engaged in 14 group aerial combats, and downed 14 enemy aircraft, of which 10 were confirmed by ground troops.

Beginning in March 1951, the FEAF command had embarked on assembling its bomber formations, having in mind to use its B-29s, together with heavy fighter escort, to destroy the network of North Korean bases that were under construction. The mission undertaken on 1 March 1951 by 18 B-29 bombers from the 98th BG, escorted by 22 F-80 Shooting Stars, was the beginning of a series of strong air raids against North Korean targets. However, the heavy losses suffered by the American side on that mission brought a halt to B-29 attacks for nearly a month in the area where MiGs were active. Only at the end of March did the American command once again send its Superfortresses into MiG Alley, but this time they were strongly screened by F-86 Sabres of the 4th FIW.

Thus, the pilots of the 151st IAD on 29 March 1951 had to repulse a major attack on Sinuiju by 27 B-29s, covered by a large group of F-86 fighters. Two squadrons from the 28th GIAP and one from the 72nd GIAP – 18 MiGs altogether under the command of Hero of the Soviet Union Lieutenant Colonel N.L. Trofimov – took part in repelling the attack. Pilots of the 72nd GIAP tied up the Sabres in combat, while Major A.I. Korobov's flight attacked the B-29 formation. Korobov made the first firing pass from below and behind, and managed to obtain hits on one of the B-29s, which erupted in flames. Captain Antonov's element also made a successful attack on the Superfortress formation, observing shell hits on the enemy bombers. Having suffered damage to several bombers and seeing that they could not break through to the target area on this occasion, the B-29 formation turned back without carrying out their assignment. The 151st IAD had no losses in this action.

Several years later, the Americans confirmed that on 29 March, the B-29 No. 45-21749 of the commander of the USAF's 19th BG Colonel Payne Jennings, Jr. was damaged by MiG fire, and while trying to nurse the crippled bomber back to its base on Okinawa, it fell into the sea, killing all 13 crewmembers aboard. This was Colonel Jennings, Jr.'s 44th mission in the skies of Korea. Thus, Guards Major A.I. Korobov did in fact down one B-29 in the 29 March battle, and the victory was a resounding one, since it claimed the life of the commander of a SAC bomber group.

On the following day, an attack was undertaken against the Supung hydroelectric station by 24 B-29 bombers from the 19th BG, escorted by 10 F-86s from the 334th FIS and approximately 40 F-80s from the 49th FBG. Here is how a participant in the engagement, Guards Senior Lieutenant V.G. Monakhov, describes the air battle that unfolded that day:

On this day, 16 MiGs of our regiment was scrambled in order to repel a B-29 attack against the cluster of hydro-electrical stations in North Korea, which was located about 100-150 kilometers northeast of our airfield in Andong. Guards Lieutenant Colonel Koliadin commanded the group. Eight MiGs led by Guards Major Bordun remained in reserve at the airbase, in order to cover our group's landing upon our return from combat.

In the air we soon encountered approximately 40 B-29s, escorted by a large group of Sabres. As we approached the enemy aircraft, Koliadin ordered the Sabres to be tied up in combat. Guards Captain A.I. Akimov's element attacked and diverted one F-86 formation of approximately 10 Sabres. Another two elements of MiGs tied up two other groups of Sabres in combat. Having chased down the main group, we saw B-29s that were flying in box formations of four bombers each. Shooting Stars were providing close escort to the bomber column. My leader, Guards Major P.B. Ovsiannikov, and I broke through the fighter screen and made a firing pass against the tail-end box of bombers, concentrating our fire on the leader. During this attack, a pair of F-80s began to emerge on our tail, but with the large reserve of speed we had accumulated in our dive, we separated from them in a climb. After the first attack, we successfully made another one against a different box, again focusing our fire on the leader. We attacked the bombers a total of three or four times and saw our shells striking the targets. In this combat we deliberately avoided tangling with the fighters.

As a result of the persistent attacks by the pilots of the 28th GIAP, the Superfortress pilots were forced to jettison their payloads before reaching the hydro-electrical station complex on the Yalu River. That is roughly what our element did during the aerial combat on this day. The gun camera footage was good, we opened fire from rather close range, but it wasn't possible to follow the further fate of the enemy aircraft that we attacked. However, in the report I turned in, I wrote that we as a pair had probably downed one B-29 and one F-86.

To what V.G. Monakhov had to say, I can only add that Guards Major Ovsiannikov was credited with two victories, one B-29 and one F-86. The Americans in turn claimed the gunners aboard the B-29s of the 28th BS [Bombardment Squadron] had downed one MiG-15, but this doesn't correspond with Soviet records, since all 16 MiGs that took part in the battle returned safely to their base at Andong.

Eight MiGs of the 72nd GIAP under the command of the regiment's deputy commander Lieutenant Colonel Trofimov also participated in this action. They also attacked the already scattered and solitary B-29s and also had accompanying duels with the F-80 and F-86 escort fighters. These pilots also observed shell hits on the targeted bombers, but didn't see any of them go down either. The American command acknowledged the loss of one of their B-29s from the 28th BS, which was being piloted by Captain Gallagher. He managed to bring his damaged B-29 No. 44-69746 back to the Itazuke Air Base in Japan, but the aircraft had been so riddled that it was written off as scrap metal. This is unsurprising, since Major Ovsiannikov conducted several passes against this Boeing and actually did turn it into a sieve. Major Ovsiannikov's other victory on this day was also acknowledged: on one of his attacks, he managed to obtain close-range hits against one of the Shooting Stars that was hindering him from attacking the bombers, but by mistake it was recorded as an F-86. In reality, this was F-80 No. 49-839 from the 49th FBG's 9th FBS, and its pilot Captain Kenneth J. Granberg went missing-in-action.

Incidentally, for shooting down a fourth B-29 Superfortress on this mission, Guards Major P.B. Ovsiannikov was awarded the Order of Lenin. However, the Americans claimed that Flight Lieutenant Levesque of the 334th FIS bagged one MiG-15, but all the Soviet pilots safely returned to their base at Andong; thus his victory was not in fact real.

This was the final air battle conducted by the pilots of both sides in March 1951. For the period February-March 1951, the pilots of the 151st IAD flew a total of 721 individual combat sorties and conducted 28 aerial combats, in which they downed 24 enemy aircraft. Their own losses amounted to five MiG-15s and four pilots. Four more MiGs received combat damage, but were restored to service by the division's mechanics. On 2 April 1951, this Guards aviation division turned over its MiGs to thrice Hero of the Soviet Union Guards Colonel I.N. Kozhedub's 324th IAD, which had arrived in Andong, and moved to Anshan, where it received the assignment to retrain the pilots of a two-regiment division of the KPAAF to fly the MiG-15. The pilots of the 151st IAD spent the time between May and September 1951 training the North Korean pilots in MiG-15s that were equipped with the RD-45 engine, which the 151st IAD had acquired from the 324th IAD. The training took place on the Anshan Air Base; during all this time the division of Guardsmen was in the 64th IAK's reserve, and sometimes the pilots of the 151st IAD scrambled on an alert. From Anshan they had the additional task to cover the takeoffs and landings of the pilots of the 64th IAK's 324th and 303rd IADs in Andong and Miaogou. There were not many such sorties, even fewer encounters with enemy aircraft, and the pilots of the 151st IAD scored no victories, but also had no losses. In addition, at the end of June 1951 one regiment of the 151st IAD began to retrain a second North Korean fighter regiment to fly the MiG-15, and to prepare it for combat operations.

According to records, by 28 July 1951 the entire flight staff of this second North Korean fighter regiment, numbering 31 pilots, had graded out as ready to conduct squadron-level combat operations in daylight hours in good flying weather, and night missions in flights up to an altitude of 8,000 meters. The regiment's technical staff had been prepared to service and repair the equipment independently, and the command staff – to lead combat operations. Simultaneously with the retraining, the unit conducted defensive combat patrols. In the course of the retraining, there were two ground mishaps with the MiG-15s involving the North Korean pilots.

On 1 August 1951, the Soviet regiment had completed the retraining of the flight and ground crews of the NKPA's 447th IAP. The North Korean regiment now had 29 pilots ready for squadron operations up to an altitude of 8,000-10,000 meters in simple meteorological conditions. On average, each North Korean pilot had 5 hours and 22 minutes of flight time during the month, including 4 hours and 24 minutes in the MiG-15. The unit suffered one air crash of a MiG-15 being piloted by the Korean pilot Ahn Eng on 20 August 1951. The causes of the crash have not been established.

In October 1951, the pilots of the 151st IAD, having completed their training of the North Koreans' IAD, handed over their MiGs to them, and then departed by train for the Soviet Union. They had carried out their internationalist and military duty with honor.

Over their entire period of combat operations in the skies of North Korea and China, the pilots of the 151st IAD between 1 November 1950 and 1 April 1951 conducted 993 individual combat sorties and became involved in 47 aerial combats with enemy aircraft, in which they officially downed 36 US aircraft (this includes only the victories of the 28th and 72nd GIAP), and were credited with 26 more probable victories. The losses of the 151st IAD over this period consisted of six MiG-16s and six pilots.

The aerial combats in February-March 1951 in the skies of Korea marked the end of the first stage of the air war in Korea. A second, more sanguinary stage, which involved twice as many aviation units from both sides as had participated in the first stage, began in April 1951.

What were the results of the first stage of the air war over Korea? The fledgling KPAAF that had started the war could not contend on equal footing with the UN and South Korean air forces, almost 90% of which came from the USAF and USNAF. In the autumn clashes, effectively the entire North Korean air force was destroyed on the ground and in aerial combats by the United States' fighters, fighter-bombers and bombers. The enemy reigned completely supreme in the skies of Korea.

The situation changed sharply with the entry of the Soviet MiG-15 fighter regiments into the fighting. In November 1950, the boundless aerial superiority of the USAF in the skies of Korea came to an end. Gradually, the Soviet pilots expelled the USAF and the allied air forces out of the territory that bordered on the Yalu River, which the American pilots quickly nicknamed "MiG Alley", and with every passing month they expanded that area. By the beginning of April 1951, the MiGs of the 64th IAK was contesting the air space as far south as the "no-fly" line drawn between Pyongyang and Wonsan.

Over the first stage of this war, the Soviet pilots drove the USNAF and the air forces of Great Britain and Australia out of their area of operations, and sharply reduced their combat activity in the zone where the MiG-15s operated. Flights by piston-engine F-51 Mustang fighter-bombers into MiG Alley greatly decreased, since they were no longer able to carry out their combat missions and were suffering heavy losses. Simultaneously, the conventional B-29 bombers also began to make rare appearances in MiG Alley; when they did show up, it was always with heavy fighter escort which still proved unable to save the B-29 formations from losses.

The F-80 Shooting Star could not fulfill its role as a fighter when opposed by the MiG-15, because its performance was inferior in every measure. Therefore with the arrival of the newer F-84 Thunderjet and especially the F-86 Sabre, the Shooting Stars switched to carrying out a ground attack role, while at the same time still requiring a strong covering force of F-84s and F-86s.

The Soviet pilots trained the Chinese pilots of several PLAAF divisions and several regiments of the KPAAF, which came to be equipped with the modern Soviet MiG-15 jet fighters. In addition, the Soviet pilots over their first five months of the war acquired valuable combat experience in the combats with the powerful and modern USAF, and adopted several new combat methods to use in their clashes with the American pilots.

Only American pilots flying the F-86 Sabre, which could take on the MiG-15 as an equal, and at the same time often held a numerical superiority in encounters between the MiGs and Sabres, became a most serious adversary in this period for the pilots of the 64th IAK. However, the Soviet pilots found new combat tactics to employ against the Sabres, using primarily their extensive combat experience and those flight characteristics where the MiG held the advantage over the Sabre, especially in climbing.

The losses of the US Fifth Air Force grew substantially with the introduction of the MiG-15. This forced the American command to strengthen the Fifth Air Force with more modern aircraft, and to transfer new aviation squadrons and groups from North America to South Korea.

THE "KOZHEDUB BOYS" ENTER THE FIGHTING

By April 1951, the front lines had largely stabilized along the old border between North and South Korea, the 38th Parallel. The fighting was mostly of local significance, and the two sides in this period conducted hardly any active combat operations. However, the conflict between the two sides in the air continued, and the frequency of aerial clashes not only rose, but also became more intense.

The US Fifth Air Force in April 1951 continued to press the offensive against the 64th IAK and had under its command at this time the 18th FBG flying F-51 Mustangs (three squadrons); the 8th FBG (four squadrons), the 49th FBG (three squadrons), and the 51st FIG (three squadrons), all equipped with the F-80C fighter-bombers; the 27th FEG flying F-84E Thunderjets; and the F-86A-5 fighter interceptors of the 4th FIW. In addition, the Fifth Air Force had two light bomber groups flying the B-26 bomber (the 3rd and 452nd BG), as well as three bomber groups (the 19th, 307th and 98th BG), each with three squadrons of B-29 bombers. The Fifth Air Force also had several reconnaissance squadrons, the 374th Airlift Group with C-54 transport planes, as well as several air rescue units. The Fifth Air Force's total numerical strength by this time exceeded 2,000 aircraft. This number does not include the separate units contributed by the South Korean, Australian, South African and Canadian air forces, which had a combined number of a little more than 100 aircraft, but had no particular significance in the air battles. In addition, USNAF, British, and Australian fighter and fighter-bomber squadrons operated from aircraft carrier groups in the Yellow and Japanese Seas, while several US Marine air squadrons were based in South Korea. The aircraft carriers contributed approximately 1,200 aircraft to the UN air presence over Korea, but these were mostly piston-engine fighter-bombers and light bombers.

All this air power was opposed by the 64th IAK alone, which by April 1951 had only three fighter divisions, each equipped with the modern MiG-15: the 151st GIAD, the 28th IAD and the 324th IAD. However, at this time the first two fighter divisions mentioned were in the 64th IAK's reserve and were occupied primarily with training Chinese and North Korean pilots. There were also nine Soviet aviation divisions in China, which were equipped with the outdated MiG-9 and Yak-17U jets, or with the piston-engine La-9, Il-10 and Tu-2, which for this reason were not employed in combat over North Korea. At the end of March 1951, it was decided to rotate the 151st IAD out of the first echelon, and for this purpose Guards Colonel I.N. Kozhedub's combat-ready 324th IAD was moved to Andong out of the 64th IAK's reserve. On 30 March 1951, the Division's 176th GIAP under the command of Guards Lieutenant Colonel A.S. Koshel' arrived on the Andong airfield. This regiment was armed with MiG-15s that were equipped with the older RD-45A engine. So by the end of 31 March, the pilots of the 28th GIAP turned over their MiG-15bis fighters to the 176th GIAP, and flew off to Mukden in the 176th GIAP's MiGs. A former instrument technician with the 324th IAD, Ivan Anisimovich Piatov remembers well how the exchange of the division on the airfield in Andong took place:

We arrived at the Andong garrison 29/30 March 1951, and on 31 March the corps commander General Belov landed in a La-9 fighter and taxied over to our dispersal area. The General climbed into a car and was driven to the command post. We accordingly started to inspect the aircraft and prepare it for takeoff again, as we'd been instructed to do. At this time, sirens started to blare from everywhere: on the airfield, in the garrison and in the town of Andong. An enemy photo reconnaissance plane was flying at an altitude of 4,000-5,000 meters, taking photographs. According to my comrade Vedernikov, who worked in the division headquarters, General Belov expressed his dissatisfaction to Kozhedub: "Why haven't you scrambled the shift on duty?" Ivan Nikitovich replied, "I'm not the boss here!" Belov then issued verbal orders: "Execute the handover of the garrison." After a two-hour discussion with Kozhedub about the combat assignment, the General flew back to his residence in Mukden, where the corps headquarters was located at the time. That's how the entire procedure of rotating the garrison wound up in Kozhedub's hands.

The pilots of the 324th IAD conducted their first combat sortie on 2 April, when six MiGs of the 2nd Squadron took-off at 1200 to intercept enemy aircraft, but unfortunately they never spotted them and returned back to base. The day of 3 April became the more intense and real combat baptism for the pilots of the 176th GIAP: first at 0910, a pair of 176th GIAP MiGs led by the regiment navigator Guards Major S.P. Subbotin (his wingman was Senior Lieutenant P.S. Milaushkin) took-off on a long-range reconnaissance flight out to the MiG's full operational radius. At high altitude they crossed all of North Korea, reached the 38th Parallel, and flew as far as Seoul. They received anti-aircraft fire and Sabres attempted to intercept them, but they were able to complete their

A pilot of the 176th GIAP Lieutenant P.S. Milaushkin (a 1945 photograph).

Hero of the Soviet Union and ace of the 176th GIAP Major S.P. Subbotin, 1952.

mission unhindered. Subbotin's element safely returned to Andong, and just as they were taxiing along the runway after landing, their MiGs' tanks ran out of fuel.

On this same day, the pilots of the 176th GIAP conducted several aerial combats with the enemy. For example, immediately after Subbotin's element departed on its reconnaissance mission, eight MiGs of the 1st Squadron under the command of Captain K. Ia. Sheberstov took-off for the area of Sonchon, where they encountered two F-84 fighter-bombers being covered by six Sabres. Having spotted the MiGs, the Thunderjets immediately turned around and headed for the sea, while the Sabres engaged the MiGs in combat. Soon another 16 F-86s arrived on the scene and American numerical superiority became evident: several minutes into the dogfight, Captain James Jabara of the 334th FIS and a future ace of the 4th FIW, shot down Senior Lieutenant Pavel Demidovich Nikitchenko's MiG; the pilot was killed in his cockpit. Here's how Jabara describes this victory:

> The first one was on April 3, when [Dick] Becker was flying as my wingman. We were two against two. We saw the MiGs first at 7,000 feet and I used 1,200 rounds, damaging the engine of one MiG that flamed out and crashed about ten miles from its home field. I damaged the other.

A half-hour later, Guards Captain A.F. Vas'ko led eight of the 2nd Squadron's MiGs to the area of Singisiu, where they were jumped by 12 F-86s, which in the course of several minutes damaged two MiGs; the MiG pilots, Senior Lieutenants A.P. Verdysh and B.G. Reitarovsky had to make forced landings under the fire of the Sabres on their Andong air field. The pilots of the 176th GIAP still had no combat experience against the modern USAF, and thus made tactical errors in their initial combat encounters with it. This resulted in their first losses on their very first day of combat experience. The weather conditions that day were difficult due to the mostly cloudy skies, which complicated the assembly of the groups and combat maneuvering. Therefore the combat came out as disorganized and chaotic; the formations broke apart into separate elements, each fighting in isolation, which the Americans exploited in order to damage two of our MiGs. Guards Senior Lieutenant A.P. Verdysh was one of the pilots that returned from the battle in a crippled MiG. Here is how he describes what happened:

> The first major battle with the Americans, in which all the regiment's pilots took part, occurred on 3 April. It was difficult to maintain formation in the clouds, and our element, consisting of Guards Captain S.M. Kramarenko and me, distracted by the search for enemy aircraft, became separated from the squadron formation led by Guards Captain Vas'ko, when we were attacked by four Sabres as we emerged from some clouds (approximately at an altitude of 4,000 meters). My aircraft took hits that knocked out the engine, but I managed for a short time to maintain enough speed to escape into some clouds behind my leader, and reported to him about the situation with my engine. However, since the engine wasn't working, I rapidly lost speed and was forced to put my MiG into a diving turn of 90-120 degrees in the clouds. Emerging under the clouds at an altitude of approximately 1,700 meters and having taken a look around, I found that I was in the area of my base and decided to make a dead-stick landing. Taking a glance to the left, I spotted three F-86s that

were rapidly closing on me. I couldn't escape from them into the clouds or perform an energetic maneuver, because my engine was dead. Just then I recalled a story of one veteran, who in the years of the Great Patriotic War [the Russian name for World War II on the Eastern Front] when once under enemy attack conducted a barrel roll with a loss of speed, causing the enemy to overshoot their target.

As I performed the barrel roll, I watched the enemy aircraft flash past me, but I had only one thought – "Don't fall into a spin!" When coming out of the barrel roll, the three Sabres were about 150-200 meters in front of my MiG's nose with their speed brakes deployed, and they began to bank to the right. They plainly wanted to watch as my aircraft crashed into the ground. But I instantly opened fire on them; everyone on the ground at the base saw this. It is possible that one of the three Sabres was damaged by my fire, which their subsequent actions indicated: they stopped their turn, pulled in their brakes, turned on their superchargers and headed back toward friendly lines in a dive.

I cannot firmly state whether or not I shot down an enemy aircraft, but I concluded that the barrel roll that I conducted saved my life. After the enemy's departure I made a forced belly landing on my airbase in my stricken MiG. The landing wasn't quite successful, but I only received a mild concussion when my head struck the gun sight.

A.P. Gogolev of the 176th GIAP's 2nd Squadron also took part in this fight, and according to him, their entire squadron scrambled in response to an order from the command post and the combat was almost in the vicinity of the airbase. The weather was poor: heavy clouds and haze up to 4,000-5,000 meters. He could only see the other MiGs in his flight. The situation was unclear, which might cause erroneous actions. Moreover, the American airplanes were equipped with radar – they might see us in the murk, while they would still be invisible to us.[2] The combat turned out to be difficult. In this, in essence its first serious combat, the 176th Regiment suffered its first losses due to the disorganization and unexpected attack. Senior Lieutenant P.D. Nikitchenko, a pilot in the 1st Squadron, was shot down and killed, and two more of the Regiment's MiGs were damaged and had to make dead-stick landings on the Andong Air Base. Senior Lieutenant A.P. Verdysh of the 2nd Squadron made a belly landing, while Senior Lieutenant B.G. Reitarovsky landed on the runway, but his hydraulics quit on him and he crashed into a revetment, breaking his leg. Both aircraft had received heavy damage and they were simply written-off.

As already mentioned, Captain James Jabara of the 334th FIS shot down Senior Lieutenant P.D. Nikitchenko in this action; Lieutenants Roy MacLean and William Yancey of the 334th and 336th FIS shot up A.P. Verdysh's MiG, while Lieutenant Colonel Benjamin Emmert of the 335th FIS damaged Reitarovsky's aircraft. From this it is evident that all three fighter squadrons of the 4th Fighter Interceptor Group participated in this battle on 3 April.

However, the day still didn't end with this action. At 0940, another group consisting of eight MiGs from the 176th GIAP's 3rd Squadron under the command of Captain V.G. Murashov was directed to the area of Singisiu, where they soon spotted a group of six Thunderjets, which the lead flight attacked. However, at this moment Murashov's flight was itself attacked by a pair of F-86s. They had to break off their attack to evade.

Captain A.L. Shipitsin's flight, which had been left behind as top cover, salvaged the situation. Having spotted the Sabres, Shipitsin led his flight in a dive upon the Sabres, and Captain I.A. Iablokov's element managed to score hits on one of the Sabres, which streaming smoke went into a dive toward the south. As is now known, Captain Iablokov managed to inflict serious damage to F-86A No.49-1173, which was being flown by Major Ronald D. Shirlaw, who had to make a forced landing in North Korean territory not far from Kaisen, after which he was taken prisoner. This was the first victory for the pilots of the 324th IAD in the skies of Korea!

That evening, the 324th IAD command, led by its commander Colonel Kozhedub, made a detailed investigation of all four combat sorties and an analysis of the unsuccessful combats earlier that day. They came to a number of proper conclusions, which were evident in the actions of the division's pilots already on the following day.

On 4 April 1951, Lieutenant Colonel E.G. Pepeliaev's 196th IAP also opened its combat score. The day began when at 0700 eight MiGs of its 1st Squadron led by Captain N.A. Antipov departed on a combat mission. In the vicinity of Sonchon they encountered a group of 12 Sabres and engaged them in battle. In the course of the ensuing dogfight, Major Edward K. Fletcher of the 334th FIS managed to damage Senior Lieutenant V.F. Kalmykov's aircraft, and he had to make a forced landing in North Korean territory. The Soviet pilot escaped with light wounds, while his MiG was repaired and soon returned to service. However, the pilots of the 196th IAP evened the score when Captain L.N. Ivanov successfully attacked a flight of Sabres and obtained hits on one of them, which limped away from the battle.

That afternoon at 1530, the 196th IAP's entire 3rd Squadron under the command of Major N.K. Shelamonov took-off on a mission. Ground controllers directed them to a group of Sabres, but the latter declined combat. When landing back at Andong, it turned out that a MiG was missing from Captain P.A. Soskovets's flight. Just when it was calculated that the MiG would be running out of fuel, Senior Lieutenant F.D. Shebanov's MiG gently landed on the runway – the pilots of the squadron had been waiting for him anxiously. The pilot climbed out of the cockpit and began to shout joyfully. "I got one! I shot down a Sabre!" On this sortie, he had fallen behind the rest of the formation on the return to base, and his lone MiG had been unexpectedly attacked from above by a pair of Sabres. However, the lead American pilot misjudged the angle of attack, overshot the MiG, and wound up directly in front of the nose of Shebanov's fighter. Shebanov only had to make a slight adjustment to line the Sabre up in his sights, and with two short bursts he shot it down. Yet although this was the 196th IAP's first victory, the squadron commander Senior Lieutenant N.K. Shelamonov dressed down the pilot for lagging behind the formation and reprimanded him, so that he would draw the appropriate conclusions from this action. Although the American command doesn't acknowledge the loss of one of its Sabres on this day, fragments of an F-86 were later found by a search team in the Anju area and were attributed to the Sabre that had been downed by Senior Lieutenant Shebanov.

After the 324th IAD pilots' more successful combats on 4 April, the mood among the Division's command and pilots improved somewhat. Division commander Kozhedub didn't restrict himself to training only the combat pilots; he also paid attention to the ground personnel and the living conditions of his subordinates. Former instrument technician of the 324th IAD's command flight Ivan Anisimovich Piatov recalls:

On 4 April (after the unsuccessful combats of 3 April), we were permitted to remain in the garrison area until 1000. We were thinking that this meant the division commander had some sort of important business in the garrison, possibly discussions with the local service staff.

So we're sitting in the mess hall, having a bite to eat. Suddenly we see the division commander emerging from the kitchen with an entourage, including two of our officers and three Chinese kitchen workers, one of them the chef. Before reaching our table, they stopped and the division commander asked, "How are they feeding you?" One sergeant ventured to reply: "They've been giving us boiled lard without any meat. Not everyone likes it, and it goes untouched." The division commander turned to the Chinese chef and said, "Lard alone is bad." The chef replied very earnestly, "Yes! A dick!" The division commander burst out laughing. Yes, this was the first Russian word that our Chinese staff had learned, and everyone started laughing. The Chinese were bewildered and couldn't understand why the Russians were laughing. Then someone explained it to them. However, the meat ration soon changed, and they began serving us more meat than lard.

The Chinese cook had arranged it in the following way: meat for the pilots' mess, while the ground staff got lard. The division commander had decided to check on the situation, because he himself had gotten sick after a meal in February, and poisoning had been suspected. Sabotage can take many forms. Thus in February it had been necessary to organize a personal security team to guard Kozhedub when traveling at night to the airfield and back again, out of our own personnel, that is, those technicians that serviced his airplane. Long after the conversation about the lard, we recalled it and smiled.

Clashes with Sabres now became a daily affair for the pilots of the 324th IAD. Each day featured on average two combat sorties and one to two encounters with the enemy, primarily Sabres, which appeared over MiG Alley in large groups of 20-30 fighters, or in two groups, one which would serve as the bait, while the other acted as the attack group. With every passing day, the pilots of both Soviet regiments accumulated that vital combat experience of aerial battles with the enemy in the skies of Korea, and with every passing day the pilots of the 324th IAD felt more confident in combat, and fought more tenaciously and intelligently against the Sabres, engaging them increasingly often on their own terms and more often emerging as the victors. To be sure, these victories didn't come easily and it was still rare when they got by without any losses of their own in the duels with the Sabre; they realized that this was a serious adversary, yet if they didn't make any mistakes in combat it was possible to dogfight with them.

An example of this became a combat on 6 April, when in the morning at 0730 eight MiGs of the 196th IAP's 2nd Squadron led by Captain B.V. Bokach encountered 16 F-86s not far from Tetsuzan, which were escorting two flights of eight Shooting Star fighter-bombers each, yet despite the enemy's enormous numerical superiority, they resolutely engaged the enemy aircraft in combat. Soon eight MiGs from the 3rd Squadron under the command of Senior Lieutenant N.K. Shelamonov came to their assistance and made the battle more equal. Shortly thereafter, flight commander Captain B.S. Abakumov shot down one Sabre from close range, and the remaining immediately broke off the combat and headed in the direction of South Korea. In this action we had no losses; only Senior Lieutenant G.A. Loktev's MiG received some light damage from the fire of a pair of Shooting Stars, but he safely returned to base with the entire group. This victory boosted the confidence of the pilots of the 196th IAP. However, the American command acknowledges no losses on this day, so it is possible that Abakumov only damaged the enemy Sabre.

BLACK THURSDAY

On the morning of 7 April 1951, the Americans launched a large air strike against the rail-road bridge over the Yalu in the vicinity of Sinuiju with 16 B-29 bombers from the 98th and 307th BG, covered by 48 F-84E Thunderjets from the 27th FEG. The entire 176th GIAP was scrambled to repel this attack – 22 MiGs took-off in response to the air raid alarm.

Six crews of the 2nd Squadron under the command of Captain A.F. Vas'ko were the first to take flight at 0850. They were followed at 2 to 3 minute intervals by two more groups from the 176th GIAP: eight MiGs of the 3rd Squadron led by Captain V.G. Murashov, then finally eight MiGs of the 1st Squadron led by Captain K.Ia. Sheberstov.

Captain Vas'ko's group was the first to spot the inbound enemy and attempted to attack the bombers, but was unable do this because of the escorting fighters. This time the Thunderjets succeeded in tying up Vas'ko's group in combat and prevented them from reaching the bomber formations.

Several minutes later, Captain Murashov's flight of eight MiGs approached the Sinuiju bridge and attempted to break through to the B-29s, which flying in flights of box forma-tions were nearing its primary target – the strategic bridge. However, Murashov's group

Major K.Ia. Sheberstov, deputy commander of the 176th GIAP.

was also unable to attack the bombers. Covering Thunderjets spotted it in time, and several flights of F-84s attacked Murashov's group. The only thing this group of MiGs managed to do was to tie up a large portion of the escorting fighters in combat and to down one of the Thunderjets – the victory was credited to Senior Lieutenant B.A. Obraztsov.

Only the 1st Squadron's MiGs led by Captain Sheberstov managed to break through to two flights of B-29 bombers and to conduct several attacks against their formations. Two flights of F-84s attempted to disrupt the MiGs' attack, but were unable to do so. Captain I.A. Suchkov successfully attacked one of the bomber boxes, concentrating his fire on the lead bomber, and saw his shells striking the aircraft, after which it burst into flames and dropped out of the formation in a dive. Back on the ground, Suchkov's wingman Senior Lieutenant D.M. Fedorov confirmed his leader's victory, reporting that he had observed the stricken B-29 turn toward the Yellow Sea, but having reached Korea Bay, it soon made a controlled crash into the water. This was B-29 No. 44-86268 of the 307th BG's 371st Squadron that fell into the bay: some of its crew had bailed out of the aircraft when it was over land and wound up as prisoners, while some were rescued in the water by USNAF SA-16 flying boats.

Captain S.P. Subbotin, flying with Senior P.S. Milaushkin as his wingman, downed another B-29 in this combat. Here's how he describes this combat:

> Waiting on the ground at Readiness No. 1, we were already listening over the radio to reports that a column of enemy bombers, covered by approximately 50 F-84s, was heading for the bridge and airfield. Soon we were given the command: "Bullet" (for takeoff), and then "Rocket" (for gaining altitude and assembling). Ten minutes after we had taken off and assembled, we saw the column of B-29 flights, being guarded on the flanks by F-84 elements. They were flying toward the bridge and the Sinuiju airfield at an altitude of 7,500-8,000 meters. The skies were clear and cloudless. We decided to attack with the entire group, since an order had arrived: "Everyone attack the B-29s; don't engage the "Crosses" [a Soviet nickname for straight-winged aircraft like the F-84]." We went into our first firing pass from out of the sun at an altitude of 9,000 meters. Subbotin and I went after the second flight of four B-29s – there were enough targets for everyone. Subbotin targeted the lead bomber, while I went for the bomber off the leader's right wing. The Thunderjets below us were startled.
>
> The initial attack was slashing and unexpected by them; I didn't even see a fusillade of fire from the B-29 gunners. The silhouette of a B-29 appeared in my gun sight, and closing on it quickly, I opened fire. The shells streaked into the B-29's fuselage and its right wing, striking both the inboard and outboard engines. I could see the shell explosions, which looked like large drops of rain hitting a puddle of water. Our speed was high, and I heard the leader's voice: "Exit [the attack] to the right." I carried out his order. The Thunderjets attempted to attack us, but they were lagging too far behind us.
>
> We executed a second attack against a group of three B-29s, but this time the gunners' fire was so heavy that I didn't manage to open fire on this pass before I heard the leader's order: "Exit to the left" – and again I followed the order, because I had to stay with my leader. Another attack, but now against a pair of bombers (one of them had dropped out of the formation). Subbotin attacked the leader, while I

selected his wingman on the right, but I had approached the bomber so closely that I involuntarily pressed the button to deploy the speed brakes and simultaneously opened fire from all the cannons. The return fire from the bombers' gunners was not as intense as it had been during the second firing pass. My shells exploded on the right wing and struck both engines. In order to avoid a collision, I continued my dive and passed below the bomber, before pulling out in a climbing right-hand turn. With this maneuver I lost track of my leader. I discovered that my cockpit glass had a bullet hole in it and I had lost cockpit pressure, but the MiG was responding well to the controls. Then I spotted another B-29 and moved to attack it, but I had exhausted my ammunition and so I withdrew from the battle. During my landing approach back at base, my landing gear wouldn't lower, so I used the emergency release and landed safely on the runway.

In this battle I damaged two Superfortresses, my leader shot down one, and several more B-29s were shot down or badly damaged by my comrades in the regiment. We had no losses in this action, though many returned from the battle with bullet holes in their aircraft.

Although additional bombers took shell hits, they apparently weren't quite fatal for these B-29s, and the regiment received credit for only two victories, which were confirmed by gun camera footage and North Korean officials; credit went to Guards Captain Subbotin and Guards Captain Suchkov. Through Suchkov's clearer gun camera footage, it was evident that he had fired at the Superfortresses from a distance of 300-400 meters. True, he also brought back his MiG with four bullet holes in it. The Americans acknowledged, in addition to the loss of one B-29 from the 371st BS, which Captain Suchkov downed, that another B-29 (No. 45-21725) from the 370th BS of the same 307th BG managed to fly back to its base at Nawa, Okinawa with heavy damage, but there it crashed upon landing and was later written-off. This was the B-29 that Captain Subbotin had damaged. However, the SAC command also claimed that B-29 gunners had shot down a MiG-15 in this action – an inaccurate claim, because the 176th GIAP had no losses at all.

As the combat was winding down, pilots of the 196th IAP were also scrambled as reinforcements, but when they arrived in the combat area, the enemy aircraft were already leaving it. Captain N.A. Antipov's group of six MiGs attempted to break through to the remaining bombers, but they were intercepted by the Thunderjets of the 27th FEG and tied up in combat. Moreover, in the course of this dogfight, one F-84 element shot up Senior Lieutenant N.E. Andrushko's MiG and our pilot had to abandon his uncontrollable aircraft. He ejected from it successfully and soon arrived back at the regiment. This was the 324th IAD's only loss on this day, and the first for the 196th IAP.

Summing up the day's results, the 324th IAD's pilots nevertheless failed to repel this B-29 attack on the bridge between Andong and Sinuiju. Only a portion of the bombers turned back before reaching the target, thanks to the attack by Captain Sheberstov's group, but two flights of B-29 nevertheless broke through to the bridge and bombed it. The bridge was damaged, but fortunately it remained standing. It was quickly repaired and once again, supplies freely flowed over it into North Korea.

After the combat ended, the commands of the 64th IAK and 324th IAD made a thorough analysis of it, which exposed miscalculations and mistakes by the commanders, and proper conclusions were drawn. In the analysis, division commander Colonel Kozhedub particularly drew attention to the fact that his regiment commanders Lieutenant Colonel A.S. Koshel' and E.G. Pepeliaev had directed their pilots' actions from the ground and hadn't personally participated in the battle, and obliged both of them to draw the appropriate conclusions.

In the following days the enemy increased his aerial reconnaissance over the Sinuiju-Singisiu area, as well as over Andong itself, and the division's pilots flew several combat missions to intercept these flights. Already the day after the Saturday battle, eight MiGs of the 196th IAP led by the regiment commander Lieutenant Colonel E.G. Pepeliaev himself were scrambled in response to an alert – Kozhedub's criticism had been effective! A RB-45 reconnaissance plane from the USAF's 91st SRS, escorted by three F-86 Sabres was on a flight route toward Andong. The RB-45 was flying at an altitude of 12,000 meters, while the Sabres were cruising 500 meters below it. However, the fighters were trailing too far behind the reconnaissance plane, and a gap had appeared between them. Taking advantage of this mistake, Pepeliaev and his wingman Iovlev emerged below and behind the reconnaissance plane, and Pepeliaev was on the verge of opening fire when his MiG got caught in the backwash of the Tornado's engines, and his aircraft did an involuntary roll and lost altitude. Having determined that he had lost his position for attacking the Tornado, Pepeliaev pounced on the three Sabres from above, after ordering the second element of Senior Lieutenant N.K. Shelamonov and his wingman Senior Lieutenant A.M. Dostoevsky to attack the reconnaissance jet.

Shelamonov quickly closed on the Tornado, conducting S-turns in order not to overshoot the target. He drew so near to the reconnaissance jet that he could see the American pilots' heads and the windows for the camera equipment on the sides of the

One of the top Soviet aces with 19 victories, Lieutenant Colonel E.G. Pepeliaev, commander of the 196th IAP, in repose at the Andong airfield, 15 August 1951.

fuselage. The lagging Sabres were quickly approaching him, so Shelamonov opened fire on the reconnaissance aircraft from all his cannons before diving away into the clouds. At this point, the combat was taking place out over the sea, because in the heat of their pursuit our pilots hadn't noticed that they had crossed the coastline. Pepeliaev's flight returned to Andong in separate elements. Shelamonov hadn't been able to see whether he had shot down the Tornado or not, nor did his gun camera film clarify the matter, because the film had simply split apart due to the extreme cold at such a high altitude. However, that evening the corps reported that the Tornado had not made it back to its base, and had made a forced landing on the coastline near Pyongyang, in North Korean territory. Thus, Senior Lieutenant N.K. Shelamonov, the commander of the 196th IAP's 3rd Squadron, received credit for a victory.

On the next day there was another encounter with a Tornado, this time involving the 176th GIAP. This time two RB-45s had appeared in the same area, but now they were being covered by 10 F-86s, so three groups of MiGs from the 176th GIAP were scrambled. The first to spot the reconnaissance planes was Captain K.Ia. Sheberstov's flight of six MiGs. The pilots of this group attempted to break through to the Tornadoes, but they were attacked by the Sabres and tied up in combat. The dogfight began unsuccessfully, because at the very start of the action, Captain G.I. Ges's wingman Lieutenant V.F. Negodaev's MiG experienced an engine flame-out, and he became a vulnerable target for the Sabres. The pilot attempted to coax his MiG back to Andong in a glide, but he had to make a forced landing in a rice field near Singisiu. Upon touching down his aircraft was completely demolished, but somehow the pilot himself escaped with only light wounds and was transported to a hospital. One element of Sabres tried to finish off Negodaev's slowly moving and descending MiG while it was still in the air,

Hero of the Soviet Union
Major G.I. Ges' (a 1955 photo).

but Captain Ges' prevented them from doing so. However, Captain Max Vaille of the 336th FIS claimed that he had shot down Negodaev's MiG, which doesn't correspond to the actual facts.

The pilots of Captain Sheberstov's group didn't manage to reach the enemy reconnaissance planes, but they did manage to divert some of the covering fighters. Captain V.G. Murashov's second group also didn't manage to intercept the RB-45s, so only the third group of six MiGs from the 176th GIAP's 2nd Squadron under the command of Guards Captain and Hero of the Soviet Union A.F. Vas'ko succeeded in attacking the Tornadoes. But the enemy had already completed its task and had turned back toward friendly territory. In pursuit, Guards Captain Vas'ko's group caught up with them, and Captain Vas'ko managed to attack one of the Tornadoes and hit it with several shells, but Sabres prevented him from making a second pass to finish it off. Vas'ko's flight engaged the flight of six Sabres in battle, and Vas'ko in one head-on pass managed to score hits against one of the F-86s, which caused it to explode in mid-air. Meanwhile Guards Senior Lieutenant I.V. Lazutin's element attempted to finish off the stricken RB-45, and Lazutin managed to draw to within close range of the Tornado, but he couldn't shoot it down because his cannons failed to fire. At that point, four Sabres pounced on Lazutin's element, and 1st Lieutenant Arthur O'Connor of the 336th FIS shot down Lazutin's wingman, Senior Lieutenant Fedor Vasil'evich Slabkin, who was killed in the cockpit of his MiG.

However, the day's aerial fighting didn't end with this: at 1410, a group of eight MiGs from the 176th GIAP's 1st Squadron took off for the area of Anju in response to an alarm, and over the target they spotted four B-26 bombers that were bombing the railroad station. Captain G.I. Ges' and S.P. Subbotin were directed to attack the bombers with their elements. Each made a firing pass against the unescorted bombers and hit two of them. As a result, B-26 No. 44-34447 from the 452nd BG's 729th Squadron never returned to base and fell in a hilly area 10-15 kilometers southeast of Anju. The second B-26 (No. 44-34547) of the same 452nd BG, plainly damaged by Captain Subbotin's fire, did in fact return to its base, but there it was written-off due to the severe damage it had received. In fact, these were two B-26 bombers were the only losses confirmed by the US Fifth Air Force on this day; the Americans still do not acknowledge the loss of either an F-86 or a RB-45.

On the next day, aerial clashes continued in the Anju area, but this time the division's pilots had more success and inflicted painful damage to him. Thus at 0700, eight MiGs from the 196th IAP's 3rd Squadron under the command of Senior Lieutenant N.K. Shelamonov departed Andong to intercept enemy aircraft. During the flight to the target area, Captain P.A. Soskovets's flight lagged behind the lead flight, which the enemy quickly exploited – a flight of six F-86s unexpectedly attacked Soskovets's trailing flight. Although the situation was unfavorable for our pilots and they were outnumbered, our pilots took on the Sabre pilots. In the course of the ensuing combat, one F-86 element at high speed attacked Senior Lieutenant V.I. Alfeev's element, but miscalculated the rate of closure, overshot their target, and wound up directly under the MiGs' cannons. Alfeev's wingman Senior Lieutenant F.D. Shebanov took advantage of this sudden turn in fortune and from short range fired a burst that struck the lead Sabre. The F-86 began to smoke and dove toward the Yellow Sea. The pilot of this Sabre, No. 49-1093 from the 335th FIS nevertheless managed to bring his stricken Sabre back to his base in Kimpo and make a successful landing there, but all the same the jet was soon written-off.

One and a half hours later at 0910, a flight of four MiGs from the 176th GIAP's 2nd Squadron commanded by Captain A.F. Vas'ko arrived in this same area. In the vicinity of Anju they spotted a flight of F-80 Shooting Stars from the 51st FIW, and having left Captain S.M. Kramarenko's flight as top cover for the attack, Vas'ko with his wingman Senior Lieutenant A.P. Gogolev attacked the trailing pair of Shooting Stars. Apparently the "Shoot" pilots never saw the MiGs, because they allowed them to approach to within murderously close range, after which both of our pilots calmly shot up the target each had selected, and both F-80s plunged to the earth.

Then finally at 1010, a group of eight MiGs from the 196th IAP led by Captain B.V. Bokach took off for the area of the Sinuiju bridge. In the vicinity of it they encountered a flight of F-80s, which exploiting the mostly cloudy weather, were trying to bomb the bridge. Our pilots spotted them in time and Captain V.A. Nazarkin's flight attacked the enemy aircraft. In the course of the action, Captain Nazarkin doggedly pursued one of the F-80 elements, chasing and firing on it for a long time, and achieved hits on one of them, but in all of the clouds they eventually managed to shake off the MiGs' pursuit.

Summing up this day's actions, the pilots of the 324th IAD fared well in three separate aerial combats, downing three F-80 Shooting Stars and one F-86 Sabre without any losses of their own. According to information gathered by the Argentinean historian D. Zampini, on this day the Americans wrote-off one of their Sabres, which had been seriously damaged by the fire from Senior Lieutenant Shebanov's MiG. Next, pilots of the American 51st FIG's 25th Squadron had come under attack by MiGs of the 176th GIAP, which shot down two F-80s (No. 49-800 and No. 49-569), one of the pilots of which was killed and the other taken prisoner. Another group of F-80s from the same 25th FIS was unlucky later that day: F-80C No. 49-1855 being flown by 1st Lieutenant Douglas Matheson was damaged by Captain Nazarkin, and although it managed to fly back to its base in Taegu, it crashed on the approach to the runway and Matheson was killed. For some reason, the Fifth Air Force command recorded that three of its F-80s were lost from anti-aircraft fire, but a day earlier, that is to say, on 9 April 1951 – here, perhaps, we're dealing with a difference in time zones?

However, all of early April 1951's aerial clashes were just a prelude to the following battle, which occurred on 12 April 1951 in the vicinity of the bridge spanning the Yalu River between Andong and Siniuju and involved the participation of more than 100 aircraft from both sides. Early in the morning, 39 (according to our records, 48) B-29 bombers lifted off the runways from their bases in Okinawa. According to American records, this mission included 8 B-29s from the 19th BG, 12 B-29s from the 307th BG, and another 19 B-29s from the 98th BG. They had a direct escort of 36 F-84Es from the 27th FEG, and in addition, three groups of Sabres from the 4th FIW – 18 fighter-interceptors which were to serve as a forward screen for the B-29 formations and were supposed to tie up the MiG groups that scrambled from Andong in combat (our records indicate that there were approximately 40 Sabres). Finally, there were approximately 20 F-80s from the 49th FBG.

The 64th IAK's ground radars picked up the incoming enemy formations, and all of the serviceable fighters of the 324th IAD were scrambled in response. Consequently, 44 MiG-15s left the runway in several "trains", as the American pilots called them.

The first to depart to repel this major formation of enemy bombers was the 196th IAP. In response to the alarm, eight MiGs of the 196th IAP's 3rd Squadron under the

Bombs Away! This striking photograph of a lead bomber was made from a B-29 Superfortress of the Far East Air Forces' 19th Bomber Group on the 150th combat mission the Group had flown since the start of the Korean war, 1951. (Smithsonian National Air & Space Museum)

command of Senior Lieutenant N.K. Shelamonov took-off at 0855, followed a minute later by six MiGs of the 1st Squadron led by Captain P.F. Tkatsky. When Tkatsky's group arrived in the area of Tetsuzan, Captain L.N. Ivanov spotted two flights of B-29 bombers approaching, which had eight F-80s serving as close escort. Having notified the leader about the enemy, Captain Ivanov decided to attack the bombers with his element. For this he maneuvered around the lead flight of "Shoots" and launched a high-side firing pass on the second box of B-29s in the formation. Greatly accelerating in the dive, Ivanov managed to close to within short range of the Superfortresses and opened fire at one enemy bomber as its image rapidly grew in his gun sight. Two engines on the left wing of his target caught fire, and the bomber dropped out of the formation and turned toward the gulf. However, it didn't manage to reach it, because Ivanov's wingman Senior Lieutenant A.M. Kochegarov, who was hot on the leader's tail, gave it another burst of cannon fire. The crew began bailing out of the burning bomber, and it fell to the earth.

The attack came as such a surprise to the adversary that neither the bombers' gunners nor the escorting fighters could do anything to prevent it. Immediately other MiG elements went on the attack against the Superfortresses. Despite the effort of the escorting fighters to disrupt the MiG attacks, this time nothing came of it; taking into account the negative past combat experience with B-29 groups, now our pilots attacked the B-29 formation in high-speed, diving passes from various directions. In the course of these slashing attacks, Captain Tkatsky succeeded in damaging another B-29. It turned back, with one engine on fire. Senior Lieutenant A.F. Gorshkov's third element didn't manage to inflict more damage to the bomber formation, since the covering fighters did manage to disrupt their attack. However, even this element didn't leave the combat area without a victory: Gorshkov's wingman Senior Lieutenant V.N. Fukin obtained hits on the tail-end Shooting Star in a flight and watched it explode upon impact with the ground.

At this time, Senior Lieutenant Shelamonov's group reached the area, where a large air battle was now underway, and spotted several more flights of B-29 bombers with fighter escort. The flights of Shelamonov's group, having split into separate elements, went for the bombers, paying no attention to the covering fighters. Shelamonov's flight attacked the first box of bombers in the column, while Senior Lieutenant P.A. Soskovets's flight correspondingly tackled the second B-29 box in the formation. Soskovets's flight had better luck against "its" box: in the course of several firing passes, it succeeded in downing one B-29 and damaging another – pilots Senior Lieutenants F.D. Shebanov and B.A. Savchenko distinguished themselves. Shelamonov's first flight also saw results from its attacks on the bombers. Senior Lieutenants P.G. Iovlev and A.M. Dostoevsky damaged two B-29s, and they both dropped out of the bomber formation and turned back with smoking engines. The covering fighters attempted to hinder the attacks by Shelamonov's group, but fighting their way through these counterattacks, the MiG pilots repeatedly broke through to the formation of bombers and attacked it until they had exhausted their ammunition.

At 0900, the commander of the 324th IAD Colonel I.N. Kozhedub scrambled two more groups of MiGs from Andong to reinforce the battle, but this time made the call to the 176th GIAP. First eight MiGs of its 1st Squadron under the command of Guards Captain K.Ia. Sheberstov took off, followed a minute later by six crews of the 3rd Squadron led by Captain V.G. Murashov.

Although both groups reached the combat area simultaneously, the pilots of Murashov's group attacked the bomber formation first, because they were at a higher altitude than Shelamonov's group. Splitting into separate elements, the pilots attacked one of the spotted B-29 boxes. Senior Lieutenant A.A. Plitkin's element was particularly successful. On the first attacking pass the leader left one B-29 burning, while on the next firing pass his wingman Senior Lieutenant B.A. Obraztsov also managed to force another B-29 to leave the formation burning and to turn back. The pilots of the other two elements in Murashov's group succeeded in damaging another B-29, for which Captain A.L. Shchipitsin received the credit, and broke up the bomber formation.

Captain Sheberstov's group in turn attacked two other B-29 boxes, employing the same technique of attacking in simultaneous high-speed firing passes made by separate elements from different directions, which allowed the fighters to penetrate the screen of covering fighters and complicated the task of the B-29 gunners. The very first firing pass was crowned with success: group leader Captain Sheberstov's fire from the close range of 400 meters left one of the B-29s burning, and it fell out of its flight's formation. On the next attacking pass, Sheberstov's wingman Senior Lieutenant G.A. Nikolaev damaged another Superfortress. They continued to press their attacks until their ammunition was exhausted, at which point they continued to feign attacks against the enemy bombers.

The second element consisting of Captains Subbotin and Milaushkin enjoyed just as much success in its attacks against the bomber box they had selected, shooting down one Superfortress and damaging two others. Here is what Guards Captain P.S. Milaushkin recalls of this action:

The pilots of our 1st Squadron encountered the enemy [Sabres] on a meeting course, so the first attack was head-on, and as soon as we flashed past each other, immediately both sides began turning and maneuvering, and a real "furball" erupted. The combat fell apart into small groups of aircraft. I was Captain Subbotin's wingman on this mission. After one turn I spotted two Sabres and called out: "Fima, attack the right one, I'll cover you!" Serafim [Subbotin] quickly reacted to my call. His attack was successful; his cannon fire blanketed the enemy element leader. The nose of his Sabre dropped and the fighter fell into an uncontrolled dive. I didn't have the chance to attack the Sabre wingman, because four more F-86s were rapidly approaching. The enemy opened fire, but we evaded it with a maneuver and went into an oblique loop. After looping twice, the enemy Sabres were no longer in sight. Just then Serafim transmitted: "Look, bombers below and to the right; attack them, and I'll cover." Without a pause to reflect, we attacked. The leader ordered: "I'll attack the leader; you take the right-hand wingman." It was a group of four B-29s, flying in a box formation. There was nobody next to them, so we went into our firing pass unobstructed. We closed on them quickly, and I saw the fuselage and engine of a B-29 growing quickly in my gun sight. I opened fire from all my cannons and saw shell hits to the bomber's fuselage and engine. Subbotin's aim was also accurate; his Superfortress began trailing a stream of white smoke. We then pulled out of our attack to the left.

The bomber box fell apart, and only two bombers remained in it. We made another firing pass; he attacked the leader, while I attacked the wingman. The silhouette of a B-29 quickly grew in my gun sight and I opened fire, but my large cannon (the 37mm) had run out of ammunition. Somehow out of the corner of my eyes, I noticed an F-84 was closing in on Subbotin. Without a pause, I banked the nose of my jet in its direction and released a stream of shells from my remaining two cannon in front of it without aiming, and the F-84 buggered off to one side. However, now I was totally out of ammunition, and I reported to Serafim: "I have no shells remaining. Attack the solitary bomber to the left and above me. I'll cover." The attack was superb and his shell hits were precisely on target – a left engine on the B-29 began to smoke, and it went into a roll to the left.

Then we attacked another pair of Superfortresses, but we didn't fire – we were now both out of ammunition. However, it was impossible to withdraw from the fight, since some of our comrades were still engaged in it, so we again went into an attacking run against three B-29s that had turned around, but came under Sabre fire ourselves. They were attacking from above, and when I glanced around, I saw a pair of F-86s with blazing noses. I shouted out over the radio: "Follow me!" and jerked my MiG into a steep, climbing turn to the right. The F-86 element attempted to pursue. We were at around 7,000-8,000 meters of altitude, but after several oblique loops, the enemy abandoned the chase.

Soon I hear the regiment commander Vishniakov's voice: "Grass for everyone", which meant it was time to return to base and land. During the rollout after touching down my engine stopped; it had run out of fuel. Serafim Subbotin's engine stopped on the landing approach, but he touched down on the margins of the airfield.

On this occasion the Sabres weren't late with covering the Superfortresses, as they had been on 7 April, but all the same not a single group of B-29s succeeded in reaching the target. Already after the initial attack, the Superfortresses began releasing their payloads and turning to the east, leading as a rule to the disruption of their formations. On this day there were additional combat sorties, but as soon as we had taken off, gained altitude, and headed off to meet the enemy, they turned around and headed back.

After the battle, that evening, we rode back to our quarters silently; we were still immersed in thoughts of the combat. Only after dinner, after our "100 grams" of vodka, did conversation and an exchange of opinions about the battle begin. The Koreans were telling us that there had been a lot of parachutes and a lot of airplanes falling. Some of the aircraft departed with smoking engines, then fell into the sea. Later the corps command informed us that according to sources, many of the B-29s crashed when making their landing on bases back in Okinawa, while some B-29s were unable to taxi after landing, and others had to make belly landings and caught fire on the ground. From the 12-man crews aboard each B-29, on average only 4-5 men remained unharmed.

The MiG attacks continued with their stinging bites, knocking one bomber after another out of formation here and there along the bomber stream. The covering fighters weren't ready for such swarming tactics and didn't have time to intercept the numerous MiG elements, so they were able to break through the fighter screen and reach their main target – the B-29s. The attacks of the second flight of Captain Sheberstov's group were also murderous for the bombers in the first box formation. Captain Ges's element managed to knock two bombers out of the box simultaneously; one bomber fell uncontrolled to the earth, the other turned back with smoking engines. The cannons of Captain Ges's MiG were responsible for the damage to both bombers. The second element of this flight also shot down one B-29 – the element leader Captain I.A. Suchkov received credit for this victory.

At 0910, yet another group of MiGs from the 176th GIAP, headed by 2nd Squadron commander and Hero of the Soviet Union Captain A.F. Vas'ko, left the runways at Andong. On the approach to the Sinuiju bridge, Captain Vas'ko's group encountered a group of eight B-29s, being escorted by eight F-80s, 15 kilometers southeast of Andong. Vas'ko directed Captain S.M. Kramarenko's element to engage the escort fighters, while he himself attacked the bomber formation. However, he fired at the bomber boxes from too great a distance and with no results. Soon he exhausted his ammunition and Vas'ko's element exited the battle. Yet Captain Kramarenko's element had to take on the flight of Shooting Stars in combat, and our pair was able to get on the tail of two "Shoots". Captain Kramarenko downed the wingman's F-80 from a range of 200 meters, while Senior Lieutenant I.V. Lazutin's fire damaged the lead F-80.

Despite the selfless attacks of our pilots, who continued to make attacking passes against the bombers even after expending all their ammunition, and despite the heavy losses, several flights of B-29 still flew bravely onward through the gauntlet MiG attacks and managed to reach the strategic bridge. Both the 64th IAK command post and the 324th IAD command post were attentively following the progress of the battle, and seeing that not all the bombers had been stopped, Kozhedub threw his final reserve into the combat – eight MiGs of the 196th IAP's 2nd Squadron led by its commander Captain B.V. Bokach. Immediately after taking off at 0922, the group went after two flights of B-29s that were already on their final approach to target, and which had two flights of fighters as top cover. The vital bridge across the Yalu River lay not far from the Andong Air Base, so there was no time for reflection. Our pilots immediately threw their MiGs into an attack against the bombers, trying to divert them from their final approach and to prevent them from bombing the bridge.

At first Captain Bokach's lead element attacked a flight of Sabres, forcing them to abandon its covering position and to dive below the bomber formation to evade. Then, having banked around, Bokach's element selected the second flight of B-29s and made several attacking passes against it, in which Bokach and his wingman expended all their ammunition. In the process Captain Bokach managed to damage one of the Superfortresses, which broke formation and headed toward the gulf. His wingman Senior Lieutenant I.V. Larionov succeeded in getting hits on a second B-29 in the box of bombers, and it was also compelled to turn away from the bridge and toward the gulf.

The second element of this flight under the leadership of Captain V.A. Nazarkin attacked the first bomber box in this formation. Nazarkin riddled the lead bomber in this box with cannon shells; within seconds, the burning bomber fell directly next to the bridge without having dropped its bombs.

Meanwhile, Captain B.S. Abakumov's flight attacked the second box in the bomber formation. Captain F.A. Iakovlev's element tied up the covering fighters in combat, while Abakumov's element went after the bombers. Here's how Boris Sergeevich Abakumov later described this combat episode:

> Early in the morning on 12 April 1951, we were gathered on the air base in our fighters' cockpits. Long before our arrival, the ground crews were busy testing the engines and preparing the MiGs for a combat sortie. The observation posts and radar stations were reporting on the situation in the air. The initial reports stated that the day would be a "hot" one. A tense silence settled over the airfield. The command post was informing us that a large group of aircraft was slowly approaching our area; their types were unknown.
>
> At the division command post, Colonel Kozhedub decided to send out a reconnaissance, so six MiGs took off from the concrete runway at Andong with a deafening roar, which shattered the morning calm. The MiGs quickly disappeared into the blue depths of the sky.
>
> Meanwhile, we were all sitting in our cockpits at Readiness No. 1. Through the chaos of the chatter and static in the air wave, in our headsets we could clearly hear the reports from the pilots of the reconnaissance flight. The scouts were reporting that they had spotted a group of bombers over the sea, heading in the direction of the Yalu River delta in a column of box formations. The B-29s were being covered by a dense ring of F-84 jet fighters. They estimated that more than 100 American aircraft were involved in this air strike. On our side, every available MiG in Andong, 44 fighters altogether, was scrambled.
>
> Now we were in the air. Kozhedub handled the combat from his command post, directing all of us toward the approaching bombers, and now already arcing smoke trails extending toward the earth traced the fatal plunge of the first of these enormous aircraft. The American fighters, in no rush to bail their fellow brothers out of trouble, buzzed around in an enormous orbit around the bombers and waited

for the moment when they could catch one of us in their sights. The bombers were unable to withstand our attacks, aimlessly dumping many tons of bombs. One of the bombers sharply swerved from its bomb run and with its every machine-gun turret blazing, headed in the direction of our airfield, which had no one left to cover it. I quickly banked my aircraft into an attack upon it and gave it a burst from my cannons – which streaked behind the target. Time was short. I attacked again, corrected my aim, and fired all my ammunition into the enemy aircraft's tail – the Superfortress's tail disintegrated in front of my eyes. The crew abandoned the bomber and took to their parachutes. My MiG almost struck one of them, but I managed to swerve and avoid him. The battle continued. Fighters flashed past right in front of me, and in this "carousel" the earth and sky jumbled together.

A Sabre element dropped into position behind me and opened fire from a range of 300 meters; each Sabre carried six 12.7mm machine guns. I immediately sensed this when their bullets began a drumbeat on my aircraft. After my energetic maneuver, the Sabres lagged behind me a bit. My crippled MiG, listing heavily to the right, hurtled toward my airfield, and the Sabres attempted to catch it.

I landed safely, but for the next mission they gave me a different MiG – division commander Kozhedub's own fighter. The mechanics and technicians took several days, but were able to return my own MiG to service.

Captain Iakovlev's element at that time was dueling against a flight of F-80s. Iakovlev managed to damage one of them, after which having carried out his order to tie up the enemy's fighter group in combat, Iakovlev's element returned to base.

The result of this largest battle in the skies of Korea to that point in the war was woeful for the Americans, though at the time they diligently concealed the heavy losses, announcing that only three B-29s had been lost. However, over time the true extent of the losses has become revealed. According to the latest research conducted by Diego Zampini, according to different sources the Americans in this battle actually lost 10 of their B-29s and two more F-80 Shooting Stars.

To this point, here is what we know about the fate of some of the B-29s: Two of the bombers downed by the MiGs fell in the combat area: B-29 No. 44-86370 fell into the sea and all 12 of its crew was killed; B-29 No. 44-69682 crashed and all of its crew perished as well; another B-29, No. 44-62252 received heavy damage on the approach to the bridge and a fire erupted on-board the bomber, forcing seven members of its crew in the back of the plane to bail out; they were taken prisoner. However, the commander of this Boeing, Captain James M. Chenault managed to extinguish the on-board flames and to nurse his crippled bomber back to the Suwon Air Base. The bomber was so badly damaged, however, that there wasn't even a thought about attempting to land it, so the remaining five crew members on board took to their parachutes, and the distressed bomber crashed on the edge of Suwon. Another damaged B-29 from the 30th BS, No. 44-61835, flew back to Suwon as well, but its crew managed to bring the bomber down safely on a runway there. However, the bomber was quickly written-off as scrap metal. Two of its crew had been killed, while almost all of the remaining crew members suffered wounds of various degrees of severity. B-29 No. 44-87618 made a landing in Seoul, but it was also written-off as scrap metal because of the damage it had received from MiG cannon fire. The list goes on: B-29

No. 44-65369 managed to fly with smoking engines all the way back to its base in Kadena, Okinawa, but the bomber crashed upon landing and burst into flames on the runway. The crew managed to escape the burning aircraft, but their Boeing was fully consumed by the flames. B-29 No. 44-27314 also made it back to Kadena, but it also crashed upon landing, but was written off as junk.

Many of the returning B-29s had varying degrees of combat damage and some of them were subsequently written off, while others were patched up and returned to service. The crews of the 93rd BG, which received the MiGs' full attention, particularly suffered in this battle. This bombardment group is known to have lost five bombers and two full complements of crews. Many crewmen aboard the other B-29s of this group were killed or wounded in the air. The 307th BG also lost two B-29s in this battle, and only the Superfortresses of the 98th BG, according to American records, had no losses.

In their turn, the Americans claim that B-29 gunners supposedly downed seven MiG-15 fighters. In addition, Thunderjet pilots of the 27th FEG claimed three "probable" kills of MiG-15s, while the pilots of the 4th FIW claimed four victories over MiGs. However, all 44 MiGs returned to base, though many of them did come back with bullet holes in them. They were quickly patched up and returned to service.

Apparently, Captain Abakumov's MiG, which did take hits in this battle, was added as a victory to the score of a future top ace of the USAF in this war, Captain James Jabara of the 334th Fighter Squadron. Here is how he describes this mission:

That day the MiGs showed that they are more aggressive against B-29 formations than against fighters. We were at a disadvantage because of slowing down for proper escort. By the time we drop our external tanks and get up speed, a MiG can be roaring through the bombers with his cannons blazing.

We counter this by keeping four plane elements together and take our chances on superior gunnery. The MiGs feint, hoping we'll follow and leave the bombers unprotected. We stick. And shoot.

… If we're outnumbered, or the fighting gets too rough, then we maneuver around and wait for the enemy to make a mistake. Thank God, he makes more than his share of them.

Like the one he made in the big scrap on April 12: I was at 25,000 feet (7,500 meters), and he was 5,000 feet beneath me, heading for the B-29s. That advantage in altitude was my break, and I used it to get speed. I caught him just as when he was in range of the B-29s. The bullets saddle-stitched his fuselage, but he went into loops and rolls. He was badly crippled. Another burst got his engine, and I saw him crash trying to leg it across the Yalu.

After a close analysis of this 12 April battle, according to the gun camera film, the pilots' reports and confirmation from the ground, the 324th IAD was credited with 10 downed B-29s. Of this total, seven went to the score of pilots of the 176th GIAP: Guards Captains K.Ia. Sheberstov, S.P. Subbotin, I.A. Suchkov, G.I. Ges' and P.S. Milaushkin, and Guards Senior Lieutenants A.A. Plitkin and B.A. Obraztsov. Another three Superfortresses were credited to pilots of the 196th IAP, Captain V.A. Nazarkin and Senior Lieutenants F.D. Shebanov and A.M. Kochegarov. In addition, pilots B.S. Abakumov and P.G. Iovlev of the 196th IAP, and Senior Lieutenant A.L. Shipitsin of the

176th GIAP did not receive official credit for their victories over B-29s, which although damaged made it out to the Yellow Sea but probably never returned to base, or possibly crashed upon landing.

At least four fighters of the covering screen were damaged by fire from MiG cannons. Guards Captains S.M. Kramarenko, I.V. Lazutin and S.P. Subbotin of the 176th GIAP each put in claims for downing or damaging a "Cross". Senior Lieutenant V.N. Fukin claimed another "Cross". The Americans confirm the loss of only two of their F-80s from the 36th FBS: the pilot of one of them, Sherwood Avery, although he managed to fly back to Suwon in his F-80 No. 49-1842 and land the damaged plane there, it was later written-off as scrap metal. The pilot of the other Shooting Star, Swenson, was able to bring his damaged "Shoot" to a point over the gulf, where he ejected from the doomed aircraft. Most likely, these were F-80s struck by the fire from the MiGs of Captain Kramarenko and Senior Lieutenant Fukin.

Thus, the overall results of this battle on the American side are 10 B-29 bombers and four fighters downed, with another five B-29s and one F-86 as probable kills. On our side, only two MiG-15s received damage beyond a few bullet holes.

However, the fighting on 12 April 1951 didn't end with this major clash. In the afternoon, at 1350 eight MiGs of the 196th IAP under the command of B.V. Bochkov took off to make a patrol over the Andong-Sinuiju bridge. This time our pilots didn't spot any bombers, but they were jumped by six F-86s. One Sabre element got in behind Captain F.A. Iakovlev's MiG and opened fire from close range, damaging the aircraft and wounding the pilot in the back. Captain Iakovlev managed to make a forced landing in a rice field not far from Singisiu, after which he was sent to the hospital, while his MiG was recovered and repaired. Iakovlev's wingman Senior Lieutenant P.M. Zykov was also attacked, but he managed to evade it with a sudden maneuver that put him into position to counterattack. He opened fire on one Sabre, scoring hits on it and forcing it to exit the battle. With this, the flurry of action finished and both sides left the combat area and returned to their bases.

Most likely, Captain Iakovlev's MiG was damaged by the experienced commander of the 336th FIS, Lieutenant Colonel Bruce Hinton, who was credited with a victory on this mission. Captain Howard Lane of the same squadron was also credited with downing the other MiG in the element they jumped, but plainly the sharp maneuver by Zykov's MiG to dive away from the attack was taken by Howard Lane as a sign that the MiG had been fatally damaged, so upon return to base he claimed a victory that in fact didn't happen.

However, whatever the Americans might claim about this battle, subsequent events only confirm the thrashing that the Americans took that day. For almost a week after 12 April 1951, the Americans licked their wounds from this defeat. In addition, the US Bomber Command announced that it had dropped 25 B-29 bombers from its roster: eight of them would remain forever on North Korean soil, while the other 17 returned to airfields in South Korea, Okinawa and Japan with such extensive damage that they had to be written-off. To be honest, General Stratemeyer did manage quickly to rebuild the strength of his three heavy bombardment groups to as many as 99 bombers, which from 17 April 1951 again appeared in the skies of North Korea and struck North Korean airfields until 23 April. However, these airfields were still under construction, and were located south of the Pyongyang-Wonsan line, that is to say, beyond the authorized reach of the 64th IAK's MiGs. For a long time, the B-29s from the US SAC opted not to enter MiG Alley.

In the subsequent days of April 1951 after "Black Thursday", the intensity of combat sharply fell. Although there were just as many combat sorties as before, encounters with the enemy became rare, because the enemy avoided them.

Sometimes small groups of F-80 fighter-bombers would appear within the operational zone of the Andong MiGs, but as soon as MiGs were spotted, they would immediately flee the given area. Thus in the second half of April, the pilots of the 196th IAP's 3rd Squadron were fortunate to encounter enemy fighter-bombers only once, and it is difficult to call what resulted a battle. On the morning of 16 April, a six-ship flight of MiGs commanded by Captain B.V. Bokach was scrambled in response to an alarm, and it intercepted a group of F-80s. However, the Shooting Star pilots spotted the MiGs in time, and having halted their attack on the ground target, made haste toward the salvation of the gulf. Only the trailing F-80s of this group came under some long-range fire, but it was inaccurate and all the Shooting Stars got away unpunished this time. A few hours later, another six MiGs from the 3rd Squadron led by Senior Lieutenant N.K. Shelamonov took off in response to an alarm – a small group of four F-80s had popped up from the direction of the gulf and had begun to attack anti-aircraft positions around the Singisiu airfield. At tree-top level, Shelamonov's six-ship flight hopped over to the Singisiu airfield where North Korean Il-10s were parked, and intercepted the four Shooting Stars over the base. Spotting the MiGs, the F-80s immediately halted the attack and tried to escape toward the gulf. During the pursuit one of the F-80s, evading Shelamonov's attack, in a sharply banking turn just above the water caught a wingtip on a wave and cartwheeled into the water. Afterward, at low tide the tail of this F-80 stuck out above the water, like a cross above the pilot's grave. As is now clear, however, in this combat the pilots of the 196th IAP were dueling not with Shooting Stars, but with Thunderjets from the 27th Fighter Group's 524th Squadron; its F-84E (No. 49-2396) was the one Shelamonov was chasing and its pilot Thomas L. Hilton's body was never recovered, so he's officially considered missing-in-action.

The other "Crosses" managed to get away, but after this encounter they made no further appearances in the area for a long time. In addition, even the F-51 Mustangs that continued to work over targets in the area switched from operating in pairs to operating in four-ship groups due to the increasing North Korean anti-aircraft defenses (for the month of April 1951, the North Korean anti-aircraft gunners claimed 25 F-51D, 13 F-80 and 2 F-84).

Only the Sabres of the 4th FIW continually intruded into MiG Alley, and often engaged the MiGs in dogfights. In the latter half of April, several serious clashes occurred between the Sabres and the MiGs. The first of these took place already on 16 April 1951, when on this day Captain Bokach's and Senior Lieutenant Shelamonov's pilots had to endure two unpleasant scraps with the pilots of the 4th FIW. In both cases, ground radar operators were late in detecting groups of F-86s and didn't have time to alert our pilots that were already in the air. Therefore the Sabre attacks were unexpected for our pilots, which immediately put them on the defensive in the ensuing combats. However, our pilots' experience of prior combats against the Sabres already showed, and the adversary was unable to extract any sort of results from his initial advantage. In these combats only one of our MiGs received light combat damage, but its pilot Senior Lieutenant I.V. Larionov safely landed back at base, and his MiG was quickly repaired.

The next tussles of the MiGs with the Sabres took place on 18 April: eight MiGs of the 196th IAP's 3rd Squadron tangled with a group of 16 Sabres. An intense dogfight flared up in the Tetsuzan area, in which our pilots, despite the enemy's numerical superiority, dictated how the fight went. Our pilots forced the enemy to conduct the combat in verticals, where the MiG clearly had the advantage over the Sabre, and emerged as victors: the group leader Senior Lieutenant N.K. Shelamonov, as well as Senior Lieutenants P.A. Soskovets and F.D. Shebanov all put in victory claims when they returned to base, and all three received credit for kills. However, these proved to be spurious, because American records show that all the Sabres that participated in the fight returned to their base at Suwon. Only one Sabre (No.49-1227) got caught by MiG fire in this combat, when a 37mm shell struck the tail of the Sabre and blew off part of its rudder. However, its pilot 1st Lieutenant Bernard Moor safely flew back to Suwon and brought his Sabre down on the runway, and after repairs it returned to service. Most likely, it was Senior Lieutenant Shebanov that damaged the rudder on 1st Lieutenant Moore's Sabre, so that is his accomplishment in this fight!

A more serious battle took place on 22 April 1951, when the same adversaries came together: pilots of the 196th IAP and of the 4th FIW. The fight developed in the afternoon at 1500 in the area of Singisiu, and it continued for an hour. By the time it ended, the fight involved 20 MiGs from the 196th IAP and 16 MiGs from the 176th GIAP against the same number of enemy Sabres. After it opened, both sides threw additional fighters into the fight. First, eight MiGs from the 196th IAP's 3rd Squadron took off for the indicated area, and they soon spotted 16 Sabres from the 334th FIS, commanded by the 4th FIG commander Lieutenant Colonel Glenn T. Eagleston. The combat was a heated one, and according to claims on the American side, they downed four MiGs without any loss to themselves. On the other side, the Soviet pilots claimed two kills in this fight, both of which were confirmed and added to the regiment's score.

In reality, only one MiG-15 was lost in this clash, and another one was damaged. Pilots of the 4th FIW had detached several elements of "hunters", which lay in wait for our pilots as they returned to Andong and attacked several elements of our MiGs. Senior Lieutenant Shelamonov's element was jumped by Sabres as it approached the airfield. Shelamonov, as soon as he heard the bullets hammering into his aircraft, immediately threw his MiG into an abrupt maneuver to avoid any additional hits, and then immediately pulled his aircraft into a rapid climb to escape further attacks. He soon brought his MiG into Andong safely, but with six .50 bullet holes in it. Meanwhile his wingman Captain E.N. Samusin was less fortunate, and his MiG took more Sabre fire – his fuel tanks were penetrated and his engine stopped, so the pilot had to eject.

Apparently, the one and same James Jabar was the American pilot who downed Samusin's MiG. Here is how he described this fight:

> Numerous circumstances were against us in this combat, when the MiGs outnumbered our 12 Sabres by approximately three to one. I got behind one of them and began to fire at him in short bursts. I was using my air brakes for all they were worth and continually firing at him. I pursued the MiG until it fell, but I didn't note how it went down, because I almost crashed myself. It was real hell; while diving after this MiG, my cockpit instrument showed I was pulling 9 Gs. I momentarily blacked out when pulling out of the dive. This was my fourth victory in the skies of Korea, but it didn't come to me easily.

Senior Lieutenants P.A. Soskovets and Senior Lieutenant F.D. Shebanov both celebrated victories over a Sabre in this clash. The American side denies the loss of a Sabre
on this day. However, the Argentinean historian Diego Zampini, who has made a
close study of the air combat losses in Korea, assumes that Senior Lieutenant Shebanov
managed to inflict serious damage to F-86 No. 48-232, which was recorded as lost due
to "unknown causes" on 27 April 1951, though it is known that on this day, there were
no dogfights between MiGs and Sabres. All the remaining skirmishes between MiGs
and Sabres on this day involving the other pilots of the 324th IAD ended without results.

One noteworthy aspect of this battle is the fact that the new commander of the 176th
GIAP, Lieutenant Colonel S.F. Vishniakov, who had just taken command of the Guards
regiment on that day, participated in it. Guards Lieutenant Colonel A.S. Koshel' had
been relieved of command of the regiment by division commander Guards Colonel
Kozhedub, because of leadership mistakes Koshel' had made and because of his reluc-
tance to fly combat missions. Vishniakov, the former deputy regiment commander,
assumed command of the 176th GIAP, and his position as deputy commander was taken
by Captain K.Ia. Sheberstov, who had been commanding the 1st Squadron. Guards
Captain G.I. Ges' took over command of the 1st Squadron.

On 24 April still another battle took place, involving pilots of the 176th GIAP's 1st
and 3rd Squadrons against a group of F-86 Sabres of the 4th FIW. The battle occurred
around 1500 in the Sonchon area, when the first group of 8 MiGs that had taken off
under the command of Lieutenant Colonel V.F. Vishniakov engaged eight Sabres.
During a sweeping left turn, Captain V.G. Murashev's flight, which had been trailing
on the left, was switching to a position behind and on the right. At this time Murashev

Major General of Aviation S.F.
Vishniakov – former commander of the
176th GIAP (a 1957 photo).

observed two F-86s that were attacking Lieutenant Colonel Vishniakov's element and firing on it. Murashev attacked these fighters and from a range of 400 meters shot down the element's leader. However, at the same moment he was attacked from below and behind by two F-86s, as a result of which Murashev's aircraft took heavy damage and became uncontrollable. Our pilot ejected and landed roughly in his parachute in the Sima-ri area, injuring his spine in the process.

The injury to his spine incurred during his parachute landing disabled Captain Murashev. No longer able to fight, he returned to the Soviet Union for treatment and rehabilitation. This was the Guards regiment's only loss in combat on this day. Lieutenant Colonel William J. Hoyd, the only one among the 4th FIW's pilots to put in a claim for a victory over a MiG on this day, had it confirmed and the MiG was added to his score. Thus the clash ended in a 1:1 draw, although the Americans in fact do not acknowledge the loss of its F-86 on this day.

The final battle in the month of April between the MiGs and Sabres took place on 25 April, but it ended without any results for both sides. Thus the April battles, in which the Soviet pilots gained valuable combat experience, paying for it with the lives of two of their comrades, finally came to an end. Despite the fact that in April 1951 the Soviet side had many victories, its triumph in the battle of 12 April 1951 entered military aviation history.

THE CREATION OF THE UNIFIED AIR ARMY

By the spring of 1951, thanks to the selfless work of the Soviet pilots from the second-echelon aviation divisions, four PLAAF divisions and one KPAAF fighter division had been formed and trained on PRC territory. However, until May 1951, the Soviet pilots for all practical purposes carried out the combat operations in the skies of Korea alone, without any assistance from its allies.

Between January and March 1951, only two fighter regiments of the PLAAF, the 7th and 10th IAP equipped with MiG-15s, helped our pilots. But with the arrival of the 324th IAD, even they left Andong and merged into newly created aviation divisions of the PLAAF.

In February 1951, two fresh aviation divisions equipped with MiG-15 fighters with the RD-45A engine were ready for combat. On their basis, in March 1951 the Unified Air Army (UAA) [also referred to as the Joint or Combined Air Army] was formed up for combat operations in Korea.

This UAA included the aviation formations of the Chinese and North Korean air forces, which were operating from PRC territory over North Korean territory. Initially the UAA had five aviation divisions, but only two were equipped with jet fighters. The 8th BAD consisted of two regiments (the 22nd and 28th) and was armed with piston-engine Tu-2 bombers. A North Korean ShAD had Il-10 ground attack planes, and still one more aviation division, the Chinese 2nd IAD, had the 4th IAP armed with 36 La-11 fighters (of which six were unserviceable), and the 6th IAP equipped with 32 MiG-9 jets (of which two were unserviceable).

However, the most vital components of the UAA consisted of two fighter divisions equipped with MiG-15s, the 3rd and 4th IAD. At the start of April 1951, the 3rd IAD, commanded by Xi Chen had two fighter regiments (the 7th and 9th IAP), which were equipped with a total of 56 MiG-15s (of which 11 were unserviceable). By the same time, the 4th IAD, commanded by Fang Ziyi, was also ready for combat operations. This division also had two fighter regiments (the 10th and 12th IAP) with a total of 50 MiGs (of which 45 were combat-ready).

As of 1 April 1951, it was credibly possible to call upon 318 fighters for combat operations against the UN air forces, of which only 304 were combat-ready at the time. Of combat-ready fighters, 157 belonged to the UAA, which included three fighter divisions, and of this total, 103 were MiG-15s, while the remainder consisted of MiG-9s and La-11s. The Soviet 64th IAK had two fighter divisions armed with 147 MiG-15 and MiG-15bis jets.

Chinese aviation units comprised the bulk of the UAA, since of its five aviation divisions, four were Chinese and only one, a ground attack or possibly a combined aviation division, was from the KPAAF. Therefore the Chinese general Liu Zhen was appointed to command the UAA. Air Force Major General D.P. Galunov served as the Soviet adviser to the commander. The KPAAF was headed by Wang Lian, and his Soviet military adviser was Colonel A.V. Petrachev. The UAA command post was situated just 50 kilometers from the command post of the 64th IAK in Andong, and from the beginning of combat operations by the UAA, both of these headquarters and formations closely cooperated with each other. It is true that the UAA's divisions operated independently of the 64th IAK, but in the initial stage of their combat operations, pilots of the 64th IAK covered the combat sorties by elements of the UAA. At first, only the Chinese 4th IAD began operations under the UAA command in April-May 1951. The Chinese pilots flew much fewer missions than the Soviet pilots, and operated primarily in small groups and under the cover of pilots of the 324th IAD. The Chinese pilots primarily targeted small enemy air groups, focusing on the enemy's bombers and fighter-bombers, while the Soviet pilots usually engaged the Sabres.

The PLAAF 4th IAD, as noted previously, was commanded by Fang Ziyi, an experienced commander who had years of combat service in the ground forces, who then graduated from the flight school in Urumqi (Xinjiang) in 1942. Most of its pilots came from the Shanghai PVO, and quite a few of them had combat experience in flying piston-engine aircraft like the La-9. Alongside the experienced pilots, there were many young pilots who had recently completed Chinese flight schools in the Yak-11. Pilots of the 151st IAD by December 1950 had re-trained the flight staff of the 4th IAD's two regiments in the MiG-15 jet. After the forming of the 4th IAD, 15 advisers from the 151st IAD were sent to assist the division's command staff. The senior in this group of advisers was the former commander of the 72nd GIAP Guards Colonel A.I. Volkov, who became the adviser and alternate to the division commander Fang Ziyi. The adviser to the 4th IAD's chief of staff was Guards Lieutenant Colonel Doroshenko, and another 10 Soviet advisers were officers of the technical staff and rear services.

Here is how Alexander Ivanovich Volkov, the former Soviet adviser to the commander of the Chinese 4th IAD recalls the start of its combat operations:

> In the latter half of April, I and the rest of the 4th IAD moved to the forward airfield in Andong, where I.N. Kozhedub's fighter division [the 324th IAD] was already based. The division's command post was set up together with the 64th IAK command post, and both began working out cooperation in combat operations. We dedicated quite a lot of work to forging friendly relations and mutual

understanding between the Soviet and Chinese Volunteer pilots. The pilots ate together and spent free time together. I especially want to note the creation and training of the 4th IAD's command staff for independent command and control in a very short time. A very fine combat command team, equipped with radars, radio communications and other equipment was created. A remote command post was also set up within North Korea in the area of the active combat operations of both sides. At the same time it is important to note that General Liu Zhen's division was given a large quantity of the latest US-built radars and radio sets, which had been captured by the People's Liberation Army during its campaign against the Guomindong Nationalist forces in south China.

It is also important to add that Fang Ziyi's excellent knowledge of the Russian language helped him carry out his duties successfully, yet he also had the assistance of fifteen or so translators that were attached to my group, who'd been former students at Harbin University. They had a solid grasp of aviation terminology, which facilitated our cooperative work and mutual understanding.

As soon as the regiments received their assigned sector of the airfield, the division's pilots were placed on active duty jointly with the Soviet pilots. However, for several days the pilots of the 4th IAD sat in the cockpits of their aircraft from sunup until sundown, never being scrambled, while the Soviet pilots were flying two or three missions a day. In the end, in response to one alarm one of the Chinese regiments, without orders, at its own initiative conducted a group sortie to the combat area, which ended without any problems. Only after this did the UAA command allow the more active use of the 4th IAD in combat operations over MiG Alley. The Chinese pilots were given the combat assignment to take on the enemy fighter-bombers at altitudes up to 6,000-7,000 meters, while Soviet pilots engaged the covering enemy fighters.

After this the division began to conduct active operations intended to destroy or chase away the fighter-bombers. In so doing, however, shortcomings in the pilots' training were revealed:

1. The ability to stay together in elements and flights;
2. The ability to conduct maneuvers at the upper limits of permissible speed;
3. The ability to use collimator sights, and a whole host of other deficiencies.

On one of the missions on 31 May, the division's best pilot and the commander of the 12th IAP Zhao Dahai was shot down while making a slow-speed pass against an enemy B-29, which had a strong impact on the flight staff's morale, and soon the division was withdrawn to Liaoyang for rest.

Upon their arrival in Liaoyang, the command and flight staff began very actively to eliminate their shortcomings, especially their cohesion in elements and flights, and rehearsed vertical and horizontal maneuvers at high speeds. At the same time, I and Stroikov conducted flight tests of all the MiGs, checking for any tendency to perform an involuntary roll at high speeds.[3] By this time, of the Heroes of the Soviet Union, only Stroikov remained in the 4th IAD, because Borovkov at the end of April departed for the Soviet Union due to illness.

On the whole, the Soviet specialists didn't rate the combat capabilities of the Chinese and North Korean pilots very highly. Their inadequate training was telling, as was their hot-headedness – when attacking, they often lost situational awareness and became victims to American counterattacks. Therefore, in the majority of cases their combat sorties were overseen by Soviet fighters. Recalls a former pilot of the 324th IAD B.S. Abakumov:

> During the day, the Koreans and Chinese also operated from our base. Their MiGs were parked on the opposite end of the runway from ours, and they would take off in our direction. They would take off first, and we would follow them, taking off in the opposite direction. We would catch their group in the air en route and provide them with top cover. The North Koreans and Chinese operated at low altitudes. They were even permitted to fly out over the sea, where they encountered the enemy bombers, which were circling out there, waiting for the moment when our fighters would begin to run low on fuel. The Chinese, who tended to be strong-willed, would fly missions without our cover. Once, having taken off independently and without having notified our command post to obtain cooperation, they lost one of their regiment commanders. This regiment made contact with a group of Superfortresses out over the Yellow Sea. The regiment commander sharply reduced his speed to a point where he was flying no faster than the bombers for the sake of making attacking passes. The other pilots, being chased by Sabres, flew past their commander at high speed. The regiment commander downed first one, then another, and then a third bomber, but then he himself was shot down over the sea. They never found his body. His MiG sank to the shallow bottom of the sea, not far from the coastline, and at low tide you could see the tail of it rising above the water. A group of North Koreans was sent to the crash site, in order to strip the weapons from the fighter and to toss some grenades into the cockpit.

This story with the attack on B-29s by the Chinese is apparently connected to the episode of the commander of the 12th IAP Zhao Dahai's last battle, but it is doubtful that he downed even one B-29 in this battle, since the American side reported no B-29 losses on this day.

Over one and a half months of not very active combats, the pilots of the 4th IAD lost three MiGs and one pilot (regiment commander Zhao Dahai) in combat. Two of the MiGs were lost in combat on 22 April, and one on 31 May. While resting on the Liaoyang Peninsula, the 4th IAD participated in command and tactical flight exercises to rehearse cooperation among various types of aircraft. In these exercises, pilots of the 3rd IAD, the 5th ShAD and the 8th BAD also participated – more than 180 aircraft. These exercises ended on 16 June 1951. The pilots of the 4th IAD returned to the front only in the middle of September 1951, reinforced and more prepared. The 3rd IAD in its full complement entered into the combat operations in the skies of Korea only at the end of October 1951, but more on its experiences later.

THE FAILURE OF OPERATION "LASSO"

During any military conflict, the contending sides conduct intensive surveillance on each other, and hunt for any new types of equipment or weapons on the enemy's side. In order to gather examples of new enemy equipment, special groups of military special-ists with one or another technical expertise are created, who by various ways and means search for opportunities to seize examples of new enemy equipment. The Korean War was no exception to this practice. The Americans were very interested in acquiring a new MiG-15bis Soviet fighter; if not an intact example, then at least fragments of one. The problem was that the MiGs were operating strictly over territory hostile to the Americans, and thus any downed MiGs could only be found deep within North Korea. For this purpose the Americans dispatched groups of specially trained agents into North Korea, and one of their assignments was to capture downed MiG pilots and to collect equipment from crash sites.

However, it was impossible to gather the full picture of the technical capabilities of the MiG-15 from bits and pieces of the aircraft. For this an intact MiG was necessary. On 11 July 1951, the prize itself came into the hands of the Americans – a solitary MiG-15, which was flying in from the sea, and was intercepted by Sabres. However, the MiG pilot (Senior Lieutenant I.V. Larionov of the 196th IAP) refused to yield to the American pilots, and in order to prevent him from escaping, they had to shoot him down. The crashed MiG-15bis was raised from the bottom of the Yellow Sea by a joint UK-American team, but the trophy was in no condition for pilots to test it.

In the summer of 1952, a report arrived that a nearly intact MiG-15 had made a forced landing in the hills just to the north of the front lines. An entire expedition was organized to find and retrieve it: an H-19 helicopter carrying specialists, escorted by F-86 and F-51 fighters, flew to the site where the MiG came down. When the team reached the location, it turned out that the H-19 helicopter was unable to lift the entire MiG. The decision was made to disassemble it, but because of the lack of proper tools, it was impossible to do this. The Americans were forced to blow off the wings of the MiG with hand grenades, and only then could the helicopter lift pieces of the fuselage and carry them back to South Korea. After this unsuccessful attempt to seize a MiG, the Americans were compelled to announce a $100,000 award for any North Korean pilot who would deliver an undamaged MiG.

However, during the war none of the pilots of the 64th IAK or any of the pilots of the UAA betrayed their army and people. Only after the war ended, or more precisely on 21 September 1953, did a North Korean pilot named No Kum Sok desert to the Americans in his MiG-15bis No.2057. He flew into South Korea and landed on the K-14 (Kimpo) Air Base. He received the promised award, while his MiG was sent to Eglin Field in Florida, now displaying American markings and a new number (No. 616), for full-scale flight tests.

In addition, back in 1950, during the UN offensive deep into North Korean territory, the Americans captured three fully intact aircraft of the KPAAF at the Pyongyang and Wonsan Airfields: two Il-10s ground attack aircraft and one Yak-9T fighter. All three airplanes were sent back to the United States, where one Il-10 (No. 55) was disassembled for close study, while the other Il-10 (No. 44) was used for flight tests at an airfield in Buffalo, New York. The Yak-9T fighter with the side number 27, which it would seem was manufactured in the USSR at the aircraft factory No.286 in Kamensk-Uralsk (but the VK-107A engine was produced in Ufe at the aircraft factory No. 26) was also flight tested back in the United States with the new identification number of T2-3002.

Soviet military specialists also tried to acquire the latest military examples in the realm of aircraft construction on the opposing side. They had access to much richer bounty than did the Americans, since almost the entire territory of North Korea was strewn with the fragments and wreckage of downed American aircraft.

With the appearance in the skies of North Korea of the most up-to-date American fighters, the F-86 Sabre, attempts were undertaken to obtain an example of this combat aircraft, if possible in a more or less intact condition. Approximately 20 of these fighters were downed by Soviet pilots of the 64th IAK between December 1950 and April 1951, and search teams were able to collect enough fragments of this new American jet fighter. However, this was inadequate for a comprehensive and in-depth analysis of this aircraft in our scientific-research institutes; a complete example of a Sabre was needed for studying it in flight. For this purpose, a special group "Nord" was formed in Moscow at the beginning of April 1951, which was given a specific combat assignment: to force an intact Sabre to make a landing on one of the airfields of North Korea or northeast China.

Another of the urgent tasks given to this group was to obtain the apparatus that enabled the work of the pressurized flight suits worn by the American pilots. Soviet Air Force scientific-research institutes had already received such suits from Korea, since many American pilots wearing such suits had ejected from crippled aircraft and been taken prisoner by the North Koreans, but the mechanism that operated the flight suit was onboard the aircraft itself, and given the crash of the downed aircraft, they naturally were rendered non-operational.

The given group was created in Moscow by an order from the Main Command of the Soviet Air Force, and it consisted of nine experienced air force pilots, four test pilots and three engineers, for a total of 16 men headed by Lieutenant General A.S. Blagoveshchensky (who at the time was the chief of the Air Force Scientific Research Institute). The group of air force pilots, who were led by Lieutenant Colonel P.A. Perevozchikov, consisted primarily of pilots from the 16th Air Army in Germany and the Moscow region: Lieutenant Colonel Dziubenko, Majors A.I. Mitusov and F.I. Guliaev, and Senior Lieutenants N.V. Babonin, N.K. Serdiuk, I.K. Semenenko, Tikhomirov and Alikhnovich. The test pilots, headed by Engineer-Major V.P. Trofimov, included Engineer-Captain V.N. Makhalin, Engineer-Captain A.P. Suprun and Engineer-Captain L.N. Kurashov. Group Nord's chief of staff was Lieutenant Colonel Rosliakov.

They arrived at the Mukden Air Base in China on 24 April 1951, and already at the beginning of May they were familiarizing themselves with the area of combat operations. At the end of May, Group Nord flew into the Andong airfield, where they immediately began work to carry out their assignment. They prepared independently for combat operations, using MiGs of the 324th IAD. So for this purpose, the 196th IAP, to which Group Nord had been attached, received 13 brand-new MiG-15bis fighters on 19 May, in which the pilots of Group Nord embarked upon training flights. They didn't prepare specifically for combat, since they didn't believe they'd be involved in any prolonged dogfights, and they began flying missions without even questioning the pilots of the 324th IAD about the specific features of aerial combat in the skies of Korea or about the appropriate tactics to employ when engaging Sabres. For this they would later pay a price.

The pilots of the 324th nicknamed the pilots of General Blagoveshchensky's Group Nord "lassoers". Despite the heavy secrecy that enshrouded the operation, the Group's task to force a Sabre to make a landing on a North Korean or Manchurian airfield soon became known to everyone.

The Group conducted its first combat sortie on 31 May 1951 when at 1330 the entire complement of 12 MiG-15s took off on a combat mission. On this flight, the commander of the 324th IAD Guards Colonel I.N. Kozhedub from his command post directed Group Nord toward two B-29s flying in the area of Anju. Having sighted the Superfortresses flying without any apparent fighter cover, both six-ship flights of the Group rushed into the attack. However, it turned out that 10 F-86 Sabres were flying top cover for the bombers. Exploiting the mistake made by the Group's pilots, the Sabres pounced on the Soviet MiGs in a diving attack. On the very first pass, they shot down the MiG of the group commander Lieutenant Colonel Perevozchikov, and soon thereafter damaged Senior Lieutenant Alikhnovich's MiG. Lieutenant Colonel Pavel Andreevich Perevozchikov ejected from his crippled MiG, but while descending in his parachute, for some reason he fell out of his parachute harness and was killed. Senior Lieutenant Alikhnovich managed to nurse his MiG back to Andong and land it safely. In a brief dogfight that followed the American surprise attack, Engineer-Captain Makhalin managed to damage one Sabre, which withdrew from the combat.

In this action, the pilots of Group Nord were attacking two B-29 bombers from the 19th BG's 28th Squadron. 1st Lieutenant Bobby Smith of the 335th FIS was responsible for downing Lieutenant Colonel Perevozchikov's MiG, while his squadron mate 1st Lieutenant Otis Gordon mistakenly claimed Alikhnovich's MiG as a kill. The Americans assert that gunners aboard one of the B-29s also shot down one MiG, but the pilots of Group Nord only conducted a single pass against the B-29s and actually never managed to close to within short range of them, so thus they had no losses from the fire of the B-29 gunners.

Most likely, as they were returning from their target, these same B-29s were attacked by a group of MiG-15s from the Chinese 4th IAD, since there is evidence that at the end of May 1951, the Chinese regiment commander Chou Dahai was shot down and killed during an attack on a B-29. Possibly, it was precisely his MiG that Sergeant Michael R. Mattochia, a B-29 gunner, received credit for downing.

After such a disastrous initial combat sortie, Kozhedub gave time to Group Nord for rehearsing formation flying and studying the tactics of aerial combat against the Sabre, so for the following week its pilots trained intensively and conducted mock dogfights. On the return from one such training dogfight, a tragedy occurred. When landing, Lieutenant Colonel Dziubenko allowed his wingman Major Guliaev to pass in front of him and during the maneuver, accidentally wound up in the backwash from the engine of Guliaev's MiG. One wing of Dziubenko's MiG dropped, but because the altitude was very low, the MiG's wingtip struck the concrete runway. The MiG slid down the runway upside down and exploded. The pilot, the former commander of the 133rd GIAP Lieutenant Colonel Dziubenko was killed. This occurred on 6 May 1951 at the Andong Air Base. After this catastrophe, it was decided to disband Group Nord, since it was unable to handle its combat assignment. The group of test pilots returned to Moscow to the Air Force Scientific Research Institute. The air force pilots were scattered among the regiments of the 324th and 303rd IAD as replacements: Major F.I. Guliaev and Senior Lieutenant N.K. Serdiuk wound up in the 176th GIAP; Major A.I. Mitusov went to the 324th IAD's 196th IAP; Senior Lieutenants N.V. Babonin and I.K. Semenenko were sent to the 303rd IAD, the former to the 18th GIAP and the latter to the 523rd IAP. Lieutenant Colonel Rosliakov and two other pilots of the former Group Nord were transferred to the Soviet Air Force's Fighter Aviation headquarters.

After the combat and defeat of Group Nord on 31 May 1951, a little joke circulated among the pilots of the 324th IAD: *Gruppa Ukh, razbita Pukh* ["Group of whoops, pounded into fluff"]. Throughout that summer, the pilots referred to this group as Group Fluff.

Only in October 1951 did the pilots of the 324th IAD's 196th IAP get their hands on the first intact Sabre in this war. On 6 October, pilots of the 196th IAP under the command of regiment commander Lieutenant Colonel E.G. Pepeliaev tangled with a group of 30 Sabres. The battle was fierce. In it Pepeliaev downed two Sabres and damaged another, and that one made a belly landing on the coast of the Yellow Sea. Unfortunately, staff officers of the 64th IAK mistakenly assigned this victory to Major K.Ia. Sheberstov of the 176th GIAP, although on his gun camera footage there was no sign of any enemy aircraft. This Sabre No.50-0671 from the 336th FIS made a forced landing on the beach, and the pilot was picked up by the USAF Rescue Service. The Sabre, however, with only insignificant damage was delivered to the Andong Air Base almost fully intact, and was then shipped to Moscow for analysis.

On 13 May 1952, anti-aircraft gunners of the 64th IAK damaged another Sabre, which had to make a forced landing in PRC territory. Its pilot was the commander of the 51st FIW's 16th FIS, Colonel Walker "Bud" Mahurin, a World War II ace with 15 victories, plus three more over North Korea. Mahurin wound up as a prisoner of the Chinese, while his only lightly damaged Sabre was also sent to Moscow. Such were the results of the hunt for a MiG or a Sabre, which both sides continued until the end of the war.

To all the above it is necessary to add that several attempts to seize one of the American combat helicopters for analysis were undertaken by the Soviet side with the assistance of its allies, the Command of the Unified Army. The first attempt was made back in the summer of 1951, when an operation was conducted in the area of Pyongyang, which was organized by its Soviet adviser and chief of staff Colonel General Sozinov and his deputy Razuvaev. A Navy S-51 helicopter was lured into a trap set by the Soviet advisers, and approached the area where a downed airman was located. Nearby, a heavily camouflaged anti-aircraft battery opened fire, hitting the helicopter. The pilot had to make a forced landing on the nearest available piece of terrain suitable for one. North Korean soldiers quickly surrounded the helicopter, and its crew of two was tracked down and captured. The pilot and observer were immediately turned over to the North Korean authorities, while Soviet specialists began examining the helicopter.

The helicopter was disassembled at the place where it came down, packed into containers and sent back to Moscow. A Professor Ruzhidsky oversaw the disassembly and packing process. Any factory labels on the components that contained information were removed from the helicopter, which was essentially undamaged. In August 1951, the helicopter arrived in Moscow, and both the various components and the body of the helicopter itself were sent on to three different research institutes for detailed analysis. However, having found out that a dated helicopter model had fallen into their hands, the Soviet specialists quickly lost interest in it.

This operation was conducted on 3 July 1951. The Soviet intelligence officers had obtained a Navy HO3S-1 rescue helicopter from HU-2. The pilot J. Koelsch eventually died in captivity and was awarded the Congressional Medal of Honor.

Two other attempts to seize an American military helicopter were unsuccessful. The next attempt was undertaken by the North Korean special services on 3 February 1952, when at a signal from agents, the NKPA's special services attempted to lure a HO3S Marine helicopter into a trap, but it ultimately didn't prove successful! Back on 14 December 1951, an AD-4NL from VS-35 had been downed by ground fire while on a mission. The crew, pilot Harry Ettinger, navigator McElroy and gunner Gill, bailed out successfully, but they were all taken prisoner by the North Koreans. North Korean intelligence agents used the Skyraider pilot, Harry Ettinger, as bait. A coded rescue signal was transmitted, and on 3 February 1952, a light HO3S helicopter from HU-1 headed into enemy territory to pick up the downed pilot. The helicopter was being flown by CPO Duane Thorin; his observer was Lieutenant A. Naylor-Foote. A trap was waiting for them on the ground, which the North Koreans organized under the direction of Soviet military advisers. However, when the Skyraider pilot Harry Ettinger, who'd come running up, climbed into the cockpit of the two-seat light helicopter, which had landed on a rice paddy beam, its center of gravity shifted, causing the helicopter to list and tip over. The spinning helicopter blades struck the ground and flew apart. Thus, in addition to Ettinger, two more Americans fell into North Korean hands.

This operation was conducted in the Wonsan area under the leadership of two Soviet intelligence advisers, Colonels A. Glukhov and L. Smirnov, who devised and conducted this operation to seize a US military helicopter. For their service, the Presidium of the Supreme Soviet on 22 February 1952 awarded A. Glukhov with the Order of Lenin and L. Smirnov with the Order of the Red Banner. With the participation of a military adviser Colonel A. Dmitriev and a translator Senior Lieutenant Nekhrapov, the helicopter was delivered to the Andong Air Base. Unfortunately, they discovered that it was the same type of helicopter that they had previously obtained, so it wasn't sent back to the USSR.

Soviet and North Korean intelligence agents attempted to repeat a similar operation on 22 May 1952. Another captured American pilot, Captain Charles Spath of the 334th FIS, who'd been shot down in aerial combat and taken prisoner back on 3 February 1952, was used as the bait. Information was passed on through a turned South Korean agent that Charles Spath was alive. The message gave his location in North Korea and said that he could be picked up. For this purpose, on 22 May, the 3rd Air Rescue Squadron dispatched an H-19 rescue helicopter from the K-14 base, which was being flown by Captain Gail Poulton, who was to carry out this dangerous assignment in North Korean territory. Everything worked out according to the plan devised by the Soviet intelligence agents, until the moment the helicopter was coming in to land at the designated place. Risking his own life, the captured pilot Captain Spath transmitted a warning over the radio that he'd been given by the enemy intelligence officers, alerting Poulton that this was a trap and to get away. Captain Poulton terminated the mission and flew away, thereby avoiding falling into enemy hands.

It is possible that the Soviet and North Korean intelligence services undertook other attempts in the future to capture different types of US military helicopters. Perhaps to this point these attempts haven't been worth revealing?

ENDNOTES

1 The Air Combat Information Group's website at www.ACIG.org, which presents extensive data bases on the combat air-to-air victories in the Korean War for the participants on all sides, does have an entry that gives Richard S. Becker credit for downing Savinov's MiG on 24 March 1951.

2 This is a reference to the US radar ranging gunsights that began equipping Sabres only in December 1950-January 1951, and which had only limited tracking capabilities.

3 The MiG-15 sometimes betrayed flight instability at high speeds, which would send the jet into a *valezhka*, or an involuntary roll. This was a very dangerous phenomenon, particularly for inexperienced pilots, which sometimes ended in fatal crashes.

3

The 64th IAK gathers strength

The lack of success of the air attacks, undertaken on 12, 16 and 18 April 1951, prompted the US Fifth Air Force command to shift its squadrons to forward airfields in the Suwon and Taegu areas and to begin planning the systematic bombing of the North Korean airfields that were under construction. The implementation of this plan began on 9 May 1951, when at around 1400 five groups of ground attack aircraft and fighter-bombers simultaneously struck airfields at Sinuiju, Wonsan, Pyongyang, Sinian, Anang, Ongjin, Kondo-myn and elsewhere. In May, intense aerial combats between the 64th IAK's fighters and American strike packages sometimes flared up in the areas of Pyongyang and the Yalu River.

At first, however, following the April battles, at the beginning of May there was a brief lull in combat operations in the skies of Korea. This stemmed from the fact that after the heated April battles, both sides conducted a regrouping and strengthening of their air forces in Korea. The Americans particularly reinforced its attack aviation: as before, three groups of F-80 fighter-bombers, the 8th and 49th FBG and the 51st FIG, as well as the Mustang-equipped 18th FBG, were flying missions. In May, they were joined by F-84E fighter-bombers from the US National Guard's 136th FBW. This National Guard wing received all of its F-84E Thunderjets and a large number of its air and ground crews from the 27th FEW. The new fighter-bomber wing conducted its first sorties over Korea on 24 May 1951.

Just one fighter wing, the 4th FIW with its F-86A-5 Sabres, was providing the cover for the ground attack aircraft. On 21 May 1951 it was sent back to Japan for a pilot rotation and for refitting; at the end of May 1951 it returned to bases in South Korea. Its new complement of pilots had their first clash with MiGs on 31 May, when they had successfully attacked the Soviet pilots of Group Nord, shooting down one MiG-15 and damaging another.

Also as before, three B-29 bomber groups – the 19th, 98th and 307th BG – were operating from bases in Japan and Okinawa, but now in small groups with heavy fighter cover, and outside of MiG Alley. Two light bomber groups, flying the B-26A Invader from bases in South Korea, were operating simultaneously with the B-29 bomber groups. They were the 3rd BG (Light) and the 452nd BG; the latter switched to flying only night missions over North Korea in May 1951.

USAF airpower in Korea, which in the spring of 1951 had numbered 1,441 aircraft, grew to more than 1,600 aircraft in the summer of 1951. In addition, the 2nd Marine Air Wing under the command of Major General Harris, equipped with F4B-4 Corsairs, AD-2 Skyraiders and F9F-2 Panthers, was staging active operations from bases in South Korea. From the sea, carrier-based aircraft of the US Navy Seventh Fleet's Task Force 70 and Task Force 77, consisting of up to 800 F4U-F Corsairs, AD-2 Skyraiders and

F9F-2 Panthers launched strikes against targets in North Korea, joined by Royal Air Force and Royal Australian Air Force naval air squadrons. Only the 64th IAK and the recently created weak and inexperienced UAA, which had three fighter, one bomber and one ground attack aviation divisions consisting of two regiments each, opposed all this enormous airpower.

True, already on 4 April 1951, the strong and experienced 303rd IAD under the command of Colonel G.A. Lobov restaged to Mukden from the Far East. Before its arrival in the Far East, this elite division had been based near Moscow and served as the "parade" division of the Moscow District PVO, participating in all the ceremonial flyovers above Moscow. The division had the full three-regiment complement, all equipped with the upgraded MiG-15bis. Its flight personnel had more flight time in the MiG than the average Soviet fighter regiment, and moreover approximately 50% of the pilots had World War II combat experience, which of course enhanced this division's combat effectiveness. It was this division that was being readied to reinforce the 64th IAK in June 1951. But already on 8 May, the 303rd IAD's 18th GIAP, commanded by Guards Lieutenant Colonel A.E. Belostotsky, flew from Mukden to the Andong Air Base in order to reinforce the 324th IAD as a temporary attachment.

A new airfield being constructed for the 303rd IAD in Miaogou, 20 kilometers northwest of Andong, was completed at the end of May 1951. However, while the 303rd IAD prepared for combat, the reinforced 324th IAD continued to fly missions over MiG Alley alone. Encounters with the enemy were uncommon, but tended to spark prolonged and intense action.

Lieutenant Colonel G.A Lobov (first on the left) – a 1944 photo.

The first such combat took place already on 1 May when at 1100 a group of eight MiGs from the 176th GIAP under the command of Guards Lieutenant Colonel S.F. Vishniakov took off on a combat patrol. On this sortie our pilots weren't vigilant and were caught off-guard by an attack of 10 Sabres from below, which scattered the regiment's formation. Our fighters were attacked as they were conducting a turn in the area of Sonchon, during which Captain S.P. Subbotin's trailing flight lagged behind Vishniakov's lead flight. Small groups of F-86 tried to attack Subbotin's flight, but all the attacks were driven off.

Vishniakov's lead flight was attacked by four Sabres as it was swinging around over Taechon. On their first pass the Sabre pilots succeeded in downing Senior Lieutenant P.F. Nikulin's MiG, and also heavily damaged the one flown by Lieutenant A.F. Golovachev, who was forced to exit the combat with a head wound.

Here is how it happened: spotting an opening, two Sabres had dropped onto the tail of Vishniakov's MiG. The commander's wingman, Guards Senior Lieutenant P.F. Nikulin accelerated to cut them off and counterattacked them, forcing them to break off the attack and sending one of the Sabres out of the battle, trailing smoke. However, at that moment the second Sabre element attacked, catching Nikulin in a disadvantageous position and unable to counter them. Nikulin's MiG took a full volley and burst into flames. The engine began to sputter, the instrument panel was smashed, and the pilot himself was lightly wounded. Our pilot safely ejected just before his MiG exploded in mid-air. Nikulin floated down to earth in his parachute and was soon picked up by a CPV patrol and brought to the hospital in Singisiu, where he spent approximately a month.

Meanwhile, the dogfight continued. Captain I.A. Iablokov, having already lost his wingman Golovachev, also attempted come to the regiment commander's aid, but fell into a spin and returned to base. Now all alone, Colonel Vishniakov parried the Sabre attack before evading them in a zoom climb, and then returned to Andong. The remaining scattered pilots of the 176th GIAP returned to Andong in ones and twos. In this action, the pilots of the 176th GIAP clearly suffered a defeat, having lost one MiG and two wounded pilots.

Their adversary in this combat had been a group of Sabres from the 336th Fighter Squadron. 1st Lieutenant Simpson Evans was given credit for destroying Senior Lieutenant Nikulin's MiG, while the commander of the 336th Fighter Squadron Lieutenant Colonel Bruce Hinton damaged Lieutenant Golovachev's fighter.

After the 1 May battle, right up until 9 May encounters with the enemy were episodic and usually resulted in no combat, because the enemy sought to avoid tangling with the MiG. In addition, the weather conditions were poor, and nearly constant rainfall curtailed the aerial activity of the opposing sides. However, on 9 May 1951, the Americans launched the largest raid yet against the North Koreans' largest airfield at Singisiu. The attack featured 312 USAF and USNAF combat aircraft: F-80Cs from the 8th and 49th FBG and the 51st FIG, F-51s from the 18th FBG, as well as carrier-based F4U Corsairs and F9F-2 Panthers from the US Seventh Fleet. Sabres of the 4th FIW and F-84E Thunderjets of the 136th FBW provided top cover for the mission.

According to the journal *Flight* (No. 2208, 1951), the given armada reached Singisiu without any opposition and inflicted a heavy attack upon the airfield and the town itself, destroying no less than 50 North Korean aircraft on the ground. In the course of the raid, the journal writes, approximately 50 MiG-15s were sighted over Andong, but only

15 of them crossed the Yalu River in an effort to interfere with the attack, but they were quickly attacked by UN fighters.

Other sources say that during the attack on the Singisiu airfield at 1400, the Americans destroyed 38 Yak-9, La-9/11 and Il-10 aircraft, and destroyed or damaged 106 buildings and 26 supply dumps. The Americans put their own losses at one damaged F-84, which was hit by anti-aircraft fire. However, the American records are not quite accurate.

In the course of the day, the enemy's fighters displayed high activity above the territory of northwest Korea. Up to 100 enemy aircraft took part in this attack on the airfield and town of Singisiu, which lasted from 1150 to 1240: F-51s, F-80s, F-84s and F-86s. The F-80s and F-84s operated in waves of 16-24 aircraft with an interval of two to three minutes between each attacking wave, which came in at low altitudes down to near ground level. Groups of 8 to 16 F-86s were echeloned above them in altitude.

Several groups of MiGs from the 324th IAD were scrambled to repel this attack. Pilots of the 196th IAP were the first to enter combat against the enemy: at 1150, the regiment dispatched 14 MiGs, flying in two groups, to intercept the enemy. However, the enemy spotted the first group under Senior Lieutenant N.K. Shelamonov, but only attacked the element of Shelamonov and his wingman Dostoevsky. Approaching the vicinity of the Singisiu airfield, the Soviet pilots sighted a flight of four Thunderjets, which were already making its egress away from the target. Leaving Captain Soskovets's element as top cover, Shelamonov and his wingman Senior Lieutenant A.M. Dostoevsky conducted a high-side attack against the Thunderjets. In the initial pass, Shelamonov misjudged the attack angle and never got an F-84 in his sights, but his wingman sent one of the Thunderjets spinning into the ground. They didn't succeed in making another pass, because by that time the F-84s had already reached the sanctuary of the Yellow Sea. Captain Bokach's second flight, which arrived after Shelamonov's, did not encounter any enemy aircraft.

However, on their return to base, as Nikolai Konstantinovich Shelamonov later relayed in a conversation with this author, he bumped into a flight of piston-engine attack aircraft – according to Shelamonov, they were Mustangs. Despite the strict order not to pursue UN aircraft across the coastline, he attacked the enemy aircraft out over the sea and sent one plunging into the water. Since what he'd done was forbidden, he didn't report this victory once he returned to base and it was never entered into the regiment's documents. Presumably, his target may have been a Corsair, rather than a Mustang, especially since the Americans acknowledge a loss of two Corsairs on the following day; most likely, his victim was F4U No. 97445 from VMF-214, the pilot of which was killed "by hostile activity". The historian Diego Zampini believes instead that Shelamonov downed F-51 No. 44-63400 from the South African 2nd Squadron, which was registered as lost two days later, on 11 May 1951. As military representatives of the South African Air Force acknowledge today, this Mustang was lost due to MiG fire.

Pilots of the 176th GIAP, which took off for the Singisiu area at 1250 with a complement of six MiGs under the command of Captain K.Ia. Sheberstov, had better luck. In the area of Sonchon they intercepted a group of four F-80s, and in the course of a lightning attack Captain Sheberstov and Captain G.I. Ges' each downed a Shooting Star, both of which crashed in the Chongju area. One of the victims was F-80 No. 49-1852 from the 8th FBG; its pilot 1st Lieutenant Frank Bay was killed. The second downed

Shooting Star, No. 49-471, was from the 49th FBG. So the assertion that the UN air force had no losses on this day, putting it gently, isn't quite accurate!

Despite the foul weather, the days of 11 and 12 May also featured several short clashes between MiGs and Sabres. For example, at 1035 on 11 May, six MiGs of the 176th GIAP led by regiment commander Lieutenant Colonel Vishniakov took off on a combat patrol. In the area of Sonchon they sighted a pair of Sabres. Vishniakov's lead element attacked them head-on and opened fire, after which the Sabres sharply reversed course and dove away for the sea. With this the combat ended, and since the MiG pilots had opened fire from great range and didn't see any results from their firing, there were no victory claims. However, according to the American side, a Sabre of the 336th Fighter Squadron was damaged. The pilot of this F-86 No. 49-1089 1st Lieutenant Morris Pitts reported that his Sabre had been hit by an anti-aircraft shell, which struck a .50 caliber ammunition bay and caused an explosion that damaged his fighter's hydraulics. The pilot returned safely to his base in Kimpo, but since he couldn't lower his landing gear, he had to make a belly landing. In the process his Sabre received so much damage that it had to be written off, but the pilot was unharmed. Most likely, it wasn't an anti-aircraft shell that hit 1st Lieutenant Pitts' Sabre, but a solitary 23mm shell from Lieutenant Colonel Vishniakov's MiG, which Pitts' fighter had caught during the head-on pass, and which became the cause of all his subsequent troubles. It was simply more beneficial for Pitts to claim that he'd been struck by an anti-aircraft shell, than to acknowledge that a MiG pilot had hit him, especially with such long-range fire.

There was another encounter with a pair of Sabres on 12 May, but the combat with them ended without any results for the pilots of the 176th GIAP. After this clash, there was another long pause in combat operations in the skies of Korea, due to weather that grounded all the aircraft. During this period the 196th IAP, which prior to then had been flying the less powerful MiG-15 equipped with the RD-45A engine, received new MiG-15bis fighters. The regiment turned over its old MiGs to the Chinese.

It was the pilots of the 196th IAP in their new MiGs that dueled with the pilots of the 4th FIW on 20 May 1951. The events of this day began at 1450, when 10 MiGs under the command of Captain P.N. Antonov from the recently arrived 18th GIAP of the 303rd IAD, took off to intercept enemy aircraft in the Changseong [Changsung] area. In the Sonchon area they met and engaged eight F-86s, but the clash ended with no results for either side. In this, their initial combat against the F-86 Sabre, the pilots of the 18th GIAP didn't get rattled and handled the action confidently, forcing the Sabres to leave the area.

For the one and a half weeks after arriving in Andong on 8 May 1951, the pilots of the newly attached 18th GIAP had prepared for combat: they had studied the area of combat operations, the enemy's tactics, and rehearsed formation flying. They had conducted their first sortie on the day they had arrived in Andong, when MiGs from the 18th GIAP were ordered to patrol over the Singisiu bridge and the Supung hydroelectric station, which passed without any encounter with the enemy. For the next several days, this remained the 18th GIAP's assignment – to cover the bridge and pontoon bridges in the Singisiu area and the Supung power station. Beginning on 12 May, the pilots of Lieutenant Colonel Belostotsky's regiment began to conduct combat sorties to intercept enemy aircraft, but none of these had resulted in enemy contact until the 20 May 1951 mission.

However, let's return to the further events that took place on 20 May: at 1505, a group of eight MiGs from the 196th IAP under the command of regiment commander Lieutenant Colonel E.G. Pepeliaev took off for the same area, followed into the air by another eight MiGs from the 196th IAP's 3rd Squadron under the command of Senior Lieutenant N.K. Shelamonov. In the region of Tetsuzan, the group sighted two flights of F-86s and engaged them. Regiment commander Pepeliaev was the first to attack, choosing the enemy's lead flight as his target. The Sabre pilots also spotted the MiGs and attempted to evade the attack with a high-G turn. One element managed to do this, but the other element hesitated before banking into the turn and came under Pepeliaev's attack: having pulled within 200 meters of the wingman's Sabre, he opened fire and scored hits, sending it into a dive while trailing smoke.

At that moment the remaining three Sabres counterattacked Pepeliaev's element, but their attack was disrupted by Captain B.V. Bokach's element. Bokach put his MiG into a zooming climb after his firing pass, but his wingman Senior Lieutenant P.M. Zykov when attempting to follow him, emerged directly in front of the Sabres, thereby becoming a superb target for these Sabre pilots. As his MiG passed through the Sabres' machine-gun fire, it took several hits, and one round penetrated his cockpit canopy and drilled into his right shoulder blade. The wounded pilot managed to shake off his pursuers after a high-speed chase at low altitude and safely brought his MiG home with 10 bullet holes in it.

Captain V.A. Nazarkin's second flight attacked the trailing flight of Sabres, but at this moment it was jumped by a third flight of F-86s which had just arrived on scene. Evading the Sabres attacks, both Narzakin and his wingman pulled excessive G-forces, and unable to manage the strain, both pilots' MiGs fell into spins, from which only Senior Lieutenant A.D. Litviniuk was able to recover, and he immediately returned to base. His leader Captain Nazarkin was a little less lucky: a pair of Sabres attacked his MiG as he was recovering from the spin and shot up his flight controls, forcing him to eject from his uncontrollable aircraft. His parachute deployed and he landed safely.

In its turn, the second element of this flight, led by Captain B.S. Abakumov, attacked the flight of Sabres that had jumped Nazarkin's element. However, another flight of Sabres dove on Abakumov's element, and only the skill and tight cooperation of our pilots bailed them out of their predicament. When pulling out of one attack in a zoom climb, Abakumov's MiG stalled and went into a spin. As he was recovered from the spin, a pair of Sabres attempted to shoot him down, but they in turn were attacked by Abakumov's wingman, Captain N.K. Kirisov, who latched so tightly onto their tails that he forced them to break off the attack with several bursts of cannon fire. They headed toward the Yellow Sea, but Kirisov still managed to chase down the lead Sabre and expended all his remaining ammunition against him, scoring several hits on the enemy aircraft from 150 meters, after which the Sabre dove away, trailing smoke.

The sudden appearance of Senior Lieutenant Shelamonov's group, which immediately plunged into the battle, bailed Pepeliaev's group out of this difficult and disadvantageous situation. Shelamonov's flight engaged one Sabre flight, while the Senior Lieutenant P.A. Soskovets's trailing flight spotted a new flight of F-86s, which was aiming to make an unseen attack on Shelamonov's flight from below, and dove to intercept them. In the flurry of maneuvering and firing passes that ensued, our pilots demonstrated that this time they were better-skilled than the American pilots and managed to register hits on three of the Sabres and to force the remaining to abandon the area. In the process, the pilots Senior Lieutenants V.I. Alfeev and F.D. Shebanov of Soskovets's flight both received credit for downing one Sabre each, while the group leader Senior Lieutenant Shelamonov damaged the other F-86.

A participant in this combat, the future ace of this war James Jabara related in an interview that on this day he as part of his squadron, numbering 14 Sabres encountered and were surrounded by a swarm of up to 50 MiGs in the area of MiG Alley, but despite this he and his comrades boldly engaged them, and he personally downed two of them, while his comrade Milton Nelson shot down another MiG. The combat occurred above Sinuiju around 1700. Here is how Jabara describes this battle:

> I was in the second wave of F-86s. I tacked on to three MiGs at an altitude of 35,000 feet, picked out the last one and bored straight in. My first two bursts ripped up his fuselage and left wing. At about 10,000 feet, the pilot bailed out. It was a good thing he did because the MiG disintegrated. Then I climbed back to 20,000 feet to get back into the battle. I bounced six more MiGs. I closed in and got off two bursts into one of them, scoring heavily both times. He began to smoke. Then when my second burst caught him square in the middle, he burst into flames and fell into an uncontrolled spin. I had to break off then, because there was another MiG on my tail.

In this battle, Jabara actually did shoot down Captain V.A. Nazarkin, a pilot in the 196th IAP's 2nd Squadron, who ejected from his damaged aircraft. But Captain Jabara's second victory didn't happen: plainly it was he who had damaged Zykov's aircraft, but his "victim" successfully returned to base, while his MiG was quickly repaired. Meanwhile Captain Nelson had mistakenly perceived one of the MiGs that fell into a spin as a victory, which he claimed back on the ground, for which he shouldn't have received credit.

In their turn the pilots of the 196th IAP claimed that in this battle, in which not 50 MiGs participated, but only 16, they had downed three Sabres and damaged another, but regiment headquarters granted victories to all four pilots: regiment commander Lieutenant Colonel E.G. Pepeliaev, Captain N.K. Kirisov, and Senior Lieutenants F.D. Shebanov and V.I. Alfeev. Incidentally, according to Alfeev's report, he damaged Captain Jabara's Sabre in this combat, but it is known that Jabara safely returned to Kimpo. By the way, it was in this action on 20 May 1951 that one of the top Soviet aces of this war, Lieutenant Colonel Pepeliaev, scored his first victory.

According to recent research by Diego Zampini, victory in this well-known aerial clash nevertheless went to the Soviets. As has been established by documents, in this battle 28 Sabres of the 335th and 336th Fighter Squadrons of the 4th FIW took part, and they were only opposed by 16 MiGs of the 196th IAP. In the course of the dogfight, Lieutenant Colonel Pepeliaev damaged Captain Milton Nelson's F-86A No.49-1080 of the 335th FIS, and although he flew back to Suwon in it, the damage was so heavy that it was immediately written-off. Captain Kirisov inflicted serious damage to a different F-86A, No.49-1313, which was flown by Captain Max Weill of the 336th FIS, and although Captain Weill was also able to return to the base in Suwon, his Sabre with the unlucky Bureau Number was simply sent to the base's boneyard to serve as a source of spare parts for other Sabres of his squadron.

Although Senior Lieutenant F.D. Shebanov also didn't succeed this time in shooting down his opponent, he nevertheless damaged Captain Morris B. Pitts' Sabre, forcing him to exit the battle and return to his base. Some American historians and veterans of this war surmise that Captain Jabara's F-86A Sabre No.49-1339 was also damaged in this combat, a fact which has been kept concealed for a long time. For the sake of justice it should be noted that Captain Jabara's and Captain Pitts' Sabres were both repaired and again returned to service.

From everything laid out above, it turns out that the pilots of the 196th IAP scored two victories and damaged two more Sabres, with the loss of one MiG destroyed and one MiG damaged in return – a ratio of 2:1 in favor of the Soviet pilots. It is a blessing that all of the participants in this major clash survived it!

This was the 4th FIW's final day of combat before its departure to Japan. After this battle, the pilots of the 4th Fighter Interceptor Group departed to undergo a pilot rotation and refitting in Japan. In the skies of Korea between 15 December 1950 and 21 May 1951, the pilots of the 4th FIG's initial echelon conducted 3,550 combat sorties and claimed 22 confirmed victories, while losing just seven of their Sabres in return.

The 4th FIG's new complement of pilots conducted its first combat with MiGs on 28 May 1951, having returned to Korea from Japan. The battle proved to be a hard one for both sides, but especially for the pilots of the 18th GIAP, since they were outnumbered 3 to 1 in it. They yielded to a numerically superior opponent in this combat, and even though they achieved no victories in it, they also didn't suffer any losses. The Americans were unable to score any victories due to their lack of combat experience; for the majority of them, this was their initial taste of combat in the skies of Korea. The fresh complement of pilots for the 4th FIG obtained their first victory only in their next combat with the MiGs on 31 May 1951, which has already been described above when discussing Group Nord's failed attempt to force down a Sabre. True, it should be noted that even after 20 May, the pilots of the 324th IAD had encounters with Sabres: there were brief clashes with F-86s on 23 and 24 May, but the Sabre pilots declined active combat with the MiGs and, in essence, these were familiarization flights over the area of combat operations by the new pilots of the 4th FIW.

On the afternoon of 28 May, genuine combats between the MiG and Sabre pilots resumed. In the "clarification of the relationship", pilots of the 176th IAP and the 18th GIAP participated on the one side, while approximately 20 F-86s took part on the other side. However, this encounter resulted in no damage at all to either side.

As if sensing the beginning of a new confrontation in the skies of Korea, the 64th IAK command on 28 May 1951 sent the 523rd IAP from the 303rd IAD to the just completed base at Miaogou, and already on 1 June the given regiment initiated its combat operations. A little later, on 11 June 1951, the 17th IAP joined the 523rd IAP in Miaogou, and the 303rd IAD in full strength began to operate over MiG Alley.

THE BEGINNING OF OPERATION STRANGLE

Starting on 31 May 1951, the USAF increased its attacks against the PLA's supply network. The territory of the PDRK was divided into 11 zones, in which 172 targets were to be destroyed: 45 railroad bridges, 12 road bridges, 39 railroad sectors and 63 supply dumps. At the order of General Ridgeway, the commander-in-chief of the US forces in

Korea, the aviation units concentrated their efforts on bombing the main supply arteries. If they would be able to paralyze the movement on them, as the Americans supposed, then the CPV armies would be cut-off from their rear supply centers and become easy prey for the UN ground forces at the front. Aerial operations would create the conditions for a turning point in the war by concentrating on the strategy of paralysis and restricting supplies, as opposed to the direct support to the ground troops, which in the first phase of combat operations in Korea had proved to be less effective than anticipated.

The task to destroy the traffic movement along three interior routes was laid upon the Fifth Air Force and the Marine pilots, while two routes along the coast were to be interdicted by the carrier aviation units under the command of Task Force 77. Ten months of sustained, round the clock bombing began on 1 June, the main victim of which became the civilian population of North Korea. This operation significantly surpassed the aerial campaign of the summer of 1950.

On 1 June 1951, four B-29 bombers of the 98th BG twice attacked the railroad bridge southwest of Sinuiju. The first mission encountered no resistance and carried out its assignment, but during the second raid, the bomber group was attacked by a solitary MiG-15, flown by Guards Lieutenant Evgenii Stel'makh of the 18th GIAP's 3rd Squadron. This was the 18th GIAP's first day of combat operations in MiG Alley. The pilots of this regiment conducted two combat sorties on 1 June, the first by a single squadron and the second with the full strength of an entire regiment. Ten MiGs of the 3rd Squadron took off first at 0835, led by squadron commander Captain P.N. Antonov, in order to cover the railroad in the Andong-Pyongyang sector. In the area of Uiju at an altitude of 7,000 meters they spotted a formation of four B-29 bombers, which were at a significantly lower

Hero of the Soviet Union
Senior Lieutenant
E.M. Stel'makh – killed
in Korea 1 June 1951.

altitude. However, at this moment several Sabre elements attacked Captain Antonov's lead flight and scattered its formation, before tying up its separate MiG elements in combat. While Senior Lieutenant F.M. Malashin's element was evading one attack by a pair of F-86s, they spotted another flight of enemy aircraft and went on the attack against it. But as it turned out, this wasn't the enemy, but the 3rd Squadron's second flight commanded by Senior Lieutenant N.L. Kornienko. While our pilots were trying to figure out who was friend and who was enemy, the leader of the second element in Kornienko's flight, Senior Lieutenant E.M. Stel'makh, having grasped the situation more quickly than anyone else, together with his wingman broke away from the "combat" with Malashin's element and immediately spotted the B-29s below him.

Stel'makh shouted out to his wingman that he was going on the attack and dove on the bombers. However, it turned out that his wingman Senior Lieutenant V.I. Murav'ev didn't hear Stel'makh's message and simply lost track of his leader. Thus no one saw where Stel'makh went, and they all returned to the base at Miaogou without him.

Stel'makh, still thinking that his wingman was providing top cover, unconcernedly went on the attack alone against the four B-29s, and on the very first pass chewed up the wing of one B-29 with a volley from his cannons. The big bomber disintegrated in the air and fell in the vicinity of Uiju. In his second pass, Stel'makh damaged another B-29, and with a burning engine it dropped out of the formation and began to turn back to its own territory. But at this point Stel'makh himself was unexpectedly jumped by a pair of covering Sabres from the 335th FIS, which latched onto the tail of the solitary MiG. With his fire, Captain Richard Rensbott knocked out the rudder control linkages on Stel'makh's MiG, and therefore Evgenii had to eject from his stricken aircraft. However, according to one version of the story, upon landing in his parachute the Soviet pilot had to engage in combat again, but now on the ground, since one of the enemy's diversionary groups was approaching the place where he came down, hoping to take the pilot prisoner. Seeing that he was surrounded by armed men wearing unfamiliar uniforms, Stel'makh attempted to hide, but the approaching enemy opened fire from their rifles. The Soviet pilot returned fire with his pistol, and continued to fire until he was down to his final cartridge, at which point he shot himself in the heart in order not to be taken alive by the enemy. According to a different version, North Korean soldiers thought he was an American. Similar cases took place during that time, when North Korean soldiers fired indiscriminately at all the pilots who had ejected from their damaged aircraft. Such incidents came to an end only after Kim Il Sung issued a special order, which banned all fire from any of North Korea's air defense weapons against parachutists descending below white canopies (the Americans had orange, red and blue parachute canopies).

According to American records, just one bomber from the 98th BG's 343rd Squadron was shot down by MiGs on this mission. In turn, the Americans claim that gunners aboard the Superfortresses shot down two MiGs, while another two MiGs were downed by Sabres from the 4th FIG's 335th Squadron.

In actual fact, Evgenii Stel'makh in his first firing pass managed to devastate B-29 No.44-86327, and 10 of its crewmen perished in its fragments. On his second pass he managed to inflict heavy damage on B-29 No.44-86335, which to be honest was able to make a forced landing at the base in Taegu (South Korea), but was immediately written off as beyond repair. Sabre pilots managed to shoot down Evgenii Stel'makh's MiG, which was credited to Captain Richard Ransbottom. Lieutenant Simpson Evans of the 336th Fighter Squadron received victory credit for downing another MiG, but in reality he didn't shoot down Senior Lieutenant N.A. Argeev's MiG, but only damaged it. Although it received 21 bullet holes, Argeev safely brought his MiG back to his base, where it was quickly patched up.

Who the Superfortress gunners shot down in this combat is unknown. Most likely, it was just a figment of their imagination, since only a single MiG attacked their formation, and it experienced no problems from the gunners aboard the B-29s.

At any rate, the B-29s suffered serious losses on this mission. Thus it was on this same day of 1 June that the command of the US Fifth Air Force prohibited bomber flights over this area without robust fighter escort.

The Superfortresses downed by Guards Senior Lieutenant E.M. Stel'makh on 1 June were the first credited to the score of the 18th GIAP, but wasn't the final success of this regiment's pilots on this day. Later that day at 1305 during a regimental sortie to intercept enemy aircraft, the 18th GIAP's 1st Squadron, which took off with a complement of eight MiGs headed by Captain A.F. Maznev, spotted six F-51 fighter-bombers at low altitude. Captain Maznev's flight remained at altitude to provide top cover, while Captain A.A. Kaliuzhny's flight attacked the Mustangs, which were flying at an altitude of just 600-800 meters. The leader of the second element Senior Lieutenant L.K. Shchukin on the very first attack managed to pull to within 80 meters of the tail of one of the Mustangs in a sharp turn to the left and with a short burst sent the leader of the trailing Mustang element in a violent dive to the earth. The remaining three F-51s hugged the ground and began to retreat. The terrain was mountainous, which restricted maneuvering. Captain A.A. Kaliuzhny's lead element went in pursuit of the Mustangs. Unable to maneuver like his adversary, Captain Kaliuzhny got behind one of the Mustangs and

Deputy squadron commander in the 18th GIAP Captain L.K. Shchukin in China, 1951.

fired on it from a range of around 300 meters. The Mustang began to stream smoke after the first burst, while Kaliuzhny continued to shed altitude and closed to within 150 meters of the F-51 before giving it another two bursts – the Mustang abruptly dropped its nose and plunged into the sea not far from the coast in a shallow dive. The other Mustangs managed to escape to the sanctuary of the Yellow Sea, so the squadron's pilots returned to Miaogou, having achieved two victories, without any losses of their own. The American side recognizes the loss of one of its Mustangs (No.44-74614) from the 18th FBG, the pilot of which was killed. The other Mustang lost on this day was from the South African Air Force's 2nd Squadron, and its pilot was taken prisoner.

Thus, the pilots of the 18th GIAP opened their combat score, and that of the 303rd IAD as a whole, in the skies of Korea on 1 June 1951. On this same day, pilots of the 523rd IAP, under the command of Hero of the Soviet Union Lieutenant Colonel A.N. Karasev, also made their first combat sortie from the base at Miaogou – one flight of the regiment covered the landing of pilots of the 176th GIAP on the Andong Air Base (with no enemy encounter).

The pilots of the 176th GIAP also became involved in two aerial combats on 1 June, but only the first one had any results. According to a daily report, around 0600 in the area of Sonchon, four MiGs led by regiment commander Lieutenant Colonel Vishniavsky engaged four F-86s, and Captain N.M. Goncharov scored several hits with his shells from his 23mm cannon on one of the Sabres. According to NKPA troops, his target fell into the sea. In fact, the American side reports the loss of its F-84 No.49-2324 from the 27th FEW's 522nd Squadron shortly after 0700, so it is most likely that in this combat, the pilots of the 176th GIAP were dueling with Thunderjets, and not Sabres.

On 2 June, three groups of MiGs from the 176th GIAP flew off to the Anju area, but only six MiGs from the 2nd Squadron under the command of Captain S.M. Kramarenko encountered the enemy – a six-ship flight of Sabres. In the course of the ensuing scrap, the group leader Captain Kramarenko succeeded in getting behind a Sabre element, and from a range of 600 meters hit the wingman's aircraft with several shells. Streaming smoke, it headed in the direction of the sea. This occurred around 1311. According to research by the Argentinean historian Diego Zampini, Captain Kramarenko in this action managed to inflict serious damage upon F-86A No.49-1130, which was being flown by 1st Lieutenant Thomas K. Hanson of the 336th Fighter Squadron. He managed to nurse his crippled Sabre back to the base at Suwon, but it crashed as the pilot attempted a forced landing, and Hanson was killed. The pilots of the 18th GIAP flew two other missions that day, the first in the morning in squadron strength, and the second in the afternoon by another squadron to the Haeju area, but neither sortie made any contact with the enemy.

The next day heavy rains began over North Korea and continued right until the middle of June, and the weather became unacceptable for conducting flight operations. Only on 6 June did a squadron of MiGs from the 18th GIAP encounter four F-80s from the 51st FIG in the area of Sonchon near the end of the day (between 1830 and 1900), and they began to stalk them. Seeing that they were outnumbered 4 to 1, the Shooting Star pilots sped toward the sea at low altitude. However, only one of the F-80 elements managed to reach the sanctuary of the sea. First Captain P.N. Antonov downed one of the "Shoots" from short range, which fell in the Sonchon area, and then one F-80 was attacked in succession by the Smorchkov-Os'kin element and the Shchukin-Akatov element. Although this Shooting Star managed to reach the sea, it fell 20 kilometers south of Chongju. The Americans acknowledged the loss of F-80 No.49-737, the pilot of which was rescued. Most likely, this was the aircraft downed by Captain Antonov. The other F-80 was apparently written off several days later, on 14 June.

On 15 June, the weather over Korea began to improve, and soon it became possible to continue combat operations in the skies over North Korea. Flight operations resumed on the morning of 17 June, and this day truly became a black one for the 4th FIW: first at 0200 its base in Suwon was attacked by two KPAF Po-2 night bombers which accurately struck a Sabre parking area. Their bombs completely destroyed F-86A No.49-1334, and four other Sabres were damaged by bomb fragments. Later that morning at 0820, 16 MiGs of the 18th GIAP under the command of regiment commander Lieutenant Colonel A.E. Belostotsky departed on a mission, and just 30 minutes later engaged 16 F-86s in the area of Sonchon. The dogfight proved to be rather intense and lengthy. In the course of it, when repulsing an attack on the regiment commander Belostotsky, his wingman Captain D.P. Os'kin hit one Sabre with his cannon fire, which headed in the direction of the sea. In their turn, the Sabre pilots managed to damage Captain A.D. Skidan's aircraft, but he was able to return safely to his base. Then Senior Lieutenant L.K. Shchukin succeeded in damaging another Sabre, but a moment later Shchukin himself failed to spot an attack from above by a pair of Sabres, which riddled Shchukin's MiG with .50 caliber bullets and inflicted such damage to it that the pilot had to abandon his aircraft and take to the parachute. Captain Samuel Pesacreta was credited with this victory. In his turn, Shchukin had downed F-86A No.49-1335, which according to American records was lost due to "unidentified hostile action".

Eighteen MiGs of the 176th GIAP which had flown off together with the 18th GIAP's group failed to encounter the enemy, with the exception of Captain S.P. Subbotin, who on his route back to base downed a solitary F-86, which was fleeing to the south at top speed. Subbotin himself spotted this Sabre, and separating from his group, attacked and downed it. Presumably, this was a reconnaissance RF-86A, the loss of which the American command prefers not to acknowledge.

Finally, in the middle of the day, or more precisely at 1120, one more combat between MiGs and Sabres took place in the area of Sonchon. This dogfight involved six MiGs from the 176th GIAP under the command of Captain Kramarenko and 11 F-86s. Captain Kramarenko's flight engaged eight of the Sabres, while Senior Lieutenant I.V. Lazutin's element dueled with the other three F-86s. In the course of this action, Captain Kramarenko became separated from his wingman and alone had to face three F-86s, which were being piloted by aces of the 4th FIW. The commander of the 336th Fighter Squadron Lieutenant Colonel Bruce Hinton was in the cockpit of one of the Sabres, while another of the F-86s was being flown by the commander of the 4th FIG himself, Lieutenant Colonel Glenn Eagleston. Future Hero of the Soviet Union Sergei Makarovich Kramarenko not only survived this unequal fight, he also scored a rather resounding victory, which became known 50 years later. In the course of the swirling maneuvering, Kramarenko managed to get one of the Sabres in his sights and registered hits on it; his target began to shed altitude and headed back to friendly lines. As is now known thanks to the efforts of Diego Zampini, in this battle Captain Kramarenko seriously damaged F-86A No.49-1281, in which the commander of the 4th FIG Lieutenant Colonel Glenn Eagleston was flying. The commander managed with difficulty to bring his stricken Sabre back to its base in Suwon, where he had to make a forced belly landing. Although Lieutenant Colonel Eagleston escaped unharmed from the landing, his Sabre was no longer suitable for flights and was written off.

Thus, in the course of 17 June 1951 alone, the 4th FIW lost three of its F-86s due to enemy action, while at least another five Sabres received damage. The losses of the 64th IAK comprised a total of one MiG-15 destroyed and one damaged.

The pilots of the other regiments of the 303rd IAD were gradually drawn into daily combat operations against enemy ground attack aircraft, which under heavy Sabre cover were conducting air strikes against military and civilian targets located in MiG Alley. Every day pilots of the 523rd and 17th IAP flew two combat sorties and spotted enemy aircraft, but their first combats with the Americans took place only in the latter half of June 1951 against Sabres of the 4th FIW, which began appearing in MiG Alley in large groups of 20 to 24 aircraft each.

The pilots of the 523rd IAP achieved their first victory in the skies of Korea in a combat on 18 June. It was scored by Captain M.S. Ponomarev, the deputy commander of the 3rd Squadron. Here is how he described it in his memoirs:

On this day, we as a regiment were conducting a routine flight around the area of combat operations. The lead flight under the command of regiment commander A.N. Karasov and the flight under the command of Senior Lieutenant I.I. Iakovlev were both part of the attack group. My element had been assigned the role to cover it. There were diffuse clouds along our group's flight path. I led my element below the lowest clump of clouds, so that I could keep the main group in sight. As we were leaving the zone of combat operations, six F-86s attempted to attack the main group. They were flying in a compact formation. They didn't see my element, because we were concealed by the thin clouds. Thus, the Sabres wound up between our main group and my element, which is to say that I was in position behind the Sabres at a range of 500-600 meters. I only had to close the distance, take aim and open fire, which is what I did. One of the F-86s began to smoke and started to fall out of control, while the remaining F-86s scattered in every direction. In this combat, one more Sabre was downed by Hero of the Soviet Union regiment commander Lieutenant Colonel A.N. Karasev, who took advantage of the confusion in their ranks. We had no losses in this action.

Senior Lieutenant I.I. Iakovlev managed to hit one more Sabre in this battle, in which 10 MiGs of the 523rd IAP and approximately 20 Sabres took part, though his own MiG took hits as well. His MiG was attacked from behind by a Sabre flight. His wingman was unable to disrupt their attack and Iakovlev's MiG was damaged, but he managed to avoid any further hits and returned his aircraft back to his base in Miaogou, bringing it back with 10 bullet holes in it. This dogfight occurred in the Chongju-Pakchon-Kusong area between 0932 and 1000, but the American side doesn't confirm the loss of its Sabres in this action.

Incidentally, on this day there were several other aerial clashes in MiG Alley between pilots of the 64th IAK and the American 4th FIW, as both sides were contesting fiercely for control of the air space in the given area. According to American records, in one of these combats 32 Sabres collided with more than 40 MiGs. At the end of the day, the Americans claimed five victories (1st Lieutenant Ralph Gibson alone of the 335th Fighter Squadron claimed two of the victories). Their own losses: one F-86A, and its pilot Captain William D. Crone was killed.

According to a report of the 64th IAK headquarters, on this day pilots of the 176th GIAP became involved in three dogfights with Sabres. First, the flight of Captain G.I. Ges' encountered the enemy, numbering 16 F-86s, in the area of Sonchon and became involved in a brief skirmish with them, which ended without any results. Then eight MiGs led by Captain K.Ia. Sheberstov, which took off a little bit later, at 0935 also encountered 16 Sabres in the area of Sonchon and engaged them in combat. The regiment's navigator, Captain Serafim Pavlovich Subbotin particularly distinguished himself in this combat by downing one of the Sabres by ramming it.

Here is how this combat unfolded: Sheberstov's group met the 16 F-86s in the area west of Anju and tied them up in combat. Subbotin's element attacked the lead element in the first Sabre flight. He fired from a range of 500 meters down to 100 meters, as a result of which the Sabre went into an uncontrolled dive and exploded in the air. After this Subbotin was himself attacked by two F-86s; despite this Subbotin went to the assistance of his comrade, who was being pursued by another Sabre element. Subbotin intercepted it before it could open fire on his comrade, but his MiG received heavy damage from the fire of the two F-86s, which opened up on him instead. Fuel began to pour into his cockpit from a ruptured fuel tank and the MiG's engine stopped. Subbotin attempted to gain separation from the Sabres with a steep dive, but his effort was unsuccessful: one Sabre pulled to within 50 meters of him and started photographing his MiG from the left and right sides. Subbotin made a quick decision to throw off his cockpit canopy and then by slowing his MiG by popping its speed brakes, to force the pursuing Sabre to collide with it, only after which he would eject from it. Having deployed the speed flaps, Captain Subbotin felt a strong thump and saw that the F-86's right wing had struck the tailfin of his MiG, as a result of which the Sabre's right wing and his own aircraft's tailfin sheared off. The Sabre spun downward out of control, struck the ground and exploded, while Subbotin's MiG pitched down into an inverted dive. At an altitude of 4,000 meters, Subbotin ejected from his aircraft and came to earth 10-15 kilometers south of Chongju. His landing was rough and he received a concussion and bruises to his body.

Both F-86 fighters downed by Captain Subbotin were confirmed by the NKPA command: one F-86 fell into the sea, which was witnessed by Chongju's chief of police, while at 1110 a second F-86 was seen falling into the sea in the area of Simbi-do, which was observed by a local police officer. The second Sabre that plunged into the sea was downed by Senior Lieutenant A.A. Plitkin, while in the cockpit of the F-86 that collided with Subbotin's MiG and crashed in the Chongju area, the remains of the American pilot were found. It was the 34-year-old Captain William D. Crone.

The 176th GIAP's final action of the day occurred in the afternoon in the Anju area, when six MiGs led by Captain S.M. Kramarenko briefly dueled with a group of 12 F-86s. The maneuvering ended without any results for either side. Pilots of the 303rd IAD's 18th GIAP finished the combat that the 176th GIAP's pilots had started, shooting down one more Sabre before returning to Miaogou without any losses. In this combat in the area of Anju, 14 MiGs under the command of Lieutenant Colonel A.P. Smorchkov had come across 10 Sabres and engaged them in battle. Captain D.A. Tarasov scored the victory. As a result of the numerous clashes with Sabres on 18 June, according to the records of the 64th IAK command, seven F-86s were destroyed or damaged. The corps' own losses amounted to one lost MiG-15, with an additional one damaged. The American command acknowledges the loss of only one Sabre on this day, F-86A No.49-1307 of the 334th Fighter Squadron, in the cockpit of which Captain Crone was killed. The Americans do not confirm the loss of the other Sabres, despite the fact that members of the NKPA testified to the fact that they had witnessed their crashes.

Aerial clashes continued in MiG Alley almost daily for the rest of June 1951. On 19 June, 10 pilots from the 17th IAP under the command of Major G.I. Pulov, experienced in essence the regiment's first serious combat in the skies of Korea against a group of Sabres. Four Sabres attempted to attack the MiG formation unexpectedly, but they themselves came under an attack from the covering flight, led by the future ace Captain N.V. Sutiagin, the deputy commander of the 17th IAP's 1st Squadron. Here is what Sutiagin himself had to say in his report after the combat:

> The mission was being carried out by 10 [MiGs]. The attack flight was Major G.I. Pulov's; above and to the right of it was Captain S.S. Artemchenko's covering flight, while Senior Lieutenant N.Ia. Perepelkin's element was trailing above and behind Pulov's flight. I was in the covering flight with my wingman Senior Lieutenant V.F. Shulev. While in a left-hand turn in the area of Sonchon, I lagged 400-500 meters behind Captain Artemchenko's element. Continuing my turn another 50-60°, I spotted a pair of F-86s below and to the left emerging onto our tail from under the lead flight. I issued the command: "I'm attacking, cover me", and made a climbing turn to the left while throttling back on fuel and deploying my speed brakes, and with a subsequent split-S I went after the Sabre element, which went into oblique

The top-scoring Soviet ace with 22 victories and the deputy squadron commander of the 17th IAP, Senior Lieutenant N.V. Sutiagin; in China, 1951.

Pilots of the 1st Squadron of the 17th IAP pose for a photograph at the Miaogou airfield. From left to right, sitting in the first row are S.S. Bychkov, V.F. Shulev, S.S. Artemchenko, N.V Sutiagin and G.F. Malunov; from left to right, standing in the second row are N.N. Kramarenko, A.S. Shirokov, N.Ia. Perepelkin, N.A. Savchenko, M.F. Osipov and N.F. Miroshnichenko.

loops. On the second loop we were already on the Sabres' tail, and in a superior position I gave the wingman two short bursts. The bursts missed. Then I decided close the range. After pulling out of their dive, the Sabre element banked hard to the right, and then rolled to the left into a climb. I stayed with them, and the range dropped to 200-300 meters.

Noticing this, the adversary performed a half-roll and dove. Releasing the brakes, we went after the Sabres at a dive angle of 70-75° in the direction of the sea. Pulling to within 150-200 meters, I opened fire on the wingman and shot down the F-86.

Just seconds later, Senior Lieutenant V.F. Shulev also downed the leader of this Sabre element. These were the first two victories for the pilots of the 17th IAP, who suffered no losses in this combat. According to an announcement from the American side in this combat just one F-86A (No.49-1298) was lost – its pilot 1st Lieutenant Robert H. Laier was killed. However a little later the Americans acknowledged that on this day they wrote off another F-86A (No.49-1171), which was noted in their documents as turned over to serve as a source of spare parts. This should be interpreted as follows: the pilot of the Sabre that wound up under Senior Lieutenant Shulev's cannons nevertheless returned to his base, but his fighter was a write-off.

In their turn, the Americans claimed that on this day their pilots damaged five MiGs. However, in the first action that morning the 17th IAP's MiGs returned with no damage whatsoever. The MiGs of the 18th GIAP, the pilots of which at 0940 had clashed with a group of 16 F-86s with no results, also had no damage. Those were the only actions involving Soviet pilots on this day. So, to put it gently, the assertion about five "damaged" MiGs has no basis in reality.

Early on the morning of 20 June, a major aerial battle flared up in the area of Simbi-do Island, involving aviation units of the UAA, the 64th IAK and both USAF and USNAF pilots. The NKPA command was attempting to stage an amphibious landing on Simbi-do Island, where an enemy radar base was located that had powerful radars for tracking the activities of the 64th IAK and UAA. It had been decided to drive the enemy from this important island.

The landing was supported by the KPAF's 1st SmAD in the form of Il-10 ground attack planes, which flew several raids against the island in order to destroy the radars and facilities of the base. One of the eight-ship flights of Il-10s was intercepted by four F-51s from the 18th FBG, and according to American claims, they downed two Il-10s in this action and damaged three more. Yak-9 fighters of the 56th GIAP were scrambled to assist the Il-10s. One six-ship flight of Yak-9s encountered four F-51s and engaged them. The Americans later claimed that in this action, 1st Lieutenant John B. Harrison of the 67th FBS downed one Yak, while the Mustangs themselves suffered no losses.

Seeing that the adversary was increasing his aerial presence over the island with the aim of destroying the landing, at 0440 18 MiGs of the 176th GIAP under the command of Guards Lieutenant Colonel S.F. Vishniakov took off to cover the landing and the actions of the United Air Army. Here is how one of the participants in this battle, Nikolai Petrovich Kravtsov later described it:

> They scrambled us early in the morning to cover a North Korean landing, which was supposed to take the island of Simbi-do. On this sortie I was flying as Captain K.Ia. Sheberstov's wingman. For some reason they were late in scrambling us, because once we arrived over the island, we could see that enemy Mustang fighter-bombers were already attacking the North Korean landing force. We went on the attack against the fighter-bombers, but Sheberstov and I for some reason wound up a little behind the element consisting of the commander of the 1st Squadron Captain G.I. Ges' and his wingman G.A. Nikolaev. Their element was already diving on the fighter-bombers. Ges' approached very closely behind one Mustang and opened fire – I only saw that the Mustang's right wing broke off. At this moment Ges' communicated that his MiG was damaged and that he was returning to base. My leader Captain Sheberstov attacked a different F-51 element and downed one of them. When coming out of the attack I spotted Sabres that were emerging on our tail. I warned the leader about this and went into a tight, climbing turn toward the sun, but as the MiG was swinging around, it suddenly refused to turn and seemingly began to level out. At that same moment I felt bullets hammering into my aircraft. The engine began to idle, even though it was receiving full fuel. I transmitted over the radio that my MiG was damaged. My leader Captain Sheberstov gave me

direction to return to base and said that he would cover me. With great difficulty I managed to bring my aircraft back to the base and made a safe landing, but later the mechanics found 14 holes in my MiG from 12.7mm [.50 caliber] bullets.

In fact, the events in this combat did follow in quick succession. At 0505 when approaching Simbi-do Island, the pilots of the 176th GIAP spotted three eight-ship formations of F-51s. The first Mustang formation spotted the approaching MiGs in time and immediately turned around and headed back to sea. The second eight-ship formation was unable to do this, since it was already under attack from Lieutenant Colonel Vishniakov's lead group of six MiGs. The first Mustang flight came under Vishniakov's fire and he managed to shoot down one of the F-51s from close range. At the same time, Vishniakov's wingman Lieutenant A.F. Golovachev downed another of the Mustangs – both of the enemy fighter-bombers fell into the sea not far from Simbi-do Island. The other flight of F-51s in this formation successfully evaded the attack by Captain N.M. Goncharov's element and escaped out to sea without any losses.

At this same time Captain K.Ia. Sheberstov's group of six MiGs was attacking the third F-51 formation, and Captain Sheberstov, as well as Captain Ges', each managed to knock down another Mustang. In fact, in this attack Captain Ges' suffered heavy damage to his MiG when he flew through fragments of his disintegrating target, which damaged his MiG's wing, jamming its aileron, and part of its horizontal stabilizer.

Ges' began to withdraw his damaged aircraft out of the battle, but at this moment his element was attacked by an arriving group of F-86s. One of the Sabres decided to finish off the crippled MiG, but the Captain's wingman Senior Lieutenant G.A. Nikolaev intercepted it and thwarted the enemy's intentions with his attack. However, Nikolaev himself wound up under attack by a different Sabre: the Sabre's machine-gun burst struck the pilot's cockpit, smashed its canopy, and fragments of Plexiglas wounded Nikolaev in the face.

Both pilots, covered by other MiGs, safely landed back in Andong. Nikolaev was immediately sent to the medical station, where his wounds turned out to be not dangerous.

At 0500, the entire 523rd IAP – 26 crews under the command of deputy regiment commander and Hero of the Soviet Union N.N. Danilenko – launched from the Miaogou airfield to go to the assistance of Vishniakov's group. However, they didn't manage to reach Simbi-do Island, because in the vicinity of Sonchon the group encountered clouds, from which separate Sabre elements began to appear and to harass the regiment's formation. The attacks from these pouncing Sabres had to be countered; in essence, these screening Sabres succeeded in delaying Danilenko's group for some time, during which the engagement over Simbi-do ended, so Major Danilenko's group returned to base.

Another group of MiGs from the 18th GIAP was scrambled into the air that morning, but they failed to encounter the enemy, though they did somehow manage to lose one of their aircraft. When returning to base, in the area of Singisiu, the group's formation was unexpectedly attacked from below by a pair of Sabres, and having downed the tail-end MiG, it immediately disappeared back into the clouds undetected. Captain A.D. Skidan had to eject from his stricken fighter. Landing awkwardly in his parachute on a rocky slope, our pilot received bruises and fractures, and he had to spend some time convalescing in a hospital.

That's how the major clash of 20 June ended. Summing up the day, the pilots of the 176th GIAP managed to down four F-51s, paying for this with three damaged MiGs and one wounded pilot. The American side acknowledged the loss of only two of their Mustangs on this day, both of which were from the second eight-ship formation of F-51s from the 18th FBG's 39th Squadron. Both of the Mustang pilots were killed: presumably Captain Sheberstov downed the Mustang being flown by 1st Lieutenant Lee Harper, while Captain Ges' shattered Captain John Coleman's aircraft with his cannon shells. It is possible that Lieutenant Colonel Vishniakov's group didn't attack Mustangs, but carrier-based Corsairs, especially because three aircraft of this type were lost on this day.

As concerns the victories of the F-86 pilots, they claimed that they had damaged four MiGs on this day, and this time the assertion of the American pilots is close to the truth. In this combat, Lieutenant Colonel Bruce Hinton damaged Senior Lieutenant Nikolaev's aircraft, while Major Franklin Fisher damaged Senior Lieutenant Kravtsov's MiG. Only 1st Lieutenant Rudolph "Rudy" Holley scored the single 100% victory on this day when he managed to shoot down Captain Skidan's MiG, but apparently the American pilot was in such a hurry after his attack to regain the concealment of the clouds after his attack that he didn't see his victim fall, so his victory was recorded as a "damaged" enemy aircraft.

On 22 June 1951, Senior Lieutenant N.V. Sutiagin added two more Sabres to his victory score, which he shot down in a single combat. He had taken off as part a group from the 17th IAP in response to a call from the 64th IAK command post to intercept an enemy air raid. A little earlier on this same day, six MiGs from the 176th GIAP's 3rd Squadron under the command of Lieutenant Colonel S.F. Vishniakov had departed on a combat mission, and it had soon encountered a group of eight Sabres. Vishniakov's six-ship formation split into elements and tied the Sabres up in combat.

Senior Lieutenant A.A. Plitkin with his wingman Senior Lieutenant B.A. Obraztsov attacked a Sabre element, but in the course of maneuvering, wingman Boris Obraztsov had wound up in a favorable position with respect to the enemy, so Plitkin gave him the command: "Take the lead and attack. I am covering you." With that, he took over the wingman's position. Obraztsov skillfully attacked the Sabre element and from close range shot down the wingman's Sabre.

At this moment, Plitkin's element was attacked from behind by a different Sabre element, and Plitkin himself came under fire; his aircraft went out of control and at an altitude of 5,000-6,000 meters, Plitkin ejected from his crippled MiG. This took place in the vicinity of Sonchon. Plitkin was shot down by 1st Lieutenant Charles O. Reister of the 336th Fighter Squadron. Senior Lieutenant Obraztsov in this action downed F-86A No.49-1276, and its pilot 1st Lieutenant Howard Miller, although able to bail out of his Sabre, was killed on the ground.

Three hours later at 0835 10 MiGs of the 17th IAP under the command of regiment commander Major G.I. Pulov took off on a combat mission. In the area of the Sinuiju bridge, they were attacked by two flights of F-86s. While banking around in a turn, four Sabres swung in behind N.V. Sutiagin's flight, but with a quick maneuver our pilots turned the table on the Sabres and wound up on their tails. Seeing this, the Americans banked to the left and went into a dive. Sutiagin opened fire on a wingman from a range of 400-500 meters. At this moment, his wingman Senior Lieutenant Shulev noticed a second pair of Sabres dropping onto their tails, and with an abrupt maneuver he evaded their attack. Meanwhile the leader of the first Sabre element, seeing that his wingman was taking fire, went into an oblique loop. However, he couldn't shake Sutiagin, who in a superior position opened fire, now from a range of just 250-300 meters. The F-86 emitted a stream of smoke and began to fall. A little later, Sutiagin shot down another Sabre, while the remaining F-86s exited the combat and departed for the Yellow Sea. On this day, a group of F-80 fighter-bombers were making an attack on the Sinuiju bridge, and taking advantage of the fact that the MiGs had been tied up by the escorting Sabres, they bombed the target without any hindrance. The Americans claimed to have downed two MiGs on 22 June (according to some sources, only one), and lost only one Sabre in return.

On 22 June pilots of the 523rd IAP also took part in the fighting, and they also dueled with a group of 16 F-86s, but this combat ended without results for either side. Fighting with the Sabres was occurring almost daily, but they didn't always end with results. However, the struggle for aerial superiority over the given area was continuing.

On 23 June 1951 the 64th IAK command halted the practice of sending small groups of MiGs into MiG Alley, and for the first time employed large, regimental-sized MiG formations to cover the important sites in the area. On this day, first two regiments of the 303rd IAD (the 17th IAP and 18th GIAP) numbering 43 MiGs were scrambled at 0830, and at 0900 the division's entire third regiment, the 523rd IAP, numbering 24 MiGs, was dispatched to reinforce the first group that had left and to cover their withdrawal from combat. The division-sized grouping of MiGs simply expelled all of the enemy aircraft from the Anju area: the American command had sent a group of 8 B-29 bombers, covered by 20 F-86s, into the area, but having spotted the large group of approaching MiGs, the bombers immediately aborted their combat mission and turned back. Separate elements and flights of Sabres tried to attack the enormous MiG group, but nothing came of their efforts. Not only were all the Sabre bounces driven off, but Captain I.I. Tiuliaev managed to down one of the Sabres, which fell in the area of Siarenken Station.

After the pilots of the 303rd IAD's 17th IAP and 18th GIAP landed, a group of 18 MiGs from the 176th GIAP under the command of Lieutenant Colonel S.F. Vishniakovsky took off. In the Chongju area eight F-86s attempted to attack them, but the Sabres themselves were jumped from above by six MiGs led by Captain S.M. Kramarenko that were covering the main group. Kramarenko managed to shoot down one of the Sabres, which plunged to the earth. The remaining Sabres immediately exited the combat area. True, however, Colonel Vishniakov's group returned to base without one of its MiGs: at 0926 Captain K.Ia. Sheberstov's six-ship formation was unexpectedly fired upon from the ground by an NKPA anti-aircraft battery, and one of the shells struck Guards Lieutenant Vladimir Fedorovich Negodiaev's aircraft. Apparently shell fragments killed the pilot, since his MiG plummeted out of control and crashed 12 kilometers northeast of Sonchon. Thus, one of our pilots was killed by friendly fire!

At the end of the day, the divisional sortie was repeated and, just as in the morning, only the pilots of the 523rd IAP became involved in a fight with eight F-86s and just as in the morning combat, Captain I.I. Tiuliaev again managed to score hits on one Sabre, which fell in the Pihyon area. In this dogfight Sabre pilots also managed to damage Captain N.I. Mitrofanov's MiG, and he returned to base with 14 bullet holes in his aircraft. Also, just before sunset the pilots of the 176th GIAP tangled briefly with the enemy, but there were no results.

The American command doesn't report any F-86 losses on this day, claiming that there were none, which is quite dubious. To be sure, the Sabre pilots also didn't claim any victories on this day, which is also strange, considering that they did manage to damage one of the MiGs.

However, a genuine battle did in fact occur the next day, 24 June 1951, between the pilots of the 8th and 49th FBG, on the one side, and the pilots of the 523rd IAP on the other. Early that morning a large group of F-80s attempted to strike one of the railroad junctions in the area of Anju. The 523rd IAP was the first to scramble in order to repulse this attack. At 0420, 10 MiGs of the 523rd IAP under the command of the regiment commander and Hero of the Soviet Union Lieutenant Colonel A.N. Karasev took off on a mission to intercept the enemy aircraft. Guided by GCI [Ground Control Intercept] controllers, the MiG group soon spotted several eight-ship formations of F-80s at low altitude, which were attacking ground targets. The strike group, consisting of two elements under the overall command of Lieutenant Colonel Karasev attacked one fighter-bomber formation, and on the very first pass, Karasev's flight downed three "Shoots", which were credited to Karasev, Captain Okhai and Captain Popov. The compact formation of Shooting Stars immediately fell apart and scattered into separate elements and flights. Seeing that MiGs were attacking them continuously and from every direction, the Shooting Star pilots began to retreat toward the sea, which they knew full well was a no-fly zone for the Soviet pilots.

In the wake of the attack by Captain Karasev's flight, six MiGs led by Captain V.E. Suslov went on the attack and also gathered their own harvest from the aggregation of enemy aircraft: Senior Lieutenant V.E. Silkin and Captain M.S. Ponomarev each downed an additional Shooting Star. As a result, the pilots of the 523rd IAP shot down five Shooting Stars and returned to their base at Miaogou without any losses.

However, the air strike didn't end with this, and new groups of F-80s continued to arrive from the direction of the sea, attempting to paralyze the movement of supplies in the Anju area. At 0813 according to information from ground radars, 16 F-80s were detected in the area of Sozan, approaching Anju at an altitude of 5,000 meters. At 0822, the 1st Squadron numbering 10 MiG-15s led by the squadron commander Guards Major A.P. Trefilov scrambled at an order from the division command post to intercept the enemy fighter-bombers. Seven minutes later, Major Trefilov, flying with his group in a left echelon of flights at an altitude of 6,000 meters spotted up to 16 F-80s 10 kilometers southwest of Anju at an altitude of 1,500-2,000 meters, which were bombing the Anju railroad station, and led his entire group into combat with them.

Major Trefilov's six-ship formation approached six F-80s, and having pulled to within 650 meters of them, his wingman Senior Lieutenant Shal'nov opened fire at the leader's left-hand wingman. The F-80s noticed the attack by our fighters and turned sharply in the direction of the sea. While pursuing the F-80 flight, Major Trefilov spotted another flight of F-80s about 2 or 3 kilometers behind them, closing to attack them. Trefilov evaded the attack of the four F-80s with a climbing turn to starboard. Coming out of the turn, Major Trefilov spotted another element of Shooting Stars about 1.5 to 2 kilometers in front of them and together with Captain S.A. Bakhaev's element moved to approach it. Closing to within a range of 550 meters from the enemy element, he opened fire on the wingman's aircraft. The pair of F-80s spotted the attack by our fighters and broke into a chandelle to the left. Major Trefilov continued to pursue them. Coming out of the chandelle, the F-80s rolled over and dove for the coast line and managed to escape. Trefilov and his wingman continued to search for enemy aircraft.

Captain Bakhaev, following Guards Major Trefilov's element, caught sight of a pair of F-80s 1.5 to 2 kilometers away to the left and turned to close upon them. Having overshot the enemy on an intercepting course, Captain Bakhaev went into a climbing turn to the port, while the F-80 element turned to the right. Bakhaev's element reversed course, dropped in behind the F-80s and having closed to within a range of 500 meters, Bakhaev opened fire at the wingman's aircraft, as a result of which the F-80 received fatal damage and plunged into the sea 15 kilometers southwest of Rakosyng. The lead F-80 spotted the attacking pair of MiG-15s and with a split-S headed toward the coast line. Captain Bakhaev pulled out of the attack into a climbing turn to port, after which he continued to scan the area for enemy aircraft.

During Major Trefilov's climbing turn to the right to evade the Shooting Star attack, Senior Lieutenant N.P. Razorvin's element saw two F-80s 1 to 2 kilometers in front of them and 1,000 meters below them, and decided to go after them. Having pulled to within 700 meters, Razorvin opened fire on the Shooting Star leader and shot him down. The F-80 wingman rolled over and dove toward the coast line. Senior Lieutenant Razorvin exited the attack in a climbing turn to starboard.

As Major Trefilov's six-ship formation closed with the six F-80s, Captain D.V. Mazilov caught sight of four F-80s, which were trying to attack Captain Bakhaev's element from behind. Captain Mazilov moved to intercept them with his flight. Having closed to within a range of 300 meters, Captain Mazilov's wingman Senior Lieutenant Shatalov opened fire on the #4 Shooting Star in the flight. His target exploded in mid-air. The other F-80s in the flight went into a climbing spiral to the left. Captain Mazilov and his flight pursued the Shooting Stars, and having pulled to within 240 meters Mazilov opened fire at the leader of the second F-80 element and downed his aircraft, which fell into the sea 20-30 kilometers southwest of Anju. The remaining pair of F-80s turned and fled toward the sea. Captain Mazilov pulled out of his attack in a climbing turn to starboard, after which he continued to search for enemy aircraft until receiving the order to return to base.

In the process of this flurry of action, four enemy F-80s were downed. There were no Soviet losses. The aerial combat took place at altitudes between 1,000 and 6,000 meters in the area of Anju and lasted for ten minutes.

The Americans claimed that in these two clashes the pilots of the 8th and 49th FBG supposedly damaged four MiG-15s and returned to base without any losses. This claim is easy to refute if one examines the gun camera footage of several of the Soviet pilots who participated in the fights. For example, on Senior Lieutenant G.T. Shatalov's film, it is clearly visible that one enemy aircraft has plunged into the water (its tailfin assembly is visible above the water). Shatalov followed it down until the enemy struck the water, barely able to avoid his enemy's fate by pulling his own MiG out of the dive at the last moment. The disintegration of one F-80 in mid-air after a volley from Popov's cannons at a range of just 100 meters is also clearly visible on Captain V.P. Popov's camera footage. The American command plainly understated its losses on this day, asserting that only one F-80 was lost. Soviet records paint a completely different picture of this day and give quite different results.

Research by the Argentinean historian Diego Zampini, who established that the Americans lost at least four F-80s on these missions, supports the Soviet version. The

Americans "spread" their losses out over the next several days, treating them as aircraft that were written off, but on 24 June 1951 they only recognize the loss of one F-80, No.49-646. Presumably, Lieutenant Colonel Karasev downed this Shooting Star from the 49th FBG, and its pilot, 1st Lieutenant Ernest C. Dunning, Jr. was taken prisoner. Senior Lieutenant Shatalov shot down F-80 No.49-1829 from the 8th FBG's 36th Squadron, and its pilot Captain Arthur J. Johnson went missing-in-action. Captain Ponomarev shot down F-80 No.49-721 from the same squadron, and its pilot 1st Lieutenant Will C. White was killed-in-action. Finally, Captain Bakhaev managed to inflict serious damage on Lieutenant Talmadge A. Wilson's F-80, also from the 8th FBG's 36th FBS and wounded the pilot. Wilson managed to fly back to his base and land his damaged aircraft, which was written off four days later. Possibly, other losses from this day will become known later? The Shooting Star pilots managed to damage only one MiG in the second clash on this morning: Senior Lieutenant G.Kh. D'iachenko aircraft returned with six bullet holes in it, but the MiG was quickly patched up.

The aerial combats on 24 June continued even after the events just discussed. A group of MiGs from the 176th GIAP under the command of regiment commander Lieutenant Colonel S.F. Vishniakov departed shortly after 0900 for a patrol over the Anju region. In the vicinity of Anju they spotted a solitary F-80 (identified by the group's pilots as

Left to right M.S. Ponomarev, S.M. Kramarenko, Shvernik and A.P. Smorchkov pose in the Kremlin on 1 April 1952 after receiving the Soviet Union's highest honors for their participation in the Korean War.

an F-94), which was conducting a reconnaissance to assess the damage after the attack by the 8th and 49th FBG. The pilot of this F-80 No.49-484 from the 8th FBG's 35th Squadron, John Murrey was unlucky; in the course of a minute he was attacked by two MiG elements. His Shooting Star received such damage that the pilot abandoned his stricken aircraft, preferring captivity to death in the cockpit of his doomed F-80. This victory was awarded to Captain N.M. Goncharov.

The final combat on this heated day of action took place at 0940, when a group of 18 MiGs of the 18th GIAP, under the command of deputy regiment commander Lieutenant Colonel A.P. Smorchkov met 12 F-86 Sabres head-on. In the course of this brief clash, Captain P.N Antonov succeeded in damaging one Sabre, after which the remaining F-86s exited the combat area, likely low on fuel. Our pilots had no losses. In the course of this day, 24 June 1951, Soviet records indicate that the pilots of the 64th IAK downed 10 F-80 Shooting Stars and damaged one F-86, without any losses. One MiG received combat damage.

On the next day, the enemy air activity subsided somewhat; plainly, the losses suffered on the preceding day had an effect on the intensity of flight operations conducted by the USAF. Thus, on 25 June pilots of the 64th IAK had only one encounter with the enemy. This took place at 0850 in the Sonchon area, when a regiment-sized group of 28 MiGs from the 18th GIAP, under the command of Lieutenant Colonel Smorchkov, clashed with 16 F-86s. The ensuing combat lasted for 10 minutes, in the course of which Captain P.N. Antonov and Senior Lieutenants V.N. Akatov, S.T. Kolpikov and N.V. Babonin each scored hits upon Sabres. In truth, none of the pilots observed the F-86s that they had fired upon fall to earth, but each pilot was credited with a victory based on their gun camera footage.

In return, a Sabre element succeeded in seriously damaging Senior Lieutenant N.A. Ageev's MiG. Though he managed to fly back to Andong, while conducting a forced belly-landing his aircraft smashed into an earthen embankment and disintegrated. Senior Lieutenant Nikolai Alekseevich Ageev perished in the crash. According to American records, the Sabres had no losses, while 1st Lieutenant Milton Nelson of the 335th Fighter Squadron downed one MiG.

The MiG activity on 25 June didn't allow the Americans to use their B-29 bombers against targets in the Anju area, but on 26 June, the Fifth Air Force command nevertheless sent a small group of its B-29 bombers to the Anju area. Once again, however, the Superfortresses failed to break through to their targets.

At 1302, two groups of MiGs from the 17th IAP were scrambled to intercept enemy aircraft that had been detected by ground radar installations. The first to take off was an eight-ship formation of the 1st Squadron under the command of Captain S.S. Artemchenko, which was followed five minute later by two six-MiG formations from the regiment's 2nd and 3rd Squadrons, led by Captains N.P. Mishakin and M.N. Shcherbakov. Once in the air, a command was issued from the division command post: "Everyone head to the Anju area", while simultaneously the group leaders were being kept informed about the situation in the air there.

At 1326, at an altitude of 11,500-12,000 meters, the pilots of Captain Artemchenko's group spotted six F-86s flying at the same altitude on a parallel course, which were trying to slide in behind their formation. Captain Artemchenko gave an order to Senior Lieutenant Sutiagin: "Attack the enemy!" while he himself went into a climb to gain altitude. Banking to the left, Nikolai Sutiagin went on the attack against the six Sabres. The enemy, seeing the attack, quickly reversed course and began to retreat below Sutiagin's flight, dragging our fighters into combat in a descending spiral. At this same time, Captain Artemchenko's lead group, having reversed course in a climbing turn to the left, spotted another group of eight Sabres below and to the left of them, flying in a column of flights with approximately 2 kilometers between the flights. Artemchenko immediately turned to port and dove on the Sabres. One of the Sabre flights evaded the attack by rolling onto their backs and pulling into a dive toward the sea, while the second F-86 flight began to emerge on the tail of Artemchenko's flight. Artemchenko's wingman Senior Lieutenant N.F. Miroshnichenko issued a warning over the radio about the enemy on their tails. Artemchenko went into a climbing spiral to port to gain altitude. On the third loop of the spiral, the enemy wound up below Captain Artemchenko's flight. Seeing their unfavorable position and realizing that they would not be able to catch the MiGs, the Sabres abandoned the chase and exited the combat in a dive.

Simultaneously, the six Sabres attacked by Senior Lieutenant Sutiagin fell into a difficult situation. After reversing course, the Sabres arranged themselves into a column of elements. Sutiagin ordered Senior Lieutenant S.S. Bychkov's element to cover his attack and then attacked the second pair of Sabres. At this moment his wingman Senior Lieutenant V.F. Shulev spotted another Sabre element below and behind them to the left, which he reported to his leader. Sutiagin broke off his attack and having reversed, attacked the tail-end Sabre element from behind and to the right. Quickly closing to within 200-250 meters he popped his speed brakes and opened fire at the Sabre leader. Vasilii Shulev stuck to his leader and also opened fire from a range of 300-400 meters.

However, because Senior Lieutenant Shulev did not deploy his speed brakes, his MiG surged in front of his leader's aircraft and he was forced to pull out of the attack in a climbing turn to starboard. Senior Lieutenant Sutiagin followed him. However, this didn't signal the end of the action: at 1325, Captain Mishakin's six-ship formation, flying toward the south at an altitude of 12,000 meters, spotted four B-29s below and in front of them to the right, approaching at an altitude of 6,000 meters with an escort of up to 20 F-84s and F-86s. The enemy bombers were in a combat box formation, while the escorting fighters were in the process of swinging from the left to the right in front of the bombers at the same altitude. Captain Mishakin alerted over the radio "I see enemy bombers" and simultaneously turned his flight around to the right and went into an attacking run against the bombers from behind at a 30° dive angle. At the moment of attacking the bombers, Captain Mishakin's flight was attacked by a Sabre element from below and to the right, which had approached from the direction of the sea. Mishakin broke sharply left to evade the attack and then went into a climbing spiral, after which he lost sight of his group.

Senior Lieutenant G.T. Fokin and his wingman Senior Lieutenant E.N. Arganovich continued their attacking run at the B-29 bombers. Having closed to within a range of 1,000 meters to the tail-end bomber, Fokin fired two long bursts from the bomber's rear. At this moment his wingman Senior Lieutenant Arganovich sped in front of Senior Lieutenant Fokin and broke up and away in a climbing, reversing turn to the left. When pulling out of his attack, Fokin's MiG was jumped by a Sabre element from behind and to the right. Fokin avoided the attack with a climbing spiral to starboard. Now both pilots of Fokin's element were alone. Leveling off after his climb, Arganovich was suddenly and unexpectedly attacked from behind by a pair of F-84s from the bombers' immediate escort, which riddled Arganovich's MiG from point-blank range. There was no one in position to defend him, and as a result of the Thunderjets' attack his MiG burst into flames and fell in an area 17 kilometers southwest of Uiju. Senior Lieutenant Evgenii Naumovich Arganovich was killed-in-action.

Captain Shcherbakov's group, consisting of six MiGs, which was then located in the Anju area at an altitude of 9,000 meters, also spotted 10 Sabres heading toward them at a lower altitude. After briefly tangling with the MiGs, this Sabre group also exited the battle, and Shcherbakov's group returned to base without any losses.

Thus the battle ended, in which the 17th IAP suffered its first loss. As a result of the battle, according to the returning pilots' post-mission debriefing, three enemy aircraft were downed: one F-86 each was claimed by Senior Lieutenant Sutiagin and Senior Lieutenant Shulev, and Senior Lieutenant Fokin claimed one B-29. A little later confirmation arrived that on this sortie Senior Lieutenant Arganovich had nevertheless destroyed one F-80, which was trying to attack his leader. Thus Evgenii Arganovich carried out his duty as a wingman to the very end of his life.

According to American records, four B-29 bombers took part in this attack, escorted by 12 F-86s, as well as four F-80s from the 8th FBG and four F-84s from the 136th FBG. The Americans don't confirm the loss of one of their B-29s on this mission, so most likely Senior Lieutenant Fokin only damaged the bomber and it flew back to base, but was out of service for a period of time. However, there is confirmation of Senior Lieutenant Arganovich's victory, since the Americans acknowledge the loss of one of their F-80C fighter-bombers (No.49-875) from the 8th FBG's 35th Squadron on this day and at the same time when Arganovich was in the air. Its pilot 1st Lieutenant Bob Lauterbach also didn't return from this battle. As is now known, an F-84 element consisting of Captain Harry Underwood and 1st Lieutenant Arthur Olinger from the 136th FBW's 182nd Squadron shot down Evgenii Arganovich. On their part, the Americans do not confirm the loss of any of their Sabres in this action.

At the same time between 1330 and 1400, but in the area of Sunchon, 10 MiGs of the 523rd IAP's 1st Squadron were involved in a dogfight with a group of 12 F-86s, in which Senior Lieutenant G.T. Shatalov downed one Sabre, which fell near Sunchon. The town's chief of police and the duty officer of Auxiliary Control Post No. 1 Comrade Krotov both witnessed the Sabre's crash. Our pilots had no losses. To be honest, however, the American command again doesn't acknowledge the loss of one of its F-86s in this combat.

On 27 June the weather again turned sharply worse, and flight operations above North Korea virtually came to a halt. However, the pilots of the 64th IAK were able to conduct one more successful aerial combat before the month's end. On the evening of 28 June, the weather slightly improved, and the Americans decided to take advantage of this circumstance: they sent a group of F-51 fighter-bombers to the Anju area without any escort or cover, in the hope that MiGs wouldn't appear in the target area in such weather. However, the Fifth Air Force command miscalculated, and several groups of MiGs from the 303rd IAD took off to intercept the small groups of fighter-bombers. Pilots of the 523rd IAP, which took off in two groups numbering a total of 18 MiGs and arrived in the area of Anju around 1835, were lucky to find the enemy. Major A.P. Trefilov's group of 10 MiGs spotted eight F-51s, which were attacking roads in the Anju area, and splitting up into separate pairs, they attacked the enemy. Not everyone managed to open fire on an enemy aircraft, because some of our pilots miscalculated the closing speed and overshot their targets, and they simply didn't have enough time for a second attack, because the Mustangs fled to the sanctuary of Korea Bay to avoid another attacking pass by the MiGs.

Senior Lieutenant G.T. Shatalov managed to down one enemy aircraft in the first attack: his leader Senior Lieutenant V.I. Surovikin overshot his target, but in his wake Shatalov managed to get his cross hairs fixed on one Mustang, and from a range of 150 meters set it on fire. Burning, it fell toward the sea, since the attack took place not far from the coast line. Just then Shatalov spotted one more pair of Mustangs and spiritedly attacked it over the sea, and managed to score hits on one more F-51.

At the same time Senior Lieutenant N.P. Razorvin's element attacked a different F-51 element also near the coast line. Razorvin attacked the leader of this element at slow speed and managed to hit the Mustang, which plunged into the sea. Other pilots of the 523rd IAP failed to attack the other Mustangs, since they were able to flee dry ground and escape to the sea, where our pilots were forbidden to fly. Thus ended the final combat of June 1951 in MiG Alley, in which our pilots at a minimum downed two enemy aircraft, without any losses to themselves.

The American command recognizes the loss of only one of its F-51s (No.44-13220) from the 18th FBG's 39th Squadron, the pilot of which Captain Charles Sumner managed to reach Seoul, but crashed upon landing. Sumner was wounded and his Mustang was written off two days later. Senior Lieutenant Shatalov was likely the Soviet pilot who damaged Sumner's Mustang in this battle. The possibility shouldn't be excluded that other carrier-based types of aircraft of the USNAF took part in this attack, and they also came under the attack from the MiGs, because on this day the American carriers lost several of their Corsairs and Skyraiders, attributing their losses to anti-aircraft fire or to failed landings. Soviet pilots poorly recognized the different types of USNAF carrier-based aircraft and either identified them all as Hellcats, which did not take part in this war, or mistakenly wrote in their reports that these were Mustangs.

After these defeats the Mustangs of the 18th FBG were rare visitors to MiG Alley, and if they did appear there, it was only under the heavy cover of Sabres.

The new month of July 1951 didn't bring with it any sort of changes in the combat situation in the skies of Korea. As before, large groups of F-80 and F-84 fighter-bombers escorted by numerous F-86s repeatedly crossed the Pyongyang-Wonsan line, attempting within the framework of Operation Strangle to paralyze road and railroad traffic on the territory of North Korea. They were actively opposed by pilots of the two fighter divisions of the 64th IAK. Pilots of the UAA in the form of the 4th IAD, which in July 1951 again entered combat from the Andong airfield, rendered active support.

Starting on 6 July, once good flying weather had returned to North Korea, the enemy began conducting daily massed raids by fighter-bombers, covered by large groups of F-86s. So the first major battle occurred already on 7 July. At a summons from the division command post, eight MiG-15s from the 18th GIAP's 1st Squadron under the command of Captain A.F. Maznev were scrambled to cover the railroad and bridge across the Yalu River in the Andong-Anju sector against an enemy air strike. Soon the group encountered 14 Sabres, which were serving as a forward screen and were to tie up the MiGs in combat. Behind the Sabres was a large group of F-84G fighter-bombers.

Lieutenant A.A. Kaliuzhny – a 1945
photo.

Understanding the enemy's scheme, the squadron commander split his squadron into two groups: Captain A.A. Kaliuzhny's flight took on the fighters, while Captain Maznev's flight went after the F-84s. Kaliuzhny's flight broke apart into elements, each locked into a separate duel with six Sabres. Here's how Captain Kaliuzhny's wingman, Senior Lieutenant A.A. Svintitsky, described this combat:

> Kaliuzhny and I, as always, flew as the tail-end MiGs. Suddenly, in the area of "Sosiski" – that's what we called a local stream – a group of six Sabres pounced on us. A carousel of aircraft started up. Four on their side became tied up in it, but one Sabre element disappeared somewhere. He [Kaliuzhny] shouted a warning: "Break, you have Sabres on your tail!" I take a look – just so, they're already hanging right behind me. I threw my MiG into a high-G spiral, thinking otherwise that they might damage my aircraft. But all the same, they scored some hits. I hear a thump, just like a stone striking an empty metal barrel. In the heat of battle, I didn't even see the bullet holes … the Sabres overshoot me and are swinging back around, while I am trying to turn into their attack. I turn more sharply and see that I won't have time. They're equipped with wing slats and can turn more tightly. I press the button to deploy the air brakes – MiGs have hydraulic speed brakes on the fuselage behind the cockpits. My MiG began to turn splendidly … of course, I slowed to 400 [km/ hour], but the turn was a thing of beauty! Right away, I see my MiG pulling right into a head-on pass. They're both hurtling toward me. I'm trying to line the leader up in my sights. I felt anger toward the leader. I gave him a burst, but hadn't quite lined him up. The tracers passed wide of him. I make another turn with the brakes

deployed. Once again I pull into a head-on attack. I didn't have anything else I could do. Accelerate away? I won't get away; they'll catch up with me and finish me off. So that's all I had left – a head-on attack. This time as well, the leader is at a slight angle from my trajectory. I aim at the wingman. I slightly fishtail and give him an aimed burst – the tracers curve wide of his tail. I give a nudge to the control stick and simultaneously push the firing trigger: I had time to see several shell explosions on the Sabre's fuselage from the air intake to the tail, and pieces flying from it … How I managed to yank the stick back to avoid colliding with him, I don't know. I literally passed just two meters above him and felt a lift from his slipstream.

I turn my MiG around again and see one [Sabre] spinning toward the earth, while the leader is wrenching his Sabre around toward me. Such is the situation – I cannot escape in a zoom climb, I don't have enough speed. I must, I think, urgently gain some speed somehow. I begin to accelerate my MiG into a shallow dive with my engine turning over at maximum while the Sabre is still in its turn. Then, once he had lost some speed in the turn, I break away in a shallow climb. I look, and he's now lagged behind me by somewhere around 1,000 meters. He tries to give me a burst, but he's now far behind me, and his tracers pass well below me. I climbed to 11,000 meters – the red light of the fuel indicator is already lit. He is now hesitating to attack me. We fly and look each other over: I'm above him, and he's about 200 meters below me. I turn a bit and he does as well. I think, "Just when will you break off?" A bit of time passed, and I look – at last he's shearing off. I dash back to base. I see a hole in one wing, right on the leading edge. I go straight into a landing, disregarding the traffic pattern. I see I'm going to be a bit short with my approach. I throttled forward, and at this instant the engine begins to sputter. I'm out of fuel. So now I'm falling directly toward some mounds about 100 meters short of the runway. But somehow everything turned out OK: my landing gear hits these mounds, my aircraft bounces back into the air, sails precisely 100 meters forward, then again drops again, but this time on the runway.

It turned out that no one was expecting me. According to their calculations, I had exhausted my fuel long ago. They had already prepared a report: "failed to return from the mission" … My armorer comes running up: "Did you fire, commander?"

"No", I answer, "I didn't fire."

"How so? – The entire nose is black!"

"Ah", I say, "I must have fired."

"Hey, you also have a hole in your wing!"

That's when I remembered that I had been in combat! I had been so stressed when landing that I'd forgotten it all!

The pilots of the other element, led by Captain V.A. Sokhan' downed one more Sabre, and soon both sides withdrew from the combat. As a result, Captain A.A. Kaliuzhny's flight shot down three Sabres without any losses of their own. Captain A.F. Maznev's flight also carried out its assignment: they broke up the Thunderjets' formation and forced them to head back to the bay without carrying out their mission. True, no one managed to shoot down one of the Thunderjets, but that wasn't important; the main thing was that the air raid was repulsed.

On 8 July there was another sortie to repel a large enemy air strike against the North Korean airfield of Kandong, which was being conducted by Mustangs of the 18th FBG. They were intercepted by 20 MiGs from the 523rd IAP under the overall command of Hero of the Soviet Union Major N.N. Danilenko. Having sighted the MiGs, the Mustangs immediately began to flee from the targeted area. The encounter occurred east of Pyongyang around 0900. Several groups of Mustangs numbering a total of 30 fighter-bombers were attacking ground targets. When the enemy was spotted, Danilenko led his attack group into a climbing turn to port, but the leader of the cover group Major A.P. Trefilov missed this maneuver and simply lost visual contact with the attack group. Danilenko at this time went on the attack against the fighter-bombers, but in doing so made a mistake – he didn't ensure that his group had top cover in case of an attack by enemy fighters, for which his group would pay dearly.

The attack against the fighter-bombers was also unsuccessful because of the rash action of the regiment's navigator Captain P.P. Pavlovsky, who without the leader's authorization left the formation and attempted to attack one of the Mustangs by himself. In doing so the flight's formation fell apart and could not conduct an organized attack.

Taking advantage of these blunders committed by the leading group of MiGs, at this moment, two eight-ship formations of Sabres led by the new commander of the 4th Fighter Wing Colonel Francis "Gabby" Gabreski pounced upon Major Danilenko's group and without any hindrance shot down two MiGs. The wing commander Colonel Gabreski himself downed one of the MiGs, killing the pilot Senior Lieutenant Aleksei Andreevich Obukhov in his cockpit. Meanwhile another future ace of the 334th FIS 1st Lieutenant Richard Becker successfully downed the MiG of the feckless Captain Pavlovsky, though he managed to parachute from his doomed fighter.

The losses of the 523rd IAP might have been even larger, but they were bailed out by the 17th IAP, which made a timely arrival on the scene with a large group of 26 MiGs. Seeing the numerical superiority of the MiGs, the Sabre pilots took no chances and exited the combat.

Afterward the Americans in fact claimed three victories, but it is reliably known that we lost two aircraft and one pilot in this battle. The third MiG, most likely, was only damaged: this was the MiG of Major A.I. Mitusov of the 196th IAP, who landed with difficulty back at his Miaogou base.

Two hours later, at 1335, another dogfight took place in the Sonchon area involving 21 MiGs of the 176th GIAP under the overall command of regiment commander Lieutenant Colonel S.F. Vishniakov against a group of 24 Sabres. Splitting his formation into three separate groups, Vishniakov gave each the order to attack its own eight-ship formation of Sabres, and then he himself attacked the leading group of Sabres with his 10 MiGs. The pilots, led by Lieutenant Colonel Vishniakov, tangled with the eight Sabres at an altitude of 11,500 meters. Vishniakov managed to down one F-86, and it fell out of control toward the earth. Meanwhile, Captain I.A. Suchkov's flight was attacking the second Sabre flight. The Sabres were flying in a compact formation, and Guards Major A.F. Vas'ko's element attacked them. One Sabre passed through a stream of fire from Vas'ko's wingman, Senior Lieutenant A.P. Verdysh, and took damage.

The attacks by the other MiG groups had no success, because the Sabres simply declined battle, and having evaded the MiGs' attack, exited the area. Thus the action ended with a victory for our pilots, who added two Sabres to their score, the fall of which were confirmed by North Korean authorities. The American in fact do not acknowledge the loss of their F-86s on this day, but knowing how painfully Americans regard losses of their top F-86 fighters, it is possible to assume that they've kept part of their losses of this type of aircraft concealed to the present day.

On 9 July there was only one clash with enemy aircraft: at 0917 18 MiGs of the 17th IAP under the command of deputy regiment commander Major B.V. Maslennikov took off for the Anju area with the assignment to cover the actions of a group of eight MiGs from the UAA's 4th IAD. On the approach to Anju they encountered a group of eight B-29s, which were being covered by up to 30 F-86s. The pilots of the 17th IAP attacked and tied up the covering Sabres, while the Chinese pilots attacked the Superfortresses. The American fighter pilots didn't fight the MiGs very actively and soon departed for the sea, avoiding MiG attacks. According to Senior Lieutenant N.F. Miroshnichenko's report, he managed to damage one F-86, but apparently it succeeded in making its way back to its base in South Korea, since our pilot was firing from rather long range.

The result of the Chinese pilots' attacks against the B-29s isn't known to this author, but the Americans claimed that they downed three MiGs: the covering Sabres downed one of them, and the other two were claimed by gunners aboard the B-29s. It is possible that the Chinese did have losses in this combat with the Americans, since the Chinese pilots tended to fight very rashly and selflessly.

On 11 July 1951, a major aerial battle occurred in the Sonchon area. That morning, 21 F-80s were attempting to strike targets in the Anju area, but they were intercepted by 26 MiGs from the 324th IAD. Sighting the MiGs, the "Shoots" immediately abandoned the area, while 14 F-86s jumped the MiGs from above. Here's what the commander of the 196th IAP Lieutenant Colonel Evgenii Georgievich Pepeliaev recalls about this fight:

> I flew off at the head of a six-ship formation. Soon we tangled with F-86s. I look – six Sabres are in front of me. The situation is advantageous. Knowing that my wingman was covering me and that I also had Captain V.A. Nazarkin's flight behind me, I started an attack. However, Nazarkin's flight couldn't support it. Later, the flight commander explained that he had lost our element in the sun; I don't know, perhaps that was the case. The Americans, taking advantage of this, immediately gave my wingman the works and soon shot him down. We were unable even to bury Larionov – his MiG plunged into the Yellow Sea. There immediately followed another burst, this time at my MiG. A second Sabre element was coming in from the right, but Nazarkin was silent. I realized that I would have no help, and not wanting to become someone else's aerial victory, I threw my MiG into a spin from an altitude of 7,000-8,000 meters. There are clouds below me, the top edge of which was around 3,000 meters. I head for them; the Sabre above me goes into a descending spiral, but the pilot doesn't have enough skill and can't catch me. I flew into a cloud, and pulled my MiG out of the spin, as they say, just above the water and headed back to base... Nazarkin never flew again; they sent him back to the [Soviet] Union.

Pepeliaev's MiG was damaged and he landed at Andong with bullet holes in it. Even before taking on the six F-86s, however, Pepeliaev had downed one Sabre, thereby taking revenge for the death of his wingman Senior Lieutenant Ivan Vasil'evich Larionov, who to the present day is still listed as missing-in-action.

Eight pilots from the 196th IAP's 1st Squadron, led by Major N.A. Antipov were also operating on this mission as part of the group. They tried to break through to the area where the enemy fighter-bombers were operating, but they were also attacked by four Sabres, which tied up almost Antipov's entire group in combat. Only one element led by the 196th IAP's deputy commander Major A.I. Mitusov, which was part of Antipov's group, managed to reach the Pyongyang area, where they sighted a group of seven F-80s and attacked it. A three-ship formation of Shooting Stars, flying at the tail-end of the overall group, came under attack, and one of them was struck by shells from the MiG flown by Major Mitusov before crashing to the earth. The remaining F-80s promptly abandoned the given area, and Mitusov's element returned to base.

On that same morning, but a bit earlier than the pilots of the 196th IAP, pilots of the 176th GIAP had tangled with the forward screen of Sabres, which numbered approximately 35 fighters, in the Siarenkan area. At 0920, 22 MiGs of the 176th GIAP under the command of Lieutenant Colonel S.F. Vishniakov had departed to intercept enemy aircraft. Twenty minutes later, they encountered a large group of Sabres from the 4th FIW, the aim of which was to tie up the MiGs in combat and screen the area where the fighter-bombers were operating. Combat flared up at different altitudes as the groups split up into separate flights and elements. As the dogfight first started, Senior Lieutenant B.A. Obraztsov succeeded in downing one of the Sabres. However when pulling out of his attack, Obraztsov's MiG was itself attacked from behind by three F-86s. None of his comrades had time to cover Obraztsov, and fire from one of the Sabres' tore into his cockpit. The pilot received serious bullet wounds in the lower back. Obraztsov released the canopy and bailed out of his MiG without ejecting, coming to ground in the Sonchon area. He was picked up by local authorities, who took him to a medical post, where he received first aid. From there, Senior Lieutenant Boris Aleksandrovich Obraztsov was placed aboard a truck from an anti-aircraft artillery unit, which set off to return him to his unit. En route to Andong, 12 kilometers away, Obraztsov passed away due to internal bleeding.

Meanwhile, the dogfight had been continuing: Captain K.Ia. Shcherbakov's eight-ship formation was locked in combat against six F-86s, and during one head-on pass, Lieutenant I.A. Zorin managed to damage one of the Sabres, which immediately exited the combat. At the same time, six MiGs under Captain S.M. Kramarenko's command were dueling with six other F-86s. In the course of the swirling dogfight, Captain Kramarenko managed to get behind one of the Sabre elements and downed one of the F-86s, which burst into flames and fell into the sea not far from Siarenkan.

Soon the fighting began to sputter out and the aircraft of both sides returned to their bases. Two of our MiGs failed to return to base on this day, and both of their pilots died – one from the 196th IAP and the other from the 176th GIAP. However, the pilots of the 324th IAD came out ahead on the ledger, adding four downed or damaged F-86s and one F-80 to their score. According to recent research by Diego Zampini, on this day the USAF lost at least two F-86s and one F-80. Captain Kramarenko's victim, most likely, was the F-86A No.48-0297 from the 335th Fighter Squadron, and its pilot 2nd Lieutenant Conrad Allard was killed. Lieutenant Colonel Pepeliaev's victim was most likely F-86A No.49-1297 from the 336th FIS – its pilot Reeves managed to make it back to the base in Suwon, but his Sabre crashed upon landing. The F-86 was totally destroyed by the crash and became a write-off four days later, while Reeves himself was able to walk away from the wreckage.

In addition, Major Mitusov managed to down F-80 No.49-1803 from the 8th FBG's 36th Squadron, the pilot of which, Cecil Moore, was killed. Thus both sides lost two pilots in the aerial fighting of this day. In turn, 1st Lieutenant Ralph "Hoot" Gibson of the 335th FIS received credit for downing Senior Lieutenant Obraztsov's MiG, while Senior Lieutenant Larionov's aircraft was downed by 1st Lieutenant Milton Nelson of the same squadron.

After this battle, the weather over North Korea again deteriorated, and this grounded most aerial operations until the middle of August 1951. Even so, at the end of July Soviet pilots clashed four more times with USAF pilots, three of which occurred on the same day of 29 July 1951.

However, over a week before this final July battle, the pilots of the 196th IAP managed on the morning of 21 July to intercept a group of enemy aircraft, which they identified as USAF all-weather interceptors, the F-94 Starfire. On Saturday 21 July the weather was dreary, with a dense cloud cover, and all the Soviet airfields were socked-in by fog. However, according to Soviet records eight all-weather two-seater F-94 Starfire interceptors took off from bases in Japan, which were supposed to conduct an aerial reconnaissance over northeast China. They were covered by 30 F-86s, which took off from Suwon. They escorted the Starfires as far as Andong, where they decided that the MiGs wouldn't take off in such weather and headed back to base. But the eight-ship F-94 formation continued their mission, flying as far as Mukden before turning around and heading back to South Korea on their return course.

Radar operators of the 64th IAK were attentively tracking their flight, but corps commander Major General M.V. Belov couldn't decide whether or not to scramble his pilots in such weather. He did, however, issue an order to the commander of the 324th IAD Colonel I.N. Kozhedub to be ready to launch his subordinates at a moment's notice. Kozhedub passed the order to the commander of the 196th IAP Lieutenant Colonel Pepeliaev to prepare the Regiment's best-trained pilots, who had the most experience with flying in difficult weather conditions, for a sortie. Pepeliaev selected nine such men and placed himself at the head of this group. They were sitting at Readiness No. 1 until the Starfires passed over the Andong airfield on their return course, by which time the fog began to dissipate. Only then was permission granted for the 10 MiGs on alert to scramble, and they were guided toward the group of enemy reconnaissance planes by ground controllers. The 10-ship MiG formation under the command of the regiment commander Lieutenant Colonel E.G. Pepeliaev, which took off at 0900, chased down this enemy group just as it was reaching the coast line. The F-94s were flying to the east at an altitude of 8,000-9,000 meters in a column of two flights, with a distance of 2-4 kilometers between each four-ship flight. Pepeliaev led his flight into an attack against the rear F-94 flight and engaged it in combat, while Captain B.V. Bokach's flight of MiG-15s attacked the lead F-94 flight. With the first pass Pepeliaev downed one Starfire from a shallow deflection angle, close to 0/4 [a no-deflection shot]. After pulling out of the attack, he caught the second F-94 in a banking turn and shot off part of its tail fin.

Senior Lieutenant A.I. Pupko fired upon a pair of F-94s in a head-on pass, and the lead F-94, evading the fire, made an abrupt maneuver and collided with his wingman – both aircraft fell into the sea. Captain B.S. Abakumov, Captain V.A. Nazarkin and, likely, L.N. Ivanov each claimed another three of the Starfires, but the latter's victory was credited to Captain N.K. Shelamonov, even though he denies participation in this combat.

That is the version of this action as laid out in the records of the 64th IAK. However, in reality, that morning the pilots of the 196th IAP instead had intercepted a group of F9F-2 Panther carrier fighters from VMF-311. The American side acknowledges the loss of only one of its Panthers (No.123464), the pilot of which, Lieutenant Richard Bell, wound up in captivity. North Korean authorities and soldiers of the NKPA managed to discover the wreckage of four Panthers and found the corpses of two American pilots, while the other three Panthers fell into the sea and remnants of them could not be located. However, the American side to the present day still doesn't report the losses of any other Panthers on this day.

The final major aerial clash of the month occurred on the afternoon of 29 July. Earlier that day, the pilots of the 17th IAP had flown two combat sorties and had become engaged with Sabres on one of them. At 1105, a regimental group of 26 MiGs of the 17th IAP under the command of Major G.I. Pulov intercepted a group of four B-29 bombers, covered by almost 40 F-86s, in the Taechon area. Having sighted the large group of approaching MiGs, the Superfortresses aborted their mission and, covered by a portion of the Sabres, turned back. The other 12 F-86s headed in the direction of Pulov's group and attacked the MiGs. A brief clash ensued, in which Captain S.S. Artemchenko and his wingman Senior Lieutenant V.F. Shulev claimed hits against two Sabres, after which the Sabres exited the combat area, while Pulov's group returned to base without any losses.

At 1116, a group of 16 MiGs from the 176th GIAP, commanded by Colonel S.F. Vishniakov, approached the Chongju area, where they collided with several groups of Sabres numbering a total of 28 fighters. Again there was a brief combat, in which the Soviet pilots celebrated a victory. Flight leader Captain S.M. Kramarenko managed to slide in behind one Sabre element and heavily damaged one of them with his cannon fire. The F-86 began to smoke and went into a violent dive as another Sabre element immediately began to cover his exit from combat. Soon the Sabres withdrew from the battle, while the pilots of the 176th GIAP returned to base without any losses.

On the third combat mission of the day, the entire 17th IAP, numbering 24 MiGs commanded by Major G.I. Pulov, took off to intercept enemy ground attack aircraft in response to a call from the division command post. The weather was most unsuitable for aerial combat, with several layers of clouds, making the airspace between the layers a scourge for the pilots. No one knows when and where an enemy aircraft might suddenly emerge.

En route to the designated area, Major Pulov sighted six F-80s approaching in a formation of two three-ship flights that were staggered in altitude, below and to the left of him. Having assessed the situation, Pulov called out: "The enemy is below us" and took his flight into an attack upon the first flight of F-80s, pursuing them until they disappeared into some clouds. At the same moment Senior Lieutenant N.V. Sutiagin went on the attack against the second F-80 flight, in response to which the enemy went into a defensive circle. Using a vertical maneuver, Sutiagin fired two bursts at one Shooting Star from the rear, and fired a third burst at a second F-80 as it was entering a dive.

Just as Major Pulov went on the attack, another F-80 flight had begun to emerge on his tail. Spotting the stalking F-80s, Senior Lieutenant V.G. Malunov attacked them, and again the enemy adopted a defensive circle. Having circled once, the enemy began to dive away to the south in a dive angle of 45-50°. Captain S.S. Artemchenko followed them, and having pulled to within 600 meters, he fired a long burst at the tail-end Shooting Star, which disappeared into the clouds below it at the same dive angle.

Major Pulov's element, having lost its first target in the clouds, spotted three more F-80s. Having maneuvered into a position for an attack against them, he initiated an attacking pass against them, but the "Shoots" slipped away into some clouds before he could close to within firing distance.

Captain M.N. Shcherbakov's flight, following behind Pulov's group and 1,500 meters above it, spotted another six F-80s below and to the left, approaching at an angle. The Shooting Stars still had their drop tanks. Swinging around to the left, Captain Shcherbakov attacked them. Having spotted the MiGs, the F-80s released their drop tanks and went into a banking turn to port, after which, having shaken out into a column, they began to dive into the clouds below them. Captain Shcherbakov, pursuing the fighter-bombers, fired a short burst at the tail-end Shooting Star as the range to it dropped from 700 to 600 meters. The attacked aircraft listed to one side and disappeared into the clouds.

Captain M.S. Ponomarev's flight, serving as the covering group at an altitude of 7,000 meters, spotted another six-ship formation of Shooting Stars below it and to the left, which were also flying in a stair-stepped formation. Ponomarev's group went into a descending turn to port toward the fighter-bombers, while the Shooting Stars simultaneously entered a descending turn to the left, taking a heading to the east of Pyongyang. As Ponomarev's flight pursued the "Shoots", one F-80 suddenly swung around and went into a head-on attack against Senior Lieutenant G.T. Fokin's MiG. The F-80 pilot opened fire first. Fokin returned fire and then pulled into a zoom climb. Observing Fokin's fire, Captain Ponomarev saw the F-80 explode. However, Fokin's MiG was also damaged just as it began to climb out of the head-on attack. Machine-gun fire struck his ammunition, which exploded and severely wounded Fokin in the right leg. Simultaneously, the aileron control cables were severed. Faint from the pain, Fokin didn't even report over the radio that he'd been wounded. He exited the combat and brought his plane back to base, where he safely landed. After landing, he was immediately rushed to a hospital, where he spent the next month recovering.

Meanwhile, Captain Ponomarev, continuing the pursuit, closed to within 250-300 meters of one F-80 element and opened fire on the wingman. The attacked Shooting Star started downward in a steep left-hand spiral. Pulling out of the attack, Ponomarev maneuvered into position to attack the lead F-80 of this element, and fired two short bursts at it from behind while employing the moving reticule of his sight. He couldn't observe the results of his fire because the enemy disappeared into the clouds.

Upon returning to base, according to our pilots' reports and the gun camera footage, four enemy F-80s were downed. Other than G.T. Fokin's MiG, we had no more losses in this battle.

As a result of this day's combats, the pilots of the 64th IAK claimed three F-86s and four F-80s destroyed. Their own losses consisted of one damaged MiG and one wounded pilot. The American command again deliberately conceals the extent of its losses of this day, though they do in fact acknowledge some of them. However, as has been the case with previous examples, they attribute these losses to anti-aircraft fire. According to research by Diego Zampini, on this day the pilots of 17th IAP on their third combat sortie engaged a mixed group of enemy aircraft consisting of eight F-80s from the 51st FIG, which were being escorted by 12 F-84E Thunderjets from the 136th FBW and a flight of F-86s. In the combat with them, Senior Lieutenant Sutiagin downed F-84E No.49-2339 from the 154th FBS, and its pilot Captain James R. Overstreet, Jr. was killed. Captain Ponomarev shot down another F-84E (No.49-2385). Senior Lieutenant Fokin downed F-84E No.49-2338 from the 111th FBS – its pilot Thomas Tremblay was also killed, but is still listed as missing-in-action. First Lieutenant William W. McAllister, who damaged Fokin's MiG, also couldn't avoid the fire from Captain Artemchenko's cannons, but McAllister managed to fly back to his base and make a successful landing there, and his aircraft was quickly repaired.

The pilots of the US 4th FIW also didn't escape without losses: the Americans confirm the loss on this day of one of their F-86A Sabres, No.49-1098, which the Americans acknowledge was damaged in a combat with MiGs. The pilot of this Sabre success-fully made it back to Suwon, but rather take any chances by trying to land his heavily damaged aircraft, he decided to bail out of it. Most likely, this was the same damaged F-86 that had been hit by Captain Ponomarev's fire.

In August, the nature of the fighting in the skies of Korea didn't change. As before, the Americans continued to attack the supply lines and chokepoints in North Korea with fighter-bombers in pursuit of the goals of Operation Strangle. These airstrikes resumed as soon as good flying weather returned over North Korea.

The next major raid by ground attack aircraft was undertaken on 9 August 1951, when a large group of F-80C fighter-bombers from the 51st FIG attempted to paralyze traffic on the roads and railroads running between Andong and Anju. At 1553, 23 MiGs of the 17th IAP under the command of regiment commander G.I. Pulov were scrambled to repulse this raid. In the Anju area they managed to intercept a group of eight F-80s, which was being covered by a group of F-86s. Having sighted the large group of MiGs, the Shooting Star pilots sped toward the sanctuary of the bay. Seven of them managed to reach it, but the eighth Shooting Star was left behind as burning wreckage on Korean ground – its pilot Captain Gerald L. Brose from the 16th FIS was killed.

Pilots of the 17th IAP 3rd Squadron securely tied up the covering Sabres in combat, preventing them from interfering with the work of the 1st Squadron's pilots. In this combat, the commander of the 3rd Squadron Captain N.G. Dokashenko's wingman, Senior Lieutenant V.M. Khvostantsev distinguished himself. In the course of the dogfight, he became separated from his leader and wound up alone. Attempting to rejoin his leader's MiG, he suddenly spotted a pair of Sabres below him, which were lining up to attack one of the other pilots from his squadron. The enemy pilots didn't see him and unconcernedly prepared to launch their attack. Taking advantage of this, V.M. Khvostantsev closed to within 150 meters of the wingman and opened up with all his cannons. Fragments began to fly off from the Sabre, and it disappeared below; the second Sabre meanwhile had time to escape out from under the attack.

An hour later, the 17th IAP's 1st Squadron, numbering 10 MiGs under the command of Major G.I. Pulov again took off at 1725 at a signal from the division's command post with the assignment to cover the return of the pilots of the 303rd IAD's 523rd and 18th GIAP from combat. Assembling into a combat wedge formation of six MiGs, flanked by a flight to the right, they crossed the Yalu River north of Andong at an altitude of 5,500 meters, after which they jettisoned their drop tanks. Information arrived from the division command post that eight F-80s were north of Simbi-do Island. Swinging around to the right after crossing over the island, Pulov's group started flying along the coast line. Captain S.S. Artemchenko spotted five approaching F-80s below them and to the right, which were flying in a shallow echelon combat formation. After alerting the rest of the group to the presence of the enemy aircraft, Artemchenko banked to the right in order to get behind the enemy, but in the process he lost sight of the Shooting Stars and took a bearing toward the Anju area.

The rest of the group began to swing around to the right. Having reversed direction, Senior Lieutenant N.F. Miroshnichenko caught sight of the same five-ship formation of F-80s, now at the same altitude and to the right, which he reported to Major Pulov. Pulov ordered Miroshnichenko to take the lead and to attack the enemy. Moving in front, Senior Lieutenant Miroshnichenko banked to the left and moved to approach the F-80s, and having closed upon them, fired a long burst. As a result of the high-speed acceleration, Miroshnichenko and Pulov passed the F-80s and pulled into a climbing turn to port. At this moment, one of the "Shoots" moved to attack Pulov's MiG. Senior Lieutenant N.N. Kramarenko, who was trailing the attacking element, opened fire on this F-80. After a long burst, the Shooting Star's right wing dropped and it spiraled downward, while Kramarenko pulled out of the attack in a climbing turn to the left.

Covering Major Pulov's attack, Senior Lieutenant N.V. Sutiagin spotted an F-80 element below him and to the right, which were circling around to the right. Coming out of their turn to starboard, the pair of Shooting Stars went into a spiral to the left, dragging the dogfight toward the sea. Following the Shooting Stars through their spirals, Sutiagin attacked one F-80 three times, firing from a range of 800 meters down to 500 meters using the moving reticule of his sight. After exiting the attack, he received a command from the division command post: "Withdraw from combat and return to base." Major Pulov took a heading of 340° and followed it back to base. En route the entire group reassembled and landed back at the base with its full complement. As a result of this dogfight, three American F-80s were shot down.

In the two clashes of this day, the pilots of the 17th IAP claimed four F-80s and one F-86, but the 64th IAK's headquarters credited the regiment with only two F-80s destroyed, which were awarded to Captain S.S. Artemchenko and Senior Lieutenant N.V. Sutiagin. The other two F-80s were registered as "damaged" by Miroshnichenko and Kramarenko. However, Senior Lieutenant V.M. Khvostantsev was not credited with downing the Sabre, even though the gun camera footage clearly showed his cannon shells striking the enemy fighter.

After a day or two of delay the American command acknowledged the loss of four of its F-80s, but as always they attributed them to either anti-aircraft fire or "mechanical bugs", not at all to the MiGs. Captain Artemchenko presumably downed Brose's F-80 No.49-838 from the 51st FIG's 16th Squadron, killing the pilot. Senior Lieutenant Sutiagin likely downed F-80 No.49-761, and its pilot, James Keiser of the 8th FBG was taken prisoner. Both Shooting Stars that were damaged by Senior Lieutenants Miroshnichenko and Kramarenko were also from the 8th FBG, but although they managed to fly back to their base, one of the F-80s (No.49-660) crashed upon landing, killing its pilot. The other pilot flew his damaged F-80 No.49-667 back to Kimpo, but took to his parachute rather than attempt to land the crippled jet.

The 335th FIS's F-86 No.49-1271, which had been damaged by Khovstantstev, also struggled back to its base, but it also crashed upon landing and was written off as scrap metal. The Americans recorded that it had been lost only on 14 August, and for some reason reported it had been lost during take-off, not when landing; moreover, 14 August 1951 featured weather unsuitable for flight operations. Thus, the losses on the American side were even larger than those actually credited to the pilots of the 64th IAK, and moreover, there were no losses on the Soviet side. Who would want to acknowledge such a defeat?!

The pilots of the 18th GIAP also conducted one combat sortie on 9 August. They were covering the railroad bridge across the Yalu as well as the Andong, Miaogou and Singisiu airbases, but they had no encounter with the enemy.

After 9 August 1951, the weather again turned bad and the combat operations of the opposing sides' air forces resumed only once the weather improved on 18 August. On that day, the pilots of the 303rd IAD had an intense dogfight with the Sabres of the 4th FIW. Around 1400, eight MiGs of the 18th GIAP's 2nd Squadron took off on the second sortie of the day to cover the Supung hydroelectric power station. During the patrol over the area, the Soviet pilots spotted fighter-bombers that were being escorted by 22 Sabres (two eight-ship formations and one six-ship formation). Our pilots attempted to break through to the fighter-bombers, but they were attacked by the Sabres and tied up in combat. A fierce, but unequal dogfight erupted, with the Soviet MiGs badly outnumbered. In view of this, the commander of the 303rd IAD Colonel G.A. Lobov at 1425 scrambled 10 MiGs of the 17th IAP as reinforcements. As Major G.I. Pulov's group was arriving on the scene, the commander of the 18th GIAP's 2nd Squadron Captain V.N. Shalev damaged one Sabre, but two other Sabres immediately attacked his element and seriously damaged the aircraft of his wingman Senior Lieutenant N.S. Gavril'chenko, who immediately exited the battle. He brought his MiG back to base with difficulty, but his fuel ran out during his landing approach. His fighter touched down next to the runway, and as it was rolling out after landing, it struck the breastwork of a trench, catapulted into the air, flipped twice, and crashed. By some miracle Nikolai Gavril'chenko survived the crash with only some bruises, and he returned to flight operations with the regiment just five days later. The hurriedly arriving pilots of the 17th IAP determinedly joined the combat and gave the pilots of the 18th GIAP the opportunity to withdraw from it.

This was in essence one of the first combat sorties by pilots of the 18th GIAP after a month-long break, because after the clashes of 7 July 1951, the 18th GIAP began making preparations to restage to the Miaogou Air Base, and the division's pilots had been granted leave until the end of the month. At that point, the poor weather descended over the area, and only on 18 August did the pilots of the 18th GIAP again resume combat operations as part of its division. Prior to this day, they had conducted only three sorties at the beginning of August (on the 5, 9 and 10 August) to cover the railroad bridge near Andong and the Andong, Miaogou and Singisiu airfields, but only one of them involved the full regiment, and on none of the missions had they encountered the enemy.

Earlier on 18 August, on the first combat sortie that morning, a second Sabre had been shot down by Senior Lieutenant A.N. Nikolaev. This was his first victory in the skies of Korea. This occurred somewhere between 0800 and 0857 in the Chongju area, when 24 MiGs of the 17th IAP headed by the regiment commander Major G.I. Pulov encountered a group of F-86s. In the course of the fight, four F-86s attacked Captain N.G. Dokashenko's flight from below and to the left. Dokashenko's flight was in an extended formation, and the Sabres overshot Senior Lieutenant A.N. Nikolaev's MiG, which was trailing behind the rest of the flight at the rear of the formation. Nikolaev had to do nothing more than bank a bit to the left, take aim and open fire in order to punish the Sabre pilots' inattentiveness. One Sabre was shot down.

The result of the day's combat was 2:1 in our favor, but again the 64th IAK headquarters credited Nikolaev with his victory, while Captain V.N. Shalev received no official victory credit. The Americans don't report the losses of any of their Sabres on this day, while 1st Lieutenant Charles Lloyd of the 334th Fighter Squadron, who had damaged Senior Lieutenant Gavril'chenko's MiG, correctly claimed to have damaged one MiG.

To be honest, the ratio of victories to losses on the following day turned in favor of the Americans. On this morning of 19 August, eight MiGs of the 1st Squadron of the 303rd IAD's 18th GIAP together with a regiment-sized group of MiGs from the 523rd IAP again joined battle against three groups of F-86s, numbering a total of 24-30 Sabres, at 0915 in the Chongju area. The pilots of the 18th GIAP came under attack by a large group of Sabres, and suffered losses while the pilots of the 523rd IAP were rushing to their assistance: Captain V.A. Sokhan' and Lieutenant V.T. Kondrashov were both shot down by 1st Lieutenant Richard S. Becker of the 334th Fighter Squadron. Fortunately both Soviet pilots managed to eject safely from their crippled MiGs and returned to their unit. Captain A.A. Kaliuzhny of the 18th GIAP's 1st Squadron in turn claimed one Sabre.

The pilots of the 523rd IAP, who had hastened to come to the aid of the 18th GIAP's 1st Squadron, allowed them to withdraw from the combat before engaging nearly two dozen Sabres in a brief but furious dogfight. According to the post-mission debriefings of the pilots, Captain S.A. Bakhaev and Senior Lieutenant V.P. Filimonov each managed to down a Sabre, while Captain I.I. Tiuliaev and Senior Lieutenant A.M. Shevarev inflicted damage on two more F-86s, all without any losses on their own side. Only Senior Lieutenant A.A. Obukhov's MiG was lightly damaged (one bullet hole), but it returned safely to its base. However, for some reason, the 64th IAK command rejected these victory claims. The American side again reports no losses of its F-86s on this day, but in addition to Becker's kills, 1st Lieutenant Gill Garett received credit for damaging a MiG.

Combat sorties resumed again only on 22 August, but they were few in number and passed without enemy contact. Storm fronts were sweeping across Manchuria and Korea, allowing only occasional days of flight operations. The weather cleared toward the end of the day on 24 August, and at 1700, a group of MiGs from the 523rd IAP scrambled to intercept enemy aircraft. At 1720 in the area of Hakchong, the 523rd IAP's group came under attack from F-86As from the 4th FIW as it was en route to the search area. Two eight-ship formations of Sabres unexpectedly attacked the regiment's formation from out of some clouds. Lieutenant G.K. Svistun and his wingman Lieutenant A.M. Shevarev were the tail-end element in the 523rd IAP's formation, and it was they who came under attack from one of the Sabre groups. Evading the attack, Svistun's element became isolated from the rest of the regiment's formation, which the Sabres immediately exploited, surrounding them on all sides. The other pilots of the regiment didn't even notice that two of their comrades had gone missing from the formation.

The two Soviet pilots engaged in an unequal battle against eight F-86s. Grigorii Svistun boldly attacked one Sabre element and downed one of them. While focusing his fire on this F-86, Senior Lieutenant Svistun was suddenly attacked from above and behind by four F-86s. The .50 caliber machine-gun fire severed his controls and his MiG tumbled downward out of control. According to evidence gathered at the site where his plane crashed, Svistun had ejected from it, but his body was discovered together with an unopened parachute that was still attached to his seat. There were no bullet wounds found on the pilot's body. The conjectured reason for the Svistun's death was loss of consciousness when ejecting, as a result of which the pilot, who never regained consciousness, plummeted to the ground and was killed.

Grigorii Karpovich Svistun had been attacked by an element of Sabres being led by Colonel Benjamin Preston of the 4th FIW. The other Sabre flight encircled Svistun's wingman, Senior Lieutenant A.M. Shevarev, and soon Captain Jack Robinson of the 334th Fighter Squadron scored hits against Shevarev's aircraft: control cables on Shevarev's MiG were severed. Because of the loss of control, the pilot ejected at an altitude of 7,000 meters. During the ejection, Senior Lieutenant Shevarev received minor injuries to his back.

On 25 August 1951, the pilots of the 303rd IAD first encountered a new enemy aircraft in combat – the British-manufactured Gloster Meteor Mk.8 jet fighter. These aircraft equipped the RAAF's No. 77 Squadron, which had been fighting in the skies of Korea since July 1950, at first in F-51 Mustangs, but in May 1951 it had been re-equipped with the twin-engine Meteors.

The Australian pilots initiated combat sorties in their new aircraft in the role of fighters in August 1951. The assignment of No. 77 Squadron was to cover the Fifth Air Force's bomber and fighter-bomber formations.

The first encounter of the pilots of No. 77 Squadron with MiGs of the 64th IAK took place on 25 August, when pilots of the 17th IAP that had taken off to repulse the next enemy airstrike encountered unfamiliar twin-engine aircraft among the covering screen of fighters. They decided to test these new enemy aircraft and their pilots in combat. As it turned out, the Meteor was inferior to the MiGs both in speed and maneuverability, which in fact determined the outcome of this first battle.

At 0758, according to information from an auxiliary control post, a group of bombers consisting of eight B-29s, covered by up to 60 fighters, was approaching on a heading of 340° at an altitude of 6,000-10,000 meters in the area 15 kilometers south of Anju. The full 17th IAP took off at 0804 with a complement of 26 MiGs under the command of Major G.I. Pulov in order to intercept the enemy aircraft in the Sonchon area. The regiment's squadrons adopted a staggered trail combat formation, with the 1st and 3rd Squadrons in the attack group and the 2nd Squadron in the covering group.

Flying on a heading of 300°, at 0837 Major Pulov sighted six twin-engine aircraft in front of him, below him and to the right, flying on a parallel heading. Having discovered the MiGs behind them, the enemy aircraft banked left and formed a defensive ring. Major Pulov, having closed to within 250-300 meters, attacked the wingman of the tail-end element from behind and above at an angle of 30-35°, after which he pulled out of the attack in a climbing turn to starboard, circled around, and repeated a second attack in the same fashion. In the course of the battle, Major Pulov conducted four attacking passes, and fired his cannons on three of them.

Senior Lieutenant Sutiagin, covering Major Pulov's element, which had become separated from the rest of its group when Pulov moved to close with the enemy, also attacked the Gloster Meteors. In the very first pass, Sutiagin fired two bursts at the leader of the tail-end element, one of which struck the target, after which he wound up in the target's turbulent backwash and fell into a spin. Pulling his MiG out of its spin, Sutiagin spotted a flight of Gloster Meteors that was in the process of forming a ring around him. Senior Lieutenant Sutiagin, yawing his MiG from side to side, accelerated and separated from the Meteors.

Captain S.S. Artemchenko's flight sighted a Sabre element and began to pursue it. Realizing that he would be unable to catch the F-86 element, Captain Artemchenko quickly abandoned the chase.

As a result of the combat, two enemy Gloster Meteor fighters had been downed. One was added to Major Pulov's personal score, while the other went to Nikolai Sutiagin.

True, the command of the RAAF No. 77 Squadron announced that the squadron had suffered no losses in the action, but most likely this is untrue, because the Australian pilots had been extremely unlucky. The point is that in this first combat test for the Meteors, they had encountered highly experienced pilots of the 17th IAP, who would eventually go on to become two of the regiment's highest-scoring pilots, and who not only handled the MiG-15 masterfully, but were also skilled combatants and superb marksmen: Regiment commander Major P.I. Pulov (this was his first victory in Korea) and Senior Lieutenant N.V. Sutiagin (this was already his seventh victory in Korea). The Australian command, just like the Americans, prefers to attribute most of its losses to either ground fire or to pilot error or engine and control malfunctions, rather than to acknowledge that they were the result of encounters with MiGs. So these two Gloster Meteors (No.77-128 and No.77-354) were recorded as being lost on 22 August due to a mid-air collision over their Kimpo airfield.

Diego Zampini, who has closely studied this air war, gives his own version for how these Meteors were lost. In his view, both of the Meteors had been damaged in combat and flew back to their base in Kimpo, escorted by their comrades, but on the landing approach they collided with each other, resulting in a catastrophe – both pilots were killed. However, in order to conceal these first two losses in combat with MiGs, they were recorded as having occurred three days earlier, even though in the report it is noted that both pilots were killed "in combat operations", where instead it would have been more sensible to state that the pilots "died in non-combat operations".

Officially, the Australians maintain that the pilots of No. 77 Squadron in their Meteors didn't have their first combat with MiGs until 29 August, when two four-ship formations of Meteors tangled with MiGs over Chongju. There was in fact a dogfight involving Meteors on 29 August, when a group of fighter-bombers, escorted by a group of Sabres and eight No. 77 Squadron Meteors, attempted at 1030 to penetrate to the hydro-electrical stations on the Yalu River, which were being covered by 24 MiGs of the 18th GIAP under the leadership of the regiment commander Guards Lieutenant Colonel A.E. Belostotsky.

The Sabre group and eight Gloster Meteors attempted to sweep the air above the Yalu River clear before the arrival of the fighter-bombers, and decided to tie up the pilots of the 18th GIAP in combat. Pilots of the 1st Squadron were the first to see the enemy, when they spotted the eight Gloster Meteors at an altitude of 9,000 meters. Believing them to be bombers, they attacked the Meteor formation. Two of the participants in this action, Lev Kirillovich Shchukin and Aleksei Aleksandrovich Svintitsky, later described it.

Lev Kirillovich states:

While covering the hydro-electrical stations on the Yalu River, the Regiment made contact with a group of Meteors at 9,000 meters. Our squadron split into separate elements, and in this manner we attacked them from different directions. The pilots of the Meteors, which were inferior to us in speed, began to employ maneuvers in the horizontal; we had to get adjusted to them, since this was the first time we had encountered these aircraft. In one of the maneuvers (a vertical with a slight change in direction), I managed to close to within 100 meters of one of the Meteors and with the fire from all three cannons hit his left engine, causing it to explode.

Thus Senior Lieutenant L.K. Shchukin achieved his fourth victory in the skies of Korea.

Aleksei Alekseevich Svintitsky was Senior Lieutenant N.V. Babonin's wingman on this sortie and witnessed his element leader's victory in this combat. Here is how he described it:

We were flying as a pair, bringing up the rear of the regiment's formation; at the start of the battle, a six-ship formation of F-86s, having emerged suddenly from the direction of the sea, ganged up on our element. Babonin turned abruptly toward the enemy – the Sabres declined combat and with a half-roll dove in the direction of the sea. Because of our abrupt maneuver, we naturally fell behind the rest of the regiment. Suddenly Babonin observed five aircraft flying along the coast line at an altitude of 11,000 meters. Thinking that they were ours, he thought, "Oh, now we'll link back up with the group." But I took a look – whose group? These weren't our aircraft! We approach more closely – they were Glosters! He attacked, and I covered him.

We closed to within 300 meters and opened fire. Fragments, pieces of metal, some sort of parts go flying ... I'm located a bit behind and off to one side, so that no one "catches" us off-guard. ... But the target continues to fly! Babonin fired and fired – and closing to within 50 meters he got caught in an engine's backwash. It flipped his MiG over and he went into a dive. Well, as soon as I became convinced that we had shot down the aircraft – the pilot ejected – I dove after him. At first I saw him at a distance, but then lost him against the backdrop of the terrain. I came out of the dive at 4,000 meters – he's nowhere to be seen. I climbed up to 11,000 meters again and saw Sabres flying below me. I crossed "the tape" – that's what we called the Yalu River – and headed for home. I hear Babonin calling for me – he's already parked on the airbase. It turns out that in the dive, he thought I was a Sabre and decided to disengage – he was totally out of ammunition.

The North Koreans caught the [enemy] pilot. They interrogated him, translating first into Chinese, and then our interpreter relayed what he was saying in Russian. ... He was the son of a wealthy American from Australia. His father purchased his first airplane for him. He crashed it. The second airplane proved to be more successful; he learned to fly in it and wound up in the war. It's a shame about this guy. The Chinese shot him.

It was later established that the pilot of the downed Meteor (A77-721) was Lieutenant Ronald Guthrie from the RAAF's No. 77 Squadron, whom, fortunately, the Chinese didn't shoot. He sat out the rest of the war in prison and returned to Australia after its conclusion.

The Meteor of R. Wilson, the commander of No. 77 Squadron, came under attack from Senior Lieutenant Shchukin's element. His aircraft received a gaping hole in its left wing from a 37mm shell. In addition, shell fragments wounded the pilot himself. With great difficulty Wilson flew back to his base in Kimpo and managed to land his damaged aircraft, but his Meteor was deemed beyond repair and was written off. Thus, in its second encounter with MiGs, the RAAF No. 77 Squadron lost two of its Gloster Meteors.

In addition to the two victories over the Meteors, the commander of the 18th GIAP Guards Lieutenant Colonel A.E. Belostotsky claimed a victory over an F-86 which was escorting the Meteors. He managed to damage F-86A No.49-1266 from the 336th Fighter Squadron. The pilot of this Sabre, Clyde R. Young, returned to base with difficulty, because his aircraft was leaking fuel from its ruptured fuel tanks, but there he ejected from the doomed aircraft.[1] We had no losses in this combat.

The final battle of the summer in the skies of North Korea occurred on the last day of summer, 31 August 1951. Toward the day's end, several groups of F-80 fighter-bombers from the 8th FBG, covered by a group of F-84E Thunderjets from the 49th FBG, undertook an attack upon the supply lines in the Anju area. Almost the entire 17th IAP, numbering 23 MiGs under the overall command of the commander of the 303rd IAD Major General G.A. Lobov, was scrambled to intercept this raid. The regiment took off at 1725 and just ten minutes later our pilots encountered several six-ship formations of F-80s in the area south of Tokchion. The Shooting Star pilots also saw the MiGs, and ceasing their attacks, hurried toward the safety of Korea Bay. Just as they were reaching the sea, the enemy aircraft were attacked. Captain M.S. Ponomarev's element attacked the trailing element of one six-ship formation of Shooting Stars, and both were struck by MiG cannon fire and fell into the sea not far from the coast. Captain Ponomarev shot down one of the Shooting Stars, while his wingman Lieutenant A.T. Bozhko got the other.

One more F-80 was downed during the chase by the division commander General Lobov himself, and this was his first victory in the skies of Korea. The flight of Thunderjets attempted to intervene in the MiGs' attacks, but they themselves were bounced by Major G.I. Pulov's element and one of them also plunged into the sea. All of our pilots safely returned to base. Major Pulov managed to shoot down F-84E No.51-526 from the 49th FBG's 8th FBS, and its pilot 2nd Lieutenant Ronald W. Reed was taken prisoner. Captain Ponomarev, who had only recently transferred from the 523rd IAP to the 17th IAP with a promotion to command the 2nd Squadron, added to his personal score in this combat by downing F-80C No.49-859 from the 8th FBG's 36th FBS, the pilot of which is listed as missing-in-action. The Americans attribute the loss of this Shooting Star to enemy anti-aircraft fire. In addition, the American side doesn't confirm any other losses in this combat, but most likely the other damaged aircraft could have been written-off much later by the clever Americans due to other causes.

One feature of the August 1951 aerial fighting was the fact that only the 303rd IAD conducted active combat operations, while the pilots of the 324th IAD were given a rest and were used only occasionally either to reinforce a battle or to cover the pilots of the 303rd IAD as they returned to base and landed. Thus the pilots of the 324th IAD had very few combat missions and even fewer combats, all of which ended without results for either side.

All of the Fifth Air Force's efforts to penetrate to the targets guarded by the MiGs of the 64th IAK in August ended without serious damage to the targeted sites, but the losses incurred from the actions of the 64th IAK and UAA were perceptible. In addition, the MiG's plain superiority over the F-80 forced the Fifth Air Force command to begin re-equipping those units using the F-80 with more modern F-84 and F-86E fighter-bombers.

In addition, at the beginning of September 1951, the 51st FIG began turning over its F-80s to other units in South Korea, and departed to Japan, where it would receive new F-86E Sabres and learn to fly and fight in them. The Group's entire flight staff underwent rotation, since most of the pilots had come from other US fighter-bomber groups in South Korea prior to going to Japan, while the rest had ended their tour of duty and returned to the United States.

Due to the poor flying weather that existed during most of the month and the resulting low number of combat sorties, August 1951 proved to be rather unproductive for the pilots of the 64th IA – only a total of 10 confirmed victories were recorded, not including several victories that were either downgraded to probable status or were not credited at all to the pilots of the 303rd IAD, against the loss of five MiGs and one pilot. Even so, this correlation of victories to losses was still 2:1 in favor of the pilots of the 64th IAK, though these numbers are naturally subject to dispute and do not reflect the American records.

THE HOT AUTUMN OF 1951

The arrival of autumn didn't alter the situation in the skies of Korea: as before the American command was striving to throttle the movement of supplies in North Korea under the goals of the ongoing Operation Strangle. The forces that had been mobilized for this purpose remained the same: six fighter-bomber and ground attack groups, one fighter-interceptor wing, two light and three medium bomber groups, two reconnaissance groups (one strategic, the other tactical), one airlift group, and up to ten separate squadrons and units.

At the beginning of September, the Fifth Air Force sharply increased its combat operations north of the 38th Parallel, in particular those conducted by fighter-bombers. Large groups of F-86 fighters from the 4th FIW again appeared in MiG Alley, the task of which was to sweep the area clear of MiGs. Thus, in the first days of September, fierce clashes with Sabres flared up.

The first September combat between this war's eternal adversaries, the MiGs and the Sabres, took place already on 1 September, when pilots of the 18th GIAP clashed with pilots of the 335th Fighter Squadron. The 18th GIAP's pilots were covering the returning pilots of the 523rd IAP from a mission, when they collided with a group of 40 F-86s and 16 Meteors. Each of the sides claimed one victory: on our side, the 3rd Squadron commander Captain P.N. Antonov received credit for a victory claim, as did the commander of the 335th Fighter Squadron Major Winton Marshall on the American side. However, according to records neither side actually had any losses in this action; the first blood was spilled in the September fighting only on the following day.

On 2 September, a large group of F-80s undertook a strike against one of the areas in MiG Alley. At 1000, the entire 18th GIAP took off to intercept it, but was unable to attack the F-80s, because the Americans fighter-bomber pilots spotted the approximately 30 MiGs that were approaching at low altitude, immediately halted their attacks, and withdrew in the direction of the sea. However, pilots of the 335th FIS in their Sabres, which our pilots estimated to be 40 F-86s, bounced the MiGs of the 18th GIAP. A heavy dogfight ensued, in which each side split into separate pairs and flights, and a "carousel" of fighters chasing other fighters began to whirl. In the initial attack, Sabres set upon Senior Lieutenant L.K. Shchukin's element. Senior Lieutenant Viktor Akatov intercepted the attack on his leader, but was shot down by Captain Ralph Gibson and his wingman. However, Lev Shchukin soon settled the score with the Americans; he in turn shot down Captain Gibson's wingman 2nd Lieutenant Lawrence Layton. This was his fifth victory in Korea, and here is how Lev Kirillovich himself described it:

> In the battle of 2 September [1951], I succeeded in downing my fifth American aircraft at an altitude of 9,000 meters, and to my surprise the victory came rather easily. When such armadas meet in the air, the aerial combats broke down into multiple dogfights, which went on at every altitude, from 1,000 meters up to 13,000 meters. The airspace became so crowded that pilots didn't pay attention to friendly aircraft or those of the enemy with which you weren't directly engaged. Apparently, it was the same for the Americans.
>
> On one of the maneuvers, for a just a moment a more quickly moving enemy F-86 appeared above and in front of me. Indeed, from his maneuver I sensed that he didn't see me. All I had to do was touch my rudder, take careful aim, and open fire from a range of 70-80 meters, after which the Sabre's nose dipped and it plummeted downward out of control. At the moment of opening fire, I saw tracers coming from my right which missed my aircraft – the pilot of a second Sabre was firing at me. However, I managed to separate from him with a zoom climb.

That's how Layton's Sabre was downed; the pilot was killed in his cockpit. Thus Lev Shchukin took full revenge for the death of his own wingman.

The weather on the morning of 2 September was unsettled, visibility was poor, and the combat was difficult for both sides. Guards Captain G.I. Gerasimenko's six-ship formation of MiGs spotted four Sabres in some gaps between the clouds and immediately attacked them, taking advantage of their superior altitude. From a range of 120 meters Captain Gerasimenko downed one Sabre, while his wingman Senior Lieutenant M.N. Kapitonov claimed another. In this battle, Guards Senior Lieutenant S.T. Kolpikov, who was Captain D.A. Tarasov's wingman, became separated from his leader when he went after a Sabre that was lining up on Kapitonov's MiG. Senior Kolpikov managed to hit it with a burst of cannon fire, but then he was immediately jumped by four Sabres – machine-gun fire stitched his MiG and set fire to it. Guards Senior Lieutenant Sergei Timofeevich Kolpikov couldn't escape his burning MiG and was killed. The commander of the 335th FIS Major Winton Marshall was given credit for this victory.

In this dogfight, the element consisting of the deputy regiment commander Guards Lieutenant Colonel A.P. Smorchkov and his wingman Guards Major D.P. Os'kin, also distinguished itself by downing two Sabres. Captain V.N. Shalev, the commander of the 18th GIAP's 2nd Squadron, claimed another Sabre.

The battle was fierce with heavy losses on both sides. The turning point came when pilots of the 17th IAP headed by the regiment commander Major G.I. Pulov arrived as reinforcements. At 1003, 16 MiGs from the regiments 2nd and 3rd Squadron had been scrambled at a signal from the division command post. They were ordered to tie up and destroy the enemy fighters. Flying in a column of squadrons at an altitude of 11,000 meters, as they were approaching the Anju area Major Pulov spotted eight F-86s in a left-echelon formation, 500 meters below and in front of them to the left. Major Pulov ordered Captain M.N. Shcherbakov eight-ship squadron to cover the attack, then directed Captain M.S. Ponomarev's flight to attack the leading flight of Sabres on the right, while he himself closed upon the trailing four Sabres with his flight. Having closed to within 1,000 meters of the enemy formation, our MiGs were spotted by the Sabre pilots, who began to drop their external tanks while simultaneously going into a turn to starboard. The left-hand flight of Sabres began to depart beneath the formation of the lead flight. During the turn, the tail-end Sabre lagged behind the rest of its flight. Pulov drew to within 400 meters of it and opened fire, sending the Sabre into a fatal plunge. His wingman Senior Lieutenant P.P. Gostiukhin confirmed the downing. Pulling out of the attack into a climbing turn to starboard, Pulov spotted another flight of Sabres above and to the left of him, which were turning toward him. He quickly reversed direction and departed with a tight turn beneath the F-86 formation; the latter in turn began to withdraw in a dive toward the sea.

Major General G.A. Lobov, who had replaced Major General I.V. Belov in command of the 64th IAK (though officially Major General Lobov didn't take command of the 64th IAK until 20 September) conducted a detailed analysis of the 2 September fight. He interviewed not only the 303rd IAD's regiment commanders, but also the subordinate pilots who had taken part in this battle, and attempted to find out why there had been such heavy losses in the recent battles. The reason was one: a single division didn't have enough strength to take on the Sabres and the fighter-bombers simultaneously. So the decision was taken to commit all five regiments of the 303rd and 324th IAD the next time the adversary launched a major attack and to give the Americans a good thrashing. However, such a battle didn't take place until 9 September 1951 in the area of Sunchon, which involved both Soviet fighter divisions and all three squadrons of the American 4th FIW.

Before then, however, the 64th IAK's pilots had several other encounters with UN aircraft, two of which had results and ended in victories for the Soviet pilots. Thus on the afternoon of 5 September, two groups of MiGs were scrambled to repel an enemy airstrike. At 1400, a group of 24 MiGs from the 523rd IAP under the command of the chief of the regiment's signals services Captain G.U. Okhai took off, followed five minutes later by a group of 26 MiGs from the 17th IAP led by regiment commander Major G.I. Pulov. The Corps' radar posts had detected a group of four B-29 bombers, which were flying with an escort of 30 fighters. The 10 MiGs of the 523rd IAP's 1st Squadron, commanded by Major A.P. Trefilov, which had taken off first, ran into a group of F-86s from the forward screen and tangled with them in combat. Meanwhile, the regiment's main group, consisting of 14 MiGs, continued on in order to intercept the B-29s, but in the vicinity of Chongju the Soviet pilots spotted six Meteors from the RAAF's No. 77

Squadron. Leaving a high cover of eight MiGs from the 2nd Squadron, Captain Okhai led his group of six MiGs into an attack against the formation of Meteors. In a quick flurry of action, Captain Okhai opened fire on two Meteors in succession from a range of 350 meters down to 320 meters, after which both Meteors lurched before going into steep dives. Captain I.I. Tiuliaev claimed another Meteor in this combat, observing it fall steeply downward. Both pilots were credited with victories over the Meteors – two for Captain Okhai and one for Captain Tiuliaev.

However, in reality only one Meteor was even struck by MiG fire in this action: cannon shells hit the tail section of Warrant Officer William Michaelson's Meteor. It was he and his leader Flight Lieutenant Ralph Dawson that came under fire from Okhai's cannons. Dawson managed to evade the fire with abrupt maneuvers, but Michaelson could not. He nursed his damaged Meteor back to base and made a landing there. However, his Meteor was so riddled with cannon shells that it was subsequently written off. The Australian pilots claimed that they had damaged one MiG in this combat, but all of the 523rd IAP's MiGs returned from the mission without any damage. A regimental group from the 17th IAP, which had hastened to join the 523rd IAP in its fight, instead ran into Sabres, with which they tangled briefly and without results, before the Sabres disengaged several minutes later and departed from the combat area.

On 8 September at 0825, the full 17th IAP numbering 26 MiGs took off to intercept enemy aircraft. Led by Major G.I. Pulov, in the area of Chongju they encountered a group of 24 F-86s from the 335th FIS and joined them in combat. In the course of this dogfight, Captain S.S. Bychkov managed to get behind a pair of Sabres and from close range scored hits against the wingman's aircraft. This F-86A No. 49-1323, being flown by the 335th Fighter Squadron's Clifford O. Thompson, was heavily damaged by the MiG's cannon fire. Thompson nursed his crippled Sabre back to Kimpo, where it was written off after a forced landing.

Finally, on 9 September 1951, an enormous clash played out in the area over Anju between 1100 and 1200, in which approximately 200 aircraft of the opposing sides took part. All five regiments of the 303rd IAD and 324th IAD participated, and one of the regimental groups was led by the commander of the 64th IAK himself, Major General G.A. Lobov. On the opposing side, the mission consisted of up to 18 B-29 bombers, up to 80 F-80 and F-84 fighter-bombers, and up to 50 F-86 Sabres, including around a dozen of the updated F-86E-10 type that the 4th FIW had received at the beginning of the month.

It is quite difficult to describe such a large aerial battle, and no one can do it better than the participants themselves. Here, for example, is how Senior Lieutenant Dmitrii Aleksandrovich Samoilov, a pilot with the 523rd IAP, describes his part in this combat:

On 9 September 1951, I flew on the first combat sortie as an element leader with Mikhail Zykov as my wingman. Zykov and I were in the group of the regiment's leader, Captain G.U. Okhai. After several maneuvers, the two other squadrons were tied up in combat, and that's when 24 F-86s attacked our six-ship formation. Our formation opened like a fan, and Zykov and I went into a climbing spiral to the left. Eight F-86s were chasing us. The encounter took place at an altitude of 6,000-6,500 meters. In the first stage of our climb, the F-86s due to their greater initial speed closed the range to us, and at approximately 1,000 meters the lead element

Hero of the Soviet Union D.A. Samoilov (on the right), credited with 10 victories in Korea, with his wingman M.A. Zykov; in China, 1951.

began to fire their machine guns at us, but then they started to lag behind, and at an altitude of around 11,000 meters first one Sabre flight and then the other gave up the chase. Having checked the airspace around us, and convinced that there were no other enemy aircraft, I rolled over and went in pursuit of the Sabres that had been chasing us. I caught up with the tail-end Sabre and shot him down. This was the first my first victory over an American aircraft.

Altogether our pilots claimed seven victories over the Sabre pilots on 9 September: two each were added to the scores of the 324th IAD's 176th GIAP and 196th IAP, while two more Sabres were credited to pilots of the 17th IAP and one to the 523rd IAP. Moreover, six MiGs from the 18th GIAP, led by the corps commander Major General Lobov, managed to penetrate to the area where the enemy fighter-bombers were operating, where they came upon 64 F-80s without any fighter cover and attacked them from above. In this pass General Lobov downed one F-80, while the others immediately fled to the sea.

We had one MiG-15 destroyed by enemy fire; the pilot from the 196th IAP Senior Lieutenant N.E. Andrushko ejected from his fatally damaged aircraft. The Americans however claim that they downed two MiGs in this battle, but most likely the second victory claim was erroneous, because everyone other than Andrushko returned to their bases in Andong and Miaogou after the action. In fact, Captain Richard Becker of the 334th FIS did shoot down Senior Lieutenant Andrushko's MiG, but Captain Ralph Gibson of the 335th FIS was unlucky – at best he only lightly damaged one of the MiGs, but didn't shoot it down. As is often the case, American records don't confirm the losses of any F-86s in this combat and only acknowledge damage to one of its new F-86E (No.51-2740) from the 335th Fighter Squadron, but its pilot 1st Lieutenant Don Jabusch managed to safely land it back at base and it was quickly repaired. This was the Sabre that Senior Lieutenant Samoilov fired upon, but evidently he only damaged it and didn't shoot it down. Only General Lobov's victory is confirmed by the American side: Lobov shot down F-80 No.49-814 of the 8th FBG, which fell in the Haeju area; the fate of the pilot is unknown.

In addition, one significant aspect of this clash on 9 September 1951 should be noted (of course, among others): the forces on the two sides were equal in strength, despite the fact that records show that all five Soviet fighter regiments took part in it. The point is that at this time, each Soviet fighter squadron only had 6-8 operational MiGs. This especially is true in the case of the 324th IAD, because it was experiencing a serious shortage of pilots. Many of the Soviet pilots had returned to the Soviet Union for a variety of reasons, but in the majority of cases due to fatigue. The combat at high altitudes and high speeds, with accompanying heavy G-forces required a lot of strength from the pilots, and their fatigue accumulated from mission to mission. To prevent the pilots from breaking down completely and to avert a fatal mistake in combat, some of the pilots had been sent in groups back to Port Arthur for one to two weeks of rest, while others had been sent back home.

Only in October 1951 did a group of 20-25 replacement pilots from the 309th IAD, which was located in Mukden, arrive in the 324th IAD. Thus in the September battles, only 6-8 pilots took part in the squadrons of the 324th IAD's regiments, and the active roster of the regiments of this division numbered 20-24 pilots.[2]

In addition, both divisions kept a reserve of one to two squadrons on the ground in order to cover their comrades as they returned from a mission and landed back at base. Thus only 6-8 pilots in the squadrons of the 324th IAD's regiments took part in the September battles, and the active roster of this division's regiments numbered 20-24 pilots. So the strength of the opposing sides in the clash on 9 September 1951 was comparable.

However, apparently neither side was able to convince the other of its superiority on 9 September, so on 10 September pilots of the 64th IAK and of the 4th FIW locked horns in two more air battles. The first dogfight, in which again all the regiments of the 303rd and 324th IAD participated, took place that morning in the Sukchon-Pakchon-Sunchon area. Pilots of the 324th IAD attacked F-80 formations, while pilots of the 303rd IAD attacked the Sabres that were covering the fighter-bombers. The action took place between 1125 and 1200.

First at 1135 in the area of Pakchon, 26 MiGs of the 17th IAP conducted a ten-minute battle with a large group of F-86s, in which Senior Lieutenant N.S. Volkov claimed one Sabre with no losses in return. While this dogfight was going on, a group of 16 MiGs from the 176th GIAP came across a group of 24 F-80s, which immediately retreated to the sanctuary of the sea, but lost one Shooting Star in the process, which was downed by Captain G.I. Ges'. Just then a group of eight Meteors was spotted, which were apparently escorting this group of F-80s. They also came under an attack from the MiGs, and again the same Captain Ges' fatally damaged one of the Meteors, while the others fled the area.

At this time (around 1150), a fighter dogfight was going on in the Sukchon-Sunchon area, involving 24 MiGs from the 523rd IAP and 26 F-86s. The Sabres were again checked and abandoned the combat area; Soviet pilots Senior Lieutenant V.I. Surovikin claimed two Sabres, while Senior Lieutenants G.T. Shatalov and D.A. Samoilov each claimed one. Our pilots had no losses in this combat.

The next battle on 10 September occurred in the area of Sunchon late in the afternoon between 1600 and 1700, when the Americans undertook another airstrike, this one conducted by F-84 fighter-bombers. First at 1614, a group of 14 MiGs from the 523rd IAP encountered a group of 18 F-84 Thunderjets from the 49th FBG's 8th FBS in the Sunchon area. The MiGs simply decimated it, taking advantage of the absence of any covering Sabres. Captains G.U. Okhai and D.V. Mazilov and Senior Lieutenants D.A. Samoilov, I.I. Iakovlev and P.Z. Churkin each put in a claim for one Thunderjet, without any losses on their own side. This was Samoilov's second victory of the day. Ten minutes later, 10 MiGs of the 523rd IAP's 1st Squadron under the command of Major A.P. Trefilov, which took off a bit later than the regiment's main group, intercepted a group of eight F-80s, and Major Trefilov managed to damage one of them – the remaining Shooting Stars immediately left the given area. A group of 22 MiGs from the 17th IAP, which had taken off at 1629 to reinforce the battle, didn't encounter any enemy aircraft in the area – the raid had been repulsed.

The 18th GIAP on these days was primarily carrying out the combat task of protecting the 64th IAK's airfields and covering the withdrawal from combat of the other regiments. Thus, it didn't have any encounters with enemy aircraft.

The fighter combat on 10 September was less intense – one could even say that they were only light skirmishes, because after the large losses in the fighting of the preceding day, the combat activity of the Sabre pilots fell sharply. The 64th IAK didn't have any losses at all on 10 September 1951. The Americans don't acknowledge losses among their F-80s and F-84s on this day, and in turn assert that the Thunderjet pilots even managed to damage four (!) MiGs, though not a single MiG of the 64th IAK had any damage. In the dogfight between the Sabres and MiGs, the Americans acknowledge the loss of only one of their F-86As (No.48-256) from the 334th FIS; its pilot 2nd Lieutenant John Burke managed to reach the sea in it, before he abandoned his crippled fighter. He was soon picked up by a Navy search helicopter. He was downed by Senior Lieutenant Shatalov. However, American records show that Surovinkin and Samoilov shouldn't have been given victory credits; they only damaged two F-86As (No.49-1227 and No.49-1139), both of which made it back to base in Kimpo and were returned to service after a period of repairs. The Australian command also doesn't confirm the loss of a Meteor on this day. However, no matter how disputable the combat records on both sides on 10 September, the combat area at day's end remained in possession of the MiGs, which had once again repulsed raids by American fighter-bombers while inflicting losses in the process.

Yet on 11 September 1951 there was more aerial combat over MiG Alley, when Fifth Air Force fighter-bombers and ground attack aircraft again tried to penetrate to supply arteries in the Anju area. The Americans launched two attacks on this day. Fighter-bombers, numbering more than 80 enemy aircraft, undertook the first strike.

The day began when 24 MiGs of the 17th IAP under the command of Major Pulov, which were sitting at the airfield at Readiness No. 1, took off at a command from the division's command post to repel a raid and intercept enemy aircraft. At 11.10, the 1st Squadron, numbering eight MiGs and led by Captain S.S. Artemchenko, lifted off the runway, followed by the remaining two squadrons of the regiment. After climbing to an altitude of 6,500 meters, the unit assembled into a staggered trail formation of elements and was directed toward the Sukchon area. The 2nd and 3rd Squadrons were in the strike group, with the 3rd Squadron 500 meters above and to the right of the 2nd Squadron, and following 500-700 meters behind it. The 1st Squadron, stepped up in altitude, followed 1,000 meters behind the strike group and 700-800 meters above it. Flying at an altitude of 7,500-8,000 meters, at 1142 in the area of Chongju Major Pulov spotted a flight of four F-84s to the front and left of his group, about 1,000 meters below it, swinging toward the MiGs in a wide starboard turn. The Thunderjets were in an formation echeloned to the right, with about 50-75 meters between each fighter-bomber. Having assessed the situation, Major Pulov decided to attack the Thunderjet flight with his group, which he transmitted over the radio, and then led his eight-ship formation to close with the enemy aircraft. The group approached in a descending starboard turn on an intercepting course. The enemy, seeing that he was being attacked, broke toward the attackers in tightly climbing left-hand spiral. Major Pulov pulled out of the attacking pass in a climbing turn to starboard. He hadn't fired, because he couldn't fix his sights on one of the Thunderjets – this was difficult to do due to the rapid rate of closure and the Thunderjets' tight turn, and the attack failed. Then Major Pulov ordered Captain M.S. Ponomarev's flight to attack, while he himself began to cover it.

Captain Ponomarev went on the attack with his flight against the F-84s, which were still in their climbing spiral, approached to within 300-400 meters behind the third Thunderjet in this flight, and fired a long burst. Shell bursts walked along the entire length of the Thunderjet's fuselage. Pulling out of the attack in a climbing turn to the right, Captain Ponomarev saw another F-84 that was firing at him. Ponomarev evaded the attack with a snap roll. Swinging around to the right, Ponomarev spotted a pair of Thunderjets 1,000 meters below him and to the right, heading in the direction of Simbi-do Island on a parallel course. Captain Ponomarev went into a pursuit curve, and closing to within a range of 450 meters above and behind them, fired one moderate-length burst, as a result of which his target burst into flames.

Captain M.N. Shcherbakov's group of eight MiGs ran into another group of F-84s north of Taechon at an altitude of 7,000 meters, flying 200 to 300 meters below them on a meeting course in a formation of flights staggered in altitude. Just 500-600 meters away, the enemy, having seen our fighters, passed underneath them in a diving turn to the right. Simultaneously, a flight of four F-86s attempted to attack Captain V.A. Blagov's trailing element from behind. Captain Blagov came out from under the Sabre attack in a climbing turn to the left, after which the Sabres flipped over and dove away to the south.

Senior Lieutenant N.G. Dokashenko's flight, located to the right of Captain Shcherbakov's flight, took over the lead of the group and in a descending turn to the right began to emerge on the tail of the F-84 flight. Shcherbakov's flight remained high to cover the attack of Dokashenko's flight. The Thunderjet pilots, noticing the MiGs closing in behind them, went into a starboard spiral. As Dokashenko closed on one of the "Crosses", the F-84 pilots tightened their turn to increase the angle of Dokashenko's attack. Dokashenko came out of his starboard turn without firing and climbed to make another attacking pass. He made three passes on this F-84 flight but was unable to catch one of the Thunderjets in his sights, so he never fired his cannons. Then, running low on fuel, he exited the combat and headed back to base. Senior Lieutenant N.S. Volkov's element attempted to obtain an advantageous position for an attack with a descending turn to port. The Thunderjets abruptly turned into this attack. Volkov rolled to the left and then moved to close on the F-84s from the rear. Having narrowed the range to 500-600 meters, he fired a long burst, after which the Thunderjets rolled onto their backs and departed underneath Volkov's element. Volkov pulled out of the attack in climbing turn to the left and observed one F-84 crashing into a knoll on the far side of Simbi-do Island.

Captain Artemchenko's squadron of eight MiGs was covering the actions of the attack group and intercepted six F-86s in combat, which were trying to attack our aircraft from above. The Sabre pilots refused combat and headed to the south in a dive.

A group of MiGs from the 523rd IAP took off to reinforce the battle. However, it encountered no enemy and soon returned to base.

The aerial action lasted for 7-10 minutes. According to the pilots who participated in the dogfight, three enemy aircraft were downed, two by Captain Ponomarev and one by Senior Lieutenant Volkov. The gun camera footage confirmed the pilots' testimony. All of our MiGs returned to base.

That afternoon, the entire 303rd IAD under the command of the new division commander Hero of the Soviet Union Lieutenant Colonel A.S. Kumanichkin took off to repel an enemy fighter-bomber raid against targets in MiG Alley. The first to lift off from the runway to intercept enemy aircraft was 10 MiGs of the 523rd IAP, which at 1525 encountered a group of F-80s in the Sunchon area. Captain G.U. Okhai attacked one flight of four "Shoots", and in his initial high-speed diving pass he downed one F-80, while Senior Lieutenant I.K. Semenenko shot down another. He had also launched a high-side attack and from short range hit the Shooting Star's fuselage between the wings; the fighter-bomber broke apart in mid-air from the salvo of all three cannons. The remaining F-80s immediately fled from the area.

At 1626, radar detected a group of up to 24 enemy aircraft inbound on a course of 360° at an altitude of 6,000-7,000 meters in the Sonchon area. At 1635, at a decision by the commander of the 303rd IAD, 26 MiGs of the 17th IAP were scrambled into the air. The 1st Squadron was trailing 1,000 meters behind and 500-600 meters above the lead 2nd Squadron. The 3rd Squadron was staggered 500-600 meters off to one side of the 1st Squadron, 500 meters above it and 1,000 meters behind. Having climbed to 4,000 meters, at an order from the division command post the group was directed to the Sukchon area at an altitude of 6,000-8,000 meters. On the approach to Sukchon, fresh information arrived from Auxiliary Command Post No. 2: "Eight enemy aircraft are in the area of Sunchon." In the area 15 kilometers southeast of Sunchon, Guards Lieutenant Colonel A.S. Kumanichkin's group spotted eight F-84s at an altitude of 5,000 meters, flying in a column of elements on a heading of 170°. Kumanichkin issued the command: "I'm attacking the enemy. Captain Shcherbakov's 3rd Squadron and Captain Artemchenko's 1st Squadron are to cover the combat." Then having reversed direction to the left, he went after the enemy aircraft in a shallow dive. Kumanichkin pulled to within 200-300 meters of the second element of F-84s and fired a long burst, as a result of which his target erupted in flames and traced a fiery arc toward the ground. The entire regiment saw the burning Thunderjet.

Captain M.S. Ponomarev's flight attacked the tail-end pair of F-84s. Having closed to within 250 meters, Ponomarev and his wingman Lieutenant A.T. Bozhko opened fire and each gave his chosen target more than a quick burst. The Thunderjet attacked by Ponomarev exploded in mid-air. After pulling out of his attacking pass, Captain Ponomarev noticed that his wingman Lieutenant Bozhko was missing. He called for him three times over the radio, but received no response. Other pilots back on the ground testified that they'd seen someone in the combat area descending in a parachute. CPV anti-aircraft artillery was also actively firing in this area. Lieutenant Bozhko had been covering Captain Ponomarev during his attacking pass, and at the moment of pulling out his attack in a climbing turn he heard Captain Ponomarev's query, but he had no time to answer, because at that instant there was a large explosion in his aircraft. Lieutenant Bozhko ejected from his MiG. From the location where he had ejected, it was determined that Lieutenant Bozhko had presumably been shot down by Chinese anti-aircraft fire.

Captain Shcherbakov's squadron and Captain Artemchenko's squadrons had been covering the combat by Lieutenant Colonel Kumanichkin's group, and in essence took no active part in the battle. The action lasted for 10-12 minutes. As a result of it, two F-84s were downed and one Thunderjet was damaged. The destruction of the F-84s was confirmed by the gun camera footage.

Having lost two Thunderjets in a matter of minutes, the other fighter-bombers immediately aborted their combat mission and headed for the sea. Other than Lieutenant Bozhko's MiG, we had no other losses on this sortie. As a result, over the day seven enemy fighter-bombers were destroyed in combat by pilots of the 64th IAK (five F-84s and two F-80s), against the loss of just one MiG.

The American command again conceals the losses among its strike aircraft, asserting that the F-84s from the 136th FBG that took part in the second mission had no losses on this day. However, one F2H Banshee from VF-172 was lost on this day, and considering that the combat took place in the area of Simbi-do Island and that the enemy aircraft arrived over the target from the direction of the sea, it is possible to conjecture that our pilots might have confused the US Navy's Banshee with USAF F-84 Thunderjets. Thus it is possible that this Banshee No.124983 was seriously damaged by Captain Ponomarev and crashed into the sea en route back to its carrier. Only the victory of the 523rd IAP's Senior Lieutenant Semenenko is confirmed by the American side: at 1528, F-80 No.49-582 from the 8th FBG's 35th Squadron was lost, and its pilot 1st Lieutenant Sterling J. Bushroe was killed when his Shooting Star exploded, though American records still list him as missing-in-action.

The next day was just as intense, since the enemy undertook another major attack with the strength of three fighter-bomber groups. The 64th IAK's two divisions were both scrambled, and were led personally into the air by corps commander General Lobov. Altogether, 80 MiGs from all five regiments of the corps took to the sky against 150 enemy aircraft. The encounter with the enemy and the subsequent battle took place between 1600 and 1700 in the Sukchon-Sunchon area.

Pilots of the 324th IAD attacked the F-80 fighter-bomber groups. The pilots of its 176th GIAP and 196th IAP descended to low altitudes, and breaking down into elements and flights, went after the four- and eight-ship fighter-bomber formations. Captain I.A. Suchkov's six-ship squadron from the 176th GIAP at 1620 encountered a group of 32

F-80s that was being escorted by eight Meteors in the Sunchon area. Senior Lieutenant N.P. Kravtsov's element stealthily approached one four-ship flight of Shooting Stars, and Kravtsov downed one of them from close range, while the other F-80s scattered in every direction. At this moment Captain Suchkov attacked a different pair of F-80s, and Suchkov managed to shoot down both of the "Shoots" – first the wingman's, and then the leader's.

At this time, Captain S.M. Kramarenko's flight arrived on the scene. Sighting a four-ship flight of F-80s, Captain Kramarenko and his wingman Senior Lieutenant A.P. Gogolev each downed one Shooting Star.

The pilots of the 196th IAP also distinguished themselves in this battle by shooting down another four fighter-bombers in this same area. Captains N.K. Shelemonov, Captain L.N. Ivanov and Senior Lieutenant A.D. Ryzhkov added three F-80s to the regiment's victory total, while Captain B.V. Bokach claimed one F-84.

At 1650, the regimental group from the 523rd IAP, which was being led by corps commander Major General G.A. Lobov himself, made contact with a mixed group of 30 F-80s and F-84s. In the course of the combat with this group, General Lobov downed one Shooting Star, while Senior Lieutenant M.A. Zykov fatally damaged a Thunderjet. Having chased away this fighter-bomber group, our group returned to base without any losses.

On this day, Soviet records indicate a total of 11 F-80 and F-84 fighter-bombers were downed, without any losses on the Soviet side. The 324th IAD had three MiGs damaged during the day, with the MiG flown by the deputy commander of the 196th IAP Major A.I. Mitusov receiving the most punishment. However, covered by Captain G.U. Okhai's element from the 523rd IAP, he was able to land his damaged MiG safely on the Andong airfield. Aircraft of the 8th, 49th and 136th FBG took part in this raid. The American command only recognizes the loss of one of its F-84E Thunderjets (No.49-2399) from the 136th FBG, which Captain Bokach of the 196th IAP presumably seriously damaged. The pilot of this Thunderjet managed to reach Cho-do Island, where he abandoned his stricken fighter-bomber and was soon picked up by the US Rescue Service. However, Diego Zampini asserts that the Americans lost at least two more F-84s on this day, No.51-666 and No.51-663 from the 49th FBG's 8th Squadron, and both pilots – Lieutenant Louis R. Miller and 1st Lieutenant Henry D. Wolz were taken prisoner. True, neither of these losses was recorded until several days later. The Americans themselves didn't claim any victories in this battle, other than claims for three damaged MiG-15s put in by pilots of the 136th FBG.

Pilots of the 303rd IAD's 17th IAP and 18th GIAP had sortied as well on 12 September, in order to reinforce the 324th IAD's regiments and to intercept enemy aircraft, but they had no encounters with the enemy. There is one more interesting aspect to this day: there were no encounters with Sabres. Plainly, the Sabre pilots had been carrying a heavy load and thus they'd been given a rest day.

The day of 13 September was a Friday, which the Americans consider an unlucky day, so they preferred not to fly. The enemy's activity sharply fell not only for this reason, but also because of the heavy losses they had suffered over the preceding days of the month. Thus there was only one airstrike on 13 September, but there was no combat. The American pilots immediately fled the targeted area, having received information that MiGs had taken off to intercept them.

Only the pilots of the 176th GIAP were fortunate to encounter enemy aircraft: at 1145 in the vicinity of the Pakchon railroad station, a group of 18 MiGs intercepted a group of eight F-51 Mustangs. Having spotted the MiGs, the Mustang pilots immediately sped toward the sanctuary of Korea Bay, but not all of them managed to reach it. On this sortie only Senior Lieutenant A.A. Plitkin's element was able to score. At low altitude, it attacked a four-ship flight of Mustangs. In the first attacking pass the leader downed one Mustang, while the others fled. Abandoning his leader, Senior Lieutenant A.P. Verdysh went in pursuit of another Mustang and quickly achieved a victory over it, but having returned to base, he received a rebuke from his leader for his lack of discipline. Surprisingly, the Americans acknowledge the loss of two of its Mustangs from the 18th FBG, but assert they were downed by enemy anti-aircraft fire. However, with a great deal of assurance one can declare that F-51D No.44-72427 was downed by Senior Lieutenant Plitkin – its pilot 1st Lieutenant William E. Jackman was killed. Also, Senior Lieutenant Verdysh shot down F-51D No.44-63886; its pilot 1st Lieutenant Leland H. Wolf was also killed.

The next major battle between the Fifth Air Force's fighter-bombers and the MiGs of the 64th IAK didn't take place until 19 September 1951, when several dozen F-84E fighter-bombers of the 49th FBG undertook an airstrike, escorted by Sabres of the 4th FIW; however, this took place in the afternoon, while those irreconcilable adversaries had already met in battle again that morning, when a regimental group of 24 MiGs from the 523rd IAP had tangled with 30 Sabres from the 334th Fighter Squadron. The combat occurred at 1045 in the Taeju area, and the commander of the 1st Squadron Major A.P. Trefilov and Captain I.I. Tiuliaev each claimed a Sabre. However, in reality this time neither side drew blood and all the participants in this dogfight safely returned to their bases. Only one F-86A (No.49-1315) was damaged in this action, but its pilot safely brought it back to Kimpo and the Sabre was quickly repaired. First Lieutenant Otis Gordon also managed to damage one MiG in this morning duel, but its pilot Senior Lieutenant N.G. Kovalenko also made a safe landing back at base. The MiG had five bullet holes in it, but it returned to service that same day.

However, the main event of 19 September occurred that afternoon between 1605 and 1615 in the Sunchon-Sukchon area. Twenty-four MiGs from the 523rd IAP under the command of Lieutenant Colonel A.N. Karasev and 24 MiGs from the 17th IAP under the command of Major B.V. Maslennikov participated in this battle. At 1605, while the regiment was tangling with 60 F-80s and F-84s in the Anju area, Captain I.I. Tiuliaev attacked one F-84 from above and behind, as a result of which the Thunderjet was downed. However, while holding the F-84 in his gunsight, Captain Tiuliaev was suddenly attacked by two other Thunderjets. As bullets ripped into his MiG, it burst into flames and went out of control. Captain Tiuliaev ejected at an altitude of 4,500 meters. The aircraft was destroyed, but the pilot was unharmed.

Lieutenant Colonel Karasev, Captain S.A. Bakhaev and Senior Lieutenant V.E. Silkin all achieved victories over Thunderjets, but Lieutenant Colonel Karasev received credit for three destroyed F-84s in one combat. Captain M.S. Ponomarev of the 17th IAP also downed one F-84.

As a result, in the second battle on the afternoon of 19 September, Soviet pilots claimed seven F-84 kills against the loss of one MiG. The American side again acknowledges the loss of only one of its F-84 Thunderjets, No.51-528 from the 49th FBG, the pilot of which managed to bring his crippled jet out over the bay before taking to the parachute. He was picked up by US Rescue Service. Meanwhile credit for the victory over Captain Tiuliaev's MiG went to Captain Kenneth L. Skeen of the 49th Group's 9th FBS.

On 20 September, F-80 fighter-bombers covered by F-86 Sabres launched fresh attacks against targets in MiG Alley. In order to repel the enemy's morning attack, 40 MiGs of the 303rd IAD were scrambled: 24 MiGs of the 523rd IAP and 16 MiGs of the 17th IAP. At 0845, a radar station in the Pyongyang area detected a group of up to 40 inbound enemy fighters at an altitude of 8,000-9,000 meters, approaching on a course of 330°. At 0849, 16 MiGs of the 17th IAP were scrambled at an order from division command post. Its main task was to tie up the enemy fighters in combat and destroy them, while 24 Migs of the 523rd IAP took on the fighter-bombers. Having taken off, the group assembled due north of Miaogou before heading south. The 523rd IAP's MiGs were flying below and in front of the 17th IAP group. They crossed the Yalu River in an area west of Andong at an altitude of 8,000 meters, before turning in the direction of Anju on a heading of 120°.

While en route, fresh information arrived from the division command post – up to 30 F-86s were over the coast line at altitudes between 6,000 and 9,000 meters. Flying on a heading of 140° at an altitude of 10,000-10,500 meters in a column of squadrons, Major G.I. Pulov sighted eight F-86s in a column of pairs to the right at the same altitude, flying on a parallel heading. Pulov called out, "I'm attacking!" At this moment, the commander of the 3rd Squadron Captain M.N. Shcherbakov, seeing another eight F-86s closing on the lead squadron from behind and below to the right, displayed strange passivity and failed to tie them up in combat.

Having caught sight of the closing Sabres, Captain Ponomarev shouted a warning to Major Pulov, "Break right, they're behind us!" Pulov went into a climbing, tight 180° turn, leaving the Sabres below him, and then dove on the lead element of F-86s. With this sudden maneuver, his wingman Major I.V. Vorob'ev became separated and lost sight of his leader. As Major Pulov closed on his target, a pair of F-86s jumped his MiG from behind. Sighting them, Pulov went into an oblique loop. The eight-ship formation of Sabres pursued him, seeing that this MiG-15 was alone. Pulov threw his MiG into a series of evasive maneuvers and eventually shook off his pursuers, at which point he headed back to base.

During the group's 180° turn to the right, Captain Shcherbakov spotted another eight-ship formation of Sabres closing on his flight from below, behind and to the right. Shcherbakov's flight shook off the Sabres with a climbing spiral to the right. At the top of this climb, Shcherbakov quickly rolled over to the left and dove on the F-86s, which were now heading in the direction of the sea in a scattered group. As he was approaching the mouth of the Yalu, an order came from the division command post: "Exit the combat", so Captain Shcherbakov broke off his pursuit.

Senior Lieutenant Dokashenko, at the moment of Captain Shcherbakov's climbing turn, spotted four F-86s just 500 meters below and to the left, which were in a descending starboard turn. Coming out of this turn, the Sabres banked left and continued to descend. Dokashenko moved to close with the trailing pair of F-86s, which had fallen behind the lead element. Noticing the approaching MiG, the Sabres pulled up into a climbing spiral. The lead Sabre broke sharply to the left, and then turned up and away to the right, passing below Dokashenko's MiG. Our pilot began to pursue him. The

Sabre banked to the left and pulled up into a climbing turn – a mistake given the MiG's superior climbing ability. Dokashenko pursued and having pulled to within 700 meters, opened fire. The tracers of the first short burst passed below and to the left of the Sabre. Dokashenko made a quick adjustment and fired another burst, as a result of which the Sabre staggered and fell.

The aerial combat lasted for 10-12 minutes. The Soviet pilots exited the battle in ones and pairs, which headed to the north at high speed.

Although the given combat with 26 Sabres ended in a victory for the pilots of the 17th IAP, in the course of it the regiment almost lost its commander. His wingman Major Vorob'ev had failed to stick with his leader during the battle and had placed Major Pulov in jeopardy. During Pulov's turn to the left, Vorob'ev had opted to pursue an F-86, losing his leader in the process.

Major Pulov had been left to fight alone against six F-86s, and only thanks to his coolness and skill did he manage to avoid getting shot down, though his MiG did receive one bullet hole in it. In addition, Captain Shcherbakov's actions in the battle had been incorrect: the leader of the cover group, Captain Shcherbakov had apparently abandoned his high covering position and had pulled his group up immediately next to the attack group, thereby allowing eight enemy fighters to close on their tail. The attack of the strike group was disrupted. Our fighters were outnumbered – 16 against 30 F-86s. American records do not acknowledge the loss of an F-86 on this day, while Captain Richard Johns of the 335th Fighter Squadron at the head of his six-ship flight of Sabres had attempted to down Pulov's MiG, but only managed to damage the 17th IAP commander's machine lightly.

In this morning combat, pilots of the 176th GIAP were carrying out the role of the strike group, which was to attack the enemy fighter-bombers. At 0940 in the area of Anju, they encountered a group of 10 F-80s and went for them. In a brief combat Senior Lieutenant N.K. Moroz downed one F-80, while Senior Lieutenant S.A. Rodionov damaged another Shooting Star – the remaining F-80s managed to escape to the bay. However, Moroz received no confirmation from the ground for his victory and thus he received no credit for it.

In order to intercept a second fighter-bomber attack, which came toward the end of the day, two regiments of the 303rd IAD were scrambled. The pilots of the 523rd IAP received the assignment to tie down the covering fighters in combat, while the pilots of the 18th GIAP attacked the fighter-bombers. Here's how a participant in this action Lev Kirillovich Shchukin describes it:

On 20 September 1951, during a regimental sortie to intercept an enemy group, we were directed from the ground toward three groups of fighter-bombers numbering a total of 24 ships. They had high cover from 16 Sabres.

The main thing was to prevent the "Shoots" from working over the [river] crossings, and this task had been given to our squadron, the lead squadron of the regimental group being led by Lieutenant Colonel A.P. Smorchkov. Our squadron commander Captain A.F. Maznev led us into a dive toward the enemy with the aim of penetrating its combat formation at high speed and scattering it, and to force them to jettison their bombs aimlessly. This we managed to do. True, at first the F-80 group leaders flew calmly, relying on good cover from the escorting Sabres.

But when they spotted us, we were already close, and one of our guys was already firing (we could see the tracers); they began to maneuver, which led to the break-up of their formation and loss of group cohesion.

With the flight consisting of me as the leader, my wingman Senior Lieutenant A.A. Astapovsky, and the second element led by Senior Lieutenant A.A. Svitinsky with his wingman Senior Lieutenant I.V. Mart'ianov, taking advantage of the enemy's confusion, we downed one "Shoot" in the very first pass – this was my kill.

The deputy commander of the 18th GIAP Lieutenant Colonel A.P. Smorchkov downed two more F-80s in this combat. Pilots of the 523rd IAP in the course of their clash with the covering 16 F-86s in the Sonchon area between 1600 and 1640 didn't claim any victories, but they successfully carried out their task of tying up the enemy fighters.

This time it is known reliably that the pilots of the 18th GIAP shot down at least two Shooting Stars. According to research by Diego Zampini, in this action Captain Shchukin downed F-80 No.49-862 from the 51st FIG's 25th Squadron, and its pilot 2nd Lieutenant Lewis P. Pleiss was killed. The second destroyed F-80C (No.49-768) was from the 8th FBG's 36th Squadron, and its pilot 1st Lieutenant William A. Pugh was also killed. To be sure, as usual the American command registered these two losses two days later and attributed them both to ground fire, but the time and location of both F-80 Shooting Stars' destruction coincide with the area where pilots of the 18th GIAP fought on 20 September.

Due to poor weather over North Korea that grounded the aircraft, there were no further large aerial combats in MiG Alley until 25 September 1951, save for one clash between several groups of MiGs and Sabres on the afternoon of 22 September between 1500 and 1540. Ten MiGs of the 523rd IAP's 1st Squadron tangled with 16 F-86s, and Captain D.V. Mazilov downed one Sabre, which crashed into a hill 15 kilometers south-west of Taegwan-dong. Meanwhile, 16 MiGs of the 17th IAP dueled with a different group of F-86s, and pilots of the 176th GIAP with still another group of Sabres. Captain M.S. Kramarenko claimed to have downed one of them. All of our aircraft returned safely to base from these dogfights. The American command recognizes only damage to its F-86A No.49-1158 in this battle, which successfully made it back to its base, where it was quickly repaired.

However, on 25 September 1951 the American Fifth Air Force command again decided to give combat to the pilots of the 64th IAK. Once again, pilots of the 4th FIW locked horns with a consolidated group of the IAK's two divisions. The sky became filled with the howl of engines and the rumble of cannons and chatter of machine guns, while a multitude of white contrails crisscrossed the azure sky, as if a giant artist was painting an abstract picture. To be sure, sometimes long black plumes from burning, falling aircraft overlaid the lovely white tangles of contrails, as warriors of this remote place of combat were making their final return to earth.

In comparison with the preceding combats in the latter half of September, this one was particularly hard-fought. Elements and flights that were running low on fuel were leaving the on-going dogfight, but the numbers involved in it didn't diminish, as fresh units would arrive on the scene. The Chinese pilots of the 4th IAD also took part in this melee and fought to their utmost against the Sabres throughout the battle. In all honesty, however, they still lacked the combat experience and necessary skill to take on the Sabres. The American pilots were better trained professionally and had enormous combat experience with MiGs, as well as many hours of flight time in jet fighters. The Chinese pilots displayed an additional shortcoming – upon sighting the enemy, they completely threw vigilance and caution to the wind. Catching sight of an enemy aircraft, they would immediately abandon their formation or their leader and attack the enemy without a second glance around, so they often were caught unawares by Sabre elements and sometimes suffered heavy losses. Plainly, the 25 September 1951 fight proved to be not very successful for the Chinese pilots, since the pilots of the 4th FIW later claimed five victories over MiGs in the battle. Since the pilots of the 64th IAK had no losses on this day, then most likely these downed MiGs were from the UAA.

This major battle took place on the afternoon of 25 September, between 1520 and 1600 in the Anju area. The pilots of the 303rd IAD were the first to sortie: At 1502, 22 MiGs of the 17th IAP under the command of Major B.V. Maslennikov took off to intercept enemy aircraft. Flying in a staggered trail formation at an altitude of 10,000 meters, they reached the Anju area, and were then directed toward Pakchon, where they ran into a group of 18 Sabres at an altitude of 9,000-10,000 meters. In the ensuing scrap, Major Maslennikov downed one F-86. After exiting this combat and en route back to base, they encountered another group of 10 Sabres at 9,000 meters in the Sakchu area. This combat lasted for 6-7 minutes and ended without results.

Ten MiGs from the 176th GIAP's 3rd Squadron came to support the 17th IAP's withdrawal from combat, and they sparred with the same group of 10 Sabres with which the 17th IAP's pilots had been fighting. These Sabres had been pursuing a group of Chinese MiGs, which were also operating in the given area. The 17th IAP's pilots had come to the assistance of the UAA's pilots and had in turn attacked the Sabres. Captain A.F. Vas'ko's element attacked a three-ship formation of Sabres, and Vas'ko managed to down one of them, which crashed in the Pakchon area.

Our pilots had aided the pilots of the PLAAF 4th IAD's 12th IAP, which had put 16 MiGs into the air under the command of Ling Wenmo. They had encountered a group of 30 F-80s, which was being escorted by 20 F-86s. A six-ship formation of MiGs led by Li Yongtai attacked the Shooting Stars, while the remaining MiGs engaged the F-86s. However, both experience and numbers were on the American side, and Li Yongtai's group itself was attacked by a squadron of Sabres, which damaged the leader's aircraft after putting 30 bullet holes into it, and downed one of Li Yongtai's subordinates. That's when the pilots of the 176th GIAP had hurried up and salvaged the situation, allowing the 12th IAP's pilots to withdraw from the battle.

At 1540, an encounter took place in the area of Taechon between pilots of the 523rd IAP and a different group of Sabres. The combat was brief and ended in a victory for our pilots: Captain S.A. Bakhaev, leading his flight in a combat against four Sabres, at a range of 400 meters in a head-on pass managed to hit his target with several 37mm shells in a vital area, and the Sabre simply exploded in mid-air. Fragments of it fell 30-40 kilometers south of Taechon. Captain G.U. Okhai's MiG was lightly damaged (one bullet hole).

In sum all five regiments of the 303rd and 324th IAD took part in this battle; rotating into and out of the battle, they continually increased their presence in the given area. In the dogfights with the pilots of the 4th FIW, the 64th IAK's pilots downed four

F-86s without any losses in return. Again, however, American records do not reflect this outcome: they indicate that only one of their F-86As flown by 1st Lieutenant Charles Lloyd of the 334th Fighter Squadron was damaged by Captain Vas'ko's cannon fire, but Lloyd managed to bring his damaged Sabre back to Kimpo and land it there. His Sabre was quickly repaired. It would only be interesting to know who flew the planes that crashed in the Taechon and Pakchon areas, from which only fragments were recovered.

Two more major clashes took place in the Anju area and in MiG Alley before the end of September 1951. On 26 September, the 64th IAK's pilots conducted two sorties, both of which resulted in combat – they were attempting to repulse a major attack by a large group of Thunderjets, which were covered by large formations of Sabres.

Early that morning, the American command launched a major attack against the railroads in the Sunchon-Anju area. Pilots of the 324th IAD were scrambled to meet the incoming raids. At 0925 they encountered 40 F-80s in formations of 6-12 fighter-bombers each over the target area.

K.Ia. Shcherbakov's element attacked six F-80s, and in his first attacking pass Shcherbakov targeted the wingman of the trailing element on the left. The F-80 broke left and went into a steep dive. Shcherbakov's wingman Senior Lieutenant B.G. Reitarovsky fired at the leader of this F-80 element, but didn't see any results of his fire. Captain A.F. Vas'ko's element attacked an F-80 flight in a head-on pass. Vas'ko fired at the flight leader but didn't observe the result. Captain S.M. Kramarenko's element attacked the lead flight of eight F-80s. Senior Lieutenant A.P. Gogolev fired at the wingman's aircraft of one element that was flanking the lead element, as a result of which he observed hits on the F-80, which began to shed altitude as it headed toward the sea.

At 0842 at the decision of the 303rd IAD's commanding officer, 26 MiGs of the 17th IAP under the command of Major G.I. Pulov took off. Its task was to cover the actions of the 523rd IAP, 24 MiGs of which under the command of Lieutenant Colonel A.N. Karasev took off at 0846 in the wake of the 17th IAP.

Over the Andong-Gisiu area, Major Pulov's group took its covering position above the 523rd IAP. In the Uiju area, the group received an order from the division command post to head in the direction of Anju at an altitude of 8,000 meters. The 17th IAP in its role as top cover for the division's combat formation took a heading of 140°.

As the eight MiGs of the 2nd Squadron under the command of Captain Ponomarev approached Anju from the north, during a starboard turn Lieutenant Kordanov spotted eight F-86s angling toward them from the right and below, which were trying to attack the covering group. Captain Ponomarev avoided the attack with a climbing turn to the right, which put them in a favorable position to attack the F-86s from the rear as they passed below. The F-86s, seeing their unfavorable position, rolled over and dove away in the direction of the sea.

Having arrived in the Anju area, the 1st Squadron, numbering 10 MiGs under the command of Major Pulov, flying in the 17th IAP's attack group, having the task to provide direct cover to the 523rd IAP, began to swing around to the right, covered by the 3rd Squadron. When entering the turn, Captain Artemchenko's flight, which was flying above Major Pulov's flight, noticed a group of eight F-86s above and to the left of them, which were dropping onto the tail of Major Pulov's flight. Artemchenko fired a burst in front of the right-hand flight of four Sabres. The Sabres broke sharply to the right. Artemchenko's flight went into a pursuit curve and tied them up in a combat, in which Captain Artemchenko from a range of 550 meters downed one F-86. As the lead element of Artemchenko's flight was banking right over Anju, Senior Lieutenant Shulev moved to separate from approaching F-86s with a climbing spiral, but seeing that he was being followed and the Sabres were firing at him, he went into a spin, from which he pulled out at 6,000 meters. Accelerating, with a climbing turn he escaped in the direction of the sun.

Major Pulov's six-ship formation, continuing to cover the pilots of the 523rd IAP and reaching the mouth of the Sonchon-po River, spotted 10-12 enemy Gloster Meteors at an altitude of 6,000-7,000 meters, flying in widely-spaced elements. Pulov gave the command, "We're attacking the enemy." With a starboard turn toward the enemy aircraft, Pulov's flight moved to close with the enemy in separate elements; Pulov and his wingman Senior Lieutenant Miroshnichenko bore down on the leading Meteor element.

The adversary, having spotted the rapidly-closing MiGs, timed their break and departed underneath Pulov's element with an energetic maneuver in the direction of the sea. Meanwhile, Senior Lieutenant Sutiagin, attacking a different element, closed to within 250-300 meters behind the Meteors and fired a long burst, as a result of which his target plummeted into the sea.

The Meteors had dragged the combat in the direction of the sea and had reached its sanctuary, making additional attacks impossible. Major Pulov issued the order, "Do not cross the coast line", and then he himself went into a climbing turn in the direction of Anju. Arriving over the town, he spotted a pair of MiG-15s locked in combat with four F-86s to the right and behind him at 1,000-1,500 meters. Rolling to his right and diving, he moved to come to the aid of the outnumbered Soviet pilots. It was Senior Lieutenant Sutiagin's element that was dueling with the Sabres. Sutiagin, getting behind one of the Sabres, closed to within 200-300 meters of it and fired a long burst, as a result of which the burning Sabre fell in an area southwest of Anju. The remaining Sabres departed in a dive toward the sea.

The eight MiGs of the 17th IAP's 3rd Squadron under the command of Captain Shcherbakov, flying in the regiment's strike group while simultaneously covering the actions of the 1st Squadron, spotted a group of eight F-86s diving toward them from the left and above. At an order from Major Pulov, Captain Shcherbakov with his eight-ship formation turned into the Sabres' attack and closed with them in a head-on pass. At the rapidly closing range of 800 meters down to 600 meters, using the mobile reticule of his sight he fired two short bursts at the leader of one four-ship Sabre flight. At the same time Senior Lieutenant Volkov opened fire, giving one burst from the range of 200 meters. After flashing past the Sabres Captain Sherbakov led his squadron into a steeply climbing turn to starboard in order to take up a position for launching a subsequent attack. The Sabre formation began to scatter into separate elements and solitary fighters. Captain Shcherbakov began to pursue the enemy with his group. One F-86, streaming white smoke, was descending in the direction of the sea. At 0915 the order arrived from the division command post: "Withdraw from combat and return to base." This combat lasted 8-10 minutes.

Meanwhile, the pilots of the 523rd IAP were locked in a tense battle with a group of 20 F-86s and six Meteors. In the course of this battle, the regiment's pilots downed two enemy aircraft and damaged one more: Senior Lieutenant I.I. Iakovlev downed one Meteor, which fell into the sea, while Captain S.A. Bakhaev sent a Sabre plunging into the sea just off the coast from Sunchon. On our side, regiment commander Lieutenant Colonel Karasev's MiG was damaged, receiving three bullet holes, but he safely returned to base in it.

In this complex morning battle, pilots of the 18th GIAP also took part; Captain M.B. Solov'ev managed to down one F-86. We had no losses.

The 17th IAP pilot Senior Lieutenant Sutiagin particularly stood out by seemingly downing two aircraft in this battle. However, as became known many years later, Sutiagin didn't actually shoot down the first of his opponents in the form of Meteor No.77-949 – he only seriously damaged Flight Sergeant Ernest Armit's ship, but the pilot managed to fly it back to his base and land his damaged Meteor there. After a period of repairs it returned to service. Yet the second adversary of our ace was not as fortunate as Sergeant Armit: the shells from Sutiagin's MiG struck the cockpit of F-86A No.49-1113, killing 1st Lieutenant Carl G. Barnett of the 336th FIS.

In the afternoon the Fifth Air Force's fighter-bombers launched a second attack against targets in the Anju area. At 1408, at first 24 MiGs of the 17th IAP were scrambled at the decision of the commander of the 303rd IAD, and then 24 MiGs of the 523rd IAP took off as well. Northeast of Andong, the Soviet group leaders received an order from the division command post: "Head to the area of Taechon and destroy enemy aircraft." Approaching Taechon, additional information came from the division command post: "Enemy fighters are at an altitude of 4,000-5,000 meters." Having received this information, Major Pulov began to descend together with the 1st and 3rd Squadrons, but ordered the commander of the 2nd Squadron to remain at an altitude of 8,000 meters. Around 7 kilometers east of Taechon Senior Lieutenant Sutiagin spotted eight F-86s below and to the right in front of them, flying northward in a column of flights. Maintaining their present course, over the town of Kaisen the group swung around to the right. Reaching the area over the mouth of the Sonchon-po River, Pulov sighted eight F-84s to the right and 300-400 meters below them, moving to intercept them in a formation of flights echeloned to the left. The Soviet group, rearranging into a column of elements, turned to meet the F-84s. The Thunderjets went into a climbing spiral to the left. Our pilots immediately moved into repeated attacks from the rear at an angle of 30-40° with a subsequent climbing turn to starboard. The pilots of the "Crosses" reacted with counter maneuvers, turning into each attack and exiting below the attacking pairs, thereby preventing the possibility of using aimed fire from a tailing position. Sutiagin and his wingman Perepelkin conducted one attack on a head-on course, firing short bursts as the range closed from 300 to 250 meters. The F-84 group dragged the combat toward the sea. Our groups pursued the enemy.

Captain Shcherbakov, flying 500-700 meters above the 1st Squadron, spotted an approaching group of up to 10 F-84s to the front and left of him, which were banked in a left-hand turn. The pilot who had spotted the F-84s, Senior Lieutenant Dokashenko, having reported to Major Pulov about the enemy, moved to close with this group of Thunderjets. The F-84 flight sharply tightened its turn to port and reversed course to meet Dokashenko's attack head-on. Subsequent attacks were met in the same fashion.

Senior Lieutenant Volkov, continuing the pursuit, closed with the lead F-84 and fired one burst before pulling out of the attack in a climbing turn to port and returning to base. Senior Lieutenant Dokashenko's element, chasing three F-84s, was attacked from behind by a pair of Thunderjets. Spotting them, Dokashenko broke off his attack. Captain Shcherbakov covered the actions of Senior Lieutenant Dokashenko's flight.

The covering 2nd Squadron was in the Sonchon area, where Captain Ponomarev was met by six F-86s, angling toward him from the front and left. Our pilots turned to meet them, but the Sabres flipped over and dove in the direction of the sea. Although the 17th IAP pilots (Sutiagin and Shulev) only managed to damage two F-84s, our attacks forced the enemy to halt their raid and leave the target area.

Simultaneously with the 17th IAP, pilots of the 523rd IAP were also tangling with a large group of Thunderjets in the same area. The 24 MiGs of the regiment had taken off to repel enemy fighter-bombers that were operating in the Anju-Sunchon area. Flying in a staggered trail formation of squadrons at an altitude of 7,000-8,000 meters above Anju, the regiment commander Lieutenant Colonel Karasev spotted a large group of fighter-bombers at an altitude of 4,000-6,000 meters, which was operating against ground targets in the area. Having checked the airspace around them and seeing no enemy fighters above 6,000 meters, Karasev committed all three squadrons of the regiment against the fighter-bombers. Thanks to his correct assessment of the combat situation, all three squadrons were employed against the fighter-bombers. Three F-84s were downed in the area of the Sinanju River – one each going to the score of Lieutenant Colonel A.N. Karasev and Captain V.P. Popov, but Senior Lieutenant P.Z. Churkin's victory received no confirmation.

Pilots of the 196th IAP also participated in this battle, and Captain N.A. Antipov managed to bring down another Thunderjet. As a result, over the day the pilots of the 64th IAK shot down nine enemy aircraft: four F-86s, three F-84s and two Meteors. We had no losses. The American side as already noted above acknowledged the loss of only one of its F-86s and one F-84E (No.50-1152) from the 136th FBG's 154th Squadron – its pilot Lieutenant Paul E. Ross bailed out and was picked up by a rescue helicopter. Presumably the commander of the 523rd IAP Lieutenant Colonel Karasev was the victor over Lieutenant Ross.

The picture repeated itself on the following day. Again there was an attack by Thunderjets in the Anju area and again both of the 64th IAK's divisions were committed to repel the raid. Only this time pilots of the 303rd IAD comprised the strike group and they attacked the enemy fighter-bombers. The F-84 pilots, left without the protection of Sabres, once again could not carry out their combat mission and departed in the direction of the sea. This time they lost six aircraft, four of which were destroyed by pilots of the 18th GIAP. Senior Lieutenant F.M. Malashov's element destroyed one "Cross" – in the turmoil of battle he spotted one four-ship formation of Thunderjets below him and dove upon them, shooting down one while the remaining F-84s rolled over and dove away.

In this morning battle, the commander of the 17th IAP Major G.I. Pulov distinguished himself. At 0908 over the mouth of the Chongchon-gang River, his group reversed course with a starboard turn. Coming out of the turn, Major Pulov sighted 10 F-84s in a column of flights at an altitude of 4,000 meters, which were approaching from below and to the right. Major Pulov issued an order to Captain Shcherbakov and Captain Ponomarev to cover the action, while he took his squadron into a starboard turn to close with the F-84s. With an energetic maneuver, the first flight of Thunderjets slid into position behind Captain Artemchenko's element and opened fire on it. Artemchenko escaped out from under the attack in a climbing starboard turn. Major Pulov swung in behind the attacking F-84 flight with a starboard turn and began to close upon the tail-end Thunderjet. Having drawn within 500 meters, he gave the "Cross" a long burst of cannon fire, as a result of which the target erupted in flames. As he was pulling out of his attack in a climbing turn to port, a pair of Thunderjets started closing on him from behind. His wingman Senior Lieutenant Miroshnichenko spotted the threat and forced them to break off their attack.

Pilots of the 324th IAD downed three US aircraft in this clash, two of which were Sabres claimed by Captain B.S. Abakumov of the 196th IAP. Again, the airstrike was repelled with heavy losses for the enemy, while our pilots returned to base without any losses. The Americans confirmed only the victory of Captain K.Ia. Sheberstov of the 176th GIAP, who downed a solitary F-80C (No.49-752) after killing the pilot 2nd Lieutenant Wilbert W. Grammer of the 51st FIW's 16th Fighter Squadron in his cockpit. Again, though, American records attribute this loss to anti-aircraft fire. In this action, an eight-ship group of MiGs under Sheberstov's command had encountered a group of 40 Shooting Stars at an altitude of 2,000 meters in the Anju area and prevented it from delivering accurate dive bombing attacks against targets, forcing them to withdraw to the sea.

In addition, 1st Lieutenant Kenneth Rapp's F-86A from the 336th Fighter Squadron was seriously damaged, though the pilot managed to nurse it back to Kimpo and landed it there. The Sabre was subsequently repaired and returned to service. Captain B.S. Abakumov of the 196th IAP was the pilot that damaged this Sabre. The American side doesn't confirm other losses on this day.

Thus the September battles in the skies of North Korea ended. The results were polar opposites. According to staff documents of the 64th IAK, pilots of the two Soviet fighter aviation divisions downed 92 enemy aircraft, losing in return only five MiGs and two pilots. This was the highest results in this war since the Soviet pilots began participation in it. The pilots of the 64th IAK destroyed in this month 47 fighter-bombers alone (28 F-84s, 17 F-80s and two F-51s). In addition, they claimed the destruction of 45 fighters, of which six were Meteors and the rest F-86 Sabres.

According to American records, over the month of September 1951 the MiG-15s had appeared on 1,177 of the sorties conducted by the Fifth Air Force in MiG Alley and conducted 911 aerial combats, in which 15 MiGs were downed (F-86s alone flew 1,119 combat sorties and downed 13 MiGs as a result of them). The Americans put their own losses in these combats as just six aircraft: three F-86s (plus three more lost due to other reasons), one F-84, one F-80 and one F-51 – these are losses in combats with MiGs that are acknowledged by the American side. According to research by Diego Zampini, in the month of September the USAF lost 20 aircraft in combats with MiGs; in addition, the Australian No. 77 Squadron lost one Meteor in combat with MiGs and had another seriously damaged. Also, the numbers for the USAF's and USNAF's damaged aircraft are incomplete. In the month of September alone, seven Sabres of the 4th FIW received varying degrees of damage from MiG fire, so wouldn't it be interesting to know the number of damaged aircraft among the fighter-bombers and bombers?

Obviously, the records on victories and losses starkly differ between the two sides; if you assume that the Soviet records inflated the number of kills twice over, then all the same 40 American aircraft remained as wreckage on the ground of North Korea from the fire of Soviet pilots alone, while more were damaged. But these are only the results of the actions of the Soviet pilots of the 64th IAK; the Chinese 3rd and 4th IAD from the UAA also fought in the skies of Korea in this period, and their pilots achieved up to 20 more victories over the Americans. Thus, the American data on their losses in aerial combat in the month of September 1951, putting it gently, appear to be greatly under-stated, which raises doubts in their veracity.

In September, the turnover rate among the pilots of the 64th IAK grew to threat-ening dimensions; many pilots were dropped from the active duty roster due to illnesses and wounds. A portion of the flight staff over the five months of fighting had accumu-lated a large amount of fatigue from the daily combats in the stratosphere with high speeds and high G-load maneuvers. After all, unlike the American pilots, the Soviet pilots had no pressurized flight suits, and the high G-forces that our pilots endured on each mission eventually resulted in injuries such as burst blood vessels in the eyes, ruptured ear drums, etc.

Because of the attrition of pilots, the squadrons were no longer flying in eight-ship formations, but in six-ship formations or as just a flight. In order to alleviate the given problem, in September 1951 10 pilots arrived in the 303rd IAD as replacements from the 151st GIAD, which was stationed in Anshan. A little later, at the beginning of October, another 16 pilots, who had recently arrived from the Baku Army PVO, were sent to the 303rd IAD from the 64th IAK reserve. At the beginning of October, the 324th IAD also received a batch of more than 20 replacement pilots from the 309th IAD, which was stationed in Gunshulin. This means that in October 1951, one-third of the pilot roster of these two first-echelon divisions had to be replaced.

On one hand, the arrival of the replacements strengthened the divisions, but on the other hand, it weakened them, because experienced pilots with combat experience in this war had departed, while 90% of the replacements were young pilots with only 60-70 hours of flight time in the MiG-15 and without combat experience. They had to be introduced gradually into action, so they would not be lost in their first days of combat.

ENDNOTES

1 The Military Aviation Incidents Report's website (www.Accident-Report.com) records that F-86A No.49-1266 was actually lost in an accident on 29 August 1951 in Takahagi, Japan. Unfortunately, there are several such inconsistencies in the Korean War records which have yet to be ironed out.

2 Interestingly, in the autumn of 1951 the 4th FIW was also experiencing difficulty with putting Sabres into the air. The AOCP (Aircraft Out of Commission for Parts) rate was very high due to an acute shortage of spare parts and drop tanks. As Larry Davis notes, it "wasn't unusual for the in-commission rate to fall below 50% of authorized strength." The situation became so dire that it caused the 4th FIW commander at the time, Colonel Harrison Thyng to go over the heads of the Fifth Air Force commander and FEAF commander to appeal to General Hoyt S. Vandenberg, the USAF Chief of Staff, for assistance in a personal message, the first line of which read, "I CAN NO LONGER BE REPONSIBLE FOR AIR SUPERIORITY IN NORTHWEST KOREA," before going on to detail the AOCP problems. See Larry Davis, *The 4th Fighter Wing in the Korean War* (Atglen, PA: Schiffer Publishing Ltd., 2001), pp. 106-107.

4

Black October – the Superfortresses recede into the shadows

October 1951 began with fierce aerial clashes in the areas of Sukchon, Sunchon and Anju. Already on 1 October, pilots of the 303rd IAD tangled with Sabres of the 4th FIW in the Sukchon area. On this day, the enemy launched one raid in the morning with his fighter-bombers to the Anju area around 0900-0930. General Lobov scrambled all three regiments of the 303rd IAD to repel the fighter-bombers. Pilots of the 523rd IAP, which took off a bit before the other regiments, made contact with a group of 16 F-86s of the forward screen in the Sukchon area. The pilots of the 523rd IAP engaged them in a dogfight that ended in losses on both sides. Senior Lieutenant D.A. Samoilov in an area approximately 15 kilometers northwest of Sukchon managed to down one F-86. However, the Regiment lost one of its own aircraft when during the dogfight Captain P.P. Poplavsky became separated from his element leader. While searching for his leader, he was jumped by two Sabres. As a result of this attack his MiG burst into flames and went out of control. The pilot ejected at an altitude of 10,000 meters. He received slight injuries to his hands and the back of his head. In this action, the 523rd IAP was dueling against pilots of the 334th Fighter Squadron, and its 1st Lieutenant Raymond Barton received credit for downing Captain Poplavsky's MiG-15.

Pilots of the 17th IAP succeeded in intercepting a group of Thunderjets from the 136th FBW and forced them to abort their mission. In the process, Captain M.S. Ponomarev shot down one of them and damaged another. As it became known later, in this fight Captain Ponomarev shot down F-84E No.49-2420 of the 111th FBS, and its pilot Captain Herbert E. Ritter was killed. There was also a brief combat with the group of F-86s that was escorting the Thunderjets, and Senior Lieutenant V.F. Shulev claimed a victory over one F-86, but never received official credit for it.

Pilots of the 18th GIAP also sortied to intercept enemy aircraft in the Anju area. However, they failed to encounter the enemy.

The day of 2 October proved to be even more heated, when the enemy again launched a major raid with F-80 and F-84 fighter-bombers. Having taken off from Taegu, the Thunderjets linked up with covering fighters from the 4th FIW, entered the Anju area from the direction of the sea, and began attacking ground targets. Forces of the 303rd IAD were scrambled to intercept them; in the period between 0840 and 0900, approximately 70 MiGs from all three regiments of the division were launched. Following the common practice, pilots of the 17th IAP, which took off with 26 MiGs under the regiment commander Major G.I. Pulov were covering the actions of the 523rd IAP's pilots.

At 0910, the 17th IAP's pilots engaged the forward screen of Sabres in the Sonchon area, while the pilots of the 523rd IAP exploited this in order to break through to the area where the fighter-bombers were operating. In the Kiojo area they sighted several small groups of F-80s and attacked them. Having spotted the MiGs, the Shooting Stars immediately broke off their ground attacks and hurried toward the sanctuary of the sea, but Senior Lieutenant M.A. Zykov still managed to down one of them.

When returning back to base from the combat mission, the 523rd IAP's 3rd Squadron encountered 12 F-86s at an altitude of 8,000 meters and engaged them. During the dogfight, Senior Lieutenant V.E. Silkin's element lagged behind the rest of his flight and was jumped by eight Sabres. The formation was loose, and the enemy fighters focused their attacks on Silkin's wingman, Senior Lieutenant C.Z. Moskvichev. One Sabre pair miscalculated the angle of attack and overshot Moskvichev's MiG; taking advantage of the opportunity, he opened fire on the wingman's Sabre and shot it down. However, while firing on his target Senior Lieutenant Moskvichev was caught in a pincer between four attacking Sabres. The pilot received a bullet wound in his left shoulder which shattered the shoulder bone, and he ejected from his MiG at an altitude of 9,500 meters.

The pilot landed unconscious next to a Chinese field hospital. Chinese doctors immediately gave him first aid, but Moskvichev had lost a lot of blood and the doctors realized that they didn't have his blood-type in the hospital. A two-seater Yak-11 trainer was urgently launched from the Miaogou airfield, which was being flown by Captain A.A. Kaliuzhny, while the chief of the 303rd IAD's parachute service, sport parachute master Colonel Svoboda was sitting in the rear cockpit with a flask of the needed blood-type. Flying at low altitude, Kaliuzhny stumbled across an eight-ship formation of F-86s, but he managed to slip away from them and reached the hospital, where a cross had been laid out with white sheets. Gaining altitude through a zoom climb over the hospital, he dropped Colonel Svoboda by parachute. Svoboda landed next to the hospital and timely delivered the vital blood supply to the doctors, thereby saving the life of our pilot. When Moskvichev regained some strength, he was sent back to the Soviet Union to recuperate from his wound.

Captain Kaliuzhny safely returned to Miaogou, and for this risky flight he was given a field promotion to major, while Colonel Svoboda was decorated with the Order of the Red Banner for his jump, which saved a man's life. Four MiG-15s from the 196th IAP under the command of Captain L.N. Ivanov flew cover for the mission.

Colonel Francis Gabreski scored the victory over Moskvichev in this action. This was his third victory in a Sabre in this war, but he obtained it in his new role as commander of the 51st FIW, the headquarters of which had recently arrived in Suwon. The bulk of this fighter wing was still back in Japan, making the transition to flying F-86E Sabres. Gabreski himself had already thoroughly mastered the Sabre and had flown many combat missions in Korea as the deputy commander of the 4th FIW, with which by the middle of 1951 he had already achieved two victories.

The pilots of the 17th IAP also carried out their mission and didn't give the Sabre pilots the opportunity to interfere with the attack by the regimental group from the 523rd IAP against the enemy's fighter-bombers. In this dogfight with the Sabres, the MiG flown by the regiment commander Major Pulov received a bullet hole in the left wing. The 17th IAP returned without any other losses or damage.

That afternoon between 1500 and 1600, the Fifth Air Force command launched a new air raid against ground targets in the Anju region. Once again, groups of MiGs from all three regiments of the 303rd IAD took off to repel this attack. This time it fell to the pilots of the 17th IAP's 3rd Squadron, flying as part of the overall group of 24 MiGs that had been sent to intercept the enemy, to make contact with the fighter-bombers. They were the first to spot eight enemy aircraft, which they identified as F-80s, and decided to attack this group. However, research by Diego Zampini has revealed that the enemy formation actually consisted of two RF-80 reconnaissance planes from the 15th TRS, which were being escorted by six Thunderjets from the 136th FBW's 182nd Squadron. In the course of the attack on this eight-ship formation of "Crosses", Senior Lieutenant N.S. Volkov and his wingman Senior Lieutenant A.N. Nikolaev made such an impetuous pass through the enemy formation that the Americans scrambled to get out of the way, and two of the Thunderjets collided in mid-air and exploded; by some miracle, Volkov and his wingman dodged all of the fragments from the exploding aircraft. As is now known, RF-80 No.45-8472, flown by 2nd Lieutenant Bruce A. Sweney and F-84E No.50-1166 piloted by Captain Adam J. Wisniewske, were involved in the collision. Sweney was killed in the explosion, but by some miracle Wisniewske survived and was picked up by an Air Rescue helicopter.

At this point, the American pilots that had come under the MiGs' attack summoned help in the form of three flights of F-86s, which attacked the 17th IAP's aircraft. At 1516 in the area over Taeju at an altitude of 9,000 meters, flight commander Captain I.N. Morozov was attacked from above and behind at a range of 200-300 meters by a pair of F-86s. His MiG burst into flames and fell 5 kilometers southeast of Ododo, which lies 24 kilometers northeast of Sonchon. Captain Ivan Nikolaevich Morozov never ejected and was killed.

Comrades from the 18th GIAP under the command of Lieutenant Colonel A.P. Smorchkov and a group of MiGs from the 196th IAP came to the rescue of the pilots of the 17th IAP and attacked the Sabre group, thereby allowing the 17th IAP's pilots to withdraw from the combat. In this battle our pilots claimed three F-86s, which were credited to Lieutenant Colonel A.P. Smorchkov, Senior Lieutenant L.K. Shchukin and Captain L.N. Ivanov of the 196th IAP. Our pilots had no other losses in this battle.

The Americans claim that on this day pilots of the 4th FIW, in addition to Gabreski, downed another five MiGs. However, the regiments of the 64th IAK only lost a total of two aircraft and one pilot. Most likely, Captain Morozov's MiG from the 17th IAP was downed by Captain George Dunn of the 334th Fighter Squadron, while 1st Lieutenant Lloyd Tomson of the 336th Fighter Squadron damaged Major Pulov's aircraft. The remaining victories by the American pilots are not reflected in Soviet records. In its turn, the Fifth Air Force command confirms the loss of one RF-80 and one F-84 on this day, and one F-86E (No.51-2746) damaged in a combat with MiGs, which apparently was hit by Shchukin of the 18th GIAP, but managed to return to its base, where this Sabre was soon repaired. It is possible that in the morning combat, pilots of the 523rd IAP fought not with Shooting Stars, but with the similar F9F-2 Panthers, and Zykov managed to down one of them. On 4 October the Americans wrote off one F9F-2 No.123593 from the roster of VMF-311, which was supposedly the victim of "enemy anti-aircraft fire".

Aerial combats continued daily in the Anju area and encounters were both frequent and fierce, with both sides suffering substantial losses. Following the pattern, on 5 October the enemy undertook two new raids against targets in MiG Alley, one in the morning and the other in the afternoon. Pilots of all three regiments of the 303rd IAD took part in repelling the first attack. On this occasion 20 MiGs of the 17th IAP under the command of Major G.I. Pulov engaged 24 F-86s of the forward screen, and in the ensuing 15-minute dogfight between 1020 and 1035, Pulov and Captain M.N. Shcherbakov each damaged one Sabre. While the 17th IAP kept the screening Sabres busy, a group of MiGs from the 18th GIAP broke through to the area where F-80 fighter-bombers were operating, and regiment commander Lieutenant Colonel A.E. Belostotsky managed to shoot one of them down before the rest escaped to the safety of Korea Bay. Pilots of the 523rd dueled with a group of Sabres in the Anju area, though with no results. Our pilots from the 303rd IAD had no losses in the morning action.

That afternoon, the 303rd IAD again took off to repulse a new enemy raid. The pilots of this division tied up the forward screen of Sabres, while MiGs of the UAA's 4th IAD, covered by pilots of the 324th IAD, operated against the fighter-bombers. In a ten-minute dogfight with 16 F-86s over the area of Sunchon between 1530 and 1540, the pilots of the 523rd IAP downed one Sabre, which went to the credit of Senior Lieutenant N.P. Razorvin. Pilots of the 17th IAP were simultaneously involved in a dogfight with another group of 16 F-86s in the same area, and Senior Lieutenant A.N. Nikolaev damaged another Sabre. Our pilots had no losses in this action.

Pilots of the 176th GIAP flew two missions to cover the Chinese 4th IAD. On the second one, 12 of them became involved in a combat with 12 Sabres that were attempting to attack the Chinese pilots, but our pilots prevented them from doing so.

Pilots of the 18th GIAP under the command of Lieutenant Colonel A.P. Smorchkov also flew an afternoon mission. They too had an encounter with a group of F-86s and in this battle group leader Smorchkov added another Sabre to his personal score. However, this victory received no confirmation from the ground and was later disallowed. The Fifth Air Force command on this day acknowledged the loss of only one of its F-80 Shooting Stars (No.49-1852) from the 8th FBG's 36th FBS, the pilot of which 1st Lieutenant Frank D. Bay was killed. Lieutenant Colonel Belostotsky was the pilot who shot Bay down.

A large battle flared up on 6 October near the coastline of the Yellow Sea, involving more than 100 aircraft from both sides. The commander of the 196th IAP Evgenii Georgievich Pepeliaev, who early on the morning of 6 October led a group of 10 MiGs on a combat patrol into North Korea's interior, was "responsible" for trigging it. In the Anju area, his MiG patrol was met by a group of 16 F-86s. Here's how Evgenii Georgievich Pepeliaev himself describes the resulting combat:

> As the battle was winding down, when the group had already broken down into separate flights and elements, a pair of F-86s attacked me in a head-on pass from a deflection angle of 1/4, and one bullet left a 30cm diameter hole in my aircraft's nose. After passing me the Sabre element went into a climbing turn to the left, which I repeated with my MiG. I then went into a climbing turn to starboard and emerged on their tails at a range of 130 meters in inverted flight. An F-86 pilot spotted my MiG behind him and rolled over into an attempted split-S, but I anticipated this, and gave him a short burst at a deflection angle of 1/4. One of my shells exploded behind the F-86 cockpit, which damaged both the engine and the ejection seat in the aircraft. I didn't follow him, because the battle was continuing. One or two minutes later I spotted a group of MiGs from the 176th GIAP below me at an altitude of 1,000-1,500 meters, which had been sent as reinforcements.

The enemy soon exited the combat, and we returned without losses to our base. After the mission I went by the photo laboratory and checked my gun camera film. On it, a Sabre at a range of 130 meters and a deflection angle of 1/4 was clearly visible, as were the results of the explosions of my shells. One could also easily see the black and white stripes on the wings, which signified that this Sabre was from the 4th FIG.

The Sabre that had been damaged by Pepeliaev came down on its belly right on the shoreline of the sea, where the pilot climbed out of his cockpit, inflated a life raft, and started paddling toward the open sea, having turned on his miniature radio beacon, for which the US Navy's Air-Sea Rescue Service was already searching. Soon rescue helicopters were circling overhead, but they were attacked by 12 MiGs of the 176th GIAP under the command of Captain K.Ia. Sheberstov. Senior Lieutenant P.S. Milaushkin and his wingman Lieutenant I.A. Ziuz' attacked a helicopter that was circling over the American pilot's raft and tried to shoot it down, but it was an unusual target for the pilots – it could hover in place. Thus all the bursts missed it, and the helicopter began to head out to sea with tight maneuvers as a second helicopter took its place over the raft.

The 176th GIAP's pilots came under attack from six F-86s, which were trying to cover the rescue operation from the air, and this they managed to do at the cost of damage to one more Sabre, which the commander of the MiG group Captain K.Ia. Sheberstov had targeted. Pilots of the 336th Fighter Squadron, who experienced some serious troubles in this encounter with the MiGs, participated in this battle. Pepeliaev damaged F-86A No.49-1319, which was being piloted by Captain Bill Garrett, and it was he who made the forced landing on the coastline 13 kilometers west of Pyongwon. The F-86E No.50-0651 flown by 1st Lieutenant Arthur O'Connor, which was covering Garrett, came under attack by Captain Sheberstov's MiG, leaving his Sabre with perforated fuel tanks, but the pilot managed to bring it back to Suwon and make a safe landing there.

This marked the commander of the 196th IAP's most successful day – he achieved two personal victories. In addition to the Sabre being flown by Captain Garrett, Pepeliaev downed F-86A No.49-1267 from the 334th FIS in this action, and its pilot with the surname of Carnes was able to take to his parachute. However, it must be noted that the Sabre he downed in the first combat, which landed damaged on the coastal mud flats near Inchon, was credited instead to the 176th GIAP commander Captain K.Ia. Sheberstov at the behest of the 324th IAD's command.

However, a half-hour earlier, pilots of the 523rd IAP and 17th IAP had also clashed with Sabres. The dogfight took place between 0850 and 0900 in the area of Sunchon, where 24 MiGs of the 523rd IAP took on 20 Sabres. In this combat Captain S.A. Bakhaev and Senior Lieutenant V.I. Surovikin each claimed a Sabre, without any losses in return. Five minutes after the 523rd IAP's action, 22 MiGs of the 17th IAP joined battle with approximately 30 Sabres. The dogfight ended at 0910 with a complete victory for the Soviet side: Major G.I. Pulov, Captain N.P. Mishakin and Senior Lieutenant A.A. Komarov each added a Sabor to their personal scores. We had two MiGs damaged in this combat: flight commander Senior Lieutenant F.G. Malunov's MiG received two bullet holes in its left wing; squadron deputy political commander Captain A.V. Bykov received four bullet holes in his MiG's left wing. Pilots of the 18th GIAP also dueled with F-86s on this day, but their clash ended without results for either side.

The Americans acknowledged damage to two of its Sabres in this morning aerial combat: No.49-1178 from the 336th FIS was probably damaged by Major Pulov, while another F-86A from the same squadron (the Bureau Number isn't given) took its damage most likely from Captain Bakhaev's cannon fire. Thus on this day pilots of the 336th Squadron, which over the day lost one Sabre with three more damaged, had been particularly caught out by the MiGs; if the lost Sabre from the 334th FIS is added to the day's totals, then the 4th FIW's losses were serious.

Having learned that an F-86E had made a forced landing on coastal mud flats and was virtually intact, an order came down from above: "Deliver this Sabre to Moscow by any means." The main advisor to the Chinese Air Force Colonel General S.A. Krasovsky, who was at the Andong base at the time, summoned an engineer from the 176th GIAP, Major of Technical Services V.A. Kazankin, and gave him an order to bring the aircraft back to Andong. Kazankin selected a team of eight technicians and set out together with them in a vehicle to carry out the given order.

The difficulty of retrieving the Sabre consisted in the fact that the area where the damaged Sabre had made its forced landing was under nearly around the clock bombing, strafing and napalm attacks by American aircraft, but fortunately the aircraft had received hardly any additional damage. The 64th IAK command had given special attention to guarding the crash site against American air raids, and conducted several more aerial combats in the course of the day, in order, as strangely as it sounds, to protect the American fighter from the American air raids. These aerial combats were fought by pilots of the 324th IAD, who were covering the actions of the UAA's 4th IAD. On this day pilots of the Chinese 4th IAD successfully attacked a small group of B-29 bombers, which were trying vainly to destroy the F-86. The Chinese pilots ganged up on one Superfortress from the 19th BG's 28th Squadron – only one crew member of this B-29 No.44-62183 survived, and he was taken prisoner.

At this time Major Kazankin arrived at the place where the Sabre had come down with a number of Chinese and North Korean volunteers from the 4th Army, and they made an attempt to extract the aircraft during a period of low tide, but the effort failed due to persistent attacks by enemy aircraft. Next he decided to disassemble the aircraft and haul it back in pieces, and thanks to his technical aptitude, over the course of the day by fits and starts he took apart the Sabre, and it was delivered in pieces to the Andong Air Base, where it was reassembled, so pilots of the 324th IAD and the 64th IAK could examine a Sabre, together with its equipment and armament, in detail.

For this work, V.A. Kazankin was given a field promotion to lieutenant colonel. The Sabre was soon disassembled again, crated up, and taken to Moscow by railroad. There, in one of the scientific institutes they placed it in a wind tunnel and obtained the Sabre's precise flight and technical characteristics, which supplemented the Soviet pilots' knowledge about their main aerial adversary – the F-86A. Thus, the first intact American F-86A Sabre was acquired in North Korea, thanks to the superb aerial gunnery of the 196th IAP's Lieutenant Colonel E.G. Pepeliaev and the team of V.A. Kazankin, an engineer with the 176th GIAP.

The next successful combat for our pilots occurred on the afternoon of 10 October. Pilots of the 18th GIAP under the command of Lieutenant Colonel A.E. Belostotsky intercepted a group of aircraft they identified as Thunderjets in the Anju area and claimed the destruction of four of the Thunderjets. The victories were credited to Lieutenant

Colonels Belostotsky and A.P. Smorchkov, as well as to Major D.P. Os'kin and Captain N.I. Gerasimenko. In reality, the pilots of the 18th GIAP had fought with F-80s from the 8th FBG and the 51st FIG, and at a minimum downed three F-80s: two Shooting Stars (No.49-1878 and No.49-544) from the 8th FBG, the pilots of which were killed-in-action, and an F-80 (No.49-746) from the 51st FIW, the pilot of which was also killed-in-action. As is common, the American side attributes these three F-80 losses to anti-aircraft fire.

On the afternoon of 12 October, pilots of the 303rd IAD once again took off to repel a raid by American fighter-bombers. All three regiments of the division participated in this battle, which occurred between 1600 and 1640 in the Chongju-Sukchon area. The 18th GIAP assumed the role of the main strike group, while 14 MiGs of the 523rd IAP and another 20 MiGs from the 17th IAP tied up 30 enemy fighters in combat. Pilots of the 18th GIAP's 2nd Squadron engaged 12 F-84s, which were being escorted by eight F-86s. The squadron's pilots conducted a swift attack against the fighter-bomber formation, as a result of which Senior Lieutenant V.I. Stepanov scored his first victory in the skies of Korea, downing a Thunderjet from close range, while the wingman of squadron commander Lieutenant N.S. Gavril'chenko targeted another F-84, fired on it and watched his shells strike home. However, he couldn't observe the results of the attack because of his high-speed pass and had no time to see what happened to the target. Presumably he damaged it.

At the same time, 14 MiG-15s of the 523rd IAP engaged the forward screen of F-86s, which consisted of 40 Sabres. Pilots of the 17th IAP arrived to assist them, and a real melee developed. The regiment's formation broke down into separate pairs and flights. Here's how a participant in this fight, Grigorii Kharitonovich D'iachenko, the deputy political commander of the 523rd IAP's 1st Squadron, describes it:

> One element jumped Bakhaev and me; we drew it into a maneuvering combat in climbing and descending spirals. Vision narrowed into a tunnel, and neither side wanted to break off combat first. After the next maneuver I went into a barrel roll first, but at the top of the roll pulled into an inverted dive and caught an F-86 in my gun sight which was flying toward me at a deflection angle of 1/4; I opened fire from my cannons, and just as I pulled out of the attack I heard the leader's voice: "Thirteen (my call sign), I congratulate you!" I glanced below and saw a ball of black smoke, falling toward the earth. My gun camera footage also recorded the hits on the enemy aircraft.

In this combat pilots of the 523rd IAP added two more Sabres to their score. They were credited to Captain G.U. Okhai and Senior Lieutenant D.A. Samoilov. In addition, pilots of the 303rd IAD's two other regiments also downed a Sabre: Senior Lieutenant N.G. Dokashenko of the 17th IAP and Captain N.V. Babonin of the 18th GIAP. The 303rd IAD's own losses amounted to just one MiG-15bis. Captain N.V. Babonin's MiG was damaged by 1st Lieutenant Joseph P. Ellis of the 334th Fighter Squadron, but he managed to eject safely from his crippled ship. This was the sole victory by American pilots on 12 October.

The Fifth Air Force command acknowledged the loss of only F-86E No.50-0682 of the 336th FIS, the pilot of which, although he managed to reach friendly territory in it, had to make a forced belly landing. The plane suffered such extensive damage that it was simply written off. Fortunately, the pilot was uninjured. Senior Lieutenant Stepanov's victory was also confirmed – F-84E No.49-2351 of the 136th FBW's 182nd Squadron, the pilot of which 1st Lieutenant Frank Kuzmech bailed out but was taken prisoner.

There were no battles in the skies of Korea on 13 October as the American pilots seemed to take the day off. However, on 14 October the Americans launched their usual raids at times that were already customary for the pilots of the 64th IAK. The first raid as always came in around 0900 and targeted the logistics hub of Anju. Again, all three regiments of the 303rd IAD responded to the attack. This time, pilots of the 18th GIAP and 523rd IAP engaged the Sabres of the forward screen, while 20 MiGs of the 17th IAP under the command of Major B.V. Maslennikov managed to intercept a large group of 30 F-84s at 0857 and attacked them. In a short ten-minute battle, F-84E No.49-2364 from the 136th FBW was downed by Major Maslennikov and fell into the sea – its pilot bailed out. The rest of the fighter-bombers withdrew.

In the fight with the Sabres, Senior Lieutenant I.I. Shavsha, a pilot in the 18th GIAP, distinguished himself by downing one F-86. On our side, Senior Lieutenant I.Iu. Krasavtsev's MiG received damage in the form of three bullet holes at the hands of 1st Lieutenant Joseph Ellis.

The next battle took place in the afternoon at around 1400, in the very same area. This time a group of 18 MiGs from the 17th IAP under the command of Major G.I. Pulov engaged a group of 28 F-86s, while pilots of the 196th IAP broke through to the fighter-bombers. In the combat with the fighters, pilots of the 17th IAP celebrated a victory when Captain S.S. Artemchenko downed one Sabre. Meanwhile, the pilots of the 196th IAP successfully drove a group of F-80s out of the target area, in the process downing one Shooting Star that was claimed by Major A.I. Mitusov. We had no losses.

As usual, the Americans do not acknowledge the loss of an F-86 on this day, but they do confirm the loss of one F-84, and one F-80 (No.49-747) from the 51st FIW's 16th FIS – its pilot bailed out and was picked up by a helicopter. Also as usual, both of these losses were recorded as being due to anti-aircraft artillery fire.

In the morning combat, Senior Lieutenant Shashva, a flight commander in the 18th GIAP's 3rd Squadron, downed an undetermined type of enemy aircraft. Shashva had spotted a solitary aircraft, which was flying above a group of F-84s, and attacked it from a range of 200-250 meters, scoring hits on it from his cannons. A stream of smoke began to emit from the right side of the target's fuselage, and it headed down in spirals. After landing and developing the gun camera footage, the pilots of the 3rd Squadron took a long time inspecting the film of the enemy aircraft that Shashva had downed but were unable to determine its type. By its silhouette it was similar to a Sabre, but some sort of white adaptations (bulges) were visible on its wingtips. The pilots concluded that they were some sort of radar-ranging device (radio altimeters).

Most likely, this was an F2X-2 Banshee pathfinder, which was guiding the F-84 group. The Americans often employed pathfinders to lead its strike groups. Moreover, it is known that on this day a Banshee (No.124951) from VMF-173 crashed when landing on a carrier, killing its pilot. Possibly, the damage it had incurred from a MiG was such that it didn't permit a safe landing on the deck of an aircraft carrier.

True, already by 16 October the pilots of the 4th FIW, primarily through the efforts of the 334th FIS, took convincing revenge in combat with MiGs by scoring nine victories over the course of the day in the Anju area. The pilots of the 334th Fighter Squadron alone downed four MiGs. Major Franklin L. Fisher from the 4th FIW's staff had a good day, downing a MiG in each of two combats over the day, for which he was awarded the Silver Star.

However, it wasn't Soviet pilots that came under attack from the vengeful pilots of the 4th FIW, but Chinese pilots of the the 12th IAP of the UAA's 4th IAD, because on 16 October the 64th IAK had no losses at all in aerial combat. Instead, pilots of the 303rd IAD in their memoirs mention the destruction of one Chinese fighter squadron, which had been jumped by a group of Sabres when approaching their base after returning from a combat mission. There was no combat in reality, but simply the slaughter of young Chinese pilots, who were caught in a difficult and disadvantageous situation without ammunition or fuel by an opponent who had a winning position. As a result, in the words of our pilots, the Sabres easily downed seven or eight MiGs before heading back to the Yellow Sea unpunished. Most likely, this occurred on 16 October 1951 on the approach to the Andong airfield.

However, the Sabres also suffered losses on this day and once again it was in combat with Soviet pilots. Thus pilots of the 196th IAP headed by the experienced regiment commander Lieutenant Colonel E.G. Pepeliaev caught American pilots that were distracted by the combat with the Chinese MiGs and downed two Sabres, one by the regiment commander himself (this was now the Soviet ace's seventh victory in the skies of Korea). One more Sabre was downed by pilots of the 523rd IAP in the vicinity of Naechongdong, which was credited to the score of deputy regiment commander Major D.P. Os'kin. Thunderjet pilots also didn't get by on this day without a loss. In the morning battle, 22 MiGs of the 17th IAP intercepted a group of eight F-84s, which were being covered by 16 F-86s, and Captain V.A. Blagov knocked down one of the Thunderjets – even the escort couldn't help it!

However, the American command recognized the loss of only one of its F-86A Sabres (No.49-1147), which Lieutenant Colonel E.G. Pepeliaev seriously damaged. The pilot of this Sabre, Nicholas Kotek, had to eject from his doomed Sabre after it suffered fuel starvation, but he was rescued. But another pilot of the 196th IAP, Senior Lieutenant A.M. Kochegarov, damaged F-86E No.50-623 in this battle, which was being flown by none other than the famous American ace Colonel Harrison Thyng, who would soon take command of the 4th FIW. Using his extensive experience, Thyng managed to bring his damaged Sabre back to base and make a landing; the F-86 subsequently returned to active service.

After 16 October, the action in the skies of Korea subsided somewhat. Both sides continued flying sorties, but encounters were rare, since the American pilots shunned active combat for several days; whenever they encountered MiGs they immediately withdrew to zones that afforded them safety, like the Yellow Sea, beyond the Chochengan line. The lull continued until 21 October, when major aerial battles once again flared up in the skies of Korea with the participation of SAC bombers and other elements of the Fifth Air Force. B-29 bombers, which made several major daytime raids deep into North Korean territory, once again dared to enter MiG Alley.

The daytime raids by the Superfortresses had been prompted by the construction of new North Korean airfields in the areas of Saamchan, Taechon and Namsi, to which a large number of jet fighters might restage at any time. These airfields were important to the UAA command, since it wanted to expand the operational radius of its MiG units, so that they could operate all the way down to the front lines along the 38th Parallel. Besides that, in October American reconnaissance had spotted the concentration of enemy aircraft on other North Korean airfields, such as 16 MiG-15s on the Eiju airfield, and 74 aircraft of the Yak-9, La-9 and Il-10 types on the Sinuiju airfield. These piston-engine aircraft would require cover against enemy fighters, and this task would have to be carried out by MiG-15 regiments of the UAA, which it was assumed would re-stage to the newly constructed bases in North Korea.

Timely sensing the threat which the completion of these new airbases in North Korea would pose, the US Fifth Air Force command decided to conduct an operation with the participation of B-29s to destroy the ten newly constructed North Korean airfields.

The first raids were conducted on 18 and 21 October, but they experienced organizational difficulties and failed to strike the primary targets. The bombers instead hit secondary targets.

On 22 October 12 B-29 bombers took off from bases in Japan for the area of MiG Alley, which had the immediate escort of dozens of F-80 and F-84s, while large detachments of Sabres prowled ahead with the assignment to tie up the MiGs in combat and prevent them from reaching the bombers. At 1403 General Lobov gave the order to scramble pilots of the 303rd IAD. The IAD launched 54 MiGs with a several-minute interval between groups: 20 MiGs of the 523rd IAP and 20 MiGs of the 17th IAP, as well as the strike group of 14 MiGs from the 18th GIAP. At 1425, the pilots of the 523rd IAP and 17th IAP engaged a large, mixed group of enemy fighters, numbering a total of 60 aircraft. Meanwhile the pilots of the 18th GIAP were directed toward a group of 12 B-29s, which had an immediate escort of approximately 10 F-84s. The MiGs went on the attack, paying no attention to the escort fighters.

Breaking through the clouds at 5,000 meters and taking up an advantageous position, the MiGs swept through the fighter screen at high speed and attacked the bomber formation. In the first pass, regiment leader Lieutenant Colonel A.P. Smorchkov destroyed one B-29 with his cannon fire, while element leader Lieutenant V.I. Stepanov damaged another Superfortress with two long bursts of fire. Having swung around for another pass, the MiGs again attacked the formation of bombers, which having dropped their bombs, had begun to turn in the direction of the sea. In so doing, Senior Lieutenant Stepanov's wingman, Senior Lieutenant V.S. Shabanov, left a third B-29 burning and smoking as it turned in the direction of the sea.

At the same time (1425-1440), pilots of the 17th IAP and 523rd IAP, which were locked in combat with the fighters of the forward screen, were thinning the formations of Thunderjets and Shooting Stars. Pilots of the 17th IAP claimed three Thunderjets, two of them at the hands of a flight commander in the 1st Squadron, Senior Lieutenant S.S. Bychkov, while pilots of the 523rd IAP claimed two more F-84s. Suffering large losses in this battle, and having failed to carry out the task of covering the bombers, the pilots of the 8th and 136th FBW, just like the Superfortresses, withdrew from the combat and departed over the sea.

Only Sabres remained in the combat area, but even they achieved no victories and failed to carry out their role of preventing the MiGs from reaching the bombers, and moreover lost two of their number in this large dogfight, which pilots of the 196th IAP downed. True, the Sabres attempted to take revenge for the defeat, and having split into small groups, they began to attack the MiGs of the 303rd IAD as they were withdrawing, low on both fuel and ammunition. Thus, the solitary pair of Shashva and Konev on their way back to Miaogou was attacked by six Sabres not far from the base. It is well that the wingman Senior Lieutenant V.A. Konev spotted them in time and warned his leader about the danger. Almost out of fuel and ammunition, our pilots were forced to conduct a brief combat, and maneuvering energetically, they were able to escape the Sabres' pincers and land at Miaogou. Both MiGs returned riddled with bullet holes – especially Senior Lieutenant Konev's fighter, in which after landing they counted 42 bullet holes. However, thanks to the selfless work of the squadron's technicians, the MiG soon returned to active service.

Also on the approach to base, Captain S.A. Bakhaev's flight from the 523rd IAP was attacked by four F-86s, which targeted the tail-end element of Senior Lieutenant N.G. Kovalenko and his wingman I.A. Rybalko. Captain Bakhaev, seeing that his flight's formation was under attack, gave the order to Kovalenko's element to switch to the right side, but the enemy continued to pursue them. When the Sabres had approached to within 800 meters, at Bakhaev's order Kovalenko's element flew straight ahead, while Bakhaev's lead element went into a left-hand chandelle. The four Sabres turned their attention to Bakhaev's element and followed it. Kovalenko saw all this clearly, and once the tail-end Sabre element went into its climbing turn, he abruptly went into a pursuit curve, closed quickly and shot down the wingman's F-86. The remaining three F-86s immediately rolled over and dove toward the sea. Our pilots couldn't chase them, since they were about out of fuel, and they touched down on their base with nearly empty fuel tanks.

As a result, in this major battle in the Anju area, which involved around 200 aircraft from both sides, 15 American aircraft were claimed (three B-29s, three F-86s and nine F-84s) by Soviet pilots, without any losses in return (the Americans pilots on this day made no victory claims). This was a major victory for the Soviet pilots and their most successful and productive aerial combat of October 1951. The Fifth Air Force command acknowledged the loss of only one of its B-29s (No.44-61656) from the 19th BG's 30th Squadron, which fell into the Yellow Sea; only some of the crew survived and were rescued. It was credited to Lieutenant Colonel A.P. Smorchkov. The other two Superfortresses received damage from the MiGs' fire, but returned to their bases. The American side also does not confirm the numerous losses among the covering fighters. It reports only the loss of F-80 No.49-695 from the 8th FBG's 35th FBS, the pilot of which 1st Lieutenant Louis T. Esposito was killed-in-action. He was presumably downed by Senior Lieutenant L.K. Shchukin of the 18th GIAP. However, the pilots of the 64th IAK were successful from the viewpoint of their most important assignment: they prevented the bombers from reaching the targeted airfield.

In this battle, five of the 64th IAK's MiGs received combat damage: those of Senior Lieutenants I.I. Shashva and V.A. Konev from the 18th GIAP, Senior Lieutenant G.T. Shatalov's MiG from the 523rd IAP (just two bullet holes), as well as the MiG flown by the commander of the 17th IAP Major G.I. Pulov, which received 12 bullet holes. In addition, the fighter flown by Senior Lieutenant A.S. Shirokov received 16 bullet holes in the wing, fuselage, engine, rudder and vertical stabilizer in this combat. Senior Lieutenant Shirokov himself was slightly wounded in the soft tissue around the lower angle of the right shoulder blade. On the whole, everything went successfully for our pilots, and soon all five aircraft were returned to active service.

There were also failures in this battle. For example, Captain S.S. Artemchenko's covering group from the 17th IAP failed to cover the actions of the regiment's attack group; having lost sight of it, at his own initiative Captain Artemchenko unsuccessfully pursued a group of enemy aircraft as far as Pyongyang. The strike group, numbering eight MiGs led by Major Pulov, attacked two eight-ship formations of F-80s at an altitude of 2,000-4,000 meters. During the dive on the targets, Major Pulov's wingman, Captain Blagov, saw his cockpit canopy fog up and he broke away from the action. After the attacking pass, Pulov, realizing that he didn't have a wingman, also exited the fight. At one point in the dogfight, Senior Lieutenant Shirokov was maneuvering against an F-84 at low altitude. A pair of F-86s jumped him, but he displayed his skill and escaped them, but not before receiving a slight wound in the back from a bullet fragment. Captain Shcherbakov left the battle without authorization, and his wingman Bykov was forced to duel alone against four F-86s, one of which he damaged. For his unsuccessful handling of the combat, the corps commander issued a formal rebuke to the 17th IAP commander Major Pulov.

On the next day, 23 October, there was another major raid by B-29s, the targets of which were the North Korean airfields of Taechon and Namsi. This Superfortress mission was covered by large groups of Sabres from the 4th FIW, as well as F-80s and F-84s from the 49th and 136th FBW. According to the Soviet pilots, the battle resulting from this raid involved 22 to 28 B-29 bombers, covered by up to 100 fighters. On the Soviet side, 58 MiG-15bis from the 303rd IAD, which comprised the 64th IAK's first echelon, were assigned to repel the raid and to attack the enemy, while 26 MiGs of the reserve 324th IAD were to serve as reinforcements and to cover the withdrawal of the 303rd IAD's pilots from combat. However, American records show that only eight B-29 bombers from SAC's 307th BG, covered by 55 F-84s and 34 F-86s, were involved in the attack upon Namsi, and that they were attacked by only 44 MiGs. The American records diverge considerably from the Soviet records. It is only clear that the enemy had superior numbers.

The raid came early in the morning (0835-0905); the cloud cover over the target and the entire area of this part of North Korea was thick and nearly total. Pilots of the 303rd IAD were at Readiness No. 1, sitting in the cockpits of their MiGs and waiting for the order to take off, since the Soviet radar operators had early on detected this armada of enemy aircraft and had immediately informed our command of its approach. At the alarm signal, all three regiments of the 303rd IAD were scrambled, while the 324th IAD remained on stand-by on the Andong base in cases of necessity.

The combat formation of the 303rd IAD consisted of a strike group and cover group, flying in a column of regiments while maintaining visual contact with each other. The 18th GIAP and 523rd IAP formed the strike group, while the 17th IAP acted as the cover group. The senior officer in the divisional group was Lieutenant Colonel A.P. Smorchkov.

At 0840, flying at the head of the strike group, the 18th GIAP, numbering 20 MiGs, encountered the enemy fighter screen, which consisted of almost 40 Sabres, approaching on an interception course in an area 20-25 kilometers east of Gisiu. Simultaneously, a group of eight B-29 bombers was spotted ahead and to the left at an altitude of 5,000 meters, flying in a line abreast formation and with the immediate escort of around 30 F-84 Thunderjets. Having assessed the situation, Lieutenant Colonel Smorchkov issued an order for the 18th IAP's 1st and 3rd Squadrons (14 MiGs) to engage the Sabres, while he led six MiGs from the 2nd Squadron against the bomber formation.

Splitting into pairs, the six MiGs made a high-speed attack against the Superfortresses, even though the Thunderjets were swarming around them like flies; they slashed through the escorts, which could do nothing with the MiGs because of their great speed. Just as in the preceding battle, the regiment leader Lieutenant Colonel A.P. Smorchkov downed one B-29, while Captain N.L. Kornienko claimed another. The B-29 formation was disrupted, as the covering fighters again had been unable to cope with their assignment; they began jettisoning their bombs and turning in the direction of the sea.

Flying at 9,000 meters above a dense layer of clouds and behind the 18th GIAP, at 0843 15 kilometers west of Taechon the regimental group of the 523rd IAP numbering 18 MiGs led by Guards Major D.P. Os'kin sighted nine B-29 bombers and up to 40 fighters 6-8 kilometers away in front of him at an altitude of 7,000 meters, moving from the Taechon area to the southeast toward Anju. The B-29s were flying with the lead flight of three Superfortresses in a compact wedge formation; the trailing group of six B-29s was following 4-5 kilometers behind the lead group and about 400-600 meters to one side, in two flights that were line abreast.

The escorting fighters were deployed as follows: eight Meteors were 2-3 kilometers in front, 1-2 kilometers to the right and 600-800 meters above the bombers. F-84s were directly covering the trailing two flights of B-29s with groups of four to eight Thunderjets, which were located in front of and to the right of the bombers, as well as behind the bomber formation at a distance of 1-2 kilometers and echeloned in altitude. Two groups of F-86 Sabres each in a compact formation of staggered flights were serving as a barrier, carrying out their patrol duties 10-15 kilometers to the right of and behind the bomber formation, that is to say, screening our fighters' likely direction of approach. Having assessed the aerial situation, Guards Major Os'kin decided to attack the enemy bombers with two squadrons, while the 2nd Squadron would cover the attack group.

Guards Major Os'kin west of Taechon at an altitude of 7,000 meters saw eight F-86s, closing in from the left to intercept them. Os'kin with his flight turned toward the approaching Sabres, but then spotted three B-29s against the backdrop of clouds, 6-8 kilometers to the left of them. Splitting from the rest of his flight, Os'kin and his wingman banked to the left to close on the B-29s. Meanwhile Senior Lieutenant Surovikin's element from Os'kin's flight briefly engaged the eight F-86s using a vertical maneuver, but after an order from the division command post exited the attack in a high-speed shallow climb and returned to base.

Os'kin's element at this time was making a high-speed pass against the three B-29s, opening fire from 1,600 meters and ceasing it at 980 meters. He fired all three cannons at the lead B-29. He watched his shells detonate on the B-29; the bomber fell out of the group and headed to the south in a dive. His wingman Guards Senior Lieutenant Samoilov also fired at the right-hand bomber, using all three cannons from a range of 2,200 meters down to 1,460 meters. Os'kin pulled out of the attack and passed over the bombers, continued straight ahead for 8-10 seconds, and then made a climbing turn to starboard into the sun. Senior Lieutenat Samoilov lost his leader in the sun and pulled around to the left for a second attack. Closing now on the bombers' tails, he chose to target the left-hand bomber and fired from a range of 1,760 meters down to 880 meters. He pulled out of this attack in a climbing turn to starboard, after which he headed back to base.

Major D.P. Os'kin, commander of the
523rd IAP, in China, 1951.

Guards Major Os'kin, having completed a 180° turn to starboard, sighted six B-29s in front of him, flying line abreast. Os'kin attacked the bomber on the extreme right of the formation, firing from a range of 730 meters down to 440 meters. He pulled out of the attack above the bombers, at which point he saw that the left outboard engine of the B-29 that he had attacked was burning. He then returned to base.

Here's how one participant in this action, Dmitrii Aleksandrovich Samoilov of the 523rd IAP, describes it when flying as the wingman to the regiment leader Major Dmitrii Pavlovich Os'kin:

> Having flown to the area where enemy aircraft had been detected, our regiment was attacked by two groups of enemy fighters. We engaged in a difficult combat with them. My commander, using a vertical maneuver, came out from under the enemy attack, and then he himself went over to the attack. Just when he, in my opinion, had closed within firing range, I caught sight of nine B-29 bombers and immediately informed the leader that we had "big ones" (as we called the B-29s) to the right and below us. Os'kin broke off his attack against the fighters and went after the B-29s, having issued the order: "Everyone is to attack the big ones!"
>
> Os'kin conducted the first attack in a converging pass, and with a salvo from all three cannons flamed one B-29. When the leader was maneuvering for a second attack, a pair of F-84s from the direct escort tried to attack him. I forced the Thunderjets to break off their attack with a burst across the front of their noses, while the leader attacked a second B-29 from behind and left it burning. Fuel was running low, and the order came to return to base. Our regiment downed several enemy fighters and bombers in this battle, while we had no losses; only one pilot had a bullet hole that he had received from a B-29 gunner.

Meanwhile the battle continued. Guards Major A.P. Trefilov saw F-84 jets in front of him and engaged them. The combat went on in the vertical plane. In short order, separate elements of F-86s arrived on the scene. Captain S.A. Bakhaev's flight encountered eight F-86s approaching from the left at the same altitude. Captain Bakhaev and his flight went around once with the F-86s, after which the Sabres straightened out and headed to the west. Bakhaev and his flight moved to close with the bombers. He attacked the B-29s from behind, firing all three cannons at the second bomber in the formation from a range of 800 meters down to 340 meters; the other pilots observed shells striking this B-29.

Together with his wingman, Captain Bakhaev passed over the bombers before pulling out of the attack in a climbing turn to port. At this time Bakhaev spotted two B-29s to the right, with eight Meteors to the right of them. Bakhaev banked to the right and launched a high-side attack against the left-hand B-29, pulled in behind the bomber and fired from a range of 1,200 meters down to 740 meters. He passed over the bombers at high speed and pulled into a climbing turn to the right, after which he headed back to base.

Captain Bakhaev's wingman, Grigorii Kharitonovich D'iachenko relates:

> After crossing the Yalu River, a large group of F-86s (up to 50 of them) met us, but we nevertheless broke through their screen. Then we tangled with the F-84s – the bombers' immediate escort. In the swirl of battle our element, which consisted of my leader Captain S.A. Bakhaev and me, saw five B-29s flying between two layers of clouds, and we all plunged down on them from altitude. The dive speed was nearing the maximum allowable, and we had to deploy our speed breaks to slow our MiGs down. To throw off the aimed fire of the B-29 gunners, I fishtailed to the left and right. I opened fire at the third B-29 with all three cannons, and saw my shells strike home, while my leader fired at the B-29 in the middle of the formation. We linked back up just above the upper layer of clouds. We turned and conducted another firing pass, this time attacking the remaining three B-29s from below. The leader shot down one, while I drove off counterattacks by enemy fighters. Soon we safely returned to base. In this battle, according to the pilots' debriefings and gun camera footage, the division's pilots downed around 20 enemy bombers and fighters. However, the corps commander General G.A. Lobov didn't believe this information, noting that our claims were too many, and disallowed a few of the victories, including my own. However, when he received official word that of the 28 B-29s only 10 returned to base [sic.], of which a few more crashed upon landing, he credited everyone with their victories, including me.

On the approach to the bombers, Senior Lieutenant N.G. Kovalenko's element, which was part of Bakhaev's flight, tied up four F-84s in combat that were trying to block Bakhaev's flight from reaching the bombers. Senior Lieutenant Kovalenko used vertical maneuvers to get behind the Thunderjets. His wingman Senior Lieutenant I.A. Rybalko fired all three of his cannons at the Thunderjets from a range of 1,550 meters down to 720 meters.

Captain Okhai's six MiGs encountered eight F-86s converging from the left at the same altitude, which they had come across prior to this while climbing. In this action, neither side could obtain an advantageous position for conducting aimed fire.

Senior Lieutenant I.I. Iakovlev closed upon the bombers with his flight and conducted an attack from above, behind and to the left. He opened fire with all three cannons from the long range of 4,400 meters and ceased firing at a range of 1,420 meters. He pulled out of the attack, passing above the bombers, with a turn to the left before heading back to base.

On its way back to base, Senior Lieutenant Iakovlev's element was taken by surprise and bounced by four F-86s in an area 15-20 kilometers northwest of Andong, as a result of which the MiG flown by Senior Lieutenant Vasilii Mikhailovich Khurtin burst into flames and fell burning into a hill 3 kilometers southwest of Gaolimyn, which lies 12 kilometers southeast of Funkhuanchen; the pilot was killed in the crash.

Senior Lieutenant A.M. Shevarev's element from Iakovlev's flight also attacked the bombers together with his wingman. Shevarev opened fire with all three cannons at a range of 1,760 meters and ceased firing as he closed to 400 meters. His wingman Senior Lieutenant F.V. Medvedev simultaneously fired all three cannons from a range of 2,200 meters down to 1,450 meters. Senior Lieutenant Shevarev passed over the bombers before pulling into a shallow turn to port, after which he spotted two B-29s. Banking to the right, he attacked one of the bombers from the left and behind at the same altitude. He fired all three cannons from a range of 1,460 meters down to a range of 440 meters. He exited the attack with a turn to the right after passing over the bombers, and then returned to base.

The aerial combat between our fighters and the enemy's bombers and fighters lasted for 12 minutes. In the course of it, five B-29s were downed, of which Guards Major Os'kin claimed two, while deputy squadron commander Captain Bakhaev, deputy political squadron command Senior Lieutenant D'iachenko and Senior Lieutenant Shevarev each downed one. One F-84 was seen going down under the cannon fire of Senior Lieutenant Rybalko by other pilots, but the gun camera film didn't confirm this.

Despite the "seething" Sabres and Thunderjets circling the B-29s, separate elements from the 17th IAP and 523rd IAP also got through to the bomber groups and conducted high-speed attacks against them, many of which scored. At 0845, a regimental group of 20 MiGs from the 17th IAP under the command of Major B.V. Maslennikov arrived in the combat area. Flying in the cover group, at an altitude of 8,500 meters they spotted a group of nearly 20 F-86s to the left and 500 meters above them, which were approaching to intercept them. Simultaneously, they sighted 11 B-29 bombers escorted by F-84s and Meteors at an altitude of 7,000 meters. The bombers were in a column formation by flights: the first flight of three aircraft were in a wedge formation, while the trailing second and third flights of four bombers each were in diamond formations. The direct escort consisted of 20 F-84 fighters and eight Meteors.

Having assessed the situation, Major Maslennikov ordered the 2nd and 3rd Squadrons to attack the screening Sabres, while he led the 1st Squadron into an attack upon the bombers. A participant in this combat Aleksei Nikolaevich Nikolaev recalls:

> We had just emerged from the clouds when we ran into enemy fighters. I and my leader Volkov somehow wound up off to one side of the dogfight. Soon I saw a group of British Gloster Meteors below and to the right, and notified my leader about this. They presented an enticing target, because the Meteors were slower and less maneuverable than our MiGs. However, the leader answered me: "We're

going after the big ones." That's when I spotted the "big ones" – the famous B-29 Superfortresses that had dropped the atomic bombs on Japan in 1945. They were flying in two groups of four, in a diamond formation. I was strongly upset that my leader opened fire on the bombers at very long range, and his fire inflicted no damage on them. Even before reaching the B-29 formation, he pulled out of the attack in a chandelle to the left. I decided to press the attack, since I didn't see any enemy fighters around. From a range of 400 meters I opened fire, targeting the left engine on one of the B-29s. The cannon fire shook my aircraft, and at maximum speed I flashed past above the bombers. I pulled out of the attack in a chandelle to the left, gained altitude, and took a careful look around. I didn't see anything other than the B-29 formation. The B-29 I had attacked had dropped out of the formation and was engulfed in flames.

I decided to attack another B-29 and went after it just as I had the first one. As I was passing over the Superfortress formation, I heard a powerful thump against my aircraft. The thought flashed through my head, "They've hit me, the swine!" However, my aircraft continued to climb steadily, there were no flames, and I pointed my MiG toward home. Several enemy fighters were rushing to intercept me, but I avoided their attacks. There was a loud din on the airwaves. I safely made my way back to Miaogou, but I had to crank down my landing gear manually, and having taxied to my place and climbed out of my MiG, I found out that the hydraulics system had been damaged, and my ammunition cases had been riddled by fragments, but fortunately all turned out well, and I added two "Fortresses" to my personal score.

Two or three days after the battle, regiment commander G.I. Pulov dropped by our barrack early in the morning, and his voice woke me up: "Nikolai, get up, a Superfortress gunner has sent you a letter." I told him that I didn't know any gunner. In response he handed me a sheet of paper, which carried a sketched diagram of a lone MiG's attack on a B-29 group and a letter in English. Here Pulov made a translation of the letter and handed it to me as a remembrance. Unfortunately, I no longer have it.

However, despite Nikolaev's claim, not all the pilots were given credit for their victories. For example, at first Captain Bakhaev received credit for his two victories over Superfortresses, but then one was stricken from his personal score; Senior Lieutenants Shabanov, Stepanov and Nikolaev received credit for the two Superfortresses that they jointly downed, but then again one was disallowed. Other pilots experienced the same thing.

As a result, according to the official documents of the 64th IAK, the pilots of the 303rd IAD on this day were credited with downing only 10 B-29s: two by pilots of the 18th GIAP (Lieutenant Colonel A.P. Smorchkov and Captain N.L. Kornienko); five by pilots of the 523rd IAP (Major D.P. Os'kin, who downed two, Captain S.A. Bakhaev, and Senior Lieutenants G.Kh. D'iachenko and A.M. Shevarev); and three B-29s by Captain S.S. Bychkov, Senior Lieutenant A.N. Nikolaev and Senior Lieutenant A.V. Bykov of the 17th IAP.

In addition, pilots of the 303rd IAD shot down three F-84s in this battle. Soviet losses amounted to just one MiG-15, which Sabres shot down already after the main dogfight ended, when our pilots were returning to base. Three more MiG-15s received combat damage: Senior Lieutenant A.N. Nikolaev's aircraft had one bullet hole in the lower fuse-lage. Lieutenant Colonel A.P. Smorchkov and Senior Lieutenant Iu.A. Ustiuzhaninov of the 18th GIAP also returned from the battle with light damage to their MiGs.

Fifteen minutes after the regiments of the 303rd IAD took off, the 64th IAK command scrambled both regiments of the 324th IAD to reinforce them. The 324th IAD also adopted a combat formation consisting of a strike group, which included 12 MiGs of the 196th IAP under the command of Major A.I. Mitusov, and a covering group comprised by 14 MiGs of the 176th GIAP under the command of Lieutenant Colonel S.F. Vishniakov. Lieutenant Colonel Vishniakov was the senior in command on this mission.

The pilots of the 324th IAD arrived in the area of Anju when the battle was already essentially winding down, so they only carried out the task of covering the 303rd IAD's aircraft as they withdrew from combat. One brief action occurred against several pairs of enemy fighters that were pursuing the 303rd IAD's MiGs, but they quickly broke off the fight. Soon all the fighters of the 324th IAD returned to base without any losses.

According to American records, only eight B-29 bombers from the 307th BG were committed to this raid, and the MiGs that had broken through to them had quickly downed two of the Superfortresses even before they could drop their bombs. A third B-29, bearing the inscription *Charlie* on its nose, was set on fire by the MiGs, but the commander Captain Thomas L. Shields coolly brought his burning bomber out over the sea and put it down in the water, thereby saving his crew. The brave commander died in the flames of his cockpit, but his crew managed to escape the burning aircraft and was soon picked up by the US Air-Sea Rescue Service.

A fourth B-29 was also left burning after a MiG attack; its crew diligently attempted to put out the fire onboard the aircraft. This B-29 crashed in South Korea due to the serious damage caused by the MiGs' 37mm cannons. Three of the remaining B-29s returned to the Kadena Air Base with dead and wounded crewmembers on board, but were written-off due to the heavy damage they had received on the mission.

The Americans themselves claimed to have downed five MiGs, two by pilots of the 336th FIS, two more by gunners aboard the Superfortresses from the 307th BG's 371st Squadron, and one MiG by Thunderjet pilots from the 136th FBW's 154th FBS. However, it is known reliably that in this battle the 64th IAK lost only one aircraft and one pilot, who was downed by Sabres; the Corps suffered no other losses on this day, and all the other victories claimed by pilots and gunners of the USAF are simply incorrect.

According to recent research by the historian Diego Zampini, nine B-29 medium bombers of the 307th BG took part on this raid, which were divided into three flights, Able, Baker and Charlie. Able Flight consisted of B-29s No.44-61816, No.44-87760 and No.42-94045, which were respectively commanded by Captains Clarence I. Fogler, James R. Lewis and Robert M. Krumm; all three aircraft belonged to the 371st BS. The second wave, Baker Flight, was headed by 1st Lieutenant William F. Reeter and his crew in B-29A No.44-86295; the rest of the flight consisted of Captain James A. Foulks' B-29 No.44-61940 and Major William R. Griner, Jr.'s B-29 No.44-27347 – all from the 372nd BS. Finally, B-29A No.44-70151 (commanded by Captain Thomas Shields) and B-29s No.44-61824 and No.44-86376 from the 370th BS comprised Charlie Flight.

The bombers of Charlie Flight were the first to come under the attack of MiGs from the 18th GIAP and Lieutenant Colonel Smorchkov managed to down B-29 No.44-70151, which fell into the sea – the entire crew perished. Another 18th GIAP pilot, Captain Kornienko, seriously damaged B-29 No.44-61824, which managed to reach its base at Kadena and make a forced landing there, after which the aircraft was written off.

Then Able and Baker Flights were attacked by MiGs from the 17th IAP and 523rd IAP: Major Dmitrii Os'kin shot down B-29 No.42-94045 from the 371st BS and on his next pass shot down B-29 No.44-61940 from the 372nd BS – both bombers plunged into the sea, taking both crews with them. After this, it was the turn for two bombers from Baker Flight, B-29s No.44-27347 and No.44-86295 of the 372nd BS, which were both seriously damaged by the 523rd IAP's Captain Bakhaev and Senior Lieutenant D'iachenko respectively. Both bombers managed to reach the Kimpo Air Base in South Korea with difficulty and made crash landings there with both dead and wounded aboard. Both bombers were written off as scrap metal.

After this, pilots of the 17th IAP took over, who succeeded in hitting the remaining three of the group's bombers from Able and Charlie Flights: Senior Lieutenant Nikolaev downed B-29 No.44-87760 from the 370th BS – some of the crew was killed, while the rest were able to bail out and were taken prisoner. Captain Bykov seriously damaged Able Flight's B-29 No.44-61816, which managed to make it back to the Kadena Air Base, but was later sent to the squadron's bone yard as a source of spare parts. Then finally Captain Bychkov damaged B-29 No.44-86376 of the 370th BS, which was the only bomber of the nine Boeings that took part in the mission to make a safe landing at Kimpo and was subsequently repaired.

In addition, Senior Lieutenant L.K. Shchukin of the 18th GIAP managed to shoot down F-84 No.50-1220 of the 136th FBW's 111th FBS, the pilot of which 1st Lieutenant John W. Shewmaker was killed. Only the commander of the 336th FIS Major Richard Creighton managed in this battle to achieve the opposing side's single victory – it was he who shot down Senior Lieutenant Khurtin from the 523rd IAP. A tail gunner aboard B-29 No.44-87760, Sergeant Jerry Webb, who was taken prisoner later, damaged the MiG of Senior Lieutenant Nikolaev from the 17th IAP.

So this major battle in the skies of Korea, which the Americans later nicknamed "Black Thursday", ended with that distribution of victories and losses. In fact, the losses of the US Bomber Command were extremely heavy in pilots and crews. However, the operation to destroy the North Korean airfields continued, and Bomber Command sent fresh groups of their B-29s against these primary targets.

More American raids were launched on 24 October, and pilots of the 303rd IAD twice took off to repel enemy air attacks. The first sortie took place in the morning, when all three regiments of the 303rd IAD took off for the Anju area; however, the adversary declined to engage the MiGs and returned to friendly territory. Yet that afternoon the Fifth Air Force command undertook an attack upon the Saamchan airfield with eight B-29s from the 98th BG's 344th Squadron, which were escorted by 16 Meteors from the RAAF No. 77 Squadron and 10 F-84s from the 136th FBW. Twenty Sabres from the 336th FIS were sent ahead as a forward screen.

Only pilots of the 303rd IAD took part in repulsing this raid. At 1406, 16 MiGs of the 523rd IAP lifted off the runway, followed by 20 MiGs of the 18th GIAP. At 1410, 19

MiGs of the 17th IAP began to take off. As on the day before, Lieutenant Colonel A.P. Smorchkov was placed in overall command of the divisional group. Once in the air, the commanders of the regimental groups were given the following combat assignments: the 523rd IAP was to engage the forward screen of Sabres, while pilots of the 18th GIAP and 17th IAP were to break through to the bombers.

At 1422, Major D.P. Os'kin, the commander of the 523rd IAP's regimental group, which was flying in a formation of echeloned squadrons, unexpectedly ran into five groups of enemy fighters, numbering up to 30 F-86s and up to 12 Gloster Meteors, at an altitude of 10,000 meters in the Sonchon area. The enemy groups were staggered in altitude between 8,000 and 10,000 meters. The regiment commander issued an order, "Fight in flights and elements." Having indicated the area and altitude of the dogfight, he managed to conserve the correlation of forces and to secure mutual cooperation between the elements.

Only Captain S.A. Bakhaev's element managed to break through to the B-29s, but once again the Sabres prevented them from attacking the bombers. Here is how Grigorii Kharitonovich D'iachenko describes this combat:

> When the fight with the Sabres began, my leader received an order from the ground to head to the Pyongyang area, where B-29s were operating. So our element headed toward there. Nearing the target, we spotted five B-29s and went on the attack. However, that's when I noticed that six F-86s were closing on us from below and behind. I warned the leader, and he broke off the attack and climbed toward the sun. The Sabres lost us in the sun's rays, but we ourselves overlooked an attack by two Sabres that had been positioned above us. Maneuvering into firing position, they opened up on me from a range of 50-100 meters, and my aircraft started to burn. I managed to turn back to the north and began gliding in my burning MiG, the engine of which was dead. I glided from an altitude of 10,000 meters down to 5,000 meters, until flames entered my cockpit. Then I decided to abandon my aircraft, and throwing off the canopy, I punched out of the MiG. I came down on a patch of level ground among the slopes of high hills, and lost consciousness when I hit the ground. I woke up to a rattle of gunfire and the hum of bullets. North Korean soldiers had taken me for an American pilot and were shooting at me. With difficulty I wiggled out of the parachute and crawled behind a nearby boulder. However, soon the firing ceased thanks to the intervention of some Chinese Volunteers, which had responded to the firing and had come to my rescue. Having bandaged me, they carried me to the bunker of the commander of the Chinese People's Volunteers in Korea, General Peng Dehuai. On the next day they drove me through Andong to a Chinese hospital; from there I was transported back to Moscow.

As D'iachenko relates, in an area 20 kilometers south of Anju he was unexpectedly attacked by two F-86s from below and behind. His aircraft's controls were damaged by the Sabre fire, and due to loss of control Senior Lieutenant D'iachenko ejected from his MiG at 5,000 meters. The aircraft was destroyed, while the pilot suffered a back injury.

G. Kh. D'iachenko, who prior to this combat had scored two victories in the skies of Korea, was shot down by Colonel Harrison Thyng, who achieved the Sabres' only victory on this day. Meanwhile, the Sabres in turn became the prey of the pilots of one element, led by Senior Lieutenant D.A. Samoilov with his wingman Senior Lieutenant M.A. Zykov, who each downed two F-86s in this battle. As a result of the combat with the enemy escort fighters, the pilots of the 523rd IAP claimed five F-86s and three Gloster Meteors.

At 1435, the pilots of the 18th GIAP chased down the B-29 group that was being escorted by Thunderjets and Gloster Meteors. The bombers had already jettisoned their bombs and were beginning to leave the area in the direction of Korea Bay. Smorchkov, assessing the situation, ordered the 1st Squadron to engage the fighters, while he took the 2nd and 3rd Squadrons against the bombers.

Smorchkov together with his wingman Senior Lieutenant V.A. Voistiny attacked one of the Superfortresses. Smorchkov closed to within short range of the B-29 and was caught in the heavy fire from the bombers' gunners. One bullet penetrated his cockpit and wounded the pilot in the leg. Despite his wound, Smorchkov completed his attack and set fire to one B-29 with a salvo from all three of his cannons. The flames quickly spread and the crew soon started to bail from the burning bomber.

Smorchkov withdrew from the battle and accompanied by his wingman safely brought his MiG back to Miaogou and made a landing there. After touching down and rolling to a stop, Smorchkov was assisted out of his cockpit and transported to a hospital, where he

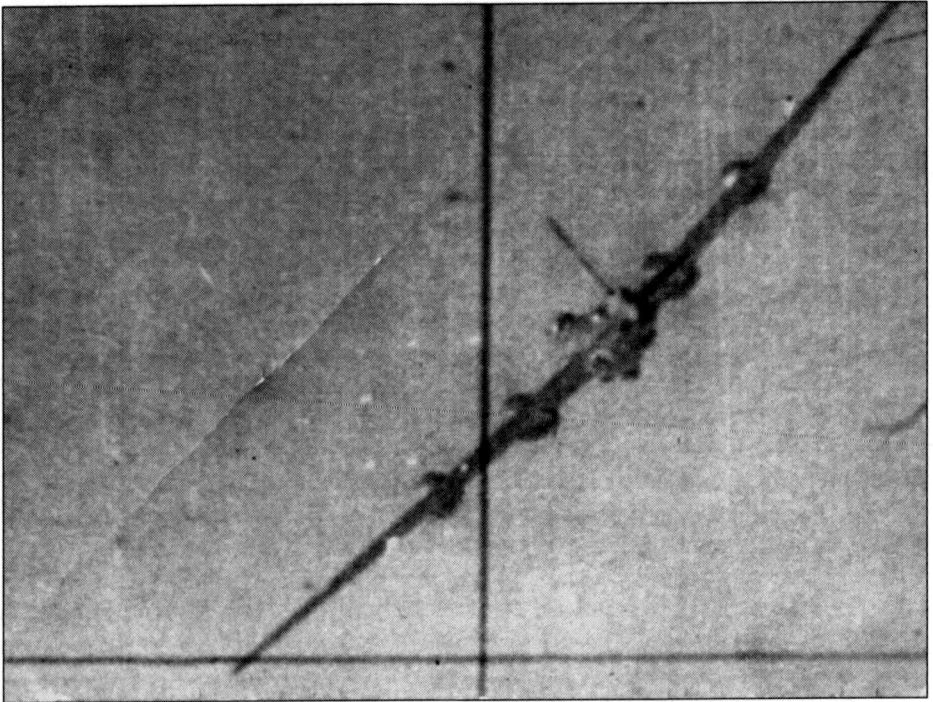

Smorchkov's victory: A frame from Lieutenant Colonel Smorchkov's gun camera footage – a B-29 is in his gunsight (October 1951).

spent a month in recovery before returning to the regiment. He went on to down three more US aircraft in the skies of Korea and pushed his personal score in this war to 12 victories.

Meanwhile, the battle continued. After the loss of one Superfortress, the remaining bombers reached the sea and returned to Kadena. The enemy fighters continued to offer combat, but the slower and less maneuverable Meteors from No. 77 Squadron could do nothing with the agile and speedy MiGs and lost the dogfight. One of these Meteors was downed by the 18th GIAP's Senior Lieutenant L.K. Shchukin. With his wingman Senior Lieutenant A.A. Astapovsky, he engaged a flight of Meteors at first with a horizontal maneuver, but then took the fight into the vertical. In a climb, where the Meteor's engine lacked sufficient power, Shchukin caught one of them and shot it down from short range. The three others withdrew from the combat. Our pilots had no losses in this combat, not including Smorchkov's wound.

In this fight on 24 October 1951, in which the B-29s had once again failed to reach their targets and had returned to their Kadena Air Base, the pilots of the 303rd IAD claimed nine enemy aircraft: one B-29, four Meteors, and four F-86s. Their own losses amounted to one MiG-15; another MiG was damaged and its pilot was wounded. The Americans recognize the loss of one B-29 (No.44-61932) from the 98th BG's 343rd Squadron. Two more bombers (No.44-27431 and No.44-86346) from the same 343rd Squadron were damaged, one of which, hit by the 18th GIAP's Senior Lieutenant V.S. Shabanov's cannon fire, made a forced landing in Taegu.

In addition, Senior Lieutenant L.K. Shchukin from the same 18th GIAP plainly damaged Lieutenant Hamilton Foster's Meteor A77-316 from No. 77 Squadron. The Australian pilot flew back to his base and made a successful landing, and the plane was soon repaired.

A pair of pilots from the 523rd IAP, Senior Lieutenants D.A. Samoilov and M.A. Zykov, delivered a thorough drubbing to the American pilots of the 4th FIW. Flying as an element, Samoilov shot down F-86A No.49-1236 and F-86A No.49-1109, and their pilots 1st Lieutenant Bradley Irish of the 334th FIS and 1st Lieutenant Fred Wicks of the 336th FIS both became prisoners of war. Zykov managed to damage seriously 1st Lieutenant Dayton Ragland's F-86A; although he managed to land his damaged Sabre in Suwon, it was soon written off.

The Americans themselves announced that they had shot down two MiGs: one by Colonel Thyng, who would soon assume command of the 4th FIW, and one by gunners of the 98th BG's 343rd BS. Mostly likely, the gunners were claiming Lieutenant Colonel Smorchkov's MiG, but it was only damaged and the wounded pilot returned safely to Miaogou.

After taking such heavy losses, the Bomber Command decided to suspend the raids for a spell, in order to recover after "Black Thursday". However, this didn't mean a halt to combat operations in MiG Alley. The fighter-bombers of the US Fifth Air Force simply took over the lead role.

There were no major clashes on 25 October. However, groups of F-80 fighter-bombers covered by Sabres made an appearance in the Anju area, while carrier-based aviation of the US Navy operated from the sea east of Anju. MiG groups from the 17th IAP and 18th GIAP were directed to intercept these groups of enemy aircraft in the area of Sonchon. In the Sukchon area, the 18th GIAP's pilots encountered several small groups of F-80s and chased them out to sea. In this action Captain N.L. Kornienko distinguished himself by adding one Sabre to his score, after which the MiGs returned to base without any losses.

Meanwhile, the 17th IAP's pilots, in addition to tangling with Sabres, also happened to bump into carrier aircraft on this day. Here's how Nikolai Grigor'evich Dokashenko, a participant in this rare encounter, describes it: "Somehow in an area east of Anju, I and my wingman encountered 12 enemy carrier fighter-bombers, which we immediately scattered, but not before downing one of them, while the rest turned back and headed for the sea. We ceased our pursuit of them, since we were low on fuel, and we returned to our base." His wingman on this mission, V.M. Khvostantsev, recalls:

> As a result of our maneuvers with the Sabres, Dokashenko and I wound up below the action. The GCI post informed us that carrier aircraft were operating under the clouds; well, the leader dove beneath the clouds into some sort of canyon, and how we avoided smashing into the mountainsides, I don't know. All my attention in this difficult meteorological condition was focused on not losing Dokashenko. Just then I saw these black piston-engine aircraft. They were flying right across our front at a target aspect angle of 4/4; I gave them a burst and followed my leader, who swung in behind one of the carrier-based aircraft and quickly shot it down.
>
> Back on the ground we spent a long time examining Dokashenko's gun camera footage. We were trying to determine the downed enemy aircraft's type from it and from our discussions. There were a lot of opinions, some saying it was a Corsair, but we decided it was a Hellcat. In this combat, other than our pair, no one else encountered carrier aircraft.

At 0700 a group of 20 MiGs from the 17th IAP under the command of Major B.V. Maslennikov had encountered a group of F-80 fighter-bombers and a flight of what they identified as F6F-5 Hellcats, which were attacking a railroad station. Flying as the third element in the 3rd Squadron's formation, Captain N.G. Dokashenko and his wingman V.M. Khvostantsev attacked four of the Hellcats angling across their front and with one burst Dokashenko downed one of them.

In reality, in this combat Dokashenko shot down a carrier-based F4U-4 Corsair (No.81576) from VF-713. Its pilot Lieutenant (jg) Leo W. Dorsey ditched his Corsair in Wonsan Harbor and was picked up by a rescue helicopter.

In addition, the aircraft downed by Captain N.L. Kornienko was likely an F-80 from the 51st FIG's 25th Squadron, which was also lost on 25 October. However it was, the US lost two aircraft on this day from the opposition of MiGs. The 64th IAK had no losses.

On 26 October 1951, the pilots of the 4th FIW took revenge for their losses on 24 October. On this day they were escorting groups of F-80 fighter-bombers. As always, the first raid was conducted in the morning around 0900. As usual, the 64th IAK's MiGs met them in the area of Anju. Pilots of the 303rd IAD's 17th IAP and 18th GIAP and of the 324th IAD's 196th IAP took off to repel the raid. On this occasion 16 MiGs of the 18th GIAP, serving as the attack group, encountered a Sabre group at an altitude of 8,000 meters and engaged it. Meanwhile, the 12 MiGs from the 196th IAP attacked the fighter-bomber groups, which were operating at low altitude. Our pilots estimated their

Lieutenant Fedor Akimovich Shebanov, future Hero of the Soviet Union of the 196th IAP who would be killed in action in the skies of Korea on 29 October 1951 (a 1948 photo).

Hero of the Soviet Union Captain N.G. Dokashenko (a 1952 photo).

overall number as 30 aircraft. Combat with Shooting Stars flared up in the Dziosiri area, in the course of which the 196th IAP's pilots downed three F-80s. However, it was in this battle that Hero of the Soviet Union and 196th IAP ace Senior Lieutenant Fedor Akimovich Shebanov was killed. At one point in the dogfight, Shebanov was attacked by three F-80s, one of which hit Shebanov's aircraft with machine-gun fire, and it fell trailing a plume of smoke about 35 kilometers southwest of Pyongyang, 7 kilometers north of the point Riuko.

A former pilot of the 196th IAP, Aleksei Antonovich Tiron confirms the story that Fedor Shebanov had become distracted by the "hunt" and had gone off on his own, which is what killed him in his final battle:

> Fedor Shebanov was always hard-headed. He always became separated from his leader, pre-occupied with a "free hunt". He'd find one and shoot it down. They were always chewing him out at every debriefing: "Do not abandon the leader!" But it was also the case that they don't punish victors. He was shooting them down after all! They awarded him with the title Hero of the Soviet Union for his victories. On his first sortie after acquiring his new title, he again left his leader and pounced on a Sabre. But on the second sortie, they got him. Koreans later brought back his remains.

The pilots of the 18th GIAP encountered a group of F-86s in the Sunchon area and engaged them in a dogfight, in which Senior Lieutenant V.I. Stepanov added a Sabre to his score, after which they returned to base without losses. Stepanov's element had attacked a flight of Sabres, and having obtained an advantageous position with a skillful maneuver, he shot up the Sabre from point-blank range.

According to research by Diego Zampini, in this battle the 196th IAP's pilots were fighting not with F-80s, but with a group of F-84s, and they downed two Thunderjets, No.51-552 and No.51-1159 from the 136th FBW; one of them was being flown by the commander of the 182nd FBS Lieutenant Colonel James Witt, who became a prisoner of war.

That afternoon at 1455, 21 MiGs from the 17th IAP intercepted a group of 14 F-80s, which was being covered by eight Sabres. Part of the regimental group took on the Sabres, while the rest went after the Shooting Stars. Regiment commander Major G.I. Pulov managed to shoot down one F-80, and through their combined efforts, the Soviet pilots drove the remaining fighter-bombers back out over the sea. Meanwhile the pilots of the 2nd Squadron, which were serving as the covering group, were locked in combat with the F-86s. At 1500 in the Sukchon area, while maneuvering against the Sabres, the MiG being piloted by Senior Lieutenant B.A. Kordanov was jumped by a pair of F-86s. As .50 caliber bullets hammered his MiG, there was an explosion in the cockpit. Senior Lieutenant Kordanov decided to abandon his stricken aircraft and ejected at an altitude of 3,000 meters, coming to earth near the village of Nampo-ri, which lies 13 kilometers west of Sukchon. Kordanov received burns to his face.

The leader Major V.P. Pravorotov had made a poor decision to descend through a cloud layer, because they had lost speed as they had cautiously let down through the clouds; an enemy aircraft, exploiting its superior speed, had quickly closed to within 100 meters and opened fire on Senior Lieutenant Kordanov's MiG.

As a result, one F-80 from the 51st FIG's 25th Squadron was lost in this afternoon combat, while we lost one MiG in return, which was downed by 1st Lieutenant Douglas Evans from the 336th FIS. According to American records, there were no F-86 losses on this day.

On 27 October 1951 there was another daytime raid by Superfortresses into the interior of North Korea, and as it turned out later, this was the final daylight raid in this war to feature an encounter between MiGs and B-29s. Eight Superfortresses from the 19th BG took off from Kadena in order to destroy the Saamchan airfield. They received heavy escort: approximately 20 F-86s, 32 F-84 Thunderjets from the 49th and 136th FBW, as well as 16 Gloster Meteors from the RAAF's No. 77 Squadron.

At 0855 Major General G.A. Lobov ordered the pilots of the 303rd IAD to repel this raid: 20 MiGs of the 18th GIAP led by Lieutenant Colonel A.E. Belostotsky were first to take off. They were followed by 20 MiGs of the 17th IAP under the command of Major B.V. Maslennikov; finally, at 0902, 22 MiGs of the 523rd IAP under the command of Lieutenant Colonel A.N. Karasev departed. This time, the pilots of the 523rd IAP served as the attack group, while the 17th IAP's and 18th GIAP's regimental groups were to take on the covering fighters. The first to become engaged were the pilots of the 18th GIAP, who ran into the forward screen of Sabres just beyond the Yalu River. The second barrier to the MiG pilots consisted of 32 Thunderjets, which the 17th IAP's pilots engaged. The 523rd IAP's pilots, who became the heroes of this battle, attacked the bombers. Therefore we'll take a close look at the actions of this regiment's pilots.

Hero of the Soviet Union
Colonel A.N. Karasev,
commander of the 523rd IAP –
a mid-1950s photo.

At 0917 while flying at an altitude of 8,000 meters, the 523rd IAP's Guards Lieutenant Colonel Karasev spotted eight B-29s and up to 64 fighters of the immediate escort 25 kilometers northeast of Sonchon at an altitude of 6,000 meters. The bombers were flying in two compact diamond formations of four each, echeloned to the left. The immediate escort fighters were arranged with eight Gloster Meteors in advance of and to the right of the bombers; 32 Thunderjets and eight more Meteors 2 to 3 kilometers behind the bombers and at a higher altitude; and two eight-ship formations of Sabres 1 to 2 kilometers to the left and above the B-29s. Having assessed the situation, Guards Lieutenant Colonel Karasev decided to attack the bombers with the 1st and 3rd Squadrons, leaving the pilots of the 2nd Squadron to cover their attacks.

At this point, the B-29 flights were to the front and left of the 523rd IAP's regimental group and now 500-1,000 meters below it, flying on a heading of 10° to 20°. Karasev's element attacked the lead B-29 from behind and above, firing with all three cannons from a range of 1,000 meters down to 600 meters, and saw his shells striking the middle of the B-29's fuselage. His wingman Senior Lieutenant I.K. Semenenko simultaneously targeted the right-hand wingman, opening fire from all of his cannons at a range of 2,500 meters and ceasing fire when he had closed to within 1,200 meters.

Karasev passed over the bombers before pulling out of the attack in a shallow turn to port, after which he reversed course and attacked the left-hand bomber in the trailing diamond from above and behind. Closing to within 1,200 meters of it, he opened fire again with all three cannons, and ceased fire at a range of 720 meters. He then pulled out of the attack above the bombers with a subsequent return to base in a high-speed climb.

On his first pass against the bombers, Karasev had been attacked from above and behind by one F-84. Back on the ground, they found one bullet hole in the upper tailfin.

Captain D.V. Mazilov, who led the trailing element in Karasev's flight, attacked the right-hand B-29 in the lead flight from above and behind. Mazilov fired all three cannons from a range of 1,200-1,100 meters, before pulling out of the attack above the bombers with a subsequent turn to port. When passing through the Thunderjet screen, Mazilov's wingman Senior Lieutenant M.D. Ovchinnikov opened fire at one F-84 as it angled across his nose. He fired from all three cannons at 110 meters and ceased fire at 550 meters, but the tracers passed to the right of the Thunderjet.

Flight commander Senior Lieutenant Iakovlev followed Karasev's flight into the attack upon the bombers, leading his flight in a column of elements against the first B-29 diamond from above and behind. He opened fire from all three cannons at a range of 1,550 meters and continued firing as the range closed to 720 meters, but led the bomber slightly with his aim. His wingman Senior Lieutenant S.D. Krupchatnikov also fired all three cannons from a range of 1,000 meters down to 850 meters. The shells all missed high.

Iakovlev pulled out of the attacking pass, passing over the bombers before swinging around for a repeat attack, which he conducted against the same B-29 flight. He opened fire at a range of 1,550 meters. Once again pulling out of the attack over the bomber formation, he subsequently climbed away and headed back to base.

The flight's second element, consisting of Senior Lieutenant A.M. Shevarev and his wingman F.V. Medvedev, attacked the lead group of B-29s from above, behind and to the right. Shevarev opened fire with all three cannons at a range of 1,200 meters. He pulled out of the attack above the bombers at high speed with a subsequent climbing turn to starboard, whereupon Shevarev fired at one F-84 from behind at the same altitude with all three cannons, opening fire at 550 meters before pulling out of the attack in a climbing turn to starboard. At this point he returned to base.

Guards Major Trefilov's six-MiG group failed to break through to the bombers and wound up tangled in combat with a group of F-84s from the B-29s' immediate escort. During the dogfight Trefilov attacked one F-84 from directly astern, firing from a range of 920 meters down to 440 meters. His wingman Senior Lieutenant K.T. Shal'nov simultaneously fired at a second F-84. Trefilov pulled out of the attack to the right and above and re-engaged the F-84s with a vertical maneuver.

Senior Lieutenant N.G. Kovalenko's element from Major Trefilov's flight also during the action attacked two F-84s from above, behind and to the right. Kovalenko fired a burst from all three cannons from long range at the leader's Thunderjet. He sprayed the fire without aiming. His wingman Senior Lieutenant I.A. Rybalko simultaneously fired all three cannons at the wingman's Thunderjet from a range of 1,000 meters. They pulled out of the attack in a climb to port, and then dove to resume the combat.

The Thunderjet pilots fired at our fighters from long ranges in head-on passes or with blocking fire from shallow intercepting headings. The B-29 gunners typically opened fire at our approaching MiGs at a range of 2,000 meters, and continued firing until our pilots had exited from the attack.

Captain V.P. Popov's six-ship group of MiGs also engaged the Thunderjets. However, Senior Lieutenant D.A. Samoilov's element managed to slip through to the bombers. Samoilov attacked one B-29 from behind at the same altitude, opening fire from all three cannons at 1,200 meters and continuing to fire until he had closed to within 440 meters. His wingman Senior Lieutenant M.A. Zykov simultaneously opened up on a second B-29 from a range of 1,100 meters down to 880 meters, but his shells all missed high. Samoilov pulled his element out of the attack, passing over the bombers at high speed before swinging around in a 180° turn to port while gaining altitude. Having reversed course, Samoilov sighted an F-84 and attacked it from behind at the same altitude, firing all three cannons from a range of 550 meters down to 410 meters. The Thunderjet abruptly staggered and fell into a violent dive.

At this time his wingman Senior Lieutenant Zykov was attacked by other F-84s from below and behind, and he received one bullet hole in the left wing and another in the left wingtip. Senior Lieutenant Samoilov then led his element back to base. Dmitrii Aleksandrovich Samoilov himself describes this combat:

On 27 October, Mikhail Zykov and I were the second element in 2nd Squadron commander Viktor Pavlovich Popov's flight. We took off as part of the entire regiment. Our squadron was given the assignment to tie up the covering fighters in combat. But for some reason we were placed at the end of the regiment's combat formations, behind the 1st and 3rd Squadrons. As we were flying toward the point of interception, I observed the following scene: a group of B-29 was heading for the sea entirely without fighter escort, while behind them a dogfight was going on; our two squadrons had been unable to break through to the bombers and were tied up in combat.

Asking Popov whether or not to attack the "big ones" and receiving an affirmative reply, I went into a tight turn to the right. My wingman and I were located on the right [of the formation], and in order to maintain position on the leader without realigning, I banked sharply. After coming out of the turn I discovered that my wingman and I were alone.

I decided to attack the bombers. I conducted the attack from behind and flamed one B-29. I should have then passed in front of the bombers and there reversed course for a head-on attack, but I instead went into a chandelle to the right in order to repeat the attack from behind. At this moment my wingman reported that his aircraft had been damaged. I advised him to break off combat. When I had reversed course, our fighters were coming toward me in order to attack the B-29s and the fighters of the immediate escort. I spotted and attacked one Thunderjet that was heading toward me on an intersecting course and downed him with nearly a full-deflection shot. In this combat our regiment had no losses.

Captain Popov's element in the meantime was using vertical maneuvers to combat the F-84s. He attacked one F-84 from above and behind, opened fire with all three cannons from a range of 1,200 down to 1,000 meters, but observed no hits. His wingman Senior Lieutenant B.L. Sinel'nikov simultaneously fired at a second F-84 from all three cannons at a range of 650 meters, but saw his shells pass behind the fighter-bomber. Captain Popov's element pulled out of this pass in a climbing turn to right and continued dueling with the Thunderjets.

Captain I.I. Tiuliaev with his element attacked an F-84 from the left and below, but missed. He exited the attack to the right, where he noticed a flight of Thunderjets were attacking Captain Popov's element. Tiuliaev began to close on the F-84s to force them to break off their attack and gave one burst from all three cannons across their front, but with his high speed he began to swing in front of them. Captain N.I. Mitrofanov, seeing that these Thunderjets might attack Captain Tiuliaev, gave them a burst, and the Thunderjets broke off the attack in a dive to port.

Captain Tiuliaev's element pulled out of their second attack to the right and above and spotted a pair of F-84s below them. He launched a high-side attack from behind, opened fire from a range of 730 meters – and his shells passed behind their target. He pulled out of this attack into a chandelle to the left. Mitrofanov at this time spotted a flight of F-84s 600-800 meters behind him and ordered Captain Tiuliaev to turn more tightly to the left, while he himself went into a descending turn to port. In the process he lost his leader, who finding himself alone, headed back to base. As Captain Mitrofanov was descending, he heard bullets striking his aircraft, so he pitched over into a dive. Leveling out at 4,000 meters, he took a heading back to base. Mitrofanov's aircraft had 10 bullet holes in his fuselage, wings, horizontal stabilizer and rudder; his cockpit canopy and gun sight had also been shot through. Captain Mitrofanov was wounded in the right shoulder by fragments.

Senior Lieutenant V.P. Filimonov from Captain Popov's group also engaged the F-84s. In the process, he attacked one Thunderjet from above and behind, opening fire from all three cannons at a range of 650 meters. His wingman Senior Lieutenant V.T. Roman'kov simultaneously fired a short burst at another F-84. Filimonov pulled out of the attack into a climbing turn to port. While heading back to base, Senior Lieutenant Filimonov saw four F-86s closing in on a solitary MiG-15, and with his element he forced this Sabre flight to break off its attack; winging over to the left, they headed for the sea in a dive. Senior Lieutenant Filimonov's element headed for their airfield.

During the aerial combat, 14 pilots fired at enemy aircraft. Two B-29s and two F-84s were downed. Lieutenant Colonel Karasev and Senior Lieutenant Samoilov each shot down one Superfortress. Samoilov also added an F-84 to his score, while Major Trefilov received credit for the other F-84.

In an early display of what later became a standard tactic, Sabres were trying to blockade the airfields in Manchuria, but were too late – pilots of the 18th GIAP had time to take off from the base at Miaogou. Eight MiGs of the 3rd Squadron under the command of Captain P.N. Antonov encountered 16 F-86s in the Sonchon area and engaged them, thus tying them up in battle.

In the clash with the fighters, the pilots of the 17th IAP downed one more F-84: Senior Lieutenant V.M. Khvostantsev shot it down at a range of 450 meters as it was approaching nearly head on and almost collided with it. Though he didn't report the victory upon his return to base, in the debriefing it was established that none of the other 17th IAP pilots fired at a "Cross"; three frames of his gun camera film also confirmed that the F-84 had been shot down. On the regiment's side the MiG-15 flown by Senior Lieutenant N.Ia. Perepelkin was damaged; in the dogfight he received one bullet through an engine turbine.

The 18th GIAP's pilots in their combat with the Sabres claimed two F-86s, which were credited to Captains P.N. Antonov and N.L. Kornienko, and returned to their base at Miaogou without any losses.

According to American records, all eight B-29s returned to their base at Kadena, but one of the B-29s was heavily damaged, and three more had received lighter damage. The Superfortress gunners claimed six MiG-15s, which doesn't correspond with reality, since all of our MiGs returned to base.

The hero of this 26 October 1951 fight was Senior Lieutenant D.A. Samoilov of the 523rd IAP, who seriously damaged B-29A No.44-62071 from the 19th BG's 30th BS; although it managed to fly back to Kadena, it crashed while making a forced landing and was written off. A victory over an F-84E (No.51-570 of the 136th FBG's 154th Squadron was also attributed to Senior Lieutenant Samoilov; its pilot bailed out over friendly territory. In addition, one of the Meteors from the RAAF No. 77 Squadron was hit by MiG fire: it was being flown by the group leader on the mission, Squadron Leader D.L. Wilson. His aircraft was hit by a shell in the cockpit area, and the pilot received a serious wound in the right leg. The pilot broke off combat and with great difficulty, bleeding heavily from his wound, managed to fly back to his base at Kimpo and make a safe landing there. Only one Soviet pilot, Captain V.N. Shalev from the 18th GIAP, fired at a Meteor in this battle from a range of 700 meters, but he thought his fire had no effect. As it turns out, however, this isn't so, and in this combat Shalev managed to damage one of the Meteors and put one of the commanders of No. 77 Squadron out of action.

The Superfortresses conducted their final raid in the month of October on 28 October, a Sunday: eight B-29s from the 98th BG took off from their base at Yakota to attack the Sonchon railroad bridge lying in MiG Alley. As always, the bombers were being escorted by several dozen fighters, F-86s of the 4th FIW and F-84s of the 136th FBW.

Several "trains" of MiGs (as the Americans called them) from both divisions of the 64th IAK took off to repel this raid. However, this time they couldn't break through to the bombers because of the strong fighter cover, and for the Superfortresses the raid went successfully without any interference from MiGs. However, the Sabre pilots had their hands full with the MiGs, in order to keep them away from the bombers. In the dogfights with the F-86s, the 303rd IAD's pilots claimed four victories, and one more victory was claimed by the commander of the 324th IAD's 196th IAP Lieutenant Colonel Pepeliaev. Captain N.G. Dokashenko of the 17th IAP's 3rd Squadron particularly distinguished himself in this battle: as part of a six-ship group of MiGs (the 3rd Squadron's entire operational strength), he engaged 14 Sabres and claimed three victories. His wingman Senior Lieutenant Khvostantsev had little to do but observe the enemy's burning aircraft, so successfully did his leader perform in the dogfight. It was one of the rare instances, when one of our pilots downed three enemy aircraft in one action, and all three were F-86 Sabres.

This dogfight occurred between 1449 and 1500, 15 kilometers east of Andong, where the pilots of the 17th IAP encountered a group of 14 Sabres of the forward screen and engaged them, which means the F-86s had set up their screen right along the border with China.

The F-86 group began to pass below our group. Captain V.A. Blagov's group jettisoned their drop tanks and went into an energetic turn to port. In the turn, Captain N.G. Dokashenko spotted a pair of F-86s that were attacking a MG-15 element from behind. Dokashenko opened fire on the Sabre wingman. At this moment, another F-86 element appeared 1,000 meters in front of Captain Dokashenko, and banking to the left to line up on them, he began to pull within firing range of the enemy fighters. Having closed to within 400 meters, he gave the Sabre wingman a long burst. The targeted

F-86 at first went into a descending turn to port, and then headed directly to the south. Dokashenko continued to pursue him, closed to within 200-300 meters, and opened fire again, when he himself was attacked from behind by an F-86 flight. Dokashenko came out from under their attack with a chandelle to the left; the enemy followed him, going into a climbing spiral to the left. While executing the first spiral, one of the Sabres opened fire, but the tracers passed below and behind him. At an altitude of 7,000 meters, the Sabres abandoned the chase and headed for the sea in a diving turn to port.

Meanwhile, Captain Blagov's element was attacked from below and behind by a pair of F-86s. Blagov with his wingman Lieutenant V.I. Bashlykov went into a climbing spiral to port. At this moment, the lead F-86 opened fire at Captain Dokashenko's MiG, while the Sabre wingman fired at Lieutenant Bashlykov. Captain Dokashenko spotted the attacking Sabres and moved to close with the wingman's F-86. Having pulled to within 500 meters, he gave it a long burst, as a result of which the targeted aircraft burst into flames. The lead F-86 flipped over to the right before heading in the direction of the sea. That's how N.G. Dokashenko acted in this dogfight according to 17th IAP documents. As is apparent from this report, only one of Dokashenko's attacks showed immediate results when he achieved hits against the enemy aircraft; his other two victories were credited to him only after examining his gun camera film.

Before this mission, only E.G. Pepeliaev of the 196th IAP had managed to score three victories in one action in the battle on 6 October 1951. All of our pilots returned without any losses. However, the Americans claimed that on this day 1st Lieutenant Robert H. Moore of the 336th FIS shot down a MiG. However, this was only a supposition, because the Soviet pilots on this day had no losses. According to research by Diego Zampini, in this combat of 28 October 1951, pilots of the 336th FIS 1st Lieutenant Douglas K. Evans and his wingman McPherson came under attack from Dokashenko's MiG, as did the commander of their group Major Richard D. Creighton – however, they all returned safely to base after the combat, but with the distinct impression that they had nearly become the victims of experienced MiG pilots. Thus, alas, for the sake of objectivity it must be stated that in this combat Captain Dokashenko didn't score three victories, or even one victory, but he gave a decent scare to the pilots of the 336th FIS! The American records also do not confirm the victories by Colonel E.G. Pepeliaev of the 196th IAP and Senior Lieutenant V.P. Filimonov of the 523rd IAP.

Finally, the 18th GIAP's pilots became involved in the final aerial combat of the month of October, when at the direction of the command post on the afternoon of 30 October they encountered what they identified as 36 F-84s in the Sunchon area, which were serving as a decoy group in order to divert our fighters from the main force, which was operating at lower altitudes against ground targets. A stubborn dogfight started up, in which both sides were testing the other's abilities in flying technique. Here's how a participant in this combat Lev Kirillovich Shchukin describes it:

> Sometimes it reached the point in separate horizontal and vertical maneuvers that the pilots nearly blacked out from the G-forces. Naturally my flight broke apart into separate elements, and the pairs were flying so close together that it almost disallowed any opportunity for the wingmen to fire. Sweating profusely, my wingman Senior Lieutenant A.A. Astapovsky and I, using a vertical maneuver, managed to cut inside the maneuver of one Thunderjet and to emerge on its tail at a range of

150 meters – the fire was accurate. In this combat one more F-84 was downed, which was credited to Captain N.L. Kornienko. However, two of our pilots, Senior Lieutenant B.P. Sapozhnikov and Senior Lieutenant I.A. Gorsky, also returned with several bullet holes in each of their MiGs.

In actuality, on this sortie the 18th GIAP's pilots had intercepted a group of F-80s from the 51st FIG and a group of F-84s from the 136th FBW, which were covering a reconnaissance mission by an RF-80 from the 45th TRS. Shchukin managed to shoot down the reconnaissance aircraft itself, RF-80 No.44-84849, and its pilot Grant Madsen was killed-in-action. Captain Kornienko shot down F-80 No.49-805 from the 51st FIG's 25th Squadron, and its pilot Captain Howard A. Wilson, Jr. was also killed. Another F-80, No.49-1823 from the same 25th Fighter Squadron was damaged, but its pilot was able to fly back to his base in his crippled aircraft, where he ejected from it. So far, no one has been able to determine who of the 18th GIAP's pilots damaged this Shooting Star.

Despite the relatively successful raid of 28 October, the losses suffered by Bomber Command's formations from the 19th, 98th and 307th BG were excessive. According to Soviet archival documents, the 64th IAK's pilots in the nearly daily aerial combats in the month of October 1951 shot down 101 enemy aircraft, including 45 F-86s, 26 F-84s, 16 B-29s, 9 F-80s, 4 Gloster Meteors and 1 F4U-4 Corsair. Our losses in October amounted to 8 MiG-15s destroyed, and about 10 other MiGs that were damaged, but due to the efforts of the ground crews, they all eventually returned to service. Three pilots were killed-in-action in the month of October: Captain Ivan Nikolaevich Morozov, a flight commander in the 17th IAP's 2nd Squadron; Senior Lieutenant Vasilii Mikhailovich Khurtin, a pilot in the 523rd IAP's 2nd Squadron; and Senior Lieutenant Fedor Dmitrievich Shebanov, a pilot in the 196th IAP's 3rd Squadron, who for his combat service in the skies of Korea was honored with the title Hero of the Soviet Union. Several more of the 64th IAK's pilots received wounds of varying severity. The losses of the UAA are unknown to this author, but according to estimates they amounted to 10-12 aircraft. According to records of the American side, in the October battles over Taechon, Namsi and Wonsan, five B-29s were lost, and another eight B-29s were damaged and subsequently written off. On one mission alone (23 October 1951), Bomber Command lost 55 B-29 crew members either killed or missing-in-action, and another 12 received serious wounds. Altogether, in October 2,573 MiG encounters were recorded, and they attacked UN aircraft on 2,166 occasions. According to American records, they downed 34 MiGs in aerial combat over the month, 24 of which were credited to Sabres of the 4th FIW, nine to B-29 gunners, and one to the Thunderjets of the 136th FBW. According to their records, only eight Sabres were lost in the month of October.

The victory and loss figures between the two sides differ widely, and this author regards the American numbers with a great deal of doubt, since now the accurate figure for losses of the Soviet side in this war are known. However, at the same time not all the claims by Soviet pilots for victories over F-86s have received 100% verification, so they must be assigned to the category of "probable victories" by the 64th IAK's pilots. According to Diego Zampini's ongoing research, in the month of October the Soviet pilots certainly downed at least 41 UN aircraft and damaged approximately 10 more. Even using these numbers, the correlation of victories and losses in the October fighting all the same remains 5:1 in favor of the 64th IAK's pilots!

The Americans reacted painfully to their B-29 losses. This was not only because the enormous, four-engined aircraft was very expensive to produce and if enemy fighter fire was destructive, the entire crew of 10-12 men went down with the aircraft, but also because the American military-political leadership could see with its own eyes that a further expansion of the war in Korea had no prospects. In the author's opinion, the American leadership came to such a conclusion in view of the fact that in Korea, its strategic air force showed that it would be unable to launch a decisive nuclear attack against the USSR and its allies. Although the B-29 had several .50 caliber machine guns and a system for automatically directing their fire, the war in Korea demonstrated their complete impotence against the MiG-15 jet fighters. The combat results in the month of October 1951 were more than convincing in this respect.

Of course, the initial B-29 losses provoked a sharp reaction on the part of the USAF command. Even relatively small groups of the medium bombers began to be covered by numerous groups of escort fighters, consisting of F-80 and F-84 jets. When this was shown to be ineffective, the enemy began to create "screens" or "barriers" of large groups of F-86s close to the Yalu River.

Summing up the results of the October fighting, it should be noted that the hard defeats and losses, suffered by the American air force, forced the American command to re-examine its combat operation tactics in the skies of Korea and to draw serious conclusions on the basis of these defeats. All this taken together forced the SAC command to cease the daylight use of B-29 medium bombers on combat missions into North Korea's interior, and to issue an order to switch its B-29 bombardment groups to nighttime combat operations using the new Shoran navigation system. The head of Bomber Command General Joe Kelly made this decision on 28 October at a meeting of the command staff of Bomber Command and the Fifth Air Force at the Itazuke Air Base in Japan. At this conference, the main conclusion was drawn that it was practically impossible to prevent MiG-15s from breaking through to the B-29 groups through the use of a large number of fighter escorts. In addition, the F-84 fighter, as well as the F-80 and the Meteor, were simply unsuitable for this role because of their inferior performance characteristics relative to the MiG-15.

Indeed, this ineffectiveness of the F-84E and Gloster Meteor fighter types as escort fighters led the US Fifth Air Force command to discontinue their further use in this role and to switch them to the fighter-bomber role. Now they themselves had to be covered by details of escort fighters. The Sabre pilots of the 4th FIW, who could oppose the MiGs on equal terms, could assume this role, but the number of F-86s in Korea was limited, and they lacked adequate strength to create impenetrable barriers against MiG attacks. The most important result of these October battles was the fact that the Americans had been unable to attain aerial superiority in the MiGs' zone of operations, and as before the MiGs proved able to contest a broad swath of North Korean territory. Later the Superfortresses conducted a few more daytime raids to support ground troops on the battlefield, but they no longer dared make a daylight appearance north of Pyongyang, that is to say, in MiG Alley.

On the whole, the October raids by the Superfortresses failed to achieve their goal. The majority of North Korean airfields and bridges had in fact not been destroyed, while the American losses were large.

In addition, it must be stated that the overall tally discussed above did not include the victories of the Chinese pilots of the UAA's 3rd and 4th IAD, which actively operated in October, although with a fewer number of combat sorties. According to certain sources, the UAA pilots did shoot down B-29s in 1951, in October as well. For example, the former commander of the 18th GIAP, Lieutenant Colonel A.P. Smorchkov, recalled an episode when a Chinese pilot who had just come back from a mission joyfully ran across the airfield and shouted that he had downed an American Superfortress; a B-29 was clearly visible on his gun camera footage, which confirmed his victory. The squadron commander with the 523rd IAP Major V.P. Popov recalled another case. On one occasion, he led a mixed group of Soviet and Chinese MiGs into combat. Our pilots were covering the Chinese on this sortie, and in the battle, one of the Chinese pilots downed one Superfortress, though to be honest, he was immediately shot down in turn. Of course, the US undoubtedly downed other Chinese MiGs, so the data on the losses of the two sides over the month of October are far from complete!

In the summer and autumn of 1951, anti-aircraft artillery played the primary role in the struggle against the night bombers; this role was carried out in part by the Soviet 87th and 92nd Anti-aircraft Artillery Divisions and the 10th Anti-aircraft Searchlight Regiment, which arrived in China from the Soviet Union at the beginning of June 1951. Upon their arrival, they immediately began to carry out combat assignments, which consisted in covering the Andong and Miaogou airbases of the 64th IAK, the North Korean Singisiu airfield, and the railroad bridge and the three pontoon bridges across the Yalu River. In September 1951, the 87th Anti-aircraft Artillery Division moved into North Korea, in order to cover the airfields under construction at Taechon and Namsi. Over the period between 8 September and 31 December 1951, the anti-aircraft gunners destroyed 50 enemy aircraft, including 10 bombers. The effectiveness of the anti-aircraft artillery in the struggle against modern jet aircraft and high-altitude bombers was shown by the combat operations in Korea to be inadequate, but the anti-aircraft gunners made a weighty contribution to repelling numerous American fighter-bomber attacks through their capable conducting of blocking fire.

The results of the active combat operations by Soviet fighter aviation and anti-aircraft artillery in the struggle against American combat aircraft in 1951 influenced the overall balance of forces in the Korean War. With the successful introduction of the CPV into the war, covered by the Soviet MiG-15s and anti-aircraft artillery, the US and its allies by the end of 1951 had lost their numerical superiority on the ground.

STRUGGLE IN THE ANJU AREA

The beginning of November 1951 was marked by new massed air raids by the American air force beyond the Pyongyang-Wonsan line in North Korea. True, they now primarily involved two F-84 groups and one F-80 group, which had begun to operate actively within the MiG's operational zone, but now more often in their new role as fighter-bombers to attack ground targets in MiG Alley.

Simultaneously with the American aviation, at the beginning of November the Australian No. 77 in their Meteors also flew numerous missions, but having lost three Meteors in two clashes with MiGs on 2 and 3 November, they sharply reduced their activity and in fact only appeared episodically in the MiG's zone of operations, and at that only in the second echelon of the American raids and with heavy Sabre escort.

The first encounter in the month of November between the two sides took place already on 1 November, but the pilots of the 17th IAP's maneuvers against a group of 14 Sabres ended without results. Sorties by other groups of MiGs from the 303rd IAD passed without any enemy encounter. Only on the following day, 2 November, did the adversaries again collide in combat. The combat sorties were intensive: the pilots of the 303rd IAD flew four combat missions as part of divisional groups over the course of the day. Thus, the 18th GIAP's pilots flew four combat sorties, two of which resulted in combat with F-84 fighter-bombers and the F-86s that were covering them, both in the Sukchon area. In one of the dogfights, Captain A.P. Antonov managed to down one F-84, while Captain N.V. Babonin attacked a flight of Meteors and shot down one of them.

The pilots of the "fraternal" 17th IAP also conducted four combat sorties over the day, which resulted in one combat action more than their comrades of the 18th GIAP experienced – all three combats were with F-86 Sabres, and all three ended without results. In addition, pilots of the 324th IAD flew sorties on this day to intercept enemy aircraft: for example, between 1449 and 1537 a group of 12 MiGs from the 176th GIAP intercepted a group of 30 F-84s in the area of the railroad and crossings in the Kaechon-Sunchon area. Having spotted the MiGs, the Thunderjets withdrew in the direction of the sea, but before they could do so, Major Subbotin managed to hit one of them.

Thus on 2 November, the 64th IAK pilots claimed to have downed two Thunderjets and one Meteor, but the Americans, like their Australian allies, do not confirm these losses. In its turn, the 64th IAK suffered its first losses in the month: in a combat with Sabres of the 334th FIS, a young pilot of the 18th GIAP Anatolii Ivanovich Shuliat'ev was killed-in-action. He had recently arrived in this Guards regiment as a replacement. In the combat he became separated from his leader, and he was caught by a pair of experienced "wolves" from the 4th FIW, Lieutenant Colonel George L. Jones and 1st Lieutenant Richard A. Pincoski, who shot up Suliat'ev's MiG at point-blank range. This was the 100th MiG-15 downed in the skies of Korea by pilots of the 4th FIW. In addition, Senior Lieutenant S.D. Krupchatnikov's aircraft received damage (1 bullet hole) in this battle, but everything turned out all right for both the pilot and the MiG.

The battles which occurred on 3 November, in which pilots of the 523rd IAP distinguished themselves, proved to be more intense. The first clash took place in the morning between 1046 and 1056 in the Anju-Sukchon-Sunchon area. We'll take a more detailed look at it.

The 523rd IAP, numbering 22 MiG-15s under the command of regiment commander Guards Major D.P. Os'kin, took off between 1034 and 1036 at an order from the division command post to repel an enemy fighter-bomber raid in the Anju-Sukchon area. The 2nd and 3rd Squadrons comprised the regiment's attack group, while the 1sts Squadron served as the covering group. Flying in a staggered trail of squadrons at an altitude of 6,000 meters, at 1046 Guards Major Os'kin encountered up to 40 F-80s and F-84s 15 kilometers south of Anju at an altitude of 4,000-4,500 meters. Before our fighters arrived, the F-80s and F-84s had been bombing and strafing the railroad and motor transport on the roads in the Anju-Sukchon area.

Major Os'kin assessed the situation in the air and engaged the enemy fighter-bombers with the 2nd and 3rd Squadrons. The 1st Squadron remained high to cover the two squadrons' actions. Os'kin attacked a pair of F-84s from behind and to the left, firing from all three cannons at a range of 500 meters. As a result of his fire, the targeted Thunderjet was downed. Os'kin pulled out of the attack with a 90° climbing turn to starboard. At this moment he spotted a flight of F-84s to the left and 300-400 meters below him, and attacked the lead element's wingman from behind and above, firing all three cannons at a range 350 meters down to 310 meters. The attacked Thunderjet wheeled out of its formation in a descending starboard turn. Captain D.V. Mazilov's element covered Guards Major Os'kin's attacks, and after receiving the order to land, returned to base with him.

Senior Lieutenant I.I. Iakovlev with his element attacked a different F-84 flight from above and behind, but the Thunderjets had time to turn into their attack. As the opposing aircraft began to close, his wingman Senior Lieutenant S.D. Krupchatnikov gave one medium-length burst at one of the "Crosses". Iakovlev pulled out of the attack into a left-hand chandelle and reversed to make a second attack on this same F-84 flight from above and behind. He opened fire at a range of 920 meters. The Thunderjets again broke sharply left in the direction of the attack and avoided any shell hits. After this, Iakovlev pulled out of the attack with a climbing turn to port, and at the order from group leader Guards Major Os'kin, headed back to base in a climb.

Captain V.P. Popov together with his wingman attacked a Thunderjet element from above and behind. He opened fire with all three cannons at a range of 550 meters: one of the Thunderjets, hit by shells, began shedding altitude in the direction of the sea. Popov exited the attack in a climb and saw another flight of F-84s below and out in front of him. He attacked them from above and behind and fired at the extreme Thunderjet on the left with all three cannons from a range of 270-220 meters, but the shells passed below the target. Captain Popov pulled out of the attack in a climbing turn to starboard and then headed back to base.

Guards Senior Lieutenant D.A. Samoilov, leading the other element in Popov's flight, led it into an attack from behind against two F-84s at the same altitude and opened fire on them from a range of 1,000 meters, but here as well his shells passed behind the target. His wingman Senior Lieutenant M.A. Zykov fired at the other Thunderjet from a range of 540 meters, but his fire also failed to hit the target. The Thunderjets broke right to come out from under the attack.

Captain I.I. Tiuliaev with his element attacked a flight of four F-84s from above and behind, opening up with all three cannons at a range of 1,000 meters. The Thunderjets began to come out from under the attack in a left-hand spiral. Captain Tiuliaev exited his attack in a climbing turn to starboard with a subsequent return to his base.

Senior Lieutenant Filimonov's element attacked yet another flight of F-84s. Closing to within 240 meters of his target, he opened fire with all three cannons and downed the F-84. Filimonov pulled out of his attack in a climb to the right, while the three remaining F-84s wheeled around to the left. Then Filimonov launched another attacking pass against these three Thunderjets from above and behind, and fired from all three cannons as the range closed from 300 meters down to 100 meters; the attacked Thunderjet began to go down in a spiral. Senior Lieutenant Filimonov went into a climbing turn to starboard and subsequently headed back to base.

Meanwhile, Guards Major A.P. Trefilov at an altitude of 5,000 to 7,000 meters covered the actions of the other two squadrons with his six MiG-15s. During the battle, nine Soviet pilots had fired at the F-84s, and five of the Thunderjets had been shot down. Claims were put in by Guards Major Os'kin for two F-84s, by Senior Lieutenant Filimonov for two more F-84s, and by Captain Popov for one Thunderjet.

That afternoon, between 1356 and 1359, two regiments of the 303rd IAD lifted off the runway to repel the next enemy air raid. The first to take off to intercept the enemy were 22 MiGs from the 523rd IAP under the command of Captain G.U. Okhai, followed a few minutes later by 20 MiGs of the 17th IAP led by Major B.V. Maslennikov. The 523rd IAP's pilots comprised the attack group and headed for the Anju area, while the covering 20 MiGs of the 17th IAP trailed 2-3 kilometers behind them and 2,000 meters above them. At 1411 in the Sunchon area, Captain Okhai sighted a flight of Meteors, which were strafing traffic moving along the roads in the vicinity. The leader decided to attack the enemy with the 2nd and 3rd Squadrons, while the 1st Squadron remained at altitude to cover their attack. However, the initial pass was unsuccessful, because Okhai opened fire prematurely from extremely long range and missed the target low. Pulling out of the attack, he noticed another 16 Meteors below him, flying in a column of squadrons. He circled over them once, then attacked one of the Meteors of the outermost pairs, but again opened fire too soon and missed his target. However, at this point he spotted yet another Meteor element below him, which was trying to escape to sea, and attacked it in a diving pursuit curve. This time Captain Okhai closed to within 300 meters of his target before opening fire, scored hits upon his target, and watched it spiral downward trailing smoke. During the enemy's withdrawal to sea, Senior Lieutenant B.L. Sinel'nikov also managed to register hits on one of the Meteors, and it also went into a dive in the direction of the sea.

At this same time, the 17th IAP's pilots engaged up to three eight-ship groups of Sabres in the Pakchon area. In this dogfight Captain N.V. Sutiagin, who twice went into an attack against a pair of Sabres and fired upon them, distinguished himself. In one of the attacks, from a range of 700 meters he landed hits on the leader's aircraft; the Sabre smoothly listed to the right and in that same list fell toward the earth. The other pilots also fired at F-86s, but their fire was not as accurate.

As a result, in these two battles on this day, the 303rd IAD's pilots claimed eight downed enemy aircraft, seven of which were credited to pilots of the 523rd IAP. In return, the division had no destroyed or damaged aircraft. According to Diego Zampini's findings, on this day Thunderjets from the 49th and 136th FBW came under attack from the 523rd IAP's pilots, and at least three of them were shot down by MiGs: thus presumably Major Os'kin downed F-84 No.49-2398 of the 136th FBW, and its pilot Lieutenant Colonel Richard Marks successfully bailed out of his burning aircraft and became a prisoner-of-war. Senior Lieutenant Filimonov most likely downed F-84E No.51-652 from the 136th FBW's 182nd Squadron – its pilot ejected after reaching Cho-do Island, and he was picked up by a search and rescue team. Finally, Captain Popov presumably fatally damaged F-84E No.51-680, which reached Pusan, where the pilot also abandoned his crippled aircraft, rather than risk landing it. As usual, the loss of the latter two F-84s was attributed to "ground fire" or "technical problems".

In addition, Captain Okhai managed to damage the Gloster Meteor being flown by Sergeant Ernest Armit, who managed to reach Kimpo in his stricken aircraft on just one engine and land it there, where it was quickly repaired. The American records do not confirm any of the other victories by Soviet pilots.

Major aerial battles unfolded on 4 November. The Americans undertook two heavy raids in the Anju area. Both divisions of the 64th IAK, the 303rd IAD and 324th IAD, were scrambled to repel these attacks, and they became involved in heavy aerial combats in the Anju region. The 303rd IAD's pilots took on the escort fighters, while the 324th IAD's broke through to the groups of F-80 and F-84 fighter-bombers at low altitude that were working over the North Korean supply lines in groups of four and eight aircraft.

The first raid came in the morning around 1000. All three regiments of the 303rd IAD and the 324th IAD's 176th GIAP were scrambled to intercept it. Twenty MiGs of the 523rd IAP were first to soar into the sky, followed by their constant "bodyguards" – the pilots of the 17th IAP, which took off in a regimental group of 22 MiG-15s led by Major B.V. Maslennikov. A little later, 20 MiGs of the 176th GIAP took off, which comprised the attack group. At 1010 50 kilometers southwest of Anju, the 523rd IAP's pilots encountered the enemy's leading fighter screen, which consisted of almost 30 F-86s, and engaged them in battle. Soon the pilots of the 17th IAP arrived to their assistance, and they took on 16 F-86s. Our opponents were pilots of the 4th FIW's 334th and 336th FIS. In the course of the dogfight, Senior Lieutenant V.F. Shulev of the 17th IAP managed to down one Sabre, which became the 400th F-86 to suffer from MiG fire in this war. The 17th IAP's Captain S.S. Artemchenko damaged another Sabre. The 17th IAP had no losses.

The 523rd IAP's pilots wound up in a more difficult fight: in the course of the 10-minute combat, Major A.P. Trefilov and Senior Lieutenant D.A. Samoilov each downed a Sabre, both of which according to their reports plunged into the sea. However, the regiment also took losses: at 1010, during the dogfight with the 30 Sabres, Captain I.I. Tiuliaev's element at an altitude of 5,000 meters was attacked by 16 F-86s 10 kilometers north of Anju. As a result of the attack, the aircraft being flown by the regiment's deputy political commander Captain N.I. Mitrofanov received several bullet holes. During the combat, one F-86 overshot Mitrofanov's MiG and wound up in front of him. Captain Mitrofanov gave it an aimed burst. While firing, he was jumped by four other F-86s. Their machine-gun fire inflicted damage to his MiG's controls. Due to the loss of control, Captain Mitrofanov ejected at an altitude of 1,800-2,000 meters 6 kilometers northeast of Pakchon. The MiG was destroyed, while the pilot suffered minor wounds and was sent to the hospital in Changtien. Several more of the regiment's aircraft received varying degrees of damage from F-86 fire, but safely returned to base.

While the 303rd IAD's pilots were dealing with the Sabres of the forward screen, the 176th GIAP's strike group headed by regiment commander Lieutenant Colonel S.F. Vishniakov arrived in the area where the enemy fighter-bombers were operating, and soon spotted a group of 30 F-80s and F-84s in the Pyongyang area. Breaking up into separate elements, the 176th GIAP's pilots attacked them from various directions. Vishniakov's element attacked one pair of Thunderjets. However, Vishniakov pulled so closely behind one of them that he wound up in its engine's backwash, so he broke off the attack. Meanwhile his wingman Senior Lieutenant I.A. Ziuz' nevertheless downed one of these F-84s, which fell at 1130 in the district of Anju.

Major S.P. Subbotin's element, pulling out of an attack against one pair of F-84s, next went after another F-84 element, but exiting that attack without firing, noticed four F-84s below and to the left of him; Subbotin attacked the leader and got him – he observed his shells striking the Thunderjet and watched it go down. Captain I.A. Suchkov's element attacked a different pair of Thunderjets and downed the leader, observing hits on his aircraft as he fired from a range of 300 meters down to 100 meters. His wingman Senior

Lieutenant A.P. Men'shikov also saw the aircraft stagger from the hits and go down. Captain N.M. Goncharov's element attacked two F-84s. At first Goncharov opened fire on the leader, and then at the wingman. He saw his shells strike one of the F-84s, which headed downward in the direction of the sea. Its fall was witnessed at 1100 by an observation post of the NKPA 5th Artillery Division. One enemy aircraft, streaming black smoke behind it, fell into the sea west of Nampo (confirmed by the chief of staff of a North Korean military unit Ho Bon-hak). As a result the 176th GIAP's pilots downed four enemy fighter-bombers and forced the remainder to flee, without any losses.

The 18th GIAP's pilots also flew one combat sortie on this day to the Anju area. There they had an encounter with a group of F-86s, but for both sides the combat ended without results.

According to research by Diego Zampini, on the morning of this day the 176th GIAP's pilots intercepted and attacked a mixed group of F-80s from the 8th FBW and F-84s from the 136th FBW. In so doing Major Subbotin presumably shot down F-80 No.49-814 from the 36th FBS, and its pilot 2nd Lieutenant Michael P. Kovalish was killed-in-action. Captain Suchkov managed to damage one of the F-84s seriously; its pilot managed to fly it back to his base at Pusan, but there he parachuted from the stricken Thunderjet, rather than risk his life by attempting to land it. In addition, Captain Goncharov presumably inflicted serious damage to F-84E No.50-1168 being flown by none other than Colonel Albert C. Prendergast, commander of the 136th FBW. He also brought his crippled Thunderjet back to a point 13 kilometers north of the K-9 Airbase in Pusan, where he also preferred to take to the parachute rather than risk landing the aircraft, but his parachute failed to open and he was killed. In addition, according to Diego Zampini carrier-based F9F-2 Panther fighter-bombers also took part in this raid, and one of their elements likely came under the attack of Senior Lieutenant Ziuz's MiG. Panther No.125090 from VF-831 received serious damage. Its pilot Lieutenant George S. Brainard nursed it back to his carrier USS *Antietam*, but when landing the crippled Panther failed to catch an arresting cable and struck another Panther parked on the deck. In the collision Lieutenant Brainard was killed. Naturally, the loss of these aircraft in the USAF's documents are attributed to a variety of reasons, just not the main one – all the damage was inflicted by MiG cannon fire!

Three hours later, around 1400, the Fifth Air Force command launched a second raid to the Anju area. Once again, pilots of the 303rd IAD were scrambled to repel the raid. Between 1415 and 1425, up to 80 enemy fighters and fighter-bombers were detected by radar in an area 20-25 kilometers south of Pyongyang at altitudes between 6,000 and 9,000 meters, flying in four groups of 8-16 aircraft each on a 340-360° heading.

At an order from the division command post, a group of 20 MiG-15s of the 17th IAP under the command of Major V.B. Maslennikov, took off from the alert status of Readiness No. 1. Serving as the division's attack group, they were to repel an enemy fighter-bomber attack in the Anju area, then were to reinforce Soviet pilots involved in an aerial combat in the Sukchon area.

Major Maslennikov's group, having arrived in the Anju area, where according to information from the division command post the enemy was operating, went into a sweeping starboard turn in order to search for the enemy. Having reversed course, Captain Sutiagin noted a large group of F-86s, about a kilometer away and above and to the right of them and alerted the group commander. However, at this moment, information arrived over the radio from Captain D.V. Mazilov of the 523rd IAP: "I'm fighting south of Anju; I'm requesting assistance." Group commander Major Maslennikov headed for the area south of Anju in a descent, but while in a starboard turn at an altitude of 7,000 meters, the group was unexpectedly jumped from above and behind by a group of up to 30 F-86s.

The 1st Squadron under the command of Major Maslennikov evaded the enemy attack with an energetic chandelle to port. Captain S.S. Artemchenko's flight, which was attacked first, began to carry out an oblique loop to the left with the aim of shaking off six F-86s that were tailing his flight. In the third loop, Artemchenko achieved an advantageous position over the enemy, and the enemy, seeing this, rolled over to the left into a dive toward the sea.

Coming out from under the attack in a chandelle to port, Captain N.V. Sutiagin's element was attacked from above and behind by an F-86 flight. Sutiagin banked steeply around to the right toward the enemy, and as they passed he threw his MiG around to the left and began to pursue them. One Sabre pair, seeing that they were being pursued, rolled over into a dive, while the other element conducted a chandelle to starboard and transitioned into a subsequent oblique loop; Captain Sutiagin went after this element. Having conducted two oblique loops in the chase, Sutiagin had closed to within 600-700 meters of the enemy aircraft and opened fire at the leader. After the third oblique loop, the Sabre wingman went into a zoom climb, reversed at the top, and dove into a head-on pass against Captain Sutiagin, who opened fire at a range of 300 meters from him, after which our pilot broke off combat at an altitude of 3,000 meters. At this moment Captain Sutiagin's wingman Senior Lieutenant N.Ia. Perepelkin was attacked by six F-86s that had pulled in behind him from the right and above. Perepelkin broke right into a climbing turn to shake off the Sabres on his tail, but the enemy began to pursue him. At this moment, Senior Lieutenant V.F. Shulev, noticing that Perepelkin was in trouble, dove on the Sabres from behind. The F-86s, noticing the MiG closing from above and behind, rolled over to the left and headed southward. Shulev, forming up on Senior Lieutenant Perepelkin's wing, returned to base.

The 3rd Squadron, under the command of Captain M.N. Shcherbakov and flying in the second echelon of the attack group to the left of the 1st Squadron, in the sweeping turn to the right over Anju at 7,000 meters altitude noticed eight F-86s converging on them from the left and 500 meters below them, flying in a column of flights. As the Sabres passed below them, at Captain Shcherbakov's command the squadron banked left and began to drop onto the tail of the Sabres. Seeing the danger, the enemy went into a leftward spiral, after which they split into two groups. One flight departed upwards in a climb, while the second flight went into a dive, which Shcherbakov's flight followed. Seeing that they were being pursued, the F-86 flight continued to dive in a tight spiral to the left. Shcherbakov's flight broke off the chase with a chandelle to starboard. In the course of this action, Captain Sutiagin managed to score hits on one F-86, which exited the combat in a dive. The 17th IAP's pilots suffered no losses or damaged MiGs in this combat.

Things weren't going as well for the 523rd IAP's pilots, who had arrived earlier in the Anju area and had been unexpectedly attacked by a large group of Sabres, forcing them to engage under unfavorable conditions. Quickly several of the MiGs received damage from Sabre machine-gun fire, and the 523rd IAP had to put out an urgent appeal for help. Although assistance in the form of the 17th IAP and 18th GIAP arrived in time, the regiment all the same was unable to avoid losses in this difficult combat. While flying in the 523rd IAP's formation, Senior Lieutenant Filimonov at an altitude of 8,000 meters over the Taechon area reported that his cockpit had lost cabin pressure, and at the direction of the 3rd Squadron commander, he headed back to base. While returning to base, at an altitude of 4,000-5,000 meters in the vicinity of Okkang-dong, his element was unexpectedly bounced by six F-86s. Filimonov came out from under the enemy fighter attack with a climb toward the sun and the Sabres lost sight of him. Leveling out and flying in a straight line for 20 to 30 seconds, Filimonov decided to bank around to the right and again descend in the direction of Changseong. At this time (1431) he was again attacked by the Sabres from behind and shot down. A search team later found the crash site and located the moving part of the cockpit canopy some distance away. Among the wreckage of the aircraft, there was no trace of the pilot's remains or of the ejection catapult, which gave the basis for supposing that Filimonov had ejected. However, Senior Lieutenant Valerii Pavlovich Filimonov was in fact never found.

In this afternoon battle, the 303rd IAD's pilots downed only one Sabre and failed to break through to the enemy fighter-bombers, while losing one of their MiGs and its pilot; several more MiGs received combat damage. Thus this combat can be rightly considered a victory for the pilots of the US 4th FIW.

Altogether over the day of fighting, the pilots of the 64th IAK claimed eight downed enemy aircraft, while in the dogfights with the F-86s, only the pilots of the 523rd IAP suffered, losing in the day's morning and afternoon actions two of its MiGs and one pilot. Another six of the 523rd IAP's MiGs received varying amounts of damage (Zykov – 3 bullet holes; Shirokov – 2 bullet holes; Roman'kov – 8 bullet holes; Parushkov – 10 bullet holes; Rybalko – 9 bullet holes; and Roman'kov – another 13 bullet holes), but they all safely returned to base and were quickly put back into service. The Fifth Air Force command denied the loss of any of its Sabres on this day and reported that its pilots downed two MiG-15s, which the Soviet side confirms. Captain William F. Guss of the 336th FIS managed to shoot down Captain Mitrofanov's aircraft, while 1st Lieutenant Alfred W. Dymock of the 334th FIS claimed Senior Lieutenant Filimonov's MiG.[1]

A brief lull arrived after this hard day, and only on 8 November did the Americans again launch its next major raid beyond the Pyongyang-Wonsan line. Once more, bitter aerial combats flared up over the Anju area.

However, two days before this, on 6 November the UAA command carried out an operation using Tu-2 bombers. A group of Chinese Tu-2 bombers covered by La-9 fighters conducted a successful bombing run over Taewha-do Island and returned to base without any losses. This island is located several kilometers from the mouth of the Yalu River, where there is a small archipelago, which the Chinese call He Dao ("dao" means island in the Chinese language) and which includes the islands Large and Small He and others. In the Korean tongue, they are known as the Taewha-do, Somni-do and Sinmi-do Islands). Despite the various names, we're talking about small clumps of dry land, which became a "bone in the throat" for our aviation commanders and the UAA leadership. On the islands the enemy had a powerful radio monitoring post, a radar station with the latest radar equipment, and a GCI post, which governed practically all of MiG Alley. A very large swath of North Korean territory was visible from them even by the naked eye with the help of a scissors telescope or just a pair of binoculars. The first operation to take Sinmi-do Island had been undertaken back on 20 June 1951. However, the main task – an assault landing and seizure of the islands by ground forces had been thwarted; a second attempt was made in November 1951. It was decided to set the start of this operation to coincide with anniversary of the October Revolution in the Soviet Union, and possibly, present the taking of Taewha-Do to the Soviet leadership as a gift, since all the preparations for it were done independently by the UAA command. The Commander-in-chief of the PLAAF Liu Yalou even flew in from Beijing to take personal direction of it.

According to Chinese intelligence, more than 1,200 communications troops were stationed on the islands, eavesdropping on the Soviet and Chinese radio communications and, most importantly, constantly busy with "subversive" activities (so called "psychological operations"). In order to destroy the enemy and to seize the islands, the CPV command decided to conduct a landing operation with troops from the Chinese 50th Army, which would be supported by the PLAAF 2nd, 3rd, 8th and 10th Aviation Divisions.

The order setting the date for the air operation was issued on 1 November. On the following day, pilots of the 2nd and 3rd IAD flew reconnaissance missions over the islands. Bombers of the 2nd Squadron of the 8th BAD's 22nd BAP were given the assignment to destroy military sites on the island and would make the first combat sortie. Thus, on 6 November, nine Tu-2 bombers (the 22nd BAP, group leader Han Yang) took off at 1435 from the Mukden (Shenyang) airfield to make the first bombing attack against Taewha-do Island. Cover was provided by 16 La-11 from the 2nd IAD's 4th IAP, which took off from the Yu Tun airfield, and 22 MiG-15s from the 3rd IAD's 7th IAP.

The nine Tu-2 bombers, led by 2nd Squadron commander Han Minyang, were each carrying eight 100-kilogram high-explosive bombs and one incendiary bomb. The Tu-2s flew to the target in a compact formation. It seems that due to the unexpectedness of the attack, the Americans simply overlooked their approach; no enemy fighters appeared in the air, but the anti-aircraft gunners got busy. The "Lavochkins" [LaGG fighters] apparently suppressed them before the bombers arrived over the target. The group leader's navigator was sufficiently experienced, and all the bombs were on target. The Chinese write that 72 of the 81 bombs (90%) successfully hit their designated targets; the bombing killed or wounded over 60 men of the UN command staff on the island, and all the intended targets were damaged. By the time several dozen F-86s finally appeared in the area, the bombers were already on their way home.

The commander of one of the Tu-2 bombers Xia Wangpin later said:

> In the course of several minutes, dozens of enemy facilities, his radar sets and one of the radio posts were burned and destroyed. Han Minyang himself acted particularly courageously. He took the most important target for himself and dove on it through a curtain of anti-aircraft fire down to extremely low altitude. All the bombs that this aircraft dropped were on-target. The enemy aviation's attempt to come to the assistance of the enemy garrison was decisively thwarted by our fighters. They didn't allow enemy aircraft anywhere near the island …

In fact there were indeed no encounters with enemy aircraft. Only pilots of the 18th GIAP took off to cover the Tu-2 bombers, but they didn't come across any enemy. Thus on this day, neither the UAA nor the 64th IAK had any losses on the mission. Nevertheless, despite the significant damage to the radar sets, they were not all completely knocked-out, since the enemy's observation posts continued to operate.

On the next day, the anniversary of the Bolshevik Revolution, the adversary displayed less activity. Only in the afternoon did the enemy undertake a raid to the Anju area, and all five regiments of the 64th IAK rose to meet it. As usual, the 303rd IAD's pilots engaged the forward screen of Sabres. At first, almost 50 MiGs of the 17th IAP and 523rd IAP tangled with approximately 30 Sabres; the 18th GIAP's pilots took off later as reinforcements, but they encountered no enemy on their sortie. Only the pilots of the 17th IAP and 523rd IAP tussled with the enemy, but the engagement ended with no results.

However, the 176th GIAP in a group of 24 MiGs under the command of Lieutenant Colonel S.F. Vishniakov came across a group of 10 Meteors in the Anju area and attacked them. K.Ia. Sheberstov went after a pair of Meteors and saw his shells strike one of them. When pulling out of the attack, he noticed a pair of attacking F-86s pursuing a different MiG, slid in behind them, and forced them to break off their attack. His wingman A.F. Golovachev fired at the wingman's Sabre, but didn't observe any results.

Captain P.A. Milaushkin's element attacked a different pair of Meteors. Milaushkin opened fire on one of them from a range of 500 meters. His wingman N.K. Serdiuk later claimed that the attacked Meteor listed to the left before entering some clouds. After this, the MiG element encountered two more Meteors; Milaushkin attacked one of them and observed hits on it, while Serdiuk fired on the other, but observed no results.

Six F-86s arrived to help the Meteors, but the Sabres could only somehow cover their withdrawal from combat. Captain Milaushkin was credited with one victory over the Meteors. His victim was the aircraft of Pilot-officer Donald Robertson, which received damage to its hydraulic system and cockpit pressurization system. Nevertheless, Robertson managed to get his damaged aircraft back to Kimpo and make a belly landing there.

New battles in the Korean sky flared up on 8 November: large groups of F-80 and F-84 fighter-bombers were going after targets in the Anju area, covered by a swarm of Sabres. Early that morning, the Americans arrived in the Anju area in several large groups from the direction of the sea, and began to attack the supply lines there. Both regiments of the 324th IAD were scrambled to repel the enemy attack, as well as the 303rd IAD's 17th IAP and 18th GIAP; the 523rd IAP was held back in reserve. Both of the 324th IAD's regiments set out on the mission with their full operational strength, numbering around 50 MiGs. The 17th and 18th GIAP also committed all of their serviceable MiGs.

Arriving over the target area, the MiG groups were attacked by Sabres, which were trying to keep them from reaching the fighter-bombers. However, they couldn't hold back all of the MiGs. Pilots of the 18th GIAP managed to break through and went after a group of 12 F-80s. Senior Lieutenant F.M. Malashin claimed to have downed one "Shoot" in this action, but he didn't receive credit for it, because on his gun camera film it was apparent that he had fired at it from extremely long range. The fighter-bombers began a disorganized withdrawal toward the sea, and the Soviet Guards pilots might have decimated this group of F-80s, had the Sabres not intervened. Two eight-ship F-86 groups unexpectedly pounced on Captain N.V. Babonin's squadron from behind, and Major William Whisner of the 334th FIS managed to score hits on Senior Lieutenant N.S. Gavril'chenko's MiG, causing him to lose control over it. Gavril'chenko had to eject from his crippled aircraft, but while descending in his parachute, the Sabres fired on him again, severing several of the parachute's lines and wounding him. After he landed, he was picked up by Chinese Volunteers and sent to the hospital, where the pilot spent two months recovering. Gavril'chenko never returned to active combat duty.

The 17th IAP with its 26 MiGs under the command of deputy regiment commander Major B.V. Maslennikov was covering the actions of the 18th GIAP. At 0927 they ran into 30 Sabres in the Anju area, which they at first wrongly identified as MiGs. Only six of the regiment's pilots fired at the enemy in this combat, and it ended without results.

According to the reports from Captain Artemchenko, Senior Lieutenant Bykov and Captain Sutiagin, the aircraft they had mistakenly perceived to be MiG-15s proved to be red-nosed F-86s (like our MiG-15s were painted). In addition, Captain Shcherbakov reported that the Sabres had a red band around the upper tailfin.

Alongside the pilot of the 303rd IAD, the pilots of the 324th IAD had a fierce dogfight with Sabres. Pilots of the 196th IAP, led by their commander Colonel E.G. Pepeliaev, particularly stood out in this battle. Pepeliaev's element downed two Sabres, both by Pepeliaev himself, but he gave credit for one of them to his wingman Senior Lieutenant A.D. Ryzhkov for the splendid job he did covering him. Another Sabre in this combat was shot down by the 2nd Squadron commander Captain B.V. Bokach.

Thus, in this morning battle, the 64th IAK pilots repulsed a large enemy fighter-bomber raid and in the process downed three F-86s. Their own losses amounted to one MiG. The pilots of the 4th FIW lost one of their own, when Captain Charles Pratt of the 334th Fighter Squadron was killed – his F-86A No.49-1338 was shot down by Colonel Pepeliaev. In addition, F-86A No.48-0259 was lost, fatally damaged through the joint efforts of Pepeliaev and his wingman Senior Lieutenant A.D. Ryzhkov, but its pilot David B. Freeland managed to fly it back to friendly territory, where he safely ejected.

In the afternoon, a second aerial combat was fought out when the Americans sent another major raid into this area of North Korea. The weather was cloudy, murky. Visibility was limited where the enemy covering fighters were loitering, while a group of F-84s was operating beneath a layer of broken clouds. The entire 324th IAD took part in repelling this raid; its aircraft was directed against the Thunderjets operating at low altitude. Groups of MiGs from the 303rd IAD's 17th IAP and 18th GIAP, which had scrambled earlier, took on the covering fighters. So, the 17th IAP's pilots engaged 30 F-86s, and the group commander Major B.V. Maslennikov managed to down one of them.

At this time, the 176th GIAP joined the fighting. Its 22 MiGs led by Major K.Ia. Sheberstov shortly before 1600 were jumped by a Sabre flight in the Kaechon area; the Sabres zeroed in on Captain A.A. Plitkin's element. He managed to evade the attack by breaking left into a tight turn, and then counterattacked these same Sabres, but saw no results. Sheberstov's group at this time caught up with six F-84s and attacked them. Sheberstov selected one of the Thunderjets, opened fire, observed hits and watched the target abruptly roll over. Sheberstov's wingman Senior Lieutenant A.F. Golovachev fired on a second Thunderjet from a range of 700 meters, but missed. Just then two F-84s opened up on them in a head-on pass, and Golovachev's aircraft received one bullet hole in its right wing.

Captain P.S. Milaushkin's element attacked a different flight of F-84s. Milaushkin managed to hit one of them from a range of 400 meters, which went down in a right-hand list. His wingman Senior Lieutenant I.S. Kutomanov attacked the F-84 group leader from the right. He fired from a range of 700 meters and saw his shells strike the target. When exiting from the attack, Milaushkin's element was attacked by a pair of F-86s. Our pilots evaded the attack with a climbing spiral.

Captain I.A. Suchkov's group, after ending the combat with the Sabres, returned to the Kaechon area, where it encountered a dozen F-84s, which were approaching the pontoon bridges in the area. The aircraft were flying in two groups: an eight-ship formation and a flight of Thunderjets. Suchkov's flight jumped the enemy and attacked two F-84s from the right with no apparent result. Two days later, confirmation arrived from members of the NKPA command staff that three enemy aircraft had crashed in the Anju area, two of which were credited to Major Sheberstov, and one to Captain Suchkov.

While the pilots of Major Sheberstov's group were engaged in this action, a little more than 20 MiGs of the 196th IAP under the command of Colonel E.G. Pepeliaev was locked in combat with a group of fighter-bombers and F-86 fighters. A participant in this clash, a former pilot with the 196th IAP Aleksandr Pavlovich Ovchinnikov, describes what happened:

> The day before this one, there had been a meeting in the regiment on the occasion of the next October anniversary; there were no sorties on 7 November. Yet the next day, 8 November, we were scrambled four times in a large group. I was flying in the

Lieutenant Colonel I.A. Suchkov, squadron commander in the 176th GIAP – a postwar photograph taken at the end of the 1950s.

lead group as regiment commander Pepeliaev's wingman. The aerial combat with a large enemy group proved to be especially difficult: [there was] a group of F-86s high and a group of F-84s low. The afternoon was cloudy and gray. The enemy aircraft were both above scattered clouds and beneath clouds. Visibility was poor, and the enemy and our own aircraft were swarming everywhere. It was difficult to figure out where your own guys were and where the enemy was, except for the dark Thunderjets and Shooting Stars that were scurrying around down below, carrying out their missions. The combat seemed to go on forever.

Senior Lieutenant Travin was flying on the extreme right of the formation; he was first to be caught by Sabres, which had circled around behind the right-hand group, and Travin wound up as a victim only because he blindly stuck with his leader Rud'ko, when he should have evaded the attack with a maneuver. There was a lot of machine-gun and cannon fire in this dogfight, and explosions of falling aircraft. This was my first combat in the skies of Korea, and I became separated from my leader, maneuvering as best I knew how in both the vertical and horizontal, in order not to be caught in an enemy gun sight. I stalled; I was behind one F-84 and fired at it, which my gun camera footage captured, but I didn't receive credit because I had fired at very long range. I returned to my base alone, and I was suffering a great deal, wondering whether I would find my commander, from whom I had strayed in battle, there. But Pepeliaev was already on the ground and in turn anxious for me, because after all it was my first combat. When I landed, he calmed down and on the whole remained satisfied with me.

In this dogfight Pepeliaev downed one Thunderjet, but we lost our own pilot Travin, who was killed in the battle. After this combat Pepeliaev suffered a heart attack – plainly, the high G-forces in the intensive combats were telling, and the doctors grounded him for some time.

In fact, in this clash Colonel E.G. Pepeliaev did down one F-84, but the regiment lost pilot Senior Lieutenant Aleksei Fedorovich Travin, who had arrived in the regiment as a replacement only in the month of October, and this was one of his first combat sorties. In sum, the 64th IAK's pilots claimed eight victories over enemy aircraft on this day, in return for the loss of two MiGs destroyed and one damaged, plus one pilot. The Americans acknowledge the loss of F-80 No.49-845 from the 8th FBG's 35th FBS – its pilot 1st Lieutenant Jerome A. Volk was killed. Presumably, he was Captain I.A. Suchkov's victim. A reconnaissance RF-80 from the 15th TRS, which took part in this raid with the assignment to photograph its results, was also struck by MiG cannon fire. It was heavily damaged, but Captain Dennis Holmes managed to reach Korea Bay and ejected over it. The opposing side doesn't confirm any other victories by our pilots on this day.

After such heavy losses, the Americans reduced their activity, though they continued to conduct raids in the Anju area; now, however, they began to send small groups of F-80s and F-84s to the area, covered by similarly small groups of Sabres. On 9 November, the 18th GIAP's pilots conducted two combat sorties, but only during the morning mission to the Kaechon area did they encounter a group of F-80s from the 8th FBG's 36th Squadron. Captain V.A. Sokhan' managed to down one of them – F-80 No.49-491 went down in flames and its pilot 2nd Lieutenant Thomas E. Hadley was killed. The

17th IAP's pilots flew four missions during the day, but all passed without any encounter with the enemy.

On 10 November, only the 176th GIAP's pilots met enemy aircraft between 1100 and 1200: this took place in the area between Pyongyang and Chinnampo, when 16 of the regiment's MiGs intercepted a group of 12 F-84s. Three of the regiment's pilots scored victories in this combat: Major K.Ia. Sheberstov, Captain P.S. Milaushkin and Senior Lieutenant A.A. Plitkin – each downed one Thunderjet. We had no losses. Confirmation of Sheberstov's and Milaushkin's victories came several days later from North Korean officials. The former was actually credited with an F-80 that came down near the village of Takha-ri, which lies 8 kilometers south of Kosia, while Milaushkin's victim fell near Chinnampo. Yet according to research by Diego Zampini, F-80 No.49-830 from the 51st FIG's 16th Squadron, which had been supposedly downed by Sheberstov, actually made it back to the K-13 Air Base in Suwon, where its pilot Captain Gerald B. Gill made a successful belly landing directly on the runway. The pilot was uninjured, but the aircraft was subsequently written off. Captain Milaushkin shot down F-84E No.51-549 from the 49th FBG's 9th Squadron, the pilot of which 1st Lieutenant Michael G. Rebo was killed.

For the next week, encounters with the enemy were rare, and the infrequent aerial sparring all ended quickly and without results. On 18 November, however, the Americans launched a new major raid to interdict sectors of the main road in the Anju area. The mission involved up to 50 F-84 fighter-bombers from the 136th FBW's 111th FBS, with cover provided by 30-40 Sabres. The entire 18th GIAP and 20 MiGs from the 176th GIAP were scrambled to repel this raid. A participant, Hero of the Soviet Union Lev Kirillovich Shchukin of the 18th GIAP, recalls what happened:

> On 18 November the Americans organized a raid against a sector of the highway in the Anju area. This raid was conducted by eight-ship groups of F-84s, which followed one after another at a distance of 2 to 2.5 kilometers. There were up to six such groups, which arrived over the target area from the sea, where we were prohibited from going.
>
> Having taken off as a regiment and arriving in this area, we spotted eight F-84s below us that were approaching the coastline. Our fuel reserves gave us little time, and regiment leader Lieutenant Colonel A.E. Belostotsky ordered our squadron and the 2nd Squadron to attack them. The 3rd Squadron went after the Sabres, which were already lurking up above.
>
> We made a slashing pass after swinging around 120° to the left and going into a high-speed dive. The adversary was flying in a tight formation at an altitude of 4,000 meters. Our 1st Squadron launched a well-organized attack against the second eight-ship group of F-84s, which allowed us to take good aim. Naturally, the [element] leaders selected their targets; I and my wingman Senior Lieutenant A.A. Astapovsky each downed one F-84 in this attack, and Captain A.F. Maznev damaged another. The exit from the attack was less coordinated, which resulted in the squadron breaking apart into separate flights.
>
> After this attack, the enemy scattered, and a maneuvering aerial combat took shape, which was very difficult to control. Each tried to take maximum advantage of a superior position. Thus, in this maneuvering combat I managed to pull close

to another F-84 and to down it; this was the only combat mission I flew during my entire time of fighting in the skies of Korea in which I managed to down two enemy aircraft.

On this day, a pilot of the 176th GIAP, Captain P.S. Milaushkin downed another F-84. Here is how he described this victory:

We took off as a squadron consisting of all six crews: G.I. Ges' and G.A. Nikolaev; A.A. Plitkin and N.A. Feoktistov; and my element with my wingman S.L. Kirichenko. The other two squadrons of the regiment took off at the same time with the same number of crews. Regiment commander Lieutenant Colonel S.F. Vishniakov, with his wingman D.M. Fedorov, led the regimental group. Our assignment was to tie up the covering Sabres in combat and thereby give the 2nd and 3rd Squadrons the opportunity to destroy the other group of enemy aircraft, which consisted of F-84s. After taking off and assembling at an altitude of 11,000 meters, we quickly encountered a group of 30 enemy aircraft. Soon the ground controller informed us that two groups of ground attack aircraft were arriving in the Anju area from the sea. Vishniakov ordered the 2nd and 3rd Squadrons to go after the fighter-bombers, while our 1st Squadron kept the Sabres busy. The battle became a melee, and the impression was that only Sabres were everywhere around.

I attacked one of the Sabres, but it was difficult to down him, because he was constantly jinking around in my gun sight, which made it impossible to zero in on him; only when you placed the reticule of the gun sight in the fixed position could you line him up. After several minutes my wingman and I became separated in this wheeling dogfight. I descended from 11,000 meters down to 4,500 meters while pursuing Sabres, but the Sabres headed to the east in a dive, and it was useless to keep up the chase.

Then suddenly I saw eight F-84s to my right, which were banking around to the right to make another run against ground targets. I turned my MiG in pursuit of them, closed to within a distance so short that I could make out the letters and stripes on the wings, and opened fire on the leader. I hit him hard; he dropped out of the formation in a tight turn and began to lose altitude steadily. I was just about to exit to the left, when I saw tracers off my left wingtip, so I banked sharply to the right into a climb, and after two oblique loops the F-84 pair behind me gave up the chase.

That's when I heard an order from the regiment commander: "Everyone, 'grass'", which meant we had to start for home, and then he immediately called for me; I responded, "I'm fighting in the 'Sosiski' area." He then issued an order: "Everyone is to head for the 'Sosiski' area." Just then they were jumped by a fresh F-86 group that had come up, and a new dogfight started up. It was a hard one for our pilots, because they were fatigued and were also running low on fuel; in addition not everyone had reached the combat area, so they had to fight in pairs against eight-ship Sabre formations.

After my attack the F-84 group began to retreat, and I remained alone. I climbed to 9,000 meters, rolled over, and in an inverted attitude I saw aircraft. I thought they were ours and formed up on their tail, and only then did I see that they were

F-86s. I immediately took aim and opened fire. The Sabre abruptly nosed down with a list to the right, though what occurred further with him I didn't see, because a pair of F-86s had slid in behind me. I pulled up abruptly into a left-oblique loop. The Sabres tracers passed below my aircraft. Soon, however, the Sabres disappeared somewhere and I was again alone. I went back to base, swinging to the left and right, so that I couldn't be unexpectedly attacked by Sabre free hunters.

The regiment returned to bases in many ones and twos, who had linked up with anyone else from the regiment that they had come across, because it was still easier and less dangerous than to head for home alone. My wingman Stepa Kirichenko made it back safe and sound. He hadn't been able to stick with me in a loop and made a mistake when swinging back around, as a result of which he fell a long ways behind me and then lost me entirely. Now alone, he had fought against a pair of F-86s.

As a result, the raid was repulsed and the enemy lost four F-84s (Milaushkin didn't receive credit for the victory over the F-86), without any losses in return. The American side confirms the loss of two of their F-84E fighter-bombers, No.51-542 and No.49-2403, both from the 111th FBS. The pilot of the second Thunderjet, 1st Lieutenant John Morse Jr., was killed, but the pilot of the first Thunderjet, having reached Cho-do Island, ejected from his damaged aircraft. The Americans believe that in this combat, a pair of F-84Es from the 111th FBS, piloted by 1st Lieutenants K.C. Cooley and J.M. Hewett jointly downed one MiG-15, but this was either a PLAAF MiG, or they merely damaged one of the Soviet MiGs, since all of the 64th IAK fighters returned to their bases.

On this same day, aviation units of the UAA suffered losses, but on the ground, not in aerial combat. A few days before this one, a Chinese MiG squadron had flown to the newly constructed airfield at Uiju, not far from Sinuiju, but hadn't yet initiated combat operations from this base. On 18 November, when returning from a patrol over MiG Alley, four F-86As from the 336th FIS led by Captain Kenneth Chandler spotted 12 MiG-15s parked on the ground out in the open. One Sabre element remained high as top cover while the second element consisting of Captain Chandler and 1st Lieutenant Ragland attacked the MiGs parked on the ramp, and with strafing fire they destroyed four MiGs and damaged four more. All of the MiGs that were destroyed on the ground were credited to Captain Chandler. Besides that, on this same mission Captain Chandler, while patrolling over the Yalu, had downed an enemy aircraft, which he identified as a MiG-9. On the next day, the remnants of the Chinese squadron, which had been largely destroyed on the ground, flew back to Manchuria from Uiju.

Back in October 1951, pilots of the 4th FIW had begun to transition to a new version of the Sabre that had just arrived in Korea – the F-86E. The process of changing over to the new fighter took several months, and the final F-86A-5 fighter interceptors left the 4th Wing in July 1952. As they were being removed, 11 F-86As of this Wing were re-equipped as reconnaissance RF-86A, which were delivered to the 67th TRW's 15th TRS based in Kimpo.

Also in October 1951 (22 October, to be precise), General Hoyt S. Vandenberg, the USAF Chief of Staff, ordered 75 F-86E Sabres to be sent to Korea, which were received by the 51st FIG. This group was based on the K-13 airfield at Suwon, and prior to this had been flying F-80s. The new equipment assigned to the 51st Fighter Interceptor Group, plus technicians and other support personnel necessary for the changeover, were delivered to Japan in the beginning of November aboard the USS *Sitko Bay* and USS *Cape Esperance*. Upon arriving in Japan, the 16th and 25th FIS received the new aircraft, and in turn handed their Shooting Stars over to the 8th FBG, which to this point had been still flying the piston-engine F-51 Mustang.

True, before they began to duel with MiGs, the 51st FIG's pilots were advised to make a few flights in the F-86A. Colonel Francis S. Gabreski, who was one of the USAF's top pilots, was appointed to command the 51st FIW. He was a Second World War veteran and had scored 28 victories in Europe, thereby becoming one of the USAF's highest-scoring aces. In Korea, he had served as the deputy commander of the 4th FIW from the spring of 1951 until October 1951, flying combat missions as part of this fighter group, and had already downed two MiG-15s in the Korean sky.

The pilots of the 51st FIG spent until December 1951 in Suwon becoming familiar with the new fighter. Meanwhile, the 4th FIG's pilots, as had been the case previously, continued to carry out the task of protecting the strike groups over MiG Alley alone. Over the months of October and November, they downed 38 MiGs and 11 aircraft of other types in aerial combats.

In October 1951, Colonel Harrison Thyng had assumed command of the 4th FIW. He was also a combat veteran of the Second World War and achieved five victories in it. Colonel Thyng scored his first victory in the skies of Korea on 24 October 1951, downing one MiG-15, and would down four more before his service in Korea ended, thereby becoming an ace in this war.

According to American official records, by the end of October 1951 the 4th FIW had lost 28 F-86As, which forced the USAF command to send a batch of replacements from the USA. Already on 1 November 1951, the new Wing commander Colonel Thyng had gotten his bearings in a sad situation regarding the condition of the equipment in the units (the squadrons' mechanics were laboring mightily to keep only 44 of the units' available aircraft in satisfactory condition for combat flying), and sent a worried dispatch to the USAF Chief of Staff on this matter. He didn't have to wait long for a reaction. The initial response, as we have seen, was the dispatch of 75 of the new F-86E for the 51st FIG. Simultaneously, the new Sabres also began trickle into the 4th FIW.

Combat over MiG Alley continued and became even bitterer. After a four-day break connected with bad weather, fighting in the North Korean sky resumed on 23 November. That afternoon the weather improved, and the Fifth Air Force command sent its fighter-bombers into MiG Alley. Between 1540 and 1545, 20 MiGs of the 18th GIAP and 16 MiGs of the 17th IAP roared into the sky. The attack group consisting of 18 MiGs from the 176th GIAP followed them into the air. In the area of Siarenkan, the 18th GIAP's pilots engaged the Sabres of the forward screen, while pilots of the 176th GIAP and 17th IAP attacked a group of 40 F-84s in the Sukchon area. Majors K.Ia. Sheberstov (of the 176th GIAP) and S.S. Artemchenko (of the 17th IAP) managed to shoot down two Thunderjets, while the remaining fighter-bombers fled the given area. Our pilots had no losses in this action.

On the next day of 24 November, pilots of the 303rd IAD took off several times to intercept enemy aircraft, but failed to encounter enemy aircraft. The pilots of the 324th IAD were luckier: in the Pyongyang area they ran into a large group of fighter-bombers, covered by Sabres, and attacked them. The 10 MiGs from the 176th GIAP attacked 16 F-84s, which were covered by a flight of F-86s. In a short combat Major K.Ia. Sheberstov and Captain P.S. Milaushkin downed two Thunderjets, while the pilots of the 196th IAP that were covering them in a combat with the Sabres shot down one of them. Our pilots suffered no losses in this battle. The Americans do not confirm the loss of their Thunderjets in this combat, yet do acknowledge that F-86A No.49-1166 was lost. The victory over it went to Senior Lieutenant V.G. Murav'ev of the 196th IAP. The Sabre pilot did manage to reach friendly territory in his damaged aircraft before jettisoning from it.

On 26 November the 64th IAK's pilots intercepted several raids by small groups of fighter-bombers from the 136th FBW, claiming one F-86 and one F-84 in the process; the Sabre was downed by Captain Nikolai Sutiagin of the 17th IAP, who was becoming known as a Sabre hunter. Here is how it happened: In the period between 1100 and 1120, a radar post detected up to 20 enemy fighter-bombers and fighters, flying on a heading of 320°, at an altitude of 8,000-9,000 meters about 50 kilometers south of Pyongyang. Another group of 16 enemy fighter-bombers and fighters, flying on the same heading, was in an area 30 kilometers to the northeast of Pyongyang at an altitude of 5,000-6,000 meters.

After taking off, our fighters in the period between 1135 and 1143 spotted 16 enemy fighters, flying on a heading of 40° at an altitude of 8,000-10,000 meters 25 kilometers southwest of Chinnampo. At an order from the division command post, the 17th IAP launched 22 MiG-15s under the command of Major G.I. Pulov from Readiness No. 1 to reinforce the 523rd IAP, which was already locked in combat in the Sukchon area.

Major Pulov's group, as instructed by the division command post, was flying at an altitude of 8,500 meters. When over Anju, Pulov noticed up to 16 F-86 fighters off to his right in the Sukchon-Sunchon area. After Major Pulov's group turned to starboard, the enemy, having an altitude advantage of 800-1,000 meters, swung around to port in order to close with the MiG group. Major Pulov ordered Major M.N. Shcherbakov to engage the left-hand, eight-ship F-86 group in the Sunchon area, while he himself went on the attack against the other eight-ship F-86 group that was coming in over Sukchon from the sea. Major M.S. Ponomarev's squadron was to cover the attack.

The two opposing groups of fighters met head-on over the Sukchon area. Letting the Sabres pass underneath and to the left of him, Pulov began to haul his MiG around to the left to go after them. Pulov pursued the Sabre flight, which departed toward the sea in a leftward spiral. At the moment of the leftward turn, Captain N.V. Sutiagin spotted another F-86 flight out in front, above and about 45°to the left, which was in the process of swinging around to the left with the aim of dropping in behind Major Pulov's lead element. Sutiagin banked to the left and climbed toward the enemy, but the enemy passed in front of him in a dive at a high target aspect angle. Sutiagin immediately banked right, then swung sharply back around to the left and went after the enemy. The Sabres were pursuing Pulov's element, while Sutiagin after reversing course to the left emerged on the tail of the F-86s, closed to within 440-200 meters and fired on the wingman of the second pair. The Sabre lurched to the right and with a list of 70-80° started to fall toward the earth. Captain Sutiagin's wingman Senior Lieutenant A.S. Shirokov fired at the leader from a range of 1,000 meters down to 800 meters. The enemy (three F-86s), noticing our fighters' fire, rolled over to the left and headed toward the sea. Captain Sutiagin's element pulled out of the attack in a climbing turn to starboard.

As Pulov was reversing course to the left to go after the Sabre flight, Major S.S. Artemchenko noticed an F-86 flight seemingly stalking them below and to the right. Artemchenko banked to the right and began to close with the enemy. The enemy, seeing the approaching MiGs, went into a split-S in the direction of the sea. Artemchenko didn't even bother to chase the enemy and went into a 360° turn to starboard. Straightening back out, Artemchenko noticed yet another F-86 flight approaching from the left and below, and turned into the attack. The enemy, seeing that they had been spotted, went into a shallow loop, but seeing that our fighters were closing on them, they turned on their afterburners and headed toward the sea.

The 3rd Squadron under the command of Major Shcherbakov, flying at an altitude of 8,500 meters to the left of the 1st Squadron in the Sukchon area, encountered eight approaching F-86s 600-700 meters below it, which with a turn to port passed underneath Shcherbakov's group. At Shcherbakov's order, the 3rd Squadron, which numbered six MiGs on the mission, began swinging around to the right while shedding altitude, in order to take up a position for launching an attack. The adversary, seeing the approach of Major Shcherbakov's group, turned tightly to port and headed for the coastline in a shallow dive. Major Shcherbakov didn't even start to pursue the enemy beyond the coastline and exited the combat in a turn to port.

The dogfight between our fighters and the enemy fighters lasted for seven to eight minutes. As a result of the combat, Captain Sutiagin downed one F-86 from a range of 400 meters down to 200 meters and a target aspect angle of 0/4 [dead astern] to 1/4.

On this day the 64th IAK lost one of its own aircraft, but it had nothing to do with enemy action. While in a dogfight with 16 F-86s in the Sunchon area, the MiG of Senior Lieutenant S.D. Krupchatnikov from the 523rd IAP suffered a flame-out at an altitude of 11,000 meters. Dropping to 6,000 meters in altitude, the pilot thought to re-start the engine, but believing that a plume would appear behind his aircraft if he opened the stopcock, thereby revealing his location to enemy fighters, he closed the stopcock, which halted the ignition. He decided to eject at an altitude of 3,000 meters and activated the emergency canopy release, but the canopy failed to free itself. Now at an altitude of 2,500 meters, Krupchatnikov decided to eject through the canopy. During the ejection he received minor wounds to the head and right arm. Our pilot safely came down in North Korean territory, and 12 days later he arrived back at the regiment and began flying combat missions.

The aerial combats on 27 November in the same Anju area, where numerous groups of F-80s and F-84s from the 49th FBG and the 136th FBG arrived from the direction of the sea, under the reinforced cover of Sabres from the 4th FIW, were particularly bitter. The dogfights involved more than 100 USAF aircraft, as well as approximately 80 MiGs of the 64th IAK. As always, the first enemy raid came in the morning, and every regiment of the 303rd IAD and 324th IAD took off to repel it. This time, however, for some reason the enemy fighter-bomber groups were not covered by swarms of Sabres, and therefore they suffered heavy losses.

The pilots of the 18th GIAP and 523rd IAP, together with the pilots of the 324th IAD's 196th IAP, arrived by squadron at low altitude in the area where the fighter-bombers were operating, and splitting into flights and elements, attacked the numerous enemy strike groups. The 196th IAP's Vasilii Dmitrievich Ostapenko describes what happened:

Having taken off in a regimental group, we soon came upon a group of F-84s. They were flying in a tight formation echeloned to the right, almost line abreast, as if on parade. In such cases only the group leader could get a full view of the air space; the remaining pilots have restricted views and can pretty much only see the aircraft flying on the left of them. When we made our first attacking pass, the extreme Thunderjet on the right separated from the formation and swung around tightly to the right. I was also flying on the outside of our formation and thought that he was going to latch onto my tail, so maneuverable were those F-84s. I banked sharply to the right to meet his attack, but as it turns out, he had simply decided to scram. My speed was high, and I quickly caught up with him and attacked. I gave him a burst, and he released his drop tanks and decided to try to shake me off with a dive. I gave him another burst, and he staggered in the air, almost as if he'd come to a stop. I shot past him and went into a climbing turn to starboard to search for [my] group, but I couldn't find it.

Usually after such a salvo, the target aircraft explodes in mid-air, but my F-84 didn't blow up; instead it fell to earth, and later a search team brought back fragments from the wreckage. I landed back at base alone, and everything ended well for me.

One more Thunderjet was downed in this action by the commander of the 196th IAP Colonel E.G. Pepeliaev. Pilots of the 18th GIAP claimed two other F-84s over the Sukchon area, while the 523rd IAP's pilots came across a group of F-80s in the Sunan region and hit it hard, downing two of the Shooting Stars.

When the Sabres finally arrived in the combat area, it was already too late to protect the fighter-bombers, but the pilots of the 176th GIAP, who were caught by F-86s from the 334th and 336th FIS, took the full blow from the vengeful Sabres upon themselves. It was a very hard fight, because the 176th GIAP was numerically small, and usually the regiment sent out just two or three six-ship MiG groups on combat missions. Thus, the Sabres' numerical superiority in this combat was almost two-fold. Climbing and diving jets filled the air, and Sabres were flashing everywhere. Here's what Aleksandr Prokop'evich Verdysh recalls of this combat:

At the time I was with the 3rd Squadron and took off as the wingman of the squadron commander Captain I.A. Suchkov. While climbing to an altitude of 6,000 meters, the ailerons' hydraulic actuators on my aircraft went out, and just when we reached an altitude of 8,000 meters, our pair was jumped by eight F-86s.

Taking advantage of my MiG's poor maneuverability due to the failure of the ailerons' hydraulics, Sabres quickly latched onto my tail and flamed my aircraft. Group leader Captain Suchkov ordered me to bail out, which I indeed did.

As I was descending in my parachute, twice enemy fighters attempted to shoot me, but I came to earth safely.[2] I'd been wounded in the left hand over friendly territory, and soon Chinese People's Volunteers picked me up and took me to a hospital. On the next day I was already back at my airfield. Incidentally, before they shot me down, I had watched as my leader Captain I.A. Suchkov shot down a Sabre in a vertical maneuver.

Another pilot of the 176th GIAP, Captain A.A. Plitkin's wingman Senior Lieutenant Aleksei Esipko, was shot down in this action, and in the words of Anatolii Alekseevich Plitkin, this is how it happened:

> We had been involved in a hard and unequal combat with a large group of F-86s and were heading home (our fuel tanks were almost empty). Suddenly Sabres jump out right in front of our nose. We fire at them (and possibly scored hits), they roll over, and suddenly I see bullets punching through my left wing. I glanced around – my "Kunak" (that's what I called Esipko) isn't there. I exited out from under the Sabres' attack and head home. Upon arriving, I reported that Esipko had been downed. The next day he showed up safe and sound, just like me and other of our comrades had before him. It was our good fortune that the Sabres were equipped with a small-caliber weapon. My wingman had to eject, while I returned with eight bullet holes in my wing, but the main thing is everything ended happily for us both.

Evidently, Captain Plitkin's flight had been attacked by Major George Davis and his wingman from the 334th FIS. Davis was one of the top pilots in the 4th FIW. He was credited with two MiGs in this combat – he downed Senior Lieutenant A.I. Esipko's aircraft and damaged Captain A.A. Plitkin's MiG, thus Davis's second victory wasn't in fact a kill. Other than Davis, two more MiGs were credited to pilots of the 336th FIS, but most likely they had downed only one MiG (piloted by Verdysh), and not two. Over the day's combats, the 64th IAK lost just two MiGs; several more MiGs were damaged, but were all quickly made serviceable again.

The pilots of the 176th GIAP put in claims for several enemy aircraft destroyed and damaged, but for a variety of reasons, they received no credit for them. The F-86 claimed by Captain Suchkov was also disallowed, as was an Australian Meteor that Captain P.F. Nikulin claimed. In this combat, having separated from the Sabres, the pair of Nikulin and Garmashov had dropped below some clouds and unexpectedly collided with a group of Meteors, which were flying in a compact formation of two four-ship groups. Nikulin immediately turned toward them, fired at the nearest Meteor to him and hit him. The remaining Meteors promptly climbed into the clouds and disappeared.

Altogether in the major battle of 27 November, the 64th IAK counted eight victories over enemy aircraft, against the loss of two MiGs. The pilots of the 18th GIAP particu-larly distinguished themselves by downing four American aircraft. On this day they had conducted an audacious and simultaneously dangerous raid to North Korea's eastern coastline. Aleksei Alekseevich Kaliuzhny, the inspector for aerial combat tactics with the 303rd IAD, flew on this mission and left a detailed account of it and the resulting combat with carrier-based USNAF aircraft:

> We were defending the North Korean airspace from Andong (PRC) and Sinuiju (PDRK) down to Pyongyang along the western coastline of the Korean peninsula bordering the Yellow Sea. However, we couldn't fly to the opposite, eastern coast-line of Korea, bordering the Sea of Japan; it was distant from Andong and we lacked sufficient fuel to fly there and return. The Americans took account of this and brought up three aircraft carriers with piston-engine ground-attack aircraft aboard to East China Bay, not far from the port of Wonsan. So from there they could

operate with complete impunity, without meeting any sort of opposition from our aviation. They were so brazen; they flew as if back over their own practice bombing area, destroying everything on the ground in succession.

When we received this information, I gave some thought to how we could teach them a lesson. I spent several days intensively studying the flight route and the engineer-navigational chart, calculating the fuel expenditures. It occurred to me that if I climbed almost to the MiG's ceiling (15,000 meters), and then dove to 3,000-4,000 meters in the Wonsan area, then I would be able to spend 8-10 minutes at this altitude. And if I was also lucky and in these minutes encountered American aircraft, then I could make one attacking pass, before climbing back up to the ceiling and heading for home. I couldn't get tied up in combat, I wouldn't have enough fuel; even if all went as planned, I would only have three or four minutes of fuel left upon landing.

I checked all my calculations with the division's engineer, Andrei Zakharovich Nesterov, and he confirmed their accuracy. Then I handed the flight plan to division commander Hero of the Soviet Union Colonel A.S. Kumanichkin, who agreed with it and in turn requested authorization for such a mission from corps commander General Lobov, who approved it.

I took a good pilot (with whom I'd flown together more than once) Senior Lieutenant Anatolii Andreevich Astapovsky; before this he had been with the 18th GIAP flying as Captain L.K. Shchukin's wingman. Together with him on 27 November 1951 I flew one combat mission as part of the entire division, in which we had tangled with some F-86s, but without result. Then that afternoon, after our MiGs had been thoroughly inspected and fully refueled, Tolia Astapovsky and I took off together.

Having climbed to an altitude of 12,000 meters while en route to Wonsan, we had moved toward the goal of our flight: a "free hunt". In the Wonsan area on the eastern coast of Korea, I went into a steep descent from out of the sun. Somewhere around an altitude of 5,000 to 6,000 meters, I saw an eight-ship formation of piston-engine fighter-bombers in front of and below us, heading in the same direction as we were. We'd been extremely lucky – not only had we immediately come across enemy aircraft, we were approaching them from above, behind, and out of the sun. I gave an order to my wingman to jettison the drop tanks and indicated the target to him.

The carrier-based F6F-5 [more likely these were AD-1 Skyraiders] were flying in a compact formation echeloned to the right. We were still 1.5-2 kilometers behind them, and in order to shoot one down we had to close to within 200 to 300 meters. We input the data into the gunsight and went on the attack against one of the aircraft flying in the middle of the formation, and the wingman on the extreme right (Tolia was flying somewhat behind me and off to the right). Only one thing worried me – whether or not they were equipped with a defensive radar in their tails, which might give them warning of our approach and spoil the attack's unexpectedness. However, they were flying calmly, with no indication that they were aware of our presence, so plainly they lacked such equipment. Our speed was close to 1,000 km/hr, and having closed to a range of 200-250 meters, I opened fire from all my cannons. After an instant, the carrier aircraft I had targeted exploded like a bomb (which was visible on my gun camera film). I was closing too rapidly and I barely had time to yank the joystick into my stomach to pull the MiG into a zoom climb to avoid running into the American formation.

At the moment when I downed my target, my wingman also downed "his" carrier aircraft, which suffered the same fate. He also hauled his aircraft into a steep climb to follow me. I didn't even begin to swing around for another attack. It was a wise decision. Having climbed up to 12,000 meters and turned back toward Andong, we safely made it back home. We went straight in for a landing; I set down my MiG and Astapovsky landed right behind me. When we checked the fuel tanks, I only had 100 liters left (enough for 2 to 3 minutes of flight time), while my wingman's fuel tanks were almost dry; of course, as the wingman he had to expend somewhat more fuel.

In the American camp, a real hubbub arose on the next day. They were trying to come to grips with what had happened. For the next several days their carrier aircraft didn't fly any ground attack missions in the given area, and then heavy details of fighters began to escort them.

When General A.S. Krasovsky (our top adviser to the Chinese PLAAF) learned about this mission, he categorically forbade the pilots from taking risks. Well, they didn't even express any gratitude to Tolia Astapovsky and me. In general, they didn't indulge our brotherhood of pilots with medals.

That was the conclusion to this uncommon and very risky raid to the area of the port of Wonsan.

According to Captain A.A. Kaliuzhny's wingman Senior Lieutenant Anatolii Andreevich Astapovsky, they hadn't encountered an eight-ship formation on the mission, but a six-ship group of F4U Corsair carrier-based fighter-bombers and they'd attacked them straight away. Having downed two of them, the remaining enemy aircraft jettisoned their bombs and scattered in every direction. That same evening, Astapovsky heard over the radio that the Americans were reporting that Communist MiGs had shot down two of their carrier fighters that day. True, this action has not been mentioned in any of the Western publications about the Korean War, which isn't surprising: Who likes to write about their own losses?!

As a result of Captain Kaliuzhny's venture, over the day of 27 November, the 64th IAK's pilots, in addition to the four F-84E and two F-80s, downed two piston-engine Corsairs. In fact the Americans do acknowledge the loss of two ground attack aircraft on this day: one of them was an AD-4L (No.123974) from VF-54, flying from the aircraft carrier USS *Essex*. It is recorded that the Skyraider was lost due to the explosion of the bomb aboard the aircraft, which also killed its pilot Lieutenant Eugene Hall. But it is obvious that the bomb on the Skyraider didn't explode on its own; it was "helped" by a shell from the cannons on Captain Kaliuzhny's MiG. Kaliuzhny's wingman Senior Lieutenant Astapovsky at that time downed F4U-4B No. 62979 from VMF-323 (aircraft carrier USS *Bedoing Strait*); its pilot Captain Charles C. Whipple was luckier – he managed to bail out.

In addition, the Americans recognize the loss of two of their F-80s, No.49-524 and No.49-531, from the 8th FBG, one pilot of which was killed, while the other managed to bail out over friendly territory. Also on this day, F-84E No.51-636 from the 49th FBG's

7th FBS was lost – its pilot Major Bernard K. Seitzinger was killed. Thus, at the very least, our pilots did down five enemy aircraft on this day.

The next day, 28 November, again proved to be a hot one, when fierce battles in which both sides suffered substantial losses erupted in MiG Alley. The full 324th IAD and the 303rd IAD's 523rd IAP took part in repelling the next raid by Thunderjets of the 136th FBW, which were again being covered by Sabres. At first, 22 MiGs of the 196th IAP, led by regiment commander Colonel E.G. Pepeliaev, engaged 40 F-86s from the 4th FIW. Next, approximately 20 MiGs from the 523rd IAP, led by the commander of the 303rd IAD Colonel A.S. Kumanichkin, came to their assistance, while 18 MiGs of the 176th GIAP attacked a formation of 30 Thunderjets in the Hugu-ri area.

The archival documents of the 324th IAD describe in detail how the events unfolded in the Chongju-Anju area, where the pilots of the 196th IAP under the command of regiment commander Lieutenant Colonel E.G. Pepeliaev fought a successful battle. This lengthy excerpt offers a good insight into the swirling nature of the large dogfights over Korea:

> At 0741, a group consisting of the following pairs of pilots took off to intercept enemy aircraft: Pepeliaev-Fukin, Bokach-Frolov, Murav'ev-Ishtokin; leading the 2nd Squadron Tkatsky-Sharokhin, with Rud'ko-Iushin, Ivanov-Tiron, and Kochegarov-Filippov; leading the 3rd Squadron Alfeev-Kapranov, with Zaplavnev-Kolpakov, Grib-Rybas, and Dostoevsky-Iovlev. These pilots comprised the attack group of the 64th IAK's overall combat formation. The group adopted a staggered trail formation by elements, and echeloned by flights.
>
> Arriving in the vicinity of Chongju, the crews spotted five groups of up to 40 F-86 fighters, flying on various headings and at various altitudes between 4,000 and 10,000 meters in compact six-ship wedge formations and eight-ship formations echeloned by flight. The regimental group, having swung around to port, engaged the enemy group in combat, which broke down into separate pairs and flights.
>
> Lieutenant Colonel Pepeliaev's group, having climbed during the turn to port, went after an F-86 flight from above and behind which, noticing the attack by our fighters, evaded it with a sudden split-S to the right. Pepeliaev's element pulled out of the attack with a chandelle to the left. At the moment of the attack against the F-86 flight, Pepeliaev's element had itself been attacked by a pair of Sabres, which Major Bokach's element warded off. After several vertical maneuvers, having closed to within 600-800 meters behind this F-86 element, Bokach opened fire from all three cannons, using long bursts against the lead F-86, while his wingman Senior Lieutenant Frolov gave medium-length bursts from the same range against the wingman's aircraft, which departed in a dive along the coastline to the south, streaming white smoke behind it. Major Bokach's element pulled out of the attack into a chandelle to port. Captain Murav'ev's element covered the attack by Major Bokach's element.
>
> After exiting his attack, Pepeliaev again spotted a pair of F-86s to the left and below his element. Going into a diving turn to port, Pepeliaev attacked this pair from above and behind, but the enemy, catching sight of our fighters, broke left into a dive and evaded the attack. Pepeliaev pulled out of this attack with another chandelle to left. While in the climbing turn, a pair of F-86s tried to swing in

behind them from above and to the left. Pepeliaev's pair evaded the attack with a vertical maneuver, and then closed with this F-86 element. Pepeliaev opened fire on the wingman from a range of 200 meters, but didn't see any results of his fire. The Sabres again went into a split-S to escape. Swinging around to the left, Pepeliaev's element caught sight of a second pair of F-86s in front and below them and attacked it. At first Lieutenant Colonel Pepeliaev gave two medium and two long bursts at the enemy's lead aircraft from a range of 500 meters down to 160 meters, and watched his shells hit the targeted Sabre, which fell off into a diving turn to left, billowing smoke. His wingman Senior Lieutenant Fukin also gave the wingman's aircraft three long bursts from a range of 650 meters down to 160 meters, and saw his shells strike the targeted aircraft's fuselage. They pulled out of this attack into a climbing turn to port. At the moment of exiting the attack, Fukin gave another medium-length burst to the lead Sabre of the now descending pair from a range of 330 meters. After exiting this attack, Pepeliaev's element sighted yet another group of six F-86s above and to the right of them, from which one element split off and began to pull in behind Pepeliaev's element. Looping twice, Pepeliaev turned the tables on this Sabre element and closed in on its tail, before opening fire from a range of 150-200 meters at the wingman's aircraft, which went down in flames. They pulled out of this attack in a chandelle to port.

While in the initial climbing turn to left Captain Tkatsky's group spotted a flight of F-86s to the right and 1,000 meters below them. Captain Ivanov's flight, reversing course to the right, attacked this Sabre flight. Only Ivanov fired, giving one long burst to the wingman of the second F-86 pair from a range of 600 meters, but he didn't see any of his shells strike the target. The targeted Sabre went into a split-S and dove away. Continuing to pursue the other three Sabres and having closed to within a range of 500 meters behind them, Ivanov opened fire on the F-86 on the right, but again saw no results from his fire. The three Sabres attempted to come out from under the attack in a chandelle to port, but Ivanov's flight continued to pursue them. Senior Lieutenant Kochegarov's element, which was covering the attacks by Ivanov's pair, at an altitude of 3,000 meters saw a solitary F-86 approaching from head-on. Kochegarov gave the Sabre a medium-length burst from a range of 250 meters, after which he again formed up with Captain Ivanov's element, which was continuing to chase the three Sabres.

During the pursuit, Kochegarov's element closed to within 870 meters of the left wingman. Touching his rudder to line up on the lead F-86, Kochegarov fired a long burst at it from a range of 650 meters, but observed no results. The Sabre leader and his left-hand wingman went into split-S and dove away.

In the combat area, Kochegarov observed one F-86 going down, trailing smoke from its left wing. Senior Lieutenant Kochegarov's element pulled up into a chandelle to port and attacked a group of three F-86s from behind and to the right. Only Kochegarov fired at them, giving them two medium-length bursts from a range of 750 meters down to 550 meters, but he didn't see any results from his fire. The three F-86s departed in the direction of Korea Bay. Captain Tkatsky's flight covered the 2nd Squadron's attacks.

Senior Lieutenant Alfeev's 3rd Squadron, flying as the regiment's covering group, when following the regimental group's initial turn to left, spotted a six-ship F-86 group below and in front, climbing to attack Captain Tkatsky's flight from below and behind. Alfeev's flight swung around in a diving turn to left and began to close upon the Sabre formation. At this moment the third Sabre element rolled over to the left and dove away. Alfeev's element continued to pursue the remaining four Sabres, and after one vertical maneuver Alfeev pulled to within firing range of them. Alfeev opened fire from a range of 600-700 meters, giving the wingman of the second Sabre element one short burst, which evaded the fire with a split-S to the right. Pursuing the leading pair of F-86s, and closing with it in a chandelle to port after several vertical maneuvers, Alfeev opened fire from a range of 400 meters at the wingman's Sabre, but didn't see any results.

At the moment of Alfeev's turn to port, Captain Zaplavnev's pair spotted six F-86s to the right and behind them, which were closing from behind to attack Alfeev's flight. Banking into a diving turn to starboard, Zaplavnev's element engaged them. After two vertical maneuvers, the six F-86s exited the combat in a dive. When pulling out of the loop, Zaplavnev's element was attacked from above and to the right by two F-86 elements.

With another vertical maneuver, Zaplavnev closed upon one F-86 pair and opened fire on the wingman with three short bursts at a range of 400-500 meters, but saw no results from his fire. His wingman Senior Lieutenant Kolpakov, covering his leader, fired one short burst across the noses of another pair of F-86s that were trying to attack Zaplavnev. At this time Kolpakov himself was attacked from above and to the right by an F-86 element. Making two vertical maneuvers and having closed to within 600 meters of this Sabre pair, he fired short bursts at the enemy wingman, but observed no results.

When pulling out of his attack, Zaplavnev was attacked by a flight of F-86s, as a result of which his MiG received six bullet holes. He shook off his attackers with a diving turn to port.

Captain Grib's element while in a chandelle to left caught sight of an F-86 pair behind it. Having executed two vertical maneuvers and closing with it, Grib opened fire on the wingman from a range of 600 meters, before pulling out of the attack in a chandelle to the right. His wingman Senior Lieutenant Rybas, covering his leader's attack, was attacked by a second pair of F-86s. He evaded the attack by banking sharply right into a climbing turn, then swung back around and attacked this pair of F-86s, which was attempting now to attack the second element of Senior Lieutenant Alfeev's flight. He gave them two medium-length bursts from a range of 600 meters, but saw no results from his fire.

Pulling out of the attack into a chandelle to the right, Rybas spotted a flight of F-86s in front of him and attacked them. Closing to within 300 meters of the tail-end Sabre in the formation, he fired two short bursts at it but observed no results. He pulled out of the pass in a chandelle to left, after which he saw another pair of Sabres in front of him and went after them. He fired one long burst as he closed from 500 meters down to 330 meters, and watched as the attacked F-86 began to fall, streaming smoke from both wing roots.

Captain Dostoevsky's pair, swinging around to the left behind Captain Grib's lead element, attacked a pair of F-86s from above and behind. After two oblique loops, he gave the wingman's F-86 long bursts from all three cannons as he closed the range from 300 meters down to 200 meters and observed his shells exploding on the target. Dostoevsky's pulled up out of the attack into climbing turn to the left. Straightening out, Dostoevsky sighted another pair of F-86s to the right and below. Swinging around to the left in a diving turn, he attacked them from a range of 200 meters and opened fire on the wingman's Sabre with long bursts, and again saw his shells strike home.

At this moment Dostoevsky's element was jumped by a flight of Sabres, as a result of which control cables on Dostoevsky's MiG were severed and its canopy was smashed; Dostoevsky himself received a fragment wound in the right arm. The pilot opted to eject from his stricken aircraft at 10,000 meters.

His wingman Senior Lieutenant Iovlev evaded the attack with a steep vertical maneuver, and after a second oblique loop he himself attacked one pair of F-86s. Closing the range from 600 meters down to 400 meters, he opened fire before pulling out of the attack in a chandelle to port.

The entire regimental group withdrew from combat in pairs and flights at an order from the group leader. They reassembled en route back to base.

The dogfight lasted for 14 minutes. In the courses of it, the regiment's pilots expended a total of 228 N-37 shells and 935 N-23 shells.

Conclusions:

1. The aerial combat was conducted tactically competently and properly. The pilots forced the adversary to exit the combat, without having carried out their mission.
2. In the aerial combat, Lieutenant Colonel E.G. Pepeliaev downed 2 F-86s; Captains I.M Zaplavnev and A.M. Dostoevsky, and Senior Lieutenants N.T. Rybas, A.M Kochegarov and V.N. Fukin each downed 1 F-86.
3. Captain A.M. Dostoevsky's MiG-15 was shot down, and two of the regiment's aircraft received damage (Zaplavnev – 6 bullet holes, Iovlev – 1 bullet hole).

In this combat, the 196th IAP's pilots claimed seven victories over the Sabres, although they did indeed lose one aircraft in return. Two more F-86s on this day were downed in the Sunchon area by the commander of the 523rd IAP Major D.P. Os'kin, but the regiment also suffered a heavy loss in this action. While covering the division's inspector for piloting technique Major N.P. Pravotorov, his wingman, Senior Lieutenant German Timofeevich Shatalov, who had five victories to his personal credit and was one of the regiment's top pilots, was killed. He was covering the commander's aircraft. During the dogfight with 14 F-86s at 0808, in the area 10 kilometers southwest of Anju Major Pravotorov's element was attacked by four F-86s. His wingman Captain Shatalov's MiG received damage to its controls, so the pilot ejected. As he did so, the pilot struck his aircraft's tailfin and he was killed. Two groups of MiGs from the 17th IAP and 18th GIAP took off to go to the assistance of the 523rd IAP's pilots, but they failed to encounter any enemy aircraft on this day.

In the course of this large battle, the 64th IAK's pilots achieved 10 victories: seven F-86s were credited to the pilots of the 196th IAP, two more F-86s went to the score of the 523rd IAP, and the 176th GIAP's pilots claimed one Thunderjet. Their own losses consisted of two MiGs and one pilot. The Americans acknowledged the loss of only one of their Sabres. At the same time, they claimed that Major Winton Marshall's element from the 335th FIS achieved two victories on this day, one by Marshall personally, and the other shared with his wingman 2nd Lieutenant Samuel Groningen. Most likely, they were the downed MiG of Senior Lieutenant Dostoevsky and Senior Lieutenant Iovlev's damaged aircraft – this was the work of the pair from the 335th FIS. Senior Lieutenant G.T. Shatalov, though, was apparently shot down by 1st Lieutenant Dayton Ragland of the 336th FIS, who also scored one victory on this day. True, Ragland's own F-86E No.50-0673 was downed in this combat; Ragland ejected, but was taken prisoner on the ground. Most likely, the commander of the 196th IAP Colonel Pepeliaev shot him down.

On this same day, 28 November, the 16th and 25th FIS of the 51st Fighter Interceptor Wing flew into Seoul from Kadena (Japan) in their new F-86Es (the 39th FIS was still forming up at this time and didn't enter combat until February 1952). Having arrived at the K-13 Air Base in Suwon, the 51st FIW's command immediately transferred 12 of the new F-86Es to the 4th Fighter Interceptor Wing as replacements, so the 51st FIW was left with 40 F-86E Sabres and 50 pilots.

On 29 November 1951, combats continued in MiG Alley with the same intensity. In the first action, the 20 MiGs of the 17th IAP attacked a formation of 30 F-84s and F-80s, and Captain Sutiagin claimed one of them, while the remaining immediately departed over the sea. At 0644, at an order from the division command post, 20 crews of the 17th IAP had taken off from a status of Readiness No.1 to intercept enemy aircraft in the Sukchon area, with the task first to engage the enemy fighters, before being redirected to repel the air strike.

Over Sukchon they didn't spot an enemy group, so they headed to Pyongyang, where they swung around to the left in a 180° turn. Coming out of the turn, the group received an order to continue on to the Sunchon area, southeast of Anju. Approaching the town of Sunchon, Captain S.S. Bychkov noticed a group of F-84 and F-80 aircraft in front of them, approaching from below and to the right, and informed group commander Captain Sutiagin of this. Captain Sutiagin, catching sight of the enemy, turned to the right 50-60° toward the enemy and issued the order: "Major Artemchenko and Major Shcherbakov are to engage the F-84s and F-80s; conduct the attack in a column of elements. Major Ponomarev will cover the area of combat."

After leveling out from the right turn, Sutiagin, having picked out a target, a flight of F-84s, allowed them to pass below them, then swung around to the left and began to close with the enemy from above and behind. The Thunderjet pilots, noticing the MiGs bearing down on them, broke into a left-hand spiral. Sutiagin's element, passing the enemy at a high angle, went into a zoom climb with a subsequent turn of 90° to port, where he spotted a pair of F-84s in front and to the left of them and 800-1,000 meters below them, which were heading away from them in a turn to port. Sutiagin banked to the left and dove on this pair of Thunderjets, and having closed to within a range of 250 meters of the wingman's F-84, he opened fire on it. The Thunderjet abruptly flipped over and fell out of control.

In trail behind Captain Sutiagin's element, Major S.S. Artemchenko's element and Captain Bychkov's pair, after the 180° turn to port encountered another flight of F-84s approaching from the right. Major Artemchenko turned toward them and swept past them head-on, after which he hauled his MiG around to the left in a climb, and again went into a head-on pass against the enemy. After this, the order came from the division command post to break off the combat and return to base.

The 3rd Squadron under the command of Major M.N. Shcherbakov, flying in trail behind the 1st Squadron, encountered the enemy on a meeting course, after which it banked around to the left, but lost the enemy in the sun. Having received group commander Captain Sutiagin's order to withdraw from combat, Major Shcherbakov and his squadron headed back to base.

Major M.S. Ponomarev's 2nd Squadron, flying as the covering group at an altitude of 7,000 meters in the area of Sunchon, encountered four F-84s approaching from its right, up to 2,000 meters below them. Ponomarev took his squadron into a descending turn to starboard and emerged behind the enemy. Captain N.P. Mishakin's flight sped in front of the rest of the squadron in the turn, and at high speed overshot the enemy and dove below them, after which the flight went into a chandelle to the left and due to low fuel exited the combat.

Ponomarev's flight, sliding in behind the enemy, closed to within 700-800 meters of them. Spotting the threat, the enemy broke left, and at this instant Ponomarev and Captain N.V. Masly opened fire from a range of 800 meters, before pulling out of the attack in a climbing turn to port.

The aerial combat between our fighters and the enemy lasted just four to five minutes. As a result, Captain Sutiagin succeeded in downing one F-84 from a range of 200 meters. While covering the actions of the 17th IAP's pilots, the pilots of the 196th IAP downed one F-86, which was credited to the regiment commander Colonel E.G. Pepeliaev.

There was a new combat that afternoon, which again involved the pilots of the 303rd IAD and both regiments of the 324th IAD. Their adversaries this time were 42 Sabres from the 4th FIW. In this dogfight, the 64th IAK's pilots claimed five victories over the F-86s without any losses in return. Pilots of the 17th IAP did particularly well, tallying three Sabres, two of which went to the personal score of Captain V.A. Blagov.

Around 1320, two squadrons numbering a total of 16 MiGs of the 523rd IAP had taken off to intercept an enemy raid in the Anju-Sukchon area. It was followed ten minutes later by approximately 20 MiGs of the 17th IAP led by Major G.I. Pulov, two squadrons of which had the assignment to cover the withdrawal of the 523rd IAP's pilots once their fuel began to run low, while one squadron was to reinforce the 523rd's actions against the fighter-bombers. Around 1345, the 18th GIAP took off with an analogous task, to reinforce the 17th IAP and to cover its withdrawal from combat.

Around 1345 our fighters sighted up to 30 enemy fighters and fighter-bombers at an altitude of 7,000-8,000 meters and 60 kilometers south of Pyongyang, and heading on a course of 340°. Another 14 enemy fighters and fighter-bombers were seen 20-30 kilometers north of Chinnampo at an altitude of 5,000 to 6,000 meters.

Major Pulov's group was flying in trail behind the 523rd IAP's regimental group at an altitude of 6,000-9,000 meters. The 1st Squadron, numbering eight MiGs, was to reinforce the 523rd IAP's group, while the 2nd and 3rd Squadrons were to cover the actions of the attack group.

Approaching the area of Chongju, the 17th IAP's covering group was tied up in combat by F-86 Sabres. The 3rd Squadron, numbering six MiGs led by Major M.N. Shcherbakov, flying at an altitude of 8,000 meters encountered up to 10 F-86s approaching from in front and flying 500-600 meters above it, which were already banking to the right to try to swing in behind Shcherbakov's group. Shcherbakov informed group commander Major Pulov over the radio that he was engaging in combat. As the Sabres flashed past,

Captain V.A. Blagov's element split off from the rest of the squadron and with a tight, climbing turn to starboard went in pursuit of a three-ship group of the Sabres. The Sabre pilots, seeing the MiGs closing in behind them, began to carry out an oblique loop to the right. In the second loop, Blagov latched onto the tail of a wingman's Sabre, and having closed to within 600-800 meters of it, opened fire: the target abruptly rolled to the left and went into an uncontrolled plunge. Blagov continued to pursue the remaining two F-86s, but the adversary conducted another three loops before heading in the direction of the sea in a dive. Blagov stayed with the Sabres, and having closed to within 400-500 meters, opened fire. The targeted Sabre abruptly yawed to the right and then began to go down in a right-hand list.

Blagov's wingman Senior Lieutenant V.N. Shestopalov began to pursue the remaining Sabre, which was continuing in the direction of the sea, and having closed to within 800-1,000 meters of it, opened fire and gave it five short bursts. The Sabre flipped over to the right and headed out over the sea. Shestapolov broke off the pursuit over the coastline.

Major Shcherbakov's element and Senior Lieutenant A.V. Bykov's element, having swung around to the right and climbed as the Sabres flew past, took up a position from which to launch an attack against the Sabres, which had shaken out into a column of elements and were still in their starboard turn. The F-86 pilots, seeing our MiGs behind them, conducted a split-S and dove away toward the sea. Shcherbakov broke off his flight's pursuit, carried out a 180° turn to port, and arrived over the Anju area, where he spotted eight F-86s in a diving turn to the left, which were preparing to attack Major Artemchenko's group. With a steep turn to port, Shcherbakov went after this group of Sabres; noticing this, the Sabres broke off their attack, banked right and headed toward the coastline. At this time, the order arrived from the division command post to return to base.

The 2nd Squadron consisting of six MiGs under the command of Major M.S. Ponomarev was trailing behind the 3rd Squadron at an altitude of 9,000 meters. At a point 10-15 kilometers northwest of Chongju, they encountered eight F-86s approaching from the right, which held a 1,000-1,500 meter altitude advantage. Having drawn even with our group, one F-86 element winged over into a dive and began to emerge on our fighters' tails. Ponomarev led his squadron in a chandelle to starboard. The other Sabre elements in turn began to drop in behind our group. Ponomarev informed Major Pulov over the radio that he was now engaged. Leveling out after the chandelle, Ponomarev went into an oblique loop to the right; pulling in behind the tail-end Sabre element, he closed to within 1,200-1,500 meters of it. The Sabre pilots, noticing our MiGs closing in from behind, rolled over to the right and headed toward the sea, where they again gained altitude to a position above our fighters, and once more attempted to attack our group. Ponomarev observed this, climbed to the same altitude as the enemy, and winging over to the left, closed with the enemy head-on. However, the Sabres, shunning a head-on pass, broke right and headed back to sea in a dive. Ponomarev's flight swung around to the left and dove after the Sabres, but broke off the pursuit over the coastline and exited the combat with a chandelle to port.

The 1st Squadron under Major Pulov's command was following in trail behind the 523rd IAP. Arriving in the Anju area at an altitude of 5,000 meters, the group began to swing around to the right. Having turned 180°, Captain Sutiagin spotted a pair of

F-86s out in front of them, above and to the right, which were rolling to the right into an attack against the 523rd IAP's tail-end squadron. Sutiagin quickly banked to the right and pulled into a climb with the aim of cutting off the enemy, and in his starboard turn began to close with the Sabres. The Sabres, having turned 180°, noticed the MiG element behind them and broke sharply to the left. Sutiagin suddenly noticed tracers streaming past his MiG, glanced back and spotted a different pair of Sabres 400-500 meters away, above, behind and to the left, which had opened fire. Sutiagin broke sharply right into a climb toward the sun, and having reached 6,000 meters in altitude, he made a 90° turn to right. As a result of the Sabres' fire, Sutiagin's wingman Senior Lieutenant A.S. Shirokov received one bullet hole in the left side of his cockpit canopy, and Shirokov was wounded in the right hand by a bullet fragment.

Major Pulov, seeing that Sutiagin had banked away to the right, began to move right to follow him, but at this moment he received a warning from Major Artemchenko; up to 24 F-86s were diving on his group from a point out in front of it, above and to the left. Then Pulov conducted a chandelle to port, before swinging further to the left and diving on the enemy below them, which was in a turn to port and trying to attack the MiG-15s from below. Pulov began to pursue the adversary, but the enemy, having noticed our closing MiGs, began to go into an oblique loop to the left. However, seeing that the MiGs were still in pursuit, they departed for the sea in a steep dive.

The aerial combat between our fighters and the enemy fighters lasted for 10-15 minutes. During the dogfight, deputy squadron commander Captain Blagov downed two F-86 Sabres from a range of 400-500 meters. Lieutenant V.I. Bashlyk damaged another F-86 from a range of 50 meters. Two of our MiGs received damage in the action: the aircraft flown by Senior Lieutenant Shestopalov received one bullet hole in the rudder, and we recall Senior Lieutenant Shirokov's close call with one well-placed bullet. Both aircraft were quickly put back into service.

The 523rd IAP's pilots also had a successful action in the Sunchon area; Captain S.A. Bakhaev managed to down one Sabre. The 18th GIAP's pilots became engaged with a group of F-80 and F-84 fighter-bombers in the Sunchon-Kaechon area, but were only able to chase them from the given area back to the sea. Finally, a group of 22 MiGs from the 176th GIAP clashed briefly with seven F-86s in the Eiju area, and Captain N.M. Goncharov claimed one F-86. In these two actions, the 64th IAK had no losses.

The Americans again claimed that they had no losses on this day, and furthermore that 1st Lieutenant Vernon White of the 336th FIS shot down one MiG-15. However, it is known with some certainty that the 64th IAK had no losses. Most likely, White received credit for Senior Lieutenant V.D. Ostapenko's MiG, which during the dogfight with the Sabres while maneuvering at high-speed, as a result of pilot error made contact with the MiG of his leader Senior Lieutenant V.N. Fukin and had to exit the combat and return to base with a damaged left aileron. Fukin continued the combat and later safely returned to base. Ostapenko's MiG was quickly repaired and returned to service that same day. However, the Americans had little to do with the incident.

The discussion of the November battles in the North Korean sky would be incomplete, if mention is not made of the operations of our allies – the pilots of the UAA. The PLAAF's 3rd IAD, which consisted of two regiments, played the primary role in the UAA's efforts in November. On 20 October 1951, this fighter division replaced the 4th IAD, which had been in active service before this, at the forward airfield and initiated combat operations already on 21 October. In this period, the 3rd IAD had 55 MiG-15s and 56 pilots on its roster.

In the first 10 days of November, the 3rd IAD's pilots were involved in five aerial combats with small groups of American aircraft, downing or damaging eight of them, while the Chinese had one lightly damaged MiG in return. In these combats, future Chinese aces achieved their first victories: the deputy commander of the 7th IAP's 3rd Squadron Zhao Baotong and the commander of the 9th IAP's 1st Squadron Wang Hai, who ended the war with nine victories. Chinese historians write that two downed and one damaged American aircraft, all achieved by Zhao Baotong on 4 November 1951, marked the beginning of the 3rd IAD's record combat score. Bringing his personal score up to seven downed and two damaged enemy aircraft (the best result in the PLAAF at the time), Zhao Baotong was nicknamed "The Dragon". He retired from active service soon after the war's conclusion and penned his memoirs, which were published in the Soviet Union in 1955 with the title *V nebe Severnoi Korei* [*In the North Korean Sky*].

The Chinese relate his story of one of his first combats, when Americans attacked his group from out of the sun as it was returning to base after a mission. At first he took them as friendly fighters, and by the time he realized otherwise, it was already too late. Trying to evade them, he attempted a loop or a split-S, but committed an error and lost speed. At this moment, having just announced over the radio, "I'm breaking off combat, cover me!" the American fighters flamed his MiG – but he still managed to land his burning aircraft at his airfield, and the flames were quickly extinguished. In the Russian translation, the description of his self-acknowledged "lessons from the first aerial combats" and acquisition of priceless combat experience "in dribs and drabs" has been presented as far more "heroic" and successful aerial battles. In the foreword to this translation, one can read that altogether over one month of combats, Zhao Baotong's squadron downed more than 30 aircraft, while his wingman Fang Wangzhan paired with him scored eight victories. Zhao Baotong mentions also the "particularly distinguished activity" of the pilot Dun Weng, who personally downed "more than ten" enemy aircraft. In the lists of Chinese aces that have been published in the CPR, such surnames are missing, and most likely Zhao was talking about Soviet pilots, but at the time it was forbidden to write about this, so therefore he had to discuss them under fabricated Chinese names.

The top-scoring Chinese squadron in the Korean War was the 1st Squadron of the 3rd IAD's 9th IAP (commanded by Wang Hai), which conducted its first combat sorties at the end of October-beginning of November 1951 (as the first of the 3rd IAD to do so). In fact, it downed or damaged 29 enemy aircraft, and 10 of this squadron's pilots had one or more victories to his personal credit. However, they achieved this not over one month and in the course of 80 aerial combats, as some historians later wrote, but over the entire war, when many of the squadron's pilots had already received promotions. Wang Hai himself at the end of 1952 was successfully serving as a regiment commander, and subsequently became a political commissar and the commander of the PLAAF.

The first success for the pilots of the 9th IAP's 1st Squadron didn't come until 8 November, when the squadron, being led by Wang Hai, having taken off on a combat mission to patrol an area approximately 40-50 kilometers behind the front lines, timely spotted enemy aircraft (according to Chinese records, "Gloster Meteors"). Having gone on the attack with two elements (including Jiao Jingwen, Zhou Fengxin and Liu Delin) and, according to some sources, having caught the enemy aircraft immediately, but according to other sources, having pursued the southward fleeing enemy for more than 100 kilometers, Wang Hai opened fire first and expended more than 200 shells, thereby damaging one enemy aircraft. Exhilarated, he pressed the trigger again, but he was out of ammunition. Then the squadron commander ordered his wingman Jiao Jingwen to attack, followed by the second element. Thus, according to these latter sources, they fired on the Americans both collectively and in turn all the way down to the 38th Parallel, beyond which they were forbidden to fly. There they halted their attacks and returned to base. The downed or damaged American jet became the first trophy for the 9th IAP.

The Chinese pilots also took part in the large battle that took place on 18 November 1951. Chinese historians write that 184 American aircraft in nine separate groups were operating in the Chongchon River area. The 9th IAP sent 16 MiGs in two groups to intercept them. Soon the first group spotted more than 60 F-84s, which were preparing to bomb the bridge across the Chongchon River. According to the Chinese, Wang Hai, who had taken off at the head of a six-MiG group, knowing that the MiG developed greater speed than the Sabre in a dive (in reality, the opposite was true), issued the order over the radio to climb and to attack from a dive. In the dive, his pilots opened fire and scattered the enemy group. After several attacks, his six MiGs downed five F-84s, two of them credited to Wang Hai himself. The rapidly flowing combat didn't last long, and the 9th IAP in total downed six American aircraft in this action.

The Chinese pilots also took part in other battles at the end of November, but this author doesn't have any information regarding them. Simultaneously with the 3rd IAD, in the autumn and winter of 1951 the 2nd IAD in LaGG fighters and the 14th IAD in MiG-15s also took part in combat operations. There is almost no information whatsoever on the 14th IAD. However, the operations of the 2nd IAD, as well as those of the UAA's 8th and 10th BAD, will be discussed below.

On the last day of November 1951, the Sabres of the 4th FIW had an atypical and simultaneously rare encounter with the enemy: they dueled with enemy piston-engine aircraft, and more precisely, with those of the UAA. On 30 November, the UAA command launched a major operation employing several of its aviation regiments. Here is what the commander of the 64th IAK General Georgii Ageevich Lobov later wrote about this operation:

> Several days before the end of November, the Chinese decided to liberate the island of Simbi-do, which was located several kilometers from the mouth of the Yalu River. One could see the approaches to this island clearly through the optical sight of an anti-aircraft gun, mounted in a clearing on a hilltop at the 64th IAK's and UAA's command posts.
>
> Eighteen Tu-2 bombers under the command of Han Minyang were assigned to this raid, which were to be covered by piston-engine La-9 fighters. Liu Yalou, the commander-in-chief of the PLAAF, arrived from Beijing to oversee the raid's organization and execution. I warned Aleksander Ivanovich (as Liu liked to be called in Russian) that we would cut-off the enemy fighters, if they appeared from the direction of land, but we were categorically forbidden to operate beyond the coastline. General Liu Yalou left with this understanding.

A previous raid by the Chinese had gone splendidly, and I had observed it personally (this was the air raid launched on 6 November, described above). Therefore several weeks later it was decided to repeat the raid, which had been widely discussed at the UAA command post. I didn't like all this chatter, personally regarding it as a bad omen. Unfortunately, these ominous forebodings were justified. The Sabres came in at low altitude from the direction of the sea. More than half of the Tu-2 bombers were downed; the piston-engine La-9 fighters, naturally, were unable to offer adequate resistance. I can only personally testify to the enormous courage of the Chinese pilots, who continued on to the target with their bombers in flames and under constant enemy attacks. The Americans couldn't have intercepted the Tu-2s through ground control radar; they must have received advanced warning through their network of agents.

The night before, on 29 November, 10 Tu-2 from the 10th BAD's 28th BAP (led by squadron commander Yao Changchuan), which had taken off from the Liaoyang airfield at 2219, bombed (without fighter escort) military ships around the Large and Small He islands, with the aim of creating favorable conditions for the following invasion operation. They arrived over the target area at 2317, but the results of the attack were considered unsatisfactory; the inexperience of the Chinese pilots with night missions was noted.

On the afternoon of 30 November, in order to support the landing operation, the third raid of the month took place against Taehwa-do Island. Nine Tu-2 bombers from the 8th BAD's 24th Regiment (group leader Gao Yueming), each loaded with seven 100-kg. high-explosive bombs and two 100-kg. incendiary bombs, covered by 16 La-11 fighters of the 2nd IAD's 4th IAP (led by regiment commander Xu Chaoweng), took off to bomb Taehwa-do. The bombers lifted off the runways of their base in Mukden at 1419. According to some sources, a Chinese MiG-15 squadron from the 3rd IAD, led by Ten' Daisu, was to provide top cover for the bombers. Judging from all that happened, they were late to link up with the bombers and were simply too distant from them, when more than 30 F-86s suddenly pounced on the Tu-2s from the direction of the sea.

The tail-end "Charlie" in the third flight of Tu-2s was shot out of the sky first, and then another as the remaining bombers scattered, but then at an order from either the group leader or from the ground, they reassembled and continued on toward the target, keeping in formation and warding off fighter attacks. The group leader went down in flames, but its place was taken by the next bomber in the formation, and this happened several times. Chinese sources written later state that the wounded radio operator and gunner Liu Shaoji downed one Sabre, thereby "initiating the destruction of the jet aircraft" (this is highly unlikely, but possibly he damaged one F-86).

The Tu-2 No.6 piloted by Zhang Fuyin took hits to one engine and burst into flames, but wrapped in flames it continued on another three minutes, and a gunner aboard continued to fire at the attacking Sabres. However, they failed to reach the target and eventually plunged into the sea, killing all aboard. The crew of pilot Bi Wubin turned out to be a bit "luckier". His Tu-2 No.4 was riddled by bullets and caught fire a bit later, when they were practically over the island. Despite an order to bail out, they continued on to the target and dropped their bombs. It isn't then clear whether they next deliberately dove into the target, or whether their fuel tanks exploded, but the entire crew perished. It isn't known how many of the bombers actually reached the target; likely, it was less than half, but according to the Chinese, they again turned Taewha-do Island into a sea of flames with their bombs.

While the bombers were fighting their way through to the target, 16 La-11 fighters were having a difficult time with the Sabres, trying to keep them at least 1,000 meters away from the bombers. The Chinese assert that the "Lavochkins" downed four Sabres and damaged three more. The Chinese historians write: "This served as the precedent of victories by piston-engine fighters over jet fighters." They assign one Sabre downed and two damaged to the personal credit of deputy squadron commander Wang Tianbao. Much later the Americans acknowledged that a La-11 damaged one F-86 in this combat, and its pilot, Major Marshall, who actually came under the cannon fire of one La-11, returned to base with a shattered cockpit. It is most interesting that even the mortal foes of the Chinese Communists, the Chinese Nationalists, recognize Wang Tianbao's "piston-engine" victory over a jet Sabre.

After the remaining Tu-2s and La-11s, licking their wounds, began straggling back to mainland China, pilots of the 523rd IAP, responding to an alarm, arrived to aid the Chinese MiGs. In truth, they arrived only after the show was over, but regiment commander Major D.P. Os'kin still managed to down one F-86. Here's how Chinese pilot Zhao Baotong later wrote about the end of this battle:

> The aerial combat broke apart into several separate actions. The fiercest was the combat over the island itself. Here our pilots had to meet with a number of problems. The point is that the Americans, striving to destroy our landing force, hurled up to 50 aircraft against it. These aircraft were keeping to low altitudes. So our aircraft were also flying at low altitudes. Thus our pilots, who were striving to provide direct cover over the landing area, were compelled to operate in unusual circumstances. It must be said that they managed to adapt quickly to the situation. Employing a combat stratagem, they broke apart the defensive ring of enemy aircraft, and then with attacks from the rear, they began to destroy the tail-end enemy aircraft. During one of these attacks, the group leader flamed one of the enemy aircraft. His wingman Sung Er at the same time attacked a second ship, but from such a close range that he himself was almost killed. His target exploded, and fragments of metal from the hostile aircraft tore into the wings of his MiG.
>
> In the course of the action, one of the enemy's groups nevertheless managed to reach an advantageous position for a strike against our landing force. Ten' Daisu, who was with our group at low altitude, noticed this. Not wasting time to climb, our pilots immediately attacked the enemy from below. The enemy wasn't expecting this attack, because the directional radar capabilities that were present on the island and normally gave advance warning of our operations had already been knocked out by the bombers. The enemy's combat formation was disrupted, and two of its aircraft burst into flames. The attacks from below didn't allow the enemy to evade our fire by diving. With successive attacks, this group was chased away from the island.

It is difficult to say how far this description of the air battle strays from the truth: a Lufbery circle of Sabres at low altitude – that's something new. However Sung Er in fact brought back fragments of an F-86 embedded in his MiG, and two Sabres were credited to pilots of the 3rd IAD.

The Chinese losses on this day, according to various sources, are estimated at four to eight Tu-2, three La-11, and one MiG-15, and 15 crew members were killed. The Chinese pilots from the other aviation units couldn't hide the bitterness of the defeat. From their saddened faces, information about the disaster even reached our pilots, who commiserated with their comrades in arms.

However, in the opinion of Soviet pilots, the main reason for the defeat was the poor cooperation between the Chinese and Soviet commands. On one occasion, returning from a mission, Pepeliaev with his group encountered Chinese in their MiGs, but from the ground he was ordered "not to interfere" in the affairs of the "neighbors" and to carry out his mission. B.S. Abakumov also recalled the same thing:

> … [Once] we were returning from a combat mission and saw below us nine bombers flying on an intersecting course. From their construction we determined that they were our Tu-2 aircraft, but we knew that there were no bombers in this area, particularly any of our own. We sent an inquiry over the radio to the command post, and the command post informed us that they were our neighbors, the Chinese, who had set out to bomb the coastal islands, where the Americans had some radar posts. From the command post we received an order to head for home. We landed … and then suddenly we saw three riddled Tu-2 aircraft with Chinese recognition symbols landing on our airbase at Miaogou, but there had been nine of them! It turned out that American Sabres, which had attacked them out over the sea during their bomb runs, had downed six of them. But what would it have cost the Chinese command to contact our command post and request air cover for the Chinese bombers? This was one more piece of evidence that the Chinese always ignored our operational assistance, right from the very beginning.

Today, the only possible justification for the UAA command's decision could be that the Soviet pilots were categorically forbidden to cross the coastline. Despite these losses in the air, the Chinese 50th Army that same evening landed on the He Dao archipelago, and for some time, all the transmissions from the American intelligence center on the islands halted, and information about the sorties of Soviet fighters and their positions in the air ceased to be passed to the American pilots. The heroic actions of the pilots have become a model of courage in the PRC, and Bi Ubin's and Wang Tenbao's exploits have forever entered the annals of the history of the Chinese Air Force.

To recapitulate, in the mission against Simbi-do Island, nine Tu-2 bombers took part, which had the immediate escort of 16 La-11 fighters, and top cover from 16 MiG-15s. Over the island of Simbi-do, where the Chinese invasion force was to land, the bombers were attacked by 31 F-86s from the 4th FIW under the overall command of the Wing's deputy commander, Colonel Benjamin Preston.

In the course of the action, part of the Sabres took on the MiGs, while the rest went after the Tu-2 bombers. According to the Americans, eight of the bombers were downed, as well as three La-11 fighters and one MiG-15. Major George Davis of the 334th FIS scored particularly well in this combat, downing three Tu-2s and one MiG-15. After this action, George Davis became the USAF's fifth ace of the Korean War, and Winton Marshall the sixth.

Soviet pilots of the 303rd IAD and 324th IAD who had been scrambled in response to an alarm arrived on scene, but there was no big battle: the Sabres were already running low on fuel. They conducted one attack against the MiGs, broke off combat and headed back to the sea. True, in the process the commander of the 523rd IAP Major D.P. Os'kin managed to down one F-86 in the Anju area, and this was the only victory for the 64th IAK's pilots on this day.

Earlier that morning, 18 MiGs of the 17th IAP had tangled with 16 F-86s, but the action ended with no results. However, in this dogfight, the MiG piloted by Captain B.E. Tikhonov received one bullet hole in the right wing. The pilots of the 18th GIAP in the course of the final day in November flew three regimental combat sorties, but they all went by without contact with the enemy.

Chinese sources give their own figures for their losses on this third raid to this island: four Tu-2 bombers destroyed and another four Tu-2s damaged, but these were able to fly back to friendly territory. Of the 16 crew members aboard the downed bombers, only four were able to take to their parachutes, three of whom bailed out over the sea and perished. Only navigator Chen Haikwan, who came down on the coastline, was saved. So a total of 15 of the 16 crewmen aboard the four destroyed Tu-2s were killed. Regarding the losses among the covering fighters, the Chinese sources are silent. As concerns their victories in this battle, the Chinese historians assert that two F-86s were downed and one damaged by the Chinese. One downed Sabre was credited to the bomber squadron's chief of communications, radio operator-gunner Lon Liu Shaoji, who though wounded, continued to fire at the attacking Sabres. The other victory over an F-86 went to Wang Tianbao, a La-11 pilot that was escorting the bombers. Both were decorated with PLAAF medals.

In one of the Chinese sources, one comes across a mention of a fourth raid against the islands of this archipelago, involving five Tu-2 bombers that took off at 1521 in order to bomb an area where a landing had been planned. However, the given source says nothing at all about the results of this raid.

With this battle over Simbi-do Island, the November fighting came to an end, but the war itself went on. So did the air war for superiority over MiG Alley with even greater intensity on both sides, as fresh battles took place in the North Korean sky in the month of December.

THE DEBACLE OF AUSTRALIA'S NO. 77 SQUADRON; FIRST COMBATS WITH THE NEW F-86s

The first day of December 1951 was marked by two events, which genuinely affected the course of the air war in the skies of Korea to one degree or another. On 1 December, pilots of the new 51st FIW flew their first combat sorties from the K-13 Air Base at Suwon in the new F-86E Sabre. The 51st FIW consisted of the 16th and 25th Fighter Interceptor Squadrons, which prior to the month of November had fought in F-80 Shooting Stars. On 6 November, the famed Second World War ace Colonel Francis S. "Gabby" Gabreski moved from his temporary post with the 4th FIG headquarters to assume command of the 51st FIW. Together with him, many experienced pilots of the

4th FIW transferred into command posts of the 51st Wing. The pilots of 51st FIW spent the month of November preparing for combat.

The 4th FIW greeted winter at full strength: in the middle of November, the 335th FIS flew into Kimpo from the Johnson Air Base in Japan. Thus, by December 1951, 127 F-86 Sabres equipping five fighter interceptor squadrons were now located on bases in Korea; another 38 Sabres were in reserve back in Japan. The UN's fighter strength had doubled.

However, the first December day of combat in the Korean sky didn't bring any victories to the pilots of the 51st FIW, nor were their more experienced colleagues from the 4th FIW able to achieve one. But the very fact of the introduction of a new USAF fighter interceptor wing into combat operations, of course, genuinely altered the correlation of forces on the aerial front, which the first battles of December demonstrated.

The other significant event of this day was the crushing defeat of the RAAF No. 77 Squadron, which had been operating as part of the UN air force from the very start of combat operations, by Soviet pilots of the 64th IAK. Here's how its organizer, the commander of the 64th IAK Major General Georgii Ageevich Lobov describes the operation to smash the Australian squadron:

In the summer of 1951, Gloster Meteor Mk. 8 aircraft had appeared in the Korean sky. As was quickly established, an Australian squadron that had arrived was equipped with these aircraft (in its table strength, the given squadron was equal to a Soviet aviation regiment operating with the 64th IAK). The very first combats against these aircraft demonstrated that they were far from being "meteors", and were inferior to the MiG-15 in every aspect of performance. The pilots' own equipment literally stunned me: from the remains of one of the pilots, it was possible to ascertain that he was some Aborigine, who was rather dark-skinned. His personal sidearm was a Smith-Wesson revolver with a crudely produced wooden handle, which had been considered out-dated even in the Second World War, since most of the main armies at that time already had automatic weapons. The Australians had no means or devices for saving or supporting a pilot who had abandoned his aircraft like the Americans had at this time, who were extremely smartly, sensibly and amply equipped.

Quite quickly the Australians became convinced that they had no chances whatsoever in a combat with MiGs, so they switched to a different use of their squadron. We quickly figured out this innovation. The essence of it consisted in the fact that the Australians fully quit using the Meteors as fighters, and switched to combat operations against ground targets. However, the illness of "MiG panic" remained, so the target and time of the Meteor missions were chosen carefully so as to avoid encounters with MiGs.

The operations they flew typically looked like this: the Australians operated "behind the backs" of the Americans during massive US air raids, which were normally launched against a group of targets in one area, and conducted by one or two fighter-bomber wings (75-100 aircraft) under heavy F-84 and F-86 fighter cover. In the process, in addition to the immediate fighter escort to and from the target area, forward screens of Sabres were deployed close to the Yalu River, in order to intercept the MiGs that were scrambled to repel the raid. That's how the Meteors were employed. They calculated that while the MiGs were tied up in combat with the Americans, the Meteors could bomb and strafe targets south and southeast of Anju.

By themselves, the Meteors had no great military significance amid the enormous number of aircraft deployed by the interventionists (primarily the USAF), but politically a crushing defeat of the US allies might give rise to a certain political repercussion.

It was decided to destroy this Australian Meteor squadron with one blow. For this purpose, a plan for a proposed massed blow that included the time and place of the Meteors' appearance, and involved a deep outflanking (from the north) of the main grouping of the USAF were all carefully worked out.

Direct guidance of the MiG-15 group to the Meteors would be provided by the auxiliary control post, which was constantly deployed in Anju. I alone did all the planning for this operation, keeping even I.N. Kozhedub [the commander of the 324th IAD] in the dark about it. I also personally issued the orders to the group that was designated to destroy the Meteors, but literally just 1.5 to 2 hours before take-off. Perhaps this was indeed excessive caution, but it ensured the 100% concealment of our intentions. I had justifications for acting this way – if only from the recent failure of the Chinese Tu-2 mission against Simbi-do Island. Of course, I couldn't imagine that one of the Soviet officers would blurt out the secret. However, as they say, God takes care of the careful.

All of our designs came to fruition. Plainly, random chance also played its role. Had the Americans started their raid an hour earlier or later, our plan would have gone to waste. Factually speaking, this is what happened: A group of 16 MiG-15s from the 176th GIAP under the command of Lieutenant Colonel S.F. Vishniakov took off at the designated time and headed north in a climb, where they loitered, using the fuel from their drop tanks, while waiting for the signal to attack the Meteors. The Australians, numbering 16 Meteors, arrived at the place and time that we had anticipated. The MiGs were precisely guided to a proper point from which to launch a surprise attack on the Meteors, and then gave the Meteors a wallop.

Only four of the enemy aircraft managed to get away, and at that only because of the proximity of the Pyongyang-Wonsan no-fly line, which we were forbidden to cross. The Americans gave no help whatsoever to the Australians. Given the losses suffered by the Australians even before this combat, the squadron could be considered fully destroyed.

Some time later, a radio listening post reported to me a broadcast from one of the US radio stations: "The awarding of US medals to the Australian pilots has taken place, the squadron of which was recently worn out in combats with MiGs, but which is now recovering its combat capability." To this I will add that right up until the end of the war Meteors never appeared again within an area where MiGs were operating.

That's how this unique operation to destroy one of the UN's air squadrons in Korea was conceived and implemented, in the words of the organizer of this operation himself, General G.A. Lobov.

The events themselves in the area of Sunchon on this day unfolded in the following manner. That morning the Americans had launched a massive raid to the Anju area with the fighter-bombers of the 8th and 49th FBG, covered by Sabres. Regiments of the 303rd

IAD, as well as the 196th IAP of the 324th IAD, departed to repel this raid. Meanwhile the pilots of the 176th GIAP remained on the ground and were seated in the cockpits of their MiGs at Readiness No.1. At 0825, the IAK's radar posts detected more than 100 enemy aircraft inbound in seven groups. Presumably, this raid was targeting the islands of Daiwa-to and Simbi-do. Since there was the serious threat that enemy aircraft might instead hit the Andong airfield complex from the direction of the sea, at 0844 20 MiGs of the 176th GIAP under the command of Lieutenant Colonel S.F. Vishniakov were scrambled to neutralize it. At the same time, a group of 16 Meteors was spotted at an altitude of 7,500 meters in an area southeast of Sunchon.

Captain Petr Semenovich Milaushkin relates:

On this day, they brought us all to the airfield earlier than usual. The aircraft had already long been readied. A few minutes later we were placed in our cockpits at Readiness No.1, the entire regiment. We were ordered not to switch on our radios and to maintain silence; the order to take off would come from the division command post in the form of signal rockets.

The sun began to rise, we started our engines, and we set out on the mission in response to the order; we assembled in the air without a single sound over the radio waves. Arriving over Andong, we heard a command from the ground, which gave us a [target] heading and an altitude of 8,000 meters. We climbed to 10,000 meters, but the ground control clarified that the target was lower, and already below us to the left. That's when we saw two eight-ship groups of aircraft, one flying in front of the other by about 2-3 kilometers. They were clearly visible against the backdrop of dark mountains and forests.

Regiment commander Vishniakov gave the order to attack them as if they were bombers (we had already worked out scheme for attacking bombers). We had 20 aircraft to their 16. There weren't enough targets for everyone, so eight MiGs remained high to cover our attack from above, while 12 of the regiment's MiGs directly attacked the Meteors.

My wingman was Stepa Kirichenko, who had arrived back in October as a replacement. For the attack, a pair from the lead squadron joined us. I radioed my wingman, "Stepa, we're attacking. You take the wingman; I'll go after the leader." That's how the entire squadron went on the attack. The enemy's speed was verging on 800 km/hr. We banked left to circle around behind them, and then attacked. The element leader appeared in my sights and I opened fire. He made no effort to evade. The shells struck his left engine, cockpit and fuselage. A puff of white smoke appeared on the enemy aircraft. When exiting the attack I gave an order to my wingman to pull out to the right, but he didn't answer.

It turned out that my wingman Stepa Kirichenko had approached his Meteor so closely that he wound up in the turbulent backwash from its engines. Stepa's MiG flipped over and he went into a spin, spun away toward the ground, and came out of it at an altitude of 500 meters. There was no enemy or friendly aircraft around him, so he headed back to base alone.

So I took fire from the wingman that Stepan was supposed to have silenced. He opened fire from his 20mm cannonns, and I saw them streaking past to the left and right of my machine; I conducted a number of oblique loops to separate from the adversary, but I couldn't shake him off. One of the other guys bailed me out of the situation; he attacked the meddlesome Meteor, and a second later the enemy aircraft was no longer on my tail. A great number of the Meteors were destroyed by us. Several Australian pilots were taken prisoner. We were told later that a day of mourning was declared in Australia due to their heavy losses in Korea.

Altogether nine of the Meteors were downed by the Soviet pilots of the 176th GIAP. Six of the nine were destroyed by the 1st and 3rd Squadrons, as well as the Regiment's command flight, and one Meteor each was credited to the regiment commander Lieutenant Colonel S.F. Vishniakov and the regiment navigator Major S.P. Subbotin. Another three Meteors were downed by the eight-ship group of Captain S.M. Kramarenko's 2nd Squadron, which was covering the combat of the main group. Convinced that there were no enemy fighters around, Kramarenko and his wingman had launched an attack against one Meteor element, both of which were shot down on the very first pass. Then Kramarenko spotted a solitary Meteor trying to escape the massacre, and catching up with him, flamed him from short range. The Meteor pilot ejected.

According to Western sources, the Australians lost a total of only three Meteors in this action; Sergeant Ernest Armit was killed, and two other of the squadron's pilots, Vance Drummond and Bruce Thomson became prisoners-of-war. One Meteor was damaged. At the same time it is maintained that pilot Bruce Gogerly officially downed one MiG-15, and another was supposedly chalked up as a shared victory. However, according to the archives of the 64th IAK and the recollections of participants in this combat, all of our pilots returned to base, and there were not even any damaged MiGs. Likely, the Australians are counting Lieutenant Kirichenko's MiG, which fell into a spin, as downed, though as we know, this doesn't correspond with the facts.

Simultaneously, Western sources have muddled the number of Meteors of No. 77 Squadron that were taking part in this mission. At first it was asserted that there were only eight of them; later this was changed to 12, and in the Polish book *Letnye kompanii. Koreia 1950-1953* [*Flight crews. Korea 1950-1953*] published in 1994, there were now 14 Meteors flying the mission. However, all of the Soviet pilots that participated in the battle of 1 December 1951 that I've questioned stated that that they saw two groups of eight Australian aircraft each approaching the ambush.

The assertion that 50 MiGs were operating against the Australians is a twice-fold exaggeration. The full operational strength of the 176th GIAP in this period did not exceed 30 crews and MiGs.

The pilots of the 64th IAK only had one more encounter with Meteors, since after 1 December the latter began to operate farther to the south, beyond the range of the MiGs. In the opinion of the Western historians, this day of 1 December 1951 conclusively settled the question as to whether the Meteors were a competent fighter. As one of them, George Odgers, who wrote a history of RAAF No. 77 Squadron entitled *Across the Parallel* that was published in 1952, claimed, "their [the Australian pilots] failure to cope with the MiG15 cannot be attributed to any lack of courage ... nor lack of resourcefulness, but to the inadequacy of the machine they flew."

As noted, the Soviet pilots only engaged Meteors once more, a year later in October 1952; this time they were escorted by Sabres, but again they didn't avoid losses (this episode will be discussed below). The UAA's pilots, who were operating near the 38th

Parallel, came across Meteors several times in 1952 and 1953. Yet these were isolated encounters: just three in 1952, and only one meeting between MiGs and Meteors of No. 77 Squadron in 1953. Thus, General Lobov was correct, when he said that Meteors sought to avoid encounters with MiGs and stayed away from their operational area.

Simultaneously with the Meteors, the Americans on this day were also caught out. According to 64th IAK records, the pilots of the 196th IAP, who repelled a US fighter-bomber raid, alone claimed to have downed four F-84Es and two F-80s. In addition, on this day pilots of the 18th GIAP flew two missions – one to cover the Andong, Singisiu and Gisiu airfields, and the second to intercept enemy aircraft. An encounter with a group of Sabres took place on the second regimental sortie, in which Lieutenant Colonel A.P. Smorchkov downed one F-86. The regiment had no losses in return.

On this same day of 1 December, pilots of the 303rd IAD flew three missions to intercept enemy aircraft, but for the pilots of the 17th IAP and 523rd IAP, these sorties ended without any enemy contact. However, pilot of the 196th IAP scored well when repelling an enemy morning raid at 1127: having taken off to intercept the enemy aircraft, Captain V.I. Alfeev's squadron formation encountered 16 F-84s in the Anju area, flying in two eight-ship formations, which without any fighter cover were striking ground targets, for which they paid dearly. Through simultaneous attacks from various directions, pairs of MiGs from Alfeev's group scattered the Americans combat formation, and having isolated individual Thunderjets, began to pick them off one by one. As a result, the regiment claimed four Thunderjets, which after developing the gun camera film, were credited to Captains Alfeev and Zaplavnev, and Senior Lieutenants Kapranov and Kolpakov.

That same afternoon, the pilots of the 196th IAP again distinguished themselves. At 1555 a regimental group of 24 MiGs, led by Lieutenant Colonel E.G. Pepeliaev, intercepted a group of 20 F-80s in the same area of Anju. Leaving one squadron at altitude as top cover, Pepeliaev with the 12 other MiGs attacked the formation of Shooting Stars from the 8th FBG's 35th and 36th FBS, and two F-80s (No.49-745 and No.49-855) were soon both lost to the MiGs' fire. Credit for these victories went to Colonel Pepeliaev and Senior Lieutenant Murav'ev. One American pilot was killed and the other was taken prisoner. The pilots of the 176th GIAP also encountered a group of 24 F-84s on this day, but the latter escaped to Korea Bay without any losses.

The Americans claimed that in this combat 2nd Lieutenant Robert E. Smith of the 8th FBG's 36th Squadron in his F-80C downed one MiG-15 – this in fact was the final victory in the Korean sky claimed by a Shooting Star pilot. However, according to existing archival documents, on 1 December 1951, all of the 64th IAK's MiGs returned to their bases – there were no losses in combat. Thus 2nd Lieutenant Smith's victory is questionable, or in this combat he only damaged a MiG.

On the morning of 2 December, the pilots of the 64th IAK again joined combat with American aircraft that were attacking ground targets in the Anju area. On this day, it was the 136th FBW that was conducting the heavy raid. Both regiments of the 324th IAD took part in repelling it. However, only the 176th GIAP group managed at 1042 to make contact with the enemy aircraft. In the Pyongyang area, 18 of the regiment's MiG-15s intercepted a group of 16 F-84s at an altitude of 4,000 meters. With the first attacking pass, the Soviet fighters split the enemy formation in two, after which the Thunderjets began to jettison their loads and head back to the sanctuary of the sea. However, in the pursuit Senior Lieutenant N.P. Kravtsov and his wingman Lieutenant N.A. Feoktistov managed to down one of the fleeing F-84s, and altogether the pilots of the 176th GIAP destroyed three Thunderjets on this day, including one by the commander of the Guards regiment Lieutenant Colonel S.F. Vishniakov. The regiment had no losses.

Pilots of the 303rd IAD also took off to intercept enemy aircraft, but they had no encounter with the latter. However our allies, pilots of the UAA, happened to clash with pilots of the 4th and 51st FIW. According to Chinese records, on 2 December 1951, the Americans sent more than 120 F-84s and F-86s to attack railroads in the Taechon and Sunchon areas. The Chinese 3rd IAD scrambled 42 MiG-15s to intercept them. In the sky over the mouth of the Chongchon River, the MiGs engaged 20 American aircraft, and claimed three enemy aircraft downed and one damaged in the action. In turn, the Sabre pilots claimed five victories over MiGs on this day, with credit for four of them going to Major James Martin and Captain Nelton Wilson of the 334th FIS, Captain Michael Novak of the 335th FIS, and the 336th Fighter Squadron's Zane Amell – all of the 4th FIW. In this combat, the pilots of the 51st FIW achieved their first victory in the F-86E; 1st Lieutenant Paul Roach of the 25th FIS opened the 51st Fighter Wing's score. According to the Fifth Air Force command, it lost no F-84s or F-86s in combat on this day.

On 3 December, pilots of the 17th IAP distinguished themselves in clashes with Fifth Air Force aircraft over MiG Alley. Over the day they became engaged in two aerial combats and downed three US aircraft. The action begain in the period between 1245 and 1252, when radar detected up to 70 enemy fighters and fighter-bombers 80 kilometers south of Pyongyang at 7,000-8,000 meters, flying on a heading of 240-350° in four groups of 12 to 20 aircraft each.

From their status of Readiness No.1, 20 MiGs of the 17th IAP under the command of Major G.I. Pulov took off at 1258 at an order from the division command post to cover the railroad bridge across the Yalu River and the Andong, Singisiu and Miaogou airfields, with a subsequent re-routing to cover the Sonchon area at an altitude of 8,000 meters. When crossing the Yalu River, Captain N.V. Sutiagin sighted a group of 16 Sabres out in front of them, to the right and above, and alerted the group commander to this. The enemy was passing from right to left in a climb. The group commander issued the order to drop their external fuel tanks and began to bank to the left toward the enemy, but from the command post came information that the group Sutiagin had spotted were friendlies, and they were to continue on to the Sonchon area to cover it. The group commander began to swing back around to the right toward the designated area, thereby exposing their tails to the enemy. As the group had begun to turn to the left toward the enemy, Captain Sutiagin had spotted another eight F-86s approaching from the left and below, which were heading for the Gisiu airfield. Captain Sutiagin reported this over the radio and went after the enemy in a diving turn to port. The enemy, noticing Sutiagin's MiG closing in behind them, went into an oblique loop to the left. Captain Sutiagin pursued them, and in the second loop, having closed to within 600 meters, opened fire at the tail-end Sabre, which banked around to the left and went into a steep dive. At this moment Sutiagin spotted another flight of F-86s diving on him from above, behind and the left. Sutiagin ordered his wingman Senior Lieutenant R.V. Khrisanov: "Swing around to the left", and having energetically hauled his MiG around to port, closed with the enemy head-on. Khrisanov attempted to stay with his leader in the tight turn to the left but fell briefly into a spin. After one revolution, he pulled his MiG out of it and headed for base at an order from his leader.

Meanwhile, group commander Major Pulov had continued the right turn toward Sunchon. At this moment, Captain S.S. Bychkov's tail-end element was jumped by eight Sabres from the right, above and behind, which continued past them in a high-speed dive and departed in the direction of the sea.

The four MiGs of the 3rd Squadron, under the command of Captain V.A. Blagov, were following in a column formation behind the 1st Squadron; during the turn to starboard Blagov noticed a pair of F-86s to the right and above them, which passed underneath his flight in a dive and emerged on the tail of the 1st Squadron's Captain B.E. Tikhonov. Captain Blagov banked to the left to pursue the enemy, and having closed to within a range of 600-700 meters he opened fire on a wingman's Sabre and gave it two bursts. Overshooting the wingman and winding up in the leader's backwash, Blagov's MiG went into an involuntary roll, after which he lost sight of the enemy.

The six MiGs of the 2nd Squadron under the command of Major M.S. Ponomarev were flying in the covering group at an altitude of 9,000 meters above and behind the 3rd Squadron. Arriving over the town of Gisiu, Major Ponomarev spotted a pair of F-86s below them and to the right, which were in the process of banking around to starboard. Ponomarev led his flight into a diving right-hand turn and went after the enemy, but at this moment heard a warning over the radio: "We're being attacked from above, behind and the right!" Ponomarev broke off his attack in a chandelle to the right, and a Sabre pair at a high deflection angle streaked past below them, where against the backdrop of the terrain they were lost from sight. When pulling into the climbing turn, Senior Lieutenant A.G. Chernozemov had noticed a pair of F-86s about 1,500 meters below and to the left of them, and he and his wingman went on the attack against them. Having closed to a range of 1,200 to 1,500 meters of them, he caught sight of six F-86s in a staggered trail of elements making a high side attack on them from the right and behind. Chernozemov directed his wingman Senior Lieutenant N.A. Zelenov to break right. The enemy closed to within a range of 500-600 meters and opened fire. Chernozemov banked to the left, and having separated by about 300-400 meters from his wingman, turned sharply back to the right to get in behind the Sabres. Noticing this, the F-86s went into a split-S to the left. However, before breaking off their attack, they had damaged Zelenov's MiG, so Senior Lieutenant Chernozemov withdrew from the dogfight.

Captain N.P. Mishakin's flight while en route to the Sunchon area sighted a pair of F-86s at a 90° degree angle to the left of them, which were in the process of turning toward his flight. Mishakin took his flight around to the left in a climb, and then dove in an attack on this Sabre element. Seeing our fighters rapidly approaching, the Sabre pilots went into a spiral to port. Captain Mishakin conducted two attacking passes, but both times he streaked past the Sabres at a high deflection angle. Then the enemy fighters rolled over to the left and dove away in the direction of the sea. Against the backdrop of the ground, the enemy disappeared from view.

The withdrawal from combat was executed in separate flights and pairs. This dogfight between our fighters and enemy fighters lasted for 10-12 minutes. As a result, Captain Sutiagin received credit for downing one F-86 from a range of 600 meters, and Captain Blagov received credit for another from a range of 550 meters.

At 1452, 18 crews of the 17th IAP under the command of Captain N.V. Sutiagin again took off from a status of Readiness No.1 to repel an enemy air strike in the Sukchon-Sunchon area. Captain Sutiagin's group received the assignment to engage the enemy ground attack aircraft in the Sunchon area. Arriving over Sunchon at an altitude of 8,000 meters, Sutiagin sighted a group of up to 36 F-84s behind and below them, which were flying to the northeast along the Seisen-ko River at an altitude of 3,000-4,000 meters. The 17th IAP's formation swung around to the left 180° while shedding altitude and went into a dive toward the enemy. Captain Sutiagin ordered, "We're attacking with the 1st and 3rd Squadrons. The 2nd Squadron will cover the combat." Having descended to an altitude of 5,000 meters, they now saw the enemy to the right and below them. Sutiagin banked to the right and began to close on the lead eight-ship formation of F-84s, which was flying in a left-echelon of flights. Having drawn to within 700-800 meters, the enemy aircraft went into a turn to starboard, and in the turn, from a range of 300-400 meters, Sutiagin opened fire on the leader of the second element, which burst into flames and fell into the hills with an explosion. Pulling out of the attack in a chandelle to port, Sutiagin swung around and made another attacking pass at a pair of Thunderjets, where he fired another burst at the lead F-84 from a range of 300-400 meters. His wingman Senior Lieutenant R.V. Khrisanov also fired at the lead F-84. When pulling out of this attack, Sutiagin noticed up to eight F-84s behind them, which were firing on his pair. Sutiagin maneuvered erratically with his joystick and rudder pedals, and having accelerated to a speed of 1,000 km/hr, left the Thunderjets far behind. Meanwhile Khrisanov, seeing that they were being attacked from behind, went abruptly into a climbing turn to port and exited the battle.

Captain Bychkov's element, flying in trail behind Captain Sutiagin's, just before Sutiagin's first attacking pass against the enemy, noticed a pair of F-84s to the front and left, and veered away from Sutiagin's element to attack them. Bychkov began to close on them, and from a range of 700-800 meters he opened fire. Pulling out of the attack into a chandelle to the left and having circled once, he spotted a flight of F-84s in front of him that were in a turn to the right, and attacked it. While closing with this enemy, his wingman Captain B.E. Tikhonov called out that there were four F-84s to the right and above. Captain Bychkov broke off his attack in a climbing turn to port.

The 3rd Squadron, consisting of four MiGs under the command of Captain V.A. Blagov, was in trail behind the 1st Squadron. While diving on the enemy, Captain Blagov felt a sharp pain in his ears and pulled out of the dive. Senior Lieutenant A.V. Bykov's element continued the dive and after banking to the right noticed eight F-84s out in front of them, which were firing at the MiG-15s ahead in the formation. Bykov attempted to force them to break off by firing short bursts from a range of 1,000-1,100 meters. The enemy, seeing the tracers, broke energetically to the right. At this point, Bykov observed an F-84, which had been fired on by the MiGs in front of him, erupt in flames and fall into the hills below them with an explosion. After driving off an attack by F-84 aircraft, Senior Lieutenant Bykov performed a chandelle to port and returned to base.

This aerial combat in the afternoon lasted for seven or eight minutes. It resulted in one destroyed F-84, which Captain Sutiagin shot down from a range of 400 meters. As rare exceptions to the normal case, the Americans sometimes acknowledged their losses in combats with MiGs, and on this occasion confirmed three victories by our pilots on this day: Captain Sutiagin in the morning presumably downed F-86A No.49-1184, and its pilot Richard Becker, having nursed his fatally-damaged jet across the Han River, ejected from it and survived. In the afternoon action, Sutiagin downed F-84E No.51-565 from the 49th FBG's 7th FBS, the pilot of which had managed to bail out before the plane crashed into the hills. He was later picked up by helicopter. Captain Blagov managed to damage F-86A No.49-1272; its pilot Martin Bambrick was able to fly it back to base, but there his aircraft was sent to the scrap yard.

On the following day of 4 December, pilots of the 303rd IAD's 17th IAP and 18th GIAP twice tangled with Sabres in the Anju area, but they both ended without results. Pilots of the 176th GIAP, which were flying in a regimental group of 22 MiGs, had better luck in a dogfight with 23 F-86s at an altitutde of 7,500 meters in the Anju area; Senior Lieutenant P.F. Nikulin shot down one of the Sabres. Over the day, the 64th IAK had no losses. This time as well the Americans acknowledge the loss in this combat of F-86E No.50-0684 from the 4th FIW, which was written off after its pilot managed to bring it back to base.

On 5 December, once again every regiment of the 303rd IAD and 324th IAD took part in repelling the next raids by the enemy's fighter-bombers in the Anju area. The regiments' pilots flew three missions during the day, almost all of which resulted in combat. Thus, on the second combat sortie at 1039, the commander of the 196th IAP Colonel E.G. Pepeliaev risked leading his regimental group of 24 MiGs beyond the Pyongyang-Wonsan no-fly line and came upon a large group of F-80 fighter-bombers numbering 16 Shooting Stars at low altitude. Attacking the Shooting Stars' formation in successive pairs, they scattered the F-80s' formation and downed three of them. However, in the course of the action, a pair of F-80s caught Senior Lieutenant Aleksandr Dmitrievich Ryzhkov's MiG at low altitude and shot it down, killing the pilot.[3] Aleksandr Ryzhkov was regiment commander E.G. Pepeliaev's wingman on this mission, had four personal victories to his credit, and had served with the regiment from the start of the 64th IAK's combat operations.

That morning, pilots of the 176th GIAP and all three regiments of the 303rd IAD took part in repulsing a raid by fighter-bombers from the 136th FBG. While the 303rd IAD's pilots dueled with the screening Sabres, the attack group consisting of 22 MiGs of the 176th GIAP attacked a group of 20 F-84s and four F-80s in the Sunchon area. The ground attack aircraft were chased back to the sea, and the regiment commander Lieutenant Colonel S.F. Vishniakov downed one F-84. This was F-84E No.49-2415, the pilot of which was killed. In addition, two of the Shooting Stars were damaged.

Pilots of the 303rd IAD distinguished themselves that afternoon when repelling the second enemy raid at 1422. In the Anju area they intercepted a group of fighter-bombers from the 136th FBW, which were being covered by Sabres of the 4th FIW. A group of 22 MiGs from the 17th IAP engaged 16 F-86s, while 22 MiGs from the 18th GIAP attacked the fighter-bombers and simultaneously engaged a different group of F-86s. One squadron from the 18th GIAP managed to harry the enemy fighter-bombers back to Korea Bay, downing two F-84s in the process – Senior Lieutenants V.I. Stepanov and V.A. Voistinny each received credit for one Thunderjet. Senior Lieuteant B.P. Sapozhnikov of the 17th IAP scored a victory over one of the covering F-86s.

In this battle the Thunderjet pilots behaved more aggressively against the MiGs, striving by doing so to force the combat's conditions onto our pilots. On this mission, the 523rd IAP's pilots encountered the following tactic: Our fighters were attacking up to 24 F-84s at an altitude of 2,000-3,000 meters, which were striking temporary bridges across the Seisen-ko River in the Anju area. During the action, one MiG flight was attacked from below and behind by four F-84s; the fighter-bombers had formed a Lufbery circle consisting of separate elements, and in these favorable conditions were able most often to ward away our fighters with defensive fire at any angle or direction of approach. Sometimes the fighter-bombers formed two defensive circles, a lower one to the right and a higher one to the left, which gave them the great opportunity to conduct blocking fire and targeted fire at our attacking fighters. This allowed the enemy aircraft here to retreat to the bay without losses.

However, the 18th GIAP suffered losses in its dogfight with the escorting Sabres. A six-ship group from the 2nd Squadron fought against superior enemy numbers, and in the course of this combat, Senior Lieutenant A.I. Baturov's MiG suffered heavy damage, so he opted to withdraw from the battle. His five comrades vigilantly covered his withdrawal against Sabre attacks, but when landing back at base, his MiG's engine flamed-out at low altitude and the pilot ejected from it. However, he was too low for his parachute to deploy fully and Baturov fell to his death. The Americans acknowledge the loss of F-86E No.49-2365 in this combat, the pilot of which Captain Horace R. Carman became a prisoner-of-war. As a result of the day's combats, the 64th IAK's records show that seven enemy aircraft were downed by its pilots, against the loss of two MiGs and two pilots.

The Americans claimed to have downed four MiGs on 5 December, two of which went to the score of the commander of the 334th FIS Major James Davis. Most likely, the other two downed or damaged MiGs belonged to the UAA's 3rd IAD. According to Chinese records, the 3rd IAD had again taken part in a major air battle. The 9th IAP was the attack group, while the 7th IAP covered it. In the combat with F-86 fighters and F-80 fighter-bombers, the Chinese claimed four victories.

In the second week of December, hard dogfights between MiGs and Sabres flared up once again. Up until 11 December, the 64th IAK's pilots downed another six F-86s, primarily F-86As, without any losses of their own. Only in a combat on 6 December did the MiG flown by Senior Lieutenant N.A. Zelenov of the 17th IAP receive combat damage, five bullet holes in the right wing and engine. The pilots of the 176th IAP scored particularly well on 8 December; in a combat involving 20 MiGs of the regiment against 44 F-86 fighters in the Sunchon-Pyongyang area, they claimed four Sabres destroyed without any losses of their own. Regiment commander Lieutenant Colonel S.F. Vishniakov, Captains P.S. Milaushkin and I.A. Suchkov, and Senior Lieutenant I.V. Lazutin all received credit for a victory.

Pilots of the UAA also participated in the combats with Sabres on 8 December. The Chinese 3rd IAD flew two group combat sorties and downed or damaged three F-86s. Around 300 aircraft from both sides took part in the battles. Historians in the PRC write, that "in an aerial combat, in which superior numbers of F-86s took part, the Chinese pilots, showing heroism, downed or damaged nine aircraft and gained experience in combats with the F-86 ...."

However, on 11 December 1951, the pilots of the 64th IAK were unable to avoid a loss. All five regiments of the 64th IAK became involved in dogfights on that day. In the first action pilots of the 17th IAP, who had taken off as the 303rd IAD's strike group for the mission, skirmished with 18 F-86s. The action ended with no results. In the second battle of the day, again pilots from all three regiments of the 303rd IAD took part, opposed by a large group of F-86s in MiG Alley. A former pilot with the 523rd IAP Mikhail Alekseevich Zykov describes the resulting dogfight:

I was shot down on 11 December on the regiment's second sortie at 1540 local time. This occurred somehow by chance. The regiment still hadn't yet been drawn into the battle, when a pair of Sabres suddenly appeared about 800 meters behind me. I was able to call for assistance to chase them away, but the Sabres, fearing to approach more closely, began to fire from this range. Usually we had no great fear at this range, but since no one yet had time to force them to break off, with their volume of fire they managed to hit me. My engine stopped, I felt a sharp jolt, and in order to escape out from under the attack I yanked the control column and … fell into a spin. While I still had a lot of altitude, I managed to check whether the aircraft was still controllable, and without any particular problem I pulled it out of the spin at an altitude of 4,500 meters. The unaccustomed silence was eerie. In the air it seemed as if no one else was around, and I began to try to re-start the engine. However, my instruments were dead, which meant I had no electrical power. At this moment my right wing took such heavy fire (apparently, from short range) that my aircraft abruptly listed to the right and went into a dive. Mountains were below me, and there was nothing else for me to do but to eject, even though I was in negative G's at the moment. Thus my seat at first was empty (the straps had been weakened), and then it slammed into my backside, which explained the blow to my spinal column.

I don't recall how I freed myself from the seat, but I consciously opened my parachute, despite the sharp pain in the small of my back. Sabres attacked me twice while in my parachute but missed me. I was saved by our squadron commander Captain V.P. Popov's element, which chased the Sabres away from me and gave me the opportunity to land safely.

I lay on the ground unconscious for around 30 minutes, but then I came to and I hadn't yet even have time to take a look around (I had landed among some boulders), when Chinese and Korean soldiers appeared and gathered me up. Soon Captain N.A. Shiliuk, the chief of the search team in this area (I had landed not far from Sei-bin) came for me, and I was sent to the hospital in Changtien.

This incident was reported as follows in the 523rd IAP's documents: While 12 crews were engaged with 20 F-86 aircraft in the Anju area, Captain Samoilov's element was unexpectedly jumped at an altitude of 10,000 meters by two F-86s. The aircraft of his wingman Senior Lieutenant Zykov received damage to the engine, as a result of which the engine stopped. The pilot made an attempt to re-start the engine, but with no success. Senior Lieutenant Zykov ejected at an altitude of 4,500 meters. The aircraft crashed, and the pilot received injuries to the small of his back and his left arm.

In this same afternoon battle, a pilot of the 196th IAP Senior Lieutenant Aleksandr Pavlovich Ovchinnikov was also shot down. Here's what he remembers of this action:

On 11 December, during the combat third sortie of the day, I was shot down when our pair was engaged by eight F-86s. On this day, the entire regiment

– approximately 30 crews – comprised our group. Deputy regiment commander Lieutenant Colonel A.I. Matusov was in overall command of the regimental group. He was leading the 1st Squadron; Captain B.V. Bokach was leading the 2nd Squadron, and Captain N.A. Antipov, the 3rd Squadron. I was flying as the wingman to the deputy commander of the 2nd Squadron Captain B.S. Abakumov. Unexpectedly Abakumov saw an eight-ship formation of Sabres to the left and below us, and informed the squadron leader that he was going on the attack, apparently thinking that Bokach and the rest of the squadron would follow him. However, Bokach couldn't follow Abakumov into the attack without an order from the regiment commander, and he continued to follow behind the 1st Squadron. As a result, we wound up alone in a daisy chain with F-86s. We were chasing the rear flight of Sabres, while the lead flight's elements were closing in behind us. Glancing back, I thought for a moment that the other pair in our flight, Senior Lieutenant A.D. Litviniuk's, was behind us, but when bullets hammered into my left wing, I realized that they were Sabres behind me, not our guys, and I began to slip out from under the attack in a climb. Abakumov transmitted that he was disengaging. It was hard to see him in the sun, but through the polarized glass of the cockpit canopy, I kept him in sight. At an altitude of 11,000 meters, because of the inadequate responsiveness of my joystick, I was unable to escape further hits to my aircraft, though Abakumov kept encouraging me. However, just then I felt that I had lost control over the aircraft and I made the immediate decision to eject. When ejecting I dislocated my left shoulder, but I didn't sense the pain until after landing. I spent three days making my way back to my airfield, but the pain in my arm wasn't subsiding, and they sent me to a hospital. Meanwhile, my leader had maneuvered successfully and unexpectedly attacked a Sabre element from behind, firing first at the leader's aircraft, and then at the wingman. Abakumov had no time to observe the results of his fire, because taking advantage of the moment he broke contact with the enemy and returned to base.

The pilots of the 196th IAP also claimed two Sabres in this combat – Captain V.I. Alfeev and Captain B.V. Bokach received credit for the victories. In addition, 22 MiGs of the 17th IAP took part in this same battle in the Anju area. They successfully engaged 10 F-86s, and Captain N.G. Dokashenko damaged one Sabre. At the same time, pilots of the 18th GIAP downed two Sabres at once in this major dogfight. Senior Lieutenant I.I. Shashva and his wingman Senior Lieutenant V.A. Konev were the successful pilots.

Both of the Soviet pilots were shot down by two pilots of the 4th FIW, 1st Lieutenant Donald Griffith from the 335th FIS and Captain Alfred Simmons from the 336th FIS. Regarding their own losses, the Americans report that on this day only F-86A No.48-0301 of the 334th FIS was lost. No details are given about the loss, other than the assertion that it was not due to combat.

The combats with the F-86s had become more dogged, and according to the assertions of our pilots who took part in the December battles, the Sabres were different and more difficult to dogfight. The losses suffered in the latest battle confirmed the pilots' reports – they were now dealing with updated Sabres. In addition, the IAK intelligence was reporting the arrival of a new Sabre wing at the front, which was evident from the greater number of F-86s that was being encountered and their greater activity.

Pilots of the 196th IAP (from left to right) P.F. Tkatskii, A.I. Mitusov and
L.N. Ivanov – Andong, 1951.

The 64th IAK command decided to test the pilots of the new wing in battle, in order
to cool their combat ardor and to reduce their activity. The commanders of both divisions of the 64th IAK visited their regiments and issued an assignment to select each
regiment's most experienced pilots for this mission – only "old men" were to head into
the combat against the new Sabres.

In the course of three days, between 13 and 15 December, ferocious aerial battles took
place between the pilots of the 64th IAK and UAA on the one hand, and Sabres of the
4th and 51st FIW on the other. The first major clash with the new F-86E occurred on
Thursday, 13 December. Prior to then, encounters with the new Sabre had been sporadic
and few, involving the small number of F-86Es that had gone initially to the 4th FIG.

On 13 December, pilots from both divisions of the 64th IAK each flew three combat
missions over the course of the day and became involved in several dogfights with Sabres.
True, the on-duty flight staff of the divisions that day didn't number more than 40-45
pilots, but they were the flower of the divisions, since primarily the most experienced
and seasoned veterans flew the missions. The full complement of the 324th IAD became
engaged in combat in all three missions, and each time both regiments were led into
battle by their commanders, Colonel E.G. Pepeliaev and S.F. Vishniakov. The 303rd
IAD's inspector of combat technique Major Aleksei Alekseevich Kaliuzhny also took
part in the fighting on 13 December, who distinguished himself in one of the actions
in the Anju-Sunchon area by downing two Sabres in quick succession. Here is how he
himself recalls the events:

I especially remember the combat on 13 December, when on one sortie I managed to down two Sabres at once. The entire division took off to intercept enemy aircraft in the Anju area. On this day, we flew three missions as a full division (but the division had no more than 40-45 crews, if not fewer). We ran into a large group of Sabres and a "carousel" of climbing and diving fighters began. In the course of it, I happened across a pair of Sabres that were plainly being flown by new pilots, who hadn't yet tasted combat. My first attack was a surprise to them. Attacking from above and behind, out of the sun, I approached to within a range of around 150 meters of the somewhat lagging wingman, and with a medium, not long, burst of fire from all three cannons, the Sabre disintegrated. Then I continued on to attack the leader still in front of me. He noticed me and hauled his aircraft into a climbing turn to port. At first the gap between us remained unchanged, but it was still too early to fire – the range was approximately 400-500 meters. But in the second half of the climb, I perceptibly began to gain on him, and when I was within 200-250 meters of him, I opened fire. I gave him several long and medium bursts, and one of them struck the Sabre. It emitted black smoke and pieces flew off of the aircraft. The Sabre fell into a spin, never came out of it, and crashed into a hill. The pilot never ejected and plainly had been killed in his cockpit.

Altogether on this day, in the dogfights with the Sabres the 64th IAK's pilots downed a record number of 10 F-86 fighters, including the new F-86E. Prior to this, never had so many Sabres gone down in one day, and this does not include the results achieved by the UAA on this day, which also engaged Sabres in the same area, though it is true, less successfully.

Pilots of the 324th IAD did especially well over the day, claiming a total of six victories over the F-86. At the same time, Captain Petr Semenovich Milaushkin of the 176th GIAP was credited with downing the 500th enemy aircraft recorded by the 64th IAK from the start of its combat operations in Korea, that is to say, 1 November 1950. Here is how Petr Semenovich recalls it happened:

On this day we flew three combat missions, two of which resulted in aerial combats. In one of them our flight was engaged with two flights of Sabres. During an attack by one of the Sabre flights, a pair of Sabres pounced on us from above and attacked my wingman Stepa Kirichenko. I shouted at him: "Break left in front of me." He reacted quickly, made the turn in my direction, and I opened fire into the space behind his jet; the enemy's leader and wingman both passed through the stream of shells from my cannons.

Back on the ground we checked the gun camera film, and on it, the Sabre leader and wingman were clearly visible as they flew through the fire from my cannons. At the time, no wreckage was spotted on the ground. However, later Captain Andrei Pil'kevich (the chief of our regiment's search team) questioned residents of the area where the aerial battle had taken place (it was the area of the reservoir of a hydro-electric power station) and learned that the Koreans had seen a large column of water rise from the reservoir surface. The Koreans began a search and soon brought up pieces of an F-86 fighter from under the water, and only then did I receive credit for a victory.

In fact, the pilots of the 176th GIAP did become engaged in two aerial combats on this day. In the first morning clash, 20 MiGs of the regiment tangled with 30 F-86s at an altitude of 5,000 meters in the Anju-Eiju area. In the afternoon action, 22 of the 176th GIAP's now took part, which in the area of Anju at an altitude of 8,000-9,000 meters successfully dealt with 38 F-86s. Both regiments of the 324th IAD and two regiments of the 303rd IAD took part in the fighting on 13 December – the 17th IAP remained in reserve and didn't fly on this day.

The 64th IAK lost only one MiG on 13 December. Senior Lieutenant I.A. Gorsky of the 18th GIAP was shot down, but he safely ejected and soon made his way back to the regiment. The Americans say nothing about their losses in these battles. However, it is known that 1st Lieutenant Charles D. Hogue's F-86A of the 334th FIS went down in the Sinanju area, but it is presumable that the losses of the Americans on this day were greater. It is now known as well that one F-86A No.49-1159 from the 336th FIS was seriously damaged on 13 December, the pilot of which managed to reach Cho-do Island in his crippled Sabre, where he bailed out and was picked up by a search and rescue team.

True, the Americans in turn claim that the pilots of the 4th and 51st FIW downed 14 MiGs, only one of which went to the pilots of the 51st FIW in their new F-86E. The commander of the 334th FIS Major George Davis particularly distinguished himself by downing four MiGs on the day, two on his first mission and two on the second. Most likely, Major Davis and his fellow pilots of the 4th FIW had feasted on the young Chinese pilots of the 3rd IAD, since the Soviet pilots on this day lost only one MiG. In total, 130 MiGs (90 MiGs from the 64th IAK and 40 MiGs from the UAA) met an equal number of Sabres from the 4th and 51st FIW in battle on 13 December. Although the Chinese pilots suffered heavy losses on this day, according to them they managed at the very least to down two F-80s from the 8th and 35th FBG, but possibly the American losses were even higher.

After such severe losses, several of the 64th IAK's top pilots were sent to the 3rd IAD's regiments to give a series of lectures to the Chinese pilots, which explained to them the tactics to use against the Sabres at various altitudes. Among those who went to instruct the Chinese in these classroom sessions were the Soviet aces Colonel E.G. Pepeliaev and Captain N.V. Sutiagin – both masters of combat against the Sabres.

The aerial combats on 14 December were just as vicious. According to archival records, the Soviet pilots downed eight F-86s, without any loss to themselves. Again the pilots of the 324th IAD stood out, claiming six Sabres on this day. Both regiments of the 324th IAD and the 17th IAP and 18th GIAP of the 303rd IAD took part in the first morning battle. Around 0800, pilots of the 17th IAP and 18th GIAP engaged a group of 32 F-86s in the Anju area. At the same time, the attack group, consisting of MiGs from the 324th IAD, ran into a large group of Sabres numbering 56 fighters in the Taegwan-dong and Taechon areas – in essence, two Soviet MiG-15 divisions were fighting two wings of F-86 fighters. The 196th IAP's pilots claimed two Sabres. The 12 MiGs of the 176th GIAP became engaged in a difficult combat, but also achieved success, downing one F-86. In the second action of the day, which took place in the afternoon, the Soviet pilots also held the advantage in the combat area when the battle ended: pilots of the 324th IAD shot down three more Sabres without any losses of their own.

Another two F-86s were claimed by pilots of the 303rd IAD, and again in one of the combats the pair of Major A.A. Kaliuzhny and his constant wingman Senior Lieutenant

A.A. Astapovsky distinguished themselves. When returning to base, they rushed to the assistance of their comrades, who were being attacked by four "free hunters" from the 4th FIG. Anatolii Andreevich Astapovsky recalls:

> After a massive aerial combat, returning together to base, Kaliuzhny and I spotted four Sabres, which were in hot pursuit of our comrades, who were flying back to base low on fuel. Without hesitation, we went straight into an attack from higher altitude; they didn't see us, and we downed one Sabre. The remaining element saved itself by fleeing.

However, for some reason the victory over the Sabre was not credited to Kaliuzhny, but to his wingman.

The pilots of the 17th IAP, which had sortied in 24 MiGs, also scored victories in this major clash: Senior Lieutenant V.M. Khvostantsev did particularly well by downing two Sabres in the dogfight. In the period between 0725 and 0734, radar had detected up to 120 enemy fighters and fighter-bombers in the Chinnampo area at an altitude of 6,000-8,000 meters, flying in groups of 8, 12, 16 and 24 aircraft in the direction of Anju. At an order from the division command post, 24 MiGs of the 17th IAP under the command of Captain N.V. Sutiagin took off from Readiness No.1 to intercept the enemy aircraft.

Captain Sutiagin's group received the assignment to engage the F-86 fighters in the Anju area at an altitude of 7,500-8,500 meters. While en route to the area, seeing that they were leaving contrails behind them at an altitude of 8,000 meters, Sutiagin decided to climb to 9,500 meters, where they would leave no contrails. Upon arriving over Anju, the group leader noticed a formation of up to eight F-86s out in front of them and to the right and higher by about 600-700 meters. However, at this same instant he received information from Major M.S. Ponomarev that a dogfight was underway behind and to the left of them.

Sutiagin decided to join the on-going fracas and ordered the group to swing around 180° to the left. Coming out of the turn, Sutiagin saw the action going on in front of them and led the entire group toward it.

As they were approaching the combat (in an area north of Taechon), Sutiagin observed a flight of F-86s off to their left and 1,000 meters below them, swinging around to their left on a course to intercept them. He gave the command: "We're going on the attack", before rolling to the right, and then back to the left into a dive upon this flight of Sabres. Having closed to within a range of 1,000-1,200 meters, Sutiagin received information from Captain S.S. Bychkov that they had Sabres behind them. Sutiagin pulled abruptly into a climbing turn to port, thereby exiting out from under the attack of these Sabres. Having conducted a low-angle spiral, he spotted four F-86s below and to the left, which were moving across their front from left to right, and having let them pass below him, he went after the enemy in a diving turn to starboard. Pursuing the enemy, Sutiagin caught sight of two F-86s that were attacking his pair from the left and behind. Sutiagin broke off his pursuit of the enemy and evaded the attack of this pair of Sabres with a climbing turn to port. At this moment, an order arrived from the division command post to break off combat, so Captain Sutiagin headed back to base.

Senior Lieutenant F.G. Malunov's element, following behind Sutiagin's element in the climbing turn to port, spotted four F-86s in front of them, to the right and below.

Malunov chose to close with this adversary, banked to the right and dove in their direction. The enemy caught sight of the closing MiGs and broke apart into separate elements. Malunov went after the left-hand element, and having pulled to within 800-1,000 meters, he opened fire. At this moment the second element of Sabres swung in behind Malunov, and he was forced to break off his attack and go into a climbing spiral to the left. At that point, the order to exit the battle arrived, and Malunov and his wingman headed back to base.

The 3rd Squadron under the command of Captain V.A. Blagov had been flying in trail behind the 1st Squadron at an altitude of 9,500-10,000 meters. After the regimental group had made its 180° turn to the left, Senior Lieutenant V.M. Khvostantsev spotted a solitary Sabre, which was surreptitiously climbing into firing position behind Captain Blagov's element. Khvostantsev, trailing behind Captain Blagov's element, closed to within 700 meters of the Sabre and gave it a short burst, but the Sabre pilot either didn't notice or he stubbornly decided not to break off his attack against Blagov. So Khvostantsev approached the F-86 even more closely, and from a range of 450 meters opened fire. His shells were on target; the Sabre flipped over and went into an uncontrolled plunge.

Captain Blagov's element began to swing around to the right, and at this moment Khvostantsev noticed another pair of F-86s off to the left, approaching at a shallow angle. He banked to the left to close with this pair of Sabres, but they, seeing Khvostantsev's element closing in on them, broke away into a leftward spiral. Khvostantsev, having pulled to within 300 meters of the wingman's Sabre, gave it a burst, and then another one as he closed to within 220 meters of the target, after which flames erupted from the Sabre's right wing. The lead F-86 rolled over to the left and dove away in the direction of the sea.

The 2nd Squadron under the command of Major Ponomarev was acting as the covering group and was trailing above and behind the 3rd Squadron. After Sutiagin had led the group into the 180° turn to left toward the combat area, Ponomarev noticed a flight of Sabres in front of and below them by 800-1,000 meters, which was approaching from the left. Allowing the enemy to pass beneath him, Ponomarev went after the enemy in a climbing turn to the right to gain more altitude. While pursuing the enemy, he heard a warning from Captain N.P. Mishakin: "Four F-86s behind us." Ponomarev broke into a climbing turn. The Sabre flight continued to pursue the group, but then after having turned 270°, fell behind and opted to head toward the sea. After coming out of the turn, the squadron group broke into separate flights and operated independently. Captain Mishakin's flight, after swinging further to the right, lost sight of the first flight and headed toward the Pakchon area. Reversing course over Pakchon, Mishakin noticed a flight of F-86s below him, approaching on an intersecting course. He banked toward the enemy and began to close with them on a head-on course, but the enemy departed underneath Mishakin's flight. At this moment, the order arrived from the group commander to break off the combat, and the flight set a course back to base.

The dogfight had lasted 10 minutes. As a result of it, Senior Lieutenant Khvostantsev downed two F-86 Sabres. Pilots Polishchuk and Blagov both observed the aircraft going down, and it was further confirmed by the gun camera footage. However, as was the previous case with Kaliuzhny of the 18th GIAP, Khvostantsev only received credit for one victory. However, the main result of the day was that our pilots had shown the enemy aces that they were also highly qualified pilots and were in no way inferior to the

American pilots and in certain respects perhaps were even better than them. Thus the victory this day was on the side of the Soviet pilots, who had once again defeated their constant adversaries in the form of Sabre pilots, without suffering any losses. On this day, only the pilots of the 523rd IAP didn't see any action – they were being held in reserve.

The Americans acknowledged the loss of two of their F-86s on 14 December: No.49-1199 from the 334th FIS went down over North Korea and its pilot (Lieutenant Charles Hogue) was killed; F-86A No.49-1191 also from the 334th Squadron was heavily damaged, but its pilot 1st Lieutenant Howard J. Schuckler nursed it back to base, where he experienced an engine failure on the approach and crashed. Schuckler was injured. The Sabre pilots on this day claimed only one victory over the MiGs, and the commander of the 4th FIW Colonel Harrison Thyng received credit for it. However, most likely Colonel Thyng only damaged a MiG, since all of the 64th IAK's aircraft returned to their bases in Manchuria, or else it was a MiG from the UAA's 3rd IAD. Incidentally, on this day the pilots of the PLAAF 3rd IAD attacked a group of fighter-bombers without interference, since all of the Sabres had been drawn into the combat with the pilots of the 64th IAK. Taking advantage of this circumstance, the Chinese pilots downed several US fighter-bombers. At the very least, the Americans confirm the loss of one of their F-84Es from the 49th FBG and one F-80 from the 8th FBG; the pilots of both aircraft were killed.

After such heavy losses the intensity of the fighting subsided somewhat. The combats became less ferocious, and the statistics of the third day of these battles in MiG Alley give evidence of this.

On 15 December, pilots of the 17th IAP became involved in a morning scrap with 40 F-86s, in which the regiment's top pilot and "Menace to Sabres" Captain N.V. Sutiagin downed his next Sabre. Around 1000 24 enemy fighters had been sighted in an area 10 kilometers south of Pyongyang at an altitude of 8,000-10,000 meters, which were flying on a course of 40°. The regimental group, consisting of 20 MiGs under the command of Captain N.V. Sutiagin, took off from Readiness No.1 with the assignment to cover the actions of the 18th GIAP in the area of Sukchon.

The group arrived in the Anju area at an altitude of 10,000 meters, where Captain Sutiagin noticed eight F-86s in front and above them, crossing from right to left. Sutiagin issued the order to tie up the enemy in combat, and went after the enemy in a climbing turn to port. The enemy noticed our group, turned, and headed out over the sea, where one flight of four Sabres remained, while the other reversed course in a right turn and headed to the northeast.

Sutiagin banked right to intercept this group, but lost sight of them temporarily. Circling around completely, he again sighted the four F-86s, which were pursuing a pair of MiGs. Sutiagin, seeing that the Sabres were 1,000-1,200 meters away and about 500-600 meters higher, went into a steep turn to the right. This time Sutiagin closed to within 600-700 meters of them, which they noticed and began to go into a tight turn to the right. Sutiagin opened fire from a range of 270 meters at a wingman's Sabre, which abruptly rolled over to the right and went into an uncontrolled plunge.

Major S.S. Artemchenko's flight was flying behind Captain Sutiagin's element. At the moment Sutiagin went on the attack, Artemchenko spotted eight F-86s to the left and in front of them at the same altitude, which were swinging around onto Sutiagin's tail. Artemchenko turned tightly to port to cut off the enemy. The Sabres, noticing this, went into a climbing turn to the left with the aim of dropping onto the tail of Artemchenko's flight, but here Artemchenko received the order to break off combat, so he disengaged and headed back to base.

The 3rd Squadron under the command of Captain V.A. Blagov was flying in trail behind the 1st Squadron. Over the area of Anju, Blagov observed 12 F-86s approaching from the left and immediately informed the group commander about this, then took his flight into a tight turn toward the enemy. In the turn he lost sight of the Sabres against the terrain below, but also lost radio contact with the group commander, so he reversed course over Anju and headed back to base.

Captain N.G. Dokashenko's flight continued on behind the 1st Squadron, then when coming out of the group's 180° turn to the left, Dokashenko noticed a pair of F-86s to the left and below them, which were turning away from them to the left. Dokashenko saw the opportunity to get on their tails, so he banked left and closed with them. He pulled to within 400-500 meters of the Sabres, but that is when the Sabre wingman spotted our MiGs, and his F-86 rolled over and dove away. The lead F-86 began to carry out a descending left turn. Dokashenko pursued it and having closed to within 600 meters, he opened fire, but the shells passed wide of the target. After this, Captain Dokashenko's flight conducted a chandelle to port and exited the combat.

As a result of this action, one F-86 fighter was downed by Captain Sutiagin, the fall of which was observed by both Captain Sutiagin and Senior Lieutenant Perepelkin. The dogfight lasted for five to seven minutes.

Altogether over 15 December, the 64th IAK's pilots shot down three F-86s without any losses. In addition to Sutiagin's victory, Captain P.S. Milaushkin got another Sabre when the 176th GIAP's pilots in a regimental group of 20 MiGs successfully engaged a group of 20 F-86s in the Neisong-Anju area at an altitude of 8,000 meters. The pilots of the 523rd IAP also tangled twice with Sabres on this day and also scored a victory, when 2nd Squadron commander Captain V.P. Popov claimed one F-86 in the Sukchon area.

The Fifth Air Force command acknowledged the loss of two of its F-86E Sabres on this day: presumably, in the morning combat Captain Sutiagin had seriously damaged one of them, No.50-0681 of the 334th FIS. Its pilot, 1st Lieutenant William F. Prindle managed to bring his damaged Sabre back to base, but when he bailed out after aborting his landing attempt, his parachute failed to open and he was killed. Also on this day F-86E No.50-0665 from the 51st FIW was lost, but its pilot James I. Wheeler was picked by up a search and rescue team.[4]

According to records of the American command, on this day a pilot of the 116th FBW's 158th FBS, Captain Paul Mitchell, downed one MiG-15 – this was the Thunderjet's final official victory of the war. Since on this day the pilots of the 64th IAK had no combats involving enemy fighter-bombers, then most likely the 116th FBW's pilots were dealing with MiGs from the UAA, and their adversaries were pilots of the 3rd IAD and 14th IAD that were still acquiring combat experience. However, if the Thunderjet pilots managed to down one MiG, the Chinese pilots were able at a minimum to shoot down three USAF fighter-bombers: one F-84E and one F-80 from the 49th FBG, and one F-84E from the 136th FBW – all three pilots of the aircraft were killed.

After this day there was a lull in operations, which lasted almost until the end of December. Only on 27 December 1951 did aerial battles in MiG Alley resume with fresh intensity. However, between these peaks of activity, there were several raids into the MiG's zone of operations by American aircraft, and there were brief skirmishes with the American pilots on 18 and 23 December. When repelling a morning raid on 18 December, pilots of the 17th IAP and 196th IAP distinguished themselves. Both regiments were involved in successful actions against Sabres. At 1124, 18 MiGs of the 17th IAP under the command of Captain N.V. Sutiagin at a command from the division command post took off from Readiness No.1 to repel an enemy air strike in the Chongju-Anju area.

Flying as part of the division's attack group at an altitude of 8,500-9,000 meters, in the area of Chongju the 17th IAP's 2nd and 3rd Squadrons were attacked by enemy F-86 fighters and tied up in combat. The 1st Squadron, numbering six MiGs under the command of the group commander Captain Sutiagin continued on to the Anju area, where it swung back around in a descending turn to the right. Having reversed course, at an altitude of 6,500 meters Sutiagin spotted six F-86s to the right front and above them, which were flying in a column of elements and in a descending starboard turn with the aim of getting behind our group. Sutiagin issued the command: "Turn to the right!" and his six-ship squadron conducted a climbing turn to the right. Sutiagin's element was now on the left of the squadron formation and during the starboard turn became the tail-end element. Having turned by 90°, Sutiagin caught sight of a pair of Sabres out in front of them, above and to the left, which was going on the attack against Senior Lieutenant F.G. Malunov's element. Sutiagin swiftly rolled his MiG to the left and opened fire across the path of the lead Sabre, which noticed this and broke sharply to the right to avoid the fire. Continuing his turn to the left, Sutiagin spotted a different F-86 flight 500-600 below and to the left, which was carrying out an oblique loop to the right. Sutiagin, allowing the enemy to pass below him, went after them with an energetic starboard turn and, having closed to within 600-700 meters of them opened fire on the second pair's wingman. Observing no hits, he closed to within a range of 400-450 meters and opened fire again. The attacked Sabre listed abruptly to the right and fell into an uncontrolled dive toward the earth.

At this moment Senior Lieutenant N.Ia. Perepelkin, Sutiagin's wingman, warned over the radio, "A pair of Sabres has opened fire on you!" Sutiagin banked right toward the sun, and with a climb and a side slip began to put distance between his MiG and the enemy. Having separated from them, Sutiagin swung around 180° to the right, where he noticed a six-ship formation of MiGs above and to the left of him, which at Sutiagin's order descended into the combat area and covered the withdrawal from combat.

Perepelkin, having spotted the two Sabres that were attacking Sutiagin, began to fire across their front to force them to break off. The enemy, seeing the tracers, conducted a split-S and dove away. Ceasing fire, Perepelkin glanced behind him, only to see two other F-86s that were firing at him. Perepelkin, jinking his MiG erratically, climbed toward the sun to escape the enemy. Having separated from the enemy, Sutiagin and Perepelkin joined back up with their flight.

In the same morning battle with the Sabres, the deputy commander of the 196th IAP Lieutenant Colonel A.I. Mitusov also downed one Sabre. In the second clash with Sabres that afternoon, the pilots of the 17th IAP again did well. The regiment commander Lieutenant Colonel E.G. Pepeliaev led 18 MiGs of the regiment into battle with a group of 16 F-86s, in which Captain V.A. Blagov downed one Sabre. Our pilots again had no losses. The American command confirmed the loss of one F-86E No.51-2730 from the 51st FIW's 25th FIS, the pilot of which Lieutenant George M. Pistole bailed out and was picked up by a US search and rescue team.

Due to bad weather, the 64th IAK's pilots flew no combat sorties again until 23 December. The enemy pilots were also grounded, so as it happened, both sides received several days of enforced rest. On 23 December, through the efforts of the 303rd IAD alone, a not very large raid by F-84s with Sabre cover was repulsed. The pilots of the 523rd IAP and 18th GIAP took on the covering fighters, while the 17th IAP's pilots broke through to the Thunderjets. Attacking one eight-ship group of F-84s, Captain N.V. Sutiagin damaged one of them, and the remainder immediately turned and headed toward the sea.

Here's a more detailed description of what happened on that mission. In the period between 0947 and 0953 radar had detected up to 60 enemy fighters and fighter-bombers at an altitude of 7,000-9,000 meters in the Chinnampo – Kosei-gun area, flying in groups of 12-16 aircraft on a heading of 330-350°. In response, 18 MiGs of the 17th IAP under the command of Captain N.V. Sutiagin at an order from the division command post took off to repel the enemy raid in the Sukchon-Eiju area. Heading south as part of the division's attack group at an altitude of 8,500-9,000 meters, in the Anju area they made a 60-70° turn to starboard and started to descend. Having descended to an altitude of 6,000 meters, Captain S.S. Bychkov sighted a group of eight F-84 Thunderjets below and in front of them and alerted group commander Captain Sutiagin of their presence, who led the group into a dive toward the enemy. The Thunderjets, obviously seeing the closing MiGs, went into a starboard spiral. The 1st Squadron numbering six MiGs and led by Captain Sutiagin overshot the enemy at high speed and at a high angle, after which it pulled into a climbing turn to port, swung back around, and came back at the F-84s head-on.

Streaking past the Thunderjets, Sutiagin conducted a chandelle to port and began to pursue the enemy, which was attempting to draw the combat to the south, beyond Pyongyang. Sutiagin, accelerating, closed to within 600 meters of the tail-end pair of F-84s, which responded by going into a starboard turn. Sutiagin followed them into the turn and having pulled to within 300 meters of the element leader, opened fire before exiting the attack in a climbing turn to port.

Captain Bychkov's element, trailing behind Sutiagin's element, attacked a different pair of F-84s at a high deflection angle and opened fire from a range of 1,000-1,500 meters, after which they pulled out of the attack in a chandelle to port. The remaining element in the 1st Squadron, Senior Lieutenant F.G. Malunov's, trailed behind Captain Bychkov's element. Follow-up attacks were not made in view of the fact that the adversary had crossed the no-fly line for the Soviet pilots, and the 1st Squadron headed back to base in a climb.

Tangling with Sabres on 23 December, Soviet pilots downed two more F-86s, one of which was shot down by the 18th GIAP ace Captain L'vov Kirillovich Shchukin. Here's how he described this action:

> On the second sortie of the day, I took part in a dogfight with Sabres. We had taken off as a division, but only part of the regiment's pilots engaged the F-86s. The situation wasn't very complex, but the F-86 pilots we met were good ones and

tied us up in such a "carousel" that we had to pass a serious test. Nevertheless, my wingman Tolia Astapovsky and I forced a Sabre flight to go into a vertical maneuver, and having closed to within 120 meters of them in a climbing starboard spiral, I managed to shoot down one Sabre.

Twenty MiGs of the 17th IAP also took part in this same battle, which occurred around 1500, and in a tussle with 20 F-86s, the regiment also scored a victory – Senior Lieutenant F.G.Malunov downed one Sabre. We had no losses on this day, and the Americans didn't claim a single victory by their pilots on 23 December. However, the American command also doesn't confirm the loss of their F-86s on this day. Two days later, though, they wrote off two F-84s from the 49th FBG, one of which was likely so damaged by the fire from Sutiagin's cannons that it was unable to get back to base.

Between 27 December and 29 December, dogfights between MiGs and Sabres again flared up in MiG Alley. On the first day of the new round of fighting, the Soviet pilots claimed three victories – all three F-86s fell to the pilots of the 324th IAD. Two of them were downed by Captain P.S. Milaushkin of the 176th GIAP in a dogfight in the Taechon area with a group of 24 F-86s. The pilots of the 303rd IAD also took part in the two combats of this day. On both missions, the 18th GIAP and 523rd IAP were in the division's attack group, while their actions were covered by the pilots of the 17th IAP, who twice engaged Sabres in combats that ended with no results, but the 17th IAP carried out its assignment. The fighting of 27 December resulted in no losses for the 64th IAK. However, the Americans claim that in one dogfight on 27 December, two pilots of the 51st FIW's 25th FIS, 2nd Lieutenants Clifford F. Brossart and Kenneth A. Shealy, each downed one MiG-15. We must conclude that either the Americans shot down two Chinese MiGs of the UAA, or else they in the best case only managed to damage a couple. In return, the Americans also don't recognize the loss of any of their F-86s on 27 December, so perhaps the Soviet pilots only damaged their targets.

On 28 and 29 December, primarily only the pilots of the by now substantially worn out 324th IAD clashed with the Sabres of the 4th and 51st FIW in MiG Alley. However, despite their fatigue, in the aerial combats with the F-86s over these two days, they added eight more Sabres (four each day) to their score, without any losses.

Here's how a former pilot of the 196th IAP Senior Lieutenant Petr Grigor'evich Iovlev describes his part in a dogfight on 28 December 1951:

On this day, we took off in a regimental group of 12 MiGs. I was flying as Captain V.I. Alfeev's wingman. The encounter with the enemy took place at an altitude of 10,000 meters on a meeting course. We engaged 48 F-86s. Our pair was attacked by a Sabre flight. Lacking sufficient speed for the attack, three of the Sabres passed underneath us, but one Sabre strayed in pursuit of a different target. Diverted by his new target and in a climb toward it, the Sabre pilot seemed not to notice us. Captain Alfeev wasn't able to attack him, but I had a favorable position. I nudged my MiG a bit to the right, lined the target up in my gunsight and opened fire. The range was approximately 200 meters, and one of my 37mm shells struck the right wingroot; the wing broke off and the Sabre, spinning around its axis, began to fall. The pilot didn't bail out.

In this combat, Iovlev's leader Captain V.I. Alfeev later claimed a Sabre. The pilots of the 196th IAP were assisted in the dogfight by 18 MiGs of the 176th GIAP, which with three squadrons engaged a group of F-86s between 0831 and 0929. In the Charyongwan-Sonchon-Chongju area at an altitude of 8,000-12,000 meters, the unit encountered 32-36 F-86s, which were operating in groups of 4-8 aircraft. Altogether, four of the 176th GIAP's pilots fired on Sabres in this dogfight. According to the post-mission debriefings, Captain I.A. Suchkov shot down an F-86, which fell in the Chongju area. In the second action of the day between 1250 and 1349, the three squadrons of the 176th GIAP in the Kaechon-Anju area encountered 19 F-86s. This time, three of the regiment's pilots fired their cannons at enemy aircraft. According to pilot testimonies, in this combat Captain N.M. Goncharov downed one F-86 south of Kaechon, and Senior Lieutenant N.K. Moroz was credited with a probable victory over another Sabre.

All three regiments of the 303rd IAD also took part in these two dogfights, though their part in it was less successful and they suffered a loss. At 1300, pilots of the 17th IAP were covering the return of other of the IAK's MiGs from a mission. At 1320 Senior Lieutenant V.N. Shestopalov while en route back to his base at an altitude of 10,000 meters in an area 25-30 kilometers southeast of Pakchon was jumped by a pair of F-86s. As a result of the attack there was an explosion in the engine. Shestopalov felt a blow to the back of the head, after which he decided to punch out of his crippled jet – he had injuries to the back of the head and the left shoulder. This was the 64th IAK's final loss in the month of December, and hence, of the year 1951.

The Americans claimed two victories on this day. Pilots of the 51st FIW Lieutenants Paul E. Roach and Biffle Pittman were credited with the MiGs, and Pittman's was the first victory for this Wing's 39th FIS, which had only recently arrived from Japan after forming up. As in other cases, the Americans don't confirm the loss of any Sabres on this day.

In the final day of aerial combat in 1951, 29 December, pilots of the 196th IAP distinguished themselves, claiming four Sabres without any losses of their own. Captain Evgenii Nikolaevich Samusin relates:

> On this day I took off as part of an eight-ship squadron formation under the command of the deputy commander of the 196th IAP Lieutenant Colonel A.I. Mitusov. Coming across our eternal adversaries, Sabre pilots, we engaged them in combat. In the course of the dogfight, a Sabre flight, not seeing us, went after Mitusov's flight, placing their tails right in front of us, and if our flight commander Captain I.M. Zaplavnev hadn't opened fire prematurely, we would have downed all of them, because each of us had our own target. When Zaplavnev opened fire, they all rolled over into a dive. However, at the moment I had a Sabre framed in the central leaf of my gunsight, and as the range closed, the Sabre filled the sight's reticles, which were set for a minimum range of 180 meters. Thus, as my Sabre began to roll over, I lead him with a roll of my own and opened fire simultaneously from my cannons, and the Sabre passed through my burst of fire. As it passed through it, I noticed it interrupted the stream of tracers, and I leveled out my aircraft, since I had no intention to try to stay behind him. An attempt to do so might have ended badly for me, since the Sabre had powerful air brakes, and my MiG might have

simply overshot him. But my wingman Senior Lieutenant N.T. Rybas went after the Sabre I had damaged and finished it off an accurate burst, so later he received the credit for this F-86.

The 303rd IAD's pilots, as they had done on the previous day, flew two missions to intercept enemy aircraft and became involved in one dogfight with Sabres, which ended with no results. However, they did a splendid job tying up the Sabres in combat, and most importantly, without any losses.

The American command at last confirmed the loss in the morning battle of only one of its F-86A (No.49-1083) from the 335th FIS. Its pilot 1st Lieutenant Ward L. Starkweather was killed.

On 31 December the final two combats of the receding year took place with the American pilots. Both combats occurred in the afternoon. Pilots of the 303rd IAD took off to intercept an enemy raid. At 1415, 12 MiGs of the 18th GIAP under the command of Lieutenant Colonel A.P. Smorchkov departed on a combat mission; they encountered 30 F-80s in the Anju area and promptly attacked them. Here's how the 18th GIAP's Lev Kirillovich Shchukin recalls his final combat of 1951:

On 31 December, we were scrambled into the air. The Americans were checking our vigilance on New Year's Eve. Having sortied as a regiment, we headed out to meet the enemy, but for some reason they shunned combat and headed for home. We had already blocked access to the Anju area, and as we began to run low on fuel we turned back toward base. At an altitude of 9,000 meters I spotted Shooting Stars scurrying around below us against the backdrop of terrain. I reported this to the squadron leader. Major A.F. Maznev authorized our flight to attack them for as long as our fuel would allow.

I and my wingman Astapovsky, together with the leader of the second element Captain A.A. Svintitsky went into a split-S and dove, curving to the right to line up on the fighter-bombers. But at this moment, Svintitsky's wingman Senior Lieutenant I.V. Mart'ianov reported that he didn't have enough fuel to make it back to base, so Captain Svintitsky immediately broke off the attack and set a course back to the airfield.

Now alone, my element pursued the trailing pair of F-80s through a notch in the hills, at an altitude lower than the hilltops on either side. I attacked the F-80 element leader, not seeing his wingman. The enemy wasn't expecting this and was flying calmly (apparently, they had already completed their mission). At very high speed I closed with the F-80 and shot it down quickly. His startled wingman opened fire as I sped by, and his tracers passed 50-80 meters wide of me. We pulled out of the attack into a climb toward the setting sun and headed back to base. Our remaining fuel no longer allowed us to fly back to Miaogou, so we landed at Kozhedub's base at Andong.

In addition to Shchukin's element, the remaining pilots of the group attacked the flights of Shooting Stars, including the group leader on this sortie Lieutenant Colonel A.P. Smorchkov, despite the low fuel reserves. Other than the F-80 downed by Captain Shchukin, the Americans don't recognize the F-80s that were claimed by Lieutenant

Colonel Smorchkov and Captain N.I. Gerasimenko. These three downed F-80s were the final victories of the 64th IAK in 1951.

In the other aerial combat on 31 December, a group of 16 MiGs from the 17th IAP led by the 1st Squadron's deputy commander Captain S.S. Bychkov engaged a group of 24 F-86s. The group had been scrambled between 1405 and 1408 at a call from the division command post. Captain Sutiagin was supposed to lead the group, but his cockpit canopy became coated with a spray of oil as it began to accelerate down the runway, so he and his wingman Perepelkin aborted the take-off and he gave an order to Bychkov to lead the group into combat. Chernozemov and his wingman Zelenov also returned prematurely from the mission because of a break in the hermetic seal around the cockpit of Chernozemov's MiG.

Although this action ended without results for the 17th IAP's pilots, the group carried out its task by repulsing the enemy raid and covering the actions of the 18th GIAP's pilots. The latter pilots downed three enemy aircraft. The commander of the 303rd IAD expressed his gratitude to all the pilots of both regiments, while Captain Bychkov was held up as an example and given a monetary bonus of 150 rubles. A day later the Americans acknowledged the loss of two of their F-80s from the 8th FBG's 80th FBS in this final clash of 1951 – one of the pilots was picked up by a search and rescue team, but the second became a prisoner-of-war, and for him, the war was over.

ENDNOTES

1   The Air Combat Information Group's on-line Korean War database reverses the responsibility for these two kills.

2   Often, a Sabre pilot would capture gun camera footage of an enemy pilot descending in a parachute by firing to one side of him, in order to obtain clear evidence of his victory. Perhaps not surprisingly, the Soviet pilots often felt like they were being targeted in their parachutes.

3   There is inconsistency between the Soviet and American accounts regarding this victory. The Soviet pilots flying the mission assert that Ryzhkov was in fact shot down by an F-80 Shooting Star, but the American records indicate that of the four victories claimed on this day over MiG-15s, all went to the credit of pilots of the 4th FIG flying in their F-86s. So according to the Americans 2nd Lieutenant Robert E. Smith's victory on 1 December 1951, is the final victory by an F-80C Shooting Star pilot over a MiG-15, though the Soviet pilots suffered no losses on this day. Thus, Smith's victory must have been over a Chinese or North Korean MiG-15.

4   The Aviation Archaeological Investigation and Research website lists this F-86E as lost on 14 December 1951.

5

The results of the aerial conflict in 1951

The just concluded year of 1951 was a successful one for the 64th IAK's pilots and proved to be their highest-scoring year of the entire war (see Table 1). According to Soviet records, altogether over the year, the 64th IAK's pilots became involved in 307 group and 16 solitary daytime aerial combats, resulting in 532 downed enemy aircraft (including two night victories) of the following types: 236 F-86, 119 F-84, 82 F-80, 42 B-29, 27 Gloster Meteor, 11 F-51, 8 F-94, 3 B-26, 3 piston-engine ground attack aircraft and 1 RB-45 (these figures excluded damaged aircraft). The figures regarding the F-84 and F-80 can be questioned, since at the start of the war the Soviet pilots often confused these two types in the air and filed mistaken claims when back on the ground. A total of 107 MiG-15s of the 64th IAK received combat damage over the year of 1951, and not quite half as many, 58, were downed. Of those that returned with damage, 36 had damaged engines that continued to work and seven which stopped in the air. All seven of these aircraft with dead engines, thanks to the skill of the pilots, were safely force-landed short of their airfields. Of the damaged aircraft, 96.5% were repaired and returned to service. Thus, the total aircraft losses of the 64th IAK over the year of combat operations, including those downed in combat, destroyed in accidents or later written off, amounted to 70. Among the IAK's aircrews, 29 were killed in combat or flight accidents, and more than 10 received combat wounds.

The number of F-86s lost in 1951, reported by the American side (23 lost in combat, 15 lost due to other reasons, for a total of 38 Sabres) is also not beyond criticism, all the more so given the classification system that was used to produce the figure. The Americans didn't consider an F-86 that fell into the sea or crashed in South Korean territory as downed by combat, but instead assigned these aircraft to the category of "damaged aircraft" that were unable to return to base. In addition, a number of Sabres that received heavy damage in aerial combat from the MiG's powerful cannons, even though they did make it back to base, were subsequently written off as beyond repair.

The Americans and their Western colleagues often exalt the high degree of training and skill of the American pilots, as well as their pugnacious spirit. However, no less experienced Soviet pilots, the majority of whom had passed through the furnace of the Great Patriotic War, opposed the American aces in 1951. The Soviet pilots for the most part were the flower of the Soviet Air Force! Take for example the two fighter aviation divisions, the 303rd IAD and the 324th IAD, which for the greater part of 1951 were assigned to the 64th IAK and bore the main burden of fighting during the year. Both of these divisions had achieved splendid records in the years of the Great Patriotic War, downing hundreds of Luftwaffe aircraft, and their ranks included several dozen pilots

Table 5.1 Results of the combat operations of the 64th IAK in 1951 (according to 64th IAK records)

Division	Subordinate units	Victories	MiG losses	Pilot losses	Period of Combat Operations
324th IAD	176th GIAP	97	13	4	04.51 – 01.01.52
	196th GIAP	100	12	5	04.51 – 01.01.52
303rd IAD	17th IAP	89	5	2	06.51 – 01.01.52
	18th GIAP	85	14	6	05.51 – 01.01.52
	523rd IAP	96	15	5	06.51 – 01.01.52
	Command flight	9	–	–	06.51 – 01.01.52
151st GIAD	28th GIAP	29	3	2	10.01.51 – 01.04.52
	72nd GIAP	4	2	2	01.03.51 – 01.04.51
50th IAD	29th GIAP	14	1	1	01.01.51 – 25.01.51
	177th IAP	9	–	–	01.01.51 – 04.02.52
Totals:		532	65	27	

who were Heroes of the Soviet Union, while many more than 100 of their pilots had achieved five or more victories and became aces in those years. In the 324th IAD alone, approximately 15 Second World War aces fought in the skies of Korea, while more than 20 pilots in the 303rd IAD had earned this status. The regiments of the two divisions were led by five Heroes of the Soviet Union, who had earned this title in the Great Patriotic War, and the 324th IAD was commanded by one of the top aces and pilots of the Soviet Air Force, thrice Hero of the Soviet Union Colonel I.N. Kozhedub. In both divisions, 90% of their pilots at the start of their combat operations in the Korea sky were veterans of the Great Patriotic War or the brief war with Japan.

In addition, both divisions were among the elite of the Soviet Air Force and were "parade" aviation divisions of the Moscow Military District, which took part in all the ceremonial flyovers above Moscow until their departure to China at the end of 1950. Back in 1948, the pilots of these divisions had switched over to flying jet aircraft, and they were the first in the Soviet Air Force to master the early MiG-9, Yak-17, La-15 jet fighters before switching to the up-to-date MiG-15. Thus, these pilots (with the exception of those of the 17th IAP) had accumulated a considerable number of hours of flight time in jet aircraft before the war and were in no way inferior to their American counterparts.

In the course of combat operations in the skies of Korea, the Soviet pilots developed new tactical methods and combat formations, which together with their superior equipment in the form of the MiG-15 fighter allowed them to meet all the assignments given to them and to combat the enemy's aviation successfully. This despite the numerical superiority of the UN air forces and the numerous restrictions under which the Soviet pilots flew and fought.

According to a number of performance indicators (acceleration, rate of climb, ceiling and armament), the MiG-15bis was superior to all the American types of combat aircraft used in the aerial battles of 1951, including the vaunted F-86A-5 – the MiGs' main adversary in 1951. Only the new version of the Sabre, the F-86E, which didn't begin to appear until the end of the year, was comparable to the MiG-15bis across a number of main performance indicators, but still not superior to it. Primarily, the course and outcome of a straight fight between the two fighters was decided by the pilots sitting in the cockpits of the MiGs and Sabres.

Therefore it is odd to read the works of some Western historians, in which they write about the USAF's losses in this war in combats with MiGs, when such losses were plainly understated by the USAF command. In the opposite direction, the US official records exaggerate the number of victories over MiGs by B-29 gunners.[1] It is reliably known that just two MiG-15s (only one of them Soviet) were lost to the fire of B-29 gunners in 1951, and two or three MiGs were damaged, but safely landed back at base. The Americans however assert that their Superfortress gunners downed 24 MiG-15s in 1951, which is plainly out of line with the actual figures.

The other main types of aircraft used by the USAF, USNAF and US Marine Air Wing in the war in Korea had a similar negative score in the combats with MiGs. The official records of the 64th IAK pilots' victories demonstrate this.

Owing to the active and skillful operations of the 64th IAK, the northwestern portion of the North Korea, in which the MiG-15 operated, became known as MiG Alley. American pilots entered this area with some trepidation, knowing full well that if they encountered MiG-15s, a fierce aerial combat awaited them. By the end of 1951, the Americans entered MiG Alley only in large groups with heavy fighter cover, which nevertheless didn't prevent them from taking heavy losses in combats with the MiGs. Primarily all of the military and industrial sites in the northern area of North Korea, as well as in northeastern China, were reliably covered from the air and thanks to the self-less actions of the 64th IAK's pilots continued to function throughout 1951.

Over the year, the 64th IAK command established an extensive network of radar stations and auxiliary control posts throughout the territory of North Korea in the IAK's zone of responsibility. This perceptibly enhanced the ability of the 64th IAK command to direct its units in combat and facilitated the detection of enemy air groups.

Here's what the radar chief at one of the GCI [Ground Control-Intercept] posts, Senior Lieutenant Mikhail Shats, had to say:

> If previously individual reconnaissance aircraft "visited" the controlled area, with the start of combat operations their flights greatly increased in frequency. Special aircraft regularly dropped off and picked up saboteurs. In the initial period, the penetration of combat aircraft into the area of MiG Alley was episodic, but after a certain amount of time it became the primary combat arena. Enhanced radar sets, which arrived to replace the old ones, from the start of the war secured thorough coverage of enemy air operations to the entire depth of combat operations out to a radius of 200 kilometers over the territory of the PRC and the PDRK.

The network of airfields closer to the North Korean border was also expanded. For example, at the beginning of 1951 all of the 64th IAK's units were operating from just the Andong airfield alone, on the territory of neighboring Manchuria. In May 1951, a new airfield at Miaogou became operational, and at the end of the year, construction of the Dapu airfield was completed, which expanded the 64th IAK's possibilities and facilitated the staging of combat missions over North Korean territory.

Also in 1951, the young PLAAF, which supported the operations of the CPV and NKPA forces on the ground in North Korea, entered the fighting. The UAA, which included the aviation units of the re-born KPAF and the PLAAF, was estalished. Although in 1951 only two divisions of the PLAAF (the 3rd IAD and 4th IAD) primarily took part in combat, the introduction of these two divisions into combat operations somewhat eased the burden on the 64th IAK, though we'll note that the number of combat sorties conducted by the Chinese pilots in the course of any month was three to four times fewer than those of the Soviet pilots. The young Chinese pilots fought courageously and selflessly, acquiring invaluable combat experience of fighting in jet aircraft against the powerful and modern US aviation. True, their losses were high, but became fewer with each passing month, while their number of victories grew.

Soviet pilots in the years 1950-1951 on PRC territory not only trained several hundred Chinese pilots to fly the jet MiG-15s and how to use them in combat, which strengthened the combat power of the fledgling jet aviation of the PLAAF, but also shared with them the combat experience that they had acquired in the Great Patriotic War and in the modern conditions of jet warfare in Korea. The Soviet Union had military advisers posted with every UAA regiment and division.

The language barrier, the absence of leading domestic aviators, and a number of other factors complicated the training of our allies' pilot recruits. In these conditions, the fledgling pilots of the Chinese and North Korean aviation divisions became easy prey for the American aces. Thus, at the request of the UAA leadership, Soviet pilots prepared them for combat operations and then covered their combat missions. Our pilots assumed the burden of repulsing the major enemy groups of bombers and fighter-bombers, flying under heavy F-86 cover. The fighter units of the UAA primarily conducted combat operations only against small groups of enemy aircraft that lacked the Sabre cover. During massive enemy air raids, which were the primary way the enemy operated in the area covered by the 64th IAK, the UAA fighters were not scrambled. Our aviators continued to carry out the more complex missions even when the UAA's aircraft park at the forward airfields of Andong, Miaogou, Dapu and Dagushan exceeded the number of MiGs in the 64th IAK.

To equip the UAA, in 1950-1951 the Soviet Union delivered more than a hundred jet MiG-9s, Yak-23s and Yak-17Us, as well as several hundred combat MiG-15s, which in 1951 equipped six new fighter aviation divisions of the PLAAF and one aviation division of the KPAF. True, in April 1951 only two Chinese IAD, the 3rd and the 4th, each of which by the end of the year had 50 combat-ready MiG-15s, entered combat. It was not until October 1951 that the KPAF's 435th IAD receive its MiG-15s from the Soviet 151st GIAD, the pilots of which were engaged in training the North Korean pilots to fly the MiG-15. However, because of the Korean aircrews' low-level of flight and combat training, the North Korean aviation division stayed in reserve.

Measures to increase the production and delivery of aircraft to the conflict area were undertaken by the Soviet leadership in the summer and autumn of 1951, in order to bring the number of combat-ready MiGs in the Soviet military contingent up to 100, which led to a change in the correlation of forces in a direction better for North Korea. With the completion of the Miaogou airfield in the summer of 1951 and the arrival of the three-regiment 303rd IAD from the USSR, the 64th IAK's combat strength swelled from 60 to 150 combat-ready MiGs.

To this it can also be added that as of 1 July 1951, the 64th IAK had 304 combat-ready and 14 unserviceable MiG-15bis, and from the middle to the end of 1951 approximately 450 jet MiG-15s fought in the Korean sky, although in the largest aerial battles of 1951, at the most up to 100 MiGs took part simultaneously. However, even this was a rare exception, since in the course of such large battles, normally the 64th IAK rotated units into and out of the combat area. As one unit was leaving due to low fuel and ammunition, a fresh unit would arrive to replace it, thereby extending the duration of the MiGs' presence in the area of the raid until the raid was repulsed.

American historians in various publications mislead the reader and report that just a "handful" of F-86s, numbering 150 fighters (each fighter interceptor wing had 75 F-86 Sabres), was opposing this Red "armada", and at that, the Americans only reached this number of Sabres with the introduction of the 51st FIW in its new F-86Es into combat in December 1951. However, besides these two fighter wings, five fighter-bomber groups of F-80 Shooting Stars and F-84 Thunderchiefs, one fighter-bomber group of F-51 Mustangs, two groups of B-26 light bombers, and three groups of B-29 medium bombers flew missions into MiG Alley, and this doesn't include the Fifth Air Force's reconnaissance and airlift units in South Korea. This also excludes the 300 aircraft from the other UN participants in the war (Australia, Canada, Great Britain, South Africa and South Korea), and all of the US Navy's and Marine Corps' air units. Thus, taken altogether the UN air forces in Korea amounted to more than 2,000 combat aircraft alone, the raids of which were opposed by a total of 400-450 MiGs of the 64th IAK and the UAA.

However, despite the quantitative superiority of the UN air forces over the 64th IAK and the UAA, their loss of aircraft in Korea in 1951 was rather palpable and consisted of several hundred USAF and USNAF aircraft lost in aerial combats with the MiGs. Even though the Americans assert that their combat losses due to the MiGs were insignificant and didn't exceed several dozen over the year (for example, only 38 Sabres were lost on combat sorties in 1951, according to American records), all these data don't square with those reorganizations that shook up the US Fifth Air Force in South Korea in 1951.

If the losses in combats with MiGs were really so insignificant, and the superiority of the Fifth Air Force's fighter units in equipment and pilot training was so significant, as some Western historians have asserted in their works, then why were piston-engine aircraft withdrawn from the area of MiG operations, like the F-51 fighter-bomber groups, followed by the B-29s? Why did the US Navy's carrier-based aircraft cease making raids within the 64th IAK's operational zone? Why were two fighter interceptor wings equipped with the latest fighter, the F-86, urgently hurried to the theater of combat operations? It was precisely in order to defend the bulk of the UN air force in Korea from MiG attacks, because without the protection of Sabres, the remaining types of UN aircraft were simply unable to carry out their combat missions without incurring heavy losses. Clearly, it was because the losses suffered by the air units that were equipped with aircraft other than the F-86 were quite heavy in combats with the MiGs, and the American command plainly had no wish to risk the lives of its pilots needlessly.

Thanks to the successful operations of the Soviet MiGs of the 64th IAK, by the end of 1951 those UN air units equipped with F-51 Mustangs had been fully driven out of the

IAK's operational zone, and except for the 35th FBG, they were re-equipped with F-80 Shooting Stars, as was the case with the 8th FBG and the 18th FBG. Indeed, factually speaking, all of the Mustang units were then restricted to operating in the southern areas of the PDRK, which were outside the 64th IAK's zone of operations.

The losses in the medium bomber groups that were equipped with B-29 bombers (these were the 19th, 98th and 307th BG) were so heavy, especially in the month of October 1951, that General Vandenberg banned all further daytime flights by B-29s, and was forced to acknowledge in November 1951: "Although superiority in the air over North Korea has not by any means been lost completely, it has now ceased to be as complete as it once was." From the end of 1951, the B-29 bombers flew combat missions into MiG Alley only at night. The creation of an anti-aircraft defense of the PDRK, which gradually extended southward from the Yalu, significantly restricted the use of the B-29 squadrons.

With the aim of strengthening its tottering superiority in the air, the USAF command in November 1951 stripped 75 of the new F-86E Sabres from the roster of the US Air Defense Command and sent them to Korea, where they were delivered to the 51st FIW to replace the F-80C fighters and F-84E fighter interceptors, which had proven to be ineffective in combats with the MiG-15.

The F-80 Shooting Stars themselves began to be employed only as fighter-bombers, and at that, only with heavy immediate escort by F-84E Thunderjets and cover of F-86 Sabres. The F-84E Thunderjet fighters, which had arrived in December 1950, had also been unable to cope with its role as a covering fighter. By many measures, they were inferior to the MiG-15 in combat and also suffered heavy losses in aerial combats. Thus, in June 1951 the single Thunderjet wing, the 27th FEW, was re-designated as the 138th FBW and began to fly missions as fighter-bombers that were also covered by F-86E fighter interceptors. Further, in order to boost the attack strength of raids into MiG Alley, the new 116th FBW with its F-84Es arrived in South Korea in December 1951 and joined the Fifth Air Force, to replace piston-engine strike aircraft that had been dropped from active operations.

In addition, in 1950-1951 three squadrons equipped with the piston-engine F-82 Twin Mustang escort fighter, the 4th, 68th and 339th All-Weather Squadrons, operated as part of the Fifth Air Force in South Korea. Two of them flew the F-82 only until December 1951, and then because of the low effectiveness of the Twin Mustangs in combat operations in Korea, both of them were withdrawn from the Fifth Air Force and departed South Korea. All three of these F-82 squadrons were active only in November 1950, but after several unsuccessful encounters with MiGs, and seeing the complete fruitlessness of using the given fighter type as an escort fighter in an area where MiGs were operating, they were all redirected to operate against ground targets as fighter-bombers in the southern portion of North Korea, where there was less of a chance of running into MiGs.

Concluding this review of the combat results of 1951, a few words must be said about the US allies in this war. Great Britain in the Korean War was represented only by several air squadrons that flew from Royal Navy aircraft carriers, which actively launched raids into the area protected by the 64th IAK only in November-December 1950, but in 1951 they shifted operations to the area of the 38th Parallel beyond the MiGs' operational radius. The South Korean 1st Squadron and the South African Air Force's 2nd

Squadron, which flew F-51s in 1951, appeared in the area of the Yalu River together with other Mustang-equipped squadrons from the USAF under heavy cover from American fighters, but this didn't save them from heavy losses due to anti-aircraft fire, as well as in encounters with MiGs. In regard to the Royal Australian Air Force's sole combat air squadron in Korea, No. 77 Fighter Squadron, it can be said safely that in the summer-autumn combats of 1951 with MiGs from the 64th IAK, it was simply decimated, and after the heavy losses of 1 December 1951, it fully shifted to operations against ground targets in the southern areas of North Korea, closer to the 38th Parallel, and was reclassified as fighter-bomber.

Since the beginning of 1951, the strength of the 64th IAK by the middle of 1951 had almost doubled, which genuinely altered the course of the air war in the skies of Korea. An end was put to the superiority of the USAF and its allies in the sky over the PDRK and, especially in the zone of responsibility of the Soviet 64th IAK, to the impunity of the unrestrained bombing of North Korean territory. Although this sphere of influence and control over the area of combat operations didn't extend to every corner of the PDRK, the territory contested by the UAA and the 64th IAK expanded ever further to the south, to the Pyongyang-Wonsan no-fly line, and presented a genuine obstacle to the successful completion of combat missions by the air forces of the United States and its allies. Granted that the UN retained a quantitative superiority in Korea, this component no longer gave them complete sway in the Korean sky, which compelled the US Fifth Air Force to change its tactics and strategy in the oncoming year of 1952.

ENDNOTE

1. The author is obviously relying upon dated Western sources to make this point. Recent scholarship on the Korean Air War has been far more objective and recognizes the qualities of the MiG-15. As for exaggerated claims by bomber gunners, this was a problem in every air force in the Second World War. When multiple gunners are firing on the same target and it seems to go down, each gunner will likely file a victory claim for the same target. Even if the target was damaged, the enemy pilot not uncommonly was able to recover from the spin or plunge at a lower altitude. So while the American claims likely are exaggerated, this is not a cynical or deliberate manipulation of the figures.

6

The final combats of the "parade" divisions

The New Year began with fresh aerial battles in the Anju area, since war has no scheduled days off or holidays. The 64th IAK entered January 1952 with its same roster of two fighter aviation divisions, one of which was organized according to the two-regiment table of organization. However, the regiments of these two divisions were barely still combat-capable with respect to both equipment and pilots. While equipment shortages could be replaced rather quickly, the situation with the aircrews stood much worse. Over the four autumn-winter months of the previous year, which were glutted with active combats in MiG Alley, the intensity of the combat operations and the enormous burden that lay on the shoulders of each of the IAK's pilots were simply immeasurable. The stresses in combats with the enemy air force were very high, and many of our pilots were now no longer physically able to withstand such heavy loads and were breaking down. Here, for example, is a list of incidents in December 1951 alone in just the 17th IAP, all of which were related to the to the pilots' deteriorating condition:

1. At an altitude of 12,000 meters, Senior Lieutenant Kramarenko blacked out and fell into a spin. He regained consciousness at 6,000 meters and pulled his MiG out of the spin.
2. Captain Ponomarev was fading into and out of consciousness at an altitude of 7,000 meters as he was flying in the group, lost his ability to judge space, and maintained his position within the formation only with great difficulty by guiding on his wingman.
3. On one mission, Senior Lieutenant Bashlykov vomited directly into his oxygen mask, and he almost collided with the group leader Major Pulov.
4. Senior Lieutenant Polianichko suffered a heart attack after landing his MiG.

However, this is only a small sample of the manifestations of pilots becoming incapacitated by the accumulated stress and physical burdens; their total number was much higher.

If one looks at the size of the regimental groups that flew the missions in December 1951, then it is obvious that by this time the number of crews committed to a combat sortie had dwindled by a third, and in the 324th IAD, by almost half. This is in fact understandable; after all, the pilots of the 324th IAD had entered combat in the skies of Korea two months prior to those of the 303rd IAD; hence the greater number of incapacitated pilots. Many of the Soviet pilots by this point were flying at the limit of their physical strength, and their doctors were constantly giving them injections to boost their strength. However, this situation couldn't continue for long, and the question about the need to replace the 303rd IAD and 324th IAD with fresh fighter aviation divisions had long since become ripe. This could not be done quickly, though, and required time; thus the January battles drained the aviation divisions of the 64th IAK of their final strength.

Their coalition allies, the pilots of the UAA, did give the Soviet pilots help in January. The 3rd IAD and 4th IAD, which left at the end of December 1951 for rest and refitting, were replaced in December and the beginning of January 1952 by the UAA's 6th and 15th IAD, which were both equipped with MiG-15 fighters. The new IAD for the most part operated in large groups, trying to deprive the enemy of aerial superiority between the Yalu and Chongchon Rivers. Chinese historians have not forgotten to mention that the commander of the US Far Eastern Air Force Lieutenant General Weyland had to acknowledge that it was becoming increasingly difficult to interdict the supply lines. Of the departing Chinese aviation divisions, the 3rd IAD had performed the best: over 86 days in the autumn of 1951 the 3rd IAD downed or damaged 64 American aircraft. In return, it recorded 23 MiG-15s as destroyed or damaged.

Already on 1 January 1952, the pilots of the 303rd IAD flew their first three combat sorties of the new year, with the pilots of the 18th GIAP and 523rd IAP participating in all three missions, while the 17th IAP took part in two of them. The latter two regiments both encountered Sabres on one of their missions. Thus, 12 MiGs of the 523rd IAP became involved in a brief but fierce dogfight with a group of 18 F-86s in the Chongju area between 1020 and 1030, in which deputy regiment commander Major G.U. Okhai, who was leading the regimental group, and the 1st Squadron commander Captain S.A. Bakhaev each claimed one Sabre. The regiment returned to base from this mission without any losses.

However, the day didn't go by without a loss in the division, unfortunately. In the first morning battle of the day, which took place around 0900 and involved 20 MiGs of the 17th IAP and a group of Sabres, 1st squadron flight commander Senior Lieutenant F.G. Malunov was shot down by hits to his engine. Something struck his head, which caused his vision to dim, and bullets also shot up his instrument panel, knocking out many of his instruments. Malunov ejected at 11,000 meters, then fumbled for his oxygen mask, which had been ripped off during the ejection, and put it back in place. Freeing himself from his seat, he waited until he dropped to an altitude of 4,000-5,000 meters before opening his parachute. He came down in the vicinity of the Kaechon airfield. Strangely, no one in the 4th or 51st FIW took credit for this victory; apparently, the victor or victors believed his MiG was only damaged. But the Americans do confirm the loss of F-86E No.50-0635 of the 51st FIW's 16th Squadron. Its pilot with the Ukrainian surname 1st Lieutenant John Lagoyda was killed in action on this first day of the new year. Most likely, Captain Bakhaev of the 523rd IAP shot him down.

In general, the entire month of January 1952 was marked by bitter dogfights only with F-86A and F-86E fighter interceptors from the 4th and 51st FIW. This resulted from the arrival of the 51st FIW, now equipped with the new F-86E. The Americans were trying to seize the initiative in MiG Alley, thereby securing favorable conditions for their fighter-bombers' operations. Therefore, they would send out several groups of Sabres of the wings in advance of a major fighter-bomber raid in order to tie up the MiGs of the 64th IAK in combat, trying to prevent them from reaching the fighter-bombers.

Thus, in January 1952 even before the arrival of the large raids by fighter-bombers in the area of MiG Alley, savage combats were occurring between the pilots of the 303rd IAD and 324th IAD on the one side, and the pilots of the 51st FIW on the other, who were hungry for victories. The first clash of the 51st FIW's pilots with MiGs on 1 January 1952, as already noted above, ended with the death of one of its pilots. Yet on 3 January, the top ace of the 4th FIW Captain James Jabara came under attack from a MiG; his F-86A No.49-1318 was damaged and he brought it back to his base in Suwon with difficulty. Senior Lieutenant N.S. Volkov damaged Jabara's Sabre in an afternoon combat that involved 20 MiGs of the 17th IAP and 30 F-86s of the 4th FIW. This was the regiment's most notable victory!

On 5 January while repelling a morning enemy raid (at 1039) in the Sukchon-Chongju area, a group of 16 MiGs from the 523rd IAP intercepted a pair of F-84s that were on their way back to base after participating in a strike against a ground target. Lieutenant Colonel A.N. Karasev and his wingman Senior Lieutenant D.A. Samoilov attacked the Thunderjets and damaged both of them, which headed toward the sea in a dive. Both F-84Es were from the 136th FBG's 111th FBS. The pilot of one of them, 1st Lieutenant Ray J. Greenway, Jr. managed to fly back to his K-2 base in Taegu in his damaged F-84 No.51-674, but crashed upon landing and was killed.

The first serious clash of the new year between the adversaries took place on 6 January 1952. Groups of MiGs from all five regiments of both of the 64th IAK's divisions took part in it as each side fed more forces into the growing battle. A group of 12 to 18 MiGs was formed from each combat-ready crew and serviceable MiG in each regiment of the 303rd IAD and 324th IAD. In this battle our pilots faced their adversaries from the 51st FIW, represented by the 16th and 25th Fighter Interceptor Squadrons numbering a total of 50 Sabres.

The first to become engaged in combat were the two regimental groups from the 303rd IAD's 17th IAP and 18th GIAP, which spotted a large group of Sabres flying in groups of eight over the Anju area. In the course of the dogfight, two more groups of MiGs from the 324th IAD's 176th GIAP and 196th IAP arrived in the combat area, which finished the action that the 303rd IAD's pilots had started.

The pilots of the 17th IAP scored particularly well in this morning action, claiming six downed and two damaged Sabres, two of which fell to the cannon fire from Captain Sutiagin's MiG. Here in more detail is show this dogfight unfolded, based on the post-mission reports of the 17th IAP's pilots:

Between 0930 and 0932, radar detected up to 100 enemy fighters and fighter-bombers at an altitude of 8,000 to 9,000 meters in an area 25-30 kilometers south of Chinnampo, flying on a heading of 340-350° in groups of 8-16 and 24 aircraft. At an order of the division command post, 22 MiGs of the 17th IAP under the command of Lieutenant Colonel Pulov took off to intercept the enemy aircraft in the Anju – Sukchon – Sunchon area, with the assignment to cover the action of the 324th IAD's pilots.

Arriving in the Sunchon area at an altitude of 9,000 meters, the group conducted a 180° turn to starboard and began to descend. In the Taechon area at an altitude 8,000 meters, the group began to go into a turn to the left. Having turned 60-70°, Captain Sutiagin noticed four F-86s above and to the right that were diving onto the tail of group commander Pulov's flight. Sutiagin warned the group commander about the enemy, and Pulov led his flight into a chandelle to port. When coming out of the climbing turn,

Pulov spotted a flight of F-86s approaching from the left and below, and went into a diving turn to the left toward them. When the enemy spotted our closing MiGs, one pair went into a split-S and dove away, while the second pair went into a turn to port, which Pulov began to follow. In the second spiral, Shulev, having closed to within 600 meters of the lead Sabre, opened fire, and the Sabre tumbled out of control and began to fall.

Captain Sutiagin, having warned the group leader about the enemy, pulled out of the turn to port, allowed the enemy to pass them from right to left, and went in pursuit. Captain S.S. Bychkov's flight covered Captain Sutiagin's element. The enemy caught sight of the pursuing MiGs and began to go into a descending spiral to the left. After two turns around, the lead Sabre suddenly straightened out and Sutiagin, having closed to within 600 meters of him, opened fire. The shells found their target, and the Sabre spun downward out of control.

Having formed back up with Bychkov's flight, Sutiagin received information from Bychkov: "Four Sabres above and to the right." Sutiagin immediately issued the command: "We're going on the attack", and banking to the left in a climb, he emerged 1,000-1,200 meters behind the enemy. The lead Sabre element continued straight ahead, but the second element went into a descending spiral to the left, which Sutiagin began to follow. In the second loop around Captain Bychkov, who was turning inside Captain Sutiagin's aircraft, emerged in front of him and began to close with the Sabre element, which responded by leveling out and entering a dive of 60-70°. Bychkov drew to within 700 meters of the wingman's Sabre and opened fire. The Sabre crashed into the ground at the same dive angle.

During the pursuit, Senior Lieutenant N.Ia. Perepelkin fell behind by 700-800 meters and spotted a solitary Sabre in front of him, which was trying to attack Captain Sutiagin. Perepelkin gave the Sabre two bursts as he closed the range from 400 to 200 meters, and the target rolled over to the left into a dive. Perepelkin passed over him and lost sight of the Sabre. Captain Bychkov after the attack pulled up into a chandelle to port. While in the climbing turn, Sutiagin caught sight of two F-86s to the right that were attacking Captain Bychkov. He opened fire on the lead Sabre from a range of 350 meters and continued to fire as the range closed to 200 meters. Meanwhile, Captain Bychkov's wingman Senior Lieutenant N.N. Kramarenko opened fire on the wingman's F-86 from a range of 600 meters. Both pilots observed hits on the targeted Sabres, and both pilots claimed victories upon their return to base.

Captain N.G. Dokashenko's 3rd Squadron at an altitude of 9,000 meters in the Anju area encountered four F-86s above and to the right of them flying on a parallel course. At the direction of the group leader, Dokashenko went in pursuit of the enemy, who noticed the MiGs behind them and reversed course to the right in a dive. After coming out of the dive, the Sabres straightened out and pulled into a zoom climb, at the end of which three Sabres turned to starboard, while one Sabre split off into a descending turn to port.

Senior Lieutenant N.S. Volkov's flight began to pursue the three Sabres in their turn to right, while Dokashenko's flight swung around to the left and went after the solitary Sabre. The F-86 responded with a dive below and became lost from the Soviet pilots' sight against the backdrop of the terrain. However, at this moment Dokashenko noticed a pair of F-86s out in front of them, below and to the right, which was stalking four MiGs flying on the same heading. Dokashenko banked to the right and went into a dive onto the tail of this Sabre element, which spotting the MiGs behind them, broke right into a steeply descending spiral. After looping around once, the Sabres leveled out, and then made a starboard turn of 90°. Dokashenko led his flight into a spiral to the right while keeping an eye on the adversary. After the starboard turn, the Sabres straightened out and reversed into a climbing turn to the left, but seeing that the MiGs were still pursuing them, they went into a split-S and headed toward the south. Dokashenko pursued the Sabres to the no-fly line, after which he broke off the chase with a climb.

Volkov's flight chased the three Sabres to the coastline, after which it turned and headed toward Anju, where Volkov caught sight of a pair of F-86s that were stalking two MiGs. Volkov attempted to attack the Sabres, but their the pilots noticed this and broke off their pursuit of the MiGs with a climbing turn to the left. During the climbing turn, Volkov pulled to within 700-800 meters of the wingman's Sabre and opened fire. The Sabre flipped over and dove away in the direction of the sea. Senior Lieutenant Volkov then exited the dogfight.

The 2nd Squadron under the command of Major M.S. Ponomarev, flying at an altitude of 10,000 meters in an area 10-15 kilometers south of Pakchon, caught sight of four F-86s out in front of them, below and to the left, which were in the process of making a turn to the left. Major Ponomarev led his flight into a pursuit curve toward the enemy. When in the turn, Senior Lieutenant G.T. Fokin spotted two F-86s swinging in behind his element from below and to the right. Fokin tightened their turn and with a climb gained separation from their pursuers. After evading the attack, Fokin noticed a Sabre in hot pursuit of one MiG, and opened fire on it from a range of 200-300 meters. Fokin stayed with this Sabre, while his wingman Senior Lieutenant A.A. Komarov gave it another burst across its front in the effort to make the F-86 break back in front of Fokin's cannons. The Sabre instead went into a split-S and dove away.

Major Ponomarev and his wingman, following a Sabre flight, spotted a Sabre that was attacking a MiG. Ponomarev banked sharply to the right toward this Sabre and gave it a long burst across its path. The Sabre evaded the stream of fire with a steep turn to the right, after which it fell went into a spin, made three or four revolutions and became lost from view. At this moment Ponomarev sighted two F-86s about 500-600 meters directly in front of him and about 1,000 meters above him, flying on the same heading. Ponomarev raised the nose of his MiG and gave the wingman's Sabre three medium-length bursts. The target rolled over and dove away.

This action lasted for 12-15 minutes. As noted above, the 17th IAP's pilots claimed six downed Sabres and two damaged Sabres in their post-mission reports. The pilots of the 196th IAP in this morning battle also downed one Sabre, which was credited to regiment commander Colonel E.G. Pepeliaev.

Only the 324th IAD's pilots took part in the second dogfight of the day: 20 MiGs of the 176th GIAP and 16 MiGs of the 196th IAP had a successful engagement with a group of 36 F-86s, in which Senior Lieutenant A.P. Golovev downed one Sabre that fell in the Siarenkan area. The 303rd IAD's 18th GIAP flew one sortie to the area of Chongju, where they also became involved in a brief tussle with a group of F-86s, from which the Soviet pilots returned with no victory claims.

The pilots of the 51st FIW suffered a major defeat at the hands of the 64th IAK's MiGs on this day. According to the records of the 64th IAK's headquarters, nine Sabres failed to return to their base. The losses on our side consisted of just one MiG-15, in which flight commander Vasilii Ivanovich Stepanov of the 18th GIAP was killed. He had scored five victories in the skies of Korea prior to his death. In the course of a dogfight, his MiG was damaged and he flew back to the Miaogou airfield in the crippled fighter, but when landing the MiG, it overshot the runway, struck a protective wall, somersaulted, and Stepanov was killed in the crash.

This was the 64th IAK's sole loss on this day, though many MiGs returned from combat with bullet holes in them, but without damage that required a lot of work from the ground crews and technicians to repair. The American side claimed that pilots of the 25th FIS downed 5 MiGs on 6 January, one of which was credited to this squadron's commander, Colonel Walker M. "Bud" Mahurin, which opened his combat score in this war. However, it isn't known how the Americans reached this number. There are likely two possible explanations. Either the four extra MiGs belonged to the UAA (that is, of course, if the Chinese took part in the combat on this day, though this author doesn't have this information), or else damaged or presumably downed MiGs were registered as "victories" for the pilots of the 25th FIS.

However, the Soviet pilots may have made the same error, as the Americans only acknowledge the loss of one F-86E, No.50-0655 of the 25th FIS, and its pilot 1st Lieutenant Lester F. Page went missing-in-action. It is possible that not all of the nine F-86E claimed by the Soviet side actually fell in North Korean territory, and several of them were also probably only damaged, but of course, more Sabres were shot down than the one F-86E that the Americans assert. Here, for example, is a document received from the 87th Anti-aircraft Artillery Division's 1777th Anti-aircraft Regiment that confirms the two victories by Captain Sutiagin:

CONFIRMATION

On 6 January 1952 at 1030 in the area of an aerial combat, 2 (two) enemy aircraft of the type F-86 Sabre were downed. The aircraft were downed in the aerial combat; their fall was observed by the entire personnel of the MAIKIN pp 43769 [the postal code name and address of the unit].

In addition, EMEL'IANOV personally observed falling aircraft in the distance, and fixed the crash sites in the area of Point 770 (map scale 1:500000), 20 kilometers away from the settlement of Ododo.

/EMEL'YANOV/

/MOSKOVIN/

/SULTANOV/

/ROGOZHIN/

I confirm the authenticity of the indicated comrades' signatures
CHIEF OF STAFF OF UNIT PP 43769

/TULIN/

Authenticated: CHIEF OF STAFF OF UNIT PP 53854 [17th IAP]

/DANILOV/

13 January 1952

Two F-86s, downed on 06.01.52 by the unit's deputy commander for aerial combat technique and aerial gunnery Major Sutiagin fell near the point of Ododo, which is 17 kilometers northeast of Sunchon.

[Source: TsAMO, Op. 303 iad, 539831, D. 1 Summary combat reports, p. 118]

Of the total number of registered victories over Sabres in this battle, six were credited to the pilots of the 17th IAP, and one Sabre each was credited to the pilots of the 18th GIAP, 176th GIAP and 196th IAP. The 523rd IAP was kept in reserve. Incidentally, the Americans also confirm the loss of two of their F-84Es from the 49th FBG's 7th FBS, the pilots of which were killed, and there is the supposition that MiGs downed both of them. It is fully possible that they were shot down by pilots of the PLAAF 6th IAD or 15th IAD. If such is indeed the case, then the victories claimed by the 51st FIW's pilots were mainly over pilots of the UAA.

The next battle between the pilots of the 51st FIW and the 64th IAK's pilots took place on the following day, 7 January. The day featured only one combat with the Sabres, which involved 16 pilots of the 196th IAP headed by its commander, Colonel E.G. Pepeliaev. These men comprised all of the 196th IAP's active-duty aircrews that day, because many of the pilots had become totally worn out by the nearly daily combats with the accompanying extreme stresses and associated high G-loads; they'd either been sent to a sanatorium for rest or had returned to the Soviet Union.

Against the regiment's 16 MiGs, the Americans hurled the 51st FIW's 16th and 25th FIS, and in the resulting combat the regiment's pilots claimed four Sabres, losing just one of its MiGs in return – the 2nd Squadron's deputy commander Captain B.S. Abakumov was shot down. He was wounded in his cockpit, ejected, and came down on North Korean territory, where he was picked up by the Koreans and delivered to a hospital. Here is how Boris Sergeevich Abakumov himself describes his final victory in the skies of Korea:

> In the beginning of January 1952 one of E.Ia. Savitsky's PVO divisions [Savitsky was the deputy commander of the Soviet PVO] arrived at our base so that our regiment could be rotated out of Manchuria. It was rated as the top PVO division in terms of combat training and had received an "Excellent" evaluation from Air Marshal F.A. Agal'tsov [the deputy commander responsible for inspection with the Soviet Air Force's Main Command]. They arrived without equipment or its ground echelon, so our technicians and mechanics had to remain behind until the next rotation.
>
> We methodically and responsibly prepared our replacements for their combat performance duties. At first the training was classroom: we explained the conditions, the enemy's tactics and so forth; on 5 January I even presented a lecture on the tactics of the enemy fighters in this area. Then we began familiarization flights over the area of combat operations with them and introduced our newly arrived comrades to their combat duties.
>
> On the morning of 7 January, my wingman Nikolai Vermin fell ill, so they gave me one of flight commander Ivan Khimchenko's wingmen. I had to fly with him, because there was no other option – at this time the regiment had only 16 able-bodied pilots reporting for duty. The entire regiment took off (as eight pairs) in response to an alert. I took off leading the second element of the first flight, covering the lead element of the regiment's deputy commander A.I. Mitusov. Our flight was to be the top group and from there we were to dive on the all the Sabres below us.
>
> When we reached the combat area, our pilots were already engaged with the enemy. I checked my wingman's position and saw that he was holding very far and wide of me. I gave him the command to close up. He pulled in closer, but soon he

again fell behind and in one of the turns became completely separated from me. He formed up with the lower group and entered combat with them.

Alone, I continued to cover Mitusov's element. Our threesome flew deep into North Korea at an altitude of 12,000 meters. We saw 12 F-86s approaching us at a slightly higher altitude. As we passed them, they rolled into a split-S and tried to attack us from behind. We smoothly put our aircraft into a climb and left the enemy below us. Another eight-ship formation of Sabres appeared, closing in from a higher altitude, but they hadn't yet regained the speed that they had shed in their climb to that position. The Sabres allowed us to pass below them, before rolling in behind us in a dive. The situation had become critical; at any cost we had to regain our altitude advantage over the enemy, which would ease our entire group's combat. But we had no speed, and hence, no ability to maneuver.

I decided to engage the Sabre squadron alone, which might allow Mitusov's element to maneuver freely. I passed my decision to the leader over the radio and went into a maneuver calculated to entice the enemy, which loved to attack solitary aircraft. They remained true to themselves: all eight Sabres went for me. The altitude was around 14,000 meters. A pilot has to handle the controls a bit more gently at this altitude. I understood this, but the enemy was pressing me, so I had to go into vertical combat. I abruptly rolled over to the left into a dive in order to regain speed. Mitusov's element could now gain altitude and go on the attack, thereby bailing me out of my predicament. However, as it turned out, there was a third echelon of this enemy group above us – four F-86s, which Aleksei Mitusov and Misha Borovkov engaged. They downed one Sabre and the remaining three F-86s dived away. Now there was no more enemy above Mitusov and Borovkov, which was an achievement. Mitusov could now come to my help, but it was already too late ...

During all this time, I alone faced the squadron of Sabres. In the course of the combat, I managed to swing in behind one enemy element, went on the attack and opened targeted fire at the leader of this pair. When pulling out of the attack, I momentarily blacked out due to the high-Gs, and when I regained consciousness, the leader of the enemy element was nowhere to be seen. I had no time to look around before bullets began to drum against my left wing. I felt a strong blow against my left hand, which was on the throttle, and for some reason it became very heavy. Some sort of gray shroud arose before my eyes. I jerked the control column to the right to get out from under the fire. My cockpit lost pressure, which I could feel in my ears. I glanced back and saw another enemy element, and I barely managed to evade their fire. Coming out of that maneuver, I went on the attack against it, but received a dose of heavy-caliber bullets from a different enemy element that I hadn't seen. The enemy fighters, it turns out, had broken down into separate pairs that took turns waiting for the moment when I would pull out of an attack against the other. My instrument panel caught fire from an armor-piercing bullet. I yanked the control column back into my belly, but the MiG didn't respond to the controls. The fire in my cockpit grew. I had lost all control. The aircraft's nose rose and then fell to the left. The next burst wounded me in the shoulder. At that time I decided to eject. Koreans picked me up on the ground and took me to a nearby village, where I was brought to a hospital, because I was in a lot of pain. On 1 February the pilots of our division departed for the Soviet Union, but I had to remain for a time in the hospital, so I didn't leave for the Motherland until the end of February.

The commander of the 196th IAP Colonel E.G. Pepeliaev downed one of the four Sabres in this combat. This was his 18th victory in the skies of Korea. His victim was a pilot of the 25th FIS, 1st Lieutenant Charles E. Stahl, who was flying F-86E No.51-651 and became a prisoner-of-war. The Americans do not report any other losses. The 64th IAK headquarters summarizes this combat action in the following account:

> At 08:49, the 196th IAP encountered a group of up to 40 F-86 aircraft at an altitude of 10,000 meters in the vicinity of Pihyon. The battle lasted 15-16 minutes between the altitudes of 7,000 and 10,000 meters and drifted toward Anju. Ten of the pilots fired on enemy aircraft. Four F-86s were downed. Colonel Pepeliaev, Lieutenant Colonel Mitusov, Captain Zaplavnev and Senior Lieutenant Rud'ko each downed one enemy aircraft.

The Americans claimed two MiG-15s destroyed in this combat, but it is known with certainty that only one MiG was downed, so the Americans were plainly mistaken about the other MiG.

On the next day the 64th IAK's pilots claimed two more downed Sabres, which were credited to Senior Lieutenant B.P. Sapozhnikov of the 18th GIAP and the commander of the 196th IAP Colonel E.G. Pepeliaev. We avoided any losses in these combats. The Americans only confirm damage to one F-86E No.50-0679 from the 336th FIS, the pilot of which managed to bring it safely back to base, and the aircraft was later repaired.

The pilots of the 51st FIW had their next clash with MiGs on 11 January 1952, when pilots of the 16th and 25th FIS led by their wing commander Colonel Gabreski were covering a raid by their fighter-bombers in the area of MiG Alley. Every regiment of the 64th IAK took part in repelling this raid, and two major dogfights resulted. The pilots of the Soviet IAK took on the Sabres of the 51st FIW, while UAA pilots attacked the Thunderjet fighter-bombers. In this battle, pilots of the 196th IAP scored particularly well, claiming to have destroyed six Sabres, of which two each went to the credit of Captain I.M. Zaplavnev and V.G. Murav'ev, while one Sabre each was added to the scores of 2nd Squadron commander Captain B.V. Bokach and regiment commander Colonel E.G. Pepeliaev; this was the latter's 20th and final victory, making him the top-scoring ace of this war in the skies of Korea at that time.

Altogether on this day according to the records of the 64th IAK, eight Sabres were shot down. In addition to the six downed by the pilots of the 196th IAP, pilots of the 17th IAP claimed two more, one of which was Major N.V. Sutiagin's next victory over an F-86. According to the regiment's documents, this is what happened. At 1400, radar detected up to 24 enemy fighters and fighter-bombers at an altitude of 5,000 to 6,000 meters in an area 20 to 30 kilometers southeast of Pyongyang, which were flying on a heading of 320°. At an order from the division command post, 20 MiGs of the 17th IAP under the command of Lieutenant Colonel G.I. Pulov took off from a status of Readiness No.1 to repel an enemy air strike in the Anju-Sukchon area.

Pulov's group received the assignment to intercept the enemy raid in the Anju-Sunchon-Taechon area. Having arrived over Sunchon at an altitude of 7,000 meters, the group didn't see any enemy aircraft, so it went into a 180° turn to starboard and headed back toward Anju. In the Taechon area, Major N.V. Sutiagin spotted two F-86s to their front left and above them about 1,000 meters, which were firing at MiG-15s of the 18th GIAP from long range. Sutiagin went into a steep climb and in a right turn opened fire on the trailing Sabre from a range of 550 meters down to 400 meters. The Sabre went into a violent dive. Because of low fuel, the group turned to port and continued on to base.

During a starboard turn over the Anju area at an altitude of 9,000 meters, Senior Lieutenant V.M. Khvostsantsev's element was jumped by a pair of F-86s from above and to the left. Khvostantsev's responded to the attack with a chandelle to the left, but the enemy began to pursue them. Khvostantsev went into an oblique loop to the left, and then with a straight loop turned the table on this Sabre element and began to chase them. Khvostantsev's wingman Senior Lieutenant I.F. Polishchuk, seeing one of the Sabres straighten out into level flight, went after it, and having closed to within 800 meters, opened fire. After two bursts the Sabre rolled to the left and dove. At an order from the group commander, Senior Lieutenant Khvostantsev's element broke off combat.

The combat between our fighters and the enemy Sabres lasted just two to three minutes, and as a result of the dogfight, one F-86 was shot down. The losses of the 64th IAK amounted to only one MiG-15, but it was being flown by one of the top aces of the 18th GIAP, the deputy commander of the 1st Squadron Lev Kirillovich Shchukin, who by this time had accumulated 17 victories in the skies of Korea (15 personal and two shared). His MiG-15 took hits from a Sabre's .50-caliber machine-gun fire and fuel gushed into his cockpit, totally saturating his flight suit. Fearing the fighter would erupt in flames at any moment Captain Shchukin ejected, but suffered a serious injury when he landed. He was sent to a hospital and took no further part in combat.

The Americans claimed four victories over MiGs on this day, one of which by the 51st Wing's commander Colonel Gabreski. Most likely, three of the downed MiG-15s were from the PLAAF 6th IAD and 15th IAD of the UAA, which were operational in MiG Alley at this time, normally flying in small groups covered by the 64th IAK's pilots. Indeed, on this day pilots of the 523rd IAP took off that afternoon to cover pilots of the UAA.

The Americans put their own losses in the actions of 11 January 1952 as two F-86E Sabres from the 51st FIW's 25th FIS; F-86E No.51-2742 was shot down and its pilot was picked up by search and rescue, while F-86E No.50-0612 was damaged in the afternoon. Although it managed to reach the sanctuary of Korea Bay, it could go no further and plunged into the Yellow Sea. Its pilot 1st Lieutenant Thiel M. Reeves is listed as missing-in-action.

Pilots of the UAA also managed to down at least two enemy fighter-bombers, the loss of both of which on this day was acknowledged by the Fifth Air Force command. One F-80 from the 8th FBG's 36th FBS was shot down and its pilot went missing-in-action. An F-84E Thunderchief from the 136th FBW's 154th Squadron was also lost, the pilot of which 1st Lieutenant Joseph F. Green became a prisoner-of-war.

The next combats between the 64th IAK's pilots and the pilots of the 51st FIW erupted on 12 January in the area of the Supung hydroelectric complex on the Yalu River. Up to 30 MiG-15s of the 17th IAP and 176th GIAP took part in the first combat that morning. The 17th IAP's pilots clashed with 14 F-86s but filed no victory claims back on the ground. But Captain S.M. Kramarenko and Senior Lieutenant N.K. Moroz of the 176th GIAP each downed one F-86. That afternoon, the pilots of the 176th GIAP between 1246 and 1353 engaged up to 20 F-86s in the Sunchon – Taechon area. Three of its pilots fired at enemy aircraft. Captain S.M. Kramarenko claimed his second F-86 of the day, and Senior Lieutenant I.N. Guly downed another Sabre.

Here's what Ikar Nikolaevich Guly himself recalls about this dogfight, in which he flew as wingman to the 176th GIAP's 2nd Squadron commander Captain S.M. Kramarenko:

We engaged a group of enemy F-86s in the vicinity of the Supung hydroelectric power station. In the course of the dogfight, it broke down into separate elements. Suddenly I caught sight a pair of F-86s that was flying a little bit below us, with a solitary Sabre trailing behind them. I was in a very advantageous position and decided to attack it. Over the radio I asked my leader to cover me and went on the attack. Dropping in behind the lone Sabre, I shot it down with a salvo from my cannons and pulled out of the attack in a climb. I spotted a pair of aircraft from a neighboring division above me (most likely these were MiGs from the 523rd IAP) and requested to form up with them, because a query to my leader had gone unanswered.

While moving to join with this element I discovered that one F-86 was firing at me. I began to maneuver frantically with a dive from 11,000 meters, in order to give him no opportunity to catch me in his sights. I leveled out my aircraft at approximately 10,000 meters and saw that the F-86 had broken off its chase of me and was now under attack from one of our MiGs (it was my leader's, Kramarenko). As a result of his attack, the Sabre was shot down and fell into the sea. We again linked up and then returned to base.

As a result, over the day's combats the pilots of the 64th IAK claimed four F-86s (all to the score of the 176th GIAP) without any losses in return. One of our MiGs, being flown by the 523rd IAP's Senior Lieutenant I.Z. Churkin, was damaged in combat. He returned safely back to base with nine bullet holes in his aircraft. Most likely, his MiG was damaged by Lieutenant Colonel George Jones of the 51st FIW, who put in the only claim for a MiG on this day, but as it turned out, Churkin's plane was only damaged.

The Chinese pilots also on this day managed to down one F-84 from the 136th FBW's 182nd FBS, the pilot of which Captain John D. Beers was taken prisoner. The Americans don't report any F-86 losses on 12 January 1952.

After two relatively quiet days, on 15 January once again the pilots of the 64th IAK clashed with Sabres of the 51st FIW. The pilots of the 303rd IAD conducted two sorties during the day, while the pilots of the 523rd IAP flew three missions. The 303rd IAD had two successful encounters with the Sabres. In the morning between 0848 and 0900, 20 crews of the 17th IAP under the command of Major N.V. Sutiagin engaged 16 F-86s in a dogfight over the Anju area, in which Captain B.E. Tikhonov downed one F-86 and Senior Lieutenant F.G. Malunov damaged another. In this combat, the regiment didn't even have any damaged MiGs.

After lunch that day, around 1500 the full 303rd IAD took part in a major battle with a large group of F-86s. The 20 MiGs from the 17th IAP alone engaged an equal number of Sabres. However, it was the pilots of the 18th GIAP that distinguished themselves in this combat, who without any losses of their own downed two Sabres, one by Lieutenant Colonel A.P. Smorchkov and the other by the commander of the 1st Squadron Major A.F. Maznev. Unusually, the command of the US Fifth Air Force acknowledged these losses, which were sustained by the 51st FIW in this final combat of the day with the MiGs. The 25th FIS lost two F-86E Sabres, No.50-585 and No.50-630, and it can be stated with confidence that they were downed by the 18th GIAP's pilots. Both of the pilots, 1st Lieutenant Vernon L. Wright and 2nd Lieutenant Daniel D. Peterson bailed out, but were captured and became prisoners-of-war. On this mission, 2nd Lieutenant Peterson was the wingman of Colonel Bud Mahurin, the commander of the 25th FIS. Peterson's Sabre was hit in the Sonchon area and he headed back to base in it, but over the Pyongyang area he had to eject and was taken prisoner. According to Mahurin, a third Sabre of his squadron was damaged on this day, but the Americans recognize only the loss of these two F-86Es.

The Americans staged another fighter-bomber raid against targets in the area of MiG Alley on 16 January. Once again, they sent ahead a large forward screen of Sabres from the 51st FIW, with groups of F-84E Thunderjets and F-80C Shooting Stars following in its wake. Both divisions of the 64th IAK participated in rebuffing this raid. In the first morning clash, which occurred around 0800, 14 MiGs of the 523rd IAP encountered a flight of F-86s in the Taechon area at an altitude of 10,000 meters and attacked it. However, that is when several more Sabre flights, numbering a total of 18 Sabres, came up, and suddenly the numerical superiority swung to the opposite side. Then pilots of the 18th GIAP propitiously arrived and took on part of the enemy fighters. However, by the time the 17th IAP arrived in the combat area, the dogfight was already over and the 523rd IAP's pilots were already on their way back to base. In this combat, Major G.U. Okhai downed one Sabre that fell into the sea. Another Sabre was downed in this action

A.P. Smorchkov, Miaogou airfield,
autumn of 1951.

by the 18th GIAP's Senior Lieutenant B.P. Sapozhnikov, but then his MiG came under attack from a pair of F-86s led by Lieutenant Colonel George Jones from the 51st FIW's command, and Sapozhnikov was shot down – Boris Petrovich Sapozhnikov was killed-in-action. In the 523rd IAP's regimental group, Senior Lieutenant V.I. Kovalev's MiG took light combat damage, receiving two bullet holes in it.

The second battle on 16 January took place before 1300, and again regiments from both of the 64th IAK's divisions took part in it. The pilots of the 17th IAP engaged a group of 12 F-86 in combat, while the 176th GIAP's regimental group encountered another group of Sabres in the Chongju area and dealt with it successfully. Between 1232 and 1238 Major K.Ia. Sheberstov shot down one F-86, which fell 10 kilometers east of Fujo-ri, and Captain S.M. Kramarenko shot down another, which exploded on the ground in an area 10 kilometers east of Chongju. This was Captain Kramarenko's 13th and final victory in the skies of Korea. Altogether, five of the regiment's pilots fired at enemy aircraft in this action. Incidentally, this was also the final combat for the pilots of the 324th IAD that yielded any results, and the pilots of the division scored no additional victories prior to their departure back to the Soviet Union.

Around the same time (at 1232), 16 MiGs of the 523rd IAP intercepted a group of 14 fighter-bombers in the Anju-Sukchon area, which the pilots identified as F-84s (but were in fact F-80s), and attacked it. Six of the regiment's pilots fired on the fighter-bombers (Okhai, Mazilov, Timofeev, Semenenko, Krasavtsev and Rybalko), but only one of them succeeded in hitting his target. An F-80 hit by Senior Lieutenant I.A. Rybalko crashed and exploded. In this afternoon action, the 64th IAK had no losses.

The American command confirmed only the loss of one of its F-80s (No.49-1880) from the 49th FBG's 80th Squadron, which in fact Senior Lieutenant Rybalko shot down. The pilot of this Shooting Star, 1st Lieutenant Richard L. McNulty was killed when his aircraft was hit at low altitude and exploded upon impact with the earth. However, the Fifth Air Force command doesn't confirm the loss of any of its F-86Es.

However, on the next day, 17 January 1952, the pilots of the 51st FIW took revenge for their defeat of the previous day by downing two of the 64th IAK's MiGs. While on a combat patrol mission, a group of MiGs from the 176th GIAP was jumped by a group of F-86s from the 51st FIW's 25th FIS and the 4th FIW's 334th FIS. With the help of the surprise attack from out of some clouds, the 2nd Squadron commander and Hero of the Soviet Union Captain S.M. Kramarenko was shot down in combat. As he recalls:

> In the course of the dogfight, I managed to get behind one of the Sabres and shot it down, but then I felt hits against my MiG. The MiG began to spin and the controls wouldn't respond – they'd been severed. So I decided to eject, which I did without any injuries. The Sabre that had downed me made another pass at me and fired at me, but missed high – his tracers passed above my parachute. The Sabre didn't have time to make another pass, because by then I had disappeared into some clouds. I came to ground safely, took a look around, gathered my parachute, walked over to the nearest road and headed toward the sea in the Anju area. Along the road I met a Korean driving a two-wheeled cart, and he conveyed me to the nearest village. Soon Korean police showed up there; they checked whether I was an American pilot, but having been convinced that I was Soviet, they gave me something to eat, brought up a vehicle and took me back to the regiment. This was my final combat

sortie of the war, since after bailing out of my MiG, they gave me a bit of rest, during which my division's time in Manchuria came to an end.

In this same combat, Senior Lieutenant Aleksandr Vasil'evich Filippov, a young pilot who had recently arrived as a replacement, was shot down. He had become separated from his element leader, and on his way back to base he was jumped by a pair of Sabres and shot down. He ejected, but was already dead when he came to earth. A participant in this action, a former pilot of the 196th IAP Aleksei Antonovich Tiron recalls, "I remember how Sania Filippov was killed – they shot him down in a head-on pass. We had descended into some clouds and the visibility greatly deteriorated. He didn't have time to open fire. The American opened fire first." Also in this combat, the MiG-15 of Senior Lieutenant V.V. Leonov, who had also recently arrived as a replacement in the 176th GIAP, was seriously damaged, but he managed to bring it back to base and made a safe landing there.

S.M. Kramarenko's wingman on that mission, Senior Lieutenant I.N. Guly, offers a different story about how Kramarenko came to eject from his MiG. According to him, this combat took place in the Anju area at an altitude of 11,000 meters; below was a light layer of clouds approximately 2,000 to 3,000 meters thick. They had spotted a pair of Sabres and attacked them, but in the ensuing maneuvering they went into a spin, from which Kramarenko could not recover and he had to eject.

However it happened back then, the 64th IAK lost two MiGs and one pilot in the combat, while the Sabre claimed by Kramarenko was not credited to the regiment's score, because no one could confirm his victory. The Americans in turn registered Leonov's

Hero of the Soviet Union Captain S.M. Kramarenko poses together with his ground crew next to the nose of his MiG-15 on the Andong airfield, 1951.

MiG as a victory, though in reality only two Sabres were downed. In this combat, the pilots of the 4th FIW shot down their first MiG-15 of the new year, which was credited to Lieutenant Colonel James B. Raebel of the 334th FIS; the other two MiGs were credited to pilots of the 51st FIW's 25th FIS, Frank B. Robison and William F. Sheaffer.

On 18 January 1952, the 64th IAK's pilots had another encounter with fighter-bombers from the 49th FBG. On this day, small groups of F-84Es were operating not far from Andong, having arrived over the target area from the direction of the sea. Recalls a former pilot of the 523rd IAP Senior Lieutenant Konstantin Timofeevich Shal'nov:

> On 18 January 1952 I took off together with Captain Bakhaev to cover our airfield and those of our aircraft that were returning from a mission. Once all the aircraft had landed Stepan Antonovich Bakhaev and I searched the area extending about 60 kilometers to the south. Unexpectedly we came across a flight of Thunderjets, which were on their way back out to sea after completing a mission. Bakhaev attacked a target that he had picked out, while I was lagging a bit behind and spotted a nearby, solitary F-84 that was directly under my nose. I went after him and quickly shot him down. I regret now what I did back then. He was plainly inexperienced and probably quite young. He didn't even see me, because he made no attempt to evade whatsoever.

Captain S.A. Bakhaev also didn't miss his target and sent it plummeting to the ground. However, while they credited Bakhaev with his victory, Shal'nov's F-84 went unconfirmed, apparently because they never found the wreckage of his victim, though it is noted in the flight log that on 18 January 1952, Senior Lieutenant K.T. Shal'nov downed an F-84. This combat occurred in the Sukchon – Anju area, when at 0745 a group of 16 MiG-15s under the command of Major A.P. Trefilov encountered a group of 10 F-84s. Only Captain Bakhaev and Senior Lieutenant Shal'nov fired their cannons at enemy aircraft. In the course of the dogfight, Senior Lieutenant V.M. Timofeev lost cabin pressure in his cockpit, but the pilot safely landed his MiG back at base.

Bakhaev had inflicted serious damage to F-84E No.51-669 from the 49th FBG. Although its pilot managed to reach his base back in Taegu, he crashed when landing.

After the aerial combat on 18 January, prior to the end of the month the pilots of the 64th IAK had over 10 additional clashes with the Sabres of the 4th and 51st FIW, in which they scored a total of 10 victories over the F-86s, seven of which went to the credit of the 17th IAP's pilots. However, these victories came with even greater stress on the bodies of the aircrews, and also with greater losses. Because of the rising incidence of pilots becoming incapacitated due to physical exhaustion and illnesses, sorties by pilots of the 324th IAD had been halted and the pilots began to prepare to depart back to the Soviet Union. Thus the entire burden in the second half of January lay upon the shoulders of the 303rd IAD's pilots, whose endurance was also nearly at the end of its rope. Only 50-60 percent of its flight staff was combat-ready at any given time, so each regimental group normally didn't exceed 12 to 14 crews for any one sortie; rarely, 16 to 20 of the regiment's pilots might be capable of flying a mission. The constant fighting at high altitudes and with high G-loads was making its negative influence felt. All of this had an affect not only on the pilots' combat effectiveness, but also on the division's loss rate.

The combat day of 19 January was typical. Between 1343 and 1348, radar detected six groups of enemy fighters and fighter-bombers, numbering up to a total of 56 aircraft,

Hero of the Soviet Union Captain S.A. Bakhaev (on the left), posing together with his constant wingman Senior Lieutenant G.Kh. D'iachenko – Miaogou airfield, 1951.

70-100 kilometers south and southeast of Pyongyang, which were flying in groups of 8-16 aircraft each in the direction of the Anju – Chongju area. At 1347 in response to an order from the division command post, 16 MiGs of the 523rd IAP under the command of the regiment's assistant commander Guards Lieutenant Colonel A.P. Trefilov took off as the division's covering group to intercept enemy aircraft in the Anju – Sunchon area.

At 1410, Major V.P. Popov and his flight, which was flying last in the unit's combat formation and trailing 6-8 kilometers behind the rest of the regiment, while in a turn to starboard sighted four F-86s 10-12 kilometers out in front of them and to the right, with around a 200 meter altitude advantage, flying in the direction of Siojio with the second element staggered to the right and behind the lead element. Having reported this to the group leader, Popov moved to close with the Sabres and attacked them as the range dropped to 600-800 meters. Major Popov fired at the leader of the final element, and Captain N.I. Mitrofanov at its wingman. The Sabre fired upon by Popov staggered sharply to the left and went into an uncontrolled dive. The remaining three Sabres went into a starboard spiral, but after one time around the spiral they headed in the direction of the sea in a steep, high-speed dive.

Major Popov pulled out of the attack into a chandelle to the right and spotted six F-86s that were 5-6 kilometers out in front of them, approaching in a formation with its elements echeloned to the right. He accepted a head-on pass with the entire flight and fired as the range closed quickly from 800 meters down to 300 meters. Exiting the attack straight ahead, he caught sight of six more F-86s 5-6 kilometers away, also in a formation with its elements echeloned to the right, approaching from dead ahead at the same altitude. As the two hostile formations closed, the Sabres flinched first and broke off into a spiral to the left, before accelerating away in a dive to the south. Popov followed the Sabres around the spiral, but because of low fuel, broke off the pursuit and returned to base. The remaining pilots of the regimental group, which had been assigned to cover the attack groups, had no encounter with enemy aircraft.

The aerial combat took place in the Kusong – Taegwan-dong area at altitudes of 11,000 to 13,000 meters and lasted for six to eight minutes. Only two of the regiment's pilots fired their guns: Major Popov fired at two F-86 aircraft, and Captain Mitrofanov fired at one. Major Popov was credited with downing one F-86 and damaging the other.

As the attack group, formations of MiGs from the 17th IAP and 18th GIAP also took part in this battle. The 17th IAP had launched 20 MiGs, which became engaged with 12 F-86s. Although Captain V.F. Shulev succeeded in downing one Sabre, the regiment also lost one of its own aircraft. At 1419 in an area 15 kilometers south of Sukchon at an altitude of 8,000 meters, flight commander Senior Lieutenant F.G. Malunov, while maneuvering against enemy F-86s, was attacked from above and behind by a different Sabre element. As a result of the attack, his MiG received 11 bullet holes in the engine, wing and tail flap. Malunov headed back to Manchuria to make a forced landing at the Andong base. On the way there, his engine flamed out, and Senior Lieutenant Malunov had to make a forced landing in an area 5 kilometers northeast of Andong. The aircraft was demolished and was unsuitable for repair, but Senior Lieutenant Malunov received only light injuries when putting the aircraft down.

1st Lieutenant Iven C. Kincheloe, Jr. of the 51st FIW's 25th FIS was the victor over Senior Lieutenant Malunov. In their turn the Americans don't confirm the loss of their Sabres, but do acknowledge the loss of one of their F-84Es from the 49th FBG. Possibly, our pilots were mistaken when they asserted that they had tangled with F-86s, and in fact engaged a group of F-84s. Or perhaps pilots of the UAA downed this Thunderjet?

On 20 January, pilots of the 17th IAP conducted three combat sorties and in the morning became engaged in one combat with 12 F-86s, in which Captain N.G. Dokashenko claimed one Sabre destroyed. This was the 64th IAK's sole victory of the day, and to be honest it in turn wasn't able to avoid a combat loss. In a dogfight with Sabres of the 51st FIW, the MiG of Captain N.V. Babonin from the 18th GIAP was shot down, but our pilot took to his parachute. Major Donald Adams of the 16th FIS shot down Captain Babonin.

On 21 January, the 303rd IAD flew just one mission with its entire complement and had one brief clash with Sabre pilots. In this action, Major N.V. Sutiagin, the top ace with the 303rd IAD, scored the only victory, and this was his 22nd and final victory in the skies of Korea, leaving him as the war's highest-scoring ace!

Between 1425 and 1433, radar was tracking up to 66 enemy fighters and fighter-bombers in an area 110 kilometers south of Pyongyang, which were flying in three groups in the direction of the Anju – Sunchon area at an altitude of 6,000 meters. At an order from the division command post, 20 MiGs of the 17th IAP under the command of Lieutenant Colonel G.I. Pulov took off from Readiness No.1 as part of the division's attack group in order to intercept the enemy in the Sukchon – Eiju area. Though part of the strike group, the 17th IAP was responsible for covering the attacks by pilots of the 523rd IAP.

A.P. Smorchkov and G.I. Pulov, enjoying a well-earned rest in the sanatorium in the city of Dal'nii, autumn of 1951.

Lieutenant Colonel Pulov's formation was flying in the attack group's second echelon to the right of the 523rd IAP. At an altitude of 9,500-10,000 meters, in the vicinity of Eiju eight F-86s were sighted out in front of them, moving in the same direction but in the process of banking to the right. The 523rd IAP's attack flight went into a pursuit curve to close with the enemy. The Sabres, noticing the approach of our MiGs, jettisoned their drop tanks and went into a descending 180° turn to starboard.

Major Sutiagin, who was located on the formation's right flank with his wingman, closed to within 600-700 meters of the trailing flight of four Sabres in the right turn and opened fire. The enemy began to escape below in a steep diving turn, but leveled out at an altitude of 6,000 meters. Sutiagin, pursuing the enemy, noticed a single MiG behind, above and to the left, which was firing long-range bursts. The target Sabre, seeing the tracers, performed a split-S. Sutiagin reversed course to the right and noticed two Sabres passing him on the left, so he reversed course to port and started to pursue them. The enemy, spotting the MiG behind them, energetically reversed course to the right and turned into Sutiagin's attack. Sutiagin fired at the F-86 wingman as the range rapidly closed from 700 to 190 meters, then hauled his MiG around to the right to go after the enemy. As he closed to within a range of 700-800 meters, the enemy began to break left, and Sutiagin at a range of 500 meters again opened fire on the wingman's Sabre, which began to emit smoke from its left wing. Major Sutiagin, hearing the order from the division command post, broke off combat and headed back to base.

The rest of the group flew as far as Pyongyang, and failing to encounter the enemy, returned to base at the order of the division command post. The action between our fighters and the enemy fighters lasted for 5-6 minutes, and Major Sutiagin received credit for downing one F-86. The 64th IAK on this day had no losses, but the Chinese lost one of their MiG-15s in a dogfight with those same pilots of the 51st FIW. True, the Chinese pilots managed to down two F-84Es on this day, evidence that they were gradually acquiring combat experience, which resulted in more success in combats with the USAF.

On 23 January, the 303rd IAD's pilots flew two combat missions and took part in one dogfight, which took place that morning in the Anju area between 1017 and 1027. Pilots of the 17th IAP, 20 crews of which had taken off under the command of Lieutenant Colonel B.V. Maslennikov distinguished themselves in a combat with 20 F-86s. In this dogfight, the commander of the regiment's 2nd Squadron Major M.S. Ponomarev and Senior Lieutenant N.S. Volkov each claimed one Sabre. The combat was very hard-fought and intense, to which the fact that three of the 17th IAP's MiG-15s received combat damage testifies. Senior Lieutenant I.F. Polishchuk's MiG-15 returned to base with three bullet holes in the right and left wings. The MiG piloted by Senior Lieutenant R.V. Khrisanov returned with two bullet holes in one wing. However, the MiG-15 flown by Senior Lieutenant A.T. Bozhko suffered the most damage; it had 12 bullet holes in the wings, fuselage, engine compartment, rudder and tail fin. However, they all returned safely to base in their damaged MiGs, which were quickly repaired.

The Americans acknowledge the loss on this day of only one of their F-84E Thunderjets from the 136th FBG, and maintain that they had no losses among their F-86 Sabres. However, pilots of the 51st FIW's 25th Squadron claimed their next two victories over MiGs. Yet if on this day the Chinese pilots had no encounters with enemy Sabres, then most likely, these MiGs were not downed, but were the damaged MiGs of the 17th IAP.

After a rare day off on 24 January, in which there were no sorties, the pilots of the 17th IAP again scored well on 25 January in two clashes with the Sabres. In the first morning combat that occurred between 0838 and 0850 in the Pakchon area, all 14 combat-ready crews of the regiment on this day tangled with 12 F-86s. Captain A.V. Bykov downed one Sabre.

Almost six hours later between 1529 and 1550, the same 14 pilots of the 17th IAP under the command of Lieutenant Colonel B.V. Maslennikov engaged a large group of 42 F-86s. In this unequal combat, Senior Lieutenant N.S. Volkov nevertheless downed one Sabre while Captain N.G. Dokashenko damaged another, but the regiment in turn couldn't avoid a loss. At 1529 in an area 8 kilometers southwest of Pakchon at an altitude of 6,000-7,000 meters, while locked in a dogfight with the Sabres, the MiG-15 flown by Senior Lieutenant R.V. Khrisanov was jumped from above and behind by a pair of F-86s while in a turn to starboard. The F-86 element leader opened fire from a range of 200 meters, and the burst tore through the aircraft's cockpit. Khrisanov began to claw for altitude in a spiral, but the F-86 element followed him. Khrisanov reached 10,000 meters in altitude, after which as a result of a second burst from the F-86 element leader, Khrisanov lost control of his aircraft. The MiG-15 flipped over onto its back, and at that point Khrisanov decided to eject. He did so from the inverted position at an altitude of 10,000 meters and came to earth in his parachute in an area 10 kilometers southeast of Pakchon. After landing, Khrisanov was picked up by NKPA ground units and brought to the hospital in the town of Andong. As a result of the Sabre attack, Senior Lieutenant Khrisanov received five fragment wounds in the right leg, but the pilot's condition was rated as good by the doctors.

On this day pilots of the UAA's 6th IAD and 15th IAD participated in a large battle with fighter-bombers of the US Fifth Air Force, but also with pilots of the 4th and 51st FIW. The Americans acknowledge that on 25 January they lost four F-84s and one F-80 on one mission, although they seem unaware of the fact that they were lost in combat with Chinese MiGs of the UAA. However, these victories came at a very high price for the Chinese pilots, if one judges from the victory claims of the F-86 pilots. The 51st FIW alone claimed six victories over MiGs on this day, while pilots of the 4th FIW were believed to have downed three more. Since the 64th IAK lost only one MiG-15 on this day, the remaining eight MiGs must have belonged to the UAA.

The single Sabre that was downed on this day, by the 17th IAP's Senior Lieutenant Volkov, was F-86A No.48-251 from the 334th FIS, the pilot of which Captain Philip E. Coleman managed to reach the K-14 base in Kimpo in it, but there the engine flamed out and the Sabre crashed. The aircraft was written off, while the pilot was injured in the crash and sent to a hospital.

In the final combats of January 1952, the pilots of the 18th GIAP did well, downing one Sabre each day in combats on 29 and 31 January. On the 29th, the commander of the 18th GIAP's 1st Squadron Major A.F. Maznev downed F-86E No.50-590 from the 51st FIW's 16th FIS in the vicinity of Chongju – its pilot 1st Lieutenant Charles W. Rhinehart bailed out, but an extensive search only recovered his parachute and he remains missing-in-action. On the final day of January Captain A.A. Svintitsky managed to down another Sabre, F-86E No.51-2724 from the same 16th FIS, but the pilot of this Sabre Captain Richard D. Starke was luckier. His Sabre flamed out over friendly territory, and he was picked up by a search and rescue team. Here is how Aleksei Aleksandrovich Svintitsky himself recalls this combat:

Somehow once my wingman Ivan Mart'ianov and I caught two Sabres – they were free hunters. We had been the last element of the regiment to take off. Then at one "splendid" moment, a six-ship formation of Sabres pounced on us. They were emerging on our tails. I turned around into the direction of the attackers and climbed. They quickly fell behind and then withdrew in the direction of the sea. However, during this time, I lost sight of the regiment.

I climbed higher, thinking that I needed to look around for the regiment. I look – and I see two aircraft out in front of us. "There we go", I think, "We'll catch up and continue as a foursome. I approach a little more closely – Sabres! They were flying a bit lower than me, and I'm approaching from behind. When you fly just a bit above the horizontal stabilizers (as it appears from the Sabre cockpit), it becomes very difficult for the pilot to spot you. He can see anywhere else he wants, but not there. I close, not shedding speed. From 800 meters I gave it a first burst in order to line it up. I check – [the target was] too distant. The tracers' trajectory passed below the target. But neither the leader nor the wingman sees them. They just keep flying straight ahead. I approach more closely. From a range of 300 meters I give the wingman another burst. The shells strike home, right up the jet's exhaust nozzle. The Sabre immediately streams black smoke ... I hear my wingman: "Sabres behind us!" He distracted me; I take a look – they're still not close. "Quiet, let me concentrate," I answer. The stricken Sabre, listing to one side, is falling in a steep trajectory; the pilot is trying to wrestle his aircraft toward the coastline, but I'm already lining up the leader in my sights. I was literally a second too late. Just an instant before I pressed the trigger, he abruptly rolled over into a dive and literally escaped out from under the tracers ... We flew back, and the deputy commander of the division comes rolling up. We report: what, how. It turned out that these very "hunters" had previously caught several of our fighters.

On 30 January, the pilots of the 523rd IAP had an encounter with a group of F-84s. At 0930, 14 of the regiment's MiGs headed by Major D.P. Os'kin came across 12 F-84s, but they were only able to chase them away from the target back to the sea.

The only loss in these last days of January occurred in the 523rd IAP; this also marked the final death of a 303rd IAD pilot in this war, and it was not even a combat loss. When returning from a mission on 30 January 1952, just before touching down, the wheels on Senior Lieutenant P.I. Parushkov's MiG struck the top of his element leader's MiG; the latter bounced hard off of the runway, veered wildly and slammed into a revetment. In the collision, the legs of its pilot, Senior Lieutenant Ivan Ivanovich Iakovlev, became trapped beneath the instrument panel, and a fire broke out. The ground crews were unable to free the pilot from the smashed cockpit, and the pilot burned to death inside the flaming wreckage. It was painful that one of the regiment's best pilots, who had achieved four victories in the skies of Korea, had to die in such a cruel and needless way, and one can imagine the psychological effects on Senior Lieutenant Parushkov, who had only recently arrived in the regiment.

On 30 and 31 January, the pilots of the 17th IAP were given two days' rest. On these days, the regiment's technical staff worked to help ready the 523rd IAP's MiG-15s for flights.

According to American records, altogether over the month of January 1952 the pilots of the 4th and 51st FIW downed 31 MiG-15s in MiG Alley. Pilots of the 51st FIW flying their new F-86Es claimed 25 of these kills, while the other six went to the pilots of the 4th FIW.

The Soviet pilots of the 324th IAD flew their final combat missions in January 1952. Already after the combat on 17 January, the 176th GIAP turned over its MiGs to the 148th GIAP of the 97th IAD, which had arrived in China in December 1951. The pilots of the 196th IAP followed suit on 20 January, yielding its aircraft to the 97th IAD's 16th IAP.

The flight staff of the 324th IAD had become worn out in the final months of 1951, and many of its pilots had been discharged and returned to the Soviet Union due to the excessive emotional and physical burdens they'd been carrying. The remaining pilots were fighting at the end of their strength, which led to the declining number of victories and the growing number of losses. Although in November 1951, 20 replacements had arrived in the division's regiments, but they lacked combat experience and primarily flew as the wingmen of the division's experienced pilots. They simply didn't have time over two and a half months to take leadership positions in the division's regiments and to have any real influence on the regiments' combat performance.

Senior Lieutenant D.A. Samoilov, one of the 523rd IAP's highest scoring aces (a postwar photograph).

The same picture arose in the 303rd IAD as well. Writing about the final months of the tour of duty, a former flight commander in the 523rd IAP's 2nd Squadron and Hero of the Soviet Union Senior Lieutenant Dmitrii Aleksandrovich Samoilov observes:

> In this period, the division and 64th IAD commands began to accuse the pilots of slacking off in their combat activity; the number of downed enemy aircraft was declining. We in turn pointed to the fact that the Sabres had become different. It had become more difficult to catch them in dives and to escape them in climbs. The command didn't much believe us, thinking that we were making excuses. However, the Sabres really were different. One of the downed American pilots, taken prisoner by the Koreans, revealed during an interrogation that they had received the new F-86E, an updated version with a more powerful engine.
>
> Besides that, obviously, our physical and psychological fatigue was telling on our performance. Our ranks were thinning, and pilots were being held back from missions due to illnesses as well. In January, there were only enough pilots to create two eight-ship groups for missions, and in February, primarily enough for only one. Of the regiment's initial flight staff, which had arrived in China in 1951, only half – 16 pilots, plus six pilots who had arrived in the regiment as replacements, departed for the Motherland on 20 February.

Only pilots of the 303rd IAD, and at that, only 12-16 crews of the 17th IAP, 8-12 crews of the 523rd IAP, and never more than 12 crews of the 18th GIAP, flew combat missions in February 1952. The latter regiment's pilots were exhausted physically and suffering low morale, which is not surprising, since they had entered combat operations over Korea a month before the other regiments of the 303rd IAD.

Although this regiment together with the entire division departed for the Soviet Union on 24 February 1952, it still flew up to ten combat missions and became involved in several aerial combats in February, though without scoring a single victory or losing a single aircraft or pilot. The pilots of the 17th IAP and 523rd IAP had several more combats prior to 20 February 1952 and were primarily sharing their combat experience with the arriving pilots of the 190th IAD, who were to replace them, and simultaneously covering their first combat sorties in the Korean sky.

The first combat action in the month of February took place in the afternoon on 1 February and involved 12 MiGs of the 523rd IAP led by Captain G.U. Okhai. They had an encounter with 12 F-84s, but the fighter-bombers managed to escape an attack from the MiGs by reaching the sanctuary of Korea Bay. This was the final encounter that the pilots of the 303rd IAD had with enemy strike aircraft in this war!

The next day, 2 February, proved to be more successful, when pilots of the 17th IAP and 523rd IAP in the morning successfully engaged a group of F-86s in the Chongju – Pakchon area. Between 0746 and 0753, 14 MiGs of the 17th IAP took on 12 F-86s, and Captain N.G. Dokashenko damaged one of the Sabres. Meanwhile, pilots of the 523rd IAP were tangling with a different group of F-86s in the same area, and in this dogfight Major G.U. Okhai shot down one Sabre. It was F-86E No.51-2770 from the 4th FIW's 335th Squadron, the pilot of which was picked up by a search and rescue team.

On 3 February between 1310 and 1320, 14 crews of the 17th IAP under the command of regiment commander Lieutenant Colonel G.I. Pulov engaged a group of 24 F-86s successfully, with the regiment commander downing one Sabre. This was F-86A No.49-1223 from the 335th FIS, and its pilot 1st Lieutenant Charles R. Spath was taken prisoner.

Pilots of the 18th GIAP clashed with a group of F-86s in the Anju area on 4 February, but returned without results. The pilots of the 17th IAP on this day became involved in two combats with Sabres, but they also ended without results. This pattern repeated itself on the next day, 5 February when pilots of the 18th GIAP again encountered a group of Sabres in the Anju area and came away with no victories or losses.

The 17th IAP and 523rd IAP spent 7 February covering the railroad bridges in the Andong area. For the pilots of the 17th IAP, all the sorties passed without any encounters with the enemy, but 12 MiGs of the 523rd IAP had one dogfight with a group of F-86s, in which Major D.P. Os'kin downed F-86E No.50-686 from the 336th FIS. Its pilot 1st Lieutenant John P. Green nursed the crippled aircraft back to friendly territory, but had to bail out 20 kilometers north of the K-14 base at Kimpo.

On 9 February pilots of the 17th IAP and 523rd IAP had another brief skirmish with a group of 26 Sabres in the area of Kiojo, which ended with no results. However, on 10 February, the pilots of the 303rd IAD achieved their next success: between 1535 and 1550, 12 MiGs of the 17th IAP became involved in a dogfight with 30 F-86s, in which Captain V.F. Shulev damaged one F-86. This was the 17th IAP's final combat action in the skies of Korea. Between 13 and 16 February, pilots of the 17th IAP flew another six combat sorties to cover the newly arrived pilots of the 190th IAD's 494th IAP and 821st IAP, but they all ended without any enemy encounters. The 18th GIAP conducted three sorties on 10 February to the Anju area and had one combat with F-86s, but it ended with no blood drawn.

During the month up until 20 February, the pilots of the 303rd IAD had downed a total of six Sabres, of which three went to the score of the 17th IAP and three to that of the 523rd IAP. As it happened, the final victory achieved by the division's pilots in this war, as well as its final combat loss, both occurred in the same action on 11 February 1952. The hero of the day was a pilot of the 523rd IAP, Senior Lieutenant K.T. Shal'nov. As he recalls:

On 11 February I was Captain S.A. Bakhaev's wingman; I took off on a mission and was in the covering group. The skies were clear. Our altitude was 11,000-12,000 meters. After carrying out the assignment without encountering the enemy, our group returned to base to land. Captain Bakhaev and I circled over the airfield, covering our comrades' landings. However, we extended our circle about 20 kilometers to the south. Just then at an altitude of 12,000-13,000 meters, we unexpectedly encountered eight F-86s, which moreover were still higher than us. Having coordinated what we would do, Bakhaev and I accepted combat. At such a high altitude, the radius of a turn was 10-15 kilometers, and as we were turning, we noticed a pair of Sabres was turning to meet us. Neither we nor they could get on the others' tail, so the attacks were conducted head-on. As always in the thin atmosphere at such an altitude, I involuntarily fell some distance behind my leader, and at this moment the lead Sabre made a successful maneuver and was preparing to fire on Bakhaev. Because I was lagging behind my leader, in a flash I successfully set my sights on the Sabre, opened fire as we closed rapidly on a meeting course and shot it down. At the same time, the wingman's Sabre evidently caught me squarely in his sights and his fire fatally damaged my MiG. There was nothing left for me to do but to abandon my burning aircraft.

It wasn't the wingman of the downed Sabre that shot down Shal'nov, but a pair of Sabres from the 16th FIS, flown by 1st Lieutenants James E. Arnold and Raymond E. Steinbis, who shared the credit for the victory over Senior Lieutenant Shal'nov. Most likely, Shal'nov in this combat shot down F-86E No.50-615 from the 334th FIS, which managed to reach Korea Bay where its pilot 1st Lieutenant Paul G. Ridgeway successfully bailed out and was picked up by a search and rescue helicopter.

This was the final aircraft downed by the 303rd IAD, and after 20 February the division, leaving behind its MiGs for the pilots of the 190th IAD, ended its tour of duty with the 64th IAK and returned to the Soviet Union. The pilots of the 18th GIAP had only one more encounter with enemy aircraft before departing: on 17 February while covering the pilots of the 190th IAD's 821st IAP, the Guards pilots had a fleeting skirmish with a group of F-86s, which ended with no results. The 523rd IAP's pilots also had their final combat action on 17 February with a group of F-86s while covering their replacements of the 190th IAD – this combat also ended without results. The pilots of the 18th GIAP and 523rd IAP flew their two final combat sorties on 20 February, once again covering the pilots of the 190th IAD.

In sum, over their tour of duty in China, participating in combat actions in the skies over North Korea between 1 April 1951 and 20 January 1952, the pilots of the 324th IAD shot down 216 US aircraft in combat (12 B-29, 118 F-86, 33 F-84, 26 F-80, 11 Meteors, 8 F-94, 6 F-51, and 1 RB-45). Of this total number of enemy aircraft downed by the division, 109 went to the credit of the 196th IAP's pilots, while the pilots of the 176th GIAP finished their war with 107 official victories. Their own losses, both combat and non-combat, amounted to 27 aircraft and nine pilots. Of these totals, the 196th IAP lost 12 aircraft and had four pilots killed, while the 176th GIAP had five pilots killed and lost 15 MiGs. In addition, for one month the 196th IAP included the special group "Nord", which lost two MiG-15s and two pilots.

According to its logbook of operations, the 303rd IAD during its time in Manchuria conducted 12,980 individual combat sorties with an aggregate flight time of 10,685 hours. Of these individual combat sorties, 10,906 were to repel enemy air raids from an alert status; 1,726 were to cover the railroad bridge at Andong, the hydro-electrical station in the Siojio area, and the Andong, Singisiu and Miaogou airfields; and 286 were to cover operations by the Chinese and North Korean air forces. Only 40 of these individual combat sorties were "free hunts", and 22 were launched to cover PLAAF bombers on missions.

The 303rd IAD became engaged in 222 group aerial combats, of which 70 involved the entire division. The pilots of the division were credited with downing 305 aircraft: 18 B-29, 155 F-86, 67 F-84, 41 F-80, 16 Gloster Meteors, 5 F-51 and 3 F6F5. Their own losses were 16 pilots and 40 aircraft. Updated and revised data to include the period between the middle of January 1952 and 20 February 1952 yields the following victory totals: 315 in all, including 18 B-29, 162 F-86, 69 F-84, 42 F-80, 16 Meteors, 5 F-51, and 3 carrier-based F4U-2 Corsairs, which had been mistakenly identified as F6F5 Hellcats in the 64th IAK's records; several more enemy aircraft were damaged. Their own losses grew to 44 MiG-15s and 18 pilots.

Colonel Kumanichkin, the commander of the 303rd IAD, was awarded the Order of the Red Banner, while the deputy division commander Lieutenant Colonel Karasev was decorated with the Order of the Red Banner and the Order of Lenin. The division chief of staff Colonel Petr Trofimovich Iurakov was awarded with two Orders of the Red Banner.

Order No.0027 "On the results of the 303rd IAD's combat operations" from the commander of the 64th IAK General Lobov, dated 24 February 1952, gives revised numbers. According to it, 21 of the 303rd IAD's pilots downed five or more enemy aircraft:

Major Sutiagin – 22
Major Os'kin – 15
Major Shchukin – 15
Lieutenant Colonel Smorchkov – 12
Major Bakhaev – 11
Major Okhai – 11
Major Ponomarev – 10
Captain Samoilov – 10
Captain Dokashenko – 9

Lieutenant Colonel Pulov – 8
Lieutenant Colonel Karasev – 7
Captain Shulev – 7
Captain Volkov – 7
Major Antonov – 7
Major Artemchenko – 6
Captain Kaliuzhny – 5
Captain Bychkov – 5
Senior Lieutenant Stepanov – 5
Captain Kornienko – 5
Captain Shatalov – 5
Major Popov – 5

Lobov's order indicates that 106 of the division's pilots were awarded with Orders, of which 20 were twice-decorated. The division didn't forget about the hard-working ground crews and technical staff, 23 of which received Orders and medals. The 64th IAK commander expressed his gratitude to all of the 303rd IAD's personnel.

Meteorological conditions over our bases as well as the opposing side's bases also affected the nature of combat operations. Of the 229 days of the 303rd IAD's combat work, 71 were days with weather unsuitable for flight operations that kept the MiGs on the ground, which comprises 31 percent of the division's days staging from the Miaogou airfield.

By month, the following list shows the number of days that the 303rd IAD's Miaogou Air Base was socked-in by bad weather.

June, after 14 June 1951: 1 day
July – 19 days
August – 20 days
September – 6 days
October – 7 days
November – 8 days
December – 7 days
January 1952 – 3 days

From the given figures, it is evident that in the region, the months of July and August were the most unsuitable for combat operations, when only approximately 30 percent of the days featured weather good enough to fly missions.

The pilots of the 17th IAP finished with 108 victories, while losing a total of four pilots (two of which were killed not in combat, but in training crashes) and 10 aircraft (again, two of which were lost in the training crashes). The pilots of the 523rd IAP achieved 105 victories in the skies of Korea, while losing 16 MiG-15s and six pilots killed-in-action. The 18th GIAP was the least productive regiment in the 303rd IAD, finishing with 93 victories, while also losing the most aircraft (18) and pilots (eight).

The command staff of the 303rd IAD scored an additional nine victories in aerial combats. In particular, division commander Colonel G.A. Lobov (who subsequently was promoted to major general and assumed command of the 64th IAK) downed four

F-80s on his combat sorties with the division, while Hero of the Soviet Union Colonel A.S. Kumanichkin, who replaced Lobov in command of the 303rd IAD, shot down one F-84. Another four American aircraft fell in aerial combat to the division's inspector for aerial combat tactics Captain A.A. Kaliuzhny.

In total, these two Soviet fighter aviation divisions over their nine-month period of participation in the Korean War as part of the 64th IAK destroyed 531 enemy aircraft in the skies of Korea, while losing 73 aircraft and 29 pilots. These two "parade" divisions that left the IAK in January-February 1952 were the highest-scoring of all the Soviet IAD that ever joined the 64th IAK over the entire period of combat operations in the war. It is not coincidental that it was just in this period and from among just these two divisions, there emerged a constellation of stellar jet aces, who through their combat achievements contributed bright pages to the history of the Soviet Air Force. Many of these jet aces in 1951 became Heroes of the Soviet Union. They included S.P. Subbotin, G.I. Ges', S.M. Kramarenko, B.A. Obraztsov (posthumously), E.G. Pepeliaev, F.D Shebanov (posthumously), G.A. Lobov, G.I. Pulov, N.V. Sutiagin, M.S. Ponomarev, N.G. Dokashenko, A.P. Smorchkov, D.P. Os'kin, L.K. Shchukin, E.M. Stel'makh (posthumously), G.U. Okhai, S.A. Bakhaev and D.A. Samoilov.

Several dozen more pilots of these two divisions who became Korean War aces were awarded with other high honors of the Motherland – the Order of Lenin and the Order of the Red Banner. Thanks to the skill and heroism of these aces and the other pilots, the 64th IAK's successful combat operations in 1951 were assured and more than a few glittering victories were achieved, which on the whole sharply reversed the UN air forces' superiority in the Korean sky.

7

The Soviet High Command's mistake

By the end of 1951, the Soviet Air Force high command faced the problem of replacing the pilots of the 64th IAK, who by this time had become physically and psychologically worn down by the daily combats with the accompanying extreme stresses on the pilots. The Soviet Air Force leadership decided at the beginning of 1952 to replace the 64th IAK's battered fighter divisions with fresh divisions from the Soviet Union.

Essentially, they repeated the mistake that they had made in the spring of 1951, when the previous rotation of divisions out of Manchuria had taken place. For all practical purposes, back in April 1951 over the course of just one week the 324th IAD had been thrown into the fighting without any sort of preparations for the combat conditions of this war, and already in its first combat actions, two pilots had been killed and five MiG-15s were lost. Owing to the fact that this was an elite Soviet Air Force division, and that nearly all of the pilots had flown in the Great Patriotic War and had many hours of time in jet aircraft, the losses were not as great as they might have been otherwise. The pilots rather quickly adapted to the situation, and soon mastered the area of combat operations and the enemy's tactics, and on this basis, began to engage the enemy raids far more effectively.

The very same process occurred two months later with the introduction of the 303rd IAD into combat. There were the same initial losses, and then the rapid adaptation to the war's new conditions and the acquisition of new combat experience with a subsequent reduction in combat losses.

The American system of replacing pilots at the end of their tours of duty was both more carefully considered and rational. When fresh air units or new pilots arrived in the Fifth Air Force, they were gradually introduced into the fighting, and only after a compulsory, thorough study of the area of combat operations and the enemy's aerial combat tactics and methods. This process lasted for one to two months. Our adversary had the Sabre-equipped 4th and 51st Fighter Interceptor Wings fighting for aerial superiority over North Korea; rather than rotating entire squadrons and groups into and out of the combat zone, they replaced individual pilots. A pilot left the rosters of these fighter-interceptor groups only after completing 100 missions, or because of wounds or traumas. Therefore fresh replacement pilots assigned to the fighter squadrons came under the wing of more experienced colleagues, who were very familiar with the area of combat operations and the enemy's capabilities and tactics, and only after several weeks of training flights and close study of the combat area did they take part in combat missions. Even then, they didn't participate in the first few combats, but instead observed them from the side, before they received the go-ahead to partake in active combat operations as the wingman for a more experienced pilot. After completing half the missions necessary for a ticket home and participating in several dozen dogfights, the pilot would then become an element leader or flight leader and in turn begin instructing the latest batch of pilot replacements. Thus, for the duration of the entire period of combat operations of the Korea War, these two fighter groups were never rotated out of the theater of combat operations and served right up until the end of the war. Through their ranks passed not only the best pilot cadres of the USAF, but also pilots of the USNAF and Marine Air Force on temporary assignment, as well as British and Canadian fighter pilots, who were acquiring invaluable contemporary combat experience in aerial combats.

The Soviet command took an alternative path, which was mistaken and not only led to growing losses, but also undermined the ability of the 64th IAK to offer the same level of resistance to American air power as it had in the battles of 1951. This blunder is plainly apparent when one examines the combat results of the 64th IAK's new divisions that arrived in early 1952.

The Moscow-area's 97th IAD PVO under the command of Hero of the Soviet Union Colonel Aleksandr Grigor'evich Shevtsov was the first to arrive, which included two of the oldest PVO regiments: the 16th IAP under the command of Hero of the Soviet Union Colonel Nikolai Fedorovich Kuznetsov, and the 148th GIAP headed by Colonel Mokhnatkin. Both of the division's regiments had distinguished combat records in the years of the Great Patriotic War, defending Moscow and other Russian cities against Luftwaffe air raids.

The division arrived in China at the beginning of January 1952 and received the MiG-15s of the departing 324th IAD in the middle of the month, as well as all of the ground service and repair personnel of Kozhedub's division, since it had arrived without its own ground crews and technicians. The division's initial familiarization flights over MiG Alley were covered by pilots of the 303rd IAD. Introduction into combat consisted of three to five flights into the area of combat operations (without becoming engaged in them) and talks given in the regiments by the most experienced pilots of the departing 324th IAD. Both regiments were based on the Andong airfield.

The 97th IAD's regiments flew their first combat sorties on 16 January 1952. On this day, 28 MiGs of the 16th IAP conducted an overflight of the area of combat operations, during which they encountered 16 F-86s, but on this occasion both groups parted peacefully.

A little later at the beginning of February 1952, another Soviet fighter division arrived from the Soviet Union's Maritime District – the 190th IAD under the command of Colonel A.S. Kornilov. It had three regiments, the 256th IAP (commanded by Hero of the Soviet Union Lieutenant Colonel I.I. Semeniuk), the 494th IAP (commanded by Lieutenant Colonel A.E. Man'kovsky) and the 821st IAP (commanded by Hero of the Soviet Union Lieutenant Colonel G.F. Dmitriuk).

The 256th IAP was based on the Miaogou airfield together with a Chinese IAD of the UAA, while the 494th IAP and 821st IAP operated from the Andong base. The division obtained some of its MiGs from the departing 303rd IAD, while the rest were new MiG-15bis fighters straight from the factory.

Only two of the 190th IAD's regiments had served in the Great Patriotic War and the brief war with Japan as part of this division – they were the 494th IAP and 821st IAP, but not more than 10% of the aircrews of these regiments were pilots with combat experience. The remainder consisted of young pilots who hadn't yet seen battle. The 256th IAP was an "old-timer" of the Soviet Far East and transferred from the 32nd IAD to the 190th IAD in 1951. The 190th IAD switched to jets only in January 1951 and its pilots didn't have many hours of flight in them (by February 1952, it didn't exceed 50-60 hours per pilot).

This was the new roster of the 64th IAK in early 1952; with no intention to slight the former pilots of the 97th IAD and the 190th AD, it is clear that they were lacking the combat skill and experience of the departing pilots of the 303rd IAD and 324th IAD. To this it must be added that the PVO pilots in this period had trained for a combat role that differed from that of the Soviet Air Force pilots.

The PVO pilots were primarily responsible for covering important military and industrial sites and targets in the country's rear from possible enemy bomber attacks during a nuclear war. Thus the PVO pilots had been trained to intercept solitary bombers and reconnaissance aircraft of the likely enemy and to repel attacks by small groups of enemy bombers against rear sites in the depth of the country. This means that little attention had been paid to preparing them to take on the more agile enemy fighters and fighter-bombers, since these were the responsibility of the Air Force pilots in the frontal zone of combat operations; hence the PVO pilots had little experience with fighter combat maneuvers. Thus it was plainly a mistake to send PVO divisions, the pilots of which had not been trained for contemporary aerial combat, and moreover had accumulated relatively few hours of flight in the jet fighter, to Manchuria.

The leaders of our Air Force and PVO didn't take into account the fact that the situation in the skies of Korea had greatly altered, and that now enemy jet fighter-bombers had assumed the primary role of conducting air strikes in this war. The enemy's fighters in Korea had also changed their tactics and had been reinforced. All of these miscalculations indeed led to heavy losses in both of these divisions and to the loss of the initiative in the 64th IAK's zone of responsibility.

However, the decision had been taken, and the fresh complement of divisions was already dispersed among the airfields of northeastern China. They, like their predecessors in the 64th IAK, had the same combat mission: to defend important sites on North Korean territory down to the Pyongyang-Wonsan no-fly line, and the hydro-electrical stations, bridges, airfields and towns along the bordering Yalu River; and to intercept enemy aircraft penetrating into the IAK's zone of responsibility and destroy them.

Although the pilots of the 97th IAD first entered combat in the middle of January 1952, its regiments didn't achieve their first victories until 3 February. The pilots of the 16th IAP scored first when Senior Lieutenant A.N. Ivanov, a flight commander in the 2nd Squadron, downed one F-86 in a fleeting combat. It occurred on a regimental sortie with all three squadrons when they encountered a large group of F-86s. Although the victory was on the side of the 16th IAP, many of the regiments' MiGs returned from this dogfight with bullet holes in them. Senior Lieutenants M.N. Kazdoba and V.M. Abramov came back with light damage to their MiGs, but Senior Lieutenant G.V. Oleiniko's aircraft was in worse condition with 10 bullet holes in it.

Pilots of the 148th GIAP also distinguished themselves on this day. On a full regimental sortie around 1100, the 1st Squadron was leading the formation, followed by the 2nd Squadron, with the 3rd Squadron flying a little above and behind the first two squadrons. They encountered the enemy over the Pyongyang area. A flight of

F-86s (numbering 12 Sabres) spotted the 1st and 2nd Squadrons and tried to attack them from the rear, failing to see the eight MiGs that were flying above and behind them. Thus the Sabres placed themselves in a very vulnerable position, which the 3rd Squadron pilots unhesitatingly exploited by counterattacking the F-86s from above. However, only one of the Sabres was shot down, while the remainder exited combat in a dive. Flight commander Guards Captain P.S. Dubino scored the victory. Here's how Prokopii Sergeevich himself recalls his first victory in Korea: "For some reason, squadron commander Dudnichenko didn't attack the enemy; possibly he didn't see them. But I caught sight of the closest Sabre flying practically right next to me, separated from the squadron formation, attacked this Sabre and shot it down." This was F-86E No.50-644 from the 25th FIS – its pilot 1st Lieutenant John W. Hatchitt was killed.

Thus the pilots of the 97th IAD had opened their combat score in the skies of Korea. However, serious combats still lay ahead, since according to the 97th IAD's pilots themselves, the Americans were well aware that fresh fighter divisions had rotated into the 64th IAK, so seemingly they were checking out and studying the new adversary, not knowing yet what they faced. This explains the Americans' caution in the first combats with the 97th IAD and 190th IAD.

However, a 16th IAP pilot Senior Lieutenant Igor' Il'ich Troitsky was shot down and killed in the next dogfight with a group of Sabres. This happened on a regimental sortie on 9 February 1952, and was both the regiment's and the division's first combat loss. Soon, however, the 148th GIAP's pilots, who took off as a regimental group with 24 MiGs under the command of Major V.M. Dudnichenko, took revenge for the death of their comrade. Senior Lieutenant G.A. Nikiforov shot down a Sabre in the period between 1340 and 1410 in the area of Taegwan-dong, but the first death of one of their combat comrades, of course, anguished all of the pilots of the division. Curiously, the Americans don't report any victories on 9 February, but their first victories in the month of February were achieved by the well-known American ace Major George Davis on 10 February, so perhaps it was Major Davis who shot down Senior Lieutenant Troitsky.

On this same day of 9 February, pilots of the 190th IAD's 494th IAP made their first overflight of the area of combat operations. The pilots of the other two regiments of the 190th IAD conducted their initial flight over MiG Alley on the following day.

However on 10 February, the 97th IAD's pilots fully squared things with the offending parties of the 4th FIW. That morning, pilots of the 16th IAP took off on a combat mission under the command of the 2nd Squadron commander Major N.D. Zinchenko and became engaged with a group of F-86s near Anju. The deputy commander of the 16th IAP's 3rd Squadron Captain Petr Vasil'evich Minervin recalls:

On this sortie, Major Zinchenko, the 2nd Squadron commander, was leading our group. The combat broke out unexpectedly. A group of enemy aircraft, apparently, was flying above the clouds and decided to drop below them. The Sabres began to emerge through an opening in the clouds in pairs, but to their misfortune, our group was right there below the clouds. Whether they wanted it or not, they had to accept combat, and a "carousel" of climbing, diving and turning fighters began. The average altitude was 7,000-7,500 meters. At first I didn't see any Sabres around me, but then suddenly a pair of Sabres popped out of some clouds right in front of my aircraft. Moreover, one of them had deployed his speed brakes; evidently, the pilot was decelerating. I throttled forward and accelerated, closed with him, and gave him a long burst with all three cannons from a target aspect angle of 1/4. The Sabre's nose quickly dropped and it headed toward the earth trailing a long plume of black smoke. It struck the ground not far from the Korea Bay coastline and exploded. I arrived back at base as a pair, since in the course of the action I'd become separated from the group.

This action occurred in the period between 0806 and 0859, and the F-86 downed by Minervin fell in the vicinity of Romge, which Korean authorities confirmed.

However, a bit earlier, in a different battle Senior Lieutenant A.N. Ivanov had caught another Sabre underneath the clouds and downed it – this happened between 0654 and 0710, and the downed Sabre fell near Naechongdong. This was his second victory in the skies of Korea in the course of a week. All the regiment's aircraft returned to Andong.

On this same day, the pilots of the 148th GIAP also did well, and their prize was none other than the famous American jet ace and commander of the 4th FIW's 334th FIS Major George Davis. This is what happened in the words of a participant in this action, the 2nd Squadron commander Captain Leonid Ivanovich Savichev:

On this day there was a regimental sortie involving all three squadrons; altogether the group numbered 22 MiGs. We flew in a stair-stepped formation: the 1st Squadron led by Captain P.P. Motorin was the low squadron; the six MiGs of my 2nd Squadron were flying just a bit above it; and Major V.M. Dudnichenko's 3rd Squadron was the high squadron. The deputy regiment commander Lieutenant Colonel Zamarashkin was leading the entire group. We were flying under a layer of clouds, covering the Supung hydroelectric station. Suddenly a pair of Sabres dropped out of the clouds, and not seeing the MiGs of my 2nd Squadron above them, went on the attack against the low 1st Squadron. I immediately led my six MiGs to its assistance and successfully latched onto the tail of the Sabres that had turned up, and started to fire at the Sabre leader from a range of 800 meters. Suddenly I caught sight of shell casings raining down around my MiG from somewhere up above; I glanced up and saw the MiG of my deputy political leader Senior Lieutenant Mikhail Averin a bit in front and above me, who was also firing at the Sabre. His fire was more accurate – fragments started to fly off the Sabre's rudder and it went into a dive and soon crashed on the ground, while his wingman fled. Two days later confirmation arrived about the downing of the ace George Davis, and the credit for it went to Mikhail Averin.

All of our pilots returned safely to base.

According to the Americans, on this day Major Davis and 18 F-86As of the 334th FIS were escorting fighter-bombers, which were attacking the railroad line in the vicinity of Kunu-ri. Their group was attacked by 12 MiGs. In the course of the dogfight Major Davis downed two MiG-15s, constituting his 13th and 14th victories, but one of the MiGs managed to catch him and shoot him down. In reality the claim that Davis scored two victories before being shot down and killed is likely a lovely legend, conceived by the USAF command in order to adorn the death of the Fifth Air Force's top ace in Korea at the time. After all, prior to his final mission, Major Davis had been credited with

12 victories in the skies of Korea, in addition to the 7 victories he accumulated in the Second World War in the Pacific. However, on 10 February the 64th IAK didn't lose a single one of its aircraft, so the only way somehow to confirm Major Davis's final two victories on 10 February is to say that they were achieved in a combat with a group of Chinese MiGs prior to his encounter with the pilots of the 148th GIAP.

Considerable controversy has arisen between China and Russia over who should get credit for downing Major George Davis. The Russian historian A.A. Demin has laid out the Chinese version of Davis's death:

> ... On this day Major Davis was leading a group of 18 F-86As that was escorting a group of fighter-bombers ... 12 Chinese MiGs suddenly attacked his group, and he managed to down two of them before his death. They believe that the victor over their best pilot was the Chinese pilot Zhang Jihui, and this was only his first victory over an F-86.
>
> The Chinese, naturally, have accepted this story unreservedly, and having noted all of Davis's accomplishments (he had more than 3,000 hours in the cockpit and was considered unsurpassed in jet aircraft, and in their expression, "hadn't become fatigued in 100 combats"), they report that Zhang Jihui had only a little more than 300 hours of flight time in various aircraft, and just 30 in jets. The Chinese pilot downed the F-86 from long range (approximately 600 meters) in his second attack; the first was unsuccessful, because Davis had successfully maneuvered and evaded the fire. His Sabre fell just a few meters away from an infantry position.

The Chinese pilot Zhao Baotong's account of this combat, which has been translated into Russian, goes like this:

> ... my friend Zhang Jihui shot down the famous American ace, Major George Davis. On this day, more than a hundred enemy fighters were providing top cover for a large group of light bombers, which were preparing to attack positions of our ground troops. The leader Li Wen-mo ordered Zhang Jihui's squadron to attack the approaching group of hostile aircraft. The haze allowed our pilots to close stealthily with the enemy and then attack them at top speed. The attack was lightning-like. The enemy group scattered. Zhang Jihui got on the tail of the group leader. The adversary was experienced. He easily carried out the most difficult maneuvers one after the other. But as soon as the Zhang Jihui's tracers streaked closely by his aircraft, he became nervous. The enemy aircraft caught fire. The American extinguished the fire with a sideslip, but Zhang Jihui attacked him again. Our ground troops found this Sabre not far from Pyongyang. According to an inscription on the helmet and the documents found on the body of the pilot, it was established that this was the group commander, the masterful pilot Major George Davis. The infantry later handed his pistol to Zhang Jijui.
>
> Having witnessed the death of their leader, the remaining pilots of this group of enemy aircraft immediately split into separate elements and began to flee the combat area. However, several aircraft still tried to penetrate to Hill 1211. They immediately headed in the direction of the sun and in doing so placed our pilots at a disadvantage. The danger had arisen of losing the enemy. Then Zhang Jihui

led his group on a course parallel to the enemy aircrafts' heading. Thus our pilots could keep an eye on the enemy, and using the high performance characteristics of their aircraft, they gradually closed with them, after which with a sharp turn they attacked them. Having carried out the first task, Zhang Jihui's group became involved in the general battle. With the attack out the turn, with the tracers of their MiGs' bursts it scattered the group of Shooting Stars that were preparing to attack our artillery positions. Having prevented the enemy from launching a heavy strike against our forces, we destroyed on this day more than 10 enemy aircraft.

The Chinese later with unconcealed satisfaction repeatedly cited their newspaper *Renmin Ribao* [the voice of the Chinese Communist Party's Central Committee]. This newspaper had published an article shortly after the events happened, which related that the FEAF commander Lieutenant General Weyland had been forced to acknowledge that the death of the jet ace George Davis had "created a gloomy mood among the American air force pilots serving in Korea."

Thus there are competing claims for the victory over the top American ace, and it still isn't fully known who first engaged Davis's group – the Chinese or the 148th GIAP. However, a single detail nevertheless leaps to the eye: Zhou Baotong's stories were recorded by a *Krasnaia zvezda* [Red Star] newspaper correspondent, Lieutenant Colonel P. Starostin, who was known for his vivid descriptions of Second World War aerial combats. So in the given case he somehow wanted to dramatize this aerial clash above the heads of the infantry "in this nameless village on a nameless hill".

I don't want to cast any doubts on the merits of Zhang Jihui, who together with his wingman reportedly destroyed five aircraft in two February 1952 dogfights. According to Zhao Baotong, in those days "… dozens of our pilots, like Zhang Jihui, Liu Min, Lu Wen-mo, Li Tzuchen were models of courage, valor and skill in numerous aerial combats." Among Zhang Jihui's other victories there was also a "twin" victory on one mission. Having expended all his ammunition and having downed one fighter-bomber, his MiG received three bullet holes; out of ammunition, he went after the "perpetrator" and began to chase him, feigning attacks. This ended when the American crashed into a hill when trying to pull out of a dive. Zhang finished the war with four victories; there were 27 such "almost aces" among the Chinese pilots – nearly a full aviation regiment. Nevertheless, Zhang Jihui was the single one of the 27 to be awarded with the country's highest military honor, the Military Hero, First Degree, thereby joining a select list of only several of the 12 Chinese aces who were so honored – that's what the victory over the American ace George Davis meant to the Chinese. In contrast, you will not find the name of M. Averin among the list of our 22 aces who became Heroes of the Soviet Union during the Korean War.

Whatever happened back then, on 10 February the pilots of the 97th IAD downed three Sabres without any losses, and moreover Captain V.F. Shulev of the 17th IAP shot down one more F-86, which was that regiment's final victory in this war. Moreover, the famous American ace Major Davis had been killed; the Americans announced three days of mourning and the day of 10 February 1952 became a black one in the history of the USAF. In this morning battle, the 4th FIW lost two of its F-86Es in combat with MiGs. Major Davis was killed in F-86E No.51-2752, while the other Sabre No.50-645 received heavy damage and was later consigned to the scrap heap.

On the left is Captain V.F. Shulev, an ace of the 17th IAP, with a MiG-15
in the background on the Miaogou airfield in China, autumn of 1951.

For the next two weeks, right up until 16 February, the 64th IAK's pilots had no
further combats, because the Americans didn't show much activity. So it was on these
relatively quiet days that the pilots of the 190th IAD began to fly their first combat
sorties. Between 9 February and 16 February, the pilots of this division, covered by the
pilots of the 303rd IAD, flew familiarization flights over the area of combat operations.
On 13 February, pilots of the 821st IAP conducted their first combat sortie to intercept
an enemy group, but it failed to make contact with it. On the next day, 14 February, the
entire 190th IAD flew a mission for the first time: the 494th IAP and 821st IAP were
in the attack group, while the 256th IAP flew as the cover group. Incidentally, the day
passed without any encounters with the enemy.

However, on 16 February, a stretch of days featuring savage dogfights erupted between
the Americans and the pilots of the 97th IAD and 190th IAD. Though at first things
went well, the pilots of these two divisions were plainly unprepared for the fierce battles
with enemy fighters, which appeared in the area of MiG Alley in large groups. On 16
February, 14 MiGs of the 16th IAP under the command of Major A.P. Tarzudin had a
successful combat in the Chongju area, in which Captain N.D. Zinchenko downed one
Sabre, and our group returned with no losses.

However, things didn't go particularly well for the pilots of the 190th IAD, who
had only started to fly combat missions over Korea on 13 February. They came under
immediate pressure from the experienced pilots of the 4th and 51st FIW. Already on
17 February the 190th IAD's pilots flew two missions as a divisional group to the Anju
– Pyongyang area and opened their combat score in the skies of Korea – a pilot in
the 256th IAP's 3rd Squadron Senior Lieutenant A.M. Zvorykin downed a Sabre in a
combat with a group of F-86s. However, in this same action the regiment lost its first

Aces of the 821st IAP: Regiment commander Hero of the Soviet Union Lieutenant Colonel G.F. Dmitriuk back on the ground in China after a successful dogfight uses his hands to demonstrate his victory to deputy regiment commander Major A.P. Prudnikov (on the left) and the assistant regiment commander for aerial gunnery Major A.A. Olenitsa (on the right), 1952.

MiG – in a combat with eight F-86s, the Sabres flamed the MiG of Senior Lieutenant G.D. Kotovshchikov, who brought his aircraft down with difficulty in a North Korean rice paddy. The pilot was uninjured, but the MiG totally burned out.

The Americans on this day claimed four MiGs, three of which apparently belonged to the UAA. Meanwhile, Zvorykin shot down F-86E No.51-2800 from the 336th FIS, the pilot of which Captain Chuck Owens managed to bail out.

The pilots of the 190th IAD scored only one more victory until the end of February. On 18 February, the full division flew one sortie, but the pilots of its 494th IAP had two combat sorties over the day and encountered a group of Sabres on one of them. Senior Lieutenant Ia.K. Kriuchkov downed one F-86. The division and 64th IAK had no losses in these combats. Thus, the 190th IAD's victory score in the February combats stood at two downed F-86s. However, its own losses were more than twice as great: three of the 190th IAD's MiG-15s were shot down in combat and one pilot was killed, and two MiGs were lost as a result of an accident. On 20 February 1952 in a combat with Sabres of the 51st FIW, Senior Lieutenant V.F. Tarakan of the 494th IAP was shot down, though the pilot managed to eject safely. On 27 February, however, when the division's pilots flew 2-3 missions over the day, in a combat with Sabres of the 4th FIW, Senior Lieutenant Leonid Petrovich Derevianko was shot down and killed by Major Felix Asla, Jr. of the 334th FIS. Moreover, on 24 February 1952 while carrying out a mock dogfight for training purposes over the Andong airfield, two MiGs of the 821st IAP collided in mid-air. The deputy regiment commander Lieutenant Colonel A.N. Vasil'ev was killed, while the other pilot, Senior Lieutenant E.T. Mazikin of the regiment's 3rd Squadron was able to eject and survived.

The 97th IAD suffered even more substantial losses as the month progressed. In one dogfight on 19 February, Senior Lieutenant S.I. Muskantsev of the 148th GIAP was shot down as he was pulling out of a spin; the pilot managed to bail out. On 21 February, the 16th IAP suffered heavy losses: pilots of the 2nd Squadron were jumped by Sabres of the 4th FIW, and pilots Senior Lieutenants Vasilii Nikolaevich Shershakov and Aleksei Pavlovich Kozhevnikov were both killed-in-action; the latter was struck by a bullet in the head. They were shot down by Captain Brooks J. Liles of the 336th FIS and Billy B. Dobbs of the 335th FIS. The day before, on 20 February, the pilots of the 16th IAP had been involved in a successful combat with pilots of the 51st FIW, in which the regiment's 2nd Squadron commander Captain N.D. Zinchenko downed one Sabre, while 3rd Squadron commander Major A.P. Tarzudin damaged another Sabre. So as it happened, on 21 February, the pilots of the 4th FIW had taken full revenge for their colleagues in the 51st FIW by downing two of the 16th IAP's MiGs without any losses of their own.

Then, finally, on 22 February when six MiGs of the 16th IAP's 3rd Squadron were flying a patrol, during a turn flight commander Major Evgenii Pavlovich Savinov's MiG went into a spin from which the pilot couldn't recover. There had been no combat, so this pilot's death wasn't a combat loss for the regiment. On this same day, the 190th IAD's pilots flew two combat missions, and on one of them in the area of Anju they engaged a group of F-86s in a fleeting combat which ended with no results.

However they occurred, the results of the initial February 1952 combats were not comforting. Over the month, the pilots of the 97th IAD claimed seven US aircraft destroyed and another two damaged (all F-86s), but lost five of their own MiGs and four pilots. For the 190th IAD's pilots, who had only become active in mid-February, the balance of victories and losses were totally on the negative side: two F-86s had been downed, but the losses were five MiGs and two pilots (including the non-combat losses).

These numbers show that the hasty commitment into combat operations without adequate preparation told negatively on the results of the initial combats in the Korean sky; moreover, the pilots of the 64th IAK's new divisions had less preparation (and indeed, training that wasn't relevant to air-to-air dogfights) than the previous divisions, and the pilots of the 97th IAD PVO and 190th IAD had no combat experience in the jet age. All these things taken together led to the more modest combat results and the heavy losses.

The Americans claimed that in the February fighting, the pilots of the 4th and 51st FIW shot down 17 MiGs, of which 11 went to the credit of the 51st in their new F-86Es, while the other six went to the score of the 4th Wing's pilots, some of whom were still flying the old F-86A-5 Sabre. The Americans place their own losses at just two F-86s. Of the total of 17 victories claimed by the Americans, only seven belonged to the 64th IAK (another three destroyed MiGs were non-combat losses), so the remaining 10 evidently belonged to the UAA. At the end of February, the 39th FIS began to form, which was to receive new F-86Es and join the 51st FIW, but this wouldn't happen until the beginning of summer 1952.

THE NEW SHIFT ACQUIRES COMBAT EXPERIENCE

Already on the first day of spring 1952, the pilots of the 190th IAD's third fighter regiment, the 821st IAP, opened their combat score. The commander of the 821st IAP's 1st Squadron Major V.A. Lazarev shot down one Sabre. Another Sabre was damaged in the same dogfight by the 821st IAP's assistant commander for aerial gunnery service, Major A.A. Olenitsa. On this day the pilots of the 190th IAD conducted two sorties as a divisional group, and during both of them the pilots of the 821st IAP ran into Sabres. Pilots of the 494th IAP also dueled with F-86s on this day, and in this action Senior Lieutenant A.N. Cherny's MiG was damaged. It arrived back at base with numerous bullet holes, but the aircraft was patched up and returned to service two days later.

More intense aerial combats erupted on 3 March 1952 over the main hydro-electrical station on the Yalu River at Supung. Numerous aerial clashes involving the pilots of the 97th IAD and 190th IAD went on above it during the day. At first, pilots of the 148th GIAP became involved in a combat above the dam, and although they beat back an American air strike on the dam, in a combat with four F-86s of the 51st FIW's 16th FIS, this regiment's 2nd Squadron commander Captain L.I. Savichev was shot down. Savichev managed to escape his doomed MiG-15. True, once on the ground, Chinese took him for an American pilot (he was wearing an American flight jacket) and were on the verge of battering him with clubs, but everything turned out okay for our pilot.

Pilots of the 256th IAP, who over the day flew three combat missions, became involved in a fiercer dogfight. Here's how a participant in it, Nikolai Efimovich Smirnov, describes it:

> On 3 March, the regiment commander Hero of the Soviet Union Lieutenant Colonel I.I. Semeniuk led the regiment on a combat patrol over a hydro-electrical station. I was his wingman on this sortie. Sabres showed up over the target and we engaged them in combat. The regiment commander sought to attack the lead Sabre group, while I stuck with him. During the regiment commander's attack on this group, it broke apart into separate elements. However, the commander stubbornly continued to follow the lead Sabre element, managed to close with it, and he opened fire. One of the Sabres immediately began to emit smoke and headed toward the sea. Enemy aircraft repeatedly opened fire at me during the action, but I vigilantly stayed with my leader and didn't abandon my position. Soon the enemy group broke off combat and headed out to sea. Having returned to our base at Miaogou, I discovered 12 bullet holes in my aircraft. However, the damage wasn't serious and soon the technicians repaired my MiG.

In this combat, in addition to the Sabre damaged by Lieutenant Colonel I.I. Semeniuk, Senior Lieutenant I.S. Mel'nik shot down another Sabre. However, the regiment also suffered a loss: Senior Lieutenant A.I. Prokhorov's MiG-15 was shot down, but he managed to eject safely from the aircraft. The Americans, however, claim to have downed three MiG-15s on this day.

The pilots of the 821st IAP flew four combat sorties on 3 March, all of them as a full regiment. They had three skirmishes with small groups of Sabres in the areas of Anju, Chongju and Pakchon.

Over the next several days the 64th IAK's pilot had a few minor dogfights with Sabres, in the process downing three F-86s without any losses. For example, on 4 March in the period between 1100 and 1140, a group of 16 MiGs from the 16th IAP under the command of deputy regiment commander Major P.K. Zhuravlev successfully engaged a group of Sabres over the Pihyon, Taegwan-dong and Sonchon area. In this dogfight the 16th IAP's shot down two F-86s without any losses of their own: the group leader Major Zhuravlev claimed one Sabre, which fell in the vicinity of Naebin, while credit for the second Sabre, which fell in the Sinanju area, was shared by several pilots. On the same day, the 190th IAD's pilots conducted two combat sorties as a group and also ran into groups of F-86s in the Sakchu, Taegwan-dong area, but these encounters ended without results. On 5 March the pilots of the 821nd IAP tangled with a group of 12 F-86s in the vicinity of Kiojo, and Captain I.P. Vakhrushev received credit for damaging one Sabre.

However, it should be said that the records on the American side do not at all correspond to the losses of F-86s claimed by the Soviet pilots in the first week and a half of March 1952. Instead, over the first 10 days of March, the US Fifth Air Force lost only fighter-bombers of the F-84E type, as many as nine of the aircraft, not considering losses among their F-80s. Possibly, in their initial combats with US aircraft, our pilots were still mixing up the different types of American aircraft they encountered in the air and recorded all of the downed aircraft as Sabres. If so, perhaps there were actually two or three F-84s among the four Sabres claimed in combat by our pilots over the first 10 days of March?

The other Thunderjets most likely were downed by pilots of the UAA. However, the UAA pilots, who lost up to 20 of their own MiGs in aerial combats in these days, took a real working over from the American pilots in return. For example, on 5 March pilots of the 4th and 51st FIW downed seven MiGs in aerial combat, and just as many were shot down in dogfights on 10 March. Pilots of the 190th IAD also clashed with the forward screens of Sabres on 5 March. The 494th IAP's pilots flew two missions on this day to cover the Supung hydroelectric power station and the Andong Air Base, but came across no enemy aircraft. The 821st IAP's MiGs also took to the air to cover the Supung power station, and here's what one of the participants on this sortie Aleksei Ivanovich Romanov had to say about it:

On this day there was a regimental sortie; having arrived in the patrol area, the regiment split up into separate pairs and flights and began searching for enemy aircraft. My wingman and I were also scanning for enemy aircraft, when I unexpectedly saw a Sabre cruising up from my right, which took up a position off of my right wingtip; I could even see the American pilot's face. Glancing behind me, I discovered that my wingman wasn't there, but instead a second Sabre was hanging behind me at a range of 100-150 meters. As later became revealed, the F-86 element had attacked our pair from above, and my wingman, instead of protecting me, immediately abandoned me by departing in a zoom climb once he caught sight of the Sabres, without even warning me of the danger. That's how I wound up under the convoy of this Sabre element.

While I was still trying to digest the predicament I was in, the Sabre right off my wingtip began to nudge me in the direction of South Korea, and I understood why the Sabre behind me wasn't firing – this pair of Americans wanted to escort me back to their base in South Korea. I understood that if I didn't come up with something quickly, they would either lead me away to hostile territory or shoot me down. I abruptly rolled over and went into a dive, but there weren't novices sitting in the Sabre cockpits; they immediately copied my maneuver and in so doing, both of them wound up on my tail and opened fire on my aircraft. One of the Sabres hit my MiG with the first burst. As I found out later on the ground, five .50-caliber bullets had struck my aircraft, two of which hit the vertical stabilizer and damaged my rudder control. One bullet severed the fuel line, another punctured the nose wheel, and the last one penetrated the fuselage. Kerosene being pumped by the turbo compressor began to gush into the cockpit, soaking me. I donned my goggles in order to shield my eyes from the fuel and began to control my MiG chiefly through my ailerons. The Sabres were continuing to fire at my aircraft, but I could make little sideslips that threw off their aim, and their tracers streaked closely by my MiG without hitting it. I descended to an altitude of 3,000 meters and struggled toward the border with China, where our anti-aircraft batteries were deployed, so that they could brush off my pursuers. However, the Sabre pilots were also aware of the anti-aircraft guns in the given area, and once I entered their zone, the Sabres turned around and headed toward the bay.

After this I calmly flew back to Miaogou and didn't get nervous until the landing approach, being unsure about how to land my damaged aircraft. I touched down normally, but leaked fuel immediately began to spray from the front wheel well, and in a cascade of sparks I found myself on the iron rim of the front wheel heading toward a hardstand. In order not to start a fuel fire on the runway for the regiment's other MiGs waiting to land, I turned my MiG off the runway and onto an unpaved area, and then my MiG came to a stop. Later because of the stress I had experienced, the regiment's doctor sent me off for a rest and I didn't fly for about a week, during which time the technicians put my aircraft back into working order.

That's how this sortie ended for one of the 190th IAD's pilots. This was a mission to the Kiojo area, where they encountered 12 F-86s. In the ensuing action, the 821st IAP's 1st Squadron commander Captain I.P. Vakhrushev damaged one Sabre. Perhaps Senior Lieutenant Romanov's aircraft wound up among those seven MiGs that were counted as downed by the pilots of the 4th and 51st FIW on this day?

Combat missions were flown almost every day, if the weather conditions allowed it. The 64th IAK's pilots began to encounter enemy aircraft rather frequently: on 6 March, the pilots of the 821st IAP clashed with 18 F-86s in the Sakchu – Siojio area, while pilots of the 494th IAP on the same day had one combat with a group of F-86s, but all these encounters ended with no aircraft lost on either side.

However, on 11 March, major aerial battles flared up again in the Anju area that involved the Soviet pilots. The pilots of the 97th IAD and 190th IAD each flew three missions on this day; all the sorties were in division strength. Two of them resulted in combat with enemy aircraft. The 97th IAD's pilots took on the forward screen of Sabres, while the 190th IAD penetrated to the region where the F-80 and F-84 fighter-bombers were operating. The pilots of the 16th IAP did particularly well dueling with the Sabres; in the first action, which occurred in the period between 0654 and 0715 over the Kusan area, they damaged two F-86s, while in the second battle of the day, involving 16 MiGs led by the 2nd Squadron commander Major N.D. Zinchenko with 40 Sabres of the 4th FIW in the Sakchu – Pihyon area, another F-86 was damaged and one was shot down. The group consisted of three flights, one from each of the regiment's squadrons: From the 1st Squadron, Captain V.V. Vlasov commanded the first flight, Major N.D. Zinchenko himself headed the second flight from the 2nd Squadron, and 3rd Squadron commander Major G.K. Zenov led the third flight. From out of the clouds, a pair of Sabres unexpectedly jumped Zinchenko's flight. Vlasov with his flight intended to get behind this pair of Sabres, but then they spotted an approaching formation of

Pilots of the 16th IAP. Seated in the first row from left to right are A.S. Boitsov, 3rd Squadron commander G.K. Zenov, the 16th IAP's deputy political commander G.A. Ziuzikov, and an unidentified pilot; standing from left to right are flight commander V.M. Abramov, I.P. Kozin (the regiment's engineer for special equipment), flight commander M.N. Kazdoba and the 1st Squadron's deputy political commander A.I. Manshukov – May 1954.

eight Sabres and engaged it instead. Meanwhile, the Sabre element from behind and below attacked Major Zinchenko's element, which didn't see them, and shot up the aircraft of his wingman Senior Lieutenant Ivanov. Apparently, the bullets struck the MiG's ammunition because there was an explosion. Ivanov ejected, but apparently his parachute failed to deploy fully and he was killed when coming down on a hill. True, it didn't take the 16th IAP's pilots long to even the score. In the clash with the eight Sabres, Vlasov managed to latch onto the tail of one of them and shot it down – the Sabre plummeted into the sea. At that point several more Sabre flights arrived on the scene, and the dogfight flared up with renewed strength, but the riled pilots of the 16th IAP were no longer spooked by the enemy's numerical superiority and soon another Sabre plummeted to the earth in the Yongsan area, the victim of Major G.K. Zenov's cannons. This dogfight occurred in the period between 1520 and 1548. Thus the regiment has suffered a heavy loss: the 2nd Squadron pilot Senior Lieutenant Aleksandr Nikolaevich Ivanov, who had already during the short time of his service destroyed two F-86s, was shot down by Sabres and killed.

The 190th IAD's pilots also did well on this day. On the first morning sortie, the 821st IAP's pilots engaged 24 F-86 in the Siojio area and Captain I.P. Vakhrushev damaged one Sabre. On the second mission, the 821st IAP's pilots intercepted a group of eight F-80 fighter-bombers covered by eight F-86s in the Pakchon area and attacked them. In the process, the group's leaders each scored a victory by downing an F-80: the commander of the 821st IAP Hero of the Soviet Union Lieutenant Colonel F.G.

Dmitriuk, the regiment's assistant commander for aerial gunnery service Major A.A. Olenitsa and the 1st Squadron commander Captain I.P. Vakhrushev.

On an afternoon sortie while patrolling an area, a regimental group from the 821st IAP headed by the regiment commander Lieutenant Colonel F.G. Dmitriuk encountered a group of fighter-bombers consisting of eight F-80s approaching on a meeting course. The regiment's pilots immediately attacked the enemy group head-on, and as the MiGs and Shooting Stars closed rapidly, with a burst from all three cannons Senior Lieutenant I.F. Denisov simply blew apart one F-80 and then by some miracle flew right through the angry burst of the explosion without taking a single hit by a fragment from the disintegrating target.

The remaining Shooting Stars were saved thanks to the arrival of 24 F-86s from the 4th FIW, which attacked Lieutenant Colonel F.G. Dmitriuk's group. A swirling dogfight ensued, which an arriving group of MiGs from the 494th IAP also joined. In this action a pilot of the 821st IAP's 1st Squadron Lieutenant A.M. Bushnev claimed one Sabre. Another F-86 was downed by Senior Lieutenant A.A. Alekseenko of the 494th IAP. In their turn, the Sabre pilots managed to damage heavily one MiG from the 494th IAP, and its pilot Senior Lieutenant Nikolai Ivanovich Zenakov was killed when attempting a forced landing.

The results of the fighting on 11 March 1952 were as follows: four F-80s and three F-86s were downed and another four Sabres were damaged, of which four F-86s were credited to pilots of the 16th IAP, while four F-80s and the other F-86 went to the score of the 821st IAP. Soviet losses consisted of two MiG-15s and two pilots. This was the first major victory for the pilots of the 64th IAK's new divisions. The American side acknowledged the loss on this day of only one of its F-80s and another F-84E No.50-1126 from the 49th FBG, the pilot of which managed to reach his base in South Korea, where the Thunderjet crashed upon landing. The Americans also recognize the loss of another F-86E No.50-604 from the 16th FIS; its pilot 1st Lieutenant James E. Arnold managed to reach Cho-Do Island where he was killed when making a crash landing. True, three days later another F-84E from the 136th FBW and one F-86E from the 335th FIS were written-off. According to American records, both of their pilots were killed "in non-combat actions". Knowing the tendency of the Americans to conceal their combat losses in dogfights with MiGs in this manner, one can assume that both of these two USAF aircraft were actually lost in the battles on 11 March (on 14 March 1952 the 64th IAK's pilots didn't fly any combat sorties). In their turn the pilots of the 335th FIS claimed two MiGs on this day, while the pilots of the 336th FIS claimed victories over two more. However, the 64th IAK's records only confirm two of these victory claims. Apparently, in the best case the pilots of the 4th FIW only damaged two of the 64th IAK's MiGs, but didn't destroy them.

Already on the following day the pilots of the 4th FIW's 335th and 336th Squadrons managed to catch a group of Chinese MiGs from the UAA and claimed four victories over MiG-15s. However, in this same action the young Chinese pilots shot down one of the Sabres – its pilot RAF Squadron Leader Graham E. Hulse, who was on temporary duty with the 336th FIS, is officially listed as missing-in-action. Also, while carrying out a reconnaissance flight on 15 March 1952, an RF-86 from the 15th TRS was shot down. This was also most likely the work of the young Chinese pilots of the UAA.

Gradually the pilots of the 97th IAD and 190th IAD were becoming accustomed with the theater of combat operations, testing the tactics of their primary aerial adversaries, the

USAF's 4th and 51st FIW, and with each passing day they were handling the combats in MiG Alley more confidently and skillfully, which was reflected in their combat results. Here, for example, is what a pilot with the 821st IAP Aleksei Ivanovich Romanov had to say about the changing tactics that the Soviets were employing:

> Our regiment commander Hero of the Soviet Union Major G.F. Dmitriuk, after the initial unsuccessful or fruitless combats with the enemy, re-examined the tactics of the regiment's operations, and instead of three eight-ship squadron formations, the regiment began to send four six-ship formations headed by the regiment's leadership out on combat missions, thereby increasing the number of groups in the regiment's formation. They were also allowed more freedom when maneuvering against the Sabre formations and this immediately had an effect on our productivity as measured by downed enemy aircraft.

The aerial combat conducted by the 64th IAK on 16 March 1952, in which all the regiments of the 97th IAD and 190th IAD took part in turn as they rotated in and out of the action, serves as an example of the growing confidence of the divisions' pilots in their abilities. In the morning, the 64th IAK launched every serviceable aircraft at its disposal to repel enemy air raids in the Taegwan-dong area, where the pilots clashed with approximately 70 F-86s. The 821st IAP's pilots took on 32 F-86s in combat, while the pilots of the 494th IAP tangled with 34 F-86s. The pilots of the 190th IAD particularly distinguished themselves; in the two dogfights on this day, they claimed the destruction of nine Sabres, while a pilot of the 148th GIAP Senior Lieutenant M.A. Averin shot down another Sabre in the period between 1004 and 1020 – the enemy aircraft fell into the sea south of Pihyon. Thus, the total number of Sabres downed in these dogfights reached 10, while the Soviet side's losses amounted to one aircraft: the MiG of the 256th IAP's 3rd Squadron commander, Captain A.I. Roi, was set on fire by a burst from a Sabre's machine guns. In his burning aircraft, he flew back to his airfield and set it down on the runway, and was barely able to escape the burning cockpit once the MiG rolled to a stop. The aircraft was consumed by the flames, and the pilot himself suffered burns and was sent to the hospital.

Here's how a pilot of the 256th IAP's 1st Squadron Senior Lieutenant Aleksei Fedorovich Bondarenko describes this dogfight:

> Our next combat mission took place on 16 March. We arrived in our assigned quadrant at an altitude of 10,000 meters, but there was no enemy aircraft at this altitude. We received an order to descend to 4,000 meters and to attack F-80 fighter-bombers that were on this day striking North Korean troop locations. Having descended to 4,000 meters, though, we engaged Sabres in combat, which were also taking part in attacking the ground troops.
>
> Our flight successfully got in behind a flight of Sabres. I very rapidly began to close with one of the enemy aircraft because of a difference in our respective speeds. The Sabre pilot had spotted me on his tail and had abruptly throttled back and popped his speed brakes. He was expecting that I would overshoot his aircraft, but I also quickly throttled back and deployed my speed brakes. I moved in right behind him and began to take aim at the Sabre, but my arms and legs were shaking and I couldn't line him up in the sights. A moment later, I calmed down. I quit shaking

and began to frame the enemy aircraft within the reticule of my gun sight. The first burst, and the tracers passed wide of the Sabre, but he continued in a straight line; a second burst had the same result, but with my third burst the outer third of its left wing broke off (which was visible on the gun camera film – the range was 200 meters). The Sabre rolled into a dive toward the earth and the pilot never bailed out. I pulled up into a tight, climbing turn to port and headed back to base.

Everything inside me began to sing; I felt boundless joy over my first victory. The sortie was somewhere toward the end of the day. Therefore after the regiment's landing and the post-mission debriefing, we immediately drove off to our quarters in the town.

I entered the room where I was living, and I felt like I had to be alone to go back over the events of the day in my mind. Then I grabbed a towel and headed for the showers, but there was no one in the room when I entered it. The victorious pilots were raucously celebrating in the mess hall, and there were 10 of them including me. This was a big victory of our division.

Yes, this was actually a big victory for the 64th IAK's pilots, in particular those of the 190th IAD, and as it later turned out, this was the highest-scoring day for the given divisions over their time in Manchuria; moreover, the losses were minimal. I would add that Aleksei Fedorovich Bondarenko gives a good description of how the young pilots greeted the victories, the psychological stress that the pilots experienced in each combat, and what nervous tension was required for achieving victories over the great American pilots.

On 16 March our pilots battled with pilots of the 4th FIW's 335th FIS, who claimed four MiG-15s destroyed on this day, as well as with pilots of the 51st FIW. Apparently in this dogfight, several of the 64th IAK's MiGs were damaged, which according to the evidence on the gun camera film, were credited to the American pilots as downed MiGs. This wasn't the case, however, as the damaged MiGs all returned safely to base. The Americans themselves acknowledged the loss of only one F-86E No.50-668 from the 25th FIS, which was being flown by an officer of the RAF John R. Baldwin, who was on temporary assignment with the 51st FIW. He was killed on this mission. In addition, two F-84s of the 49th FBW were lost on this day; most likely, they were also downed by pilots of the 190th IAD, who mistakenly took them for Sabres. However, it seems that the American losses on this day were even greater.

On 17 March the pilots of the 97th IAD, or more precisely, of its 148th GIAP stood out. In the next dogfight with Sabres, they managed to destroy three without any losses of their own. This battle took place in the afternoon between 1626 and 1640 in the area of Sokha-dong. The victorious pilots were Senior Lieutenants E.V. Filippov, G.A. Nikiforov and V.A. Taravkov. In this dogfight Senior Lieutenant N.K. Sirotinin was lightly wounded, but he managed to return to base safely. The 190th IAD's pilots also conducted several regimental combat sorties and had several fleeting brushes with Sabres, all of which ended without results.

On 19 March, Lieutenant F.S. Krasulin with his wingman Senior Lieutenant A.A. Leonov had a combat against four Sabres right over the airfield, which were trying to catch someone either taking off or coming in for a landing. However, Lieutenant Krasulin's element disrupted their plan and not only chased the Sabres away from the airfield, but also downed one of them – Lieutenant F.S. Krasulin got the victory credit.

The next major battle between the 64th IAK's MiGs and the Sabres of the 4th and 51st FIW took place on 20 March. Our pilots took off to repel a raid by enemy fighter-bombers and as always tangled with the forward screen of Sabres, while the Unified Air Force "worked over" the fighter-bombers.

Pilots of the 97th IAD's 148th GIAP and squadrons from all three regiments of the 190th IAD took part in the battle – the 16th IAP was kept in reserve. The battle occurred in the Pihyon – Kusong area between 1600 and 1620. The 148th GIAP's 1st and 2nd Squadrons initiated the dogfight. Having spotted a group of 40 Sabres above them that were angling across their front from right to left, they pulled up into a climbing turn to the left. As a result of the maneuver, they found themselves within approximately 200 meters of the enemy fighters. In this attack, the commander of the 1st Squadron Captain P.P. Motorin's element attacked one Sabre pair, and Captain Motorin's wingman Senior Lieutenant V.F. Korochkin shot down the right-hand Sabre.

Soon another 20 Sabres arrived and joined the action, but the pilots of the 148th GIAP also received help from the pilots of the 190th IAD, who claimed four Sabres in this dogfight, while losing one of their own aircraft. On this mission, the 821st IAP was flying top cover for the 494th IAP, which was operating at low altitudes, and in the area 20 kilometers west of Taegwan-dong they tangled with a group of F-86s. The MiG of Senior Lieutenant S.I. Kolesnikov of the 494th IAP (which opened its combat score in this action) was hit by Sabre fire, and he made a belly-landing in his damaged aircraft back at base. The pilot was unhurt, but the MiG had to be written off.

Six MiGs from the 148th GIAP's 3rd Squadron, led by its commander Hero of the Soviet Union Guards Major V.M. Dudnichenko, ended this combat on a victorious note. Here's how this was expressed in the regiment's documents:

On 20 March 1952, six MiG-15 fighters headed by the 3rd Squadron commander Hero of the Soviet Union Major V.M. Dudnichenko were scrambled to cover the bulk of the regiment and to secure its withdrawal from combat. Having climbed to an altitude of 10,000 meters and arriving in its assigned area, Major Dudnichenko caught sight of six F-86s to the left of him. Swinging his squadron around to the left, Dudnichenko attacked three F-86s in a head-on pass, thereby covering the attack by the element consisting of his political deputy Major A.T. Bashman and Lieutenant A.I. Krylov. From behind and to the right at a range of 200-300 meters, they fired on two F-86s at a target aspect angle of 2/4 and shot down both of them – this occurred between 1620 and 1629 in the Kaisiu – Tetsuzan area.

The element led by Senior Lieutenant Kh. Musin attacked a pair of Sabres from an enemy six-ship formation that had arrived to bail the first group out of trouble. After an attack from the front at an angle, with a subsequent turn and a yo-yo maneuver, our pair closed with the enemy fighters and from a range of 350 meters downed one F-86. Thus, the 3rd Squadron's pilots destroyed three enemy aircraft on one combat mission.

In reality, though the pilots of the 148th GIAP did down three aircraft in this combat, the 3rd Squadron only received credit for two victories. For some reason that is still unknown, Senior Lieutenant Krylov didn't receive credit for his victory.

As a result, during the day of 20 March 1952 the 64th IAK's pilots repelled two enemy air raids and destroyed seven F-86s in the process, while losing only one aircraft in return. The Americans assert that on 20 March their Sabres downed five MiG-15s. In reality, the 64th IAK lost only one aircraft on this day. However, the American records for this day include the two MiGs lost by the 64th IAK on the next day, 21 March. The 821st IAP's Senior Lieutenant G.T. Tiutikov was shot down by Sabres, though the pilot ejected safely, and the 494th IAP's Senior Lieutenant B.S. Smirnov made a dead-stick landing at the Andong Air Base. In a combat with Sabres, bullets had riddled his fuel tanks and all his fuel had drained away. The pilot was able to walk away from the crash, but his MiG had to be written off. Apparently, these two victories were credited to the Sabre pilots as having occurred on 20 March according to Washington time, not to local time.

In addition, on 21 March Senior Lieutenant G.M. Viazikov's MiG was damaged in a dogfight with Sabres – his cockpit canopy was smashed and steering controls damaged. However, with the help of his MiG's trim flaps he was able to return to base safely and make a landing there. Apparently, the Americans also recorded Viazikov's MiG as a 20 March victory. The remaining two MiGs that the Americans claim on 20 March are either figments of imagination or Chinese MiGs from the UAA. The Americans again acknowledge the loss of one F-86E (No.50-628) on 20 March from the 334th FIS, which was heavily damaged in one of the combats; the pilot succeeded in reaching his base, but his Sabre did a ground loop when landing and had to be written off. The pilot was unharmed.

The next major aerial combat in the skies of Korea took place on 24 March 1952, when the Americans again launched large fighter-bomber raids into the zone of the MiGs' operations. As usual, there were two enemy raids, one in the morning and the next in the afternoon. Violent dogfights developed in various sectors; having broken apart into small groups, the aircraft of both sides became entwined in tangles of contrails at high altitudes.

The full complement of the 97th IAD departed first to repel enemy aircraft that had been detected by ground radar. Pilots of the 16th IAP launched from the Miaogou airfield, while the 148th GIAP's pilots took off from the Andong runways. A column of the three squadrons from the 148th GIAP led the way, with the 1st Squadron in front, the 2nd Squadron trailing, and the 3rd Squadron positioned at higher altitude behind the other two squadrons. Approaching the area where the enemy fighter-bombers were operating, the pilots spotted a group of 12 F-80s and attacked them. However, the Shooting Star pilots were on the alert and began to avoid the MiG attacks with a tight climbing turn in the direction of the bay, while simultaneously calling for help. When beginning to level out from the turn, one of the F-80s was fired upon by Senior Lieutenant V.F. Korochkin, who could clearly see his tracers disappearing into the center of his target and the explosions of his shells. What happened next with the F-80 he didn't see, as he quickly overshot it, and further events prevented him from observing what became of the Shooting Star (on his gun camera footage, the target was barely visible, so Korochkin didn't receive credit for a victory).

During the attack, the 148th GIAP's MiGs closely approached the coastline, and at that point our anti-aircraft gunners opened up on both the enemy aircraft and our own MiGs. The MiG-15 of Senior Lieutenant A.P. Fedoseev from the 148th GIAP's 1st

Squadron was struck by this friendly fire, and he was forced to eject from his burning aircraft. He came down in his parachute on the muddy coastal flats when it was low tide, and Chinese soldiers picked him up.

Simultaneously, arriving MiGs from the 16th IAP also attacked the Shooting Stars, and its 1st Squadron commander Major G.K. Zenov managed to catch one of the F-80s and downed it cleanly; his victory was confirmed in every possible way. However, at that point Sabres of the 4th FIW showed up and went on the attack against the 148th GIAP's leading 1st Squadron. Senior Lieutenant E.V. Filippov's flight was jumped by a Sabre squadron, and one of the Sabre pilots, unable to handle the rapid acceleration of the dive, collided with Filippov's MiG. There was an explosion, and both aircraft plummeted to the earth; flight commander Senior Lieutenant Evgenii Viktorovich Filippov, who had already scored two victories in the Korean sky by this day, was killed in the cockpit of his MiG.

According to the version of events offered by the other pilots of the 148th GIAP who took part in this battle, everything went just the opposite: the collision didn't happen when the Sabres jumped Filippov's flight, but in the ensuing dogfight, when Filippov himself steered his aircraft toward the lead Sabre and rammed it. However, the first version of this episode that I have laid out is more plausible.

However it happened back then, two MiGs had already been lost and the Sabres were continuing to press. Left without his wingman (Fedoseev had been shot down by the Soviet anti-aircraft battery), Captain P.S. Liubovinkin was being harried by a pair of Sabres and he was calling for help, but in the helter-skelter of the dogfight no one responded. Liubovinkin raced toward his base, but on the approach to Andong the Sabres nevertheless finished him off, and he and his aircraft crashed not far from the town.

The unlucky 148th GIAP pilot Aleksandr Pavlovich Fedoseev, whose MiG was struck by friendly anti-aircraft artillery fire, offers a vivid description of what happened on this unhappy mission:

> For our regiment and me, 24 March 1952 became a "black day". I recall this day in quite a lot of detail and I've never forgotten it. As usual we took off in response to an alarm, and having assembled in the regiment's combat formation, we climbed to 10,000 meters and set out from the Andong airfield and took a heading along the North Korean coast toward the Pyongyang-Wonsan no-fly line. The regimental group's leader was the regiment's inspector of piloting technique Major A.M. Balabaikin.
>
> The regiment's formation was as follows: the 2nd Squadron was in the attack group; the 1st Squadron was flying a bit to the right and at the same altitude in its normal position, while approximately 500-800 meters above and behind was the regiment's 3rd Squadron. On this sortie, the division command post was issuing certain unreliable orders and kept re-directing us and changing our altitude in order to guide us to the enemy. For some reason we never encountered them, and as a result the 1st Squadron wound up over the very coastline itself. We were categorically forbidden to enter the airspace over the sea, just as we couldn't cross the Pyongyang-Wonsan line. Just then an order arrived over the radio from the group commander for the squadrons to split into opposite turns of 180°, so the

2nd Squadron banked around to the left and receded from the coastline, while the 1st Squadron wheeled to starboard and wound up over the seashore. In particular Liubovinkin and I during the turn became the squadron group's extreme pair on the left, and he and I wound up to a certain extent out over the sea.

I believe this maneuver was wholly unsuccessful. At that point we received an order from the corps command post to descend to 5,000 meters, and as it happened, our squadron commander Motorin began a tight, descending turn of 180° -- in other words, he was carrying out the order from the corps command post.

Here it must be said that one of the Sabre's favorite tactics was to catch us in a turn, when the wide radius of the turn at high altitude and maximum speed gave them the opportunity to turn inside us and quickly close for an attack. The Sabres were superior in horizontal maneuvers and could turn more tightly than the MiG, and when we were coming out of the descending turn, I heard the voice of the pilot Sirotinin over the radio: "I'm alone." I thought that he had lost his leader Filippov and that he was trying to link-up with someone; such cases did happen,.

As I was continuing to descend over the fringe of the coastline, trying to catch up with my leader Liubovinkin, who was himself lagging behind the lead pair of Motorin and Korochkin, I caught sight of bursting anti-aircraft shells out in front of me and at a lower altitude. The second burst was just a bit below me and closer, and I didn't even see the third burst. The force of its explosion abruptly flipped my MiG onto its back; a large piece of Plexiglas was driven out of the right side of the canopy, and a small fragment of it dug into my head after penetrating my winter headset. I managed to roll my MiG back over into level flight. I glanced down at my instruments and saw that there were all sitting at 0, my hydraulics were gone, and the needle on my engine's RPM indicator was steadily moving downward; in addition, my radio wasn't working and everything was silent.

That's when I decided to abandon the aircraft while I still had altitude. There couldn't even be any talk about pondering a forced landing – there was only the sea and the mountainous terrain. As I'd been taught, I pulled back the lever of the catapult's safety-lock and placed my feet on the seat's footrest, after which the cockpit's canopy was supposed to fly off and open the cockpit to the outside air. But this didn't happen. The canopy only twisted a bit and that was all. With the fingers of my right hand I began to press on the rollers of the cockpit's slide, and just as I had given up all hope, the canopy tore free. Well, I immediately pressed the launch button, sensed my seat settled a bit, and then it abruptly shot upward. At first the forces pushed me back into the seat, and my head and neck scrunched down into my body, but a second later everything went in reverse. My body began to sprawl and after a second or two, my seat separated from me with a jerk – my automatic belt release mechanism worked. I began tumbling in a free fall through the air.

When I pulled the parachute's ring with my right hand, through inertia my left arm also jerked away from my body; as the canopy opened, a strap caught my left arm, jerking it violently upwards and backwards, and dislocated my left elbow. Thus, only my right arm continued to function and I felt a strong pain in my shoulder.

When I checked below to see where I would land, I saw that I was going to come down approximately a kilometer out to sea. The parachute was a "Rocket", consisting of separated linear panels, had a high rate of descent (11 meters a second), and had been especially designed for ejecting at high speeds. It had one more peculiarity: as it dropped, it would slowly spin. As it was spinning, whenever I saw dry ground I would say to myself, "We're going to survive", but when my face had turned toward the sea and I saw its boundless expanses without a single ship visible, then I said to myself, "And no one is going to know where my grave is."

However, fate was kind to me on this day and didn't let me drown in the sea. The point was that it was low tide … At great speed I plopped down into the ooze. I didn't have time to collapse my parachute, which yanked my legs and body out of the muck, but left my boots behind. After sliding through the muck on my belly for several dozen meters, the parachute collapsed. I stood up on my feet, which were now clad only with socks. That's when I saw a file of Chinese soldiers, about seven of them, advancing toward me according to combat doctrine. A young Chinese soldier carrying a rusted submachine gun of unknown manufacture was out in front, coming toward me with a tentative step. I had a holstered TT pistol hanging from the belt around my waist. The file stopped about 50 meters away from me, while this young soldier approached to within about five meters from me and began to motion to me with trembling hands to unfasten my belt and hand him my pistol. My belt was coated with muck and there was no way I could unfasten it with one hand. Yet there he was, right in front of me, pointing the barrel of his submachine gun at my belly, while I agonizingly tugged at my belt and his hands with the submachine gun shook more and more. I even gave a thought for God to prevent him from losing patience and squeezing the trigger. I didn't want to die from this rusted submachine gun.

At last I unfastened my belt, pulled the holster with the pistol off of it and tossed it at his feet. Then the rest of the Chinese soldiers walked up to me. Their commander could comprehend Russian, and when I said "*Sulen muzha*" (Soviet man), he offered me his hand, I grabbed it with the hand of my good arm, and in this fashion we made it back to dry ground. We arrived in one of their villages, from where an hour or two later we set out with four submachine gunners in a 3/4 ton Dodge truck further into the interior of their territory. We drove for a long time and only stopped when we reached a small settlement in the mountains – they had a hospital there. Once inside, they laid me on an operating table, placed a mask over my face, gave me chloroform, and I fell asleep.

I woke up the next morning; my arm had been wrapped against my body with bandages and the pain had subsided. The next day, when I could walk around freely on my feet, they handed me a cardboard tag, a receipt given when turning over personal clothing to a storage facility. I read the name on the receipt – Filippov. At first I couldn't understand how this receipt had wound up here. An interpreter asked whether I knew this man. I told him, "Yes!" They then called me out into the yard, where I saw the body of Zhenia Filippov wrapped in a parachute.

From the inquiries of the Chinese, I understood that Zhenia had ejected from his MiG at low altitude, and his parachute hadn't had enough time to open. A day later one of our vehicles arrived with a paramedic and an aircraft technician. From them I learned that on this ill-fated mission, my element leader Pavel Liubovinkin had been killed. Remaining alone after my MiG went down, he for some reason didn't link-up with the lead element of Motorin and Korochkin, but headed back to base at medium altitude alone – this was his crude blunder that cost him his life! The point is that the American pilots had undertaken a systematic blockade of the Andong airfield. Situated out over the sea, they would monitor our MiGs' landing approaches after a combat mission. To counter this, we had worked out a tactic to arrive over the airfield at high altitude, and from there to conduct the landing as quickly as possible, without making any turns around the base; in other words, to go straight in for a landing. That's why they had been able to catch Pasha Liubovinkin over the airfield.

Many observers on the ground saw what happened. The anti-aircraft artillery was putting up blocking fire. They got him just as Liubovinkin's aircraft was suspended at the top of an oblique loop. According to the eyewitnesses, he managed to eject normally, but as he was descending in his parachute, this Sabre pair that was out for blood opened fire on him. As a consequence, Liubovinkin was already dead when he hit the ground.[1]

They sent me to a hospital in Changchun, where I spent a month, and then on to a sanatorium in the Soviet city of Dal'nii, where I spent another month. I returned to the regiment only in the middle of July, and quite soon the regiment withdrew to the rear airbase at Mukden, and we began to prepare for our departure back to the Motherland.

As a result, in this combat on 24 March 1952, the 148th GIAP suffered its heaviest losses during the entire time of its participation in this war: three aircraft had been destroyed, another MiG had been damaged, two pilots had been killed, and another had wound up in a hospital. This was indeed a "black day" for this Guards regiment.

To assist the pilots of the 97th IAD, two groups of MiGs from the 256th IAP and the 821st IAP (the 16th IAP was in reserve) arrived in the combat area and immediately joined the dogfight, thereby allowing the pilots of the 97th IAD to break off combat – they were already running low on fuel and ammunition. The pilots of the 190th IAD became involved in a vicious combat, in the course of which they reported downing four F-86s. The 821st IAP's command flight claimed two of the Sabres (one each going to the credit of regiment commander Lieutenant Colonel G.F. Dmitriuk and the regiment's assistant commander for aerial gunnery service Major A.A. Olenitsa); the other two went to pilots of the 256th IAP, one of which was credited to the regiment navigator Captain V.E. Kolmanson. However, the 190th IAD lost two MiGs in return. Senior Lieutenants V.M. Mandrovsky of the 256th IAP and I.M. Omel'chenko of the 821st IAP were both shot down, but both ejected safely and soon returned to their regiments. Aleksei Ivanovich Romanov relates how his wingman Omel'chenko was shot down on this mission:

We arrived in the patrol area with a regimental group of 24 MiGs. Our 2nd Squadron consisting of two flights led the way, while the other two squadrons trailed above and behind us. Vasilii Molokanov's flight was bringing up the rear of the 2nd Squadron, and my pair was the squadron's tail-end element. Suddenly I saw a pair of Sabres stealing up on us from below, seeking to get onto our flight's tail. But I spotted them in time and reported this over the radio to the flight leader, before going into a sharp turn in the direction of the regiment's other squadrons, in the hope of placing this Sabre element under an attack from our MiGs, but this didn't happen. Omel'chenko, instead of following my maneuver, passed under my MiG in order to re-align our formation, and in essence, popped out in front of the Sabres, which took advantage of this favorable situation and shot up Omel'chenko's aircraft from point-blank range. He ejected, and while descending in his parachute was again attacked by this pair of Sabres, which fired at him, but fortunately missed.

As a result, on 24 March 1952 the 64th IAK's pilots, while repulsing fighter-bomber raids by the USAF, shot down four F-86s and one F-80 (another F-80 was listed as a probable victory), but their own losses were also high: five MiG-15s had been downed (one not by the enemy, but by friendly anti-aircraft artillery), another MiG had been damaged, and two pilots were killed and two wounded. Besides that, the 64th IAK also had two non-combat losses on this day: while rolling out after making a dead-stick landing at the Andong airfield, Senior Lieutenant N.I. Chernikov's MiG from the 821st IAP swerved off the runway because of a punctured right wheel and ran into some parked MiGs. The pilot was injured, and his MiG was completely demolished and written off. As a result of this accident, three more of the regiment's MiGs were damaged, one of which also had to be written off. Thus, on 24 March 1952 the 64th IAK lost a total of seven MiGs – its greatest single-day losses since the start of the war.

The Americans claimed that on 24 March the Sabres of the 4th FIW shot down two MiGs and pilots of the 51st FIW's 16th FIS downed one more. This is a rare case when the records of victories and losses coincide between the two sides. In addition, neither side recorded in their plus column the enemy plane destroyed in the collision. The Americans didn't record the loss of their Sabre in the collision as being the result of ramming by a MiG, and they pass over in silence the destruction of the MiG and the death of its pilot Filippov when counting their victories on the day. The Americans themselves acknowledged the loss of just one F-86A No.49-1140 – in the collision with the MiG, 1st Lieutenant James D. Carey of the 334th FIS was killed. Most likely, the pilots of the 821st IAP on this day tangled with a group of F-84 fighter-bombers and downed two of them (one credited to regiment commander G.F. Dmitriuk and the other to regiment navigator Major A.A. Olenitsa), but mistakenly recorded them as Sabres. If so, these were the two Thunderjets noted by the Americans as lost on this day, F-84E No.50-1119 and F-84E No.51-540 from the 49th FBG – the pilot of one of which, Harry L. Collins, Jr., was killed, while the fate of the other pilot is unknown. Yet Major G.K. Zenov of the 16th IAP also damaged F-80 No.49-649 from the 8th FBG's 80th Squadron, the pilot of which managed to fly it back to his base, but crashed his aircraft when attempting to land it. The pilot survived unharmed, but the Shooting Star was written off. Thus, the day was a costly one for both sides.

The last major battle in March took place on the 25th. Once again, the pilots of the 16th IAP and the 190th IAD collided in combat with a large group of Sabres from the 4th FIW. The 16th IAP's pilots did well, downing two Sabres in the area of Pihyon. Senior Lieutenant B.M. Abramov particularly distinguished himself; he not only shot down an F-86, but shot it off the tail of Senior Lieutenant A.V. Molodtsov's MiG, thereby saving his squadron comrade. In an afternoon dogfight with 30 Sabres in the Taegwan-dong area, pilots of the 494th IAP downed another F-86, with the credit for the victory going to Senior Lieutenant A.A. Alekseenko in a combat with eight F-86s. Our losses consisted of one MiG: Lieutenant G.M. Viaznikov of the 821st IAP was shot down by Captain Brooks J. Liles of the 336th FIS. American records show that two F-86As of the 335th FIS were lost in combat on 25 March: F-86A No.49-1066 was shot down and its pilot ejected, but F-86A No.49-1088 was only damaged and its pilot managed to bring it back to his base at Kimpo, where he landed it safely, but his plane had to be written off.

Summing up the results of the March fighting, both sides report the following victories and losses. The pilots of the 64th IAK over the first spring month claimed to have downed 48 enemy aircraft, including 42 F-86s, five F-80s and one B-26. Of these, 28 aircraft were credited to the 190th IAD, 19 went to the score of the 97th IAD, and the one B-26 was shot down at night by pilots of the Separate 351st Night Fighter Aviation Regiment [NIAP]. Their losses (including non-combat losses) amounted to 16 MiG-15s; four pilots were killed-in-action, and several more pilots were wounded or injured when ejecting.

This list does not include three probable victories by pilots of the 97th IAD (credited to A.I. Krylov, V.F. Korochkin and A.V. Molodtsov). Several words are necessary about the probable victory of the 16th IAP's Senior Lieutenant A.V. Molodtsov. According to him, he scored a victory at the beginning of March. The group encountered eight F-86s and tied them up in aerial combat. Molodtsov made several head-on passes with Sabres, and in one of them he managed to reverse course sharply and in a spiral fired at the wingman of a Sabre element. He saw his shells hit the Sabre's wing and watched as it abruptly nosed down into a dive. He couldn't observe what happened to the damaged Sabre, because the combat was continuing. Later after the combat according to intelligence information it became known that the Sabre Molodtsov had damaged fell into the bay and its pilot ejected. Molodtsov didn't receive credit for this Sabre; instead it went to the tally of his regiment. Most likely, this occurred on 4 March 1952, when pilots of the 16th IAP downed two F-86s: one went to the credit of the 16th IAP commander Major P.K. Zhuravlev (who had taken command of the regiment at the end of February, after the departure of Lieutenant Colonel N.F. Kuznetsov due to illness), but the second was credited to the regiment as a shared victory.

For their part, the Americans claimed that their Sabre pilots downed 39 MiGs in the month of March, while losing only three F-86s and two F-84Es in aerial combat with MiGs. If we take into account that of this number of downed MiGs included only 12 that belonged to the 64th IAK, then the remaining MiGs, or more likely only part of them (since not all of the American victories are confirmed by the Soviet and Chinese side) likely belonged to the units of the UAA.

Such heavy losses in the UAA were caused by the introduction of an additional three new fighter divisions into combat operations by the month of March 1952. In addition to the two combat-seasoned Chinese 3rd IAD and 4th IAD, which had been operating in the skies of Korea since the spring of 1951, the 6th IAD and 15th IAD, both equipped with the MiG-15 entered combat in December 1951. Finally, the 2nd IAD, which was equipped with piston-engine La-11 and Yak-9 fighters flew into the Siniuju airfield in March 1952. However, the level of training of the young Chinese pilots was lower than that of the experienced American pilots, which explains the large Chinese losses in the initial combats with Sabres. It is known, though, that in these first combats the pilots of

A Lavochkin La-11 piston-engine fighter, a type used by the 64th IAK in the Korean War.

the 6th and 15th IAD also achieved a number of victories over the F-86, but primarily they operated against the F-80, F-84 and F-51 fighter-bombers under the cover of the Soviet pilots of the 64th IAK.

It was Chinese pilots who shot down one F-51 of the South African 2 Squadron on 20 March 1952: on this day, an eight-ship group of F-51D fighter-bombers were operating against the railroad line between Suchon and Kau-dong. They were attacked by six Chinese MiG-15s and the Mustang flown by David Taylor, who was killed in his cockpit, was shot down. One can assume that this wasn't the only victory in the month of March scored by the Chinese pilots.

Also in March 1952, all the regiments of the 64th IAK received new MiG-15bis fighters fresh from the factories; most of the worn out MiGs and those in the repair shops, which had been obtained from the previous divisions before they rotated out of the theater of combat operations, were handed over to the UAA and to the 83rd IAK stationed on the Liaodong Peninsula. However, several dozen of the "old" MiGs that were in still good condition remained with the Soviet regiments, but at the end of spring 1952 even they were replaced by the new MiG-15bis arriving from the factories.

The intensity of the fighting in MiG Alley in the month of April 1952 differed little from that of the month of March, but the largest aerial battles took place in the first week of April. According to records of the 64th IAK command, its pilots destroyed 26 F-86s and one F-51 in combat in this week.

The MiG-15bis, the primary fighter used by the 64th IAK's squadrons in the Korean War.

On 1 April, the pilots of the 64th IAK repeated their success of 16 March, though this time they downed one Sabre fewer – nine F-86s. This was largely due to the pilots of the 190th IAD, who claimed eight of the nine Sabres. Four of the F-86s were downed by pilots of the 494th IAP, while the other two regiments of the division claimed two each. The 494th IAP's pilots flew two missions to intercept enemy aircraft, and both resulted in dogfights. In the first action they engaged 40 F-86s in the Pakchon area, and the second dogfight involved 16 F-86s and occurred in the Sunchon – Kusong area. In these two combats, the regiment's pilots Captain B.V. Lavrinovich and Senior Lieutenants A.P. Kargin, F.P. Shevchenko and A.A. Alekseenko shot down one Sabre each. The regiment in these two dogfights lost one MiG piloted by Senior Lieutenant G.S. Mil'chutsky, but he was able to eject safely from his crippled fighter. The pilots of the 821st IAP conducted three group sorties to intercept enemy aircraft and clashed with Sabres on two of them. Senior Lieutenants N.K. Levichev and I.F. Boldin each shot down one F-86, but the regiment also lost one of its own aircraft, in which Senior Lieutenant Nikolai Ivanovich Chernikov was killed.

In one of the combats on 1 April, the MiG of Senior Lieutenant V.I. Mukhreev of the 821st IAP was also seriously damaged. In this mission he was flying as deputy regiment commander Major A.P. Prudnikov's wingman. As they were starting their landing approach, they were jumped by a pair of F-86s that flamed Mukhreev's aircraft. Our pilot managed to come out from under the Sabre's fire with an abrupt maneuver, and then a pair of MiGs that were covering the Andong airfield came to his assistance. Mukhreev managed to put out the flames and brought his MiG in for a safe landing. The technicians later counted 26 bullet holes in Mukhreev's MiG; three of the bullets had penetrated his cockpit canopy, and the pilot was lightly wounded in the neck by fragments of the Plexiglas. This wound didn't prevent Mukhreev from continuing to fly combat missions, and his aircraft was quickly repaired.

One Sabre on 1 April was downed by pilots of the 16th IAP, who with 14 MiGs took on 20 F-86s in the Sakchu area. Our total losses over the day, then, consisted of two MiG-15s and one pilot.

For their part the Americans claimed that on 1 April, five MiGs had been shot down by pilots of the 4th FIW, and just as many by pilots of its rival 51st FIW. Its commander Colonel Francis Gabreski claimed one victory over a MiG-15. Major William H. Westcott of the 25th FIS shot down two MiGs in two combats on this day. The Americans place their own losses on this day at one F-86E No.50-586 from the 335th FIS, the pilot of which 1st Lieutenant John E. Dews bailed out over Cho-Do Island and was picked up by an H-19 helicopter. He soon returned to his squadron. Two more F-86E Sabres (No.50-602 and No.50-632) from the 51st FIW were damaged by MiGs. Both Sabres returned to base, but the Americans don't reveal their further fate.

On the next day the 64th IAK's pilots claimed six more F-86s in aerial combat. Pilots of the 148th GIAP particularly distinguished themselves: having taken off at 0840 as a group of 18 MiGs under the command of Lieutenant Colonel V.M. Dudnichenko, at 0915 they ambushed four F-86s in the Sakchu area and attacked them. Lieutenant Colonel Dudnichenko, Major G.Z. Finogenov and Captain A.T. Bashman each shot down one F-86, while the regimental group escaped any losses of its own. Dudnichenko downed his F-86 from a range of 300 meters, and it exploded in mid-air – fragments of it were found on the banks of the Yalu River west of Supung-dong. Captain Bashman also got his Sabre from the short range of 200 meters, and it fell 8 kilometers northwest of Supung-dong.

Pilots of the 190th IAD claimed two more Sabres, but its 494th IAP also suffered losses on 2 April. This regiment's pilots sortied twice on this day to intercept enemy aircraft, and twice they became involved in combat with Sabres of the 51st FIW. On the first mission they fought with 20 F-86s in the Taegwan-dong area, while on the second group sortie they clashed with 24 F-86s in the Kiojo area. In the course of these two dogfights the regiment lost two MiGs, and in one of them Senior Lieutenant Aleksandr Iakovlevich Voronov perished, while the other pilot Senior Lieutenant V.F. Tarkan managed to eject from his aircraft. The 494th IAP did manage to down one F-86 on this day – credit for it went to Senior Lieutenant G.P. Kriuchkov.

The 256th IAP also added to the victory total on this day. In a dogfight between eight MiGs of the regiment and 12 F-86s, Captain A.M. Arkhipov and Senior Lieutenant A.M. Zvorykin destroyed one Sabre each.

The Americans claimed to have shot down three MiGs on this day, but plainly one of them was only damaged. As on the previous day, the Americans report losing only one F-86E (No.50-592) from the 25th FIS on this day, the pilot of which 1st Lieutenant Joe Cannon bailed out south of Cho-do Island and came down in the sea, but he soon returned to his squadron. Two more F-86Es (No.50-0676 and No.51-2755) were damaged, but again, their further fate is unknown.

On 3 April, the pilots of the 148th GIAP had a successful dogfight, downing four F-86s without any losses in return. But the 190th IAD's pilots weren't as lucky. Returning from a combat mission, two of the division's MiGs were caught and shot down as they approached Andong by Sabres of the 4th FIW's 336th FIS. The pilots Senior Lieutenant N.I. Kozlov of the 256th IAP and Senior Lieutenant B.S. Lavrinovich of the 494th IAP both bailed out successfully. They were shot down by Captain Robert H. Moore and 1st

Lieutenant Charles G. Carl – these were the Americans' only two victories on this day. In its turn the Fifth Air Force command doesn't acknowledge the loss of any Sabres on 3 April.

On 6 April, dogfights again erupted in MiG Alley. The pilots of the 190th IAD were scrambled three times on this day to repel fighter-bomber raids. In a morning clash in the Kiojo area, the deputy commander of the 821st IAP's 3rd Squadron Captain V.N. Zabelin downed one Sabre. In the second combat of this day in the Sonchon area, the 821st IAP intercepted a group of F-51 Mustangs, and Major A.A. Olenitsa managed to shoot down one of them before they fled to the safety of the bay. Then in a combat with Sabres that had hurriedly arrived on the scene, Captain Zabelin got his second victory of the day by downing one F-86. In these actions the regiment had no losses.

Pilots of the 148th GIAP scored especially well in battles with the Sabres of the 4th FIW, claiming five of the F-86s. The victors were Captains A.T. Bashman and S.I. Muskantsev, as well as Senior Lieutenants A.I. Krylov and V.N. Razumovsky, and Lieutenant V.A. Fortuchenko. The 64th IAK lost only one MiG in return: when approaching Andong for a landing, four Sabres caught the MiG of Captain E. Konoplev of the 148th GIAP and damaged it. The Soviet pilot was already low on fuel, but he managed to escape the Sabres and set his plane down on the Andong runway straight away. He landed at high speed, and losing control of the MiG, he rolled off the runway and crashed. The pilot received serious injuries and spent a long time recovering in a hospital, while the MiG was written off.

The 190th IAD's top ace with 9 victories
Major V.N. Zabelin – a photo taken at
the end of the 1950s.

The Americans claimed that on 6 April they shot down four MiG-15s, but most likely these were Chinese MiGs of the UAA, which was operating against the fighter-bombers. On this day the Americans again acknowledged the loss of only one F-86E (No.51-2733) from the 16th FIS, the pilot of which 1st Lieutenant John H. Laskey managed to fly back to his K-13 Suwon Air Base, but crashed 600 feet short of the runway when trying to land the Sabre. Laskey was killed in the crash. In addition, the Americans recognize the loss of three F-51 Mustangs for various reasons, but most likely Major Olenitsa's victim was F-51 No.45-11643 from the 18th FBW. Its pilot reached Cho-do Island, where the Mustang crashed and was written off. Also on 6 April the Americans lost one F-86E from the 136th FBW, the pilot of which was killed, but the Americans claim the Thunderjet was shot down by ground fire. More likely, it was shot down by a Chinese fighter pilot.

After a week-long break due to weather that kept the aircraft grounded, on 13 April the pilots of the 51st FIW and the 64th IAK again met over the Yalu River in battle. Beating back the next raid by enemy fighter-bombers, the Soviet pilots took on the covering Sabres, while the UAA's pilots attacked the groups of Shooting Stars and Mustangs. The combat was vicious and the losses on both sides were substantial: the 64th IAK's pilots downed four Sabres, while losing three of their MiGs and one pilot in return. A pilot of the 494th IAP Senior Lieutenant Vladimir Mikhailovich Shebeko was killed in the combat. In addition, when returning from a combat mission, the commander of the 16th IAP Lieutenant Colonel P.K. Zhuravlev's MiG was attacked over the airfield by four Sabres and shot down. Fortunately, Zhuravlev was able to bail out, but he received injuries when ejecting from his crippled MiG and spent around a month in the hospital convalescing.

True, the pilots of the 16th IAP quickly evened the score. On this same day, eight MiGs of the regiment's 3rd Squadron encountered 24 F-86s at an altitude of 9,000 meters in the Taegwan-dong area. The commander of the second flight Captain A.S. Boitsov was the first to spot the enemy, and taking advantage of the favorable situation, launched an attack. Captain Boitsov with his wingman V.A. Shchipalov jumped a flight of F-86s and on the first pass Captain Boitsov shot down one of them; evidently, the Sabre pilot never saw the approaching MiGs and made no attempt to evade. The star-tled remaining Sabres refused combat and headed toward Korea Bay. This was Captain A.S. Boitsov's first victory in the skies of Korea. Subsequently he would add five more victories to his total and become the 97th IAD's top-scoring pilot. A little later by a 14 July 1953 decree he was awarded the title Hero of the Soviet Union for his combats in the skies of Korea.

Pilots of the 148th GIAP also did well on this day; 18 MiGs under the command of Lieutenant Colonel A.M. Balabaikin took off to repel an enemy air raid in the Pihyon – Sunchon area and encountered a group of F-86s at an altitude of 8,000 meters. In the ensuing dogfight Lieutenant Colonel Balabaikin downed one F-86, and the remaining Sabres left the combat area. Our regiment had no losses.

On this day a large air battle took place in the Anju area, in which pilots of the 494th IAP clashed with a group of 16 F-86s, while pilots of the 821st IAP took on 18 other Sabres. The 494th IAP lost two MiGs in this combat: Senior Lieutenant D.S. Varfolomeev managed to bail out of his stricken aircraft, but Senior Lieutenant V.M. Shebeko was killed-in-action. The 494th IAP's pilots managed to down only one F-86, the credit for which went to Senior Lieutenant E.A. Pomaz. The 821st IAP's pilots also claimed one F-86 destroyed without any losses in return. Again, Captain V.N. Zabelin received credit for the victory.

The Americans claimed that they downed seven MiGs on 13 April, two of which were shot down in one action by Major William Westcott of the 25th FIS. The commander of the 51st FIW Colonel "Gabby" Gabreski shot down another MiG. This was his sixth and final victory in Korea, for soon he returned to the United States. The Americans acknowledged the loss of two of their Sabres on this day: F-86E No. 50-0636 was shot down and its pilot Major George V. Wendling was killed. F-86A No.49-1316 from the 336th FIS was also damaged in the dogfight, but returned to base. In addition, pilots of the UAA shot down an F-84E from the 136th FBW.

On 18 April 1952, the Americans undertook another attempt to destroy the hydro-electrical station on the Yalu River, but this effort also failed thanks to the courage and skill of the pilots and anti-aircraft gunners of the 64th IAK. On this day the pilots of the 821st IAP flew two missions to intercept enemy aircraft and wound up encountering F-86s on both of them. In the morning brush with 20 F-86s in the area of Kiojo, the two sides parted peacefully, but on the second group sortie, when the regiment was covering the 64th IAK's other pilots as they withdrew from combat and were coming in for a landing, the regiment engaged 20 F-86s, in which the regiment commander Lieutenant Colonel G.F. Dmitriuk downed one Sabre. The deputy commander of the 148th GIAP Lieutenant Colonel V.M. Dudnichenko downed another F-86 that morning in the period between 0715 and 0725, which fell 10 kilometers north of Sakchu. Thus on this day, two of our Heroes of the Soviet Union both scored victories!

The aerial combat of 21 April in the area of the Yalu River proved to be especially savage. The eternal rivals, pilots of the Soviet 64th IAK and pilots of the USAF 4th and 51st FIW once again met in combat. This action was indicative as well of the new combat tactic used by the Sabre pilots against the Soviet pilots, which they adopted in April 1952.

Seeing that victories against the 64th IAK's MiGs in aerial combat came at a high price, the pilots of the 51st FIW decided without the knowledge of their higher command to cross the Yalu River border surreptitiously and conduct "free hunts" over the airfields of northeastern China, in particular the bases at Andong and Miaogou. Already back in March, Sabres had begun to stalk the IAK's MiGs that were returning from combat low on fuel and ammunition, shooting them down as they made their landing approaches, after which the Sabre pairs and flights would immediately make for the nearby Korea Bay, avoiding punishment for their unauthorized act. For example, Sabres had shot down Captain P.S. Liubovinkin of the 148th GIAP as he was coming in for a landing at Andong. In April 1952, the MiGs of Lieutenant Colonel P.K. Zhuravlev of the 16th IAP, E. Konoplev of the 148th GIAP, and of other pilots were shot down or damaged as they came in for landings. Notables such as Colonel Francis Gabreski, Colonel Walker "Bud" Mahurin, Lieutenant Colonel George Jones, Major William Whisner and a number of other lower-ranking American pilots were especially fond of prowling over the area of the Chinese airfields.

On 21 April, pilots of the 190th IAD's 821st IAP and 256th IAP came together in battle with pilots of the 4th and 51st FIW. The dogfight with 30 F-86s took place in the Siojio area. The division's pilots claimed three F-86s in the action, two of which were credited to Senior Lieutenants P.M Veshkin and G.T. Tiutikov of the 821st IAP. Captain Iu.D. Obraztsov of the 256th IAP shot down the other Sabre. However, this victory came at a high price: the 256th IAP lost four Migs and two pilots on this day. In the dogfight itself, only Senior Lieutenant S.S. Lubman was shot down; wounded, he was able to eject from his burning aircraft. The other three pilots of this regiment were caught by Sabres as they were returning to the Miaogou airfield low on fuel to make a landing. The 1st Squadron's Senior Lieutenant Aleksei Fedorovich Bondarenko recalls what happened:

The combat was continuing, but my fuel was running low, so I broke off combat alone (earlier my wingman had become separated from me during the aerial melee). Suddenly I caught sight of another solitary MiG flying in the same direction off to one side of me. Its pilot gave his call sign and requested permission to join up with me. I granted his request and radioed him that we were heading back to base. This pilot Semen Tolmatsky, as I later found out, was from a different squadron. We went into a circle over the airfield; everything was quiet. Our final landing approach was from the direction of the bay. I began to go into the approach, but heard the other pilot's call sign and a request to permit him to land first, because his fuel tanks were almost dry. I gave him the OK, he took the lead, and I followed him at a range of 200-300 meters. He made the final turn and began to glide in for the landing, while I was just entering the final turn, having reduced my speed to 350 km/hr. Just then I heard an order: "Warning! Sabres approaching the circle!" I immediately shoved my throttle forward and put my MiG into a horizontal left turn. Out of the corner of my eye, I saw tracers streaking toward the MiG-15 in front of me – the fighter nosed down and plunged into the ground. Then I saw that my right arm was broken, but I didn't feel any pain at the time. I realized I was wounded.

I instantly grabbed the control stick with my left hand and began to act. However, it was impossible to escape the attack. They were sitting within firing range; I had little speed, my altitude was low (somewhere around 300-400 meters), and I was badly wounded. A second burst of machine-gun fire followed the first, and I felt a strong blow to my left shoulder. After a third burst, I had wounds in both legs (the left thigh and the right knee).

I won't even try to hide the fact that my life was flashing in front of my eyes at that moment. I decided to eject, threw aside the canopy, placed my feet on the footrest, stuck my middle finger through the parachute ring, and pushed the lever on the right arm of my seat. However, the explosive charge beneath the seat didn't ignite – I couldn't eject.

Later I realized that I was a lucky fellow; if I had been able to eject back then, I likely would have been killed. In the first place I would have lost consciousness from the loss of blood given the high G-forces when ejecting from the aircraft, and in the second place my altitude was too low for my parachute to open before I hit the ground. I hadn't ejected simply because the catapult had failed, and I couldn't bail out on my own, because my wounded right arm wasn't functioning. Then I grabbed the control stick with my left hand and began to make three turns above the airfield. Over the radio I called for assistance. Before entering the third turn I cut my speed and lowered my landing gear, but at this instant there was a strong explosion. However, my aircraft continued to respond to my controls, and I began to carry out the third turn. I could see a plume of yellow smoke trailing behind my aircraft. I raised my landing gear and switched on the anti-fire system. Simultaneously I conducted the final turn, entered the glide path and told the ground: "I can't see well, give me guidance." There was silence in response.

I'm gliding, there's nothing from the control tower, and my landing gear is retracted. I needed to land my aircraft to the left of the runway, but now the MiG isn't responding to the control stick and is heading for the concrete runway. The thought flashed through my mind that I would burn to death on the runway. I gently eased my stick over to the left and kicked left rudder. Miraculously, when there was only around 50 meters remaining to the ground, my MiG began moving to the left. Now I'm leveling out to the left of the runway and soon my MiG's belly is touching down. I was thrown forward against my belts several times, then the aircraft stopped, and that's when I heard an order: "Get out of the aircraft!" I unfastened my belts, leaped from the cockpit together with my parachute to the ground, ran about 70 meters away from the MiG and collapsed. I had no strength left. My MiG had come to a stop not far from an anti-aircraft battery, and the anti-aircraft gunners that came running up grabbed me and dragged me away from the MiG, which was continuing to burn, while there was still some ammunition aboard it. They immediately took me to a hospital, and then about a month later I was sent to Changchun (PRC) for further treatment and recovery. For this "landing", I was given a field promotion to "captain".

That's how Senior Lieutenant A.F Bondarenko's MiG of the 256th IAP's 1st Squadron was damaged and he was badly wounded, while the pilot Israel' Alekseevich Tolmatsky of the same regiment's 2nd Squadron was killed. Another pilot of the 256th IAP, Senior Lieutenant Dmitrii Stepanovich Selivanov was shot down and killed when coming in for a landing. Here's how this happened in the words of the squadron engineer Viktor Georgievich Verkhovsky:

When Selivanov died, I was at the Miaogou airfield. This occurred on the day's final mission. The uninvited "guests" arrived as the last aircraft were coming in, and one of the F-86 latched onto the tail of Selivanov's MiG. Having no time to turn his MiG toward the sun, Selivanov went into a nearly vertical corkscrew climb. The enemy seemingly began to lag a bit behind, while continuing to pursue and firing sporadic bursts. But then Selivanov's MiG began to run out of fuel (it was apparent from the interruptions in the contrail), and at an altitude of 9,000 meters the aircraft faltered, where it was fired on for the final time. After this, Selivanov ejected, but apparently he fell through the Sabre's machine-gun fire, because his parachute never opened. Selivanov's MiG, on the other hand, didn't plummet to the earth, but it began to fall tail-first and then somehow leveled out, seemingly stopped, and began to rock from wing to wing and from tail to nose, and fell as it teetered from side to side and back to front. We began to think that the aircraft was going to come down on a hardstand of our aircraft (it had been shot down over a section of the runway). However, at an altitude of approximately 30 meters, it rocked forward and fell nose-first into the ground before flopping over onto its tail assembly. Of course, the aircraft was badly crumpled, but the fact is it wasn't torn apart into pieces. It fell east of the runway about 150 meters from the road leading to our quarters.

In addition, for the first time the Sabres employed the tactic of sealing the 64th IAK's airfields to prevent take-offs. Six Migs from the 16th IAP's 3rd Squadron were scrambled to assist the pilots of the 190th IAD, but during take-off they were unexpectedly attacked by four F-86s from the direction of the bay, which shot down the tail-end pair led by Captain Nikolai Ivanovich Naumov. Both pilots ejected, but Naumov didn't have enough altitude and he was killed when he struck the ground, while his wingman Senior Lieutenant A.I. Chivragov safely landed and remained unharmed. This was the first incident when the 64th IAK's aircraft were attacked while taking off (usually it had been during landings) and suffered losses.

As a result, on 21 April the 64th IAK downed four F-86s (two by pilots of the 821st IAP, and one each by pilots of the 148th GIAP and 256th IAP). Eighteen MiGs of the 148th GIAP had taken off to cover the Manchurian airfields. When returning from the mission, at an altitude of 3,000-4,000 meters, four F-86s attacked the leading element of the Major A.M. Balabaikin's regimental group. However, his wingman Senior Lieutenant A.I. Kashtanov timely detected their approach and gave warning to him. Major Balabaikin reacted instantly: he broke sharply left into a tight turn, and circled around in behind the tail-end pair of Sabres and shot down one of them.

The 64th IAK's losses were also heavy: six MiGs were destroyed and three pilots killed, and two more pilots suffered serious wounds. This was one more "black day" for the pilots of the 64th IAK's current roster.

The Americans claimed to have shot down seven MiGs on this day (one, plainly, was only damaged), of which two went to the score of the 51st FIW, and five to the 4th FIW. Captain Robert G. Love of the 335th FIS distinguished himself by downing two MiGs. The Americans acknowledged the loss of two F-86s: both were shot down, and the pilots 2nd Lieutenant Vance R. Frick (flying F-86A No. 49-1178) of the 336th FIS and 1st Lieutenant Michael E. De Armond (flying F-86E No.51-2787) of the 335th FIS were both taken prisoner. The F-86E No.51-2760 of the 334th FIS was also seriously damaged, but its pilot Captain Jore J. Lewis was able to return safely to his base at Kimpo.

The final major aerial battle in the month of April 1952 took place on 30 April. The high command headed by the commander-in-chief of the USSR's PVO forces, Lieutenant General E.Ia. Savitsky and the commander of the 64th IAK Major General G.A. Lobov had visited the Andong base. They gave the pilots of the 16th IAP an order to conduct an outflanking maneuver deep into North Korean airspace in order to emerge in the area where the enemy fighter-bombers were operating and to attack them unexpectedly. In order to carry out this risky mission, it was decided to send six MiGs from the 16th IAP's 3rd Squadron, led by the squadron's deputy commander Captain S.S. Tokarev. They took off on this mission with the following crews: Captain S.S. Tokarev with his wingman Senior Lieutenant A.G. Levin, Captain P.V. Minervin with his wingman Senior Lieutenant L.P. Morshchikhin, and Captain A.S. Boitsov with his wingman Captain L. Tolubensky. They flew under an order of strict radio silence, and were directed toward their target from the ground. They flew with drop tanks to the area of interception at an altitude of 10,000 meters. Finally, an order came from the ground: "Turn right. A group of Americans will be out in front of you; attack them." The ground control was being executed from the auxiliary control post in the Anju area by Major A.R. Prudnikov. Coming out of the turn, our pilots spotted a group of 24 F-80 and F-84 fighter-bombers without any escort at an altitude of 6,000-7,000 meters. Jettisoning their drop tanks, our fighters went on the attack. The Shooting Stars, seeing the approaching MiGs, scattered their bombs and headed for the sea. All three of the element leaders, Captains P.V. Minervin, S.S. Tokarev and A.S. Boitsov, each shot down two F-80s. All six MiGs safely returned to base, though Boitsov's element did so only after stopping at the reserve Singisiu airfield in North Korea to refuel. For this successful mission, each participant was given a promotion in rank, and all except for Captain Boitsov were awarded the Order of the Red Banner, while now Major A.S. Boitsov received the Order of Lenin. Here's how a participant on this mission, Lev Pavlovich Morshchikhin, described it in an interview with the author:

> In April, the regiment took off with six crews. Zamykin's flight was on duty the night before and didn't take part in the day's missions. Many of the pilots were sick: the stresses of the February and March combats were telling. We sortied 3-4 times a day, and this was always at high altitude and with maximum speeds.
>
> On this day we had just finished breakfast when they announced Readiness No.1. We hurried to our cockpits and barely had time to fasten our belts when a green rocket soared into the sky from the launch command post. Over the radio there was the calm voice of Major Tarzudin: "Take off as soon as possible." More due to the launch sequence and for checking radio communications, Sergei Sergeevich Tokarev led the six-ship formation; I was Abramov's wingman in the left-hand element. Already in the air, the main radio gave the command: "Proceed to the area of the 'Boot'."
>
> All of the prominent landmarks had been given code names. We climbed to 10,000 meters; the command post gave us the aerial situation and then the order: "You will be working downstairs." This meant at low altitudes.
>
> Oh, not good at all … Oh, how unfortunate … We were used to working up near the ceiling, and not downstairs. Too bad … we began to descend. My head was swiveling around a full 360°. Goosebumps started to run along my spine. Altitude and speed … those were our trump cards, the superiority of our MiGs. Flying at low altitudes, we were no better than the Sabres. From the command post came the report: "Look, below you, 'Shoots' and Thunderjets are working over the ground – your target."
>
> The Shooting Stars and Thunderjets were one of the first jet fighter-bombers. They had a speed of 900-1,000 km/hour. For MiGs, they presented no problem. To fight with them was like fighting back in the Great Patriotic War in our Yaks and LaGGs against the Ju-87 *Laptozhniki* ["Baste shoes", referring to the wheel fairings on the Stuka, which resembled baste shoes]. That's what we called the Stukas. The present situation was suggesting that the Yanks had come up with some clever ploy. We're flying just above the hilltops at an altitude of 2,000-3,000 meters. We don't see any "Shoots". In several locations the hills were on fire. The "Shoots" had

struck with napalm. We don't see the arsonists. The hills are green and the "Shoots" are camouflaged in the same color.[2] The main radio was cutting in and out. The anti-aircraft gunners helped us spot our targets. They were prompting: "Look, we have the same target." There were no Sabres, and the gunners were working against the fighter-bombers. Shell bursts were all around us, but not any Shooting Stars. Even the silk scarf around my neck isn't helping things. It is chafing my neck. My head is spinning now not 360°, but a full 720°. But no "Shoots" are visible. We headed toward some anti-aircraft shell bursts, and the artillerymen joked, "Don't interfere!"

Suddenly I see a Thunderjet just off my left wing and a little below me. I shout over the radio: "'Shoots' below us!" There followed a storm of radio chatter: "There they are, strike them!" "The target's below us!" A complete din. The whirl of combat. The main radio cut everyone off: "Cease the chatter, work quietly, there are no Sabres, everyone be silent." Our appearance, plainly, was a surprise for the enemy. The Thunderjet was so nearby that I had no way of turning toward it, and besides, my speed was too high. Out of fright, the Thunderjet pilot went into a split-S at the moment we appeared beside him. I saw the yellow belly of the aircraft, glimpsed a detached wing tumbling among the flames on the ground, followed by an explosion. Our altitude was low, and there was nothing the pilot could have done. So he had smashed into a hillside. All this happened so quickly that I only had time to say over the radio "One more" – and then I was already in a 180° turn to get in position for another attack.

As I came around, I saw in front of me the black puffs of anti-aircraft artillery, and directly on my heading a dozen Shooting Stars and Thunderjets, and further in the distance, another dozen. Having spotted us, the fighter-bombers had re-formed into a defensive ring, with one aircraft following behind another – an effective way of defending themselves. However, we also had something ready as a way to attack them. The anti-aircraft gunners were firing selectively, in order not to hit us. In the heat of battle we paid no attention to their fire, or to the fact that we hadn't yet jettisoned our drop tanks. The main radio reminded us: "Swallows, swallows, check your valves." Translated from our everyday language: "MiG pilots, drop your tanks." They weren't needed – we'd already used up the fuel in them, but in order to jettison them, you had to be in horizontal flight. But where's that when the swirl of combat is going on? The "Shoots" were firing at us, we were firing at the "Shoots", and all of this was going on at extremely low altitude and near the speed of sound. I barely managed to find a time to level out and told my wingman, "Vitek, valve", and his and my drop tanks tumbled toward the earth. But the main radio was now crackling with an order from the command post, "Swallows, hit the trail"; in other words "Return for a landing", and then in the open: "Look after your fuel. Everyone hit the trail … the trail."

Our fighters in such combat conditions at low altitude had enough fuel for 40 to 50 minutes of flight. The "Shoots" and Thunderjets, having formed three or four defensive circles, rearranged into one, which then stretched into a single file toward the water – to the sea, which to their good fortune was visible in the distance, while the water for us was a no-no, categorically forbidden. They were afraid that one of us might be shot down, and then our presence would be revealed to the United

Nations. Officially, we Soviet pilots weren't there. "Stalin's falcons" weren't participating in a filthy war.

Tokarev issued an order: "Shrubby, keep watch above us." Kolia Naumov had thought up such a call name for me, not because of any dense thatch of hair on my head, but because of my male pattern baldness that had noticeably progressed recently. It had to be assumed that the call name was due to what I'd been experiencing.

It's no sin to hide that it was a bit terrifying. Whether you're brave or not, each man wants to live. By some unknown effort or willpower you could keep this fear hidden, so that no one around you would suspect its presence. As much as possible you put on a brave face.

"Shrubby, look so that they don't snooker us." The concerns were legitimate: so far this combat action had gone quite easily and productively. In the regiment, Tokarev, Naumov, Oleinik, Molodtsov and I were still sharp-eyed and we often could spot enemy aircraft far in the distance before the other pilots. You see the enemy first – and half the battle is won, and on the attack it virtually guarantees a victory. It had been a gamble to tangle with the fighter-bombers, if only because of the proximity of the sea, but now we also had the blinking red light on the instrument panel – the signal that only enough fuel for 15 minutes of flight remained. The division command post was issuing a persistent demand: "Swallows, hit the trail. Carry it out immediately. Everyone hit the trail." Finally, unable to hold out any longer, it issued the order in the open: "Fuel is running low. Everyone is to land."

Vitek Abramov ordered: "Our element will bring up the rear. We're going home." Our six ships assembled into formation on the way back to base. Boitsov and his partner Leonid Tolubensky landed at Singisiu, where the Koreans had an airfield on the other side of the river. They didn't have enough fuel to make it back to base. Abramov and I landed together with dead engines. We were lucky. The group leader Tokarev's engine stopped as he was rolling out after touching down. All six MiGs had fired, but the gun camera footage confirmed only four victories. Observers on the ground confirmed the fall of nine aircraft. The anti-aircraft gunners claimed two of the aircraft for themselves. Later counter-intelligence clarified that 11 enemy aircraft had failed to return to base. This was on 30 April. After this combat, the enemy didn't fly again over North Korea until 5 May. The break was to our advantage. In May we could take off with a larger complement.

I must add only one correction to Lev Petrovich's story; he forgot that on this mission, his element leader was not Viktor Abramov, but Captain Petr Vasil'evich Minervin.

In truth, on this day the regiment also lost one aircraft. While landing at the Andong airfield, Captain A.I. Manushkin's MiG of the 1st Squadron was shot down by Sabres, but he safely ejected. Also on this day, eight crews of the 494th IAP also successfully engaged a group of 12 F-84s. They intercepted the Thunderjets and chased them back to sea, downing one of them in the process. At the same time the regiment had a fleeting aerial skirmish with a group of Sabres that had hurried to the scene, downing one F-86 without any losses of its own.

The Americans claimed that on 30 April 1952, the pilots of the 4th and 51st FIW shot down six MiG-15s in aerial combat. It is possible that on this day, that in addition to the combats with Soviet pilots, they tangled with pilots of the UAA. The Americans recognized the loss of only one F-80 (No.49-680) from the 8th FBW's 36th FBS, the pilot of which 1st Lieutenant John W. Zwiacher became a prisoner-of-war. True, the Americans also acknowledge the loss of one F-84E No.51-536 from the 49th FBG's 8th FBS, the pilot of which 1st Lieutenant George H. Hansen was killed-in-action. Mostly likely, he was shot down by Senior Lieutenant G.P. Kulakov of the 494th IAP.

The results of the April 1952 combats were as follows: the pilots of the 64th IAK claimed 48 American aircraft downed in aerial combat, including 40 F-86s, six F-80s, one F-84 and one F-51. Of these, 24 aircraft were destroyed by the pilots of the 97th IAD, while the remaining 24 victories went to the credit of the 190th IAD. Their own losses amounted to 17 aircraft; in addition, six pilots were killed-in-action and several more were wounded or received various types of injuries. The Americans claimed that their pilots of the 4th and 51st FIW downed 44 MiG-15s in April, plus two Yak-9s that were destroyed on the ground. The Americans place the combat losses of these two wings in April 1952 as four F-86s. Altogether in the month of April, the Fifth Air Force lost 243 aircraft for various reasons, and another 290 were damaged.

The two Yak-9s that had been destroyed on the ground belonged to a North Korean IAD, which was stationed on the Sinuiju airfield. On 22 April 1952, returning from a mission, a pair of F-86s from the 51st FIW's 25th FIS, flown by Captain Elmer Harris and Captain Iven Kincheloe, spotted 24 Yak-9 fighters parked on hardstands of the Sinuiju airfield and strafed them. Each pilots destroyed one of the piston-engine fighters during their single pass over the base. Incidentally, in the month of April one MiG-15-equipped IAD of the KPAF, which was part of the UAA, joined combat operations for the first time.

In addition, the 64th IAK's victory list for the month of April does not include two probable victories by pilots of the 148th GIAP. On one of the regimental sorties that month, Captain V.M. Osipov and his wingman Senior Lieutenant V.F. Korochkin had pounced on four F-86s, which had moved to attack the lead flight of the 1st Squadron without noticing Captain Osipov's element trailing a bit above and behind, and had thereby placed themselves under their cannon fire. The Soviet pilot's counterattack was skillful and accurate – the two flanking Sabres on either side of the formation were both shot down. Ground observers confirmed the fall of two enemy aircraft, and no one else in the regiment had fired on these two Sabres, but neither pilot was credited with a victory because of the poor quality of the gun camera film, on which the results of the firing wasn't clear.

Pilots of the 821st IAP scored the first victory in the month of May. On this day they conducted one regimental combat sortie and took on a group of F-86s in combat, in which they damaged one F-86. As is known now, F-86E No.51-2786, which was being flown by Colonel Albert W. Schinz, was shot down by a MiG, although the pilot managed to fly it out to sea before ejecting from it. Schinz swam to a nearby island, where he remained concealed for 30 days before being rescued by a US Navy ship on 1 June 1952. It still isn't clear which one of the Soviet pilots fatally damaged Colonel Schinz's Sabre, since our pilots didn't claim any victories on this day, but it had to have been one of the 821st IAP's pilots.

Despite this success, the month of May started extremely badly for the pilots of the 64th IAK, because the Soviet pilots suffered heavy losses in the first two aerial battles. To be honest, half of the losses resulted from the actions of the "free hunters" from the

4th and 51st FIW. By now, several elements or flights of F-86 were constantly present over Korea Bay off the coast from the Miaogou and Andong airfields, which were just several kilometers from the coast line. Whenever these Sabres spotted MiGs launching from the airfields, they would immediately attack them as they were taking off. They would also watch for MiGs returning from a combat mission and attack them as they came in for landings.

For example, on 3 May 1952 a pilot of the 148th GIAP Captain X.F. Musin was shot down over the Miaogou airfield while coming in for a landing by a prowling Sabre flown by 1st Lieutenant Albert G. Tenney of the 51st FIW's 16th FIS. However, 1st Lieutenant Tenney also didn't return to base: he was shot down in turn directly over the Miaogou base before he could reach the sanctuary of the sea by Senior Lieutenant E.T. Mazikin of the 821st IAP. The American pilot ejected from his F-86E No.50-0652 at low altitude and was killed when he hit the ground, because his parachute hadn't had time to open fully. His body was collected by Soviet soldiers. This occurred on the afternoon of 3 May around 1630. More details regarding this episode can be found in a document of the 64th IAK headquarters:

> Captain Abitkovsky's group from the 821st IAP had the assignment to cover the airfields at Andong and Miaogou. The 1st Squadron led by Major Vakhrushev (from Lieutenant Colonel Olenitsa's group) at 1629 ran into four F-86s in the Singisiu area at an altitude of 8,000 meters. The enemy wanted to decline battle and turned toward the south. Our fighter group began to pursue the foe. Then Lieutenant Colonel Olenitsa transmitted over the radio that he was engaged with eight F-86s in the vicinity of the airfield. Major Vakhrushev halted the pursuit of the enemy and returned to the area where Lieutenant Colonel Olenitsa was tied up in combat. At 1638 Senior Lieutenant Mazikin caught sight of two F-86s in front of him, which were chasing a single MiG-15 on the approach to the Miaogou airfield. Senior Lieutenant Mazikin attacked the adversary and shot down one F-86. The pilot's body was found in the wreckage of an F-86 which had been downed in the vicinity of the Miaogou base. From his personal documents it was established that the pilot was Captain Gilbert [sic.] Tenney, who belonged to the 51st Fighter Interceptor Group.

Yet in other encounters with Sabres on 3 May, the pilots of the 494th IAP were particularly unlucky. They came under a surprise attack by Sabres and lost three aircraft simultaneously. Senior Lieutenants G.P. Kulakov, G.I. Unanov and M.I. Efimov were the victims of this attack. The first two pilots managed to bail out, but Senior Lieutenant Mikhail Ivanovich Efimov was killed-in-action. True, pilots of the 256th IAP on this day managed to down one F-86; Senior Lieutenant F.S. Krasulin was the victor. As a result, on 3 May the 64th IAK lost four MiGs and one pilot, while downing only two F-86s in return. The Americans claimed that on 3 May they downed five MiGs, not including 1st Lieutenant Tenney's victory.

On 4 May 1952, the Americans used F-86s in the role of fighter-bombers for the first time. Pilots of the 51st FIW were the first to do this. At the beginning of May, 12 F-86Es of this fighter interceptor wing were converted into fighter-bombers (a drop tank was attached to one wing and a bomb was attached to the other), and Colonel "Bud"

Mahurin, the commander of the 4th FIG, assumed command of this group. On 4 May 1952, these 12 strike Sabres, escorted by regular Sabres, bombed the Siniuju airfield, where a North Korean IAD was based, and pilots of the 25th FIS Major Elmer Harris and Captain Iven Kincheloe together destroyed five piston-engine Yak-9 fighters on the ground. The aircraft of this North Korean fighter division attempted to take off from the blockaded airfield, but two of them were shot down during take-off by Captain Richard H. Schoeneman and 1st Lieutenant James A. McCulley of the 16th FIS.

On this same day, a different group of Sabres from the 4th FIW's 335th Fighter Squadron, in order to prevent MiGs from reaching the Sabre fighter-bombers, block-aded both airfields of the 64th IAK and did so quite successfully. Over the airfield at Miaogou, the Sabres downed three MiGs from the 256th IAP, which was staging from this airfield. All three of the Soviet pilots, Senior Lieutenants V.V. Pidunov, N.I. Kozlov and M.P. Blagov, safely ejected; the Sabres suffered no losses.

Vladimir Fedorovich Korochkin, who was a pilot with the 148th GIAP's 1st Squadron at the time, recalls what happened over the base on that day:

> Starting approximately from the month of April 1952, Sabres began to attack us during take-offs and landings. They took position over the sea not far from the bases, and seeing MiGs rolling down the runway for take-off, they would dive on the launching aircraft and frequently shot them down in front of our eyes. Why wouldn't a small group of experienced pilots secretly take off from other bases or already be in position for this same purpose, in order to assure the safety of our aircrafts' take-offs and landings and to deprive the enemy of this easy booty? By the way, that's how my commander Petr Motorin was shot down on 4 May. That morning we were taking off as a flight. I don't know why, but I was the tail-end MiG and Senior Lieutenant Osipov's wingman. Immediately after lifting off the runway, having initiated the process for retracting my landing gear, I glanced behind me and caught sight of four Sabres right on our tails that were attacking us. Without stopping to think, I broke sharply left and swung around into their attack, which forced them to turn away to avoid a collision, so their first attacking pass was fruitless. However, since we hadn't had time to accelerate and it was practically impossible to throw the MiG into energetic maneuvering, we had to accept combat under quite unfavorable circumstances. The result of the combat was woeful: the Sabres managed to shoot down the aircraft of the 1st Squadron commander Captain Motorin, who was able to eject, and to damage my aircraft. In the action I received bullets in the MiG's fuselage and wing, but I safely landed my MiG and the technicians soon repaired it. We had been taking off from the Miaogou airfield, which had become our new base just the day before.

On this day Sabres shot down one MiG over the Andong airfield, three over the Miaogou airfield, and damaged two more. In return, the Americans lost one of their own Sabres, which was downed by a pilot of the 148th GIAP Senior Lieutenant G.A. Nikiforov, and another of the "hunters" received damage. In sum, the Sabres of the 335th FIS shot down four MiGs over the 64th IAK's bases in China. However, the Americans registered only three victories over MiG-15s on 4 May, while they recorded the other victory as having happened on 3 May.

On 6 May, a pilot of the 16th IAP Captain Arkadii Boitsov distinguished himself, having received authorization to lead his element on a free hunt. In the area of Siojio at an altitude of 8,000 meters, he spotted a flight of F-86s, which he surprised with a rapid attack and destroyed one of them. The remaining Sabres fled the area. The downed F-86 was being flown by Robert MacTaggert [or McTaggert], who was killed in the cockpit of his aircraft.[3]

Only the pilots of the UAA took part in repelling the next enemy fighter-bomber raids in the area of MiG Alley on 8 and 9 May 1952. They clashed with fighter-bombers, as well as with Sabres, without support from the Soviet pilots. According to the Chinese pilots' claims, they shot down approximately 10 enemy aircraft in these actions. The American acknowledged losing three F-80s of the 49th FBG and three F-84s from the same 49th FBG and the 136th FBW over North Korea on these two days. One F-86E from the 336th FIS was also lost. However, the Americans attribute these losses to a variety of reasons, with the exception of combat with MiGs, but at least half of these losses could be accurately described as due to MiG fire. The Chinese pilots paid for these successes with the loss of two MiGs, which were shot down on 8 May by pilots of the 335th FIS.

Beginning in May 1952, the pilots of the 97th and 190th IAD began staging free hunt sorties as pairs and flights, as well as squadron-sized sorties to intercept enemy aircraft. For example on 13 May 1952, the new Sabre fighter-bombers of the 25th FIS launched another strike against the Siniuju airfield together with groups of F-80 and F-84 fighter-bombers. However, this time the Americans didn't have the same success as they had enjoyed back on 4 May, because small groups of MiGs from the 148th GIAP and 821st IAP took off to meet them. Moreover, the group of MiGs from the 148th GIAP was led by a Soviet Air Force inspector Colonel Pakhomov from the 64th IAK command staff. The 148th GIAP's pilots encountered a group of F-80 Shooting Stars en route to Sinuiju, and conducting several attacking passes against them, scattered their formation and forced them to retreat to the bay without having completed their mission. In the process, Colonel Pakhomov and a pilot of the 148th GIAP V.A. Taravkov shot down one "Shoot" each. This occurred between 0905 and 0950 in the Wonsong-dong area.

Pilots of the 821st IAP led by deputy regiment commander Major A.P. Prudnikov came across a group of F-84s, which shunned the encounter with the MiGs and exited the Sinuiju area in the direction of Korea Bay, but lost one Thunderjet in the process. Senior Lieutenant P.N. Veshkin achieved the victory.

Another group of 821st IAP MiGs engaged a group of F-86s from the 4th FIW, and Major Prudnikov shot down one of them, while our group had no losses in return. However, the Sabres took a bit of revenge for the general lack of success on the day by catching a squadron of the 494th IAP that was covering the Andong airfield and downing the squadron's deputy political commander Captain E.A. Pomaz, but he safely ejected from his stricken MiG.

As a result, while repelling the enemy's fighter-bomber raids against Siniuju, the pilots of the 64th IAK claimed four US aircraft destroyed, while losing one MiG in return. Fighters of the UAA also took part in repelling the raids on 13 May; since the Americans claimed to have downed five MiG-15s, four of them possibly belonged to the UAA. However, the Americans also suffered a serious loss. In the action over the Siniuju airfield, the commander of the 4th FIG Colonel Walker "Bud" Mahurin was shot down. He was compelled to make a forced landing in his F-86E No.51-2789 on North Korean territory and was taken prisoner by the North Koreans. In truth, it still isn't known precisely who shot the American commander down. Mahurin himself asserts that he was shot down by ground fire over the target area, but according to other sources, he was shot down in aerial combat by a pilot of the 190th IAD, though perhaps it was Major A.P. Prudnikov of the 821st IAP. Moreover, Mahurin's forced landing on North Korean land was so skillful and successful that his Sabre reached the 64th IAK almost wholly intact. Technicians of the 97th IAD specially drove into North Korea to pick up the F-86 and returned to the Andong airfield with it, but then it was transported to the Soviet Air Force's scientific research institute in Moscow for detailed analysis. In addition, on this day the Americans also lost two F-80s (No.49-734 and No.49-669) of the 8th FBG. The pilot of one of them, 1st Lieutenant William B. Slade, was killed-in-action, while the other pilot 1st Lieutenant Jack Berry was injured when he crash landed his Shooting Star at the K-13 base.

In May the UAA command deployed two new fighter divisions, both consisting of two regiments. They were the 12th IAD and 17th IAD, each equipped with 45 combat-ready MiG-15s. However, once again the pilots of these divisions, lacking any combat experience against the American jets and pilots, suffered painful losses in their initial clashes with Sabres. For example in one dogfight with Sabres of the 335th FIS on 15 May, they lost three MiGs. In this action, 1st Lieutenant James Kasler particularly stood out, downing two MiGs at once. To be sure, the Chinese pilots also showed their teeth: they managed to damage seriously one F-86E from the 25th FIS; its pilot quickly had to bail out from his crippled Sabre and was picked up by a search and rescue team. At a minimum one F-84E from the 49th FBG's 9th FBS was also shot down and its pilot 1st Lieutenant Vernon R. Huber became a prisoner-of-war.

The Americans launched a rather large raid on 17 May, consisting of F-84E Thunderjets. Our ground control operators did a splendid job directing 20 MiGs of the 821st IAP under the command of Lieutenant Colonel G.F. Dmitriuk to intercept them. At low altitude they reported encountering an unescorted group of 12-16 F-84s in the Changseong – Sonchon area. More likely, the Sabres were at a higher altitude than the F-84s, above the low cloud cover, and they simply didn't see the MiGs. Taking advantage of the surprise, the 821st IAP's pilots made two attacking passes against the Thunderjet formation, and having downed five of them, broke off combat. Our pilots returned to Andong, while the surviving Thunderjets headed toward the bay. The Sabres simply didn't have time to come to the Thunderjets' assistance. It was primarily the regiment's leadership that scored well in this action: regiment commander Lieutenant Colonel G.F. Dmitriuk, 1st Squadron commander Major I.P. Vakhrushev and 3rd Squadron commander Major V.N. Zabelin each claimed one Thunderjet, while the regiment's assistant for aerial gunnery Lieutenant Colonel A.A. Olenitsa shot down two F-84s in this combat. Pilots of the 494th IAP, who hurriedly arrived on the scene, downed another of the Thunderjets; Senior Lieutenant V.G. Krutskikh received credit for this victory.

On this same day the pilots of the 190th IAD also tangled with enemy fighter-bombers. In an afternoon mission, pilots of the 821st IAP were directed by ground controllers to what they identified as a group of F-51 Mustangs, but were more likely F4U Corsairs; thanks to their maneuverability the fighter-bombers were able to escape to the bay, but Major A.P. Prudnikov was nevertheless able to shoot down one of them, while Lieutenant Colonel Olenitsa damaged another. In a combat with Sabres that soon arrived on the scene, Captain I.F. Denisov shot down one of the F-86s, while the remainder exited the battle. However, on their way back to base they came under attack by pilots of the 148th GIAP. The Sabres were attempting to slip away below the group of MiGs, but the Soviet pilots spotted the enemy fighters in time and dove on them. Senior Lieutenant Korochkin succeeded in getting one of the F-86s on the outside of their formation in his sights, which decided its fate. The Sabre's fall was confirmed by a report from the ground, and the gun camera footage was clear – the Sabre was destroyed. This occurred between 1145 and 1150 and the Sabre fell 10 kilometers west of Sionan.

In total, on 17 May the pilots of the 190th IAD downed eight US aircraft (six F-84s, one F-86 and one reported F-51), with seven of them going to the credit of the 821st IAP. One more F-86 was shot down by a pilot of the 97th IAD's 148th GIAP. This day of combat was all the more successful because the 64th IAK didn't lose a single MiG. The chief of the 821st IAP's aerial gunnery service Lieutenant Colonel A.A. Olenitsa enjoyed a memorable day by downing two F-84s and damaging one piston-engine fighter-bomber. The Americans don't report any victories on 17 May 1952.

The F-84s of the 49th FBW were the ones that came under the attack of the 821st IAP. It lost three of its aircraft from MiG fire on this day: F-84E No.50-1114 was shot down and its pilot Captain Chester A. Shaw was taken prisoner; F-84E No.51-518 was also shot down, but its pilot bailed out and eventually returned to his unit; finally, F-84E No.50-1230 was seriously damaged by a MiG, and its pilot managed to reach his K-14 Base at Kimpo, where he crashed upon landing. The fate of this pilot is unknown. The 136th FBW's 154th Squadron also lost F-84D No.48-760, the pilot of which 1st Lieutenant James M. Smith went missing-in-action. As noted above, it likely wasn't Mustangs that the 821st IAP's pilots came across on this day, but carrier-based Corsairs. One of these from VF-64 (No.81079) exploded in mid-air and its pilot Lieutenant (j.g.) John A. De Masters is listed as missing-in-action. Thus, of the nine victories claimed by Soviet pilots on 17 May, the American side confirms six.

On 20 May 1952, pilots of the 4th FIW's 335th FIS, led by the new wing commander Colonel Harrison Thyng, had a successful dogfight in the area of the Yalu River not far from Andong and downed three MiG-15s of the UAA. Thyng himself got one of the victories. This same group then attacked MiGs as they were coming in for a landing at the Miaogou airfield, and shot down and killed the 256th IAP's navigator Captain Viktor Emmanuilovich Kalmanson directly over the base. On this day some of the 256th IAP's pilots were shuttling a batch of new MiG-15bis over the short hop from Andong to Miaogou, and this incident took place as this group was coming in for a landing. Here's how one of the eyewitnesses, squadron engineer Viktor Georgievich Verkhovsky, describes this tragedy:

> As the shuttle pilots were coming in for a landing from the north, they were attacked by a "Sabre hunter", which had popped up from behind the hills to the northwest. Kalmason's MiG was at an altitude of 60-70 meters; at this time we were standing next to the radio, waiting for our aircraft to come in. The Sabre, in a steep, diving turn to starboard, opened fire with some deflection. Kalmason had time to utter over the radio, "Oh, the bastards, they've got me ....", just before the .50-caliber bullets stitched his aircraft. The MiG dropped its nose and struck the ground at the start of the runway, but there was no explosion. The impact triggered the catapult

and launched Kalmason from the cockpit onto the concrete. One of the bullets had struck him in the back of head and had drilled through his entire torso. We buried him in Port Arthur.

To be sure, the pilots of the 190th IAD quickly evened the score – Major V.N. Zabelin downed one of those fond of doing a little hunting in the Andong area. His victim was Captain John F. Lane of the 336th FIS, who according to American records went missing-in-action on this day. His F-86A No.49-1255 fell at 1220 in an area 10 kilometers south of Sakchu.

On the following day of 21 May, pilots of the 821st IAP fully got even for the death of their comrade from the brotherly 256th IAP by downing three Sabres in a dogfight with a group of 10 F-86s in the Sonchon – Serikan area, without any losses in return. The victories were achieved by Major V.N. Zabelin, who was becoming a specialist in downing Sabres, and his comrades Major V.A. Lazarev and Senior Lieutenant E.T. Mazikin. The Americans acknowledged the loss of two of their Sabres from the 4th FIW: F-86A No.49-1327 of the 335th FIS, the pilot of which 2nd Lieutenant Alfred M. Miller, Jr. managed to fly back to Kimpo, but crashed a half-mile short of the runway at K-14 (the pilot was uninjured, but the F-86 had to be scrapped); and F-86A No.49-1317 of the 334th FIS, the pilot of which 1st Lieutenant Ronald A. Berdoy successfully ejected after his aircraft went into an unrecoverable spin several miles north of his K-14 base (Berdoy was rescued, but his Sabre had to be written off).

On 25 May 1952, there was a major raid by USAF fighter-bombers, in cooperation with carrier-based strike aircraft of the US Navy against CPV and NKPA supply lines in the Anju area. Groups of MiGs from the 190th IAD's 256th IAP and 821st IAP, as well from the 97th IAD, were scrambled to repel strikes by small groups of enemy fighter-bombers and ground attack aircraft.

On the first combat mission of the day, initially pilots of the 821st IAP were directed to the Taegwan-dong area. Here's how one of its participants, the former commander of the 821st IAP's 1st Squadron Major I.P. Vakhrushev, describes this regimental sortie:

> On this mission, our regimental group was accurately directed by ground controllers to a group of F-84 fighter-bombers, which was operating at low altitude in the Taechon area. My element (Senior Lieutenant V.I. Gorodiansky was my wingman) was leading the squadron, because at the low altitude it was difficult to keep the group closed up, so the other elements were trailing somewhat behind. In addition, we had a poor view of the terrain below us on this day because of the smoke at low altitude (there were numerous fires on the ground). When coming out of one maneuver, I unexpectedly saw a group of F-84s out in front of me, which having shaken out into single file were one after the other attacking some ground target. They hadn't seen me yet, so using the factor of surprise, I attacked one of the Thunderjets as it was pulling out of an attack and shot it down. The remaining fighter-bombers immediately halted their runs on the ground target, and exploiting the poor visibility, headed toward the bay to avoid attack by the other elements. However, the 3rd Squadron commander Major V.A. Lazarev nevertheless overwhelmed another F-84. Our pilots returned from this combat with not a single bullet hole in their MiGs.

A group of MiGs from the 148th GIAP were directed against a different group of F-84s and also attacked the fighter-bombers successfully by downing two of them and chasing the rest back to the bay. One of the regiment's flights was being led by Captain P.S. Dubino, who spotted a group of F-84s as they were attacking a railroad station. Here our pilot made a mistake that almost cost him his life: separating from his flight, he closed on one of the Thunderjets and settled in behind it, before hitting it so heavily with his cannon shells that it exploded in mid-air. Suddenly his intuition told him to turn around and check behind him, and when he did so, he saw a Sabre latched onto his tail, ready to open fire. With an abrupt maneuver he avoided the attack and headed back to base alone.

Pilots of the 256th IAP on this day were unlucky. Major V.G. Sevast'ianov's squadron headed out on a combat mission and in the Anju area they encountered a group of F-84s that were being covered by Sabres. Major Sevast'ianov split up his squadron and led part of it against the F-86s, while the rest of the squadron attacked the fighter-bombers. In the process Senior Lieutenant N.E. Smirnov managed on the initial pass to damage the leader's aircraft, which started to stream smoke and head in the direction of the sea. N.E. Smirnov doesn't know its fate, because as he was pulling out of his attack at an altitude of 9,000 meters, a flight of Sabres attacked him and flamed his MiG. Smirnov ejected and came down safely on North Korean territory, but he was injured during the jump and had to spend approximately a month in the hospital in Andong.

While returning to the Miaogou airfield, Senior Lieutenant I.S. Mel'kin's MiG ran out of fuel and he was forced to put his plane down on North Korean territory. The pilot emerged alive and unharmed, but his MiG had to be written off.

On a different mission on this day, four MiGs of the 256th IAP's 2nd Squadron under the command of Captain Iu.D. Obraztsov were searching for a group of fighter-bombers, when in the smoky atmosphere they were unexpectedly jumped by a flight of F-86s. Senior Lieutenant Fedor Semenovich Krasulin's MiG was shot down; he ejected, but his parachute must have failed to deploy fully, because he was killed when he hit the ground.

Also on 25 May, pilots of the 148th GIAP engaged a group of carrier-based Corsairs and Senior Lieutenant G.A. Nikiforov downed one of them, while the rest scattered. A different group of pilots from the 148th GIAP, having encountered a group of F-84s covered by Sabres, also drove away this group, downing one F-84 and one F-86 without any losses of their own.

As a result over 25 May 1952, the 64th IAK's pilots claimed seven US aircraft, including five F-84s, one F-86 and one F4U-4, and damaged another F-84. Pilots of the 148th GIAP scored particularly well, downing five enemy aircraft on this day without any losses. The IAK's total losses for the day were three MiGs from the 256th IAP and one pilot.

According to the American side, the pilots of the 4th FIW scored four MiG-15 kills in these actions on 25 May 1952, although the 64th IAK's combat losses were only two MiGs. In their turn the Americans claim that on this day they had only one damaged Sabre, F-86A No.49-1973 of the 334th FIS, the pilot of which brought his damaged jet safely down on the base at Kimpo. They also acknowledge the loss of one of their F9F-2 Panthers, which crashed when landing on its aircraft carrier, and one of their AD-2 Skyraiders, the pilot of which bailed out.

Three days later, on 28 May 1952 the Americans gained revenge for their losses of 25 May, when pilots of the 51st FIW claimed three MiG-15s. Two of the MiGs were shot down in one action by Major Elmer Harris. The 64th IAK's losses on this day amounted to only one MiG-15 – a pilot of the 821st IAP Senior Lieutenant P.T. Makhonin was shot down, but he safely ejected from his damaged aircraft. However, a bullet had smashed a bone in his right arm, and after he was picked up by CPV troops, he was sent to a Soviet hospital. The other two MiG-15s most likely belonged to the UAA. In return, the pilots of the 821st IAP's 3rd Squadron claimed one Sabre in a dogfight with the F-86s.

The last battle of the spring 1952 campaign took place on 31 May, when the Americans launched a raid against Singisiu with carrier-based aircraft. Eight MiG-15s of the 148th GIAP were scrambled to intercept and repel this raid. One of the 148th GIAP's flights was led by the 2nd Squadron commander Captain L.I. Savichev, and the other flight by Major A.T. Bashman of the 3rd Squadron. In the Singisiu area they encountered blunt-nosed carrier fighter-bombers which they identified as F4U-2 Corsairs and attacked them. However, with their extremely high rate of closure they were unable open fire before overshooting the slow-moving targets. True, they broke up the enemy fighter-bomber formation; ceasing their ground attacks, the fighter-bombers began to depart for Korea Bay. However, our pilots, considering the difference in speeds and their mistake in the first pass, throttled back and attacked again. This helped – four of the piston-engine fighter-bombers were shot down. They were added to the combat scores of Major A.T. Bashman, Captain L.I. Savichev, and Senior Lieutenants A.I. Krylov and V.P. Burdin. We had no losses in this action, because the fighter-bombers had been working over the target without Sabre protection.

For some reason the staff documents noted that these downed enemy aircraft were F-51 Mustangs, but most likely they were carrier-based Corsairs of VF-113, two of which were written off on 1 June and 2 June 1952 (one pilot was killed, the other rescued), and British carrier-based Sea Furies of the Fleet Air Arm 802 Squadron, which our pilots mistakenly identified as Mustangs. Three of these Sea Furies were written off several days later.

A group from the 821st IAP intercepted another group of piston-engine F-51 Mustangs as they were leaving the target area and managed to down one of them. It disintegrated under the cannon fire of 2nd Squadron pilot Senior Lieutenant V.M. Molokanov. This was RF-51D No.44-84638 from the 18th FBG's 12th Squadron, the pilot of which 1st Lieutenant Paul R. Kniss was taken prisoner.

This victory has a little prequel, which a former pilot of the 821st IAP Aleksei Ivanovich Romanov wrote about in a letter to the author:

> In our 2nd Squadron, Captain Abitkovsky and Captain Molokanov had victories in aerial combats. Molokanov shot down his F-51 just a day after he'd been rebuked at a Party gathering for the fact that as a flight commander he'd been unable to shoot down an enemy aircraft for such a long time! Well, after this "pep talk", on the next regimental sortie on 31 May his flight encountered a group of F-51s and he shot down one of them.

Romanov himself also had one encounter with four F-51s, which were painted in a lighter shade (which meant they couldn't have been carrier aircraft) and moved to attack them, while they, having sighted the MiGs, immediately formed into a circle, just like our Il-2s used to do in the Great Patriotic War. However, he didn't succeed in attacking them, because at that moment Sabres pounced on our MiGs, and they had to abandon the F-51s and take on the F-86s.

However, the pilots of the 821st IAP also had a heavy loss on this day: a flight commander in the 1st Squadron Captain Ivan Fedorovich Denisov, who had two victories to his credit in the skies of Korea, was killed-in-action. Here's how deputy political commander of this squadron Vasilii Ivanovich Gorodiansky relates what happened:

> I recall 31 May; that morning I led a flight almost all the way down to Pyongyang. Returning back to base at an order from the command post, I heard that a large group of Sabres was blockading the airfield. Captain Denisov's flight took off from the blockaded airfield and tied up the Sabres in combat. All of this, if you will, might have gone well, if Ivan Denisovich had been able to retract his landing gear. He couldn't do so, however, because the landing gear toggle switch wasn't activated. Denisov didn't know that the regiment commander's aircraft that he'd been given for the mission was of a given series which were equipped with toggle switches as a safeguard.
>
> The crew chief had failed to warn the pilot about this detail, and this ended tragically. After take-off his landing gear were still down, and from the command post, realizing what the problem was, a message prompted the pilot to hit the toggle switch to raise the gear, but it was already too late. His MiG had by now reached a speed of 400 km/hr, which made it impossible for him to retract the landing gear fully. He also couldn't reduce his speed below 400 km/hr. An unequal combat had started up, in which Denisov's MiG had become a target sleeve, although Ivan was maneuvering it as much as he could to avoid aimed fire. Incidentally, I'll say that according to the regiment's records, almost all of its combat losses were not in the course of dogfights, but occurred when our pilots were returning from a mission low on fuel, and Sabres were waiting for them to land. The Americans loitered over the bay about 30 kilometers from Andong, and seeing our aircraft taking off or coming in for a landing, they would dive on the almost helpless aircraft and fire at them – it wasn't any great feat to shoot down an aircraft with deployed speed brakes or lowered landing gear. I recalled that the squadron and regiment leadership proposed a discussion of measures to reduce the losses in the area of the bases to General Lobov. A meeting did take place, but there was nothing with which to cover the airfields.

Captain Denisov was shot down by a pair of Sabres from the 335th FIS, since on this day its pilots downed two MiG-15s. Credit for these victories went to Lieutenant Colonel Francis J. Vetort, who probably downed Captain Denisov, and Major William K. Thomas. The results of the last day of aerial combats in May 1952 were as follows: the 64th IAK officially recorded victories over five F-51 Mustangs (or more likely F4U Corsairs), while its own losses were one MiG-15 and Captain I.F. Denisov of the 821st IAP, who was killed.

The total results for the month of May 1952 were as follows: the 64th IAK claimed victories over 35 enemy aircraft, including 12 F-84, 13 F-86, 2 F-80, 6 F-51, 1 F4U-4 and 1 B-26. The 190th IAD was credited with 20 of these victories (plus two damaged US aircraft) and the 97th IAD with 13. The victory over the B-26 was achieved at night

US B-26s bombing North Korea. (US Air Force)

by pilots of the 351st NIAP, and Colonel Pamokhov from the 64th IAK headquarters downed one F-80. However, just two fighter regiments, one in each IAD, achieved the vast majority of the victories. For example, 18 of the 190th IAD's 20 victories were achieved by the 821st IAP alone, while of the 13 victories added to the 97th IAD's record, 12 went to pilots of the 148th GIAP.

The total losses of the 64th IAK in the month of May amounted to 17 aircraft destroyed and four pilots killed-in-action. In May 1952 the 190th IAD had ten aircraft that returned with combat damage, of which two had up to 20 bullet holes in them, two with up to 40 bullet holes, and one MiG made it back to base with 154 bullet holes in it! The Americans claimed that the pilots of the 4th and 51st FIW destroyed 27 MiG-15s, one Yak-9 and 1 Tu-2 in the month of May 1952 in aerial combat, and another three Yak-9s on the ground, for a total of 32 aircraft, while losing just five F-86 Sabres in return.

The Meteor pilots of the Australian No. 77 Squadron also enjoyed a good month in May 1952. This squadron was now operating in the Pyongyang area, outside of MiG Alley, and had two MiG encounters. On 4 May, a pair of Meteors engaged a group of nine MiG-15s, and Pilot Officer J. Surman shot down one of the MiGs. On 8 May, in another clash with MiGs over the Pyongyang area, Pilot Officer Bill Simmonds downed another MiG – its pilot ejected. Both MiGs were from the UAA, since only the Chinese operated in this area with small groups of MiGs. The losses of No. 77 Squadron in the May dogfights with MiGs aren't known, but according to the data on total results by pilots of the UAA, two Gloster Meteors were shot down in 1952, and possibly both of these were indeed downed in the May fighting. The Australians acknowledge the loss of three Meteors in the month of May; one of them (No.A77-385) was damaged by MiGs and crashed upon landing – it was written off on 12 May 1952. Another two Meteors were lost on 15 and 16 May, and the loss on the latter date was Meteor No.A77-936, which was probably lost due to MiG fire. Thus the Chinese pilots fought successfully against the Meteors, even though they didn't score as well against them as the Soviet pilots had!

ENDNOTES

1   It should be pointed out that Fedoseev is relating what he heard on the ground and this story is not what the author has said happened. It is more likely that Liubovinkin had been mortally wounded in his cockpit when the Sabres shot his MiG down, and the Sabre pilots had made a pass at his descending parachute and fired to one side in order to capture clear evidence of their victory on their gun camera film. However, the author has maintained in a personal correspondence with this translator that there were occasions when American pilots did fire on Soviet pilots suspended from parachutes after bailing out.

2   Some Soviet Korean War pilots have claimed that American jets in Korea wore camouflage colors. Shooting Stars and Thunderjets in Korea had a natural metal finish, which was greatly dulled in the Korean environment.

3   I have not been able to find the American pilot's name or his squadron on any Internet database devoted to the Korean Air War, nor is Boitsov's victory on 6 May 1952 noted in the Air Combat Information Group's Korean War database.

8

Another hot summer

THE 64TH IAK IS REINFORCED

In addition to the two new fighter aviation divisions that had joined the Unified Air Army, one more Soviet PVO fighter division from Iaroslavl' joined the 64th IAK and entered combat operations in May 1952 – the 133rd IAD under the command of A.R. Komarov. This was a full-strength IAD, consisting of three fighter regiments: the 147th GIAP (commanded by Lieutenant Colonel M.I. Studilin), the 415th IAP (commanded by Hero of the Soviet Union Major P.F. Shevelev) and the 726th IAP (commanded by Lieutenant Colonel L.D. Goriachko). The given PVO division had departed for China back in March 1952, but without its equipment. Having arrived at the Mukden-West Air Base in China at the beginning of April, the division soon received new MiG-15bis fighters and began conducting training flights and studying the area of combat operations.

Pilots of the 415th IAP were the first to fly combat missions, staging from the Mukden-West airfield to cover the take-offs and landings of fighters at the Andong airfield. On 29 April the 415th IAP transferred to Andong, from whence it flew several combat missions in May to the area of the Supung hydroelectric station. The 147th GIAP, which had also spent the entire month of April at the Mukden-West Air Base, was the next to begin combat operations. The regiment's pilots flew their first combat mission and had their first combat action on 5 May 1952, having taken off to sweep the airspace over the Andong base of enemy fighters. They had a fleeting skirmish with a group of F-86s, which ended without results. In May 1952, while still in the 64th IAK's second echelon, the 147th GIAP kept two squadrons on combat alert status at the Mukden-West Air Base, while the third squadron, the 2nd (Night) Squadron, flew to the Miaogou airfield and initiated nighttime combat operations.

Both of these regiments of the 133rd IAD, which were still in the 64th IAK reserve in this period, flew several dozen combat missions in May and had several encounters with enemy aircraft, but they all wound up without any results. The single loss in the 133rd IAD in May resulted from an accident on 27 May. There was a low layer of clouds that day, and the deputy division commander Colonel A.N. Barabanov was carrying out a training flight. The weather abruptly deteriorated and he came in for a landing, but he forgot to lower his landing gear and made a belly landing – the aircraft burst into flames and became fully consumed by them; fortunately Barabanov had time to scramble out of the cockpit and run away from the MiG. He survived intact, but got a little banged up during the belly landing and wound up in the hospital.

During this time, the 133rd IAD's 726th IAP didn't take part in combat operations. It continued to train at the Mukden-West airfield. As a result, in June 1952 only two regiments of the 133rd IAD participated in combat operations: the 415th IAP from the Andong airfield, and the 147th GIAP with two squadrons from the Mukden-West base

US Air Force F-80 Shooting Star fighter-bomber involved in an air strike over Suan, North Korea, in the largest air strike of the Korean Conflict on May 8, 1952. (US National Archives)

and one night squadron from the Miaogou airfield. In June, another Soviet PVO division arrived in China, the 216th IAD under the command of Hero of the Soviet Union Colonel A.U. Eremin. This division arrived at Mukden from the Baku District PVO without its equipment, and it began preparing for combat operations at the end of June 1952, after receiving new MiG-15bis fighters. It also consisted of three full-strength regiments: the 676th IAP (commanded by Lieutenant Colonel V.E. Gol'tsev), the 518th IAP (commanded by Lieutenant Colonel Litvinenko) and the 878th IAP (commanded by Lieutenant Colonel S.D. Dronov).

In the month of June, the new Dapu airfield, which was located not far from Andong, became operational; it was presumed that it would ease the congestion at the Andong Air Base, which was jammed with the regiments of the 97th IAD and 190th IAD, as well as Unified Air Army units. Already in the middle of June, the 133rd IAD's 415th IAP was the first to fly over to the Dapu airfield and began to conduct combat operations from this new base.

A certain lull in the operations of the 64th IAK in the skies of North Korea arrived in June 1952. This was brought about by the changeover in its complement of fighter divisions and the time spent preparing the new fighter divisions for combat. The rosters of the 97th IAD and 190th IAD had significantly thinned: several dozen of their pilots had been killed in combat, received wounds or injuries after ejecting, or had departed for the Soviet Union due to fatigue or illnesses. Therefore in May 1952 a batch of approximately

50 young replacement pilots had arrived from the Soviet Union. This group had been formed from pilots who had recently converted from piston engine aircraft to the jet MiG-15, at Lieutenant General E.Ia. Savitsky's direction. They were sent off to this war with the aim of checking the quality of combat training in the units; on average, each of these pilots had only 20-30 hours of flight time in jet aircraft.

The 16th IAP alone in the month of May 1952 received 13 young pilots as replacements, while another 15 wound up in the 148th GIAP. Almost the same number of young pilots arrived in the 190th IAD. In connection with the fact that the flight personnel of the 97th IAD was now significantly younger, already at the end of May its 16th IAP departed for Mukden for supplemental flight training with its newly arrived replacements. Great emphasis was placed primarily on making combat maneuvers as pairs and flights at high speeds and at high altitudes. In June the 148th GIAP also rotated back to Mukden for the same purpose, so only regiments of the 190th IAD and 133rd IAD remained at the Andong and Miaogou airfields.

As of 1 July 1952, the Unified Air Army had six full-strength Chinese fighter divisions – the 3rd, 4th, 12th, 15th, 17th and 18th IAD, which numbered 275 combat-ready MiG-15s and MiG-15bis, plus another 28 under repair. The Soviet fighter divisions on this day had another 302 MiGs. Of this number, 37 MiG-15s and 56 outdated MiG-9s of the 15th IAD were not activated for combat; primarily, they and the 2nd and 14th IAD guarded rear sites in northeast China and kept busy with training pilots.

On 2 June Unified Air Army pilots flew a mission to intercept US aircraft, but it ended in failure: a group of F-84s from the 49th FBG's 7th FBS during a strike against the Siniuju – Chongju pounced on four Chinese MiGs. In this combat 2nd Lieutenant Leonard A. Guilton damaged one of the MiGs.

Despite the reduced activity in June 1952, Soviet pilots nevertheless continued to fly combat missions, and already on 4 June pilots of the 190th IAD again took off to repel enemy fighter-bomber raids in the Anju area. On this day pilots of the 494th IAP flew four group combat sorties and almost all of them made contact with enemy aircraft. On the final mission of the day, the pair of 2nd Squadron commander Captain Zamiatin and his wingman Senior Lieutenant F.P. Shevchenko was attacked while taking off. Shevchenko's aircraft was targeted by one "Sabre hunter" and his MiG fell from low altitude not far from the end of the runway. When the MiG struck the ground Shevchenko's head slammed against the gun sight and he was knocked unconscious. He was dragged out of his smashed aircraft and sent to a hospital. The pilot came away with bruises while his fighter was written off. This was the 64th IAK's first loss in the month of June. Apparently it was so obvious that the MiG had been shot down just as it was taking off from the Andong airfield, and so evident on the American pilot's gun camera film, that he didn't even file a victory claim, so it is still unknown who it was that shot down Shevchenko. According to the claim of his squadron mates, earlier on this day Shevchenko also had at least one victory over an F-86, but for some unknown reason he received no credit for this victory.

On 6 June the pilots of the 97th IAD staging from the Andong airfield had their last battle of the month. True, it wasn't a battle as such, but its 148th GIAP suffered its two final losses in the skies of Korea: the regiment had scrambled in response to an alert in order to support the 494th IAP, which was engaged with a group of enemy aircraft in the Anju area. However, on take-off, the regiment's tail-end pair of Captain V. Ivanets and his wingman Senior Lieutenant V.N. Naumenko was jumped by six F-86s, which had been loitering over the bay near Andong. At high speed, they dove on the MiG element as it was climbing immediately after taking off, and downed both of them on the first pass. Fortunately, both Soviet pilots managed to eject safely.

Pilots of the 494th IAP under the command of Lieutenant Colonel A.E. Man'kovsky on this day had been successfully directed to a group of F-84 fighter-bombers, which were operating at low altitude in the Anju area, and attacked them from the approach. In the course of the action three F-84s were downed, while the others were chased back to the bay. However, when returning to the Andong airfield to land, the MiG formation was again attacked by Sabres of the 4th FIW, which shot down two of the regiment's aircraft: Senior Lieutenants G.S. Mil'chutsky and Iu.K. Garin both successfully ejected. Here's how Iurii Kirillovich Garin himself relates what happened:

> Concerning the ill-fated day of 6 June 1952, then of course I remember it well. That morning our squadron had been at Readiness No.2, so we were sticking close to our aircraft. The command to take off came from the division command post. As we were taking seats in our cockpits and starting our engines, the order came to stand down. We hadn't even had time to turn off our engines when the order came again to take off. However, the leader of our eight-ship squadron deputy squadron commander Captain S.A. Ableev had already switched off his engine, so he wasn't able to take off immediately. Captain G.S. Mil'chutsky assumed command, and we took off as a six-ship formation consisting of the elements Mil'chutsky-Fedoseev, Potylitsin-Tiurichev, and Alekseenko-Garin. Two minutes later Ableev and Briuzgin lifted off the runway, but a pair of Sabres attempted to attack them while they were taking off; they had to take evasive action and then flew to a different base.
>
> Once in the air we received the assignment to repulse a raid by F-84 fighter-bombers against the road and rail network 90 kilometers away from base. As we were flying to the targeted area, we received a report informing us that approximately 100 F-84 and F-86 aircraft were over the target area. Descending, we jettisoned our drop tanks and accelerated to a speed of more than 1,000 km/hr. Alekseenko was the first to spot the fighter-bombers and reported this over the radio. I also spotted Thunderjets that were coming in from the direction of the sea and diving on a column of vehicles. Mil'chutsky issued the order: "We're attacking." Our speed was greater than that of the F-84s, and Alekseenko swiftly opened fire on one fighter-bomber and shot it down. Captain Mil'chutsky and Senior Lieutenant Tiurichev – the squadron's youngest pilot – also downed one enemy aircraft each.
>
> But we also couldn't avoid losses: both Mil'chutsky and I were shot down. When pulling out of an attack, after reversing direction, I suddenly felt a machine-gun burst striking my aircraft. My engine's thrust fell somewhat and my cockpit canopy was shattered. Overhead, Fedoseev's aircraft flashed across mine. He was attempting to force the Sabres to break off their attack. I didn't see who was firing at me, but I quickly hauled my aircraft into a climbing turn to escape the stream of fire and announced over the radio that I'd been hit. When coming out of the chandelle, two Sabres again attempted to attack me from above, but I managed to turn into their attack. We passed within approximately 50 meters of each other. I turned

toward base and managed to climb to an altitude of 9,000 meters, but then my engine flamed out. I decided to bail out, since the airfield was still distant. There was nowhere to land the MiG – the terrain as mountainous, and it was also a dangerous maneuver to attempt with a dead engine. So I ejected.

The fight didn't end for me with this, however, though it is hard to call this a fight. After my parachute opened, a pair of Sabres attacked me, but it was apparent that they weren't firing at me, but only filming me. In this action I received fragment wounds in the left arm and neck. Even now I'm walking around with a "souvenir" from a 12.7mm bullet in my neck. In the hospital where they delivered me I met Mil'chutsky; he'd also been wounded, in the head.

On 6 June, it was Thunderjets from the 49th FBG's 7th FBS, which were conducting a strike against Chongju, that came under the attack of the MiGs from the 494th IAP. According to the report of the American pilots, three MiG-15s attacked them. The F-84 flown by 2nd Lieutenant W.G. Heath was damaged, but he flew back to his base and landed it there with 80 holes in it, including one in the Thunderjet's right wing that measured 30 x 50 centimeters. The Sabres of the 4th and 51st FIW in total downed eight MiG-15s on 6 June over the Andong airbase complex, of which four belonged to the Unified Air Army. In their turn the Chinese pilots shot down two F-86Es from the 51st FIW – both Sabre pilots Ensign and Mann took to their parachutes and were picked up by search and rescue teams.

After this battle the 97th IAD departed to Mukden, and primarily regiments of the 190th IAD and two regiments of the 133rd IAD continued to carry out combat operations. On 10 June 1952, pilots of the 147th GIAP opened their combat score – this was done by pilots of the regiment's 2nd (Night) Squadron, which had been operating from the base at Miaogou since the end of May. On the night of 10 June, B-29 bombers from the 19th BG were conducting a mission against Kwaksan and were attacked by two MiG-15bis fighters from the 147th GIAP and four MiGs from the 351st NIAP. In this night action, Captain A.M. Karelin of the 351st NIAP downed one B-29 and inflicted serious damage on another one. The commander of the 147th GIAP Major M.I. Studilin attacked another Superfortress caught in the glare of searchlights and shot it down – this was the first victory in the skies of Korea for this regiment and the 133rd IAD.

The Superfortresses flew another mission on the night of 14 June. Night fighter pilots from the 147th GIAP's 2nd Squadron and the 351st NIAP again took off to intercept them. Only Captain F.S. Volodarsky of the 147th GIAP's 2nd Squadron was lucky enough to detect and attack a target, as a result of which one more burning B-29 was sent plummeting to the ground.

In these first two weeks of June 1952 there were few combat sorties, but after the 97th IAD's departure on 6 June, sorties were a rare sight – a short pause in the fighting arrived. On these days of rest, primarily units of the Unified Air Army continued to fly missions, and they had several combats with the UN air forces. For example on 7 June and 8 June, pilots of the Unified Air Army shot down two F-86Es, the pilots of which 1st Lieutenants Richard S. Drezen, Jr. and Robert S. Chesney both bailed out over the Yellow Sea and were rescued by Navy search and rescue. In turn the pilots of the 4th FIW succeeded in taking revenge against the Unified Air Army pilots by downing three

Chinese MiG-15s on 11 June, two of which went to the credit of 2nd Lieutenant James F. Low of the 335th FIS.

The 64th IAK's pilots resumed flying combat missions on 15 June, but because of the blockade over our bases by enemy aircraft, these sorties brought only losses to the IAK. The days of 15 and 16 June proved to be unfortunate for the pilots of the 494th IAP, when three of the regiment's MiGs were shot down by Sabres in aerial combat over MiG Alley and in the vicinity of the airfields: on 15 June Senior Lieutenants A.P. Kargin and I.A. Omelaev were shot down; these victories went to Lieutenant Colonel Stephen Stone of the 334th FIS and 2nd Lieutenant James Low of the 335th FIS. On 16 June, Senior Lieutenant G.P. Kulaev was shot down by Captain Francis A. Williams of the 51st FIW's 25th Squadron, though this victory was recorded as having occurred on 15 June. All of the Soviet pilots safely ejected, and the Americans had no losses in these actions.

On the eve of these events, there was a change in the command of the 51st FIW: on 13 June, Colonel John Mitchell assumed command of the Wing in place of Colonel Gabreski, who had returned to the United States. Colonel Mitchell was an ace of the Second World War, in which he had attained 11 victories in the Pacific theater. At the same time in this change of command, the fully trained and equipped 39th FIS arrived from Japan to join 51st FIW from Japan, and already in the month of July 1952, this squadron began to receive the first new F-86Fs.

On 20 June 1952, two dogfights occurred in the Andong area, both involving North Korean pilots flying the piston-engine La-9 and Americans of the 4th FIW in their F-86s. According to some sources, four North Korean aces, masters at the controls of their aircraft who had solid combat experience, arrived at the Andong airbase in the month of June. They were supposed to study the aerial combat tactics of the latest rotation of Soviet pilots, flying their jet aircraft, because soon the North Korean pilots of the given regiment were to convert to flying MiG-15s.

Lt Col Richard F. Turner, one of the USAF F-86 Sabre jet pilots serving with the US 4th Fighter Interceptor Wing in Korea. (Smithsonian National Air & Space Museum)

Hero of the Korean People's Democratic Republic Major Paek Ki Rak was commanding this group. He had received this high honor for his service back in 1950. On the morning of 20 June, Major Rak and his wingman took off on a training flight and unexpectedly encountered 10 F-86s in the vicinity of the airfield, which immediately attacked the LaGGs and forced them to accept combat. Using the La-9s superior maneuverability, the Korean pilots in the resulting turning, twisting combat downed two F-86s according to records of the NKPA command, but only Major Rak returned to base. His wingman became the victim of Captain Frederick "Boots" Blesse of the 334th FIS.

A little later that day, a second element of La-9s under the command of Captain Kim were also conducting a training flight when they were also attacked by a different group of Sabres from the 4th FIW in squadron strength. The dogfight lasted for 18 minutes, in the course of which Captain Kim and his wingman Kang Sung Hung reportedly each downed one F-86, but the Sabres in turn shot down first Senior Lieutenant Kang, who was killed in this action, and then later flamed Captain Kim's fighter, though he managed to bring his burning La-9 down safely in a field. Pilots of the 336th FIS Colonel Royal N. Baker and 1st Lieutenant George J. Woods shot down the two North Korean fighters.

According to the NKPA command, in these two actions three La-9 fighters were downed and two pilots were killed. According to the same report, their pilots shot down three F-86s, and one American Sabre pilot, whose last name was Farler, was taken prisoner.[1] However, the Americans report no losses in the dogfights with the LaGGs on 20 June.

In the final days of June, almost all of the clashes between MiGs and Sabres took place in the area of the Andong and Miaogou bases, when Sabres inbound from the bay attempted to attack the MiGs of the 64th IAK and the Unified Air Army as they were taking off or returning to base from combat missions. Thus, on 21 June Sabres of the 25th FIS shot down one Chinese pilot in his MiG-15 as he was coming in for a landing. In return, on the same day a pilot of the 494th IAP Senior Lieutenant G.T. Shishov brought down one of these "hunters". Here is how this event happened according to documents of the 64th IAK headquarters:

> At 1555 hours, Senior Lieutenant Chistiakov's group encountered four F-86s in the Singisiu area at an altitude of 7,000-8,000 meters.... The enemy shunned battle and sought to escape out to sea, when they were subjected to an attack by our fighters. Two pilots actually fired at enemy aircraft. Senior Lieutenant Shishov shot down one F-86. The pilot of the downed aircraft, 2nd Lieutenant Frick from the 4th FIW, was taken prisoner by our Korean comrades.

The destroyed Sabre was F-86A No.49-1178 of the 336th FIS, which was shot down not far from Uiju around 1600. Its pilot 2nd Lieutenant Vance R. Frick bailed out, but couldn't evade capture.

On 23 June 1952 as a result of a massed raid by 284 F-80, F-84 and F-51 fighter-bombers, the Supung hydroelectric power station was knocked out of operation for two months. On this day, pilots of the 64th IAK were unable to take off to intercept the enemy aircraft due to poor weather conditions – the IAK's forward airfields were shut down by enormous thunderheads. The Americans took advantage of this situation and launched a major attack against the Supung hydroelectric station. The Americans noted the odd absence of MiGs in the air that day. However, on occasion the 64th IAK opted not to attempt to repel individual enemy airstrikes due to a variety of reasons: unsatisfactory meteorological conditions in the area where our units were based; a particularly strong Sabre presence in the vicinity of the Andong airfield complex; the remoteness of the area where the enemy fighter-bombers were operating; and sometimes even to economize strength in order to carry out the 64th IAK's main task – protecting strategic targets in Northeast China.

Senior Lieutenant A.A. Alekseenko of the 494th IAP scored the final victory of the month of June 1952 on 24 June by downing one Sabre in the vicinity of the Miaogou airfield, when the MiGs' fuel tanks were almost empty. The Sabre was F-86E No.50-0669 from the 335th FIS, which was shot down in a morning dogfight with MiGs. Its pilot 1st Lieutenant Albert B. Smiley managed to fly his crippled aircraft back to the K-14 Base in Kimpo, but there it crash-landed. The pilot was not injured, but his Sabre had to be written off.

On 25 June, a flight of MiGs from the 256th IAP engaged four F-86s in the area of their airfield; although there were no results, the "hunters" were chased back to Korea Bay. However, two days later on 27 June the 147th GIAP suffered its first loss. In response to an alarm, a pair of MiGs led by Captain P.S. Petraev scrambled from Mukden to fly to Andong in order to cover the IAK's MiGs that were returning from a combat mission. In the Andong area they were jumped by four F-86s, and in the ensuing combat Senior Lieutenant Vladimir Alekseevich Pozhidaev's MiG was damaged. The pilot was forced to make a wheels-up crash-landing, in which he was killed. Captain John Spalding of the 25th FIS received credit for shooting Pozhidaev down. This was the first loss of the given regiment in combat operations, and of its parent 133rd IAD.

The Americans prior to the end of June shot down two more Chinese MiGs. On 21 June, an element consisting of 1st Lieutenants William D. Angle and Donald A. McClean of the 336th FIS shot down one MiG-15, while on 25 June 1st Lieutenant Robert L. Goodridge of the 335th FIS downed another.

Thus the month of June 1952 featured relatively low aerial combat activity and ended with little loss of blood. According to 64th IAK headquarters' records, its pilots shot down a total of 10 US aircraft and damaged one more, including 4 B-29, 3 F-84, 2 F-86 and 1 B-26. The damaged aircraft was another B-29. The pilots of the 494th IAP achieved five victories, while the 351st NIAP recorded four kills and one damaged (all at night). The 147th GIAP's 2nd (Night) Squadron also scored two victories at night. The losses in June were rather significant: eight MiGs were destroyed and one pilot was killed.

The Americans claimed that in June their air forces shot down 21 enemy aircraft, of which 18 were MiG-15s and three were La-9s. Their own losses they report as six F-86s, of which only four were lost in combat. In addition, Marine Corps pilot 1st Lieutenant John Andre of VMF-513, flying an F4U-5NL Corsair, shot down a North Korean Yak-9 in aerial combat on 7 June 1952.

However, according to a claim by Major Petr Vasil'evich Minervin of the 148th GIAP, in June 1952 flying from the Mukden airfield, pilots of his regiment achieved several victories, including two by Minervin himself. Here's how he describes the June fighting:

> In the middle of June, early one morning I was scrambled at the head of an eight-ship
> formation. There had already been a passing rain shower that morning; you could

feel the humidity and clumps of clouds were beginning to form. As we climbed after take-off, we headed in the direction of the Supung hydroelectric station, and having reached an altitude of 9,500 meters, we emerged from the clouds. From the ground we received a command to take a heading of 120°, which I in fact did – it was quiet and peaceful in the air. About three minutes later, a fresh order came from auxiliary control post: "'Crosses' are operating below you (F-80s or F-84s); they're at an altitude of 1,000-1,500 meters, and they do have cover." I began to descend and cautioned my pilots over the radio to increase their watchfulness. Having shed 2,000 meters in altitude, I spotted a group of F-80s; they were bombing ground targets. I gave an order to flight commander Senior Lieutenant Krylov to remain at this altitude and to make sure that he kept me in sight, and then I began to descend to the altitude where the fighter-bombers were working; we were somewhere around Kujang.

The Shooting Stars were targeting a pontoon bridge about 90-100 kilometers east of Kujang. I established that there were eight F-80s attacking the bridge, and I didn't yet see any covering fighters. I focused the attack on this group's tail-end element. I reformed my group into a right echelon formation and went on the attack. However at that moment my wingman reported that four F-86s were closing on us from the right and below, and we had to break off the attack on the "Crosses" and turn into the attack of the approaching Sabres. Closing, we passed each other at a high angle of separation and then lost each other. Krylov's flight, monitoring the situation, guided me toward the four F-86s. A fine dogfight began. Having made two unsuccessful attacks, I headed in the direction of the sun and saw that the adversary was agitated, having lost sight of me. I took a close look around and that's when I spotted a solitary Sabre; having closed quickly with him at a shallow deflection angle, I opened fire from all my cannons at a range of 250-300 meters. The Sabre erupted in flames in the air and several seconds later exploded. In the meantime, the enemy fighter-bombers had broken off their attack and drawn away back to their bases. I also assembled my pilots and headed back to our airfield. This was my fourth victory in Korea.

At the end of June 1952 my flight was scrambled to cover our airbase; a group of aircraft returning from a mission was approaching to make a landing. Having climbed to 11,000 meters, I took a look around; everything was quiet and calm. I looked all around me; the visibility was excellent. Then I heard an order from the ground: "Take a course of 100°." I set out on this heading, but two or three minutes later, my wingman reported that below and to the right, in the area of "The Boot" (code name for the Supung hydroelectric station) there were six F-86s that were energetically closing with my flight.

At this moment I had a favorable position, with the sun at my back, plus I was 500-600 meters higher than the enemy. I kept careful watch over the enemy; it turned out that because of the sun they didn't see me, while at the same time their contrails were giving their position away. Thinking briefly, I turned sharply to the left and dove on the enemy. But the Sabres somehow received a warning and changed their altitude. The contrails disappeared and I lost sight of them for a spell. From the ground I received a new heading and an instruction to descend to 7,000 meters, and soon I was directed to the village of Sakchu, which lies 15 kilometers to the east of the Supung hydroelectric station. In this area I encountered six F-84 aircraft, which had no cover. I moved to attack them, but I was spotted by the enemy – they went into a defensive circle to the left. It was nothing for me to arrange to smash this circle with my flight and we downed two Thunderjets – I shot down one and Senior Lieutenant G.A. Nikiforov claimed the other. We had no losses on this mission. This took place on 27 June 1952, my birthday, and this action brought me my fifth victory in this war.

That's how the former chief of aerial gunnery services Major P.V. Minervin of the 148th GIAP described two of the aerial combats at the end of June. However, most likely Petr Vasil'evich mixed up the dates of these two actions. The author suggests that the combat with the F-84s, or more accurately, the F-80s in the area of Sakchu that involved Minervin and his comrades took place on 23 June, because it was on this day that F-80s from the 8th FBG conducted a raid against targets in MiG Alley. Two F-80s (No.47-558 and No.49-758) received damage and flew back to their base, but the first of them crashed upon landing, while the second had to be written off because of the extensive damage to it. Because of the fact that both of these F-80s made it back to South Korea, there was no confirmation or evidence from ground troops, so neither of these victories were credited to the pilots of the 148th GIAP.

However, on his birthday of 27 June, Petr Vasil'evich did in fact shoot down his solitary Sabre – it was RF-86A No.48-0217 from the 15th TRS, the pilot of which Major Jack P. Williams was killed. However, for some reason even this victory was not credited to Minervin's score!

In June 1952, the Americans registered 292 combat sorties by MiGs. According to American records, in June four F-86s were shot down, while 20 MiGs were destroyed in air-to-air combat.

A FATAL DAY FOR THE 190TH IAD

At the end of June, the 97th IAD returned to the Andong airfield, but it flew missions from there only briefly; at the beginning of July it restaged to the Mukden-North airfield once again and from there it conducted combat operations for the next two months, while located in the 64th IAK reserve. The main task of the pilots of the 97th IAD was to cover the take-off and landing of aircraft of the IAK's first echelon and to free the airspace over the IAK's forward airfields at Andong, Miaogou and Dapu.

The pilots of the 190th IAD also served briefly in the first echelon, flying missions from the Andong and Miaogou airfields in the month of July. The transfer of this division into the 64th IAK reserve was hastened by a day that was disastrous for the division's pilots – 4 July 1952.

On this day, the USAF launched a major raid by fighter-bombers in the area of the Supung hydroelectric power station, and in order to repel this raid, the entire 190th IAD was gradually scrambled in order to augment the forces in the air. The first to depart to intercept the enemy aircraft were pilots of the 494th IAP and 821st IAP. Here's how a former pilot of the 494th IAP, the commander of the 3rd Squadron Captain Nikolai Petrovich Chistiakov describes this battle:

I scored my only victory in the skies of Korea on 4 July, when I took off at the head of the regiment (three squadrons had been scrambled) on a combat mission.

The assignment was to cover the Supung hydroelectric station against a raid by US ground attack aircraft. While flying to the vicinity of the dam, we were several times redirected by ground control to adopt a higher altitude or to descend to a low altitude and repeatedly switched between targeting the covering Sabres or the fighter-bombers. Finally, we were led against a group of F-84 fighter-bombers, which were flying at low altitude, and once we detected them, we immediately went on the attack against them with the entire regiment – and overlooked an attack by a large group of Sabres from above (the ground control also missed them and didn't even warn us about the danger), which attacked our formation without any hindrance and simultaneously shot down seven of the regiment's MiGs. Fortunately, all seven pilots survived, having ejected from their damaged aircraft. Two pilots were shot down in my own 3rd Squadron – Senior Lieutenants A.F. Genai and M.I. Kosynkin.

Only my element managed to reach the fighter-bombers, and I hit one of the outermost Thunderjets in the formation. I then immediately broke off combat and returned to base.

Sabres of the 4th and 51st FIW took part in this stunning blow against the 494th IAP, and this was the most successful and stealthy approach by such a large group of Sabres toward a target. The effect of surprise played its role and on the first attacking pass seven MiGs were shot down simultaneously (a very rare case in this war). The following pilots of the 494th IAP were shot down, but managed to eject safely: Senior Lieutenants M.I. Kosynkin, A.F. Genai, E.I. Galmanov, A.N. Chernykh, I.P. Potylitsin and Iu.V. Tiurikov, and Captain B.V. Lavrinovich. The pilots of the 494th IAP managed to down only one Sabre in return – it was shot down by Captain V.P. Krutskikh of the 3rd Squadron at 1127 in an area 20 kilometers south of Sakchu at an altitude of 1,500-2,000 meters, but this was of small comfort when viewed against the regiment's disastrous losses.

Pilots of the 821st IAP, which had been scrambled for assistance, also had a bad day. They came under an attack by a different group of Sabres in the vicinity of the airfield, and having lost three MiGs, they abandoned their mission. Senior Lieutenants M.V. Nikiforov, P.V. Aleksandrov and V.V. Shmagunov were all shot down – the first two were able to bail out and were rescued, but Vladimir Vasil'evich Shmagunov was killed in the cockpit of his aircraft. He was the only pilot of the 190th IAD lost on this day, and it was the only death of a pilot of the 64th IAK in the month of July 1952.

Only a group of MiGs from the division's 256th IAP, which at 1125 had hurriedly arrived on the scene in the Gisiu – Pihyon area and had attacked, shooting down one Sabre in the very first pass (the victory was achieved by Lieutenant V.M. Mitin), forced the remaining Sabres to abandon the combat area. Pilots of the 97th IAD also took part in the battle of 4 July, launching from their airfield in Mukden. Several groups of MiGs from both of the division's regiments were scrambled. During a dogfight with F-86s in the vicinity of the Supung hydroelectric station, a pilot of the 16th IAP Senior Lieutenant M.N. Kazdoba was shot down – he successfully ejected from his stricken aircraft at an altitude of 9,000 meters, and soon he was picked up by North Koreans and delivered back to his airfield. This was the last loss of the 97th IAD in this war.

Major Petr Vasil'evich Minervin of the 148th GIAP, one of the participants in this battle, claims he scored a victory on this day:

> On one of the days of July, there was an accident at the Supung hydroelectric station and the turbines had to be shut down. The Americans hastily sent their fighter-bombers against the station with the aim of destroying it.
>
> The regiment had just returned from a mission and was in the process of refueling and taking on ammunition. Then suddenly there came an order: "Scramble as many aircraft as you have ready." My flight had been resupplied with everything necessary, so we were launched and immediately after lifting off the runways we were given a heading toward the hydro-electrical station. As I approached the dam, I saw a flight of four Shooting Stars in the air below me, which were preparing to dive on the station's machinery building. I quickly decided to attack it. Having closed on the enemy's tail-end aircraft, from a range of 200-250 meters I opened aimed fire on the F-80 from all my cannons – the enemy fighter-bomber's right wing dropped and with a black plume of smoke it headed toward the earth.
>
> The leader of the F-80 flight jettisoned his bombs wildly, which fell into the Yalu River, and at tree-top level he retreated from the area of the hydro-electrical station. We arrived back at base after carrying out the mission without any losses. This was my sixth and final victory in this war.

This author, however, still hasn't been able to find confirmation of Major Minervin's victory in July.

On this day pilots of the 190th IAD conducted two combat missions to repel raids by enemy aircraft. On both missions they became involved in hard dogfights.

The Americans were unable to destroy the Supung dam on 4 July, and this was the achievement of the pilots and anti-aircraft gunners of the 64th IAK, although it came at a very heavy price. In the course of the day, 11 MiGs were lost in action and one pilot was killed. In return, they managed to down only two F-86s and one F-84; another F-80 was recorded as a probable.

The American side confirms the loss on this day of two of their F-86E Sabres, both from the 335th FIS. The first, F-86E No.51-2769, was shot down by Captain Krutskikh, and its pilot Captain Clifford D. Jolley successfully bailed out over Cho-do Island and was eventually picked up by an H-5 helicopter. However, the pilot of the second F-86E (No.50-0683) 1st Lieutenant Austin W. Beetle, Jr. was less lucky. He also bailed out over Cho-do Island, but he drowned before search and rescue could reach him. The 49th FBW's 8th FBS lost one F-84 (No.51-572) and its pilot 1st Lieutenant Robert H. Warner was killed. However, this wasn't a combat loss. The Thunderjet experienced a malfunction shortly after take-off, and the pilot made an unsuccessful crash landing in a river bed 3 miles west of his K-2 Base.

For the American pilots, this was the most successful day of combat since the start of the war in Korea, when in one large clash nearly a dozen MiGs were shot down almost simultaneously; moreover, these were Soviet MiGs, not MiGs of the Unified Air Army, which enhanced the value of the day's victory. True, the Americans claimed that they downed 13 MiGs on 4 July, but plainly two of them were only presumed to be victories (or were simply damaged in this action), since it is reliably known that the 64th IAK lost 11 MiGs on 4 July. Of the 13 MiGs credited to the Sabre pilots, seven went to pilots of the 4th FIW, which only recently had completed replacing its squadrons' old F-86A Sabres with the more powerful F-86E. Thus only Sabres of the E version fought in this battle. The other six victories went to pilots of the 51st FIW, two of them going to pilots of the 39th FIS which had just joined the 51st Wing. In essence, this was their first combat with MiGs in the skies of Korea and their first victories in this war. In addition, this was the first time that the 51st FIW fought in the skies of Korea with its full complement of squadrons – the 16th, 25th and 39th Fighter Squadrons.

Incidentally, the 39th FIS already possessed several of the latest version of the Sabre, the F-86F-1 with the new J45-GE-2y engine. It also had a larger drop tank that could hold 727 liters (instead of the 445-liter drop tanks carried by the F-86E), which increased their radius of combat operations up to 200 kilometers, which meant they could linger longer over MiG Alley.

After these losses, the 190th IAD was withdrawn into the 64th IAK reserve in Mukden. To replace it, at the beginning of July two squadrons of the 147th GIAP (the 1st and 3rd Squadrons) flew over to the Andong airfield from Mukden and began to fly combat missions from this forward base. At the same time, the full 415th IAP was conducting combat operations from the Dapu base. At the end of June, the 133rd IAD's 726th IAP restaged to Andong from Mukden, and from the beginning of July the regiment began standing on combat alert, while its pilots began to fly combat sorties.

In addition, on 5 July 1952 the 216th IAD's 518th IAP and 878th IAP flew over to the Miaogou airfield from Mukden, while the third regiment of this PVO division, the 676th IAP, restaged to the Dapu airfield. The 133rd IAD entered active combat operations in the middle of July 1952, while the 216th IAD didn't initiate them until the beginning of August 1952.

Prior to this, these two divisions of the 64th IAK's second echelon in Mukden had been primarily responsible for covering the Andong, Miaogou and Dapu airfields, which at the same time gave the pilots of the 133rd IAD the opportunity to familiarize themselves with the area of combat operations during their initial combat sorties from these airfields. For example, on 11 July a group of MiGs of the 16th IAP, which had taken off from the Mukden-West airfield to sweep the airspace over the Andong complex of airfields, encountered four F-86s; Major A.S. Boitsov's element shot down one of the Sabre "hunters", while the rest immediately withdrew from the area of the bases. A group of MiGs led by the commander of the 821st IAP Lieutenant Colonel G.F. Dmitriuk also shot down one F-86 over the Andong airfield; credit for the victory went to the regiment commander himself. In these clashes the 64th IAK's pilots had no losses. However, the American side reports that it had no losses among their F-86s on 11 July, which seems very strange.

On the following day, 12 July, the very same Major A.S. Boitsov of the 16th IAP shot down another of those American pilots who sought easy prey – it was his sixth victory in the skies of Korea and simultaneously the final victory of the 16th IAP and of the entire 97th IAD. Major Boitsov's victim was F-86E No.50-0597 of the 16th FIS. Its pilot, Captain Patrick M. Ellis, took to his parachute north of Cho-do and was rescued by an H-19 search and rescue helicopter.

The pilots of the 415th IAP under the command of Hero of the Soviet Union Major P.F. Shevelev scored their first victories on 13 July: a flight commander in the 2nd

Squadron Senior Lieutenant V.P. Lepikov shot down one Sabre, while his wingman Senior Lieutenant V. Chernomorets damaged another Sabre. Most likely, however, Lepikov shot down an F-84 Thunderjet from the 8th FBS, which Americans records show was lost on this day. Apparently, the pilots of the 133rd IAD were also unable to identify accurately the types of enemy aircraft they encountered in their first battles in the skies of Korea!

Three days later on 16 July, the pilots of the 726th IAP also opened their combat score by also downing one F-86 and damaging another. The 1st Squadron commander Major V.Ia. Fedorets achieved the victory, while Senior Lieutenant I.I. Kapunov was only credited with damaging a Sabre. In this action, F-86E No.51-2797 was shot down, and its American pilot 1st Lieutenant Richard S. Drezen, Jr. of the 25th FIS was killed when his Sabre exploded in mid-air.

The pilots of the 64th IAK had a more successful day on 20 July, when pilots of the 415th IAP downed three Sabres without any losses in return. Pilots of the 256th IAP covered them as they returned for a landing, and the new commander of 256th IAP Major V.N. Zabelin shot down one Sabre "hunter" over the Dapu airfield (this was our ace's ninth and final victory in this war; Zabelin had achieved eight victories previously while with the 821st IAP). According to the summary report of the 64th IAK headquarters, the action of the 415th IAP's pilots unfolded in the following manner:

> Between 1604 and 1620, the 415th IAP, consisting of two squadrons and one separate element encountered a group of 20 F-86s at an altitude of 8,000-10,000 meters in the area of Sinuiju and Sakchu. Eight of the pilots fired their cannons at the enemy. According to the pilots' briefings and the evidence on the gun camera footage, Senior Lieutenant Lepikov shot down one F-86. A search team was sent out to locate the downed aircraft. Later, in Document No.00202, the search team reported that a pilot of one of the F-86s that were shot down on that day, 1st Lieutenant John Ellis of the 4th Fighter Wing's 336th Fighter Interceptor Squadron, was taken prisoner.

According to the same Document No.00202 from the headquarters of the 64th IAK in Andong:

> On 20 July between 1612 and 1620, Major Zabelin's group (the 256th IAP), flying at an altitude of 7,000-13,000 meters in the Uiju – Pihyon area encountered four separate groups numbering a total of 24 F-86s. Major Zabelin shot down F-86E No.51-2401, which crashed 12 kilometers southeast of Sinuiju. The F-86E pilot was killed and the aircraft was totally destroyed.

The Americans don't recognize the loss of an F-86E with the Bureau Number 51-2401 on this day. They do confirm the loss of 1st Lieutenant John G. Ellis's F-86A No.51-2828 of the 336th FIS, which was shot down by MiGs, and the pilot was captured by North Korean soldiers. James B. Selkregg of the 39th FIS was shot down while flying F-86E No.50-0664, though the Americans wrote it off as a non-combat loss; Selkregg bailed out and was picked up by a search and rescue helicopter. Most likely, this was the Sabre that Major Zabelin shot down. Another F-86A (No.49-1210) of the 336th FIS was damaged, but returned to its base. The Americans also acknowledge the loss of three of their F-84Es from the 49th and 136th FBW, but the Americans report that all of them were the result of ground fire or technical malfunctions. However, Sabre pilots on this day escorting the Thunderjets also tangled with Chinese MiGs and even shot down one of them, so it is possible that the "technical problems" on one or two of these F-84Es were due to the cannon fire of the Chinese MiGs.

Pilots of the 821st IAP achieved the final victory in the month of July 1952. On 22 July, Senior Lieutenant V.S. Badrudinov shot down one F-86. Most likely, this was F-86A No.49-1252 from the 4th FIW's 336th FIS, which was written off as a "non-combat loss" only on 28 July.

After their highly successful action on 4 July 1952, the American pilots shot down only four more MiGs that month, one each on 12, 14, 16 and 20 July. All of these MiGs belonged to the Unified Air Army, since after the losses on 4 July, the Soviet pilots incurred no further losses in the skies of Korea for the rest of the month.

In sum, the pilots of the 64th IAK destroyed 14 US aircraft in day and night aerial combats in the month of July: 12 F-86, 1 F-84 and 1 RB-50. Two more F-86s were damaged and one F-80 was recorded as a probable victory. The 190th IAD scored six of the victories, while the 97th IAD added two and the newly arrived 133rd IAD contributed five victories and two probable victories to the total. Losses were also high: 12 MiGs were lost in combat and one pilot was killed. The 190th IAD particularly suffered, having lost 10 aircraft over the month, seven of which were from the 494th IAP.

The Americans claimed that their pilots in July 1952 destroyed 18 MiG-15s, with the loss of six of their F-86s in return, five of which were lost in combat. By their estimate, the MiGs flew 404 combat sorties in the month of July.

In the month of July, the British Fleet Air Arm also suffered losses at the hands of MiG pilots: on 26 July 1952, a group of MiGs from the Unified Air Army pounced on four Sea Furies and four Fairey Fireflies in the area of Chinnampo, and in the ensuing combat they shot down one Firefly, which fell into the Yellow Sea. An additional Firefly was damaged and made a forced landing on dry land, and finally a third Firefly limped back to its aircraft carrier HMS *Ocean* with combat damage. The English claimed that there were no losses among the Firefly crews.

In July 1952, the Fifth Air Force's Air National Guard fighter-bomber groups underwent paper reorganization. On 10 July 1952, the Air National Guard's 136th FBW became the 58th FBW. The Wing's squadrons also received new designations: the 111th, 154th and 183rd FBS received new identities as the 69th, 310th and 311th FBS respectively. Analogous changes on paper occurred in another group, the 116th FBW. It became the 474th FBW, and its three squadrons, the 158th, 159th and 196th FBS were re-designated as the 428th, 429th and 430th FBS respectively. Both fighter-bomber wings retained their aircrafts' previous markings and identification numbers.

Soon after the reorganization, the 474th FBW was transferred from its base in Japan to the K-8 Base in Kusan, where by this time the upgrading of this airfield's runways had been completed. In July 1952, the 49th FBW was the first in the Fifth Air Force to receive the new F-84G Thunderjet. By October 1952, the remaining fighter-bomber groups were re-equipped with the new Thunderjets.

THE NEW SHIFT ENTERS THE FIGHTING

On 31 July pilots of the 518th IAP and 878th IAP conducted their first familiarization flight over the area of combat operations, and already on 1 August all the regiments of the 216th IAD initiated active combat operations. On 3 August 1952, pilots of this division had their first encounters with the USAF, but they ended with no results.

Back on 1 August, pilots of the 726th IAP had experienced a difficult dog fight. That day, a large group of F-86s attempted to breakthrough to the Supung hydroelectric station, but 24 MiGs of the 726th IAP led by the regiment's chief of the aerial gunnery services Lieutenant Colonel V.I. Chizh were being directed by ground controllers to intercept it. Our group was flying at an altitude of 10,000 meters, but the enemy's F-86s appeared unexpectedly, and they enjoyed an altitude advantage over our MiGs. The Sabres quickly exploited the superiority they had in both altitude and surprise. Thus, from its very beginning the action proved unfavorable for our pilots in every respect. In the words of Lieutenant Colonel Chizh, who later took command of this regiment, the combat was also handled unsuccessfully due to the fault of the regiment's pilots themselves, who broke formation to chase individual targets, thereby losing all cohesion and the ability to come to each other's relief in the combat.

The result of the dogfight was sorrowful. Despite the fact that the regiment's pilots managed to down two Sabres that were credited to Senior Lieutenants P.G. Kolotov and N.I. Sychev, the 3rd Squadron commander Captain Valentin Stepanovich Gorobchenko and flight commander Captain Andrei Alekseevich Kostin were both shot down and killed. The 2nd Squadron's Senior Lieutenant Lev Mikhailovich Tsvetkov was also shot down; he managed to eject successfully, but didn't have enough altitude for his parachute to deploy fully, and he plummeted to his death. The deputy commander of the 2nd Squadron Captain N.I. Ivanov somewhat sweetened the bitter pill of this dogfight. When returning to base alone, he was jumped by a pair of F-86s led by Major Felix Asla, Jr., the commander of the 336th FIS.

Here's how Nikolai Ivanovich Ivanov himself describes the day's action:

> As the deputy squadron commander, I was leading the second flight in the second eight-ship formation. Over the radio they were constantly informing us that Sabres were all around us, and that there were a lot of them. I, of course, was an old bird, but I hadn't yet participated in these dogfights. I felt very tense, just like anyone else who doesn't see the enemy, but knows they are somewhere nearby.
>
> The first thing I saw were drop tanks tumbling through the air, trailing streams of kerosene. Then I heard my wingman transmit: "I'm switching to the left" – though I hadn't given him such an order. Apparently however he believed that it would be safer there; the tanks were falling to my right.
>
> I saw the dropping tanks, and then the aircraft that had jettisoned them – Sabres. They were already moving in our direction. Our altitude was around 10,000 meters, while they were above us and had almost already intercepted our group. I glanced to the left – where was my wingman Lev Tsvetkov? Now there were already Sabres on my left. Generally speaking, we had nodded off a bit …
>
> Right away I faced the question: "What's to be done?" I decided I had to act. My tension disappeared and a real rage came over me … Whenever I met the enemy, I

always calmed down, because now I knew where danger was threatened. I shouted something to my wingman over the radio, something like "Lev, hold on!" and I began to turn for dear life in order to throw off the Sabre pilots' aim. I maneuvered energetically to escape the Sabres that might latch onto my tail. Then it so happened that in this duel, my aircraft went into a spin. I in fact often went into spins and took my pilots into spins, so I knew what one was. Of course this time I hadn't anticipated going into a spin, but I didn't lose control over the situation.

I began to come out of the spin and saw a Sabre lining up on me, so I threw my MiG into another spin, this time deliberately. I was feeling a lot of anger, but I couldn't figure out what to do. I didn't have a lot of altitude left now. I can't say exactly how much, but it couldn't have been much. So then I pulled my MiG out of the spin, and one of the Sabres overshot me. I didn't even begin to check around – I might or might not be shot down – and went right after him. I took aim, gave him one burst and then another, and I saw right away that he's going down. Just as I began to level out, a second Sabre flashed past just above me. Apparently he had been firing at me, but I hadn't gone down and he pulled out above me out in front of me. I performed some sort of maneuver ... He was above me, and I roughly pulled lead and fired at him. For some reason I remember precisely – I set my gun sight in the fixed position in order to do everything somehow more quickly and as a result I indeed shot down a second Sabre. Returning to base, I found out that my wingman Lev Tsvetkov and two other comrades had still not returned; it really was a hard fight.

For this action Ivanov was awarded the Order of Lenin. Soon the wreckage of a Sabre bearing the identification number 51-2767 was found by a search team; it had nine victory stars painted on the side of it below the cockpit, five of which had not been filled in with paint, which meant that the pilot had shot down four enemy aircraft and damaged five others. The body of Major Felix Asla, Jr. of the 336th FIS was found in the cockpit of the smashed aircraft.

A group of MiGs from the 147th GIAP led by Captain N.I. Shkodin was covering the pilots of the 726th IAP as they were breaking off combat. It intercepted the more zealous of the Sabres, damaging one of them in the process; the remaining F-86s withdrew from the combat.

As a result of this clash, four F-86s were shot down and one was damaged. Soviet losses consisted of three MiGs and three pilots. The Americans claimed that in this battle, pilots of the 4th FIW shot down four MiGs (one victory was plainly only conjectured), while they put their own losses at one F-86E, in which Major Asla, Jr. was killed.

The beginning of August was marked by two events that took place in the 64th IAK. In the first days of August, two regiments of the PVO's 216th IAD began active combat operations, and on 4-5 August they had their initial clashes with the USAF in the skies of Korea. The second event was the completion of combat operations by pilots of the 190th IAD, who were making their final combat sorties over MiG Alley. Up until 10 August, pilots of the 190th IAD scored their final two victories over American pilots in the Korean sky, losing six of their own MiGs and two pilots in return.

On 4 August 1952, a six-ship formation of MiG-15s of the 494th IAP's 3rd Squadron under the command of Captain N.P. Chistiakov took off on a combat mission toward the port of Chemulpo. In flight to the target area, the group was attacked by a pair of

F-86s, but they had jumped the leading flight of MiGs without noticing Captain V.P. Krutskikh's trailing pair, thereby placing themselves under attack. Taking advantage of this opportune moment, Krutskikh moved to attack them from above, but he failed to take into account the difference in speed. Due to his rapid acceleration in his attacking dive, he didn't have time to fire at the Sabres and instead overshot them. 1st Lieutenant Henry A. Crescibene of the 335th FIS, seeing the MiG out in front of him, retracted his speed brakes and shot Krutskikh's MiG up. The Sabres didn't linger and immediately headed toward Korea Bay. Vasilii Romanovich Krutskikh ejected from his stricken aircraft, but lacked sufficient altitude for his parachute to open and was killed.

This was not the 64th IAK's only loss on this day. An unpleasant incident occurred that almost ended tragically. Pilots of the 216th IAD's 676th IAP were making their first combat sortie. Eight MiGs of the 1st Squadron under the command of Hero of the Soviet Union Major I.F. Gnezdilov were patrolling over MiG Alley, when they were unexpectedly attacked by eight MiG-15s of the 32nd IAD's 913th IAP, which had only recently arrived in China and were in the 64th IAK reserve. Led by the 913th IAP's chief of aerial gunnery services Major I.I. Rukakov, who was also making his first combat sortie in the skies of Korea, they confused the 676th IAP's MiGs for American F-86s. At an altitude of 10,000 meters, Rudakov attacked the leader of the second flight Captain M.P. Zhbanov. The group commander Major Gnezdilov, who noticed that Zhbanov was in jeopardy, saved him with a timely order, shouting over the radio: "Break left!" However, despite this abrupt maneuver, a burst of cannon fire from Rudakov's MiG struck Zhbanov's aircraft in the right wing and fuselage. As a result, the ailerons were knocked out, the right wing and instrument panel were damaged, and shell fragments penetrated the cockpit canopy. Fortunately, the pilot wasn't wounded, and with difficulty he was able to nurse his stricken MiG back to base and make a successful landing there. Squadron technicians needed a week to repair the aircraft. So this woeful episode ended without any lasting repercussions.

On 4 August 1952 pilots of the 64th IAK achieved just one victory: Captain S.K. Ivanovsky of the 726th IAP damaged one Sabre. The Americans on this day also scored only one victory.

On 5 August the pilots of the 216th IAD's 518th IAP experienced their first combat action, though it wound up being unsuccessful. Senior Lieutenant I.V. Iakovlev, flying as the wingman to the 1st Squadron deputy commander Captain M.I. Mikhin, was shot down, though the pilot safely ejected. In addition, the 2nd Squadron's deputy political commander Captain N.Z. Brozhenko's MiG was damaged. The Americans of the 336th FIS had no losses. In addition, pilots of the 133rd IAD on this day also tangled with Sabres, damaging two F-86s in the process, but once again this took place in the vicinity of our Manchurian airfields. One of the Sabre "hunters" was damaged by the commander of the 415th IAP, Hero of the Soviet Union Lieutenant Colonel Pavel Fedorovich Shevelev, who recalls:

> We took off on a combat mission as two squadrons. The mission passed without any combat, but as we were already returning for a landing at the Andong airfield, we were attacked by Sabres, which had stolen up on us from the bay. Major Petrov's 3rd Squadron was covering our landing from above, but its altitude was too high, so they didn't see what we had going on down below. My wingman Senior Lieutenant

A.A. Dedikov landed first, but as he was rolling out after touching down, Sabres fired on his aircraft and flamed it. I immediately accelerated to go around again and retracted my landing gear. Having completed a tight circle, I spotted a Sabre that appeared right next to me; without thinking long, I swung in behind him and hit him with a fusillade right over the IAK's command post. The Sabre began to smoke, the right landing wheel strut dropped, the flaps opened, and it immediately departed toward the bay. I was directed to head toward the Dapu airfield, because pairs of Sabre "hunters" were still roving over Andong.

Shevelev received credit only for damaging this Sabre, though later that day it became known from IAK intelligence officers who were monitoring radio traffic that it had plunged into the sea. They overheard the shouts of the American pilot that his fighter was heavily damaged, and he ejected from it. The flames aboard Dedikov's aircraft were quickly extinguished by technicians that had hurried to the scene, and it was soon returned to service. The pilot himself wasn't wounded by the machine-gun fire. One more Sabre was damaged on this day by Captain V.A. Marenich of the 726th IAP. The pilots of the 133rd IAD had no losses in these clashes.

However, the 97th and 190th IAD, which had taken off from Mukden to sweep the airspace over the Andong airfield clear of prowling Sabres, did suffer losses. Pilots of the 16th IAP were attacked by a flight of F-86s over Andong, and the recently arrived young pilot Lieutenant Sergei Semenovich Iazev was shot down by them; he ejected from his stricken aircraft, but unfortunately he died when hitting the ground. This was the final loss and the last victim in this war of the 97th IAD and of the 16th IAP in particular. Yet another clash with the Sabres concluded with the downing of Captain V.D. Golushkov, the 494th IAP's chief of aerial gunnery services, but he successfully abandoned his crippled MiG-15 and parachuted to safety.

As a result, on 5 August the 64th IAK's pilots damaged two F-86s (one was actually shot down), but lost three of their own aircraft and one pilot in return. Two more MiG-15s were damaged that day. The Americans claimed that on this day they shot down five MiGs – two by pilots of the 336th FIS, the other three by pilots of the 39th FIS. However, in reality, only three MiGs were destroyed, while the other two MiGs were damaged.

On 6 August the 878th IAP conducted its first regimental sortie to the Singisui – Anju area. On the way out the regiment failed to encounter the enemy, so when returning to base their attention slackened, for which they in fact paid dearly. As the regiment was coming in for a landing, its formation was unexpectedly attacked from the direction of the bay by several small groups of F-86s, which first shot down Senior Lieutenant Mikhail Ivanovich, who was killed in the cockpit of his MiG on his very first combat mission. Next Senior Lieutenant V.I. Prilepov's MiG was damaged, and the pilot had to make a forced belly landing next to the airfield; in the process the MiG was damaged beyond repair and Prilepov received injuries. The Sabres immediately slipped away back to the sea unpunished.

That afternoon the Americans launched their next massed raid in the strength of 24 F-84Es from the 49th FBW's 69th FBS against the Sapyong railroad station. Sabres of the 4th FIW were covering them. Pilots of the Unified Air Army and of the 216th IAD's 518th IAP and 676th IAP took off to repel this raid. As always, the Soviet pilots took on the covering Sabres while the MiGs of the Unified Air Army attacked the Thunderjets.

The pilots of the 676th IAP had their first fierce aerial combat in the skies of Korea, in which 1st Squadron flight commander Captain V.I. Belousov opened the regiment's combat score by downing one Sabre; the chief of the 518th IAP's aerial gunnery services Major V.S. Mikheev damaged another Sabre in this action. True, one of the regiment's MiGs, being piloted by Senior Lieutenant A.T. Topol'sky, returned from the battle with bullet holes in it.

Pilots of the 133rd IAD's 415th IAP, who were covering the landings of the 216th IAD's pilots, had a short tussle with Sabre pilots looking for easy prey – Captain A.I. Tkachev damaged one of these F-86s, and it headed toward the bay in a dive.

Even earlier, pilots of the 190th IAD, who flew two combat sorties on this day, had taken off to sweep the airspace over the Andong airfield. Pilots of the 256th IAP and 821st IAP in fact had several dogfights with F-86s. In one of them, the aircraft of the commander of the 821st IAP's 2nd Squadron Captain V.V. Abitkovsky was seriously damaged. He was forced to abandon his aircraft, which he did in an unusual manner, without using the catapult. Instead, he released the canopy, unfastened his belts and simply rolled the MiG upside down and fell out of the cockpit. He couldn't eject because he'd been wounded. He came safely down to earth in his parachute. Here's how a participant in this battle Aleksei Ivanovich Romanov recalls it:

> I had an experience when Sabres almost caught us during a landing. This happened on 6 August 1952 when I, as the wingman to the squadron commander Captain Abitkovsky, was returning to base after completing a combat mission. Just as we were approaching our airfield, we were attacked by a pair of Sabre "hunters", but we spotted them in time and managed to evade the attack, and compelled our adversaries to fight in the vertical. Repelling an attack of one Sabre against the leader's aircraft, I went into a spin and came out of it at low altitude. I found myself right next to the Andong airfield, where I came in for a landing. Meanwhile my leader was nevertheless shot down, but he managed to abandon his stricken aircraft in a parachute; he landed next to the Miaogou airbase.

Pilots of the Unified Air Army also had a successful fight with the Thunderjets. They scattered the F-84s, downing 2nd Lieutenant William L. Fornes of the 69th FBS, who was killed on this, his 50th combat mission in Korea. An F-84E from the 474th FBW was also shot down, the pilot of which was taken prisoner.

In sum, on 6 August the 64th IAK lost three aircraft and one pilot, and one more MiG was damaged. In return, its pilots shot down one F-86 and damaged two more Sabres. The Americans report the loss of two of their F-86Es, which were written off on 7 and 8 August. The first of them was F-86E No.50-0685 from the 334th FIS, which was being piloted by 2nd Lieutenant John Ridout. Flying his damaged Sabre back to the K-14 Kimpo Air Force Base, he was too low on the approach and crashed into a hilltop short of the runway. The aircraft was demolished and Ridout was injured. The second F-86E (No.51-2754) from the 16th FIS was also damaged, and its pilot 1st Lieutenant James I. Bonini was forced to bail out near Cho-do Island, where he was picked up by search and rescue. The American command doesn't consider either of these as combat losses, but most likely both Sabres had been damaged by the cannon fire from MiGs of the 216th IAD. The Americans claimed that on 6 August they shot down six MiG-15s, three of which most likely belonged to the Unified Air Army. Captain William J. Ryan particularly distinguished himself by downing two MiG-15s in one action.

On 7 August 1952 the 64th IAK's pilots didn't have any victories, but they lost two aircraft. The 190th IAD conducted two combat sorties to sweep the airspace above the 64th IAK's forward bases and had several combats with Sabres. One MiG-15 was lost in a battle with the F-86s; the pilot, Senior Lieutenant V.M. Mandrovsky of the 190th IAD's 256th IAP successfully bailed out. The other MiG-15 wasn't lost in combat: in mid-flight Senior Lieutenant R.N. Gol'dshtein of the 415th IAP had to abandon his aircraft because a wing tank became stuck and wouldn't release, which made continuing the mission or trying to land the plane dangerous. The pilot ejected and parachuted safely down to earth.

The Americans claimed that they shot down four MiG-15s on 7 August 1952. Likely, the American pilots recorded damaged MiGs from the 676th IAP as victories. On this day, pilots of the 676th IAP twice tangled with F-86s. First, between 1046 and 1129, eight MiG-15bis engaged 28 F-86s in a combat, in which two of the regiment's fighters were damaged: Captain F.A. Bodin's aircraft received three bullet holes, and Senior Lieutenant Gubenko's MiG returned with one bullet hole in it. Then at 1705 that afternoon, eight MiG-15bis of the 1st Squadron dueled with four F-86s, and Captain M.P. Zhbanov's aircraft received two bullet holes in the right wing. All the damaged aircraft successfully returned to base.

The next day, 8 August, the Americans primarily fought with pilots of the Unified Air Army and claimed three kills over MiG-15s. The 64th IAK had no losses on this day.

On 9 August, the 190th IAD suffered its final loss in the skies of Korea. While sweeping the airspace over an airfield, Senior Lieutenant Khalitov of the 256th IAP was shot down in a dogfight with a group of F-86s by 1st Lieutenant Heber M. Butler of the 16th FIS. The pilot safely ejected. However, this time the pilots of the 64th IAK evened the score with the Americans – pilots of the 216th IAD shot down one F-86 and damaged another without any losses in return. A Sabre damaged by Captain Mikhin of the 518th IAP plunged into the bay, but its fall wasn't seen from the land and he was given credit only for damaging the Sabre. Meanwhile Captain V.I. Belousov of the 676th IAP was downing his second F-86 in this war. Most likely, this was the first F-86F lost in the war, No.51-2908 from the 39th FIS. Its pilot safely abandoned his aircraft and was picked up by a search and rescue team. This loss was actually recorded by the Americans on 13 August, but this date was in a stretch of almost 10 days in which there were no combats in the skies of Korea with MiGs, so it is more probable to assume that this Sabre had been downed by Captain Belousov, but it wasn't officially recorded by the Fifth Air Force command until 13 August.

After this battle, as mentioned there was a ten-day lull in the fighting over MiG Alley. Both sides used the time to bring themselves back into good fighting trim and to prepare for new clashes. In this period, two divisions of the 64th IAK's second echelon, the 97th IAD and 190th IAD, which had fought in the skies of Korea for more than a half year, returned to the Soviet Union. Over this period of service, which extended from 4 January to 10 August 1952, pilots of the PVO 97th IAD conducted 4,189 individual combat sorties, engaged in 164 group air battles, shot down 68 enemy aircraft and damaged 17 more, while suffering the loss of 21 MiGs destroyed, 35 damaged, and 10 pilots. In their turn the pilots of the 190th IAD completed 4,615 individual combat sorties in the skies of Korea, had 199 group aerial combats, and downed 85 enemy aircraft and damaged 39 more. Their own losses amounted to 64 aircraft and 15 pilots. Only one pilot in this rotation, Major Arkadii Sergeevich Boitsov, became a Hero of the Soviet Union for personally downing six US aircraft and for his successful combat on 30 April 1952.

Major A.S. Boitsov, with six confirmed victories, and Major A.T. Bashman of the 148th GIAP, with five confirmed victories, were the only aces in the 97th IAD. One more pilot of this division, Major P.V. Minervin, had three confirmed victories and three probable victories. In the 190th IAD, all of the aces served in the same regiment, the 821st IAP. The regiment commander Lieutenant Colonel G.F. Dmitriuk and the regiment navigator Major A.A. Olenitsa had five victories each, while a squadron commander in this regiment Major V.N. Zabelin achieved nine victories in this war, eight of them with while serving in this regiment. He scored his ninth victory after becoming the commander of the 256th IAP.

During this respite in the action, the Americans replaced old aircraft with newer versions. Thus, in August-September 1952, all of the fighter-bomber wings flying Thunderjets were re-equipped with the newer F-84G model, and by autumn 1952 they now had 193 aircraft in three fighter-bomber wings of the USAF (the 49th, 58th and 474th FBW). In the 4th and 51st FIW there now remained only F-86E Sabres, but already in August 1952 the first F-86F Sabres, which featured the more powerful J47 engine and a new, larger "6-3" wing design that offered better maneuverability at high speeds, arrived in the 51st FIW.

Two fighter-bomber groups of the Fifth Air Force were still flying the F-80C Shooting Star. These were the 8th FBG and the 35th FBG. In addition, the 18th FBG continued to use the F-51D Mustang fighter-bomber in Korea.

A 12th FBS North American F-51D-25-NA Mustang s/n 44-84602 in Korea.
(US Air Force)

The fighter-bombers of the Fifth Air Force constituted the UN air force's main strike element in Korea in 1952-1953 and they were given the most difficult and important combat missions in the skies of Korea. Thus, it was this grouping of the Fifth Air Force that received all the emphasis in strengthening and modernizing in 1952.

Parallel with these reorganizations and reinforcements of its combat strength in the groups and squadrons of the Fifth Air Force in Korea, the 64th IAK and Unified Air Army also worked to enhance their capabilities. On 1 July 1952, the 64th IAK had 636 combat-ready aircraft (of which 302 were in the first echelon) and 28 aircraft under repair; the given MiGs belonged to the 97th IAD, 133rd IAD, 190th IAD, 216th IAD and the 351st Separate NIAP. However, in August the 64th IAK's first echelon underwent changes: the 97th and 190th IAD rotated back to the Soviet Union, and their place was taken by the 133rd IAD and 216th IAD, plus the night-fighting 351st Separate IAP. In the middle of July, the new 32nd IAD from the 54th Maritime Air Army arrived in China, which had three full-strength regiments. Colonel G.I. Grokhovetsky commanded the division, which included the 224th IAP (commanded by Hero of the Soviet Union Lieutenant Colonel D.V. Ermakov), the 535th IAP (commanded by Lieutenant Colonel Smirnov) and the 913th IAP (commanded by Lieutenant Colonel V.A. Marchenko). All of these regiments were equipped with new MiG-15bis fighters.

The division immediately deployed to the Mukden (the 224th IAP and 535th IAP) and Anshan (the 913th IAP) airbases, and at the beginning of August, it began to prepare for combat operations. Because the 32nd IAD had not received its jets until the spring of 1951, its pilots only had an average of up to 20 hours of flying time in them and were still poorly prepared for combat. Although the backbone of the leadership at the division and regiment level were experienced officers who had flown in the Great Patriotic War and the war with Japan, most of the flight personnel were young and lacked combat experience. The first to begin combat operations, while still in the 64th IAK's second echelon, was Lieutenant Colonel V.A. Marchenko's 913th IAP from the Anshan airfield. On 20 August 1952, the regiment conducted its first familiarization flight over the area of combat operations, and already at the end of August it was primarily covering the takeoffs and landings of aircraft at the forward airfields in Andong, Miaogou and Dapu.

Then that same August 1952 the 518th Separate IAP of the Pacific Ocean Fleet's air force under the command of Lieutenant Colonel V.T. Dobrov arrived in China with the 64th IAK in order to gain combat experience. It came only with its pilots and had no equipment.

The Unified Air Army on 1 July 1952 had eight Chinese and North Korean aviation divisions, but only six of them engaged in active combat operations in this period: the 3rd IAD (47 combat-ready and four unserviceable MiG-15bis), the 4th IAD (45 combat-ready and six unserviceable MiG-15bis), the 12th IAD (56 combat-ready and six unserviceable MiG-15bis), the 15th IAD (37 combat-ready and three unserviceable MiG-15bis and 59 combat-ready MiG-9s), the 17th IAD (44 combat-ready and six unserviceable MiG-15s) and the 18th IAD (46 combat-ready and three unserviceable MiG-15s). In total, the Unified Air Army on 1 July 1952 had 275 combat-ready and 28 unserviceable MiG-15s and MiG-15bis, not including the 56 outdated MiG-9s. The two other fighter aviation divisions (the 2nd and 14th IAD) didn't participate in combat and were primarily responsible for protecting rear sites in northeast China and were busy training their pilots.

Two Soviet technicians pose in front of a Soviet MiG-9 fighter in China, 1951.

In sum, in August 1952 the allied 64th IAK and Unified Air Army had approximately 600 MiG-15 and MiG-15bis jet fighters operating against the US Fifth Air Force in Korea. They were staging from four airfields: Anshan, Andong, Dapu and Miaogou.

Fighting resumed over MiG Alley only on 19 August in the Singisiu, Sonchon and Changseong areas. On this day only the 216th IAD fought against F-86E Sabres. In these clashes pilots of the 518th IAP distinguished themselves by shooting down one F-86 and damaging another, without any losses in return.

The combat on 20 August proved to be more serious, when the enemy undertook an air strike in the Changseong – Pyongyang area. Pilots of the 133rd IAD and 216th IAD took part in repelling it, but the pilots of the 726th IAP, which had taken off at 1216 with 18 MiGs led by regiment commander Colonel L.D. Goriachko, collided with a large group of enemy aircraft in the Koto region, consisting of Thunderjets covered by Sabres.

In the ensuing bitter combat, the pilots of this regiment shot down one Sabre, but lost two aircraft in return. The commander of the 2nd Squadron Major A.A. Shekhovtsov, while already coming in for a landing at the Andong Air Base, was attacked by four F-86s. He engaged the flight of Sabres, but chose poor tactics in the ensuing dogfight, opting to go into a turning combat, rather than rely on the MiG's superior climbing performance. This was unwise, because the F-86 could out-turn the MiG-15, and in fact Shekhovtsov's mistake cost him his life. A pair of Sabres caught him in a turn and shot down his MiG, killing Major Aleksandr Alekseevich Shekhovtsov, and that of his wingman Senior Lieutenant V.M. Leletsky, who was able to eject successfully.

At 1242 in the Eiju – Sunchon area at an altitude of 5,000 meters, Colonel Goriachko and his wingman Major Sova encountered four F-84s approaching at an angle and attacked them. The regiment navigator Major Sova from a range of 700 meters at a 2/4 target aspect angle shot down one F-84, which fell burning into the sea 4 kilometers off the coastline. The remaining Thunderjets were driven back to the bay.

In this air battle pilots of the 726th IAP had dueled with Sabres of the 334th FIS, and Majors Edward Bellinger and Frederick Blesse shot down the two MiGs of the 726th IAP. Another MiG-15 was shot down by pilots of the 51st FIW's 39th Fighter Interceptor Squadron, but apparently it was a Chinese MiG. The Americans acknowledge the loss of F-86E No.50-0643 from the 334th FIS in this battle, the pilot of which 1st Lieutenant Norman Schmidt bailed out over Korea Bay and was picked up by a search and rescue helicopter. Captain N.I. Ivanov shot down this Sabre, his third victory in the Korean sky, but the Americans claim that Schmidt's Sabre flew through debris of a blown-up MiG, and his engine failed after ingesting some of the pieces. Major Sova shot down F-84E No.51-574 from the 474th FBW on this day, the pilot of which bailed out and soon returned to his unit, but again the Americans attribute this loss to an engine flame-out, which caused the jet to catch fire, crash and burn.

On 22 August the 64th IAK's pilots had several dogfights with Sabres, in which pilots of the 518th IAP shot down one F-86, while another F-86 went to the score of pilots of the 133rd IAD's 415th IAP. There were no Soviet losses in these air battles. Senior Lieutenant M.N. Ignatov shot down F-86F No.51-2866; its pilot Major Deltis H. Fincher of the 39th FIS was killed. Ignatov shot the Sabre down from long range, approximately 600-800 meters, and at first didn't receive official credit for it, but after the wreckage of the F-86 was discovered, his victory was confirmed. According to documents of the 64th IAK headquarters:

> From preliminary reports and gun camera evidence, 1 F-86 was shot down and 1 F-86 was damaged. According to intercepted radio messages, 2 F-86s were shot down and 1 F-86 was damaged. A group of pilots of the 518th IAP were conducting a combat mission to the Kaechon, Anju and Sunchon area. Captain Frolov's flight engaged six F-86s at 0950 in the Hamisan area at an altitude of 11,500 meters. Captain Chernavin's flight covered the attack of Captain Frolov's flight. Two pilots fired at enemy aircraft. Senior Lieutenant Ignatov shot down one F-86 from a range of 500-600 meters at a target aspect angle of 1/4. The enemy aircraft crashed in the Kaechon area; the aircraft was located and the pilot was dead.

Meanwhile the commander of the 415th IAP's 1st Squadron Major G.I. Bodganov on this day shot down another F-86 (No.51-2860) from the same 39th FIS. Here's how this happened:

> On 22 August 1952, at 1506 the 415th IAP's 1st Squadron numbering eight MiGs under the command of squadron commander Major Bogdanov took off at 1506 from the Andong Air Base on a "free hunt" to the Gisiu, Sonchon, and Changseong area. At 1529 in the Sonchon area at an altitude of 8,000 meters, the commander of the lead flight Major Bogdanov while in a turn spotted four F-86s, which he attacked from above, behind and from the left together with his wingman Captain

Polivaiko. Major Bogdanov fired at three F-86s from a range of 700 meters at a target aspect angle ranging from 3/4 to 2/4. The F-86 leader of the second pair burst into flames and fell 12-13 kilometers east of the Neiben bridge.

The Americans on this day had no victories. So the sorties into the area of our forward airfields didn't always end successfully for the Sabre pilots – we had triumphant days as well!

After the fighting on 22 August there was another pause that lasted for about a week, and only at the end of August did several more clashes with Sabres take place, which led to losses on both sides. The final dogfights of summer occurred on 29 and 30 August.

On 29 August the 64th IAK's regiments flew two missions to the Changseong – Kaechon area, where combats took place between small groups from both sides. Our pilots departed on the missions in groups not larger than flights or eight-ship formations, which the Americans did as well. During these small skirmishes each side lost one aircraft. A flight of MiGs from the 518th IAP under the command of the regiment's chief of aerial gunnery services Major V.S. Mikheev while on one patrol spotted four F-86s, and taking advantage of the fact that they hadn't yet been seen by the Americans, they launched a high side attack. Mikheev down one of the Sabres from close range. After pulling out of the attack into a steep climb, his wingman Senior Lieutenant L.N. Pankov lost sight of Mikheev and began to search for his leader. Spotting a solitary jet, he decided that it was his leader, and he moved to join it. However, closing to within 300-400 meters of the aircraft, he determined that it wasn't a MiG, but a Sabre. Quickly thinking, Pankov banked to get the target in his sights and fired at the Sabre; according to the pilot's report, the Sabre erupted in flames and headed toward the bay, but since he was forbidden to cross the coastline, he returned to base. In fact, only Major V.S. Mikheev was given credit for a victory, while Pankov's victory was never confirmed.

The Americans soon outplayed the young pilots of the 913th IAP, who were covering the landings of the 216th IAP, and they shot down one of the regiment's youthful pilots, Senior Lieutenant N.V. Nevrotov. He was shot down by a surprise attack from behind and forced to abandon his stricken aircraft. At the time, the six Soviet pilots were flying with their drop tanks still attached, and they were caught by the Sabres and Nevrotov was shot down before they even had time to jettison their external fuel tanks. This was both the 913th IAP's and the 32nd IAD's first combat loss. 1st Lieutenant Charles Gabriel of the 51st FIW's 16th FIS took the credit for the victory over Nevrotov. On this same day, the commander of the 133rd IAD's 147th GIAP Lieutenant Colonel I.G. Bannikov was severely wounded. He had become the regiment commander in July 1952, after the previous regiment commander Lieutenant Colonel M.I. Studilin had been promoted to deputy commander of the 133rd IAD. Ivan Grigor'evich Bannikov recalls:

On 29 August 1952 I allowed my constant wingmen Captain Kostin's element to rest. In its place I took the chief of the regiment's aerial gunnery services Major Dmitrakov's element; his wingman was the regiment navigator Captain Kravchenko.

We flew the first mission of the day without any encounter with the enemy. We were sent off on the second sortie of the day at an order from the IAK command post around noon. We took off as an eight-ship formation: I was leading the first flight, while the commander of the 3rd Squadron Captain N.I. Shkodin led the second flight. As we were arriving over the area we were to cover, the formation became extended, and a large gap appeared between the two flights. Together with my flight I entered some clouds and began to climb through them. After emerging above the clouds at an altitude of 10,000 meters (there were cirrus clouds), we were attacked by a group of F-86s from behind and above (they had spotted us through their radar gun sights and as we were exiting the clouds, they were already prepared to jump us). I gave Dmitrakov the order to try to repel the attack from the left, while with an energetic turn to the right I began to escape out from under the attack of the element that had attacked me and threatened the pair of Sabres that was attacking Dmitrakov's element. Dmitrakov's wingman obeyed my command and out of the turn opened fire at a Sabre that was attacking my element. Coming out of my turn at 11,000 meters, I spotted my wingmen and the Sabres, but that's when I saw tracers, and then the firing Sabre as well, which was attacking my aircraft from out of the sun. As a result of the fire from this Sabre, I received a bad chest wound. One of the Sabres (there were two of them) overshot me and began to roll over into a split-S. I lined him up and gave the Sabre a burst, but I'm not confident that I hit it.

Checking my aircraft's controls and engine, I convinced myself that everything was working, so I headed in the direction of the airbase and warned the command post to cover my landing, since I was coming in wounded. I lowered my wheels and extended the landing flaps using the backup system, because the hydraulic fluid had leaked out of the main system. I made my landing normally and taxied into a revetment. But I couldn't climb out of the cockpit myself; technicians had to remove me from it, because I no longer had any strength.

My wound was severe – the top of my left lung had been devastated, and pleurisy had developed in the right lung. After an operation in the Andong hospital, I spent the next 24 days laying in a semi-comatose condition, and only after this did everything begin to heal.

The Americans acknowledge the loss of F-86E No.50-0658 of the 335th FIS on this day. Its pilot 1st Lieutenant Walter S. Druen successfully bailed out and was rescued uninjured. After Bannikov's wounding, Lieutenant Colonel K.S. Erko, who arrived from the 726th IAP, assumed command of the 147th GIAP, though he commanded the regiment for only around a month before falling ill and returning to the Soviet Union.

The day of 30 August was more successful for the pilots of the 51st FIW, as well as pilots of the 4th FIW's 334th FIS. Combined, they shot down five MiGs on this day, while losing only one Sabre.

Captain Ia.N. Zhurin's flight of the 676th IAP's 3rd Squadron came under an attack by a group of Sabres, and two of his flight's pilots were shot down. Here's how Zhurin recalls this unsuccessful dogfight:

My first air battle took place on my third mission. When I lifted off the runway together with my flight, they informed us over the radio that four American aircraft were heading toward the airfield on some special mission. We were given the order to prevent them from reaching the base.

Climbing after take-off, we discovered that the information from the command post didn't reflect the real situation. Instead of a single American flight, we ran into four flights. I informed the ground that I was engaging them. I wanted to tie the enemy up in combat. Alas, that didn't happen. Their numerical superiority allowed Sabres to plant themselves on our tails. Leading the flight, I tried to separate from our pursuers. Two pilots of my flight for some reason didn't follow me into the turn to the left, but turned away to the right. My wingman lost his head, unable to handle the speed, and became an easy target for the Americans. So I remained alone against four enemy fighters that were sitting on my tail. They opened a furious fire on me. I had to maneuver. Spotting a cloud, I entered it and went into a steep dive. I managed to plunge from 12,000 meters down to around 3,500 meters. How much time all this took is difficult to remember. In any case, when I landed on the runway back at base, I had just 10 liters of fuel left in the tanks. Several minutes after me, a pilot of my flight Nikolai Fedorchenko touched down on the runway with a dying engine. There were three bullet holes in his MiG's fuselage. The other two aircraft were shot down: pilots Boris Opredelennov and Leonid Solov'ev managed to eject and by evening they had both returned alive and unharmed to our base. That's how my first aerial combat in the skies of Korea ended.

A pair of Sabres from the 334th FIS consisting of Captain Lewis Blackney and his wingman 1st Lieutenant Ronald Berda shot down another pilot of the 676th IAP Senior Lieutenant A.T. Topol'sky of the 2nd Squadron directly over the Dapu airfield; within sight of the entire regiment, A.T. Topol'sky ejected and safely came to earth within the airfield's perimeter. The pilots of the 676th IAP in these clashes on 30 August managed to shoot down one Sabre and damage another. Pilots of the regiment's 2nd Squadron Captain M.F. Iudin and Senior Lieutenant I.V. Efimov scored the successes. Captain Iudin damaged F-86E No.51-2794 from the 335th FIS, which returned to base and was possibly repaired.

On 31 August there was no fighting above MiG Alley, but the 64th IAK still lost one aircraft as a result of the catastrophic explosion of a drop tank during take-off. The deputy commander of the 518th IAP's 2nd Squadron Captain Fedor Stepanovich Eremchenko – an experienced combat pilot – was killed. Here it must be said that due to the poor quality of the supplied drop tanks, in 1952 and 1953 the 64th IAK lost several aircraft, which resulted in the death of several pilots.

Over the last summer month of 1952, the pilots of the 64th IAK downed a total of 15 enemy aircraft (14 F-86 and one F-84) and damaged another 10 US aircraft (nine F-86 and one B-29). Of these, pilots of the 133rd IAD shot down seven and damaged six while losing seven aircraft and four pilots in return; the pilots of the 216th IAD shot down another six aircraft and damaged four, losing seven aircraft and two pilots in return. Finally, pilots of the 190th IAD in August shot down two enemy aircraft, while losing six aircraft and one pilot. In addition, in the August fighting both the 97th IAD and the 32nd IAD lost one aircraft, and the 97th IAD pilot was killed. As a result, in August 1952 the 64th IAK lost 22 aircraft and eight pilots, while eight more aircraft were damaged and several pilots were wounded. If you also consider that a portion of the US aircraft damaged in the August fighting didn't make it back to base, then the losses on both sides could be reckoned as equal – 1:1.

For the first time in August 1952, pilots of the Unified Air Army began to struggle actively against the UN carrier aircraft in the Yellow Sea, sending small groups of MiGs out over the sea in order to intercept inbound aircraft launched from carriers. The first encounter of the carrier aircraft with Unified Air Army MiGs had taken place on 26 July 1952, when four MiG-15s had jumped four Fireflies and damaged three of them. One of the damaged Fireflies ditched in the water and began to sink – its crew was saved by search and rescue.

The next encounter took place on 9 August 1952 in the Hanchon – Chinnampo – Pyongyang area, when a flight of MiG-15s attacked four Sea Furies from 802 Squadron. In this action, Lieutenant Clark's Sea Fury was damaged, and in return Lieutenant M.H. MacKearney damaged one MiG-15. However, a more intense combat occurred elsewhere on the morning of 9 August, when four Sea Furies from the same 802 Squadron was attacked by an eight-ship formation of MiGs north of Chinnampo. In this action, pilots Lieutenant P.S. Davies, and Sub-Lieutenants B.I. Ellis and P. Heine damaged two MiG-15s, plus another MiG-15 over Cho-do Island, while Peter "Hoagy" Carmichael shot down one MiG-15, which crashed into a hillside and exploded – this was the first victory over a MiG-15 by a piston-engine aircraft of the UN air force in the skies of Korea, and this was achieved by a lieutenant of the Royal Navy's Fleet Air Arm, Peter Carmichael. The Englishmen had two damaged Sea Furies, one of which made a landing on the HMS *Ocean*, while the other piloted by Lieutenant Robert H. Hallam made a wheels-up landing on Cho-do Island; the pilot was rescued.

On the next day of 10 August, Lieutenant Carmichael's same flight of four from 802 Squadron engaged eight MiG-15s and damaged two of them in the ensuing combat, one of which according to the post-mission debriefings of the British pilots was burning. In this air battle the MiGs shot down Carmichael's Sea Fury and he landed on the water and was quickly rescued. On 11 August there was another meeting between MiGs of the Unified Air Army and Fireflies of 825 Squadron, but this encounter passed without any losses to either side. However, the Fireflies aborted their mission when they spotted the MiGs.

ENDNOTE

1   Captain Hugh P. Farler was actually a crewmember of B-29A No.44-86327 of the 98th BW's 343rd Squadron, which was shot down by MiGs on 1 June 1951 while on a mission to bomb the Kwaksan railroad bridge. I've been unable to find a Sabre pilot bearing the surname Farler. It is possible that the North Koreans had Captain Farler's identification papers and chose to use his surname to create a fictitious Sabre pilot that they had shot down.

9

The fighting intensifies

ANOTHER BLACK DAY FOR THE FIFTH AIR FORCE

September 1952 was marked with bitter fighting in the air. At the beginning of September, the Sabre pilots sharply increased their presence over our forward airfields on Chinese territory and in general began to practice "free hunts" over the territory of northeast China.

On 1 September 1952, pilots of the 133rd IAD and 216th IAD in the first autumn dogfights claimed two F-86s without any losses. However, the first serious clashes with the enemy occurred on 4 September. Pilots of the 133rd IAD and 216th IAD had several heated combats in the area of the Supung hydroelectric station. To repel an incoming enemy raid, Major V.I. Frolov's 1st Squadron of the 518th IAP departed first, and in the vicinity of the reservoir it encountered a group of F-86E fighter-bombers from the 25th FIS, covered by Sabres of the 16th FIS. Initially Major Frolov's eight-ship formation engaged the Sabres, but soon they were joined by arriving MiGs from Lieutenant Colonel P.F. Shevelev's 415th IAP. The opposing side also fed reinforcements into the fight in the form of several additional groups of Sabres from the 4th FIW. Then at 1500, eight MiGs of the 676th IAP's 2nd Squadron under the command of Captain M.D. Karatun joined the large dogfight.

Meanwhile, several small groups of Sabres of the 4th FIW were blockading the Dapu and Andong airfields. While taking off from the Dapu airbase as reinforcements for the growing air battle, eight MiG-15s with drop tanks from the 518th IAP's 3rd Squadron were jumped by Sabres, and two MiGs piloted by the squadron commander Major I.D. Khromov and Lieutenant P. Basalaev were shot down. Both pilots safely ejected. The group abandoned its mission and landed at a different airfield.

In the course of the "furball" itself, the deputy commander of the 518th IAP's 1st Squadron Captain M.I. Mikhin again stood out. Over the reservoir he attacked a pair of Sabres and from close range shot down one of them. This was his second victory in the war. True, a pilot of his flight Senior Lieutenant L.N. Pankov, spotting a different Sabre element, left the formation to attack it, but the Sabres was already retreating toward the sea. His wingman B.V. Korshunov shouted over the radio, "Break off the attack, they're attacking you!" Pankov, though, continued to close on his targets and soon flamed the wingman's aircraft. However he himself was fired upon by a different pair of Sabres, and quickly he smelled the odor of kerosene in his cockpit and lost control of his MiG. Several seconds later he ejected at an altitude of 3,000 meters and descended in his parachute into the Supung reservoir. He was rescued by Chinese fishermen: they pulled him out of the water just as Pankov was running out of strength to keep his head above the surface.

In this battle pilots of the 676th IAP's 2nd Squadron, which came under the attack of several pairs of F-86s in the Sonchon area, seriously damaged two Sabres, one by squadron commander Captain M.D. Karatun himself. However, in this action one of the squadron's pilots Senior Lieutenant V.K. Tatarov was shot down by a Sabre element. The pilot was lightly wounded in the back, but he was able to eject from his stricken MiG. Wounded, Viacheslav Tatarov landed in the mountainous terrain and for the next 24 hours fled from groups of South Korean infiltrators, who were trying to capture him alive. Only on the following day did he reach a position held by Chinese People's Volunteers, who immediately transported him to the Soviet hospital in Andong. He spent a month there recovering, after which he returned to his regiment and resumed flying combat missions. Senior Lieutenant V.K. Tatarov was awarded with the Order of the Red Star for his courageous action.

In a different action on this day, the deputy political commander of the 3rd Squadron Senior Lieutenant N.F. Kizim's MiG was also damaged, and he was compelled to make a forced landing short of his base. One of the sorties of this day conducted by pilots of the 415th IAP ended tragically. An electronics technician assigned to service the regiment's command flight, Eduard Aleksandrovich Adamchevsky, relates what happened in the vicinity of the Dapu airbase:

> The day of 4 September 1952 was a hard and tragic one for the regiment. On this day, three regiments were scrambled from our Dapu airfield to intercept enemy aircraft: our 415th IAP, the neighboring 676th IAP, and one of the Chinese fighter

North American F-86F Sabre jet, 1953. Conventional weapons that could be carried included a pair of 1000-pound or smaller bombs, two 750-pound napalm tanks, or eight 5-inch HVAR rockets. (US Air Force)

regiments. Once in the air, the Chinese in their MiGs assumed the high position in the combat formation; a little below them were the MiGs of the 676th IAP, while our regiment's MiGs took the low position and flew at low altitudes.

When returning to their Dapu base, as the pilots of the 415th IAP were circling to come in for a landing they were running out of fuel – a result of the regiment's higher rate of fuel consumption in the denser air at low altitudes. However, just then four Sabres approached, and in the final turn before landing, Senior Lieutenant A.I. Titov's MiG was attacked after he had already lowered his landing gear, and his aircraft was riddled with machine-gun fire in the full view of everyone on the ground – the MiG's nose dropped abruptly and it plummeted into a hill next to the airbase and exploded. The Sabres went into a zoom climb and headed back toward the bay. But even as they did so, several more pairs of Sabres arrived from the bay to replace them, and lining up behind the Chinese and our MiGs that were coming in for a landing, began to shoot them up. Some of our pilots, despite the fact that they only had a few liters of fuel left in their tanks, tried to counterattack the enemy. Mikhail Zatolokin was one of them; from higher altitude he attacked the Sabre element nearest to him and at point blank range fired his cannons at one of them. The targeted F-86 disintegrated in the air. Its pilot ejected and was taken prisoner. Zatolokin immediately came in for a landing as his fuel was running out, but he miscalculated and overshot the runway, touching down at the very end of it. The MiG bounded over three barriers and struck a trench breastwork – the MiG's landing gear were torn away and its nose with the machine guns was completely smashed. As was later shown, Zatolokin hadn't attached his shoulder belts, and when crashing against the breastwork, his head violently slammed against his gun sight and his skull was fractured. He passed away as his ground crew members that had come running up were pulling him out of the cockpit. Thus, Mikhail Zatolokin's death was senseless.

This didn't satisfy the Sabres and they continued to chase the MiGs that were coming in for a landing from various directions without fuel. Thus, they managed in the vicinity of the Dapu airfield to shoot down another six MiGs of the Chinese fighter regiment. A pilot of our regiment Vladimir Gutchenko also came under an attack by a pair of Sabres, and he, evading the attack, went into a steep climb, so that in case his engine stopped he would have sufficient altitude to eject. However, just then one of the Sabres that had attacked him passed in front of his aircraft's nose. He quickly reacted to this and fired the final remaining shell of his ammunition load at the Sabre and struck it. It disappeared somewhere, while Gutchenko immediately went in for a landing and safely touched down.

Later we learned that the pilot of the Sabre Gutchenko had damaged became disoriented when trying to return to base and flew off toward the Liaodong Peninsula, to the vicinity of our Port Arthur, where because of the lack of fuel he ejected and was taken prisoner. As was later determined the shell from Gutchenko's cannon hit the F-86 and smashed its generator, knocking out the Sabre's electronics. Without functioning instruments and a working radio, the pilot became confused and flew in the wrong direction.

After the cause of Zatolokin's death had been established, a strict order immediately went out to the entire division for every pilot to fasten all his belts in his aircraft's cockpit. Already on the following day this measure saved the life of the regiment's pilot Captain Viktor Filippov.[1] He took off on the morning of 5 September to assess the weather, but just as he was making his final turn for a landing after returning to base, his engine suddenly flamed out, and although he attempted to glide, he nevertheless roughly came down nose-first just beyond the airfield's perimeter. The fact that the pilot had fastened all his belts was just what saved his life. Filippov walked away from the crash with only a light scare, while his MiG took heavy damage and had to be written off. An investigation revealed that a ground crew member had forgotten to refuel Filippov's aircraft, and his fuel ran out on the final turn. That technician also got off lightly, with only a stern rebuke.

The official account of the 64th IAK headquarters indicates the following:

> On 4 September 1952 at 1441, the 415th IAP consisting of 24 crews under the command of the IAP's deputy commander Major Nosov took off to intercept and destroy enemy ground attack aircraft in the Sonchon, Anju area. At 1510 while landing at the Dapu airfield, our aircraft were attacked by F-86 fighters. Pilot Senior Lieutenant Titov in an air battle over the Dapu Air Base shot down one F-86, which fell into Korea Bay, 25 kilometers southwest of Dugam-po.

On this day Aleksandr Ivanovich Titov scored his first victory in the skies of Korea, but alas, he was killed over his own base when returning from the mission.

In sum, in the air battle of 4 September, the IAK's pilots claimed five Sabres, but received credit for only three of them; Pankov and Zatolokin didn't receive credit for their victories (possibly Zatolokin's victory was assigned instead to Major P.G. Nosov, the regiment's navigator), because their gun camera film burned up together with their aircraft. In addition, three F-86s were damaged. One of them was being flown by 2nd Lieutenant Roland W. Parks of the 51st FIW, whose gyro-radio compass was knocked out by his Sabre's loss of electricity. As indicated above, he became disoriented and mistakenly arrived over the Liaodong Peninsula, where MiGs of General Iu.B. Rykachev's 83rd IAK took off to intercept his F-86E No.51-2801 and came up along either side of him. Seeing that death was unavoidable if he attempted to escape, he ejected from his Sabre over Port Arthur without combat and was taken prisoner.

In addition to this Sabre, three more F-86E fighters were lost. F-86E No.51-2722 of the 335th FIS, which was being piloted by 1st Lieutenant Ira M. Porter, was damaged by a MiG and the pilot had to eject over the Yellow Sea, where he was picked up by a US search and rescue SA-16 flying boat. F-86E No.51-2763 from the 25th FIS, being flown by 1st Lieutenant Laverne G. Stange, was also damaged by a MiG; having reached the Yellow Sea, this pilot also ejected and was rescued by a helicopter. Finally, F-86E No.50-0678 from the 334th FIS, piloted by Theodore S. Coberly, suffered hydraulic failure after being damaged by a MiG; the pilot managed to reach his base, but crash landed there – Coberly survived, but the Sabre had to be written off.

On our side, six aircraft and one pilot (A.I. Titov) were lost in combat; three of the aircraft were shot down over the Dapu airfield. Another MiG was lost as a result of pilot error (Zatolokin), so it wasn't recorded as a combat loss.

The Americans claim that they shot down 13 MiGs on 4 September 1952, eight of them going to pilots of the 4th FIW and five to the 51st FIW. 1st Lieutenants Justin W. Livingston and Ira M. Porter (who our pilots then dumped into the Yellow Sea) of the 335th FIS each received credit for two victories in one combat. If you subtract the six MiGs of the 64th IAK from the total number of victories achieved by the Americans on this day, then the remaining seven MiGs must have been from the UAA, six of which were also shot down while attempting to land at Dapu.

On 5 September, pilots of the 133rd IAD shot down two Sabres and damaged another. However, Captain N.I. Ivanov of the 726th IAP, who already had three victories over F-86s at this point, didn't receive official credit for the Sabre he shot down. On this day, there was a squadron sortie, and the first to take off was Ivanov and his wingman Rusakov. As they were taking off, a pair of Sabres approached from the bay and an order came from the command post to abort the take-off – too late, because our MiGs had already lifted off the runway. Ivanov managed to jettison his drop tanks as soon as his MiG was in the air and by some miracle avoided the Sabre machine-gun fire. Then he himself attacked the Sabre pair from behind as they overshot him. One of the Sabres erupted in flames and fell into the bay, which everyone in the regiment saw. However, since Ivanov was firing at the Sabres from below, into the sun, his gun camera footage was spoiled, and because no identification tag could be taken from the aircraft that fell into the sea, Ivanov didn't receive credit for the victory. Here's how Nikolai Ivanovich himself describes this victory:

> As I was taking off, I kept one hand on the ejection lever. On my takeoff run I jettisoned my drop tanks. They never teach this and I never spoke with anyone about this, but when they shouted to me over the radio, "You're being attacked!" I'd already just lifted off the runway and I had no choice. There was no way to stop – I'd crash into the hills, so I pressed the button to release the drop tanks. Perhaps it was just this that saved me. Those, who were on the ground told me later that my take-off made a great impression on them. I don't know … it didn't make an impression on me.
>
> Fortunately everything turned out all right. Only one bullet hit my aircraft, while my wingman joined me in the air without taking a single bullet. On that day the cloud cover was 5-6 [on a scale of 1 to 10]. I climbed through a cloud, and just as I emerged from it there was a pair of Sabres passing just overhead – they were heading toward the bay. I went after them and soon I was firing at one and probably shot it down. This was over the airfield itself and everyone saw it.

However, since this aircraft fell into the sea, as already mentioned Ivanov didn't receive credit for it.

A little while later, Sabres of the 4th FIW gained revenge in the vicinity of the Miaogou airfield by shooting down one MiG of the 878th IAP as it was landing – Senior Lieutenant Gonchar successfully ejected. The pilots of the 878th IAP on this day had flown a regimental sortie to the Gisiu – Anju area, where they had a brief and fruit-less combat with a group of F-86s, but while coming in for a landing they came under an attack by Sabre "hunters". The Americans claimed four victories on 5 September, three of which they plainly achieved over UAA pilots. The Americans admit the loss of one of their reconnaissance RF-86A jets bearing the Bureau Number 48-0246 from the 15th TRS, the pilot of which 1st Lieutenant William C. Sney bailed out and was rescued. Most probably he was shot down by Senior Lieutenant V.S. Poskrebyshev of the 147th GIAP, while Major M.E. Vorontsov damaged another F-86 which was apparently escorting this reconnaissance jet. In addition, a F-84E from the 49th FBW's 7th FBS was lost on this day, the pilot of which was killed – most likely, he was a victim of one of the pilots of the UAA.

After 5 September, combat missions followed one after another, and each day there was from one to three combat sorties, depending on the enemy activity, and almost each sortie resulted in dogfights with Sabres, which were operating very actively. This account will only linger on those combat sorties that led to results for our pilots or the American pilots.

On 6 September at 1020, six MiGs under the command of Captain M.F. Iudin engaged six F-86s. As a result of this action, Captain Iudin managed to down one F-86, which fell into the bay just off the coast.

The next day 24 MiGs of the 32nd IAD's 535th IAP and 913th IAP took off to cover the Andong, Miaogou and Dapu airbases. For the pilots of the 535th IAP, this was their first combat sortie, but unfortunately it was unsuccessful. Here's how a former squadron commander of the 535th IAP Kirill Ivanovich Sema describes the mission:

On 7 September, a familiarization flight over the area of combat operations was planned for the squadron. The deputy commander of the 535th IAP Lieutenant Colonel Akimov was designated as the leader; his wingman was the regiment's navigator Major V.V. Isakov. I and my wingman Ivan Shikunov were covering them. Senior Lieutenant F.I. Masleev led the second flight. We had traversed the entire territory of North Korea and were already approaching the border with China when above and behind us I noticed a flight of Sabres that was closing in on our flight because of the black plumes of smoke from their afterburners. I warned the group leader Akimov about this, but he replied, "We'll proceed", and then began to climb. Our altitude was 12,000 meters and I again warned the leader that the enemy was approaching and demanded that we reverse course for a head-on attack, but the leader again replied, "We'll proceed." At this time my wingman Ivan Shikunov reported over the radio that he was being fired on. I abandoned the lead element and circled around sharply to the right, to go to the assistance of my wingman. I gave him an order to break left, but instead of this he began to turn to starboard, by which he complicated my task of repelling the attack. I opened fire while pulling lead and drove away one F-86, but they still had time to flame Shikunov's aircraft. He ejected (this occurred over the Dapu airfield) and seemed to land safely. However, when the emergency aid reached him, it turned out that he was dead. Apparently, at the moment of ejection he bowed his head, and the force of the ejection broke his neck. So my wingman Vania Shikunov tragically perished on his first combat sortie. This was the only death of a pilot in my squadron during our entire period of service in Manchuria.

The 64th IAK had no other losses on this day.

Apparently, it was the pair of 1st Lieutenant William Powers and his wingman 2nd Lieutenant Paul Kauttu of the 51st FIW's 16th FIS or the pair of Captain John Taylor and his wingman 1st Lieutenant Edward Powell of the 4th FIW's 335th FIS that shot down Ivan Mikhailovich Shikunov, since they each claimed one MiG-15 on this day while flying "free hunts" (each pair shared the credit for a victory). In total, however, the Sabre pilots, according to their claims, shot down three MiGs on 7 September.

The 64th IAK's pilots also downed a Sabre on this day and damaged another. Pilots of the 216th IAD's 878th IAP distinguished themselves. After the first morning combat mission, the regiment's 1st Squadron took off under the command of the regiment commander himself, Lieutenant Colonel S.D. Dronov, to cover the Miaogou airfield. Over the base, Dronov and his wingman Selivestrov intercepted a pair of Sabre "hunters" at an altitude of 7,000 meters and attacked it. Unexpectedly for the Sabres, the commander of the 1st Squadron Captain V.M. Selivestrov hit one of the Sabres from a range of 200-300 meters, and trailing smoke, it fell into the sea just offshore (at low tide its tail assembly was visible). However, the victory was given to the regiment commander, who also fired at the Sabre element, although from long range. A flight commander in the 3rd Squadron Captain A.E. Lomasov also damaged another Sabre on his first combat sortie. However, the Americans deny the loss of their F-86s on this day.

The day of 8 September proved to be not so successful for the 64th IAK's pilots. There was a raid by enemy fighter-bombers to the Anju area, and pilots of the 216th IAP took off in groups of eight to ten MiGs to repel it. During the ensuing clashes, Captain M.I. Mikhin of the 518th IAP attacked a flight of Thunderjets and shot down one of them. In a tussle with Sabres, pilots of the 518th and 676th IAP who had hastened to join them shot down one Sabre and damaged another. However, the Sabres downed three MiGs: the 676th IAP's 3rd Squadron commander Major G.V. Mishchenko, Lieutenant A. Shchelkunov of the same squadron and Senior Lieutenant V. Lobyshev of the 518th IAP were all shot down. They all successfully bailed out. The 676th IAP's 3rd Squadron was particularly hard-hit. In addition to the two downed comrades, in this combat the MiGs of the squadron's deputy political commander Senior Lieutenant N.F. Kizim and of the squadron deputy commander Captain A.F. Iurchenko were damaged. Kizim with difficulty flew his crippled MiG to the North Korean airfield at Gisiu and made a belly landing there, and had time to get out of the burning aircraft before its ammunition exploded. Captain Iurchenko also made a forced belly landing – the pilot survived, but the aircraft had to be written off. Thus, the entire leadership of the 676th IAP's 3rd Squadron was shot down in one dogfight, but fortunately they all remained alive and unharmed!

In addition, Senior Lieutenant D.I. Chepusov was shot down by "free hunters" in the vicinity of the Miaogou airfield. Fortunately, he also safely ejected.

As a result, on 8 September the 64th IAK lost six aircraft in combat, while downing two enemy aircraft and damaging another, so this day can be chalked up to the group of pilots of the 4th and 51st FIW, which received credit for five victories on 8 September 1952. Major Frederick "Boots" Blesse of the 334th FIS particularly stood out on this day, having downed two MiGs in one combat. In fact, the 4th FIW's 334th Squadron scored all the victories on 8 September. One of the two kills claimed by the 64th IAK on 8 September was F-84E No.51-596 from the 49th FBG's 9th FBS, which was shot down by Captain Mikhin.

A major air battle took place on 9 September 1952 in the area of Taegwan-dong. Both sides fed additional forces into the initial clash, and eventually 60 F-84s covered by 40 F-86s from the US Fifth Air Force and approximately 100 MiGs from the 133rd IAD and 216th IAD took part in it.

The raid began after 1000 and the first to take off to repel it were approximately 50 MiGs from the 216th IAD's 676th IAP, 518th IAP and 878th IAP, with each regiment contributing 16-18 aircraft. They tied up the forward screen of Sabres from the 51st FIW in combat, which gave 18 MiGs (two squadrons) of the 726th IAP under the command of regiment commander Lieutenant Colonel L.D. Goriachko an opportunity to penetrate to the fighter-bombers. According to the 64th IAK headquarters' official account:

> At 1049 18 crews of the 726th IAP led by the IAP commander Lieutenant Colonel Goriachko took off to intercept and destroy enemy ground attack aircraft in the Taegwan-dong area. At 1054 in a region 10 kilometers southwest of Taegwan-dong, the regiment encountered up to 60 F-84 fighter-bombers covered by up to 40 F-86 fighters. Flight commander Senior Lieutenant I.I. Katunov shot down one F-84 from a range of 700 meters at a target aspect angle of 1/4-2/4, which fell in an area 11 kilometers south of Taegwan-dong.

The pilots of the 726th IAP came across a large group of F-84Gs lacking any fighter cover and furiously attacked the Thunderjet formation. Thunderjets, coming under fire from the MiG cannons, fell to the earth one after another. As a result, only a portion of the F-84G fighter-bombers were able to flee to the bay, while 14 of them remained on North Korean soil. The enemy fighter-bombers hadn't suffered such heavy and painful losses since the autumn of 1951. Here's how former participants in this turkey shoot, Mikhail Arsent'evich Katashov and Lev Ivanovich Rusakov describe it. Says M.A. Katashov:

> We scrambled in response to an alert to repel a massive enemy raid against a hydro-electrical station. After flying 50-60 kilometers, we encountered a large group of F-84s at altitudes of 3,000-4,000 meters approaching on an intersecting course. The regiment reported the detection of the enemy to the ground and received an order to attack and for each pilot to select a target independently. That's when everything started ... We had some advantage in altitude and conducted the attack from above and behind after a turn to port toward the fighter-bombers. After this pass, the fighter-bomber formation scattered, and then we started choosing our own targets and shooting down the enemy.
>
> I began to pursue a pair of F-84s, which were wildly jettisoning their bombs. They tried to flee through a valley between hills, but they couldn't escape because of the low altitude. So using my favorite approach, a dive, I caught them and shot them down. Other pilots of my flight, Senior Lieutenants V.I. Motonakh and M.S. Grechin, each bagged two F-84s in the same fashion.

Lev Ivanovich Rusakov had this to say about the action:

> The most memorable of all the regiment's battles took place on 9 September 1952. We took off as two squadrons – eight MiGs of the 2nd Squadron and 10 aircraft of

the 1st Squadron. Regiment commander Lieutenant Colonel L.D. Goriachko was leading the group. While we were climbing over Chinese territory, at an altitude of 6,000-7,000 meters we received an order to jettison our drop tanks and to fly to Zone 21 while descending to 1,000 meters. Having executed the order, on the approach to the zone we spotted a large group of "Crosses" (F-84s) approaching at a higher altitude, leading a group of Sabres, and it was being directly escorted by two F-86 elements. The order arrived: "Everyone is to choose a target. Attack!" and it started … The action took place at low altitude above hilly terrain, with large G-forces to the point of blacking out.

When the Yankees began to yell that they were under attack, Sabres of the aerial screens (as the Americans' zones of patrol were called) began to pounce on us. Later they calculated that there were two groups of F-84s in this combat (around 100 aircraft) and almost as many Sabres. As a result it was established that we shot down 15-16 F-84s and one Sabre. But our losses were also heavy – my comrade was killed – my classmate Ivan Kapunov and the regiment navigator Major I.K. Sova (a bullet struck him in the head). The combat was bloody and fierce; it was us or them.

Subsequent events unfolded in the following manner. After the heavy losses the Thunderjets began to retreat to the bay, with our MiGs of the 726th IAP in dogged pursuit. The F-84 losses would have been even heavier, had not a new group of Sabres of the 51st FIW arrived to their assistance. It in turn attacked the Soviet pilots of the 726th IAP who were focused on the chase and shot down Senior Lieutenant Ivan Ivanovich Kapunov. Now the table had turned against the pilots of the 726th IAP, since the Sabres had both numerical superiority and a better position for attacking. Moreover, the regiment's formation had split into separate elements, so there was no longer a well-organized group, which the Americans indeed exploited.

The "brotherly" regiments of the 133rd IAD – two eight-ship formations of the 147th GIAP and just as many MiGs from the 415th IAP – which hurriedly arrived on the scene, saved the situation. They then attacked the Sabres who were now distracted by their own pursuit of the scattered MiG elements. The battle flared up with new intensity, and a carousel of turning, diving and climbing MiGs and Sabres began to spin, and from which burning aircraft of both sides were falling. We have a couple more eyewitness accounts from participants in this combat who recall how it went. The former commander of the 147th GIAP's 3rd Squadron Captain Nikolai Ivanovich Shkodin remembers:

The 415th Regiment flew off first in response to an alarm, and then we were scrambled in two eight-ship formations. The overall group leader regiment navigator Major Kravchenko led the first squadron, while I headed the second. After a few minutes in the air, I spotted a gigantic dogfight involving several dozen jets; the combat was in full swing. A Sabre element attacked and shot down Captain K.P. Pronin's aircraft from Captain Kaliuzhny's flight. I went on the attack against this Sabre pair, and from close range I shot down one of these "pirates", thereby taking revenge for the death of a comrade.

In this dogfight N.I. Shkodin's wingman Captain Fedor Gavrilovich Afanas'ev also distinguished himself. Here's what he has to say about his victory:

"Hunters", experienced US pilots, were often waiting for us to come in for a landing. One such "hunter" decided to go on a hunt alone in the area of the Miaogou airfield and selected as his target my leader Captain N.I. Shkodin. Seeing this, I cut my speed in order to increase the interval between Shkodin and myself while calling for Shkodin over the radio to turn to port, and began to bank to the left in order to decrease the radius and get in behind this Sabre. He understood me and turned, while I accelerated and closed in behind the Sabre, which was already firing at Shkodin, and gave it a burst. The Sabre pilot immediately broke off his pursuit of Shkodin and turned away to the right. I followed him into the turn and in the pursuit shot him down, and his Sabre crashed to the ground.

These were Shkodin's and Afanas'ev's first victories in the skies of Korea.

However, Sabres of the 4th FIW managed in the area of the Andong base to swing in behind the 726th IAP's 1st Squadron commander Major K.N. Degtiarev's MiG as he was circling to come in for a landing and shot him down. However, he was able to bail out and quickly again returned to the regiment.

Pilots of the 415th IAP also downed one Sabre. A hero of this day Evgenii Ivanovich Polivaiko relates:

It was a sortie to the area of the Yalu River to repel an enemy air strike. I was flying in a flight of the 1st Squadron as the wingman to squadron commander Major G.I. Bogdanov (Captain Timofei Akimov was leading the second element). There was a big air battle, an enormous dogfight. In one of the maneuvers Bogdanov gained a very advantageous position over a pair of F-86s. But then something happened with Bogdanov's gun sight, and the burst he fired missed the target wide. The Sabre jinked to one side and wound up directly in my sights, and I fired at him with all my cannons from pointblank range. It began to smoke, then erupted in flames and fell on the bank of the Yalu River (I saw the flash of the explosion). But at that moment a different pair of Sabres jumped me, while Bogdanov was in no position to help, since he was out in front of me. The Sabres caught me in pincer and were firing at me from two directions. Akimov's element saved me. They heard my call signs and bearing, which I was shouting over the radio. By this radio guidance Akimov's element was able to find me, and they attacked the Sabres that were tormenting me. They together broke off the attack in a dive, leaving me alone. I took advantage of the moment and found refuge in a cloud, having received several bullet holes in my aircraft. However, everything turned out all right for me. Later it was established that the American pilot I had shot down was a black man.

However, in this battle the 415th IAP also suffered losses. Two of the regiment's pilots, Senior Lieutenants G.A. Burin and M.E. Sergeev, were both shot down. Happily, they both managed to eject from their doomed MiGs and quickly returned to the regiment.

As a result, in this major clash the pilots of the 133rd IAD downed 17 enemy aircraft, including 14 F-84G Thunderjets claimed by pilots of the 726th IAP (another two F-86s were presumably downed, but the regiment didn't receive credit for them). The 147th IAP shot down two F-86s, and one Sabre was shot down by pilots of the 415th IAP. The division's losses were also heavy: six MiGs were destroyed and three pilots were killed

– Konstantin Pavlovich Pronin, Ivan Kuz'mich Sova and Ivan Ivanovich Kapunov. In addition, in the dogfight with Sabres of the forward screen, pilots of the 216th IAD claimed four F-86s and damaged another, without any losses in return. Pilots of the 676th IAP claimed two of the Sabres: first in a large morning air battle in the Taegwan-dong area involving six MiGs led by Captain M.F. Iudin against a flight of Sabres, the captain shot down one Sabre, which fell 8 kilometers southeast of the village of Sinhung-li. Captain Iudin discussed this victory in more detail in his report:

> On 9 September 1952, at 1103 I took off as part of a group of six aircraft as the leader of the second flight in order to destroy F-86 fighters, which were covering strike aircraft that were operating in the Taegwan-dong region. On the approach to the area where the strike aircraft were working over ground targets, at 1114 I spotted a flight of F-86s to my left at 5,000 meters, approaching us at an angle. I informed the squadron commander Captain Korotun, who moved toward the lead pair, while the tail-end pair of F-86s latched onto the tail of Senior Lieutenant Kalinkin's MiG. The F-86 leader opened fire, but the bursts were inaccurate and passed behind Senior Lieutenant Kalinkin's aircraft. I took an angle to cut him off and got in behind the wingman's F-86. Closing from above in a left turn, I opened fire at a range of 300-400 meters and a target aspect angle of 2/4. The first two bursts passed in front of the F-86 and forced him to swerve to one side, but the following two long bursts struck the target, and the final burst hit the central part of the fuselage around the cockpit. The F-86 smoothly went into a normal turn to the left and headed down below. At this moment, my wingman Senior Lieutenant Efimov informed me that four F-86s were attacking us from above and behind. An attack from above and behind by Captain Mikheev forced the Sabres to break off the attack, and they headed toward the bay.
>
> I observed the fall of the F-86. I assume that the F-86 crashed in an area 10 kilometers southeast of the village of Taegwan-dong.
>
> I expended the following amount of ammunition: 40 N-37 shells and 160 N-23 shells.
>
> The cloud cover was 5-6, and the clouds peaked at 6,000-7,000 meters; visibility was 15 kilometers.

Then in a later combat action at 1545 Major G.A. Bolotin's group of eight MiGs engaged two flights of Sabres. Major Boldin shot down one F-86, which fell 15 kilometers northeast of Gisiu.

Pilots of the 518th IAP also shot down an equal number of Sabres. Captain M.I. Mikhin of the 1st Squadron had a good day – he shot down one F-86 (his third) and damaged another. The "damaged" Sabre actually plunged into the bay, but since there was no physical evidence, it was considered only damaged. Senior Lieutenant E.I. Stadnik also added one Sabre to his combat score.

Incidentally, regarding all the confirmed victories of 9 September 1952, all of the F-84s shot down by the 726th IAP were found on the ground and their factory identification tags were obtained. It wasn't necessary to confirm some of them, since on the gun camera film, as for example, that of the commander of the 726th IAP Lieutenant Colonel L.D. Goriachko, who downed two F-84s simultaneously in this action, the explosion in the air of one of the F-84s was plainly visible, so in this case other evidence wasn't even necessary. The outcome of this day of heavy combat was as follows: the 64th IAK shot down 21 enemy aircraft (plus two more listed as probable victories) and damaged one enemy aircraft (more accurately, downed it); 14 F-84Gs and seven F-86s were shot down. Its own losses over the day of fighting amounted to six MiGs and three pilots.

The Fifth Air Force command acknowledged the loss of six of its F-84s and one F-80. However, the Americans admitted the loss of only four of the F-84s directly on 9 September. These were F-84E No.51-688 from the 49th FBG's 7th FBS (the pilot of which 1st Lieutenant Jimmy H. Alkire was killed); F-84E No.51-687 from the 9th FBS of the same Group (the pilot of which Captain Warren E. O'Brien was killed); F-84E No.51-490 from the 58th FBW's 69th FBS, the pilot of which 2nd Lieutenant William H. Suffern, Jr. was killed; and finally F-84G No.51-776, the fate of the pilot of which is unknown. Another F-84E (No.49-2410) from the 58th FBW's 310th FBS was written off on the following day; its pilot 1st Lieutenant Albert E. Plecha was killed. Finally, three days later F-84G No.51-10357 from the 49th FBW's 8th FBS was written off, the pilot of which 1st Lieutenant Robert L. Dunne was also killed.

In addition, in this major battle on 9 September, F-86A No.49-1139 of the 4th FIW was lost, the pilot of which in fact returned to his unit, as well as two F-86Es (No.50-0666 and No.50-0672) from the same 4th Fighter Wing. The pilot of the first F-86E, Dennis A Dunlop crashed when landing at his base, but survived, while the fate of the other F-86E pilot isn't reported.

The Americans claimed that in this air battle, pilots of the 51st FIW shot down five MiG-15s, of which three went to pilots of the 25th FIS and two to pilots of the 39th FIS. Ernst Glover, a Canadian pilot who was on temporary duty with the 4th FIW's 334th Fighter Interceptor Squadron, also shot down one MiG (it was probably he who shot down Degtiarev in the Andong area). This is a rare instance, when the losses of the 64th IAK coincided with the number of victories claimed by pilots of the 4th and 51st FIW in this battle.

THE "SAILORS" ENTER THE FIGHTING: THE FIRST VICTORIES OF THE MARITIME PILOTS

After the major battle on 9 September, the enemy took several days off until 14 September. Pilots of the 518th IAP and 676th IAP had a few minor skirmishes with Sabres on 12 and 13 September, but these ended with no losses on our side. However, on 12 September pilots of the 518th IAP distinguished themselves by downing one F-86 and damaging another – Senior Lieutenant M.I. Mikhin got the victory, while Senior Lieutenant N.I. Kas'ianov registered the damaged F-86. Senior Lieutenant I.P. Kalinkin of the 676th IAP also added another Sabre to his personal score. How this victory happened was told in detail in the report filed by the 2nd Squadron commander Captain M.D. Korotun:

> On 12 September 1952 I took off with a group of six aircraft to carry out a combat mission. As we were approaching the combat area in a combat formation of staggered elements on a heading of 110°, at 0944 in the area of Sakchu I noticed four F-86s on the same heading to the left of our group at an altitude of 10,500 meters. The group and I turned in the direction of the enemy and closed with them, flying at a higher altitude at a speed of 900 km/hr.

We spotted two more pairs of F-86s at an altitude of 9,800 meters, which were in position to attack my wingman Senior Lieutenant Efimov and Captain Iudin's wingman Senior Lieutenant Kalinkin from both sides, so I attacked the F-86s, which were closing on Captain Iudin's pair from the left.

Seeing that the F-86 leader was rapidly approaching Captain Iudin's element, I went after this F-86. At the moment that I opened fire at it from a range of 500-600 meters, I myself was attacked by the F-86 wingman. After receiving information from Senior Lieutenant Kalinkin that an F-86 was attacking me, I broke off the attack into a tight turn to the right. At this time Senior Lieutenant Kalinkin opened fire at the F-86 that was attacking me, from a range of 300-200 meters and at a target aspect angle of 1/4. Being in a higher position, I observed Senior Lieutenant Kalinkin's fire, which struck the right wing and rear portion of the F-86, after which it flipped over and went into an uncontrolled plunge.

At this moment, Senior Lieutenant Kalinkin's aircraft went into a spin. I continued to observe the falling F-86 aircraft until the moment that Kalinkin's aircraft came out of the spin.

I think that the aircraft attacked by Senior Lieutenant Kalinkin was shot down, because it was damaged and was streaming black smoke as it fell, though I didn't see the place where it crashed, because at that time I was maneuvering to avoid the attack of a different F-86 element. I didn't notice any hits on the F-86 that I attacked, but this was captured on my gun camera film.

I expended 7 N-37 shells and 28 N-23 shells in the combat.

On 14 September the 878th IAP's 1st Squadron had a successful combat with a group of F-86s in the Singisiu area, in which flight commander Senior Lieutenant M.I. Chumachenko did well, downing one Sabre and damaging another. The 676th IAP's 2nd Squadron, consisting of eight MiGs led by Captain M.D. Korotun, which hastened to the aid of the 878th IAP, bagged two more Sabres, which were credited to Senior Lieutenant Topol'sky and I.G. Dezhkin. True, the Sabre pilots in turn managed to inflict heavy damage to Senior Lieutenant Dezhkin's MiG in this combat, and he had to make a landing at the airfield in Liaoyang.

In the afternoon, the 676th IAP's 1st Squadron consisting of eight MiGs led by Hero of the Soviet Union Major I.F. Gnezdilov took off to intercept enemy aircraft, and at 1550 it spotted a flight of F-86s and engaged it. Gnezdilov and flight commander Captain Iu.A. Varkov each claimed a Sabre in the Kiojo area, while losing the MiG piloted by Senior Lieutenant A.M. Antipov, who safely ejected. In their turn Sabres conducted a blockade of the Miaogou airfield, downing a MiG-15 of the 518th IAP being flown by flight commander Captain Vladimir Sergeevich Chernavin, who came down in the hills beyond the runway together with his aircraft – the pilot was killed. The Sabres got away unpunished.

The results of the day favored the pilots of the 64th IAK. Five F-86s were claimed by pilots of the 216th IAD and another one was damaged, of which four F-86s went to the score of the 676th IAP's pilots. Their own losses over the day amounted to two aircraft, while Captain V.S. Chernavin of the 518th IAP was killed; one more MiG-15 received combat damage. The Americans claimed three victories, but evidently they counted Senior Lieutenant Dezhkin's MiG as downed, though in reality it was soon repaired and returned to service. In contrast, the Americans in one of the rare cases admit to heavy losses among their Sabres in the fighting on 14 September. Thus they acknowledge the loss of five of their Sabres, three of which were F-86Es with the Bureau Numbers 51-2725, 51-2727 and 51-2820 – the pilot of the second Sabre 1st Lieutenant John J. Breen of the 16th FIS bailed out north of Cho-do after his engine caught fire and was rescued by an SA-16 flying boat, while the pilot of the third Sabre 2nd Lieutenant Paul C. Turner of the 25th FIS was less lucky; he bailed out but couldn't evade being captured. Two of the new F-86F fighters of the 25th FIS (No.52-4536 and No.52-4555) were also lost, but the Americans don't report the fate of their pilots. Thus the opposing side confirms all of the victories claimed by our pilots.

The next day of 15 September was noteworthy because for the first time Soviet naval pilots of the Pacific Ocean Fleet, who had recently arrived in the 64th IAK, flew their first combat mission. The command of Soviet naval aviation had decided to test its pilots in combat, with the aim of giving them valuable combat experience in the conditions of modern warfare, as well as to assess the level of training and skill of the Pacific Ocean Fleet's pilots. The choice fell upon the Pacific Fleet's 7th IAD, which was commanded by Colonel Koreshkov. The 578th IAP under the command of Major V.T. Dobrov was selected from this division's roster of units. Altogether 52 men were picked: 12 officers of the headquarters' flight and 40 pilots. Since the regiment was experiencing a shortage of officers, 13 pilots from the 305th IAP of the Pacific Ocean Fleet's 165th IAD transferred to the 578th IAP as replenishments. Between 5 August and 18 August, the pilots of the 578th IAP underwent a special course of flight training, and on 18 August they were sent to China aboard a railroad train.

The regiment's leadership staff and pilots arrived at the Anshan airfield on 20 August 1952 without any airplanes, as well as without any of their ground crews and technicians. It was decided by the 64th IAK command that the 578th IAP would be attached to the 133rd IAD, and the "sailors" would replace one of the division's regiments for a period of a week to 10 days, thereby giving that regiment a short rest, while the naval pilots would fly the aircraft of the given regiment and carry out the same missions that were being flown by the pilots of the replaced regiment.

Until 1 September, the pilots of the 578th IAP spent their time becoming familiar with the 64th IAK's other airfields (Miaogou, Dapu, Mukden and others), flew around them in squadron-sized formations, and familiarized themselves with the area of combat operations. On 3 September the regiment's pilots restaged to the IAK's forward base at Andong. The 578th IAP's pilots operated from this base until 25 December 1952.

The first to fly a combat mission were eight pilots of Captain Vasilii Danilovich Andriushchenko's 3rd Squadron, who were joined by MiGs of the 726th IAP's 3rd Squadron. Here's how Vasilii Danilovich himself describes this inaugural combat sortie by the naval pilots:

> On 15 September 1952 my first sortie on a combat mission took place. On this day the Americans had decided to launch a massive air raid against strategic targets in North Korea. Several dozen strike aircraft and almost as many covering Sabres took part in the raid. The fighter-bombers were flying in groups that were echeloned in altitude between 5,000 and 12,000 meters, covered by Sabres. We were sitting on the ground in the cockpits of our MiGs and we could clearly see the black waves of

hostile aircraft as they came rolling in over the Korean coastline from the direction of Korea Bay. Almost all of our fighter regiments were scrambled to repel this raid.

The time arrived for our eight-ship formation to take off as well. I took off first. My wingman was holding tightly in formation next to me. Another pair was launched after us, and after that, another one … I retracted my trailing edge flaps and landing gear and pointed my aircraft toward the railroad bridge in the vicinity of Singisiu. It was now our squadron's turn to guard this important strategic target.

One of my pilots turned back to base because his landing gear wouldn't retract. There were now seven of us. We would operate in two groups, a group of five in the lead and a trailing element. Our altitude was 6,000 meters; the bright ribbon of the river and the railroad bridge were beneath my wing. Having reversed course to the right, I spotted a squadron of eight Sabres almost directly crossing our front. It was descending headlong in the direction of the sea and still hadn't seen us. Likely, someone had already spooked it. I gave the signal: "We're attacking" – and pointed my aircraft directly at an enemy flight leader. While I was trying to catch the turning Sabre in my sights, I myself was attacked. Three short bursts from all my cannons and the hostile aircraft began to smoke and went into a violent dive. But my situation was also critical; a flight of Sabres that had hastened to the scene was already giving me aimed bursts of fire. I shot a quick look for my wingmen – there was no one around me. There was only one hope left, to separate somehow from the enemy. Our MiGs were superior to the F-86 in climbs. I knew this well from my colleagues. So I took advantage of this. The Americans escorted me with fire all the way up to 15,500 meters!

I landed at a reserve airfield. I couldn't reach my own base; my fuel ran out and my engine stopped. Later, when analyzing our actions, I realized that I was barely able to tie the enemy up in combat; our five-ship group couldn't keep pace with his fast-moving, dazzling maneuvers and simply fell apart. That's where our lack of training in maneuvering sharply as a flight and in dogfighting at enormous speeds and extreme G-forces was telling.

We lost two aircraft in this our first combat: Senior Lieutenant Zubchenko landed his burning fighter in the first patch of open, reasonably level ground that he could find and survived by some miracle, while Senior Lieutenant Nikitin reached his base and made a wheels-up landing in his burning aircraft and was injured.

Thus ended the first air battle for the pilots of the Pacific Ocean Fleet's 578th IAP, which they didn't handle well, losing two of their aircraft. Captain V.D. Andriushchenko was only credited with damaging his Sabre, because it fell into the bay. Senior Lieutenant E.G. Kravtsov managed to damage another F-86 in this combat with eight F-86s, but on the whole the battle was handled poorly and resulted in senseless losses.

With a great deal of confidence one can assert that in this combat, the pilots of Captain Andriushchenko's 3rd Squadron encountered pilots of the 4th FIW's 334th FIS. The future ace Captain James Robinson Risner celebrated a victory over one of the pilots of the Pacific Fleet's 578th IAP, scoring his third victory in this battle. In Risner's account, in this action he attacked four MiGs and damaged one of them; trying to finish off this MiG, he conducted a rather lengthy pursuit of it all the way to the Miaogou airfield, where he finally made sure of his victory by knocking the MiG down with a final burst, sending it crashing to the ground in the area of the base.

On 15 September pilots of the 216th IAD and 133rd IAD conducted two to three combat sorties to intercept enemy fighters in the Singisiu – Changseong area. Taking on the covering fighters, they cleared the way for the Chinese pilots of the UAA to work over the fighter-bombers. Pilots of the 726th IAP distinguished themselves in one clash with Sabres, downing one F-86 and damaging another. Pilots of the 147th GIAP also shot down one Sabre, without any losses of their own.

However, trouble was now almost always waiting for the 64th IAK's pilots in the area of their own airfields. This day was no exception; Sabres intercepted pilots of the 676th IAP as they were taking off from the Dapu airbase and shot down two of the regiment's MiGs, while damaging two more. When a ground observation post reported that a group of Sabres were heading toward the base, the regiment's 2nd Squadron was supposed to scramble into the air. However, for some reason the regiment commander delayed with the order to take off, and by the time the long-awaited command finally arrived, the Americans were already over the base. After taking off they had to climb through a ravine, so there was practically no possibility to maneuver. The Americans first shot down Senior Lieutenant Ivan Vasil'evich Efimov, the wingman to flight commander Captain M.F. Iudin. Machine-gun bullets directly struck his cockpit and sent the MiG smashing into one of the ravine's walls. The blast wave of the resulting explosion tossed Iudin's aircraft upward, and this saved his life. A burst of machine-gun fire intended for him passed harmlessly below him. Iudin jettisoned his drop tanks and went into a zoom climb. The element led by squadron commander Captain M.D. Korotun took off next, and it also came under the attack of Sabres, which shot down Captain Korotun's MiG and seriously damaged the aircraft of his wingman Senior Lieutenant I.P. Kalinkin. Captain Korotun managed to eject safely, while Kalinkin managed to land his burning MiG on a neighboring airfield. Only Captain Iudin's MiG remained in the air, and things would have been hard for him in the midst of the swarming, firing Sabres had an approaching storm front not offered him sanctuary. Entering the storm, Iudin shook off his pursuers, and having popped out of the cumulonimbus cloud in a different place, he came in for a landing back at base. However, on the approach to the runway a new problem arose: his landing gear wouldn't lower; apparently the hydraulics system had been damaged. Iudin made a couple of sharp porpoise maneuvers, and finally shook the landing gear free. On top of everything else, after touching down the aircraft began to veer off the runway – it turned out that the tires had been shot through. But again Iudin was lucky: the passing tropical downpour had soaked the ground and the aircraft, slipping off the side of the runway, quickly bogged down in the mud. The ground crew members that came running up counted 27 bullet holes in the fuselage and wings of Iudin's MiG, but in a short period of time they fully repaired the aircraft.

At this point in the day, the correlation of victories and losses in the 64th IAK was 1:1, that is, two enemy aircraft had been shot down and two of our own MiGs had been destroyed. However, the trouble for our pilots didn't end here. At the end of the day, eight MiGs of the 878th IAP's 3rd Squadron under the command of Hero of the Soviet Union V.V. Egorov were scrambled in response to an alarm in order to cover the base. The weather was bad, a thunderstorm was approaching, and low heavy clouds were suspended over the airfield. However, eight Sabres were already loitering in the vicinity of the airbase, and they immediately went on the attack against Egorov's squadron. Egorov made a tactical blunder and instead of evading the Sabre attack and clawing for altitude, he led the group into a dive to escape it, which only worsened their situation. Senior Lieutenant N.M. Zameskin's element was bringing up the rear, and it was the first to come under Sabre fire, but it was rescued by the fact that the enemy opened fire from excessive range and the tracers arced well below the targets. Zameskin didn't hang around for the opponent to close the range, and leaving the formation, he went into a climb. The eight-ship formation of Sabres followed him, and it so happened that he had diverted the eight F-86s away from the rest of the 3rd Squadron group, which allowed the rest of the pilots to escape. Clouds rescued Zameskin's element; it plunged into them, but it turned out that these were storm clouds, and the pilots wound up caught in the turbulence. With great difficulty, and with both the aircraft and the pilots' nerves badly shaken, they separately tore away from the grip of the thunderstorm and landed at the Dapu airbase on the last drops of fuel in their tanks. When returning to Dapu, Egorov's six-ship formation also entered the violent thunderstorm, and not everyone was able to escape it. The deputy political squadron commander Senior Lieutenant V.K. Vasil'ev ran out of fuel and he decided to eject, but his cockpit canopy was jammed, so having flipped the MiG onto its back, he tried to kick it away with his feet. However, since the catapult mechanism had already been activated, it immediately shot him out of the cockpit, and he injured his spine and wound up in a hospital. Flight commander Senior Lieutenant N.V. Barannikov more successfully ejected after running out of fuel, and he came down safely on Chinese territory.

A tragedy occurred in the vicinity of the Miaogou airfield itself, where clouds draped the airfield and the ceiling was just 300 meters. When approaching the base, in the clouds Senior Lieutenant Chumachenko (the hero of the preceding day) didn't have time to avoid a hill that unexpectedly loomed in front of him in the low clouds and he crashed into it. His wingman Senior Lieutenant M. Goncharov somehow avoided the hill and set his plane down on the runway, but his speed was too great and he wasn't able to stop before leaving the end of the landing strip. His MiG struck an earthen barrier and flipped over. The pilot survived, but injured his spinal column and he also wound up in a hospital.

Thus, in total four of the 878th IAP's MiGs crashed in the difficult meteorological conditions, one pilot was killed, and two pilots received spinal column injuries and took no further part in combat. In view of this, the 64th IAK's total losses on 15 September 1952 amounted to eight aircraft (together with the losses of the "sailors" of the 578th IAP) and two pilots, though to be sure, half of these losses were not from enemy action.

The Americans claimed that on 15 September the pilots of the 4th and 51st FIW shot down eight MiG-15s, half of which thus belonged to the 64th IAK, so the other half were from aviation regiments of the UAA. Pilots of the 4th FIW bagged six of the enemy aircraft, while the other two went to pilots of the 51st FIW's 25th FIS. The Americans acknowledged the loss of three of their Sabres on this day: two F-86Es of the 4th FIW and one F-86E of the 51st FIW were shot down. One F-86E (No.50-0688) from the 335th FIS was damaged, and its pilot Lieutenant Joe A. Logan, Risner's wingman on this mission, with Risner's assistance reached Cho-do Island and ejected, but drowned when he was unable to free himself from his entangling parachute lines. Another F-86E (No.50-0667) from the 336th FIS was shot down, but its pilot 1st Lieutenant Arthur J. Cuddy was more fortunate – he bailed out and was picked up by an SA-16 rescue aircraft. The third F-86E (No.50-0641), flown by 1st Lieutenant Arthur E. Johnson of the 16th

FIS, crash landed back at its base, killing its pilot. This was likely the F-86 that Captain V.A. Marenich of the 726th IAP damaged. The two other Sabres were shot down by Senior Lieutenant V.M. Kutovoi of the same 726th IAP and Major F.G. Afanas'ev of the 147th GIAP. One F-84E of the 49th FBW's 8th FBS was also lost; its pilot became a prisoner of war. Most likely, he was downed by Chinese MiGs of the UAA.

The day of 16 September 1952 was noteworthy for the fact that pilots of the 32nd IAD, who were operating in the second echelon from the Mukden airfields, finally opened their combat score. There was yet another raid by enemy fighter-bombers of the Fifth Air Force in the Singisiu – Changseong area and primarily pilots of the 216th IAD were scrambled to repulse it. Pilots of the 518th IAP and 676th IAP flew two combat missions that resulted in fighting, while pilots of the 878th IAP conducted three group sorties. In dogfights with the forward screen of Sabres, pilots of the 676th IAP shot down two F-86s, while those of the 518th IAP added another Sabre to the day's total. The deputy political commander of the 676th IAP Captain Grigorii Mikhailovich Pivovarenko shot down one of the Sabres, and here is how he describes this victory:

> On 16 September, paired with my wingman Senior Lieutenant Matveev Sapegin, in the course of one dogfight I heard a voice from the IAK command post: "Whoever is in the air, help a wounded pilot, who has enemy on his tail." I transmitted: "Swan-21 (my call sign), understood" – and went to meet the enemy. We were red-lining our MiGs, flying at more than 1,000 km/hour at an altitude of 8,000 meters and we passed one of our MiG-15s that was being chased by two Sabres. I went into a split-S and with an unbelievable effort (we didn't have pressurized G-suits back then), I pulled my aircraft out of the dive, climbed a little and got in behind the pursuing Sabre pair. I demolished the lead F-86 from close range with fire from all three cannons, while Matvei Sapegin damaged the wingman's Sabre. Thus we rescued the wounded pilot and added victories to our score.

Only G.M. Pivovarenko received credit for a victory. In this combat the 676th IAP lost one MiG, but its pilot Senior Lieutenant V.N. Pozniakov jettisoned from his stricken aircraft at high speed, as a result of which he broke his legs. Senior Lieutenant Gubenko's MiG was also damaged, but he safely landed back at base.

On this same day the pilots of the 32nd IAD took off several times to cover the forward airfields of the 64th IAK. Groups of MiGs from the 224th IAP and 535th IAP took shifts covering Andong, Dapu and Miaogou, while the 913th IAP remained in reserve. The pilots of the 32nd IAD had several clashes with Sabres in the areas of the Andong and Dapu airbases and opened their combat score in the skies of Korea.

The 224th IAP's 2nd Squadron commander Major P.I. Karataev shot down the first enemy aircraft, an F-86E, over Andong. Karataev and his wingman deputy political squadron commander Captain E. Kudriashov attacked a group of Sabres, and right away Karataev broke one F-86E's fuselage in two with a long burst. Immediately Karataev and Kudriashov themselves came under attack. Their MiGs received damage. Kudriashov, tied up in combat, lost sight of Karataev. Each pilot ended the difficult combat alone. Kudriashov's aircraft had less damage, and this allowed him to escape out from under fire. However, Karataev's lost power, and his air brakes got jammed in the extended position. The machine-gun bullets created burrs as they punched through the metal skin, which restricted the movement of the rudder. In effect, his MiG had become a poorly handling glider and had become a target sleeve for the enemy, and the Sabre element gave the target everything they had. Karataev had every right to eject, but he didn't do so. He explained later, "It was flying. It wasn't falling. Why bail out? True, bullets were rattling against the armor plate behind my head, but they weren't penetrating."

The Americans, having expended all their ammunition, pulled up alongside Karataev. The major could even see the earphones on the enemies' helmets, which resembled motorcycle helmets. One gave a wave with a gloved hand and then they flew away. Karataev turned his riddled MiG for home. His MiG had 119 bullet holes in it. The rear fuel tank had exploded. Half of the engine's compressor blades had been mangled, while 16 more had been simply knocked out. The windshield glazing was smashed. One bullet penetrated the pilot's pistol holster. Karataev managed to nurse his flying wreck to the Dogushan Air Base, where a Chinese aviation division was stationed. There he made a wheels-down landing on the perforated steel matting of the runway. Here's how Petr Ivanovich Karataev discussed the episode:

> On this occasion we flew off in a formation of three eight-ship groups to intercept a large group of Sabres and Thunderjets, heading from the coastline toward the target we were protecting. We gained altitude and started to search the sky for the silhouettes of the American aircraft. When approaching the conditional "front line" – the border between China and Korea – my wingman and I encountered two Sabres. Judging from everything, they had been late to notice us. The Americans started to flee, but my wingman and I went into a dive after them. We caught the Sabres, and when the distance between us had closed, I poured fire into one of them from every cannon. The Sabre began to stream smoke and began spinning toward the ground. I pulled out of the attack in the style of Kozhedub – in a chandelle. That's when I came under fire from four Sabres, which had been flying echeloned above me. As a result my MiG received more than a hundred bullet holes, but it continued to respond to the controls, and I made a safe landing on the nearest airfield.

The MiG looked like a sieve, but the pilot climbed out of the cockpit unharmed, though one bullet had punched through his holster and had become lodge in his pistol grip. The aircraft itself was brought back to Mukden, where it spent the next 16 days undergoing repairs and had almost everything replaced. All that was left of the old MiG was its side number 228 and its nose.

In a different action on this day, pilots of the naval 535th IAP's 2nd Squadron did well, downing another F-86, thereby recording the regiment's first victory and the second one of the division. This was deputy squadron commander Captain V.A. Utkin's accomplishment. Captain Utkin's wingman, Senior Lieutenant Ivan Aleksandrovich Dovgii, had the following to say about this victory:

> Viktor called out, "I'm attacking." I saw out in front of us aircraft with yellow bands on their wings. I also saw the flames from the cannons of the leader's MiG. The Sabre burst into flames; the target disappeared in a dense ball of fire. This ball of flames seemingly splashed against a hillside. Even though this had been a foe, I was unsettled by the sight.

Unfortunately, the regiment also suffered its first loss in this action. The commander of the 2nd Squadron Captain I.K. Lebedev-Kosov was hit, but he ejected from his stricken aircraft and wound up in a hospital with a damaged spinal column.

As a result, on 16 September 1952 the 64th IAK claimed five F-86s, against the loss of just two of its MiGs. The Americans claim that their pilots downed five MiGs in return, two by pilots of the 51st FIW's 39th FIS and three by pilots of the 4th FIW. The Americans also maintain that in the dogfights on 16 September, they just lost one F-86F (No.51-2909) of the 335th FIS, the pilot of which Captain Troy G. Cope was killed.

Pilots of the 216th IAD stood out in the fighting on 17 September, engaging in several clashes with Sabres in which Captain Iu.A. Varkov shot down one and another three F-86s were damaged. These pilots of the 676th IAP, which had taken off as an eight-ship formation, engaged six F-86s between 0930 and 0950 – Varkov's victim fell in the Sonchon area, and two more Sabres were damaged in the area of Taegwan-dong. However, the American side again declares that it had no losses in the 4th and 51st FIW on this day.

On 18 September, the deputy commander of the 518th IAP Captain M.I. Mikhin again distinguished himself, claiming to have downed one F-86. However, it is more likely that Mikhin on this mission downed a Thunderjet, not a Sabre – this was F-84E No.51-1157 of the 474th FBW's 430th FBS, the pilot of which 1st Lieutenant Calvin E. Hodel was killed. However, most importantly, over these two days of September 1952, the 64th IAK didn't lose a single MiG-15.

Bitter air battles flared up over MiG Alley starting on 21 September. On this date a large group of enemy fighter-bombers conducted a strike against a chemical plant on the Yalu River. Pilots of the 133rd IAD and 216th IAD took part in repelling it. One eight-ship formation of MiGs from the 676th IAP's 1st Squadron and two eight-ship formations from the 518th IAP tied up the 30 Sabres of the forward screen in combat, while pilots of the 133rd IAD's 147th GIAP and 415th IAP broke through to the groups of Thunderjets.

The former of the 147th GIAP's 3rd Squadron Captain Nikolai Ivanovich Shkodin had this to say about the ensuing air battle:

> The 415th IAP departed first in response to an alarm to repel the raid; a little while later my regiment followed it into the air, and I saw F-84s that were bombing a chemical factory, while off to one side a fierce action was going on. My regiment hurried to assist the 415th IAP and soon I was attacking a group of "Crosses" at low altitude. At first I attacked two F-84s as they were pulling out of their bombing run and successfully latched onto their tails, but then I saw a pair of F-84s pursuing a lone MiG-15 and firing at it from all their machine-gun barrels. I abandoned my target and hastened to bail the comrade out of the predicament into which he'd fallen. Closing on the "Crosses" that were distracted by their attack, I picked off one of them and it fell to the earth. I learned that I had rescued a squadron deputy political commander of the 415th IAP, Captain E.I. Polivaiko.

In this combat, pilots of Captain Dmitrii Voroshilov's 1st Squadron also stood out by shooting down three Thunderjets, one of which was claimed by D.M. Voroshilov himself, while his wingman Senior Lieutenant Ivan Shinaev sent two more down in flames. True,

Ivan Ivanovich Shinaev himself didn't return from this sortie; he was caught by a pair of Sabres and shot down. As a result, the pilots of the 147th GIAP in this action shot down four F-84s, losing in return only one aircraft and its pilot I.I. Shinaev. A pilot of this same squadron Senior Lieutenant G.M. Krempel' shot down a Sabre, while pilots of the 415th IAP added another destroyed Sabre to the five aircraft downed by the 147th GIAP.

After this clash, another one flared up in the vicinity of the Dapu airfield, which was being blockaded by a detachment of Sabres; this one involved pilots of the 676th IAP's 1st and 3rd Squadrons, as well as eight MiGs of the 878th IAP. In this dogfight over the airbase, the MiG piloted by Senior Lieutenant V.F. Lekomtsev of the 878th IAP was damaged, and he had to make a belly landing in the vicinity of the base; the aircraft was beyond repair, but the pilot was unharmed. Another MiG-15 of the 676th IAP's 3rd Squadron was shot down, and its pilot flight commander Captain Fedor Andreevich Bodnia was killed. Most likely, Captain Robinson Risner of the 4th FIW's 336th FIS shot him down; Risner in fact claimed two MiGs on this day, thereby becoming an ace. In Risner's words, in this dogfight he encountered a Russian that he considered to be the best fighter pilot he had ever met. They locked in combat at 10,000 meters before the MiG went into a dive; the Sabre, which because of its heavier weight was superior to the MiG in this maneuver, caught the MiG in the dive and Risner hit it with a burst. The damaged MiG crossed the Yalu River and began descending toward a runway of one of the Chinese airfields, where it in fact crashed. Risner, as well as his wingman, watched all of this. One of the Sabres also went down; apparently, Senior Lieutenant P.A. Kozlov of the 676th IAP's 1st Squadron hit the F-86 with cannon fire, but he wasn't given credit for a victory, because the Sabre fell into the sea. Petr Aleksandrovich Kozlov states:

On 21 September, having sortied as usual with my wingman in the regiment's formation, I shot down an F-86, which fell in the coastal belt of Korea Bay, in a dogfight against 70 enemy fighters in the area of the hydro-electric dam on the Yalu River. In this action my aircraft received damage, and together with my partner I was forced to make a landing with 12 bullet holes in my aircraft at the reserve airfield at Anshan.

Ivan Ivanovich Tishchenko, a former member of Captain Fedor Andreevich Bodnia's ground crew, told the author how his pilot was killed:

On 21 September the regiment had a hard fight with enemy aircraft, and by the time that we had calculated that they would be running low on fuel, only some of the regiment's aircraft had returned to the base; many had to make a landing at reserve airfields. I had already lost hope of seeing my aircraft. Then approximately 40 minutes after take-off, I suddenly saw against the backdrop of the hills a low-flying aircraft with lowered landing gear, which was coming around for a landing. At this moment, two pairs of Sabres appeared from behind the hills. In this short interval of time, the airfield had no air cover. Bodnia was warned about the Sabres' appearance from the command post. Bodnia, having retracted his landing gear, began to maneuver while scrambling for altitude. A dogfight between one MiG and four Sabres began; we could hear the frequent firing of the Sabres' machine guns, as well as several salvoes from the MiG's cannons. Then suddenly another two Sabre pairs popped up over the hills, which were being followed by a group of MiGs. With the MiGs' appearance, the Sabres broke off the combat with Captain Bodnia's MiG and left the area of the base, pursued by the group of MiGs. Meanwhile Bodnia's aircraft went into a shallow dive and came to earth in a cornfield about 1.5 to 2 kilometers away. I drove with the emergency response team in a prime mover to the spot where Bodnia's aircraft had come down. Soon we spotted the MiG in the cornfield; it was sitting on its belly with retracted landing gear. The cockpit was empty and without its ejection seat. There were a few bullet holes in the rear part of the fuselage and in the tail assembly, the fuel tanks were empty, and all the ammunition had been fully expended. Having searched the area and without finding anything else belonging to the aircraft, we determined that the aircraft had landed on its own, without a pilot.

Having posted a security detail, we drove back to base. When arriving at the regiment's command post, we learned that the body of our pilot together with his ejection seat had been found on the outskirts of a Chinese village approximately 3 or 4 kilometers from the base. There the pilot's body was found without any signs of life; the pilot's hands were still in the position when a pilot ejects, his lifeless fingers still gripping the ejection levers. It was determined that the pilot had been killed when striking the ground; apparently he didn't have enough altitude for his parachute to deploy fully. No wounds from the Sabres' weapons were found on the pilot's body. Captain F.A. Bodnia was buried in the Russian cemetery in the city of Port Arthur.

According to regiment documents, the events unfolded in the following manner:

While returning to his base from a combat mission on 21.09.52, at 1346 Captain Bodnia was attacked by a pair of F-86s as he was coming in for a landing; he fought with them for 4 minutes. As a result of the unequal combat, Boldnia's aircraft was heavily damaged and the pilot ejected. Due to the low altitude the parachute didn't have time to open and Captain Bodnia was killed.

In this air battle, Captain Iu.A. Varkov's MiG was also damaged, receiving six bullet holes, but he safely returned to base. A pilot of the 32nd IAD's 913th IAP Lieutenant A.A. Aleksandrov shot down another Sabre "hunter" in the vicinity of Dapu – this was the regiment's first victory in the Korean sky.

The day's results were as follows: the 64th IAK's pilots shot down seven enemy aircraft and P.A. Kozlov probably destroyed another. Of these victories, six went to the score of pilots of the 133rd IAD (two F-86s and four F-84s). Their own losses amounted to three aircraft and two pilots, plus one MiG-15 was damaged. The Americans claimed to have downed five MiGs on this day, four by pilots of the 336th FIS and one by a pilot of the 25th FIS. The Americans place their own losses at one destroyed F-86A No.49-1227 from the 335th FIS and one F-84E No.50-1207 of the 8th FBS, the pilot of which was killed.

On 26 September 1952 there were dogfights in the Singisiu – Pihyon – Changseong region. They involved pilots of the 216th IAD on the Soviet side and their traditional adversaries of the 4th and 51st FIW on the American side. All three regiments of the 216th IAD flew two sorties on this day, both of which resulted in dogfights.

The first to depart early in the morning on 26 September was a pair of MiGs from the 878th IAP's 1st Squadron, led by the deputy squadron commander Captain V.M. Seliverstov, with the assignment to scout the weather and to use this as an opportunity to conduct a free hunt. This is what Vasilii Mitrofanovich Seliverstov himself recalls of this sortie:

> I took off on this day together with Vladimir Prilepov with the assignment to check the weather. Approaching the coastline, we unexpectedly spotted a Sabre element, which was flying along the coast, but below our pair. Taking advantage of our altitude superiority, I decided to attack the F-86 leader and pushed my MiG over into a dive. Having closed with it, I fired at the lead Sabre from a range of 400 meters and saw shell hits and their explosions on the Sabre. The American began smoking and turned out to sea, where we were forbidden to fly, and we returned home. Later confirmation of the victory arrived, since we had intercepted enemy radio traffic about the loss of a Sabre.

On the second sortie to the Singisiu – Pihyon area, pilots of the 878th IAP's 1st Squadron had a dogfight with six F-86s, in which Senior Lieutenant S.N. Skorov shot down one Sabre, but the Americans in turn downed the young pilot Senior Lieutenant Aleksandr Grigor'evich Orlov, who went down together with his MiG. After this clash the squadron landed at the Anshan airfield, because their own base at Miaogou was being blockaded by Sabres.

Pilots of the 518th IAP also flew two combat missions on 26 September, on one of which flight commander Senior Lieutenant Fedor Pavlovich Fedotov of the 3rd Squadron shot down his first enemy aircraft. This is how it happened, in the words of Fedotov himself:

> During a regimental sortie, we were flying as a squadron southward over North Korea. Suddenly the leader reversed course by 180°, back toward the airfield. I had seen Sabres that were heading toward us at approximately the same altitude, so I warned the commander over the radio that the course reversal was inadvisable. We were presenting our tail to the enemy. However, the commander didn't see them and didn't hear me. During the flight there was a lot of interference over the radio, and you couldn't catch anything anyone was saying over the radio waves, but the leader was obliged to take a look. Our two flights made the turn, but I instead broke formation and went into a climb and allowed the enemy to pass below me, before I instantly reversed course in a dive and dropped onto the tail of the Sabres. As the range closed from 200 to 150 meters, I gave a long burst to the Sabre on the extreme right, which began to disintegrate. From the surprise I even ducked my head in the cockpit as fragments of the enemy aircraft came hurtling toward me. The enemy's remaining aircraft reversed course in a dive and departed in the opposite direction.
>
> When I reported to the command post that I had downed a Sabre, they didn't believe me, since no one had seen anything, much less a combat, and that included

the commander as well. They didn't believe me or my wingman. We spent a long time examining the gun camera film. It was difficult to see what had happened – the extremely close range meant the target wasn't even in the frame much of the time, plus the strong vibration of the firing cannons made the image very jumpy. In the end, it took us three days to figure things out. I ordered the technicians to search my aircraft, since fragments of my target might have been sucked into my engine intake. I received approval from the command to partially dismantle the aircraft. We indeed found fragments that proved my victory. After this they sent a search team to the area where the plane fell, and it returned with repeat confirmation.

On this same day pilots of the 676th IAP also had two combats. On the morning mission in the 0915-0930 period, a flight commander of the 1st Squadron Captain Iu.A. Varkov damaged one Sabre in the Sonchon area.

As a result, the 64th IAK, or more accurately, the pilots of the 216th IAD downed three F-86s and damaged one more on 26 September 1952. Moreover, the damaged F-86 is debatable: although this Sabre was credited to Captain Varkov as "damaged", most likely it also didn't return to its base. Varkov's wingman Senior Lieutenant Sapegin wrote in his report that the "Sabre went straight in after Varkov's bursts", but since it fell into the sea, he only received credit for a "damaged" F-86.

The combat losses on 26 September amounted to one MiG-15 and the death of Aleksandr Grigor'evich Orlov of the 878th IAP, but the 64th IAK also had non-combat losses. During take-off on a combat mission, two MiGs of the 518th IAP accidentally collided in the air: both pilots Captain S.I. Khlopkov and his wingman Senior Lieutenant P. Basalaev safely abandoned their aircraft and soon returned to the unit. During a different sortie, another MiG-15 was lost when landing. Captain M.M. Iurin of the 133rd IAD's 726th IAP, flying MiG-15 No.527 badly misjudged his landing at Andong and after touching down didn't have enough of the runway left for braking. The pilot managed to leap out of the cockpit, and 2 or 3 seconds later the aircraft ran into an embankment and was demolished. Thus, on 26 September the 64th IAK lost just one aircraft in combat, but three due to non-combat losses; however, fortunately none of these pilots was killed.

The Americans claimed that on 26 September they destroyed four MiG-15s in air battles, two of which were achieved on one combat mission by 1st Lieutenant Cecil G. Foster of the 51st FIW's 25th FIS (possibly he received credit for the two MiGs of the 518th IAP that collided in the air), while the pair of Lieutenant Colonel Theon E. Markham and 2nd Lieutenant Glenn A. Carus possibly shot down Orlov. According to American records, pilots of the 334th FIS downed another MiG. However, the Americans make no comments whatsoever regarding their own losses, insisting that on this day they didn't lose any Sabres. In that case, how did the 216th IAD's search teams come up with those pieces of wreckage from a downed F-86 that they presented?

The 216th IAD continued its successful string of air battles on 28 September in the Singisiu – Pihyon and Taechon – Anju areas. Pilots of the 878th IAP managed to down four F-86s in two dogfights. The victories were scored by Captain N.M. Zameskin and Senior Lieutenant V.F. Korzh of the 3rd Squadron, as well as by 1st Squadron flight commander Captain Iu.V. Nikolaev and the regiment commander himself, Lieutenant Colonel S.D. Dronov. The regiment had no losses in these dogfights. Incidentally,

Nikolaev's gun camera footage plainly showed how his cannon fire blew the right wing off of his targeted Sabre.

Pilots of the 676th IAP's 1st Squadron also did well. On the first morning combat mission, eight of its MiGs engaged eight F-86s in the area of Singisiu in the period between 0910 and 0942. Here's what one of its participants, flight commander Captain Mikhail Petrovich Zhbanov, has to say about this dogfight:

> At an altitude of 9,000 meters, our eight-ship formation spotted 12 F-86s, which were lower than us and plainly hadn't seen us yet. Under the command of Major I.F. Gnezdilov, we plunged into their combat formation and scattered it. One of the elements presented its tail to me at a favorable angle for opening fire. I and my flight took advantage of this and attacked them from close range. As the results of the flight's attack, the leader of my second element Captain V.I. Belousov and I each shot down one Sabre in one pass.

The other flight commander on the mission, Captain Iu.A. Varkov, shot down another Sabre in this battle, which fell into the sea not far from Tetsuzan. This was his third victory in this war. Belousov and Zhbanov damaged two F-86s in an area 10-15 kilometers away from Singisiu; later confirmation arrived that they had both fallen in the indicated region. The squadron had no losses in this action.

True, our Senior Lieutenant I.V. Kotchenko of the 415th IAP was shot down on this day, but he safely escaped his stricken MiG using his ejection seat. This was the 64th IAK's only loss on this day. On 28 September, the Sabre pilots as always recouped their losses at the expense of the less experienced Chinese pilots, shooting down three of their MiGs. However, the Sabres didn't feel themselves at such ease in the area of our airfields, since pilots of the 32nd IAD, who'd been given the task of covering the 64th IAK's three forward airfields, were now on the hunt for them. One of the Sabre "hunters" was damaged by the deputy commander of the 535th IAP Lieutenant Colonel P.S. Akimov.

The American command acknowledged the loss of just one Sabre on this day, F-86F No.51-2911 of the 335th FIS. The Sabre was hit, but its Marine pilot, Major Alexander "Rocky" J. Gillis, who was on temporary assignment with the 4th FIW, successfully bailed out over the Yellow Sea and was picked up by a search and rescue helicopter. One F-84E from the 474th FBW and one F-80C of the 49th FBW were also lost on this day, the pilots of which were both killed. Likely, they were shot down by UAA pilots.

The last air battles of the month took place on 29 September. During dogfights (there were two of them on this day) in the area of Changseong, Singisiu, Pihyon and Anju, the 518th IAP's pilots bagged two Sabres and damaged another. The 1st Squadron deputy commander Captain M.I. Mikhin, who became an ace in the September 1952 fighting, again distinguished himself by downing one F-86 and damaging another on 29 September. This was his eighth victory in the skies of Korea. The regiment had no losses on this day.

A combat sortie by the naval pilots of the Pacific Ocean Fleet's 578th IAP on 29 September was unsuccessful. Sabres of the 51st FIW pounced on their group and shot down two of the MiGs. The regiment suffered the first loss of a comrade when Senior Lieutenant Ivan Aleksandrovich Meshcheriakov went down together with his MiG. The second pilot Senior Lieutenant V.A. Chervony managed to bail out. They were shot down by Lieutenant Colonel Albert S. Kelly, who in the summer of 1952 commanded the 51st FIG but was on this mission flying with its 25th Squadron, and 1st Lieutenant Joseph R. Butler of its 39th FIS. However, the 39th Fighter Squadron also lost its F-86E No.50-0626, the pilot of which 1st Lieutenant Thomas F. Casserly was killed in his cockpit after his Sabre came down 1,000 feet short of the runway at Suwon.

The results of the September fighting, according to the archival records of the 64th IAK's headquarters, were as follows: 71 enemy aircraft were shot down and 18 were damaged, including 52 destroyed and 17 damaged F-86s (these include the unconfirmed victories by Kozlov of the 676th IAP and Andriushchenko of the 578th IAP), 18 destroyed F-84s, and one B-29 destroyed plus one B-29 damaged (both the result of night combats). Of this total number, pilots of the 216th IAD claimed 38 enemy aircraft destroyed and 13 damaged; the 133rd IAD recorded 30 enemy aircraft destroyed and four damaged; and the recently arrived 32nd IAD shot down three enemy aircraft and damaged another. The losses were also heavy, amounting to 36 MiG-15s and 12 pilots, as well as six aircraft and one pilot lost in non-combat incidents. The Americans claimed that over the month of September, the pilots of the 4th and 51st FIW shot down 63 MiGs, while losing only nine F-86s in combat, plus another three F-86s due to non-combat reasons.

Half of these 63 MiG-15s that were destroyed in September belonged to units of the UAA. It is also known that in September 1952 there were several air clashes over the Yellow Sea involving Chinese pilots of the UAA and US Navy and US Marine Corps carrier aircraft. For example, on 7 September 1952, Corsairs from the aircraft carrier USS *Sicily* encountered MiGs over Cho-do Island, but this occasion passed without any combat losses on either side. Two days later on 9 September, two flights of VMF-312 Corsairs fought off 16 MiG-15s in the area of Hungnam, a port on the coast of the Sea of Japan. On the following day of 10 September, a pair of F4U-4B Corsairs of VMF-312, consisting of the leader Captain Jesse G. Folmar and his wingman 1st Lieutenant Walter E. Daniels were attacked by a pair of MiGs over the Taedong River. The Corsairs took the dogfight into a maneuvering fight at lower altitudes and counterattacked. Captain Folmar managed to catch one MiG-15 in his gun sights and shot it down. As the MiG was hitting the water, five more MiGs arrived on the scene and Folmar's Sabre was badly damaged by MiG fire in the left wing. He opted to bail out and was quickly picked up by a rescue plane. This was the second piston-engine carrier aircraft victory over a jet MiG-15.

On one of the days of September, a MiG squadron under the command of Teng Du Ho took off to cover coastal areas of North Korea and soon intercepted carrier bombers covered by fighters (possibly British Sea Furies and Fireflies). According to North Korean records, in this action squadron commander Teng shot down one carrier bomber, while his wingmen downed an enemy fighter that was trying to cause him to break off his attack. The remaining enemy aircraft retreated out to sea.

In September Chinese pilots responded to six massive raids against the hydro-electric station on the Yalu River at Lagushao and the bridge across the Yalu there. The Chinese, operating against "heavy" bombers (apparently referring to B-26s or B-29s), regularly sent groups of four to eight MiGs from the 3rd IAD, 12th IAD, 17th IAD and 18th IAD to areas south of Pyongyang, where they would attack the American aircraft and scatter them. In the process, they claim to have destroyed 30 aircraft and damaged six more. Through these combat operations they were disrupting US air strikes north of the

Chongchon River, thereby facilitating rail traffic along the two major railroad routes in the northern part of Korea.

WINGTIP TO WINGTIP: THE TENACIOUS AUTUMN BATTLES

The beginning of October 1952 was not as intense. Although both sides continued flying missions into MiG Alley, their encounters were rare and didn't always end in combat. Both sides were resting after the fierce September clashes and not showing much combat activity.

In October 1952 the USAF focused on supporting a two-pronged offensive against CPV positions in the Shangganglin (Sanggam-ryong) area, the so-called Triangle Hill Complex. UN pilots actively attacked supply lines leading into the area and intensified their efforts to interdict traffic across the Chongchon and Taedong Rivers. However, by this time the PLAAF had been significantly strengthened; by May 1952 seven more aviation divisions had been formed, including three fighter divisions, and two separate reconnaissance regiments. Most of the fighter aviation divisions had now been re-equipped with the MiG-15bis with its improved flight characteristics, which gave the Chinese pilots a greater capability to combat the newer F-86s on more even terms.

The first collisions in the air in the month of October between the adversaries took place on 2 October in the area of the villages Unsan, Kiojo and Singisiu. The pilots of the 878th IAP became involved in a dogfight during the second combat mission of this day with a group of F-86s from the 51st FIW and lost one MiG-15 in it. Its pilot Senior Lieutenant Sandalov bailed out. He was shot down by 1st Lieutenant Francis A. Humphreys of the 39th FIS.

However, the Soviet pilots on this day bagged a by now rare prey – they shot down a Meteor Mk.8 fighter-bomber of the RAAF 77 Squadron. A flight commander in the 518th IAP's 3rd Squadron Senior Lieutenant F.P. Fedotov claimed the victory. He describes what happened:

> Whenever our aircraft were returning to base from a combat mission, my flight was sometimes scrambled on a free hunt. On one such sortie on 2 October, when we now had no other MiGs in the air, I headed to the south with my flight in the hope of encountering the enemy, which was also hunting for us. Suddenly over the radio I heard the voice of the corps commander General G.A. Lobov, who requested that I identify myself and then reported: "You have withdrawing Meteors out in front of you, under heavy cover. Try to chase them down." I increased my lookout and soon caught sight of four Meteors in our front and below us, and above them – up to 30 Sabres. "Well, I think I'm in for it" – I had to make a quick decision while they still hadn't spotted me.
>
> Usually, US fighters provided the Meteors with heavy cover, if they were in the operational range of our MiGs. I couldn't plunge into an attack, lest I overshoot them. I decided I had to shed altitude while remaining within firing range. I performed a "wild maneuver" – I abruptly tipped my MiG onto its left wing and went into a vertical dive with a simultaneous 90° turn. I had to exert unbelievable effort, to the point of blacking out, with the use of the elevator trim tab. However, I wound up below the Meteors at a range of 400-600 meters. It was easier for me to

attack the aircraft on the right of the formation from below. I immediately gave it a long burst; the enemy aircraft tumbled over its left wing onto its back and began to fall. The remaining three Meteors went into a spiral to the left. The swarm of Sabres above me stirred. I hadn't thought about how I'd get away, but now I needed to do it. I decided to break through the Sabre formations with a chandelle to the left and simultaneously set a course back to my base. The Sabres didn't respond. I think that this was a reckless attack on my part. I think the Sabre commander was hesitant to attack and then pursue us, simply because he didn't believe that there was just one flight of MiGs around, and was afraid that other groups of MiGs would then launch an attack against them.

We had already carried out the maneuver to break off combat at maximum speed (during the mission we didn't use the throttle at all – we were at full throttle from take-off to landing) and put a lot of distance between us and the Sabres. That's when General Lobov confirmed over the radio that the enemy aircraft had been shot down and congratulated me and the flight's pilots for the victory.

Fedotov had shot down Meteor No.A77-496, being flown by an English pilot-instructor Oliver Cruikshank, who was on temporary duty with 77 Squadron.

Similar clashes between small groups of fighters took place on the next day as well, in the same area of Singisiu, Pihyon and Kiojo. Pilots of the 216th IAD took part in them – all three regiments took off in separate squadron-sized groups and conducted searches for enemy aircraft. Thusly, pilots of the 518th IAP and 676th IAP each conducted one combat sortie, and on each one engaged small groups of F-86s. In contrast pilots of the 878th IAP each flew two or three sorties and had two dogfights, though neither one ended with any results. In all of these skirmishes during the day, only the 676th IAP pilot Senior Lieutenant M.G. Sapegin managed to down one Sabre, but in return F-86s managed to damage Senior Lieutenant Boris Opredelenov's MiG, and he had to jettison from his stricken aircraft. He soon returned safely to his unit.

On this same day, the 32nd IAD's 535th IAP was activated to cover the hydro-electric dam in the Singisiu area and became involved in two dogfights with Sabres over the reservoir. Eight fighters from the 2nd Squadron led by Captain V.T. Smorgunov flew the first mission. In the area of the hydro-electric station they were unexpectedly jumped by Sabres of the 51st FIW's 25th FIS, which broke up the MiGs' formation. The Sabres immediately exploited this by separating wingman Lieutenant Boris Vasil'evich Fedorov from his leader, flight commander Senior Lieutenant I.A. Dogvy, and caught him in a pincer. The pilot called for help over the radio, but no one was able to come to his assistance, since they themselves were in a predicament. Left without help, Fedorov was shot down by a Sabre element consisting of 1st Lieutenants Craig R. Canady and Asa S. Whitehead. Our pilot successfully ejected, but came down in the reservoir and drowned before help could reach him.

On a later mission on this day, it was now the Sabres' turn to be caught in a difficult situation in the area of the dam. Fedor Il'ich Masleev, a participant on this mission, had this to say about it:

We were covering the dam. Wrapping up our mission and preparing to head home, my wingman Il'ia Sokolov and I spotted a solitary F-86, heading in the direction of the bay, about 500 meters in front of us and at the same altitude. I immediately went on the attack, pulled to within 200-300 meters of it, gave it a burst and saw the flashes of my shells' explosions on it. The Sabre rolled over to the left, after which I saw a white, and then a black plume of smoke trailing from it, and it headed downward. I reported over the radio about my victory and safely returned to my base at Mukden together with my wingman. This action occurred a bit to the northwest of Singisiu.

In his flight book, F.I. Masleev jotted down: "03.10.52 – a combat sortie to cover the hydro-electrical complex. With my pair, had a dogfight with F-86 aircraft. I personally shot down one F-86. Flight duration: 0 hrs, 48 mins. Altitude 10,000 meters." However, in all likelihood his victim fell either in the reservoir or the bay, since there was no material evidence to back up his claim. The regiment accordingly recorded this F-86 as "damaged".

Thus, on 3 October the IAK's pilots shot down one and damaged another F-86, while losing two aircraft and one pilot. The Americans claim to have shot down three MiG-15s on this day. Major Frederick Blesse downed one of the three MiGs, most likely Opredelenov's, but Blesse's Sabre also came under an attack from Senior Lieutenant Matvei Sapegin's MiG and took serious damage. He nursed his crippled F-86E No.51-2821 out to the bay, where he ejected from it. He was soon picked up by a search and rescue team.

Clashes in the air continued almost daily up until 11 October, but neither side showed much aggressiveness, since the majority of them ended with no results. In the course of this less intense week, the 64th IAK's pilots shot down only six F-86s and damaged another five Sabres. Pilots of the 216th IAD distinguished themselves: the 518th IAP's pilots shot down four of the Sabres and damaged three, without any losses in return. The deputy commander of the regiment's 2nd Squadron Senior Lieutenant V.A. Smirnov did particularly well in a dogfight on 6 October, shooting down two Sabres in one action, when a Sabre element appeared in front of him as he was breaking off combat. He pulled up right behind the wingman and shot him down, and then the leader flying next to him. The gun camera footage captured the Sabre at a range of just 30 meters. For this action Smirnov was awarded the Order of the Red Banner. Another participant in this dogfight was Nikolai Zakharovich Brazhenko, who at the time was the 518th IAP's 2nd Squadron deputy commander for political affairs. Here's what he has to say about it:

Once (6 October 1952), I was flying a combat mission as part of the 1st Squadron, which was being led by Major Molchanov. Senior Lieutenant Vladimir Smirnov's element was flying behind us, followed by other of the squadron's aircraft. We were climbing. At the next moment, to the right and above us I saw a glint of reflected sunlight. Over the radio I reported, "Probable enemy aircraft above us and to the right." After this I noticed two enemy fighters trying to get in behind us. The stress was rising, because the enemy was really moving and it was disadvantageous for me to go into a dive. The enemy plane was heavier, so the MiG-15 was inferior to the adversary in a dive.

Suddenly I heard a thump against my ship; it was enemy machine-gun fire. I informed Smirnov about this over the radio. Only he could drive away the enemy attack. Thoughts of my five-year-old daughter Valia, my wife Shura, my Mama and other relatives flashed through my head. I thought that my end was near.

At this time, firing at my aircraft ceased. My MiG's engine lost power. I began to lag behind my leader, about which I notified him over the radio. After this we began to descend. I had a sense that if I attempted to throttle back, my engine would die. I cut the throttle only after my plane touched down. The aircraft started rolling out and I cut the throttle, after which the engine seized up. I rolled off the end of the runway due to inertia. I called for assistance over the radio and received a tow back to a hardstand. It turned out that the engine's turbine had been damaged – one-third of the engine's compressor blades had been shot away.

Thanks to my timely detection of the enemy, pilot Vladimir Smirnov shot down two enemy Sabres, which were trying to shoot down my aircraft; so Smirnov bailed me out, for which I am eternally grateful to him!

On this day, a pilot of the 32nd IAD's 535th IAP Captain K.I. Sema also claimed to have shot down one F-86 in the area of the hydro-electric station, but he received no credit for it because of the long-range at which he fired at it.

Over this period, pilots of the 878th IAP shot down two F-86s and damaged two more. Over the week of low-intensity fighting, the 64th IAK lost only two aircraft and one pilot: on 4 October 1952 Captain Manuel Fernandez of the 334th FIS shot down Captain Kapralov of the Pacific Ocean Fleet's 578th IAP while the latter was coming in for a landing (the pilot safely ejected), and on 9 October Captain Carl Dittmer of the 335th FIS (who downed two MiGs on this day) shot down and killed Senior Lieutenant Aleksei Pavlovich Svichkar' of the 878th IAP in the vicinity of the Miaogou airfield. The Americans claimed that in the air battles of 4 and 9 October they bagged four MiG-15s, all by pilots of the 4th FIW. Over the week of combat the Americans admitted the loss of only one F-86E (No.52-2841) from the 334th FIS, the pilot of which 1st Lieutenant Myron E. Stouffer, Jr. was taken prisoner. He was Senior Lieutenant V.A. Smirnov's victim on 6 October. On 9 October, Captain V.G. Kazakov and Senior Lieutenant M.P. Kalitov of the 518th IAP according to their claim damaged two F-86s, but since the Americans acknowledge the loss of one of their F-84Es from the 474th FBW on this day, most likely the 518th IAP's pilots were dueling with Thunderjets in this action, not Sabres.

Pilots of the UAA also did well during this week of relatively light combat: on 4 October a flight of North Korean MiG-15 pilots under the command of Kang Jung Dok sortied to the area of the port of Hamhung on the Sea of Japan coastline, and there they intercepted six Corsair fighter-bombers covered by fighters. The pilots of this flight consisting of Hwan Su Song, Chong He Ham and Pak Chan Hung shot down five enemy aircraft and damaged two more, before returning to base without any losses. The flight commander Kang Jung Dok personally claimed two of the victories and damaged one more. The USNAF command recognizes the loss of only one of VF-884's F4U-4 Corsairs (No.80798) from MiG fire, the pilot of which Lieutenant Eugene F. Johnson was killed. True, on this same day it was noted that a carrier-based AD-1 Skyraider from VA-195 was also lost due to unknown causes and one can assume that this loss was the result of MiG action. In addition, on 7 October, the USNAF command acknowledged the loss of F4U-4 No.96770 from VA-193 due to MiG fire, the pilot of which was also killed, but it is most likely this Corsair had been lost in this same action on 4 October.

Capt. Manuel J. Fernandez Jr., of
the 34th Fighter Intercepter Wing,
became the 26th US jet ace of the
Korean War, February 18 1953.
(US Air Force)

We'll note that the pilots of the given North Korean flight were part of a regiment commanded by Shin Kang Dong. It was this regiment that Soviet pilots of the 28th IAD's 139th GIAP had trained to fly MiG-15s and prepared for combat back in 1951 in Chingdao.

On 11 October, several air clashes played out over the 64th IAK's main base, the Andong airfield complex. Already in the morning, the Americans began to arrive in the vicinity of the base from the direction of the bay in separate elements and flights at very low altitude (to avoid detection by our radar) and attempted to attack all of the MiGs that were taking off or coming in for a landing. The enemy shut down the airfield's operations.

In order to clear the airspace over the Andong complex, several groups of our fighters from the 224th IAP were scrambled from a Mukden airfield. The first to depart for the Andong area was the regiment's command flight led by the 224th IAP's deputy commander Hero of the Soviet Union Major K.V. Novoselov; his wingman on the mission was the regiment's chief of aerial gunnery services Major E.I. Goriunov, while the regiment navigator Captain F.D. Reutsky led the second element. Having arrived over Andong, K.V. Novoselov unexpectedly spotted a solitary Sabre below him, which had either become separated from its group, or was simply "bait" set out for our pilots.

Novoselov went on the attack against the loner, having shouted to his wingman Major Goriunov that he had seen an enemy aircraft and was attacking it. But Goriunov, apparently not hearing the order, didn't stick with his leader and remained with the rest of the flight. Unaware of this, Novoselov calmly continued his attack, and having closed to within firing range, shot down this Sabre, but just as Novoselov began to pull his MiG out of the attack, bullet tracers lashed his aircraft and it began to burn. Noveselov ejected from the burning fighter, but in the process fractured his elbow and lost consciousness.

He came down in his parachute on a steep, stony hillside and tumbled down the rocky slope to its very bottom. He came to a stop battered and maimed, with a multitude of injuries. North Korean soldiers found him in a woeful condition and took him to a hospital, where Novoselov spent the next two months, before being sent back to the Soviet Union for additional treatment.

The former deputy commander of the 224th IAP's 3rd Squadron Aleksandr Petrovich Anisimov recalls the mission on which Novoselov was injured:

> On the second encounter, he with his element attacked a pair of F-86s [sic.], but he failed to see a second pair of F-86s, which was above and behind the first pair. This Sabre element attacked Novoselov alone, since his wingman and Goriunov's element during the attack were widely separated from Novoselov and were in no position to help him, so Novoselov was shot down in this combat. Novoselov ejected, but as he was ejecting he broke his right elbow on the side of his aircraft and lost consciousness, and without regaining it, he came down on a very high, rocky hill, with a slope of approximately 70-75 degrees; he landed near its summit and tumbled over the rocks down to its very bottom. He was so battered by the rocks that he was black and blue all over.
>
> With D.V. Ermakov's approval, I drove to Andong from Mukden and visited him in the hospital on behalf of the personnel of the 3rd Squadron and of the entire regiment. He looked like he was crucified on the hospital bed – it is impossible to describe his condition. I'm not ashamed to admit it; even now I will say that we cried a bit together. Nevertheless, the doctors eventually put him back on his feet, but he still couldn't flex his right elbow.
>
> For this combat action he was credited with downing one enemy aircraft and awarded the Order of the Red Banner. They gave him a promotion to lieutenant colonel – and then discharged him. There's a sad story for you!

Immediately after K.V. Novoselov's flight took off, eight more fighters under the command of Major P.I. Karataev were urgently dispatched to the Andong area. One of its pilots, a former member of the 224th IAP Valerii Lazarevich Ryzhov, talks about this sortie:

> On 11 October we sortied from a Mukden airfield as a group of two flights. The 2nd Squadron commander Major P.I. Karataev led the first flight, while Captain V.G. Smorgunov, whose wingman was Senior Lieutenant S.A. Il'iashenko led the second flight. I was in the second element of Smorgunov's flight, flying as wingman to Senior Lieutenant Vasilii Rochikashvili. Soon our group received an order from the 64th IAK commander General G.A. Lobov himself to head to the Andong airfield in order to cover the base – groups of F-86s had appeared there, which were awaiting the return of our aircraft from a combat mission.
>
> Our group reversed course, went to full throttle and set off for the indicated area. During the turn the group leaders spotted a pair of F-86s approaching from the direction of the bay, which were looking for a suitable opportunity for an attack. Passing our group, they banked around to close on the tail-end element, Rochikashvili and me. Their attack was swift (they had passed us at a higher

altitude). I didn't notice them until they were already right on my tail. I didn't even have time to issue a warning that I was being attacked. I tried to throw off their aim, but bullets fired by an F-86 stitched my aircraft and it became uncontrollable. I had to abandon it.

My leader turned in the direction of the attack in order to repel it, but the Sabres were no longer interested in continuing the clash and broke off combat. At this time, it seems, another Sabre element came up and attacked Rochikashvili, who was now without cover, and damaged his MiG, wounding the pilot in the right shoulder. Rochikashvili also had to eject from his stricken aircraft.

Meanwhile, when ejecting I dislocated a shoulder and in addition came down in the Yalu River. I struggled to remain afloat for the next 15 minutes, until a Korean fishing boat picked me up. I met my leader Vasilii Rochikashvili in the hospital to where they took me, and also saw our badly injured deputy regiment commander Hero of the Soviet Union Major K.V. Novoselov. Why hadn't the other pilots of our group come to our aid? Well, because we'd received a strict order from the IAK command post to head to the vicinity of the Andong airfield urgently, and no one dared to disobey it.

In sum, over our Andong airbase as well as en route to it, Sabre "hunters" shot down three MiGs of the 224th IAP and escaped unpunished, which also left all three pilots with wounds and injuries.

Meanwhile, over Andong dogfights were continuing between MiGs and Sabres. Pilots of the 878th IAP participated in one of them. They'd also been scrambled from the Miaogou airfield in order to sweep the airspace over Andong clear of Sabre "hunters". First Captain N.M. Zameskin's element arrived in the vicinity of the Andong airfield, and he led his element toward one nearby "hunter". The combat with it took place directly over the IAK command post. Having spotted the target, Captain Zameskin held the upper hand. The opponent exerted all his skill in order to escape the dangerous situation he was in, but our pilots latched onto his tail and followed him through a cascade of head-spinning maneuvers, trying to line him up. For one instant Zameskin managed to catch him in his sights and gave him a short burst – the flashes of shell explosions were visible on it – and then smoke began to stream from underneath the Sabre. The American pilot ejected and came to earth in a hilly area. Soon an American rescue helicopter located him and picked him up.

On this same day of 11 October, 20 MiGs of the Pacific Ocean Fleet's 578th IAP also flew a combat mission; the regiment group was led by its commanding officer, Major V.T. Dobrov. However, once again the naval pilots demonstrated poor cohesion at high altitudes and speeds. The leading command flight became separated from the main group and was suddenly jumped by Sabres. The 1st Squadron commander Captain V.D. Andriushchenko left his eight-ship formation to rush to help the command flight, and with one brief salvo from his cannons shot down one Sabre. However one of our MiGs, emitting heavy smoke, was already falling together with the enemy aircraft. This was Lieutenant Ivan Ivanovich Postnikov's MiG, and he was killed in this action.

As a result of all the dogfights with Sabres on 11 October, the 64th IAK lost four aircraft and one pilot, plus three more pilots that were wounded. The IAK's pilots recorded two victories over F-86s. The Sabre shot down by Major K.V. Novoselov was

442   RED DEVILS OVER THE 38TH PARALLEL

not counted, since no wreckage from it was found; apparently, it had gone down over the bay.

The Americans claimed that on 11 October 1952, their pilots shot down six MiGs in aerial combat: three by pilots of the 335th FIS and three by pilots of the 51st FIW's 39th Squadron. The Americans also acknowledged the loss of one of their F-86Es (No.50-0679) from the 336th FIS, the pilot of which 2nd Lieutenant John E. Fagan bailed out and was picked up by a rescue helicopter – his Sabre was the one shot down by Captain Zameskin.

More intense were the dogfights with the enemy on 12 October, in which both of the 64th IAK's fighter divisions participated. Bitter combats with Sabres of the forward screen, which were covering the work of their fighter-bombers in the Anju area, flared up in MiG Alley that morning. A group of MiGs from the 216th IAD's 518th IAP were first to enter the fighting. A little later, a group of MiGs from the 133rd IAD arrived in the combat area as reinforcements.

As a result of this air battle, the 216th IAD's pilots shot down two F-86s (both of them going to pilots of the 878th IAP) and Captain N.Ia. Molchanov of the 518th IAP damaged one more. Pilots of the 133rd IAD claimed three more Sabres destroyed, of which two were shot down by pilots of the 726th IAP and one by pilots of the 147th GIAP. Even better, the 64th IAK's pilots had no losses. One of the victories on this day was achieved by Georgii Gerasimovich Iukhimenko, who at the time was a senior lieutenant and deputy political commander of the 726th IAP's 3rd Squadron. Here's how he described his victory:

> We were flying as a flight: Squadron commander M.D. Reshetnikov with his wingman Senior Lieutenant A.N. Zakharov, and I with Senior Lieutenant V.M. Mishchenko. There were many of our aircraft and Sabres in this dogfight. In the course of it, a Sabre element got behind Major Reshetnikov's lead pair and presented a mortal danger to his wingman Zakharov. With my element I immediately performed a maneuver, caught up with the Sabres that were attacking Zakharov, opened fire and shot down one of them.

In their turn the Americans claimed that pilots of the 51st FIW shot down four MiG-15s on this day, but most likely they all belonged to UAA regiments. However, the pilots of the UAA were gradually gaining experience. For example, on 12 October pilots of one of the UAA's fighter divisions attacked a flight of four piston-engine F-51D fighter-bombers from the SAAF's No. 2 "Cheetah" Squadron, which were conducting a reconnaissance between Samdong and Kowon. Four MiGs shot down 1st Lieutenant Trevor Fryer's Mustang – he bailed out but was captured by the North Koreans. One of the F-84Es of the 58th FBW was also lost, and it is fully possible that pilots of the UAA shot it down. However, the Americans categorically deny the loss of any of their F-86s on this day.

On the following day, 13 October, the Soviet pilots notched only one victory: the 676th IAP's navigator Major G.A. Bolotin, flying in a group of eight MiG-15s, at 1705 spotted a pair of F-86s and attacked it, shooting down one of them which crashed 15 kilometers southwest of Toko-ri. However, he then came under an attack by a different F-86 element and his aircraft was damaged, but he was able to make a safe landing back at his base in Mukden. Ground crew members counted five bullet holes in the MiG, the right aileron's control cable had been severed, and the pilot flew his MiG only with the assistance of the left aileron and rudder. His aircraft returned to service several days later. Although the Americans don't report the loss of one of their F-86s on this day, two days later they announced the loss of F-86E No.51-2798 of the 16th FIS; its pilot Lieutenant Colonel Carl W. Stewart bailed out near Cho-do Island and was rescued. The Americans record this as an "operational loss", but it can be assumed that this Sabre was in fact Major Bolotin's victim, since on 16 October the pilots of the USAF reported no combats with MiGs.

Major Bolotin also distinguished himself on the following day of 14 October. Early that morning at 0643, he flew off at the head of eight MiGs, and in the Sonchon area they had a clash with a flight of F-86s. In the course of the dogfight Major Bolotin got behind a pair of Sabres and shot down the wingman's F-86, while his own wingman Senior Lieutenant P.I. Prudnikov damaged the Sabre leader. With this the combat immediately ended and our pilots returned to base without any losses.

After the heated combats of 11-14 October, there was again a brief lull. Although both sides continued to fly combat missions, the two adversaries only rarely tangled with each other. In one of the clashes, which occurred on 17 October at 1152 in the Pyongyang area and involved eight MiGs and an F-86 flight, the 676th IAP's 3rd Squadron commander Captain M.F. Iudin shot down another Sabre. Likely this was F-86A No.49-1147 of the 336th FIS, which according to the American version of the events, was lost because the aircraft ran out of fuel and its pilot Nicholas Kotek had to make a dead-stick forced landing. However, most likely the cannons of Captain Iudin's MiG had damaged the fuel tanks of Kotek's Sabre, which is why he had to terminate his flight, but he fortunately survived unharmed.

Prior to the end of the month, the most serious combat clash between the two sides took place on 18 October. On this day eight MiG-15s of the 878th IAP's 1st Squadron, led by squadron commander Captain V.M. Selivestrov, had a dogfight with eight F-86s in the Kiojo area, in which the squadron's pilots claimed three F-86 kills without any losses in return.

True, the Americans claimed that 51st FIW pilots shot down two MiGs on this day, but they didn't belong to the 64th IAK. The Americans themselves acknowledged the loss of two of their F-86s on 18 October: the first was F-86F No.52-2778 from the 16th FIS, which caught fire after taking a burst of cannon fire from Captain G.N. Nikul'shin's MiG; making a forced landing, the aircraft crashed on North Korean territory and its pilot Captain Gabriel P. Bartholomew, although he survived the crash, was taken prisoner. Another F-86E from the same 16th FIS, bearing the Bureau Number 52-2878, was shot down by Senior Lieutenant S.N. Skorov.

Captain Nikul'shin's actions in this dogfight were particularly noteworthy. Sabres caught his aircraft and shot it up, shattering his cockpit canopy and wounding Nikul'shin in the face in the process. The bridge of Nikul'shin's nose was broken and blood began to fill his eyes, hindering his vision. Then suddenly the Sabres that had damaged his MiG appeared right in front of his fighter's nose. Reacting instantly, he opened fire from a range of 100 meters (on his gun camera footage, the Sabre fills the entire frame) and then swerved away, in order not to run into the enemy aircraft. Later, Nikul'shin safely landed at the Miaogou airfield despite his wounds and he was taken away to a hospital.

For this action G.N. Nikul'shin was awarded the Order of Lenin, but he never returned to the regiment. After recovering sufficiently in the hospital, he was sent back to the Soviet Union.

Between 12 October and the end of the month, the pilots of the 64th IAK conducted a total of seven air battles with Sabres in which they scored results, claiming a total of 11 F-86s destroyed. They were all "trophies" of the 216th IAD: credit for six of the F-86s went to pilots of the 676th IAP, three were shot down by pilots of the 878th IAP, and Captain V.G. Kazakov of the 518th IAP claimed two Sabres in a dogfight on 26 October. Their own losses over this period consisted of just two aircraft, neither of which was lost due to enemy action. The 878th IAP lost two MiGs in a mid-air collision on 24 October. Lieutenant P.N. Opryshko's MiG struck the cockpit of the aircraft of his wingman Senior Lieutenant V.F. Korzh below it, as a result of which Senior Lieutenant Vladimir Fedorovich Korzh was killed, while Senior Lieutenant Opryshko had to bail out. Two more MiGs were damaged in dogfights on 22 and 23 October. A former pilot of the 676th IAP's 1st Squadron Petr Aleksandrovich Kozlov recalls the mission on 22 October:

> On 22 October 1952, I flew as part of the 1st Squadron (my wingman didn't take off because of an engine malfunction). I linked up as a third with Iu. Varkov's element, which was forbidden by the command due to tactical considerations and the desire to ensure that no pilot was caught alone in combat. As we were climbing after take-off with full drop tanks, we ran into a group of up to 30 fighters that were covering a solitary RF-86, which was tasked with photographing ground targets along the Yalu River and the hydro-electrical station itself. This station, aluminum factories, as well as ground troop concentrations and military sites in the area of the capital of the PRNK Pyongyang – this is the list of targets that interested the opposing side, and where they focused their air strikes.
>
> Hurrying to jettison our drop tanks and being caught at a disadvantage, at an altitude of 7,000 meters we joined combat with this group of fighters, by which we disrupted their mission, because the reconnaissance Sabre went into a steep dive and headed back to the bay, while the rest of the group swept down on us, trying to destroy us. Although there were just seven of us, we put up fierce resistance, because each one of us faced a flight of Sabres. Having descended to almost hilltop level, we broke off combat, by which we saved ourselves, though it is true that we didn't down a single enemy aircraft.

In this combat Senior Lieutenant A.M. Antipov's MiG was damaged, receiving 12 bullet holes, but he safely landed back at base.

Another MiG of the 676th IAP was damaged the next day, on 23 October. On this day at 1315, a mixed group of eight of the regiment's crews, led by Hero of the Soviet Union deputy regiment commander I.M. Gorbunov was scrambled to intercept enemy aircraft in the Kiojo-Sonchon area. At 1325, two pairs of F-86s were spotted and Gorbunov attacked the lower F-86 element. While closing, Gorbunov himself was attacked by an F-86 element; he went into an abrupt dive and pulled out of it at 4,000 meters, where he was attacked again. An enemy burst that left 24 bullet holes in Gorbunov's MiG struck the aircraft, which jammed his rudder and severed the control cable to the right aileron. Gorbunov managed to nurse his nearly uncontrollable aircraft back to Mukden, where he safely touched down at 1402. The dogfight itself occurred in the region 15-25 kilometers southeast of Gisiu. In it, Senior Lieutenant V.P Altunin managed to shoot down one Sabre.

After 12 October the Americans achieved victories only over pilots of the UAA for the rest of the month, shooting down nine MiG-15s in aerial combat, of which six were shot down by pilots of the 4th FIW, while the other three went to pilots of the 51st FIW. According to their own admission, in the final October combats the Americans lost two more F-86s. One of them, F-86E No.51-2902 of the 39th FIS, which was claimed as a victory by Senior Lieutenant V.P. Altunin in the 23 October dogfight, was instead seriously damaged. Its pilot Lieutenant Colonel Theon W. Markham, managed to return to his base in it, but he crashed when attempting to land it; the Sabre was a total loss, while the pilot was injured, but survived. In the dogfight of 26 October already discussed above, Captain V.G. Kazakov seriously damaged F-86A No.49-1210 of the 4th FIW's 336th FIS; its pilot and his fate are still not known.

In comparison with the preceding month, the overall results of the fighting in October were more modest. The 64th IAK shot down a total of 25 enemy aircraft, including 24 F-86s and one Meteor Mk.8, and also damaged seven F-86s. In addition, the victories claimed by Novoselov, Sema and Kozlov went uncounted. The pilots of the 216th IAD were responsible for 21 destroyed and six damaged enemy aircraft. Pilots of the 133rd IAD scored three victories in the month of October, and one destroyed US aircraft went to the credit of the naval aviators of the 578th IAP. Losses over the month of October amounted to 11 aircraft and four pilots, of which nine aircraft and three pilots were lost in combat, while the remaining losses were due to non-combat causes.

The Americans claimed that in October 1952, Sabre pilots shot down 27 MiGs. Their own losses amounted to seven F-86s, of which only five were lost in action against MiGs, while the other two losses were not due to combat.

From October 1952, one squadron of the 32nd IAD's 913 IAP (the 3rd Squadron), and 224th IAP (the 1st Squadron), both operating from the same Mukden airfield, switched to night duties. From then until January 1953, these squadrons flew no daytime combat sorties.

After a short break in combat operations, November 1952 began with major fighter-bomber raids in MiG Alley, in the Changseong area in particular. To defend this target area, on 1 November several groups of MiGs from the 133rd IAD scrambled, which took on the forward screen of Sabres, while pilots of the UAA attacked the fighter-bombers and the fighters of the immediate escort.

In the ensuing dogfights, the 133rd IAD's pilots destroyed five enemy aircraft: four F-86s and one F-84, and they damaged one more F-86. Pilots of the 176th IAP did particularly well by downing three of the Sabres and inflicting damage to another one. The 1st Squadron commander Major K.H. Degtiarev shot down two Sabres in this action, thereby paying back for his defeat in the dogfight on 9 September 1952. Our pilots had no losses. Pilots of the 216th IAD also took off in order to reinforce their comrades and to cover their withdrawal from combat, but they had no encounter with the enemy. However, on this day the UAA lost two of its MiGs, which were downed by pilots of the 4th FIW. The US Fifth Air Force command denies the loss of their F-86s on 1 November, confirming only the loss of one Panther and one F-84G of the 58th FBW,

Lt. R. P. Yeatman, from the USS *Bon Homme Richard*, is shown rocketing and bombing a Korean bridge, November 1952. (US Navy)

which according to American records was lost on 2 November while making a training flight. Most likely, Major K.P. Petrov of the 415th IAP, who was the only Soviet pilot to claim a victory over an F-84 on 1 November, was the "examiner" of the Thunderjet pilot on this training flight.

Enemy air raids in the area of MiG Alley continued on 2 November, and again pilots of the 133rd IAD and the UAA were scrambled to repulse them. Pilots of the 415th IAP were particularly capably guided to one group of Shooting Stars; having found F-80s that were working over ground targets without any fighter cover, they dealt with six of the "Shoots" without any interference. The remaining F-80s managed to escape to the bay. In this action flight commander Captain V.P. Lepikov shot down two of the F-80s. However, distracted by his pursuit of the Shooting Stars, Lepikov didn't see approaching Sabres that were hurrying to the scene, and 1st Lieutenant Thomas White of the 51st FIW's 16th FIS shot him down. Lepikov safely bailed out and soon returned to the regiment – this was the 64th IAK's first loss in the month of November. The Americans admitted the loss of two of their F-80Cs (No.49-586 and No.49-885) of the 12th TRS, but only five days after the event and at that claimed that the losses were due to ground fire. One of the pilots was taken prisoner, while the other was saved by a search and rescue team. Considering that the Americans often concealed their losses in combats with MiGs in this fashion, it is possible to assume that both of these Shooting Stars were shot down by pilots of the 415th IAP.

After the intense action of the first two days of November, another lull in combat operations began on 3 November. The number of combat missions flown by both sides

Lockheed F-80C-10-LO Shooting Star s/n 49–624 of the US 8th Fighter-Bomber Group, 80th FBS, Korea, 1950. (USAF Museum)

fell by almost half, and encounters in the air were rare and not particularly fierce. To this it must be added that the weather deteriorated to such an extent between 8 November and 15 November that the aircraft on both sides were effectively grounded. Up until 15 November the adversaries avoided contact in the air, so between 1 November and 18 November the 64th IAK's pilots had only two clashes with Sabres that had any results. Thus, on 6 November pilots of the 224th IAP, while covering the Dapu airbase, had a brief dogfight with Sabres of the 51st FIW, in which Senior Lieutenant Ivan Oreshkov's MiG was damaged and the pilot himself wounded. The engine stopped. Practically over the airfield Oreshkov, separating from the enemy in a steep dive, decided to try and save his aircraft. He began to glide toward the base. It was closed on this day, and Chinese workers were cleaning the runway. Ivan didn't spot them until he had already lowered his landing gear and he now no longer had sufficient altitude to eject. The Chinese didn't notice the aircraft coming in for a landing – with its dead engine, the MiG was gliding soundlessly. In order to avoid hitting the workers, Ivan turned away from the runway. The aircraft crashed and Ivan was badly injured. With a bloody, swollen face and eyes nearly fully closed, you couldn't recognize Ivan's nationality. Unable to speak, the Chinese who found him thought he was a Chinese pilot and took him to one of their own hospitals. It took a great effort to locate Ivan, and it was even more difficult to get the Chinese to understand that he was one of ours, a Soviet pilot. In the difficult combat when Ivan Oreshkov was wounded, his wingman Nikolai Sokolov's MiG was also badly shot up. He continued to fight, however, covering Ivan's escape and forced landing.

On 9 November, a group of pilots of the 913th IAP, while flying a mission into MiG Alley, encountered a group of F-86s, but they declined battle and headed back to the bay. When returning to base, our pilots spotted a dogfight. Chinese pilots were dueling with Sabres. Our pilots hastened to aid the Chinese and helped chase the Sabres away back to the bay. In the process Senior Lieutenant L.I. Maleevsky's element intercepted one of the retreating Sabres and attacked it. During the attack, his wingman Senior Lieutenant I.D. Mukovnin had a more favorable position than the Maleevsky, so Mukovnin was the one who latched onto the Sabre's tail and shot it down. True, Mukovnin only received credit for damaging this F-86, which apparently fell into the sea. We had no losses in this action.

There is almost no information regarding how the Chinese pilots fought in the autumn air battles with Sabres. However, it is reliably known that they were no longer those fledgling pilots that used to make easy prey for the Sabres, as they had once been; they had gained hard experience in combats with the American pilots, and with each passing month victories over the UAA's became a more difficult task for the Americans. In November 1952 alone, pilots of the UAA scored 15 victories over UN pilots. The pilots of Major Wang Hai's regiment particularly distinguished themselves in the November fighting. For example, on 11 November Wang Hai and his wingman Lieutenant Jiao Jingwen, returning from a combat mission, encountered a squadron of Sabres. Using the element of surprise, they jumped the Sabre formation and on the very first pass Major Wang Hai shot down two F-86s at once, while his wingman, protecting his leader from an attack by a different pair of Sabres, shot down one of them. Then the Chinese pilots got away from the startled Sabres. The Americans confirm the loss of F-86F No.51-2875 from the 4th FIW on 11 November, but consider it a non-combat loss.

The Americans had only three victories after 2 November right up until 17 November, shooting down (or more accurately, damaging) one of the 64th IAK's MiGs and two MiGs from the UAA. True, on 17 November Sabre pilots clashed with UAA pilots and over the day of combats attained six victories, shared equally between the 4th FIW and the 51st FIW. The losses on the American side in these air battles aren't known to the author. It is known only that a pilot of the 913th IAP's 1st Squadron Senior Lieutenant V.A. Efremov shot down one F-86 on this day. Six MiGs of the 1st Squadron had taken off on a free hunt and had fought with a small group of F-86s. We had no losses in this dogfight.

A more serious clash between the opposing sides' air forces flared up on 18 November in the Kiojo, Pakchon, Kaechon area. Groups of MiGs numbering six to eight aircraft each from the 32nd IAD and 216th IAD sequentially took off for that area. Their adversaries, as always, were pilots of the 4th and 51st FIW. Thus, in one of the dogfights six MiG-15s of the 878th IAP's 3rd Squadron tangled with eight F-86s at an altitude of 11,000 meters. In this combat the 878th IAP's pilots shot down two Sabres and seriously damaged another, before returning to their base at Miaogou without any losses.

On this day, the 32nd IAD also had a successful action. Pilots of its 535th IAP, conducting a free hunt, intercepted a flight of F-86s and shot down one Sabre and damaged another. A short time later, pilots of the 224th IAP that were covering the landing of our fighters back at their base shot down another Sabre and damaged still one more. After serving the previous night on duty, Senior Lieutenant B.N. Sis'kov and his wingman Lieutenant V.I. Klimov voluntarily took part in this daytime combat sortie, even though they could have avoided it, since they were flying night missions. In this action Senior Lieutenant Sis'kov shot up one Sabre from close range and it exploded in the air. Sis'kov's aircraft entered the smoke from the explosion, and as confirmation of his victory, returned with small fragments of the Sabre he had downed in his MiG's engine intake. Possibly, it was B.N. Sis'kov who downed the American pilot 2nd Lieutenant Jack H. Turberville of the 25th FIS in this dogfight, who is reported as missing-in-action.

Altogether over the day of fighting, the 64th IAK's pilots shot down four F-86s in the day's dogfights and damaged three more, without any losses in return. The Americans, to be sure, claimed that they shot down two MiGs, but most likely they belonged to the UAA. In addition to the loss of F-86E No.51-2734 from the 25th FIS, in which Jack Turberville was killed, the 335th FIS lost its F-86E No.51-1963. This is all that the opposing side acknowledged on this day!

Pilots of the 216th IAD flew two combat missions on 19 November, both of which resulted in several small tussles with Sabre pilots. On one of them, Senior Lieutenant A.N. Brazhnikov of the 878th IAP shot down one F-86 in a combat in the area of Sunchon.

The next major air battle took place on 20 November in the Pukchin, Unsan and Kiojo area, in which pilots of the 216th IAD shot down three Sabres without any losses. Lieutenant Colonel V.S. Mikheev and Captain N.Z. Brazhenko of the 518th IAP claimed two of the Sabres. Nikolai Zakharovich Brazhenko recalls:

> Once we took off as a flight to cover the airfield, in order to secure the landing of our aircraft who were returning from a mission. Zhuravel' was the leader and I was his wingman. The second element consisted of Iakovlev and his wingman Didenko. From the ground they transmitted: "There is a pair of enemy fighters at high altitude out over the bay. Be alert!" I watched as one enemy aircraft attempted to attack my leader. The second enemy fighter was located above me by 200 meters. Its pilot wasn't given me a chance to take good aim at the Sabre that was getting in behind Zhuravel's MiG. I directed Zhuravel' to break left, while I fired a burst across the front of the enemy fighter. After my leader had made the sharp turn to the left, the enemy aircraft went into a dive, trying to escape to the bay. I also went into a dive after the enemy, knowing that the enemy would have to pull out of it before hitting the ground. At that moment I gave the enemy fighter a burst. He got away to the bay. We were forbidden to cross the coastline. Intelligence later reported that the enemy fighter fell into the bay. Thus, regiment navigator Vasilii Zhuravel' didn't became a victim of the enemy, while the MiGs approaching from a mission safely made their landings.

Captain N.M. Zameskin of the 878th IAP shot down a third Sabre; this was his fifth victory in the skies of Korea, which thereby made him an ace in this war.

On this same day, one more Sabre was damaged in the area of our forward airfields by Senior Lieutenant S.A. Dorokhov of the 535th IAP. The Americans on this day claimed five victories over MiGs, but since the 64th IAK had no losses, then plainly the American pilots were taking it out on the less experienced UAA pilots. In their turn the Americans acknowledged the loss of two of their F-86Es (No.51-2489 and No.51-2746) from the 25th FIS; both of their pilots, Major Vernon J. Lyle and 2nd Lieutenant P.D. Blakely, successfully bailed out over the Yellow Sea and were picked up by search and rescue helicopters.

Two large air battles took place on 21 and 22 November 1952. On 21 November, several dozen F-84G fighter-bombers attempted to destroy a military officers' school in the Pukchin area. Sabres of the 4th and 51st FIW escorted them. Pilots of the 518th IAP and 878th IAP tied up the covering Sabres in combat, while pilots of the 415th IAP that had been guided by ground controllers to the fighter-bombers tore into them in a concerted attack. A participant in this action, the former commander of the 415th IAP and Hero of the Soviet Union Lieutenant Colonel Pavel Fedorovich Shevelev, recalls:

> There was a regimental sortie to repel a raid on Pukchin. The regiment was scrambled rather late, and the airspace above Pukchin was full of ground attack aircraft. At first we spotted a four-ship flight of F-84s; I attacked them directly from our approach and shot down one of the Thunderjets. Then we bumped into eight F-84s and attacked them straight away. On the first pass Captain V.M. Panov shot down one F-84, and then Senior Lieutenant N.M. Sokurenko shot down a second after a short pursuit; its wing broke off as the shells struck it.
>
> To be honest, we also suffered losses because we overlooked an attack by two groups of Sabres. Thus, six F-86s unexpectedly attacked the 1st Squadron, being led by squadron commander Major G.I. Bogdanov, and shot down the MiG of Georgii Ivanovich Bogdanov, who was killed in the cockpit of his aircraft. The Sabres also managed to shoot down Senior Lieutenant A.A. Garankin, but he managed to eject successfully. However, the Sabres also weren't able to escape unpunished – Captain V.M Panov shot down one of them in this action.

Altogether in this dogfight the pilots of the 415th IAP downed five F-84s and one F-86, but for some reason two of the victory claims raised doubts on the part of the 64th IAK command. So the regiment commander Lieutenant Colonel P.F. Shevelev was credited with one destroyed F-84 and one damaged, while Captain V.M. Panov received credit for only two victories in this air battle; the third went down in the victory totals as only damaged. As a result, the IAK command officially credited the 415th IAP with three destroyed F-84s and two damaged Thunderjets, plus one destroyed F-86. The Chinese pilots put in claims for two downed F-86s. The IAK's losses over the day of combat amounted to two MiGs and one pilot.

The American command credited their pilots with downing three MiGs on this day. From the data on losses of the USAF and USNAF on 21 November, one can assume that the 415th IAP's pilots attacked combat formations of both the USAF and a group of carrier-based aircraft, since according to the information on the Americans side, two F9F-2 Panthers were shot down, as well as two F-80s from the 49th FBW's 80th FBS, which the Americans attributed to either ground fire or causes other than MiG cannon fire. It is difficult to believe that so many of the victories claimed by Soviet pilots remained without confirmation. However, the victories over the Sabres were confirmed by the American side: on this day, F-86E No.50-0627 from the 16th FIS was lost, as well as one reconnaissance Sabre, RF-86A No.48-0187 from the 15th TRS, the pilot of which Sidney W. Jones bailed out and was picked up by a search and rescue team. These two victories were credited to Captain V.G. Kazakov of the 518th IAP and Captain V.M. Panov of the 415th IAP.

Several air battles took place in the area of the Supung hydroelectric station on 22 November. Covering the region, the 32nd IAD successfully repulsed all the raids by F-86E fighter-bombers, which in small groups were trying to penetrate to the dam.

Thus, eight MiG-15s of the 224th IAP's 3rd Squadron under the command of the squadron commander Captain P.S. Mironov took off in the afternoon to cover the dam. Consisting of Captain Mironov and his wingman Captain V.N. Lazarev, Major E.I. Goriunov and his wingman Senior Lieutenant N.I. Maliutin, as well as Captain K.V. Portnov's flight, the squadron spotted a pair of F-86s in the vicinity of the hydro-electrical station and engaged it in combat. Attacking it, Captain Mironov shot down the lead Sabre, while Captain Lazarev damaged the wingman's F-86. At that moment, Major Goriunov's element, which was covering their attack, was attacked from above by a different Sabre element in a high-speed pass. Several .50-caliber bullets struck Goriunov's MiG, and one of them shattered the canopy; a shard of Plexiglass wounded the right side of the pilot's neck. However, the Sabres, having overshot the MiGs, placed themselves under attack, which Major Goriunov exploited by blasting a Sabre at point-blank range from every cannon (the burning F-86 was clearly visible on his gun camera footage). The Sabre wingman also didn't get away – Senior Lieutenant Maliutin pursued it and shot it down. After this, all of our pilots safely returned to their base at Mukden.

As a result, Mironov's flight virtually destroyed an entire flight of Sabres, escaping with only damage to Major Goriunov's and Captain Mironov's MiGs, but they were both quickly repaired. All the pilots of Captain P.S. Mironov's flight were awarded Orders of the Red Banner for this successful combat and received on the spot promotions in rank.

On the next sortie of this day, eight MiGs of the 913th IAP's 3rd Squadron, while on a patrol, came across a flight of Sabres and went in pursuit of it. Several of the squadron's pilots fired at the tail-end Sabre element and shot down one of the F-86s, which fell into the bay. Since the Sabre came down in the sea, it was credited to the regiment as only damaged and assigned to the combat score of Senior Lieutenant E.Ia. Karchevsky, whose gun camera footage was most clear.

On this same day after a month's rest, the pilots of the 216th IAD's 676th IAP took off on a combat mission. At 1325, eight MiGs of the regiment had a dogfight with 16 F-86s. In the melee with this group of Sabres they damaged two F-86s, one of which was hit by the regiment navigator Major G.A. Bolotin. However, his MiG also received damage and he was compelled to eject from his stricken aircraft.

The results of the fighting on 22 November are as follows: the 64th IAK shot down three F-86s and seriously damaged four more. Our own losses consisted of one MiG destroyed and one MiG damaged. The Americans, though, maintain that on this day their Sabre pilots achieved three victories over MiGs, while acknowledging the loss of only two of their Sabres. The F-86E No.51-2758 from the 16th FIS received combat damage (a MiG shot off its cockpit canopy), but its pilot 2nd Lieutenant Edmund G. Hepner bailed out near Cho-do Island and was picked by a USAF H-19 rescue heli-copter. The other lost Sabre, F-86F 51-12794, flown by Robert D. Hartwig of the 335th FIS, took heavy damage and had to be written off.

After 22 November, combat actions again subsided until the end of the month, and enemy encounters became rare. The most serious air battle took place on 26 November, which involved the naval pilots of the Pacific Ocean Fleet's 578th IAP. However, once again the naval pilots received rough treatment from the Sabre pilots; the 578th IAP lost two MiGs in this action. Both Captain A. Tsar'kov and Senior Lieutenant Doroshenko were shot down, but fortunately managed to eject successfully. On this mission Doroshenko was flying as wingman to regiment commander Lieutenant Colonel V.T. Dobrov and had to experience a high-altitude ejection after his MiG was shot down while covering his element leader. Having ejected, he nearly froze to death as he descended in his parachute from that high altitude, but everything came out OK. The Soviet MiGs were shot down by pilots of the 51st FIW Major James Douglas "Doug" Lindsay (a Royal Canadian Air Force exchange pilot with the 51st FIW) and his wingman on the mission, 1st Lieutenant Harold E. Fischer. Senior Lieutenant V.A. Chernovy's victory, who downed one Sabre, was of small comfort to the naval pilots.

After 22 November, over the rest of the month the 64th IAK's pilots shot down only three F-86s, while losing two aircraft in return. A pilot of the 726th IAP Senior Lieutenant V.P. Veriaskin achieved the final victory in November 1952 by damaging F-86E No.50-660 from the 334th FIS, the pilot of which 1st Lieutenant John Ferebee managed to return to Kimpo in it, but there made a belly landing and the fighter had to be written off. Over this same period the Americans (pilots of the 39th FIS) also shot down three MiGs, one of which was from the UAA.

In November 1952, in addition to "free hunts" our pilots flew missions to intercept enemy ground attack aircraft and fighters. The average length of time of an individual MiG combat sortie was 48 minutes. The 64th IAK had 83 group air battles, including one involving a regiment and 72 involving squadrons. The IAK claimed 32 enemy aircraft destroyed and 13 damaged. In the 415th IAP, the top-scoring squadron was the 3rd Squadron led by Major Petrov, which downed seven American aircraft. Unfortunately, the 64th IAK in this month lost seven of its own MiGs and one pilot, Major Georgii Bogdanov, who was killed-in-action. The most productive Soviet fighter division in November was the 133rd IAD, which destroyed 10 enemy aircraft and damaged five, while pilots of the 32nd IAD shot down six and damaged another six enemy aircraft. According to American records, their pilots in November 1952 shot down 28 MiGs, 18 of which were chalked up by the 51st FIW, while the other 10 went to pilots of the 4th FIW.

The Chinese pilots in the month of November 1952 flew 800 individual combat sorties, while the North Korean pilots flew 56. Taken together they had 22 group air battles, in which they claimed 15 US aircraft destroyed and four more damaged. Their losses over the month of November amounted to just seven MiG-15s destroyed and four MiGs damaged, while two pilots were killed-in-action.

In total over the month of November 1952, the 64th IAK and the UAA combined lost 15 MiG-15 fighters, so of the 28 victories that were credited to the American Sabre pilots, 13 were spurious. They likely resulted from claims based on hits against a MiG that was then seen to go down, but in reality was only damaged and managed to return to base – a rather frequent occurrence in aerial combat.

In addition, there was a serious international incident in the month of November 1952 that involved Soviet pilots of Soviet Air Force units that were not part of the 64th IAK: on 18 November, a US Navy carrier task force consisting of the USS *Oriskany* and the USS *Princeton* approached the Soviet-North Korean border in the Sea of Japan not far from the North Korean port of Najin, where it conducted a dawn airstrike against an industrial complex at Hoeryong. In response, four MiG-15s of the 781st IAP of the Pacific Ocean Fleet's 165th IAD, under the command of Captain N.M. Beliakov, took off from the Soviet Unashi border airfield in the Primorsky District, south of Vladivostok, in order to patrol over the area near where the carriers had been spotted. Not far from the American task force and over international waters, our fighters without any justification were unexpectedly jumped by a division of F9F-5 Panthers from VF-781 Squadron, which had taken off from the USS *Oriskany*. With the surprise attack the Panthers broke up the MiG flight's formation and damaged Senior Lieutenant Pakhomkin's MiG. Together with his element leader Senior Lieutenant Pushkarev, they exited out from under the attack with a sharp turn and left the combat area. True, only Senior Lieutenant B.V. Pushkarev's MiG returned to the Unashi airfield; Vladimir Ivanovich Pakhomkin's MiG couldn't reach the coastline because his fuel tank was leaking fuel after the attack, and he fell into the sea near Cape Lev, where he drowned. Captain Nikolai Mikhailovich Beliakov and his wingman Senior Lieutnant Aleksandr Ivanovich Vandaev were unable to escape the grip of groups of Panthers (four more Panthers from VF-721 and four F2N-2 Banshee fighters from VF-11 Squadron had arrived on the scene); fighting heroically, they were killed in this dogfight – they were shot down by Lieutenants (j.g.) John D. Middleton and E. Royce Williams of VF-781.[2] According to their records, the Americans had one Panther that was damaged in this action. The two sides exchanged notes of protest, but then this incident was long forgotten, and all the records connected with it were classified. The first information about this incident, which took place on 18 November 1952, didn't appear in the Russian press until 40 years later.

ENDNOTE

1 Captain Filippov is of course not the same Senior Lieutenant Evgenii Filippov, who was killed-in-action on 24 March 1952.
2 This has become a notorious incident that has drawn a lot of recent research. The American version of the events asserts that there were seven MiGs and that they in fact attacked the American Panthers first.

10

The third winter of the war

At the end of the autumn of 1952, in view of the steadily growing number of MiGs in Manchuria, the USAF command raised the question about re-equipping another two fighter-bomber groups with F-86F Sabre fighter-bombers. The discussion focused on the US Fifth Air Force's 8th and 18th FBG. In this fashion, the Americans wanted to resolve two essential problems with one type of aircraft, which could carry out the functions of a ground attack aircraft and simultaneously fight MiG-15s on equal terms. First, pilots of the 18th FBG, consisting of the 12th and 67th Squadrons, plus the SAAF's No.2 "Flying Cheetahs" Squadron transitioned to new F-86Fs in December 1952. Prior to this, their pilots had flown and fought in the skies of Korea in piston-engine F-51 Mustang II fighter-bombers and had suffered heavy losses. For example, the SAAF No.2 Squadron alone, while participating in combat operations in Korea in their Mustangs between November 1950 and January 1953, had lost 74 of the 95 F-51Ds with which the squadron had started the war. Thirty-four of its pilots had been killed-in-action and eight more had become prisoners-of-war. Experienced pilot-instructors from the Las Vegas Air Force Base (today the Nellis Air Force Base) had arrived in Korea to train the pilots of the 12th and 67th FBS. In addition, under the gaze of the experienced pilots of the 4th and 51st FIW, who had long been flying and fighting in Sabres, the pilots of the 18th Fighter-bomber Group began to learn the ropes of employing the F-86 in combat. The pilots of the 67th Squadron were the first to receive their new Sabres in January 1953.

Meanwhile the fighting over MiG Alley continued. The December air battles began on 2 December, but only pilots of the UAA and the Sabre pilots of the 4th and 51st FIW took part in them. The American pilots and the UAA pilots spent a week sorting out their relationships with one another. Air battles between them took place on the 2nd, 3rd, 4th and 7th of December 1952. The Americans claimed that in these dogfights their pilots shot down 11 MiGs. The day of 7 December was a particularly productive one for the American pilots, who claimed seven victories over MiGs, five of which were achieved by pilots of the 4th FIW. However, the UAA's pilots also claimed victories in these combats.

Soviet pilots of the 216th IAD also participated in the fighting on 2, 3 and 7 December, but they were small skirmishes, which for both sides ended without any losses. The pilots of the 32nd IAD in this period were occupied with only covering the airfields and had no encounters with the enemy.

The first December dogfight that ended with a result for the 64th IAK's pilots occurred on 5 December. On this day, pilots of Major I.D. Khromov's 3rd Squadron of the 518th IAP distinguished themselves. While on a patrol, in the area of Anju they encountered a group of Sabres and engaged it in battle, in which the squadron deputy political commander Senior Lieutanant Vit'ko shot down one F-86, while flight commander

Captain F.P. Fedotov damaged another (it fell into Korea Bay, so the pilot didn't receive credit for a victory). When returning to Miaogou, Captain Fedotov's flight was directed toward a pair of F-86Fs in the area of the Supung dam, which were on a reconnaissance mission, and Captain Fedotov shot down the Sabre leader with a high side attack. The Sabre pilot ejected and became a prisoner – he turned out to be Major Andrew Robert MacKenzie of the Royal Canadian Air Force, who was on temporary assignment with the 51st FIW. The 518th IAP's pilots had no losses in these actions. According to documents of the 64th IAK, the events unfolded in the following manner:

> On 5 December our fighters shot down the leader of a group of four F-86s of the 51st FIW, which consisted of exchange pilots of the Royal Canadian Air Force. Squadron commander Major Andrew Robert MacKenzie bailed out and came down in the area of Supung next to the 51st Anti-aircraft Battery. As our personnel were approaching, Major MacKenzie opened fire from his pistol. He surrendered after we opened return fire. He was handed over to Chinese authorities.

The Americans acknowledge the loss of two Sabres on this day: in addition to Major MacKenzie's F-86F-1 No.51-2906 of the 39th FIS, which was shot down by Captain Fedotov, the 39th Fighter Squadron also lost F-86F No.51-2903, which Senior Lieutenant Vit'ko shot down. The pilot of this Sabre, Major Jackson Saunders, was more fortunate – he ejected and was soon rescued.[1]

The 64th IAK suffered its first loss in the month on 8 December 1952. In the vicinity of an airfield, an element led by the commander of a squadron in the Pacific Ocean Fleet's 578th IAP Major Mikhail Marchenko was attacked when landing. A pair of Sabres damaged the leader's aircraft, wounding the pilot. While he still had enough strength, Marchenko attempted a forced landing in the countryside beyond the airfield's perimeter, but his MiG crashed. Though the pilot survived, he received numerous injuries requiring hospital treatment. Pilots of the 51st FIW's 16th FIS Major Edwin Heller and his wingman 1st Lieutenant G. Woodworth shot down Marchenko and shared credit for the victory.

There was another combat loss on 10 December. Captain V.N. Lazarev of the 32nd IAD's 224th IAP was shot down. Lev Petrovich Kolesnikov, who flying the same mission when Lazarev went down, relates what happened:

> So, we took off in the following group: Mironov, Lazarev and Portnov's flight. Over the Yalu River at 12,000 meters, Mironov spotted Sabres and attacked them. They went into a descending left-hand spiral. I was on the outside of the group, furthest away than anyone else from the point of attack, which gave me the opportunity to cut inside their turn and open fire; even if I didn't hit a target, I might force the enemy to get nervous and swerve in front of Mironov's cannons. Having opened fire, I pulled into too tight of a turn and went into a spin. My tracer shells nevertheless startled the adversary. The Sabres scattered wildly. Vasilii Nikitich darted after one of them. I successfully brought my aircraft out of its spin – onto the tail of our group that had lost altitude in the spiral, but instead of five MiGs, I saw only four. Distracted by his chase, Lazarev had become separated from us and had immediately been attacked by Americans that had rushed to save their pilot. His MiG's

rudder and throttle control were damaged. The engine continued to work at full throttle, and the uncontrollable aircraft plummeted toward the earth in an almost vertical dive. Vasilii Nikitich had no choice but to eject. When the ejection mechanism shot him out of the cockpit, the shock from the slip stream was such that even though Lazarev had his eyes closed tightly, bleeding under his cornea blinded him for several days and his face was covered with bruises. One boot flew off from the impact of the wind. Blind, he descended in his parachute ....

Vasilii Nikitich commented later, "I waited for an eternity to hit the ground."

He came down on the frozen ground. Lazarev was unable to stand up not only because of his unshod foot. The ejection at maximum speed and the incredible somersault in the howling wind stream bruised his back. So the pilot just laid there in the middle of a field. He heard footsteps and conversation. From words I was able to snatch from their discussion – "Truman?" *Zhiyuan?*" – I understood that the people walking toward me were wondering whether I was one of theirs or an American. It was worth knowing: back then we flew armed with pistols. Then Lazarev started to sing: "*Shiroka strana moia rodnaia! [My native land is wide!]*

"Ho!" – the Chinese Volunteers rejoiced, and our irrepressible deputy political commander was ceremoniously taken to a hospital. The American pilot who shot Lazarev down was 1st Lieutenant James F. Low of the 4th FIW's 335th Fighter Squadron.

More intense air battles took place in the second half of the month, starting on 15 December. True, even 15 December was just a prelude for what was to come, but the commander of the 535th IAP Major P.I. Karataev achieved a victory on that day. His wingman at the time, Vladimir Nikolaevich Lapygin, has this to say about it:

On one of the missions, returning to base as a pair with the regiment commander, we spotted a solitary enemy aircraft at low altitude (800-1,000 meters) and attacked it. The Sabre went into a turn, but having completed two complete revolutions, he grasped that no advantage was coming from it and he leveled out, trying to escape to the bay. In the level pursuit regiment commander Karataev chased him down and in the first attack sent it crashing into a hill.

However, now when heading back to base for the second time, Major Karataev's aircraft came under a surprise attack from a Sabre element and received 75 bullet holes in it. The MiG sustained a long list of damage: one of the aircraft's fuel tanks began burning, the ailerons became jammed, and seven .50-caliber bullets struck the engine. Karataev had to lead his crippled MiG to Mukden, where he made a successful landing on the Mukden-West airbase. Eight days later his MiG was back in service through the efforts of the technical personnel of the local PARM [*podvizhnaia aviaremontnaia masterskaia*, or mobile aviation repair shop].

The Americans don't acknowledge the loss of their F-86 on this day, but report the loss of one F-84G (No.51-10338) from the 49th FBW's 8th FBS, the pilot of which 1st Lieutenant John M. Corbett was killed, though they attribute it to anti-aircraft fire. Perhaps it was him that Karataev and Lapygin intercepted on this day, mistaking his aircraft for a Sabre?

The next day several savage air battles occurred between pilots of the 216th IAD and of the UAA on one side, and pilots of the 4th FIW on the other side, particularly of the 335th FIS. Dogfights developed over the populated points Pukchin, Kaechon, Pakchon, Taechon and Changseong. Pilots of the naval 578th IAP of the Pacific Ocean Fleet finally had a good day; in the area of Taegwan-dong, Major M.N. Obodnikov and Captain K.T. Kokora shot down one Sabre each in a dogfight with a group of F-86s, while the regiment suffered no losses. Eight MiG-15s of the 578th IAP's 2nd Squadron, led by Captain M.P. Shvetsov, had taken off on a combat mission, and in the area of Taegwan-dong they encountered four F-86s. Here's what one of the dogfight's active participants, Mikhail Nikolaevich Obodnikov recalls about it:

> Flying toward the border at an altitude of 10,000-11,000 meters, we dropped our external tanks and entered North Korean airspace. Smirnov's element climbed to 12,000 meters and remained there. To the question, "Where are you?" he replied that he was behind and above us. Kokora and I were flying in trail behind Captain Shvetsov's four-ship flight at approximately 10,000 meters altitude. In a turn, I lagged a bit behind and when coming out of the turn almost collided with a Sabre. A pair of "hunters", without noticing us, had gotten in behind Shvetsov's flight. I wound up flying seemingly as the wingman to the Sabre wingman, just 10-15 meters to one side and behind him. Such a situation! If I fired at the wingman, then the Sabre leader would shoot down a wingman or even two of our guys in Shvetsov's flight. Therefore I opened fire at the leader, who was just 50 meters away from me, and shot him down. Then I also stitched the wingman's Sabre with a long burst from all three cannons. I didn't begin to accompany them down to the ground, but instead headed off toward Shvetsov's flight.

This was the most successful and productive combat of the naval pilots from the 578th IAP of the Pacific Ocean Fleet in the skies of Korea. True, the command of the naval regiment decided to give one of the victories to Obodnikov's wingman Captain K.T. Korocha, but the main thing was that two enemy aircraft were downed and without any of our own losses.

On this same day, pilots of all three regiments of the 216th IAP also flew combat missions, each of which resulted in a clash with enemy four-ship or eight-ship F-86 formations, but only the pilots of the 676th IAP managed to achieve a victory in one of them. A pilot of the 676th IAP's 1st Squadron Grigorii Mikhailovich Pivovarenko relates the following about this action:

> On the morning of 16 December 1952, the squadron numbering eight MiGs under the command of Hero of the Soviet Union Major I.F. Gnezdilov was scrambled. However, something happened with the squadron commander's radio; since he couldn't hear orders, he turned back together with his wingman Senior Lieutenant Altunin and landed. I and my wingman Senior Lieutenant M. Sapegin linked up with Captain M.P. Zhbanov's flight, and the six of us headed toward the area of the Supung hydroelectric station, where eight F-86s had appeared according to information from the command post. At an altitude of 10,000 meters I jettisoned my drop tanks and soon thereafter spotted the eight F-86s and engaged them in

battle. But at this time another eight-ship formation of Sabres pounced on us from behind some cirrus clouds. As a result of their first pass against me, I was left with a damaged elevator and a shot-up cockpit; bullets had ripped through one of the legs of my trousers and my instrument panel was smashed. I ejected at an altitude of 10,000 meters. During my ejection my oxygen mask was torn off and I was seized by shivering; the temperature outside was -56 C. At an altitude of 6,000 meters a pair of Sabres made a firing pass at me and severed several parachute lines. This increased the speed of my descent and I received a concussion when I landed, as well as a broken leg and a dislocated vertebra. Soon Chinese comrades located me and carefully carried me to the area of Kuandian, where they gave me some medical assistance, and then sent me to Dapu.

In this hard combat, the squadron's pilots also shot down one F-86; credit for the victory went to Senior Lieutenant O.I. Grekov. The Americans took it out on Chinese pilots of the UAA, downing according to their claims four MiGs (plus Pivovarenko's MiG).

The day of 17 December proved to be a particularly hot one, when the enemy launched fighter-bomber attacks in the areas of Okkang-dong, Kaechon, Anju and Singisiu. The 535th IAP flew off to the Anju region with its full complement of serviceable MiGs, followed later by pilots of the 878th IAP as reinforcements. Several dozen aircraft tangled in a giant fur ball. In the course of the dogfight, Captain V.A. Utkin's element separated one Sabre from the rest of its group and put the squeeze on it. The American tried to evade the attack, but Utkin skillfully maneuvered into position and opened fire from all his cannons. The first burst virtually shot away the Sabre's entire tail, the second burst blew off its left wing, and the Sabre went tumbling crazily downward. This was Captain V.A. Utkin's second victory of the war. Lieutenant P.A. Vorob'ev of the 878th IAP damaged another Sabre, and soon the enemy fighters broke off combat. We had no losses in this action.

Another large air battle took place in the area of the Supung hydroelectric station, which F-86E fighter-bombers of the 51st FIW were trying to attack. Pilots of the 1st Squadron of the 32nd IAD's 913th IAP prevented them from reaching it. Here's how the former deputy commander of the 1st Squadron Senior Lieutenant Semen Alekseevich Fedorets describes this combat:

All three squadrons of the regiment took off in response to an alarm and received their assignments in the air over the radio. Our 1st Squadron sortied with 10 MiGs – two flights plus my element. I and my wingman Sasha Popov brought up the rear of the squadron's formation. We encountered the enemy at an altitude of 13,000-14,000 meters, and a "carousel" of fighters began to spin in descending spirals. The regiment split apart into separate groups, flights and pairs. The Sabres were under attack from the entire group, and with the decrease in altitude and a movement into a dive they began to exit the combat. The action lasted for 3-4 minutes, but over this time everything had been squeezed out of the pilots and the work put in by the ground crews. The regiment leader issued the command: "Low tide!" – the signal to break off combat. Squadron commander Major S.I. Babich led his group out of the spiral and set a course back to base in a climb.

Popov and I had driven off a couple of enemy attacks during the dogfight and had become separated from the main group, so we took our own heading back to our base. Suddenly Popov transmitted; "Take a look, a Sabre is joining up with me on my right." I immediately spotted it to the right of Popov, below and behind. I gave him an order: "Fly straight ahead and in a steady climb", and then rolled my aircraft to the right into an attack against the Sabre from above and the left. Not wasting a moment, I immediately fired a burst across his path to force him to break off the attack, but the Sabre pilot had time to fire a burst. Sasha called out over the radio: "I've been hit, my brake flaps have extended." I closed with the Sabre and gave it an aimed burst from a range of 500-600 meters. The Sabre broke sharply left and began to descend toward Korea Bay.

I quickly assessed the situation, and rolling my MiG back to the left, I went after the Sabre in a dive. After 20-40 seconds I could see that I was falling behind in the dive and that the range was increasing, so I decided to fire at the long range of 1,000-1,200 meters. I carefully took aim with an allowance for the shells' trajectory at this range and gave it one, and then a second short burst. I saw my tracers blanketing the F-86, and after the second burst, it suddenly went into a turn to port, which was just what I needed. I began to close instantly and from a range of 600 down to 200 meters I gave it another two or three bursts – I watched as my shells struck the Sabre's nose and cockpit area, and it reacted by rolling over and heading in a dive toward the direction of the bay, trailing smoke, but still 15-20 kilometers short of the coastline, it crashed into the ground and exploded.

Fedorets landed at Mukden on the last drops of fuel. His wingman Senior Lieutenant A. Popov made a normal landing back at base in his damaged MiG. True, he had to lower his landing gear manually, because the hydraulic line to them had been severed and all the hydraulic fluid had drained away. They discovered 8 – 10 bullet holes in his aircraft, but technicians quickly repaired it.

In this combat over the area of the Supung dam and reservoir, in the initial surprise attack the pilots of the 913th IAP shot down one F-86 (claimed by Captain A.I. Khoitsev) and damaged another (credited to Senior Lieutenant E.G. Aseev) before returning to base in Mukden without any losses. This was the 913th IAP's first major victory in the skies of Korea since the start of its combat operations with the 64th IAK.

As a result, on 17 December the 64th IAK's pilots shot down three F-86s and damaged two more, without any losses of its own. The Americans on this day didn't declare any victories.

Fighting flared up again in those same areas of MiG Alley on 18 December, once again involving pilots of the 64th IAK and of the UAA. From our side, pilots of the 133rd IAD took part in the fighting, which were supported by pilots of the 216th IAD's 518th IAP. In these dogfights the 133rd IAD's pilots shot down one Sabre and damaged two more F-86s. The Sabre downed by the commander of the 147th GIAP Major N.I. Shkodin was soon found by a search team with the dead pilot still seated in the cockpit. Pilots of the 518th IAP damaged another F-86. We had no losses on this day, but the Americans report one victory that they achieved on 18 December. Possibly, they intercepted the radio transmissions of a pilot of the 676th IAP Senior Lieutenant P.I. Sirotenko, who strayed far to the north during the action and had to make a forced belly landing in the countryside in the area of Tangzhichen after running out of fuel. The Americans don't recognize the loss of their Sabres between 15 December and 20 December, claiming that there weren't any. If so, then whose wreckage did our search teams of the 64th IAK locate back then?

After several days of another respite in the fighting, only on 22 December did the adversaries meet again in combat over the Pakchon area. Pilots of the 32nd IAD and 216th IAD participated in the dogfights of 22 December, but success was on the side of the 216th IAD. On one of the sorties a group of MiGs from the 518th IAP engaged a group of F-86s from the 39th FIS in combat, and wingman Senior Lieutenant Boris Vadkovsky succeeded in downing one Sabre, but he was unexpectedly jumped by a pair of Sabres from out of some clouds and his MiG was set aflame. Vadkovsky managed to bail out in time. He was shot down by 1st Lieutenant Harold Fischer of the 39th FIS. Yet Vadkovsky had managed to shoot down F-86E No.51-2864 from this same fighter squadron, and its pilot had been forced to eject, after which he was picked up by a search and rescue team.

On this same day pilots of the 878th IAP flew two combat missions, but the enemy avoided encounters and only pilots of the 2nd Squadron got lucky: they had a brief clash with a group of F-86s, in which flight commander Senior Lieutenant P.A. Vorob'ev shot down one Sabre, while the rest of them immediately fled the combat area; our pilots returned to their base at Mukden without any losses. In this action Vorob'ev shot down F-86F No.51-12966 of the 335th FIS, and its pilot 1st Lieutenant Donald R. Reitsma went missing-in-action.

However, the Sabres got even against the pilots of the 32nd IAD's 224th IAP, who on this day were covering the 64th IAK's forward airbases. Senior Lieutenant Oleg Zhadan attacked a twin-engine reconnaissance aircraft and shot it down. The reconnaissance plane was flying with heavy fighter escort, and they quickly attacked and flamed Zhadan's MiG, badly wounding the pilot. Zhadan somehow found the strength to bail out, but he spent a long time lying unconscious in a hospital bed. However, the regiment and Zhadan didn't receive credit for his victory, because his gun camera film that confirmed this victory burned up together with Zhadan's MiG. Captain Herbert Weber of the 334th FIS was the American credited with shooting down Zhadan's MiG.

As a result, on 22 December the 64th IAK's pilots downed two enemy aircraft, but they themselves lost two of their own MiGs. The Americans claimed three victories on this day and admitted the loss of two of their Sabres. However, the Americans don't confirm the loss of a reconnaissance aircraft on 22 December 1952.

Serious fighting erupted at the end of the month; the days of 24, 25 and 28 December were marked by particularly fierce air battles. On 24 December, pilots of the 133rd IAD's 726th IAP distinguished themselves by bagging three Sabres in one action with a group of F-86s. The victories were scored by deputy regiment commander Lieutenant Colonel V.I. Chizh and Senior Lieutenants A.N. Zakharov and L.I. Rusakov. The American side confirms the loss of F-86F-1 No. 51-2858 from the 334th FIS – the fate of the pilot is unknown.[2]

On Christmas Day 1952 fighting flared up over the areas of Kusong, Changseong and Singisiu, involving pilots of the 133rd IAD and 216th IAD, as well as units of the UAA. Two F-86s were shot down in these air battles and one more was damaged. The 518th IAP's chief of aerial gunnery services Lieutenant Colonel V.S. Mikheev did particularly well in this dogfight, downing one F-86 and damaging the other. The Sabre pilots tried to even the score over the 64th IAK's airfields, but our pilots didn't allow them to do even this. Taught by bitter experience, our pilots were now particularly alert when coming in for landings at their bases. Swarms of MiGs from the 32nd IAD and on-duty regiments from other of the IAK's fighter divisions now constantly patrolled over the airfields. So on 25 December, the commander of the 415th IAP Colonel P.F. Shevelev and his wingman Captain V.M. Panov were taking their turn to patrol over the Dapu Air Base. There they spotted a solitary Sabre "hunter" that was lying in wait for MiGs that were taking off or coming in for landings. They caught him in a pincer, and since the Sabre pilot didn't show any evasive maneuvers, they easily shot him down. Credit for the victory went to Hero of the Soviet Union P.F. Shevelev.

The day's results were three F-86s downed by pilots of the 64th IAK and one damaged, without any losses on the Soviet side. The American command claimed that they shot down two MiG-15s, but most likely they belonged to the UAA. In their turn the Americans deny the loss of any Sabres on 25 December, confirming only the loss of one F-84G from the 58th FBW, which was probably shot down by pilots of the UAA.

The final day of aerial combat in the departing year took place on 28 December (there was one night action on 30 December) in the Changseong – Kusong area. Pilots from all three divisions of the 64th IAK took part in the air battles, as well as UAA pilots. Pilots of the 518th IAP and 878th IAP clashed with equally-sized groups of Sabres over the given area, but the dogfights ended without results, while pilots of the 726th IAP in one of these actions shot down one F-86.

Pilots of the 913th IAP also claimed a Sabre kill on this day. How this happened is related by a participant in this combat Ivan Ivanovich Karpov:

> As I recall, there was a regimental sortie, and my wingman Petr Byvshev and I were bringing up the rear of the formation. My head was constantly swiveling; everything was calm and my wingman was where he should have been. At one point in the flight I checked my 6 o'clock again and suddenly saw a Sabre behind me; he'd already taken a quick shot to figure out the deflection. I quickly shoved the control stick to the right, but I was an instant too late, and took a burst. Apparently, at this moment my wingman realized the situation and immediately went on the attack against this "cheeky fellow", who'd alone wedged himself between us, and shot him down. However, this impudent Sabre's machine-gun fire hit my aircraft somewhere in the engine, and it began to smoke. As fast as I could fly with a sputtering engine, I turned to the west toward Anshan.
>
> In total, I flew 100-150 kilometers in my burning MiG and gently set it down on the runway, but immediately my cockpit filled with smoke, while flames erupted from the rear of it. Even as I was rolling down the runway, the heat of the flames built to a point that I could no longer withstand it, so I leaped from the cockpit and ran away from the aircraft, which was soon enveloped in flames. Chinese rushed to put out the fire, but I blocked them from reaching the aircraft, since it had the VK-1A engine.

The "cheeky fellow" who inflicted the fatal damage to Karpov's MiG was 1st Lieutenant Harold Fischer of the 39th FIS. Incidentally, Fischer returned safely to base; although Byvshev was given credit for an official victory on this day, this is just another example of the wishful thinking that inflated victory totals on both sides in the Korean War.

462   RED DEVILS OVER THE 38TH PARALLEL

However, the air battles on 28 December didn't end with this; covering an airfield, a pilot of the 224th IAP Senior Lieutenant N.I. Maliutin encountered a solitary F-86 and took it on in combat. The dogfight didn't last long and soon Maliutin sent the Sabre spinning into the ground. This was the pilots of the 64th IAK's third victory on this day and its final daytime victory of 1952. The Americans acknowledged the loss of only one F-86E (No.52-2842), the pilot of which 2nd Lieutenant Robert R. Hodge crashed "due to unknown reasons" and was killed.

Altogether in December 1952 the pilots of the 64th IAK destroyed 27 enemy aircraft, including 22 F-86 fighters shot down in daytime combats and five B-29 bombers at night. An additional 10 F-86s and two B-29s were damaged in air battles (see Table 10.1):

Table 10.1 Results of the fighting for December 1952

Units of the 64th IAK	Enemy Aircraft Destroyed	Enemy Aircraft Damaged
133rd IAD	8	4
32nd IAD	8	2
216th IAD	7	2
578th IAP of Pacific Ocean Fleet	2	2
351st Night IAP	2	1

The 64th IAK's own losses over the month of December amounted to six MiG-15s. There were no losses among the pilots.

In addition, the UAA's pilots flew 910 individual combat sorties in December, 886 by Chinese pilots and 24 by North Korean pilots. They became involved in 29 group air battles, in which they shot down 17 US aircraft and damaged two. According to Chinese records, on 2 and 3 December the 3rd IAD and 12th IAD had five dogfights with F-86s, in which they destroyed or damaged eight Sabres. Pilots of Major Wang Hai's fighter regiment particularly distinguished themselves by downing more than 10 enemy aircraft during the month. The hero of 2 December was pilot Sun Shenlu of the 1st Squadron in Wang Hai's regiment, who downed two enemy aircraft. In the same action he received combat damage (he returned with 12 bullet holes in his MiG), but he was able to come in for landing on a "friendly" airfield on his last drops of fuel. He returned to his unit on the next day and again took part in the fighting. On the next day, in an air battle on 3 December 1952, the regiment commander shot down three and damaged three enemy aircraft, while his wingman Jiao Jingwen claimed two enemy aircraft. After this battle, Wang Hai had raised his personal score in the skies of Korea to eight victories.

Several days later (probably on 7 December 1952), 12 MiGs led by Major Wang Hai engaged 44 F-86s in combat at an altitude of 12,000 meters, and Wang Hai shot down his ninth F-86, while his wingman Jiao Jingwen also downed a Sabre, his third victory in the war. On 15 December Sun Shenlu, whom the Chinese pilots nicknamed the "Sniper of air combat", again distinguished himself. The Chinese maintain that because of badly rattled nerves after returning from his latest combat mission, he could neither eat anything nor sleep, but at an order to scramble, he immediately took off. Sun Shenlu and his wingman Ma Lianiu encountered a group of enemy aircraft, and the leader "nipped off" one of them. Several days later (on 16 or 18 December), this pair was covering Wang Hai's element and in a clash with four Sabres that were attacking the commander, Sun Shenlu shot down two F-86s in one pass. Prior to the end of December, this pilot shot down two more hostile aircraft and damaged one more.

In his final dogfight on 25 or 28 December, according to Chinese records when pilots of Wang Hai's regiment together with 12 "friendly", that is to say, Soviet pilots engaged more than 40 F-86s in combat, they downed six of them. Sun Shenlu with his wingman Ma Lianiu shot down one Sabre (Sung's sixth, plus 1 damaged). After this, 10 American fighters caught him in a pincer, surrounded him, and shot him down. The "Sniper" Sun Shenlu posthumously received the honor Military Hero First Degree.

Table 10.2   Results of the fighting for the year 1952 (according to records of the 64th IAK)

Formation	Period of Combat Operations in Year	Enemy Aircraft Destroyed	Enemy Aircraft Damaged
324th IAD	01.01.52 – 16.02.52	18	1
303rd IAD	01.01.52 – 11.02.52	36	4
97th IAD	03.02.52 – 12.07.52	63	–
190th IAD	17.02.52 – 10.08.52	90	–
133rd IAD	10.06.52 – 31.12.52	73	19
216th IAD	06.08.52 – 31.12.52	78	33
32nd IAD	16.09.52 – 31.12.52	15	10
351st Night IAP	01.01.52 – 31.12.52	8	2
578th IAP (naval)	01.09.52 – 31.12.52	4	–
Total		385	69

Altogether the UAA pilots in the December air battles lost six aircraft destroyed. Another 12 aircraft received combat damage.

Chinese sources assert that in November-December 1952, 238 MiGs of the Chinese fighter divisions took part in aerial combat, 2,463 individual sorties were flown, 52 hostile aircraft were destroyed and 11 were damaged. By their efforts, "the activity of the American fighter-bombers in the area south of the Chongchon River was sharply limited."

It turns out that in December 1952, the 64th IAK and the UAA together lost just 12 MiG-15s and had approximately another 15 damaged. This means that of the 27 MiG-15s claimed by the American side to have been shot down by Sabres, only 12 were actually destroyed in air-to-air combat. The other 15 MiGs in the best case were only damaged, but weren't shot down.

According to revised data of the 64th IAK headquarters for the year 1952 found in the Russian Ministry of Defense's archives, its pilots became engaged in 868 group air battles, in which 394 enemy planes were destroyed. The 64th IAK's own losses over the year amounted to 172 MiG-15s (excluding any lost in night combat actions). Despite the fact that the overall correlation of losses was 2.2 to 1 in our favor (which was significantly lower than the ratio of 7.9 to 1 achieved in 1951), our pilots retained an edge over their counterparts on the opposing side.

In 1952 the fighter divisions of the 64th IAK had assumed the main burden of conducting the fighting, even though by the middle of the year the UAA had introduced five fighter divisions into the fighting, and by the end of the year, it had 10 fighter aviation divisions in combat operation, which were rotating two at a time in and out of combat every one to two months. However, its units only began actively fighting in the month of November.

According to American records, the pilots of the 4th and 51st FIW flew 39,342 individual combat sorties in 1952, in which they shot down 380 enemy aircraft, of which 375 were the MiG-15 and MiG-15bis jet fighters. The Americans place their own F-86 losses for the year 1952 at 80 Sabres, of which only 53 were lost in combat, while the remaining 27 were declared as non-combat losses. Of course, this is difficult to believe.

A NEW YEAR – NEW BATTLES, OLD EQUIPMENT

The year 1953 began with a decrease in combat operations. The reason was the bad weather and the fact that the majority of the UAA's pilots were not qualified to fly in difficult meteorological conditions, so they flew few missions in January 1953.

Also at the beginning of 1953, the 64th IAK's structure underwent changes. In the middle of January, the regiments of the 32nd IAD (except for one night squadron in the 535th IAP) flew from the Mukden and Anshan airfields over to the forward bases at Andong and Dapu, and replaced the 133rd IAD, which had become worn out by eight months of constant fighting. In turn, the 133rd IAD's regiments flew back to Mukden and Anshan and entered the 64th IAK's second echelon, receiving the assignments that previously the pilots of the 32nd IAD had been carrying out – covering the take-offs and landings at the forward airfields, and when necessary during an air battle, serving as reinforcements.

As before, the 216th IAD remained in the 64th IAK's first echelon and continued to conduct combat operations from the same airfields at Miaogou and Dapu. In addition to the 216th IAD, two separate aviation regiments also remained in the corps' first echelon, the Pacific Ocean Fleet's 578th IAP and the 351st NIAP.

The first combat in the 1953 between the 64th IAK's pilots and the Americans took place on 2 January. The dogfights occurred over the Yalu River. In one of the small clashes, flight commander Senior Lieutenant Anatolii Shamrai of the 224th IAP's 2nd Squadron shot down the first enemy aircraft of the new year, an F-86E Sabre. This was the 64th IAK's only victory of the day. The American pilots also opened their combat scoring of the new year when 2nd Lieutenant William R. Bowman of the 51st FIW's 39th FIS shot down one MiG-15. Most likely his victory was over a Chinese or North Korean pilot of the UAA, since the 64th IAK reported no losses on this day.

Up until 14 January, the pilots of the 32nd IAD and 216th IAD flew very few combat missions, and their encounters with the adversary are not worth mentioning. If they indeed took place, the enemy usually avoided combat. Only on 6 January did pilots of the 133rd IAD's 726th IAP damage one Sabre in the area of the Manchurian airfields; after this, there were no further enemy encounters at all until 12 January due to the poor meteorological conditions. As is now clear one F-86E (No.51-2744) from the 16th FIS was actually damaged on 6 January. However, this Sabre crashed short of the runway when attempting to land back at its base and its pilot 2nd Lieutenant Harry F. Carter was killed, while the F-86 was recorded as an operational loss. Captain S.A. Ivanovsky of the 726th IAP was the one who achieved this victory, but it was nevertheless only credited to him as a damaged enemy aircraft.

Infrequent clashes with the enemy resumed on 12 January, which ended without any results. Prior to this there were a few night actions, since B-29 bombers undertook a number of major raids to the Sinuiju, Singisiu and Andong areas at night. Intercepting these raids on 10 and 12 January, pilots of the 351st NIAP shot down three B-29s and damaged another. Pilots of the 535th IAP's 1st (Night) Squadron assisted in repelling these bombing missions and destroyed two more B-29s.

The first serious daytime clash occurred on 13 January in the Taechon and Pukchin areas, in which the American pilots shot down two of the UAA's MiG-15s. Both victories went to pilots of the 4th FIW. The first serious air battle, in which Soviet pilots participated, took place on the next day, 14 January. Aerial combats took place over the Unsan, Taechon and Keijo areas. The entire 518th IAP and 878th IAP of the 216th IAD took part in the air battles, as well as all three regiments of the 32nd IAD. All of the sorties were in regiment strength. The pilots of the 216th IAD flew two combat missions on 14 January, both of which resulted in combat. Thus, in the first action pilots of the 878th IAP dueled with 16 F-86s, and in the second, with 10 F-86s, though to be true they both ended without results. Meanwhile, the pilots of the 518th IAP in their first dogfight of the day damaged one Sabre, and shot down another F-86 in their second combat. The 3rd Squadron flight commander Captain N.I. Kas'ianov became the hero of the day for the 518th IAP and the entire 216th IAD, by getting the victory and damaging another F-86 on this day. Both dogfights ended without any losses to the 216th IAD.

Pilots of the 224th IAP had several dogfights in the area of the Supung hydroelectric station on 14 January. One of them took place during a regimental sortie with the squadrons flying in a column of flights staggered in altitude. Here's how one of the pilots on the mission, former pilot of the 224th IAP Sergei Aleksandrovich Il'iashenko talks about it:

> Our squadron under the command of Major M.G. Doroshenko took off in response to an alarm. We flew to the area of the hydro-electrical station in a column of flights, staggered in altitude. At an altitude of 11,000 meters we spotted a pair of F-86s off to our left, approaching at an angle. Doroshenko banked toward them and began to close for an attack. My leader Captain V.T. Smorgunov and I stretched behind Doroshenko (he was flying with Kudriashov as his wingman) in the column, when suddenly a pair of Sabres popped up in front of us from below. Smorgunov opened fire at the lead Sabre and the wingman's Sabre winged over to the right into a shallow dive. The Sabres broke in different directions; Smorgunov went after the leader, while I targeted the wingman. Smorgunov gave me the command to attack the wingman's Sabre, and I opened fire. At this same instant I was attacked from behind – my aircraft immediately burst into flames, my cockpit canopy was shattered, my radio was knocked out, and I ejected. In this combat my leader Captain Vasilii Smorgunov shot down his Sabre, and it seems that squadron commander Major Doroshenko damaged another.

In this same dogfight a 1st Squadron flight commander of the 224th IAP Senior Lieutenant B.N. Sis'kov also distinguished himself by shooting down one F-86. Unfortunately, in this action another MiG-15 was downed. Senior Lieutenant N.P. Sokolov from an altitude of 15,000 meters began to dive through a cloud layer in the area of the Supung dam, and when exiting the clouds at an altitude of 5,000-6,000 meters, he was unexpectedly attacked by a Sabre element and his MiG was damaged. The pilot ejected from his crippled aircraft and parachuted down onto the ice of the reservoir, but the ice couldn't hold the weight of the pilot and gave way. The pilot slipped under the water headfirst. Our pilot was unable to clamber out of the fragile ice by himself, and his parachute dragged him below the surface. Nikolai Pavlovich Sokolov drowned in the reservoir. Here's how a participant in the action Lev Petrovich Kolesnikov describes it:

> The ground below disappears. The MiGs of my comrades are bobbing in front of me and behind me, like skiffs on a light sea. The dim winter sun is illuminating the gray ice on the recently blue river. White contrails stream behind the tails of the leaders. We've entered the inversion layer. That's the layer where a host of ice crystals float. Melted by the heat of our turbines, they trace our white track through the sky. When that happens, it becomes clear our aircraft are crowding the Korean sky: three six-ship formations of our regiment, and those of other regiments. Over there, plainly, the North Koreans with their famous Kim Ki Ok are marking the sky. In that direction are the Chinese volunteers. Somewhere in their formation is the "stick it to 'em" 19-year-old youngster Wang Hai. He already has several downed Sabres to his credit. And now, there they are. Oho! White filaments, looking like

Senior Lieutenant B.N. Sis'kov
(a 1950 photo).

innocent threads, extend toward us from the Sea of Japan, the Yellow Sea and the 38th Parallel, hurrying to meet us. Down below, as always smoke billows from the hills, paddies and fields. Korea is burning.

"Canisters!"

That means to jettison our drop tanks. The little finger of the right hand touches the button on the joy stick. The aircraft leaps a bit, and the nearly empty drop tanks disappear from the wings. All around, here and there similar packages, resembling white baste shoes, go flying, spinning and tumbling, their paths marked by thin plumes. Only these aren't the results of inversion. Kerosene is streaming from them. Down below, when striking the rocky ground, some burst into flame, while other simply disintegrate into pieces, which can in fact cut someone down accidentally. It is war.

Freed from their drop tanks, the MiGs jauntily accelerate. The airspeed indicator is showing more than 1,000 km/hour. Great! A combat speed. Our altitude is 12,000 meters. It wouldn't be a bad thing to climb a little higher. But now there is no time. There they are, Sabres closing head-on. The nose of one of them is decorated with a fiery crown. You mean you're shooting, fool? One formation flashes like lightning through the other, and by some miracle they part without a collision. Mironov goes into a turn and we follow him. In the distance, a little patch of flame is spinning wildly across the sky, leaving a smoky zigzag behind it: gravity takes over and it heads downward. Someone's been shot down.

Over the radio comes an order from the ground: "Cover the canopy!" Then suddenly a single name flashes through my head: "Kolia!" A white piece of fluff is floating above the bluish ice of the reservoir. Aircraft with yellow bands on their wings are rushing toward it. Like hell! We won't let it happen!

Kolia's wingman Askol'd German is already circling the parachute. Flight commander Boris Sis'kov and his wingman Klimov join him. Doroshenko is hurrying there with his flight of six MiGs; Mironov and I are hurrying at the head of it. The Americans won't get a sitting duck. A large dogfight breaks out. It splits up into separate flurries of action. Seconds pass. More seconds, and then a report comes from the ground: "The vultures are leaving. The parachutist has landed. You are to descend. Subsequently, return home."

This was the 64th IAK's first loss of life in the new 1953 year. Unfortunately, it wouldn't be the last.

The results of the dogfights on 14 January were as follows: the 64th IAK shot down three F-86s and damaged one more. Its own losses amounted to two aircraft and one pilot. The Americans however claimed that on 14 January the pilots of the 4th and 51st FIW shot down eight MiG-15s – plainly some of them belonged to the regiments of the UAA. The Americans themselves acknowledged the loss of just one F-86F (No.51-12950) of the 51st FIW, the pilot of which Colonel John Mitchell managed to return to his base and safely land his Sabre there.

A major air battle occurred over the area of Anju on 15 January. On this day, the American Fifth Air Force command launched a major fighter-bomber airstrike against targets in the Hihong area, involving several dozen F-84G Thunderjets covered by Sabres. Pilots of the 133rd IAD's 726th IAP and of the 216th IAD's 518th IAP and

878th IAP took part in repelling this raid. Pilots of the 32nd IAD remained in reserve. Fortunately, we have the recollections of participants in this air battle. Vasilii Ivanovich Chizh, the former deputy commander of the 726th IAP remembers:

> On 15 January I had to take off on a combat mission in the role of the regiment leader to a patrol zone, where after some time passed I received an order from the command post to head to the Anju area, where F-84 fighter-bombers were headed inbound from the sea, and to disrupt their attack. Having caught sight of a large group of fighter-bombers covered by Sabres, I led the regiment into an attack against the F-84s. In these attacks, my wingman, who on this mission was Senior Lieutenant A.N. Zakharov, and I each managed to shoot down one F-84. After returning to the Anshan Air Base and the pilots' debriefing, it was established that seven F-84s were shot down, while the others turned back and headed toward the sea. However, when analyzing this operation at the corps' command post, where my wingman and I were presented shotguns as awards, we were informed that intercepted American radio messages revealed that a total of 13 US aircraft had gone down in the sea. For this combat I was recommended for the Order of the Red Banner, which I received back in the Soviet Union.

Georgii Gerasimovich Iukhimenko, the former deputy political commander of the 726th IAP's 3rd Squadron, adds his description of the battle to Chizh's story:

> On the 15 January mission, Lieutenant Colonel V.I. Chizh commanded the lead flight, while I led the second flight. My wingman on this mission was Senior Lieutenant Vitalii Mishchenko; the second element consisted of Senior Lieutenant P.G. Kolotov and Senior Lieutenant V. Panteleev. We were directed to the area of Hoeryong at low altitude, since there F-84 aircraft covered by Sabres were attacking a ground target. We attacked the enemy aircraft as they were coming out of their dives. I opened fire on one of the Thunderjets; it listed sharply and departed toward the bay. My wingman V.M. Mishchenko also shot down one F-84, but I lost him during the action and he became easy prey for the covering Sabres and didn't return to base. I really suffered over the loss of my wingman, since he was a fine pilot and a very good, modest man. In addition to me, Chizh, Zakharov, Mishchenko and other pilots of the regiment achieved a victory in this battle, and on the whole the regiment totaled seven victories.

However, the 726th IAP had a strict method for determining victories, and pilots received official credit only for those victories which were confirmed by fragments of enemy aircraft, such as identification tags removed from them. The wreckage of three F-84s were found, which went to the personal scores of Lieutenant Colonel V.I. Chizh and Senior Lieutenants A.N. Zakharov and V.M. Mishchenko; three more F-84s were only credited as damaged, since they came down in the bay and were confirmed only by gun camera footage, including the F-84 that G.G. Iukhimenko claimed to have downed.

On this day pilots of the 518th IAP and 878th IAP tangled with 22 F-86s in the Kusong area. Four F-86s were damaged in the dogfight, or which three went to the score of the 878th IAP's pilots – our pilots had no losses in return.

The result of this air battle was as follows: three F-84s were destroyed and three F-84s were damaged, as were four F-86s (a portion of these fell into the sea). Our losses consisted of just one MiG-15 – Senior Lieutenant Vitalii Mikhailovich Mishchenko was killed. He was shot down by Captain David Davidson of the 4th FIW's 334th FIS. This was the Sabres' only victory on this day. The F-84 shot down by Major Chizh came down over land, and its pilot ejected and was taken prisoner. He was 1st Lieutenant Roger Warren flying F-84G No.51-1139 of the 58th FBW's 69th FBS. Also on this day F-84G No.51-10411 from the 58th FBW was lost. The American command doesn't confirm the loss of the remaining Thunderjets.

On 15 January the 3rd Squadron of the 32nd IAD's 913th IAP flew over to Andong from a Mukden base. Commanded by Captain V.F. Semenov, to this point it had been carrying out nighttime combat duties. Now the 913th IAP participated in daytime combats at full strength. Incidentally, on 15 January 1953 the 913th IAP flew two combat missions to cover the landings of the 216th IAD's regiments, but had no encounter with the enemy.

After this costly battle, the enemy again began to avoid encounters with MiGs, and if they never the less clashed with them, it never involved more than 8 –12 aircraft. Thus the scoring sharply dropped. Fortunately, we had no losses in these combat incidents. Between 15 and 23 January, the 64th IAK lost only one aircraft and it didn't involve combat. On 19 January on a sortie with the regiment, the deputy commander of the naval 578th IAP Captain V.D. Andriushchenko's engine suddenly flamed out at an altitude of 12,000 meters. Andriushchenko went into a glide from this altitude and steered his MiG back to base for a landing, but he came down 300 meters short of the runway. As he did so, his landing gear collapsed from the impact and his MiG landed on its belly, skidded into a rocky hillock, and there it crashed to a stop. The injured pilot was taken away to a hospital, where he spent the next month.

Up until 23 January, the pilots of the 64th IAK had a total of only four productive combats, downing three F-86s and damaging another (one in each dogfight). The dogfights took place between small groups. For example, on 16 January 1953 eight MiG-15s from the 878th IAP's 1st Squadron had a brief clash with four F-86s in the area of the hydro-electric station, and flight commander Captain Iu.V. Nikolaev shot down one F-86 – this was F-86F No.51-12975 of the 335th FIS. The fate of this Sabre's pilot is unknown, because the American records don't give the name of the pilot who came under this MiG attack.[3] The combats on the 20th, 21st and 22nd of January were nearly identical.

The day of 21 January proved to be a rather stressful one for the pilots of the 32nd IAD's 224th IAP. Here's how Lev Petrovich Kolesnikov describes this day and the combat that almost became his last one:

> On 21 January 1953, the day commemorating Lenin's death, we were preparing for a short hop over to one of the forward airfields. This was due to take place that evening, but in the day we were scrambled for combat. There were six of us: Mironov, Maliutin, Goriunov, Kuan, Grisha and I. Major Svishchev's six-ship formation was flying about 3 kilometers out in front of us. At an altitude of 14,000 meters, Svishchev's group began a turn to port. It was then that Sabres appeared between the first group and our six MiGs. There were a lot of them, and they immediately damaged Iurii Borisov,

who was the "tail-end Charlie" in the first flight. Mironov, cutting off the turn, closed with the Sabre that was firing at Borisov and promptly opened fire. The Sabre emitted a "peacock's plume" of flame and began to break up. Mironov and Maliutin were immediately attacked, and the turn came for Goriunov and Kuan to fire, but then enemy attackers in turn placed their element under attack. Grisha and I instantly opened fire. The Sabre leader pulled his F-86 into a turn to starboard, while the wingman rolled over into a dive. I kept an eye on him just in case. The Americans had such a tactic: one maneuvers at altitude, while the other seemingly flees in a dive. The MiGs, which don't like to dive, go after the one that has remained at altitude, while the seemingly fleeing Sabre gains speed in the dive, and then climbs to attack the MiGs from below and behind. This one was truly scampering away.

"Follow me! Our tail is clear", I transmitted Grisha Berelidza.

The Sabre went into a dive. We went after him. Our speed increased. The arrow on the altimeter plummeted: 10,000; 8,000; 6,000! The fighter began to shake and the control stick became as intractable as a steel rod driven into the earth. The air visibly began to condense against the cockpit glass.

"Grisha, fire and then pull out!" I prompted. Hills, rocky slopes and forests threateningly reached up to meet us.

Then suddenly the American energetically pulled his aircraft out of the dive. We dropped below him, and now he himself took the role as the attacker. Our aircraft were camouflaged, and he probably lost me against the backdrop of the nearby earth – he was attacking Grisha. I lined him up and gave him a burst. The tracers just missed the Sabre's cockpit canopy. The Sabre hauled into a tight turn and I stayed with it, and then suddenly drew so close to it that I caught sight of the pilot: he was turning his head around. The glowing pip of my gun sight was resting on a foreigner's polished helmet.

In the air, airplanes look like little toys, models, and in the helter-skelter of combat I somehow forgot that living people were in those cockpits. Now I saw the man, and my finger involuntarily froze over the trigger. At that same instant, very evil little balls of light began rapidly to whiz around my head. Streaking past me, they quickly faded in the distance. I realized someone was shooting at me. But the American, whom I hadn't killed, broke suddenly to the left, and winding up off to one side and even a little behind me, again was turning toward Grisha. Then I yanked my MiG out from under one fire to under another, while Grisha was calling: "Turn with a climb to the left!"

On paper this is a few lines and a minute of reading. Back then, it was just seconds. I huddled lower under the protection of the armor shield and immediately, having heard the drum beat of bullets striking my aircraft, I performed not a barrel roll, but something more like, damn it, a "keg" with a roll around a flexed axis. The tracers fell away. Then, hauling my MiG into a climbing spiral, I checked behind me: the Sabre was hanging behind my tail and pointing its ugly snout at my cockpit.

As I later found out, I was still yelling over the radio that I was engaged and taking fire. Grisha and Svishchev both requested in unison: "Where are you?"

The ice of the reservoir, where Kolia Sokolov perished, was spinning beneath the swept-back wing of my MiG. I radioed: "At 6,000 meters over the '*vysheboika*' [literally, higher killing process]."

The Americans had nicknamed the airspace over the reservoir the "advanced school of combat" – that is where the most intense air battles took place. We caught on to their nickname, only in our own interpretation – schools of aerobatics and combat tactics [*shkoly vysshogo pilotazha i vozdushnogo boiia*], which some wit long ago had baptized as *vysheboiki*.[4]

"We're on our way," Svishchev replied, while Grisha encouraged, "Break!"

The Sabre's belly gleamed, and I pressed the rudder pedal. The MiG skidded onto one wing, and the stream of tracers from the Sabre's machine-gun burst flashed past me to one side. I deployed my air brakes and hauled back on the control stick even more strongly. In those same seconds I saw MiGs sweeping down from altitude. The Americans broke off combat. We were unable to pursue them: we had little fuel left. The ground radioed: "The vultures are leaving. You are to descend."

My MiG had punctured fuel tanks, and I trailed a plume of kerosene spray all the way back to the runway. The antenna of my radio direction finder was demolished, and on my wings and fuselage it looked like some sort of numbskull had been getting his exercise by slashing them.

Karataev told me, "In comparison with the way they worked over my MiG, here their treatment was plainly incomplete. As for your 'They're shooting at me', next time, don't yell. They have female translators sitting and listening in on us. But on the whole, I congratulate you on your combat baptism."

To Grisha I said, rephrasing Ostap Bender's famous utterance, "An idiot's dream came true. The idiot has been under fire."[5]

Later we congratulated Mironov on his latest victory. Iurii Borisov expressed his gratitude to him for saving his life, and in my turn I thanked Major Svishchev.

They rolled my MiG and Borisov's MiG over to the repair shops. The repair workers knew how to patch up damaged aircraft in a matter of hours, but they were waiting for us right away at the forward airfield. We had to fly as passengers in a transport Li-2."

The Sabre claimed by Major P.S. Mironov was from the 336th FIS, F-86E No.51-2846. The Americans again don't report the fate of the pilot of this Sabre, saying only that it was damaged in a combat with MiGs and returned to base.

True, the UAA pilots really took punishment from the Sabres, since according to American records, between 16 January and 23 January the pilots of the 4th and 51st FIW shot down a total of 15 MiGs. The UAA's regiments suffered particularly heavy losses on 21 and 22 January, when according to American records they shot down six MiG-15s on the 21st, and five more on the 22nd of the month. Captain Dolphin "Dolph" Overton III and Lieutenant Colonel Edwin Heller of the 51st FIW's 16th Squadron, who each claimed two MiG-15s in one action, particularly stood out.

On 23 January, the 64th IAK's pilots had a total of two dogfights with enemy aircraft, which weren't marked by any notable intensity, but I want to dwell on one victory on this day in particular. Here is what the local press in Mukden wrote on 26 January 1953:

On 23 January, an American aircraft that had violated China's air space was again shot down by our air force over Liaodong Province's Kuandian District. At 1145 on 23 January, four American F-86 aircraft appeared over the Kuandian District from the direction of Korea. One of them was quickly shot down by our air force. The pilot of the downed aircraft was taken prisoner. The remaining three US aircraft hastily disappeared. The downed American aircraft, F-86 No.731 (an F-86E with the serial number 52-2871) crashed upon landing in the village of Baichentsza, in Kuandian's Third District. The captured pilot is the commander of the 51st Wing's 16th Fighter Squadron of the Fifth Air Force of the American aggressors in Korea, Lieutenant Colonel Edwin Lewis Heller, Serial No. 9900-A, 34 years of age.

Let's stop and discuss this combat action in more detail, since it wasn't every day that such important persons of the opposing side's air force were captured. The actual hero of this battle, a former pilot of the 32nd IAD's 913th IAP Ivan Ivanovich Karpov, continues the tale about this action and describes how Lieutenant Colonel Heller was shot down:

The combat itself (in comparison with other dogfights) was almost insultingly prosaic. This took place on the regiment's first combat sortie around 10 or 11 AM. Petia Byvshev and I were flying as the tail-end pair. The entire group began to turn in the direction of the sun. The sun was blinding; we couldn't see anything. I no longer remember clearly, but it seems my wingman radioed me that he'd attached himself to the formation of a different squadron. It was at this moment that I spotted a Sabre crossing my heading out in front of me at a target aspect angle of 1/4 or 2/4. I made a slight turn and gave it a quick, un-aimed burst. The Sabre rolled over and disappeared somewhere. In the next moment I, continuing to turn to the right behind our regimental armada, caught sight of another Sabre to my front left at long range (600-800 meters), which was banking toward the right. The Sabre was almost in my sights and of course, hadn't seen me. I placed the pip of the gun sight on the aircraft and gave it a long burst – the Sabre gave a jerk, shuddered, and I realized that I'd hit it. I continued turning and searching for my own guys, but didn't see anyone. At this time someone started to shoot at me; I could red balls flying past me, and my aircraft started to shake like an empty tin can that someone is hitting with peas. My aircraft started to become uncontrollable, but I was trying to avoid the bursts with the pedals, while the Sabres were trying to finish me off, firing and firing. I turned around for an instant and saw two F-86s right behind me. In the next moment they completely knocked-out my controls and I decided to eject. I ejected successfully and soon I was hanging in the straps of my parachute. Later I found out that I had accidentally "run into" a Sabre flight, which was hunting for aircraft straying from the group, but they hadn't immediately spotted me. As a result I saw four F-86s, but only attacked two of them. In my opinion, I became isolated partially because of poor meteorological conditions (heavy haze and the turn toward the sun), and partially because of the insufficient cohesion and maturity we showed in combat formation flying, but also because of my own shortcomings. I hit Heller's Sabre with two shells, one in the right wing and the second in the cockpit (it seems that Heller was wounded). On this sortie I had a particularly trouble-free ejection and came down without any injuries or traumas. But as was supposed to happen after an ejection, I underwent an examination in a Changchun hospital and spent the next half-month grounded.

That is how one of the top pilots of the USAF's 51st FIW, the commander of its 16th FIS Lieutenant Edwin Heller was shot down. Prior to this day, he had scored 3.5 victories in the skies of Korea, plus another five to six German aircraft that he'd shot down in the Second World War. For I.I. Karpov, this was his first and only victory in this war.

According to documents of the 64th IAK headquarters, the events of this day unfolded in the following fashion. The first states:

> At 1130 in the Sinuiju – Dapu area, a group of MiGs of the 535th Regiment (20 MiG-15s led by Lieutenant Colonel Akimov) encountered 24 F-86s at an altitude of 10,000 meters. Six pilots fired their cannons in the course of this battle, the results of which are still unknown. Two squadrons of the 913th IAP (16 MiGs led by Lieutenant Colonel Razorenov) encountered 12 F-86s at an altitude of 12,000 meters in the Dapu – Andong – Sinuiju area. Three pilots fired at the enemy. According to the pilots' reports, Senior Lieutenant Karpov shot down one F-86. Senior Lieutenant Karpov hasn't returned from the combat mission. He ejected in the area around Benxihu.

The second, a couple of days later, reports:

> On 23 January 1953, during an air battle around Kuandian between pilots of the 51st Fighter Interceptor Wing and pilots of the 913th IAP, Senior Lieutenant Karpov shot down one F-86. The pilot ejected and was taken prisoner by Chinese comrades. He is wounded and is presently located in the hospital in Andong. The downed pilot, Lieutenant Colonel Edwin Heller, a USAF ace, is the commander of the 51st Fighter Interceptor Wing's 16th Fighter Interceptor Squadron.

On this day (23 January 1953), pilots of the 518th IAP also damaged one Sabre. American sources assert that the pilots of the 51st FIW over the day of combats shot down three MiG-15s, and I.I. Karpov was shot down by either Major Harold Herrick or Captain Dolph Overton of the Wing's 16th FIS. They each achieved one victory on this day.

The pilots of the 51st FIW had a successful dogfight with UAA pilots on 24 January, and claimed to have shot down four MiG-15s in this clash. Three of them went to the score of the 16th FIS, while Captain Cecil G. Foster received personal credit for two of them. Soviet pilots also took off to intercept enemy aircraft on this day, and only pilots of the 535th IAP and the Pacific Ocean Fleet's 578th IAP had an encounter with the enemy, though they both ended without results. However, because of an engine failure while in flight, a pilot of the 578th IAP Senior Lieutenant Zemtsov had to eject, but this wasn't a combat loss.

Just one dogfight took place on 25 January: during a patrol, a regimental group of aircraft of the 32nd IAD's 535th IAP came across a large group of F-86s and engaged it in combat. In the course of the action, the 3rd Squadron's Senior Lieutenants P.N. Blinov and F.I. Masleev fired at two Sabres from close range. Upon returning to Andong, news came from the command post that according to intercepted radio messages, one of the Sabres had fallen into the bay and its pilot had ejected, while the other Sabre managed to limp back damaged to its base in South Korea. According to this information and the gun camera footage, P.N. Blinov received credit for a victory. This was over F-86F No.51-2861 from the 335th FIS. Its pilot Captain Murray A. Winslow managed to bail out near Cho-do Island and he was rescued by an H-19 search and rescue helicopter. F.I. Masleev, however, only received credit for damaging his Sabre.

On 26 January, one productive air battle took place over the Kusong area, when eight MiG-15s from the 913th IAP's 3rd Squadron tangled with a group of F-86s. Senior Lieutenant A.I. Shliapin, as well as Senior Lieutenant A.P. Pushchin and Major A.T. Kostenko all combined to shoot down one Sabre, so it was recorded as a group victory. In this action F-86E No.51-2796 of the 336th FIS was shot down and its pilot 2nd Lieutenant Bill J. Stauffer is listed as missing-in-action, though his Sabre crashed in an inverted position.

The 64th IAK's pilots had four to five more daytime combats and three night combats before the end of the month, in which they downed seven US aircraft, including four F-86s, two B-29s and one B-26. Four more F-86s were damaged. The pilots of the 32nd IAD between 27 and 31 January recorded two enemy aircraft destroyed and one more damaged. The pilots of the 216th IAD did better, claiming three enemy aircraft destroyed and another three damaged. Finally, pilots of the 351st NIAP shot down two enemy aircraft. We had no losses in these combats, though as a consequence of bad weather, a pilot of the 913th IAP Senior Lieutenant G.M. Udovikov became disoriented and began to fly in the direction of the Liaodong Peninsula. His fuel ran out and he made a forced belly landing near Siujou. The MiG crashed as he put it down and Udovikov was badly shaken up in the process and wound up in a hospital.

On 28 January, the 535th IAP scrambled in response to an alarm to intercept enemy aircraft. However, the weather conditions were miserable – it was snowing. They had a fleeting and non-productive skirmish with a small group of F-86s. When returning to base, a pilot of the regiment Senior Lieutenant B.G. Seniutkin ran out of fuel and he was forced to make a landing prior to reaching the Andong airfield. The MiG hit the ground on its belly. The hard landing injured Seniutkin's spine, and they took him away to the Andong hospital.

The toughest aerial combats were at the end of the month, on 30 and 31 January. The pilots of the 216th IAD had a successful dogfight in the Kusong, Pakchon and Sukchon region, in which they shot down two F-86s without any losses in return. Senior Lieutenant M.F. Antontsev of the 878th IAP claimed one of the Sabres, while credit for the other went to Lieutenant Colonel I.M. Mosin of the 676th IAP. The Americans on this day recognize only the loss of F-86F No.51-12960 of the 39th FIS; its pilot 1st Lieutenant Edwin "Ed" Hatzenbuehler bailed out and was picked up by search and rescue.

On 31 January during a regimental sortie to the Changseong, Kusong and Unsan area, the pilots of the 878th IAP had a successful combat with a squadron of F-86s, and shot down one and damaged two more without any losses. The Americans claimed, though, that 1st Lieutenant Joseph McConnell, Jr. of the 39th FIS on 30 and 31 January shot down one MiG each day, while 1st Lieutenant Raymond A. Konsey of the 4th FIW's 335th FIS shot down a piston-engine Tu-2 bomber of the UAA.

Altogether in the first month of 1953, the pilots of the 64th IAK shot down 25 enemy aircraft in day and night combats (14 F-86, 7 B-29, 3 F-84 and 1 B-26) and damaged 16 more (12 F-86, 3 F-84 and 1 B-29). Their own losses over this period amounted to eight

Capt. Joseph McConnell Jr., a pilot with the 51st Fighter Intercepter Wing, talks with his crew chief while in the cockpit of his F-86 Sabre jet, "Beauteous Butch II." Capt. McConnell became the US' 27th jet ace of the Korean conflict March 9 1953, and was the top American ace of the war with 16 kills. (US Air Force)

aircraft and two pilots, of which only four aircraft and both pilots were combat losses. In addition, the UAA's losses in this month consisted of 12 MiG-15s (four pilots were killed) and one Tu-2. Thus, the total losses in January 1953 on the Communist side amounted to 17 aircraft (disregarding the 64th IAK's non-combat losses), while according to the American side, its Sabre pilots shot down 38 enemy aircraft (37 MiG-15s and one Tu-2), while losing 11 F-86s, of which only five were lost in combat. Thus only 17 of these victories can be confirmed for the American side, while the remaining 21 aircraft claimed as victories were most likely only damaged and returned to their bases.

The Chinese pilots of the UAA flew 1,520 individual combat sorties in the month of January, and the North Koreans only 12. Together they had 31 group aerial combats, in which they claim shooting down 15 enemy aircraft and damaging another two.

February also began with low intensity combat operations in the air; both sides were operating in small groups against each other. The nature of the combats suggested changes in the size and formations of the air groups. An eight-ship formation had shown itself to be too cumbersome for a dogfight. The squadron "front" formation was also unsuitable. They began to launch in six-ship formations that would assemble into wedges of staggered elements. The lead, or strike element, would fly with the wingman tucked in close to one side and behind the leader. Above and behind was the covering flight, with one element staggered to the left and the other staggered to the right. The left-side cover wingman was responsible for keeping the right hemisphere under watch. Simultaneously, he had the entire group in his field of vision. This provided security for his place in the formation. The right-side wingman, correspondingly, was responsible for keeping watch over the left hemisphere.

In the fighting, the pilots of the 32nd IAD, the 216th IAD's 878th IAP and the two separate regiments, the Pacific Ocean Fleet's 578th IAP and the 351st NIAP primarily took part. The pilots of the 133rd IAD was in corps reserve and was based on the second-line airfields at Mukden and Anshan. The pilots of the 216th IAD's 518th IAP and 676th IAP were also enjoying a breather – both regiments had restaged to Anshan. The UAA was becoming more active, and their number of combat sorties increased, which compensated for the reduction in the combat activity of the 64th IAK.

The initial air battles in February occurred on 2 February in the Gisiu area. The Americans were trying to breakthrough to the Supung hydroelectric station and attack it in small groups of F-86 fighter-bombers from the 51st FIW. Covering the dam and power station, pilots of the 224th IAP had two dogfights with Sabres. The first involved Major P.S. Mironov's six MiGs from the 224th IAP's 3rd Squadron and a group of F-86s, which ended successfully for our side. Squadron commander Major Mironov shot down one Sabre. Their six-ship formation was soon replaced by six MiGs from the same regiment's 1st Squadron led by Major P.I. Svishchev. Soon they were also directed from the ground toward 12 F-86F-30s, with which they engaged in combat. In the course of it one Sabre tried to escape into some clouds, but there was a nearby MiG, which swung in behind its tail and fired a burst at the F-86, damaging it. The Sabre pilot changed his mind and headed for the bay instead. Senior Lieutenant N.K. Olintsov was the pilot who damaged it, but he didn't receive credit for this victory. All of the raids by small groups of F-86s were repulsed, and our pilots had no losses in the actions.

However, the Americans claimed that on 2 February pilots of the 4th FIW shot down two MiGs – plainly, they were dueling with UAA pilots. In their turn the Americans acknowledged the loss of F-86F No.51-12941 of the 335th FIS, which was shot down by Major Mironov – his third victory in this war!

The next clashes between small groups from both sides occurred on 4 February, in which pilots of the 32nd IAD and the 216th IAD's 878th IAP took part. The 878th IAP's pilots did well in them, or more precisely, those of the 3rd Squadron headed by its commander Hero of the Soviet Union V.V. Egorov. At first Egorov's eight-ship formation came across a group of F-86s, and in the ensuing dogfight squadron commander Major V.V. Egorov shot down one Sabre. Returning to base after the combat action, the deputy squadron commander Major N.M. Zameskin noticed a pair of F-86s that was stealthily approaching the group from below. Zameskin reported this to the division's command post and received permission to attack. Attacking from above, from a range of 200 meters he poured fire from every cannon into an unsuspecting Sabre and it exploded in mid-air, which was captured by his gun camera film. This was his sixth victory in the skies of Korea. Our pilots had no losses in these dogfights. The Sabre shot down by Zameskin was F-86E No.51-2749 of the 16th FIS – its pilot 2nd Lieutenant Max H. Collins successfully bailed out prior to the explosion, but he'd been wounded in the attack.

The 64th IAK's first loss in the month happened on 7 February. On this day, eight MiG-15s from 913th IAP's 1st Squadron, while on a mission, were jumped by a pair of F-86s that emerged unexpectedly from behind some clouds. Having closed with the MiG group, they unleashed a fusillade of fire against one of the pairs on the outside of the formation and shot down the wingman, Lieutenant I.K. Dem'ianov before disappearing back into the clouds. Fortunately, our pilot safely ejected and soon returned to the regiment. On this day, however, the Sabres also didn't get away unscathed. In a dogfight between pilots of the 32nd IAD and a group of F-86s, one of them was damaged by the deputy commander of the 535th IAP's 2nd Squadron Captain V.A. Utkin. We had no losses in this action. The damaged Sabre, F-86F No.51-12948 of the 335th FIS was able to reach its base, where the pilot safely landed it. The Americans claimed that on 7 February, the pilots of the 4th FIW shot down two MiG-15s – one of them was I.K. Dem'ianov's aircraft, but the other was likely only damaged.

Another pause then settled over the fighting, caused by bad weather and a decline in the enemy's combat activity, which lasted until the middle of the month. Flight operations resumed on 12 February, but the first encounter with the enemy after the break took place only on the next day, 13 February. Pilots of the 535th IAP flew one regimental sortie in the neighborhood of 1000 and encountered a group of four F-86 Sabres that was escorting an RF-80. In a brief dogfight, Captain V.A. Utkin succeeded in getting hits on one Sabre, which broke off combat. Our group had no losses. As has since been established, on this day F-86F No.51-12938 of the 335th FIS was damaged in the Sinuiju area. Its pilot 2nd Lieutenant Paul J. Jacobson struggled to reach the bay in it, but there the engine stopped and the aircraft plunged into the sea; Jacobson was killed. Thus this was a complete victory for our pilot.

On 15 February, several combat encounters with the enemy took place in the areas of Uisan, Sunchon, Taechon, Sonchon and Gisiu, in which pilots of the 32nd IAD, the 216th IAD's 878th IAP, the Pacific Ocean Fleet's 578th IAP and of the UAA took part. Thus, on the second mission of the day the 535th IAP, which was being led by the regiment's deputy commander Lieutenant Colonel P.S. Akimov, engaged a large group of Sabres. In the ensuing dogfight, 3rd Squadron flight commander Captain P.N. Blinov damaged one Sabre, which managed to reach the sanctuary of Korea Bay and fell into the sea there, but its pilot ejected in time and was picked up by a search and rescue helicopter. Blinov only received credit for damaging this Sabre. In this same action, Senior Lieutenant P.P. Zabolotny's element was attacked by a pair of Sabres, and under their fire his wingman Lieutenant Nikolai Nagorny was wounded. He broke off combat and made a successful landing at Andong, after which he was hospitalized.

On this day, the naval pilots of the 578th IAP enjoyed one of their most successful combats: a squadron in the strength of eight MiGs under the command of Captain V.D. Andriushchenko in cooperation with the 726th IAP's 3rd Squadron tangled with eight F-86s in the vicinity of the Andong airfield, and the 578th IAP's deputy commander Captain Andriushchenko and Senior Lieutenant E.G. Kravtsov each downed one Sabre and the squadron returned to base without any losses. This was one of the final combats of the 578th IAP's pilots in the skies of Korea, since several days later this naval aviation regiment returned to its previous base in the Maritime District.

The USAF Fifth Air Force command claimed that pilots of the 51st FIW shot down three MiG-15s on this day, while pilots of the 4th FIW added one more; most likely, they achieved all of these victories in dogfights with pilots of the UAA. In their turn, the Americans deny the loss of any of their Sabres on this day.

On the next day several air battles took place in the Kusong – Gisiu area; the Soviet pilots were covering a local power generating station. A former pilot of the 535th IAP Fedor Il'ich Masleev relates what happened in one of them:

> We took off on 16 February to intercept a group of Sabres over the area of a dam with a complement of six MiGs, flown by Major P.I. Karataev with Senior Lieutenant V.N Lapygin; the other elements consisted of Major E.I. Goriunov with Senior Lieutanant P.P. Zabolotny, and me together with Senior Lieutenant I.K. Sokolov. At an altitude of 13,000 meters, to our front right we spotted a formation of five aircraft flying in a compact formation as if on parade; an RF-94 (or RF-80) was located in the middle of it, being closely escorted by four F-86, with two on each side. My element attacked this group from the left, but the attack was unsuccessful – we pulled out of the pass to the right of the targets and I decided to make another pass. I began to maneuver for the attack, when over the radio I heard the voice of my wingman: "125, break right, I'm under attack." I went into a tight, climbing turn to starboard and at this moment a burst of machine-gun fire from a Sabre struck my MiG. I felt a burning sensation in my right arm. I began to weave back and forth, trying to nudge my aircraft in the direction of a burst that had just passed me, but at times I could feel the bullets striking home. It is difficult to say how long this went on. My radio wasn't working. I headed toward Dapu, but in the area of Fenghuang-cheng decided to eject, since my engine was no longer working and my aircraft was trailing a long plume of white smoke; my cockpit canopy, gun sight and instrument panel had been shot up. I reached out and placed my hand on the canopy ejection lever, and at this moment saw a Sabre and its pilot wearing a helmet just 50 meters off my right wing. He obviously had fired off all his ammunition at me and had decided to take a closer look at me, to see why I was still flying. I abruptly banked my aircraft toward him to try to collide with him, but the American pilot reacted instantly by diving to the left beneath me, and that is when I saw a MiG element approaching from my right, the leader of which opened fire at the Sabre. I'm still amazed to this day that I was able to make a belly-landing on the ground to the right of the runway at Dapu with a dead engine and no instruments, just a little over 200 meters short of the arresting barrier. My right arm was wounded and blood was flowing down it. That's how my 49th combat sortie ended. Meanwhile, that Sabre that had shot me up was shot down by that MiG element. That very same day they transported me in a Yak-12 to Andong, where I was taken to the hospital.

That Sabre was "damaged" (more accurately, shot down, but was credited as only damaged) by the 913th IAP's 1st Squadron deputy commander Captain V.N. Aleksandrov.

On this same day pilots of the 51st FIW's 39th FIS scored well by downing three MiG-15s, two of which were credited to 1st Lieutenant Harold Fischer. Most likely, the 913th IAP's pilots on this mission encountered a group of carrier-based F9F-2 Panthers and attacked them. The Panther pilots summoned help in the form of Sabres, which in their turn damaged Masleev's aircraft. The Americans don't admit the losses among their Sabres on this day, but the USNAF VF-93 squadron lost two of its Panthers.

Serious battles took place on 18 and 19 February. One of the participants, the former 913th IAP deputy squadron commander Vasilii Nikolaevich Aleksandrov recalls:

> Early one morning, on the 18th of February, as usual we arrived at the airfield at 0530, where our ground crews had already completely readied our aircraft. The weather was superb; visibility was unlimited ("Million by million", as our pilots said). There was not a cloud in the sky. We sensed that this would be a stressful day. Almost daily, the enemy aircraft made their first sortie at sunrise, when its blinding rays would be right in our eyes. They always flew in from the east, and this greatly complicated the visual search for them.
>
> We were seated in our ready hut, playing dominoes, checkers and chess. An order came out over the radio's loudspeaker from the division command post: "Readiness No.1". We and our entire regiment dashed out to our waiting MiGs and climbed into the cockpits. Five or six minutes later, the order to scramble arrived. We pushed our engine throttles forward and according to the previously arranged plan the 3rd Squadron took off, followed by the 2nd Squadron and then our 1st Squadron, bringing up the regiment's rear. We knew what we had to do; climb as quickly as possible and try to use up the fuel in our drop tanks before meeting the adversary. From the directions from the ground, we knew the flight paths of the enemy aircraft and their approximate number – up to 40 aircraft at an altitude of 9,000 meters. Somewhere at an altitude of 10,000 meters, we jettisoned our drop tanks at an order from the regiment commander Major V.A. Marchenko and began to clamber for more altitude. We climbed to 12,000 meters, when someone began to shout over the radio that he could see aircraft at the same altitude as us, somewhat to the left of the sun's disc. They were approximately 8 to 10 kilometers away. We angled toward them on an interception course. We closed, and a real melee began. An ever increasing number of aircraft tangled in combat in flights and elements. Our squadron joined the dogfight a little later, because we were flying above and behind the rest of the regiment.
>
> I spotted a Sabre element and shouted to my wingman over the radio to attack. In the radio noise he delayed in reacting to my maneuver, but nevertheless stayed with me. Our favorite and well-justified tactic was to try to force the adversary to fight in the vertical plane, where the MiG was greatly superior. This we succeeded in doing; the Sabre pair rolled over and decided to go into a dive. We didn't delay in pursuing, but the distance to them was somewhat large. Then one of the Sabre pilots simply did something stupid. He was lax in pulling out of the dive, enabling us to cut off his arc and close to within 600 meters. He then tried to pull into a zoom climb (yet another mistake), and our range closed to 400-500 meters, where I pressed the trigger button. It was a burst of average length, but the hits were clearly visible. Just 20-25 seconds later the Sabre began to smoke, and another instant later the pilot ejected, but his parachute didn't open right away. I lost further sight of him. This entire mission, from take-off to landing, took approximately an hour of time, while the combat itself lasted only 3 to 3.5 minutes, and the rest of the time was just a prelude to it. The dogfight was east of Dapu, 40-50 kilometers southeast of this airfield. We landed at Andong.

In this combat the 3rd Squadron commander Senior Lieutenant A.I. Shliapin shot down another Sabre. We had no losses. However, just the day before on 17 February a pilot of the 4th FIW's 335th FIS 2nd Lieutenant John MacKey shot down the MiG being flown by Captain I.F. Zelensky, the deputy commander of the 913th IAP's 3rd Squadron, who successfully ejected. Thus, A.I. Shliapin of the same squadron squared the account with the American pilots of the FIW. To be sure, however, the Americans deny the loss of a Sabre on 18 February!

In this day's massive dogfight involving approximately 100 aircraft, the pilots of the 913th IAP shot down two F-86 without any losses. However, the Americans claim that the pilots of the 4th FIW shot down seven MiG-15s, two of which were downed by the 334th FIS's Captain Manuel Fernandez. Probably, a few of these victories came at the expense of the UAA, but a few of the aircraft were likely only damaged and returned to base.

Additional heavy aerial fighting took place on 19 February in the Kusong, Taechon and Singisiu areas, when the enemy again targeted the Supung hydroelectric power station. To repel this air raid, the entire 32nd IAD and the 216th IAD's 878th IAP were scrambled. Fortunately, we have the testimony of two pilots who participated in this clash in the vicinity of Supung.

Semen Alekseevich Fedorets of the 913th IAP recalls:

> On this mission, the chief of the regiment's aerial gunnery services Major I.I. Rudakov was leading the regiment. After take-off, the squadrons assembled in a climbing turn and took their position in the regiment's formation. After climbing to 13,000 to 14,000 meters, we set a course to intercept a group of Sabres of the forward screen.
>
> We spotted the group of Sabres a bit below us and off to our right, approaching at an angle of 60-70 degrees. With a turn of 90 degrees, we went to close with them and to attack. After several spirals this entire armada descended to an altitude of 7,000 to 8,000 meters, where the air was denser and the aircraft were more stable in high-G maneuvers. In the course of the dogfight, a Sabre got in behind Valentin Shorin in our flight, and he went into a 60 degree climb in order to break away from the enemy. At this time his leader Evgenii Aseev planted himself on the Sabre's tail and fired several bursts out in front of it. I was flying on Aseev's right and 70 to 100 meters above him, covering his attack. Suddenly Aseev transmitted: "25, approach more closely, I've run out of shells" – and banked away to the right below me. I immediately dropped onto the tail of this Sabre and struck it with a burst from a range of 400-500 meters. The Sabre pilot sensed that the situation could only end in the smell of fuel, and he rolled over into a dive. I followed his maneuver precisely and in an inverted position caught the Sabre in the crosshairs of my gun sight and gave it a short burst from 80-100 meters. I could plainly see as the large orange balls (tracers) of my N-37 shells struck the Sabre's fuselage behind the cockpit. There was a bright glint of reflected sunlight from a thrown aside cockpit canopy, while the Sabre fuselage broke apart and the two pieces headed downward.

That's how Captain S.A. Fedorets shot down F-86E No.52-2839; its pilot 2nd Lieutenant Edward G. Izbicky of the 4th FIW's 334th FIS became a prisoner. According to S.A. Fedorets, who read the transcript of the American pilot's interrogation, he was a

Top ace of the 32nd IAD with 7
victories Lieutenant Colonel S.A.
Fedorets.

young pilot, but he'd already accumulated approximately 450-500 hours in the cockpit of the F-86. He was flying his 21st mission in the skies of Korea on 19 February and he really wanted to bag a MiG, but his luck went against him and he himself was shot down and taken prisoner.

In this dogfight the flight commander Senior Lieutenant Evgenii Georgievich Aseev of the same squadron also achieved a victory. Here's how he describes it:

> I was on a sortie with the entire regiment and over the Yalu we encountered a large group of Sabres and a real brawl began. The regiment broke down into flights and elements. My wingman Sergei Tiurin became separated from me, but soon Valentin Shorin linked up with me and we headed toward the Supung hydroelectric station. As we approached it, we saw our guys already withdrawing, but a pair of F-86s had settled in behind them and was waiting for a suitable moment to attack. Shorin and I were above them and could see them well. I shouted, "We're attacking!" and hurtled downward into an attack on them. They saw us clearly and the wingman made a sharp turn away from us to the right, but the leader made a mistake: he pulled up into a steep climb and from short range I hit his Sabre with shells from all my cannons. I apparently killed the pilot, because the aircraft wasn't smoking or burning, but it simply arced downward toward the earth. Just then another Sabre element appeared and I broke off combat. In this action another Sabre was shot down by the regiment navigator Major A.T. Kostenko. The result of the dogfight was three F-86s downed, with no losses on our side. Senior Lieutenant Shorin's MiG returned with several bullet holes in it, which were quickly patched up by the squadron's technicians.

However, just a bit later a formation of eight MiGs of the 535th IAP's 3rd Squadron departed for the area of the Supung reservoir. One of the flights was being led by the regiment commander Major P.I. Karataev. They didn't encounter any enemy in the vicinity of the Supung hydroelectric station. When returning to base, Senior Lieutenant P.P. Zabolotny's wingman went missing. He didn't respond to queries over the radio. As it turned out, Senior Lieutenant Il'ia Konstantinovich Sokolov's MiG had been damaged by Sabres and he'd made a forced landing, but the impact of the belly landing triggered his ejection mechanism, which shot him through the cockpit canopy and killed him. This was the only death of a 64th IAK pilot over the entire month of February. Probably, he was shot down by Colonel Royal N. Baker, the commander of the 4th FIG. On this same day Colonel James Johnson of the 335th FIS shot down another MiG which likely belonged to the UAA, since the 64th IAK had no other losses on 19 February 1953.

The results of the fighting on 19 February were as follows: four F-86s were shot down, three by pilots of the 913th IAP and one by the 878th IAP's Captain I.G. Semenov. Soviet losses consisted of one MiG-15 destroyed and one damaged, and pilot Senior Lieutenant I.K. Sokolov was killed. The Americans claimed two victories on this day and acknowledged the loss of only one of their Sabres.

Another major dogfight took place two days later on 21 February in the Kuandian – Changseong area, as well as in the Sikisiu, Hakido, Sosan, Pukchin and Gisiu sector in the Anju area. Two regiments of the 32nd IAD (the 224th IAP and 913th IAP) took part in it on our side while its 513th IAP remained in reserve. Regiments of the 216th IAD also became involved in the fighting. A participant in this air battle, a flight commander in the 913th IAP's 1st Squadron Captain Semen Alekseevich Fedorets has this to say about it:

> On our next mission, the regiment attempted to repel a raid by F-80 Shooting Stars targeting Ryonpo in the Hamhung area (on the coast of the Yellow Sea). We were flying at an altitude of 14,000 meters at nearly maximum range. The enemy ground radars and those on one of their aircraft carriers standing just offshore of Korea in the Yellow Sea spotted our approach and gave an order to the F-80s to clear out of the target area. Our command post informed us of the situation and issued the command for us to return to base. Having wheeled around to the right, our squadron was approaching Anju. At this time I spotted out in front of us a group of F-86s that was crossing the Korean coast in from the sea at a distance of 25 to 30 kilometers and a little bit higher than us, which I reported to the squadron commander Major S.I. Babich. He replied that he understood, but hadn't reached any sort of decision about engaging in an air battle. Closing with the enemy, Captain A.I. Khoitsev's flank element on the left switched to the right side of Babich's flight, thereby making squadron commander Major Babich's pair the left-flank element. Rather than increasing the intervals between the elements, the pilots of his flight moved in closer to him. The leader of the F-86 group moved to attack his flight, but Babich directed a turn to starboard of 30 to 40 degrees, which only worsened his situation, since he was placing the tail of his aircraft under attack from the approaching Sabres at a 0/4 target aspect angle. They instantly took advantage of this. I was flying with my flight above and to the right. I could see that the situation was developing not in our favor, so I conducted an energetic climbing

turn to right, and then swung sharply back to the left and went into an impetuous attack against the lead Sabre. It managed to open fire on Babich's aircraft and damaged it. I closed with the Sabre and from a range of 300 meters I gave it one, and then from a range of 100 meters a second burst from my cannons. The Sabre rolled over onto its right wing and with a puff of smoke dove precipitously toward the ground. Major Babich's MiG was now trailing a plume of black smoke, but it was continuing to fly in a gentle descent. In his damaged aircraft Babich reached an area over a Buddhist temple and ejected, before parachuting safely to earth. The temple's members picked him up and rendered him initial first aid, and then reported to the regiment command post about him.

In addition to S.I. Babich, one more pilot of the 913th IAP Senior Lieutenant Smirnov was shot down, who also successfully ejected from his stricken aircraft. One of them was shot down by the pair of Captain Winston Stacey and his wingman 1st Lieutenant Robert Carter, while the second MiG was shot down by Major Vermont Garrison, all of the 4th FIW's 335th FIS. However, if Fedorets downed one of them, then most likely it was someone from Captain Stacey's element. According to American records, they shot down three MiG-15s in this action, but one of them failed to receive credit for his kill, since the pilot who shot it down in this battle was later shot down in return and the proof of his victory burned up in the wreckage of his fallen Sabre.

On this day pilots of the 224th IAP distinguished themselves; in a large dogfight with F-86s they shot down two of the Sabres and damaged another. Deputy commander of the 1st Squadron Captain N.D. Batrakov had a particularly memorable day. In one pass he shot down two Sabres simultaneously, though he was given clean credit for only one of them, while the other was recorded as damaged. Batrakov inflicted fatal damage to F-86F-30 No.52-4340 of the 18th FBW's 12th FBS. Its pilot Harry H. Porter bailed out and was rescued. Incidentally, this day marked the first counter-air mission of the 18th Wing's 67th FBS after transitioning to the F-86F from the F-51D and their first combat with MiGs in their new jet equipment. For this action Batrakov was awarded with the Order of the Red Banner. Our pilots had no losses in this combat. Pilots of the 216th IAD's 518th IAP also damaged one Sabre.

In sum, in the air battles on 21 February, three F-86s were destroyed and two were damaged by the 64th IAK's pilots. Our own losses consisted of two MiG-15s, but no pilots were killed. The Americans admit the loss of only one of their F-86s, Porter's.

The final air battles that winter occurred on 25 and 26 February 1953 in the Singisiu area over a local power generating station. The dogfights were primarily fleeting and low-intensity, involving small groups of fighters. A participant in one of them, a former pilot of the 535th IAP Petr Petrovich Zabolotny shares his experience in it:

On 25 February, flying as the wingman to the deputy regiment commander P.S. Akimov, we flew off to cover a power plant. We loitered over the hydro-electrical station for 40 or 50 minutes, because it had come under a bombing. Without encountering any enemy, we were given an order from the command post to return to base. When approaching the airfield, we were prohibited from making our landing, because Sabres were over the base and its anti-aircraft gunners were firing. We were directed to head to a reserve airfield. That's when I spotted a flight of F-86s that was following about 800-1,000 meters behind us. I warned Akimov, "12, Sabres beind us." He radioed me in response that they were friendlies. I repeated my warning. The Sabres opened fire. I glanced at one of my aircraft's wings and saw bullet holes, and I could also hear bullets punching through the skin of my MiG's fuselage. I glanced over at Akimov and saw that he had a Sabre with a checkerboard pattern on its tail fin right behind him, which had opened fire on him. Meanwhile this three-ship F-86 formation was all this time firing at me. I hauled my MiG around to the left in order to drive away Akimov's attacker. I gave it a burst, and then began to veer away from him in order to avoid a collision. The Sabre fired another burst at Akimov's MiG before departing beneath my MiG, trailing blue smoke, and heading toward the bay. Akimov's aircraft burst into flames and he ejected. After this I went into a climb, in order to separate myself from the persistent threesome of Sabres that were continuing to fire at me. Shortly after starting my climb, I yanked back on my control stick to increase the angle of my climb, but the controls didn't respond, because they were damaged. This happened at an altitude of 4,000 meters, my aircraft was no longer responsive, and it went into a dive. I ejected at an approximate altitude of 1,000 meters. Descending in my parachute, I watched the three Sabres fly away to the bay. I came down safely. I was immediately picked up and delivered to a hospital, where I saw Akimov – he had injured his thumb on one hand. I spent five days in the hospital and again returned to operations.

Lieutenant Colonel Akimov's element had been shot down by a flight of Sabres from the 51st FIW's 39th FIS being led by Major James Hagerstrom, a pilot of the 18th FBW's 67th FBS, which had recently transitioned to the F-86F-30. More experienced pilots of the 51st Fighter Interceptor Wing flew with the pilots of the 67th Squadron on their first combat sorties in their new mounts in order to give them greater confidence. On this mission it was in fact Major Jim Hagerstrom who shot down Lieutenant P.S. Akimov's MiG, and according to Zabolotny's account above, he damaged Hagerstrom's Sabre, but the American pilot safely returned to his base in it. In his turn Zabolotny himself came under the fire of 1st Lieutenant Harold Fischer of the 39th FIS, one of the squadron's top aces, and he himself was shot down. This was Fischer's 9th victory in the skies of Korea.

In the final combat of the month on 26 February, pilots of the 913th IAP damaged two Sabres over the area of a power generating station without any losses in return. The Americans report the loss of one F-86F-30 No.52-4348 from the SAAF No.2 Squadron, which was attached to the 18th FBG; its pilot Lieutenant R.L. Van Rooyen bailed out over the K-8 airbase and was rescued. Although the Americans claim this was a non-combat loss caused by fuel exhaustion and that the Sabre was written off only two days later, it seems more probable that this Sabre had been damaged in a combat with MiGs and that Captain V.P. Aleksandrov was the responsible party.

The results of the February fighting for the 64th IAK were a total of 12 F-86s downed and 10 F-86s damaged. This speaks to the enemy's much lower level of activity in this month in comparison with previous periods. Although the Americans in fact claimed that they shot down 26 MiGs in the month, this is a dubious figure, because the 64th IAK only lost eight aircraft in February 1953, while the UAA lost just seven MiGs. In addition, 10 MiGs received combat damage and five pilots were killed. Thus, only a total of 15 MiGs were lost in February and another 10 to 12 were damaged, which means that 11 of the total number of victories claimed by the American side were only damaged and not shot down. The Americans placed their own losses at five F-86s, of which only four were lost in combat, which seems too low in number to be accurate.

The point is that in addition to the 12 F-86s claimed by the pilots of the 64th IAK, another 10 F-86s were shot down and four more damaged in 29 dogfights with pilots of the UAA. The UAA pilots were beginning to conduct combat missions more actively. It is no coincidence that in the month of February the UAA recorded now 1,578 individual combat sorties, of which 1,226 were flown by Chinese pilots and 352 by North Korean pilots. In the winter of 1952-1953, according to assertions by the Chinese themselves, in the course of several months the PLAAF had built up its inventory of fighter aircraft (by March 1953 another two fighter aviation divisions, the 26th and 27th, had been organized), while at the same time "the combat activity of the American air force was steadily diminishing". The North Koreans sharply increased their combat activity, which is most likely connected with the better weather. In February they again took on enemy carrier aircraft. On 6 February, a flight of North Korean MiGs intercepted a pair of Fireflies from the HMS *Glory* and destroyed one of them (the English, however, assign this loss to 9 February 1953 and attribute it to flak).

As noted previously, on 21 February a new USAF formation began taking on MiGs after transitioning to the F-86 – the 18th FBW. True, at first this involved only its 67th Squadron in the purely fighter role. This squadron began conducting patrols over the Yalu River in the forward Sabre screen together with pilots of the 51st FIW. At the same time at the end of February, the pilots of the 8th FBG also replaced their F-80s with new F-86F-30s and started to retrain in them. The first to transition to the new jet fighter were pilots of the 35th Squadron. Because the pilots of the 8th FBG had previously been flying F-80 jets, they quickly adapted to the F-86F. According to the words of one of the 35th Squadron's pilots, the process of re-equipping and learning to fly the F-86F went so quickly that the engines in the Sabres were practically never switched off. However their first appearance in the skies of North Korea in the F-86F-30 didn't take place until the beginning of April 1953, and in the meantime, the pilots of the 8th FBG were still undergoing training.

In the middle of February 1953, a new airbase in northeast China became operational in the vicinity of Kuandian. This was located in a mountainous area at an altitude of 2,000 meters above sea level. It had been built next to the Supung hydroelectric power station in order to be closer to this important facility to facilitate operational coverage of it. True, the airfield did not have concrete runways, but used pierced steel planking instead. In February, the 913th IAP transferred to the new airfield at Kuandian. However, when landing on the runways, because of the poor connections linking the metal planks, they ruptured violently when Senior Lieutenant A.K. Popov's MiG touched down, causing it to crash and then erupt in flames. Fortunately, the pilot managed to escape the cockpit unharmed before it burst into flames. The MiG was totally consumed by the fire. After this calamity, the pilots of the 913th IAP flew back to Andong, while urgent work to construct concrete runways at Kuandian began immediately. Already by March 1953, it was fully restored to operational status. That month, the 913th IAP's 3rd Squadron flew back to Kuandian and operated from it until 18 May 1953, when it was replaced by a different aviation unit of the 64th IAK.

ENDNOTES

1. The Korean War Aircraft Loss database, available at http://www.dtic.mil/dpmo/korea/reports/air/ indicates that Saunder's F-86F in fact caught fire shortly after take-off and he bailed out 5 kilometers north of the K-13 Air Base. If so, obviously this F-86F was not a combat loss and was not shot down by Senior Lieutenant Vit'ko.

2. Although several Russian websites report the loss of this F-86F No.51-2858, it is not recorded in the Defense Prisoner of War/Missing Personnel Office's Korean War Aircraft Loss database, nor does this database show the loss of any F-86F on 24 December 1952. However, the website does carry an entry for F-86F No.52-1228, which was recorded as lost on 28 December 1952 after taking heavy damage from a MiG, and here too nothing is reported about the pilot flying this Sabre or his fate.

3. The Aviation Safety Network's website (http://aviation-safety.net/wikibase/wiki) states that this F-86 was damaged by MiG debris but returned to base and was repaired. F-86F No.51-12975 wasn't lost until 11 February 1953 in a crash during final approach, when it was being flown by Albert W. Beerwinkle, who was killed in the accident (according to the Aviation Archaeological Investigation & Research website: http://www.aviationarchaeology.com.

4. This is actually a very clever play on words. *Vysheboika*, which is derived from the Russian words for "higher" (*vysshii*) and "fight or combat" (*boi*) sounds very much like *vosheboika*, which was the Russian term for the process of killing lice.

5. Ostap Bender was a famous character, a witty ne'er do well and scam artist in Ilf and Petrov's classic novel *The Twelve Chairs*.

11

Spring 1953 – new Sabres enter the fighting

CHANGES IN THE 64TH IAK'S ORDER OF BATTLE

Before the onset of the spring 1953 fighting, the 64th IAK underwent changes in its order of battle: at the beginning of February 1953, both of the separate fighter regiments, the Pacific Ocean Fleet's 578th IAP and the 351st NIAP, left Manchuria and returned to the Soviet Union. The naval pilots had in fact been unable to make much impact on the course of combat operations, since the pilots of this regiment were essentially unprepared for air combat in the skies of Korea, which resulted in their low number of kills and heavy losses. In addition, the naval pilots were flying borrowed aircraft, substituting for regiments of the 133rd IAD on missions, staging from different airfields, and seemingly played second-fiddle to the other regiments of the 64th IAK, which of course negatively affected their combat performance. According to information from the deputy political commander of the Pacific Ocean Fleet's 7th IAD Lieutenant Colonel M.E. Chevychelov, the pilots of the 578th IAP destroyed at least 10 American fighter-bombers and fighters, while losing seven aircraft and two pilots in return. In addition, five of the regiment's pilots received severe injuries when making forced landings or ejections. However, according to revised archival data, the pilots of the Pacific Ocean Fleet's 578th IAP over seven months of combat operations flew 946 individual combat sorties, including 21 missions as a full regiment, 66 squadron-size missions, and two in the strength of a flight. In the process, it had 20 group aerial combats with the adversary, 18 of which involved a squadron. But their productivity in these aerial combats was very low: just four F-86s were shot down by the regiment over Korea and another two were damaged. Their own losses actually amounted to 11 MiGs and two pilots. The squadron commander, later the squadron's deputy commander Captain V.D. Andriushchenko, who shot down one F-86 in the skies of Korea and damaged another, was awarded the Order of the Red Banner, while another 10 pilots of the regiment received the Order of the Red Star.

In accordance with the plan to replace this regiment, at the end of February 1953 the Pacific Ocean Fleet's 781st IAP under the command of Lieutenant Colonel N.D. Snopkov from the Fleet's 165th IAD arrived in Andong from the Novorossiia Air Base. As was the case with their predecessors from the Pacific Ocean Fleet, the 36 crews of the 781st IAP departed on their tour of duty without their own aircraft. After a brief period of familiarization in the MiGs of the 133rd IAD and having mastered the MiG-15bis fighter, the naval 781st IAP by the end of March 1953 had on its staff 25 combat-ready pilots based on the Miaogou border airfield. This airfield served as the regiment's main base of operations until the end of its period of combat service, with the exception of the month of June, when 22 crews of the 718th IAP staged from the Dapu airfield in order to intercept enemy aircraft. Already at the beginning of March, the naval pilots began to fly their initial combat sorties under the cover of regular Soviet Air Force pilots. This time, considering the mistakes that were made in preparing the Pacific Ocean Fleet's 578th IAP for combat operations, the 781st IAP's pilots were introduced into the fighting under the stricter supervision of the 64th IAK's "old men", the pilots of the 216th IAD.

As was also the case with the 578th IAP, the pilots of the Pacific Fleet's 781st IAP represented a mixed "stew" of pilots from the three regiments of the Fleet's 165th IAD. A former pilot of the 781st IAP Vadim Petrovich Sazhin recalls how they were selected for the regiment before it departed on its assignment to China:

> I came to Snopkov's regiment from the 47th IAP. I was the youngest pilot in the regiment, with a rather low amount of flight training – a total of 250 hours of flight time back in the flight school, and just 50 hours of time in the jet MiG-15. Therefore it was necessary to bring me up to speed somehow in just the course of a week. The division's inspector, a colonel, arrived by plane. I made a couple of flights with him in a UTI MiG-15 trainer, where we deliberately went into spins. He questioned me back on the ground. "Understood," I said, meaning I understood that a spin in a MiG-15 was a rather demanding stunt, especially pulling out of one. Then there were three sorties that involved mock dogfights – and that was all. Then, with this "baggage" I headed off to war. Everything else had to be worked out on location.
>
> Snopkov's regiment was brought up to strength with men from all three of the division's regiments. Some pilots couldn't make it through the KGB's background checks, others were disqualified for some other reason; only 40 percent of the newly arrived pilots wound up in the regiment.

At the same time the 351st NIAP, which had served in the 64th IAK longer than any other regiment, from 19 June 1951 to 18 February 1953, also departed to return to the Soviet Union. Over this period, the pilots of the 351st NIAP under the command of Lieutenant Colonel I.A. Efrimov officially destroyed 15 US aircraft in nighttime actions in the skies of North Korea, including nine B-29s, five B-26s and one RB-50. They received credit for damaging seven more enemy aircraft: five B-29s and two B-26s. In addition, on 7 November 1952 Senior Lieutenant I.P. Kovalev received probable credit for destroying or damaging an F3D-2 Skynight night interceptor. Of this total number of night victories, the regiment's pilots achieved 10 of them (plus credit for damaging three more) while flying the MiG-15bis. The other five enemy aircraft (all of the B-26 type) were destroyed and three more (two B-29s and one B-26) were damaged while flying in La-11 night fighters. Its top-scoring pilot was the deputy regiment commander Anatolii Mikhailovich Karelin, who received credit for downing six US aircraft and damaging two more in night actions. By a decree dated 14 July 1953, he was awarded the country's highest title Hero of the Soviet Union. The 351st NIAP's losses in the skies of Korea over this period amounted to two MiG-15s and two La-11s, with both of the "Lavochkins" written off due to accidents, not combat. Only one of the regiment's pilots was killed-in-action; the remaining pilots all returned to the Motherland.

Another night fighter regiment under the command of Lieutenant Colonel V.A. Vasil'ev arrived to take the place of the departing 351st NIAP. This was the 298th NIAP, which consisted of three regiments, all equipped with the MiG-15bis. On 15 February this regiment flew into Andong and began to prepare for combat operations by studying the theater of combat operations and carrying out training flights. On 23 February one of its squadrons, the 3rd Squadron, restaged to the Miaogou airfield, while the two other regiments remained in Andong. At the beginning of March 1953, they began flying their first nighttime missions to intercept enemy aircraft.

In March, the 64th IAK headquarters limited the number of combat missions flown by pilots of the 216th IAD due to their fatigue, thereby allowing them a period of rest. Primarily, pilots of the 32nd IAD and those of the naval 781st IAP (from 9 March 1953) took part in the March fighting. The pilots of the 133rd IAD from the Mukden and Anshan airfields covered the 64th IAK's forward airfields and stood by as reinforcements for large air battles.

The first clash of the new month occurred on 3 March – the 64th IAK's pilots repelled a raid by enemy fighter-bombers in the Chaniangen – Andong area. Pilots of the 32nd IAD and 216th IAD took part in this battle. Here's how a pilot of the 913th IAP Semen Alekseevich Fedorets recalls it:

On this mission Lieutenant Colonel A.T Kostenko (the 32nd IAD navigator) was leading the regiment and was flying with our 1st Squadron; I was his deputy commander on the mission. We took off, climbed to 14,000 meters, and arrived in an area east of the hydro-electrical station. There we encountered a group of F-86s on an interception course at almost the same altitude. The dogfight began in spirals, but with the tighter turns and increase in G-loads, everyone descended to medium and low altitudes. Everything was going well; we were pressing the enemy, when suddenly Sergei Tiurin, the tail-end pilot in our squadron's formation, radioed: "Take a look to the right; a Sabre has gotten in behind me." I swung around to the right and gave it a burst to drive it away. The Sabre reacted by rolling over into a dive, while Tiurin headed back to base in a climb.

I looked around and saw that I was now alone. I shoved my control stick forward and went into a dive at a 60-70 degree angle. In the dive I found what I thought to be a Sabre directly in front of me. However, against the background of the terrain at such a dive angle it was possible to be mistaken. I continued to close and from a range of 300-400 meters I gave a short burst, which stitched the Sabre, but only after making sure that it actually was an F-86 and not a MiG. From its exhaust pipe I saw a white emission, and the F-86's speed sharply dropped – his engine had lost thrust. I decided to give him another short burst from a range of 100 meters and barely had time to bank my aircraft to the left so that the belly of my MiG's fuselage didn't impale itself on the Sabre's tailfin. My aircraft slipped past beneath the Sabre's left wing by just 3 to 5 meters and by some miracle I avoided colliding with it (my gun camera footage showed that I had fired my final burst at a range of just 30 meters). I can still clearly see in my mind's eye the Sabre's black exhaust nozzle.

I pulled my MiG out of its dive and at this time I heard Kostenko's voice: "Everyone is to descend" (the code signal to break off combat). I set a course back to base, where all of our pilots returned without any losses. I landed, and clambering out of the cockpit, I started walking off to one side and began to wipe my eyes. They asked me what was going on and I replied that I could hardly see anyone. I could see only silhouettes against a black backdrop. It was the Sabre's black exhaust nozzle, the image of which was still in my eyes. This condition lasted for more than two hours, and only then did it begin to dissipate and my vision returned to normal.

Senior Lieutenant V.N. Aleksandrov took part in the same dogfight:

We took off in full regiment strength. Everything was just as always. We climbed to 12,000 meters, released our drop tanks and split up into squadrons, staggered in altitude. The weather was fine for the entire day. We were already over the hydro-electrical station, began to circle, and within two to three minutes the enemy approached with a very large group.

At the very start of the dogfight, we split into separate flights and elements in order to tie up as many of the enemy fighters in combat as possible. We went round and round with one F-86 element over the combat area – no one bothered us and we didn't bother anyone else; everyone was focused on their own business. Only shouted orders over the radio suggested the intensity of the combat. After several times around the circle, my adversary rolled over and broke away toward the bay with its afterburner on. I chased him for a bit, but realizing that I couldn't catch him, began to descend at maximum speed because my fuel was already starting to run low. Then suddenly at an altitude of 4,000 meters, an F-86 appeared right in front of me from somewhere up above me, which was apparently fleeing our MiGs and hadn't yet had time to look around. I nudged my aircraft a bit to the left toward it, caught it in my gun sight and gave it a burst. It staggered to one side and began to smoke, but a pair of Sabres jumped me, or more accurately, my wingman, and I had to bail my partner out of trouble. However, everything turned out all right; we gained separation from them and they didn't even try to pursue us, because apparently they were also low on fuel.

On the ground the gun camera film showed that I had downed the enemy aircraft, and authorities confirmed the crash of an aircraft into a swamp. But I didn't get credit for this fighter; we always considered downing an enemy aircraft the goal in and of itself anyway – if we received credit, fine, but it wasn't necessary.

However, V.N Aleksandrov nevertheless did eventually receive official credit for damaging this F-86.

Pilots of the 535th IAP under the leadership of the regiment commander Major P.I. Karataev also took part in this air battle. Karataev shot down one Sabre, and in addition, Senior Lieutenant N.P. Krasnikov damaged another. Pilots of the 224th IAP joined the dogfight together with the pilots of the 535th IAP. A former pilot of the 224th IAP Lev Petrovich Kolesnikov recalls his part in this action:

On 3 March we had a big fight. Kolia Maliutin's MiG was damaged. Our six-ship formation split apart. The Mironov-Lazarev pair was somewhere. Anisimov and Maliutin were each on their own, and [Grisha] Berelidze and I comprised a separate element. The commander gave the order, "We're breaking off combat."

That's when I spotted a solitary MiG with a pair of Sabres chasing it. We were higher, so shoving the throttle forward, we closed with the enemy. Grisha gave a burst. The tracers just missed wide of the lead Sabre. Startled, he and his wingman pulled into a climbing 180° turn. Grisha followed their maneuver. I had never experienced such wild G-forces before. The oxygen mask's rubber scrunched against my face. My hands and feet became glued to the levers and pedals. My vision began to darken and narrow, but when everything became clear again, I saw the superiority of the MiG over the Sabre in climbs: we had closed to within firing distance of the enemy. Grisha again fired a burst. The Sabre quickly began to decelerate and fell off to one side. We couldn't pursue the second one: our fuel was running critically low. On the ground it became clear that Grisha had saved Kolia Maliutin. It would have been difficult for him to escape his pursuers. Kolia's aircraft was badly damaged.

In sum, two F-86s were destroyed and two were damaged by the pilots of the 32nd IAD in this battle over the Supung hydroelectric power station, though it is more likely that three were destroyed and just one damaged. The Soviet pilots had no losses in this action. On this same day, Senior Lieutenant N.M. Sokurenko of the 133rd IAD's 415th IAP shot down a Sabre "hunter" in the vicinity of the Dapu airfield. Late that same evening, a pilot of the 147th GIAP's 1st (Night) Squadron of the same 133rd IAD Captain M.E. Zalogin placed a final victorious exclamation point on the day's fighting. Having sortied to intercept an enemy aircraft, he shot down an F-94 Starfire all-weather interceptor.

Altogether on 3 March 1953, the 64th IAK claimed four enemy aircraft as downed and two as damaged, without any losses. The Americans had no victories on this day in the skies of Korea. However, they also don't confirm the victories of our pilots either, asserting that on this day they had no Sabre losses.

A new encounter with the enemy took place only two days later, on 5 March. When covering the landing of our aircraft, over one of the forward airfields a group of MiGs from the 415th IAP intercepted several pairs of Sabre "hunters", and Captain S.D. Danilov registered hits on the Sabre of one of those American pilots fond of easy victories. We had no losses.

The next air battle, or more accurately the combat of one pilot, the 878th IAP's 1st Squadron Vasilii Mitrofanovich Seliverstov, occurred on 8 March. Here's what he had to say about this particularly memorable mission for him:

There was a regimental sortie on 8 March, involving six MiGs of the 1st Squadron, followed by eight MiGs of Major G.S. Kholodny's 2nd Squadron, and then six MiGs of Major V.V. Egorov's 3rd Squadron. Senior Lieutenant Vladimir Prilepov was my wingman on this mission. In the patrol area (Chongju – Sonchon), my squadron descended together with the 2nd Squadron down to extremely low altitude, while the 3rd Squadron remained at altitude. Flying in front of the regiment, my squadron and I reached the bay and began to turn away from the coast, and that's when several groups of Sabres suddenly appeared from out over the sea. Spotting them, I shouted over the radio: "Everyone, zoom climb!" They all carried out my order but my wingman Prilepov, who tarried for a bit, and he was attacked by four F-86s. Coming to his rescue, I allowed them to pass in front of me and then from short range shot up the leader of the first Sabre element, whose F-86 immediately began streaming smoke and nosed over into a dive.

I saved Prilepov, but a different flight of Sabres separated him from me, while the wingman of the F-86 I had downed placed my own MiG under fire. Bullets struck the cockpit, smashed the canopy, and some of them hammered against my back protective armor and damaged the ejection mechanism. Fragments of heavy caliber bullets hit me under the left eye, and blood began to mist my eyes. I began to bank my aircraft around to head for home, but one four-ship F-86 flight on my left was trying to herd me back in the direction of South Korea, while I had another four-ship F-86 flight hanging off my right wing. I was caught in a pincer. To top it off, I had four more F-86s flying above me. I realized that they wanted to force me to land in South Korea. However, I was not in agreement and decided to try to break free back to my own side, whatever it might cost me. Two times I dodged the fire from first one and then another of the Sabre flights.

Understanding that I didn't want to cooperate and that I was still flying ever more deeply into North Korean territory, the Sabres redeployed into a single file and began to shoot up my aircraft. They quickly damaged the engine, which came to a stop and then began to smoke. I realized that I had to abandon my aircraft. However, the ejection mechanism was broken and my altitude was now low. So I rolled my MiG over onto its back, unstrapped myself, released the canopy, and simply dropped out of the cockpit at an altitude of 1,000 meters before opening my parachute. Furious that I was still alive, two F-86s tried to finish me off in my parachute. They had time to make a single pass at me, but I was saved by their inaccurate fire and the fact that the ground was right below me. Soon Koreans picked me up and took me back to my own guys. Next I wound up in a hospital, where I spent more than a month, and only at the end of April did I resume flying combat missions.

On this same day a pilot of the 878th IAP Senior Lieutenant Dmitrii Ivanovich Chepusov was killed. His MiG had been damaged by Sabre machine-gun fire and crashed into a hillside short of the runway when he attempted to land it. So on 8 March the Sabre pilots had their own successful day. The 64th IAK's pilots had no victories, but lost two MiGs and one pilot in return. The Americans claimed to have shot down four MiG-15s on 8 March, three of them going to the score of pilots of the 51st FIW. The Americans also don't report any sort of losses among their Sabres.

On the next day, 9 March 1953, two dogfights took place between pilots of the 32nd IAD's 224th IAP and those of the 51st FIW. According to Lev Kolesnikov, the situation on this day was difficult:

The day of 9 March 1953, the day of Stalin's funeral, was overcast and drizzly. Not all the units, especially the Chinese, had been prepared for operations in such difficult weather conditions. We, Mironov's pilots, didn't have enough training for it either. However, someone had to go in order to repel an enemy air raid. So we took off in three six-ship squadrons. Mironov was entrusted to lead them. Having penetrated a thick layer of dense clouds, we climbed out of the gloom into blinding blue skies. Just as blinding was the white layer of clouds now below us. Equally blinding white contrails streamed behind our aircraft. It clearly marked our formation. For a moment, I had a sense of strength.

Another participant in one of these battles on this day, a former pilot of the 224th IAP Valerii Lazarevich Ryzhov, recalls:

There was a regimental sortie by squadron. Each squadron took its position in the formation. Our 2nd Squadron consisted of two flights (eight crews); one flight was being led by squadron commander Major M.G. Doroshenko, while Captain V.T. Smorgunov commanded the second flight, in which I was flying with my leader Vaso Rochishkavili. We had taken off from the Dapu Air Base and climbed to 11,000-12,000 meters. Everything was going well, until we made a climbing turn to starboard. That's when Sabres unexpectedly pounced on us from every direction. I watched as Rochishkavili got in behind one Sabre and fired at it, but then machine-gun fire cut me off from my leader. I dodged the tracers and avoided any hits to my MiG. I went into an oblique loop in order to gain separation from the Sabres and did shake them off with this maneuver, but as I came out of it I couldn't spot my leader anywhere around me. Just then several bullets struck my cockpit canopy and shattered it. Obviously, they were firing from long range and still managed to hit me. So then again I found myself being chased and under long-range fire. With a climb I soon separated myself from this Sabre element and headed back to base alone. On my last remaining drops of fuel I landed on my airfield, where I learned that my leader had arrived back damaged. He had lost control over his MiG's rudder. He made the unwise decision to attempt a landing, while the ground controllers also failed to assess the situation correctly (it would have been wiser to prohibit a landing and to give the order to eject). As he was making his final approach, he lost control, and muffing the landing, he touched down briefly before bounding into the air again, overshooting the runway and crashing into a barrier. That's how my leader and fine comrade Vasilii Ivanovich Rochishkavili was killed.

In this same dogfight, the 3rd Squadron commander Major P.S. Mironov's wingman, the inexperienced pilot Vadim Nikolaevich Kuan, went into a spin at low altitude when trying to evade a Sabre attack. Because of the low altitude, he had no time to pull it out of the spin and crashed into a hillside. This young pilot had scored just one victory in Korea, but for some reason he'd never received official credit for it. In December 1952, Kuan had been flying as Mironov's wingman in place of Lazarev. The commander had latched onto the tail of one Sabre and Kuan had shot it up at point-blank range. Fragments of the exploding Sabre became lodged in Kuan's Mig. However, the enemy aircraft didn't fit within the frames of Kuan's gun camera film, so nothing was readily apparent from it.

Colonel John Mitchell, the commander of the 51st FIW's 39th FIS, and 1st Lieutenant John Goodwill of the Wing's 16th FIS each added one of the pilots of the 224th IAP to their respective combat score on 9 March. On this same day, an ace of the 334th FIS Manuel Fernandez received credit for downing a MiG, but apparently he had shot down one of the UAA's MiGs, because the 64th IAK had no other losses that day.

In their turn, the pilots of the 224th IAP also claimed two Sabres in this battle: one went to the credit of the 1st Squadron's Senior Lieutenant V.I. Piminov, while the 3rd Squadron's G.N. Berelidze, who later became an ace, achieved his first victory. He shot down F-86E No.51-2827 of the 16th FIS, the American pilot of which 1st Lieutenant Richard M. Cowden was killed-in-action.

On this same day pilots of the 518th IAP also tangled with Sabres, but this action ended without any results. The final results of 9 March 1953 as noted by 64th IAK records was two enemy aircraft destroyed, in return for two aircraft lost and two pilots killed. In fact, the naval aviators of the Pacific Ocean Fleet's 781st IAP also clashed with Sabres on this day, and according to the recollections of a pilot of this regiment, Anton Mikhailovich Kasprik, on this sortie he was flying as squadron commander Captain I.F. Klochkov's wingman. During the patrol, from somewhere up above two Sabres pounced on them, and streaking past the wingman, they went straight for the leader. However, Klochkov didn't lose his cool, counterattacked this Sabre element and with a powerful burst of cannon fire hit one of the Sabres, which exploded in the air. This was the first victory for the naval pilots of the 781st IAP, although the victory wasn't credited to the regiment, since no confirmation of it was found on the ground.

The next battle in the skies of North Korea didn't take place until 13 March. It involved pilots of both the 32nd IAD and 216th IAD. Pilots of the 518th IAP flew two combat missions on this day, though they never encountered any enemy. However, on both occasions they had taken off to reinforce a dogfight and arrived already as it was ending. From the 216th IAD, only the 676th IAP claimed no victories or had any losses after running into a large group of F-86s. In contrast, this day was a hot one for the pilots of the 216th IAD's 224th IAP and 913th IAP. They endured a difficult dogfight with a large group of Sabres. In this action Senior Lieutenant G.N. Bereldize shot down his second Sabre in this war. However, the F-86s evened the score by downing one MiG. The pilots of the 535th IAP's 3rd Squadron were the unlucky ones; they were unexpectedly jumped from above by a group of Sabres. An element containing Senior Lieutenant N.A. Khristoforov wound up in a particularly awkward situation. He drove off an F-86 attack on his leader, but as he was pulling out of his pass he came under an attack by a different Sabre element and was shot down. He ejected and landed in his parachute safely, and soon returned to his regiment and continued flying missions in the skies of Korea.

However, the Sabre pilots attempted once again to take it out on our pilots as they were coming in for landings, by sending small groups of Sabre "hunters" into the area of our forward airfields. However, the 64th IAK command, considering the bitter experience of previous losses over its own bases, now began ensuring there was a constant MiG presence in the area to cover the take-offs and landings of our fighters. That was also the case on 13 March, when a pair of MiG-15s from the 535th IAP led by regiment navigator Major V.V. Isakov scrambled to cover the airfields. His wingman on this mission was Senior Lieutenant Vladimir Nikolaevich Lapygin, who shares his experiences on this sortie:

> On 13 March, regiment navigator Major V.V. Isakov and I, flying as his wingman, were scrambled to cover our airbase, since Sabres were often arriving and attacking our aircraft during take-offs and landings. Having climbed to an altitude of 2,000

meters, we spotted a couple of Sabres that were approaching the base. Without delaying, while we still hadn't lost sight of the Sabres against the backdrop of the terrain, we went on the attack against them. However, the Sabres nevertheless noticed us and went into a climbing spiral. We followed them into it and on the third loop around I managed to catch the wingman's Sabre and shot it down. Now alone, the Sabre leader decided to get away from us and head directly to the bay at maximum speed, and he was already starting that way. However, the F-86 pilot plainly didn't consider that the MiG was just a bit faster in level flight, which was a fatal error – Major Isakov chased him down in level flight and shot him down.

V.N. Lapygin did receive credit for the F-86 that he downed, since it fell not far from the base. However, the Sabre shot down by Isakov evidently fell into the bay, and thus he received credit for only damaging it.

The results of the aerial battles of 13 March are as follows: two F-86s were downed and one more was damaged. Our own losses consisted of just one MiG. True, the Americans claimed that on 13 March 1953 they shot down eight MiG-15s, four going to pilots of the 4th FIW and four to the pilots of the newly Sabre-equipped pilots of the 18th FBW's 67th FBS in their F-86F-25s. Of the latter's victories, two were claimed by the 67th Squadron's top pilot, Major James Hagerstrom, who would later go on to become an an ace in this war. Most likely, all but one of these MiGs belonged to the UAA, since the 64th IAK lost just one MiG on this day. The Americans acknowledged the loss of two of their F-86s. First, that afternoon, F-86E No.52-2879 of the 336th FIS was shot down in a combat with MiGs – its British pilot RAF Squadron Leader Graham S. Hulse, who was on temporary assignment with the 4th FIW, went missing-in-action. He was most likely shot down by Senior Lieutenant Berelidze. The other Sabre lost on this day, F-86F-30 No.52-4394 of the 18th Wing's 67th FBS, was seriously damaged in a dogfight with MiGs, and though its pilot Archie P. "Pat" Buie managed to bring it back to his base, he crashed when trying to land it. The Sabre was demolished and officially written off a day later, but Buie fortunately survived without any major injuries. Most likely, it was his Sabre that was damaged by the pair Isakov – Lapygin of the 535th IAP.

However, the 64th IAK suffered heavy losses on 14 March. At first, a tragedy occurred during the usual morning patrol – two of the 224th IAP's MiG-15s collided in the air. While on a patrol, the belly of 1st Squadron Lieutenant E. Stroilov's MiG accidentally struck the tailfin of his element leader Senior Lieutenant N.K. Odintsov's MiG below him and broke off a chunk of the tail. Both Stroilov and Odintsov had to abandon their MiGs: Odintsov ejected safely, but Stroilov suffered a spinal column injury as he was ejecting. He wound up in a hospital and never returned to the regiment. As they were descending in their parachutes, the two pilots exchanged sharp Russian words, but once on the ground they reconciled.

Then in the middle of the day the pilots of the 518th IAP had an unsuccessful dogfight with a group of F-86s, in the course of which Senior Lieutenant Vladimir Nikolaevich Sedashev's MiG was damaged. When landing at the Miaogou base, the MiG crashed and the pilot was killed. As a result, on 14 March 1953 the 64th IAK lost three aircraft and one pilot, though only one of the MiG's was lost due to enemy action. In return, the 64th IAK registered only one "damaged" on this day, an F-86 that was hit by Senior Lieutenant S.A. Dorokhov of the 535th IAP in one action.

The Americans claim that their pilots destroyed four MiG-15s on 14 March, but only one of them belonged to the 64th IAK. The other three victories were probably achieved in aerial combats with pilots of the UAA. However, one must also consider that American pilots often received victory credit for 64th IAK and UAA MiGs that were only damaged and which still were able to return to their bases, though the same can be said about Soviet victory claims.

After 14 March, another short lull in combat operations ensued, and combats in MiG Alley ceased right up until 21 March. On that day pilots of the 4th and 51st FIW scored heavily against the pilots of the UAA, claiming eight downed MiGs in one dogfight: seven of the MiG kills went to pilots of the 4th FIW. Only pilots of the Soviet 518th IAP and 535th IAP took part in the day's action, though for our pilots all the encounters with the American Sabres ended without results for either side. However, the Americans reported that on this day one F-86F was lost and one F-86F was damaged – both from the 335th FIS. Both of these Sabres were evidently victims of the increasingly experienced UAA pilots. Incidentally, both of these F-86Fs were written off a day later. Thus, the 21 March tussle between the pilots of the 335th FIS and the UAA's pilots was not a playful one, and resulted in significant losses for both sides.

The 64th IAK's pilots first combat after the long break in action didn't occur until 26 March. On this day, eight MiGs of the 535th IAP's 1st Squadron under the command of Major K.I. Sema, which had been sent out on a patrol over the area of the Supung hydro-electric station, at an altitude of 10,000 meters encountered three groups of F-86s, with 12 Sabres in each, that were echeloned in altitude. Major Sema's first flight attacked one group of F-86s, while Captain A.G. Andreev's second flight took on a different group. Squadron commander Major Sema at the start of the dogfight successfully attacked one Sabre element, damaging the Sabre leader with his first pass, and then damaging the wingman's Sabre on the next – they both broke off combat and headed toward the bay. However, that's when Sema himself was attacked by a flight of four F-86s, but his wingman Senior Lieutenant I.P. Tereshchenko was able to ward off their attacks until he ran out of ammunition, at which point with his leader's authorization he returned to base. Immediately the four Sabres pounced on Sema and quickly damaged his MiG. However, Sema was able to escape by finding sanctuary in some nearby clouds, after which he brought his crippled MiG back to Mukden and safely made a dead-stick landing there (his fuel had run out at least 40 kilometers short of Mukden). Major Vermont Garrison of the 335th FIS damaged Major Sema's MiG, though he received credit for downing it. Apparently, he received it due to intercepted radio transmissions, because Sema over the radio openly reported to the regiment command post that he'd been hit and was struggling to return to base.

In addition, when returning alone from this mission, Major Sema's wingman Ivan Tereshchenko was fired upon by Sabres and damaged over the airfield when coming in for a landing, but everything also turned out well for him – he safely landed his damaged MiG. In this dogfight Major Sema damaged F-86F No.51-12936 of the 335th FIS, the pilot of which managed to return in his Sabre back to his base and made a safe landing there.

The days of 27 and 28 March were marked by several minor clashes between the 64th IAK's pilots and Sabres, in which our pilots downed two F-86s. Senior Lieutenant G.N. Berelidze of the 224th IAP claimed one of the Sabres on 27 March, while on the following day the naval pilots of the 781st IAP achieved their first official victory when Captain V.D. Lukovnikov received credit for downing a Sabre. We had no losses in these clashes. However, the Americans do not confirm the loss of an F-86 Sabre on either day.

The American side does claim that on 27 March, pilots of the 18th FBW's 67th Squadron shot down three MiGs, two of which were credited to Major James Hagerstrom, but since the 64th IAK had no losses on this day, UAA pilots might have been the victims of the American pilots.

However, on 28 March things went less successfully for the American pilots in combat with UAA pilots, in particular with Guards Captain Han Min Kwan's squadron of the KPAAF's 56th GIAP. On this day, Guards Captain Han's squadron engaged a group of F-86s at an altitude of 12,000 meters not far from the town of Sunchon. In the course of the ensuing dogfight, the leader of one element Guards Lieutenant Kim Hyon Hak with a successful maneuver got behind the leader of one of the F-86 groups, but then he himself came under the attack of a different F-86. His wingman Ho Ki Bok, who counterattacked and shot down this Sabre, bailed him out of the predicament. Then his leader Guards Lieutenant Kim spotted a Sabre flight that was attacking Captain Han Min Kwan's element. Kim rushed to his assistance and with a climbing turn, emerged below and beneath one of the Sabres. With a powerful burst of cannon fire, he flamed this F-86 and it plunged toward the earth. However, the dogfight continued, and soon the squadron's pilots sent another Sabre spinning into the sea, after which the adversary abandoned the combat scene. Altogether in this combat action, the North Korean pilots reportedly shot down three F-86s and damaged another, while losing only one MiG in return – it was shot down by the commander of the 335th FIS Colonel James Johnson.

The last large air battle of the month took place on 29 March. Pilots of the 32nd IAD and of the 781st IAP participated in it. Dogfights involving small groups of fighters from both sides went on all day over the area of the Supung dam and reservoir. It was a black day for the pilots of the 535th IAP. On the morning mission, in which only the 2nd Squadron took part Senior Lieutenant V.Ia. Kabanov was shot down in a clash with F-86 Sabres. He was able to bail out of his stricken MiG. Later, four MiGs took off on the second sortie in the middle of the day to the Supung area. In the vicinity of the power station, they had a dogfight with four F-86s, in which an element led by Colonel George L. Jones (his wingman was Major Braley) attacked a pair of MiG-15s and shot down Senior Lieutenant V.N. Lapygin. Wounded in the attack, Lapygin ejected from his crippled aircraft, and after a month of treatment in a hospital, he returned again to the regiment and resumed flying combat missions.

In a different dogfight, a group of MiGs from the Pacific Ocean Fleet's 781st IAP collided with a group of F-86s from the 51st FIW. In this action, Captain I.I. Popov shot down one Sabre, but the Sabres soon evened the score by downing Captain Il'inykh, who ejected from his fatally damaged MiG. Here's how one participant on this mission, Vadim Petrovich Sazhin, describes how this dogfight went:

At the time we flew off in three groups: two six-ship formations headed by Major Bakaras' in front, followed by eight MiGs from the 3rd Squadron. We were flying along the bay's coastline at 11,000 meters in altitude. I saw the Sabres out over the bay; they glinted in the sunlight, but then I lost sight of them. At the same time I saw a pair of MiGs off to our right, a bit below and behind us. It was Il'inykh with his wingman. I asked over the radio, "Who's off to the right? Take a careful look; Sabres are approaching from the bay." Il'inykh gave his call sign. Neither he nor his wingman was able to spot the Sabres – the sun was blinding. A few moments later I saw a pair of Sabres coming in for an attack against Il'inykh. I gave him a warning, but the Sabres were already close, and the lead F-86 opened fire. Il'inykh's cockpit canopy went flying and his MiG started to smoke. I shouted at him: "Jump!" He heard this command and pressed the ejection trigger. He was losing consciousness when he ejected, because fragments had severed the feed to his oxygen mask, and at an altitude of 11,000 meters, you won't live long without oxygen. Then I saw tracers from MiG cannons streaking toward the Sabre that had been firing at Il'inykh. The Sabre became enveloped by shell explosions and started to go down. His wingman rolled over and followed him; Il'inykh's wingman headed downward as well. The cannon fire had come from Captain Popov's element with his wingman Borovinsky; they had been flying behind Major Bakaras' and me. We continued flying straight ahead while the rear group tangled with the group of Sabres, and Borovinsky had to fight off F-86s. They followed him for a long time, and he had to make a landing on a Chinese airfield, not on his own.

The result of this day of fighting, unfortunately, was not in favor of the 64th IAK's pilots: over the day they downed just one enemy aircraft, while having three MiGs destroyed and one damaged in return. The Americans claimed four victories, all of which went to the score of pilots of the 4th FIW. In one combat on 29 March 1953 involving Captain Andreev's flight of the 535th IAP's 1st Squadron against one F-86 flight, Senior Lieutenant S.N. Baiushkin's aircraft took combat damage. His MiG received 18 bullet holes, but the pilot safely brought it back to base and made a normal landing there. The Americans confirmed the loss of one F-86E (No.52-2873) from the 25th FIS, the pilot of which 1st Lieutenant Allen P. Hunt was killed. Although the Americans assert that this was a non-combat loss, stating that the Sabre crashed when returning from a combat mission, one can say with high probability that this Sabre fell as the result of Captain Popov's cannon fire.

Thus, the reduced number of air battles in March 1953 is reflected in the 64th IAK's relatively low victory totals for the month. The 64th IAK recorded only 11 downed enemy aircraft: 10 F-86s and one F-94, plus five more F-86s damaged. Of these, the 32nd IAD claimed seven US aircraft destroyed and four damaged; the 216th IAD shot down two F-86s and damaged one, while pilots of the Pacific Ocean Fleet's 781st IAP received credit for downing two F-86s. The 64th IAK's losses over the month of fighting amounted to eight aircraft and three pilots, but the fighter aviation corps lost four additional MiGs and one pilot due to non-combat causes.

The American command claimed that their Sabre pilots in March 1953 shot down 35 MiGs, and put their own losses at four F-86s, plus one F-86 that was written off as a non-combat loss. However, according to archival records, in March 1953 the 64th IAK lost eight aircraft, while the UAA's losses for the month amounted to 13 MiGs destroyed and 11 MiGs damaged. Thus, the Communist side's total losses were 21 MiG-15s destroyed and approximately 15 more damaged. This means that of the 35 downed MiG-15s claimed by the Americans, in reality they only destroyed 21, while the remaining 14 MiGs were able to return to base.

In their turn in March 1953, according to Soviet records the UAA's pilots flew 1,834 individual combat sorties, of which 1,358 were conducted by Chinese pilots and 376 by North Korean pilots. The UAA pilots were involved in 42 aerial combats, in which they claimed to have downed 17 US aircraft and damaged four more. Thus, the losses of the two sides were equal (with the inclusion of our non-combat losses).

At the beginning of 1953, UN forces in an analogy with 1950 threated simultaneous amphibious landings on the east and west coasts to isolate the Communist forces. Historians in the People's Republic of China write that the "Military Council of the Chinese Communist Party's Central Committee made timely preparations to repel this landing. The volunteers' assignments also included providing air cover for the ground troops. They carried out this task." In this period new Chinese air units began flying combat missions, providing air defense for primary targets and covering ground troops.

According to Chinese records, between January and March 1953 the UAA headquarters committed 399 Chinese aircraft into the fighting, which flew 4,093 individual sorties. They shot down 50 enemy aircraft and damaged 16 more. In March 1953, a total of 123 American aircraft participated in group raids against targets in the area south of the Chongchon River, 97 of which failed to reach their targets. The total number of individual combat sorties flown by the Chinese pilots virtually coincides with our own data, but the victories have been somewhat overstated.

On 1 March 1953, the last of the separate night squadrons (Major K.I. Sema's squadron) of the 535th IAP, having restaged to the Dapu airfield, began flying daytime combat missions. Only pilots of the 298th NIAP began to conduct nighttime missions in March. All the remaining separate night squadrons of the 64th IAK's other regiments switched from nighttime duties to flying daytime combat sorties.

March 1953 signified one more change. On 16 March 1953, the pilots of the SAAF 2 Squadron, which was part of the 18th FBW, began flying missions in their new F-86F-25 Sabres.

"WE'LL SHOOT RARELY – BUT ACCURATELY"

As in the case of March 1953, the April fighting in the air was relatively light and without intensity. There were rare clashes between small groups of MiGs and Sabres over the month and only two large air battles, when the Americans launched major fighter-bomber raids into MiG Alley that were covered by Sabres. The first didn't take place until 7 April 1953, but prior to this the 64th IAK's pilots over the first week of April had two dogfights – one in the daytime and one at night. Thus, on 2 April pilots of the 298th NIAP achieved their first victory in the night sky of North Korea: Captain Vil' Viktorovich Goncharov, guided by ground radar controllers, intercepted and shot down a US F-94 Starfire. However, three days later (5 April 1953) the regiment also suffered its first loss in the skies of Korea, though it was not combat-related: the 1st Squadron's Senior Lieutenant Nikolai Shurko crashed when landing on the Andong Air Base at night. Fortunately, this was the first and only death in the regiment over its entire time of combat service.

Meanwhile, the first daytime action took place on 4 April. On this day, pilots of the 32nd IAD and 216th IAD flew combat missions, but only the pilots of the 676th IAP were able to increase their victory tally in the skies of Korea after the long break in the action. At 0850 a flight under the command of Major Iu.A. Varkov intercepted an element of Sabre "hunters" in the vicinity of Andong, and Varkov shot down one Sabre that fell into the bay 8 to 10 kilometers west of Rika-ho – this was his fourth victory in this war. On this day, one MiG from the 133rd IAD's 726th IAP was also lost. While on a combat patrol mission, Senior Lieutenant V.I. Motonakha placed excessive stress on his MiG's wings, causing one to break off. He safely ejected and soon returned to the regiment. Prior to 7 April, the 64th IAK lost two MiGs and neither loss was the result of combat.

On 7 April the Americans launched a new air raid deep into MiG Alley under the cover of Sabres. Pilots of the 32nd IAD, as well as those of the Pacific Ocean Fleet's 781st IAP, were scrambled to repel it; the 216th IAD remained in reserve. However, having detected the approach of several groups of MiGs with the help of radar posts, the strike aircraft, timely forewarned, turned back toward the bay, avoiding any encounter with the MiGs. Thus our pilots didn't meet any enemy fighter-bombers on this day, but did have several dogfights with Sabres of the forward screen.

Thus, on the second combat sortie of the day, a group of MiGs from the 913th IAP tangled with a group of F-86s, and Senior Lieutenant A.K. Popov, who was flying as the wingman to the regiment's chief of aerial gunnery services Major I.I. Rudakov, successfully got in behind one of the Sabres and began to close with it in a dive. It was cloudy in the combat area and the Sabre found sanctuary by dipping into the clouds, but Popov followed his target into them, while Major Rudakov veered away before reaching them. Now alone, Popov still managed to catch the Sabre when they emerged below the clouds and shot it down. However, he didn't see a different Sabre element that was stealthily approaching him; Popov was himself attacked and shot down. Popov managed to eject from his stricken plane successfully, and safely made it back to his regiment a day later.

In other dogfights with the Sabres on this day, the naval pilots also had success by downing one F-86. Two of the regiment's squadrons (22 MiGs) under the command of Lieutenant Colonel N.D. Snopkov engaged 16 F-86s in combat that were part of the forward screen in an area 20 kilometers to the southeast of Sonchon. In this diving and climbing dogfight that began at an altitude of 2,000 meters, thanks to precise cooperation and the mutual assistance of arriving reinforcements, Senior Lieutenant A.A. Borovinsky shot down one F-86, and the remaining enemy aircraft, their formation, having become disorganized, retreated in the direction of Korea Bay. Pilots of the 535th IAP also had some success this day, when Major V.A. Utkin damaged his next Sabre.

However, the day's most significant event took place over the Dapu airfield. The hero of this action, Grigorii Nesterov Berelidze, relates how the American ace Captain Harold E. Fischer, Jr. of the 51st FIW's 39th FIS, who by this time had 10 victories in the skies of Korea, was shot down:

> The 3rd Squadron took off on a combat mission. We returned from the mission a few minutes earlier than had been planned, and when approaching the base, I got the permission of squadron commander Major P.S. Mironov to remain with my element in the air over the airfield (just in case), while the remaining pilots made their landings. When the last airplane of our group had lowered its landing gear and was circling to land, a "guest" popped out from somewhere behind the hills at low

altitude and started to attack our MiG. At this time I was over the airfield together with Lev Kolesnikov, and I heard a command from the regiment command post over the radio: "Whoever is in the air! A Sabre is attacking our MiG in its landing pattern, help it!" Having heard the transmission, I took a look below me and saw the silhouettes of two aircraft, and naturally determined that the enemy fighter was the rear one. From an altitude of 9,000 meters, I went into a split-S and began to pull my MiG out of its dive at low altitude. As soon as my vision cleared from the effects of the G-forces, I saw that just as I had calculated, I was about 3 kilometers behind the enemy aircraft. With the high speed I had gained in the dive, I quickly closed on it. My wingman's vision had also grayed out from the G-forces, and after exiting the dive he temporarily lost sight of me. As soon as I had pulled to within firing range, I fired a burst, and having "rolled the dice", I turned abruptly away. The enemy Sabre, damaged by our fire, touched down on one "foot", but safely.

The opponent I had downed turned out to be none other than the twice-ace of the American air force Captain Harold Edward Fischer, Jr., born in 1925. For this action I was awarded with a hunting rifle.

This episode requires further discussion in more detail and in the sequence of events. When the six MiGs of the 224th IAP's 1st Squadron were landing, Major P.S. Mironov's 3rd Squadron MiGs were still in the air over the base, as well as MiGs from a Chinese IAP. Fischer without his wingman (he was experiencing engine problems, and Fischer had sent him back to base) broke through to the Dapu Air Base. He attacked Captain K.V. Ugriumov's MiG of the 224th IAP's 1st Squadron, and hit it with his first burst, leaving 22 bullet holes in it. Considering the matter finished, Fischer streaked right over the airfield. Konstantin Ugriumov, having warned over the radio that he'd been damaged and that a Sabre was at work in the landing circle, lowered his landing gear and made a safe landing. Further on, Fischer spotted a pair of Chinese MiGs that were coming in for a landing, which were being flown by Chang Niuku (the squadron deputy commander) and his wingman Han Decai, and damaged the wingman's MiG, knocking out its hydraulics. Han Decai, streaming hydraulic fluid from his MiG, nevertheless came in for a landing, and although one landing strut refused to lower, he brought his MiG down safely.

Harold Fischer asserts that on this his final combat mission he shot down two MiG-15s, bringing his personal score up to 12 victories. However, this doesn't correspond with reality, since neither MiG was seriously damaged; they were both quickly repaired and put back into action. In his turn, Fischer's F-86F No.51-2852 (according to some sources, it was F-86F No.51-2871) with the intimidating name "The Paper Tiger" struck the ground of northeast China and turned into a dying bonfire of wreckage. Harold Fischer himself became a prisoner and spent 27 months of solitary confinement in a Chinese prison as a political prisoner (he'd been shot down over Chinese territory). While he was descending in his parachute, a pilot of the 224th IAP Senior Lieutenant A.A. German feigned an attack on him in the air. From his movements, it was clear that his situation was unenviable, but German couldn't open fire ("Non-ambulatory patients are not shot"). In his testimony, Harold Fischer said that there were two Europeans present when he was captured, and this "helped" them get a reprimand for violating the orders to maintain secrecy. Two years later, Harold Fischer was released.

Continuing our discussion of this significant event, according to archival data, at 1610, six MiG-15s of the 224th IAP being led by Senior Lieutenant A.P. Anisimov had experienced a brief clash with one F-86 flight at an altitude of 13,000 meters in the Kusong area, which had ended without any results. Having returned to the vicinity of the Dapu airfield, at 1640 Senior Lieutenant G.N. Berelidze's element was directed toward a solitary F-86, which was at an altitude of 1,000-1,500 meters and was attacking Senior Lieutenant K.V. Ugriumov's MiG, and from a range of 400 meters he shot down this Sabre.

The victim of Harold Fischer's first attack, the deputy political commander of the 224th IAP's 1st Squadron Senior Lieutenant Konstantin Vasil'evich Ugriumov, recalls the action this way:

> Kolia Batrakov and I were paired together on this, the second mission of the day. There were quite a few aircraft in the air. We were returning. We knew the American tactic to try to catch us when landing. Kolia got lost and became separated from me. I was the leader. I headed further into Chinese territory, about 60 kilometers, and turned around there. I arrived over a river valley and flew along it ... I see that I'm on the approach to the base. I radioed that my approach was from the north ... when suddenly at an altitude of 400 meters someone fired on me. ... I immediately lose the feel of the control stick, it is loose. Everything else is working normally. My cockpit canopy has been smashed. I see a Sabre positioned right next to me. He was behind me. He attacked from out of nowhere. He was really moving. He fired and then overshot me. Then it was my chance to shoot at him. That's the way we went – I was firing at him, he was firing at me. He didn't want to emerge in front of me, so that I could fire at him. He wanted me to move in front. ... I shouted, "I've been hit, I'm coming in from the north, I'll be there soon." The commander said, "Come straight in ... there are Chinese flying at altitude." So I did. Suddenly there's a Chinese MiG popping out in front of me, and he (the American) goes after him. He came distracted from me. That's when Grisha Berelidze swooped in. He fired at him and shot him down.
>
> He immediately hit the silk. On the ground, he was stripped and searched; he had a lot of money and some sort of ID card, and this was taken from him. My trailing edge flaps were broken and in my damaged aircraft I made a landing; my tires had been punctured. They counted 22 bullet holes in my airplane. Bullets had also struck the protective armor behind me, but they hadn't penetrated it, so nothing happened to me. The main thing is that I landed. My aircraft wasn't written off; they patched it up and repaired it. The American was taken prisoner. He later spent a year and a half in a Chinese prison. Then he was exchanged for a Chinese general.

Historians from China and the United States have put forward their version of the story, according to which the Chinese pilot Han Decai, the deputy political squadron commander in one of the 15th IAD's regiments, shot down Harold Fischer. This is the Chinese version of Fischer's downing. according to Chinese historians:

> Han Decai was returning from a dogfight. When he was already over the airfield and covering the group's landing, suddenly a Sabre emerged from some clouds in an ambush and damaged the group commander's MiG with the side number "3",

which had already throttled back before landing. Having seen the leader's damaged aircraft Han Decai attacked the enemy and destroyed him. The Sabre pilot bailed out and was taken prisoner.

However, this is just the version that the Chinese and the Americans have disseminated to this very day, but the reality is that Soviet pilots played the main role in shooting down Harold Fischer and his resulting capture, and this was their achievement on this day!

As a result on 7 April 1953 the 64th IAK's pilots in return for one MiG destroyed and one MiG damaged shot down two F-86s and damaged one more (the F-86 shot down by A.K. Popov wasn't credited to the regiment). The Americans claimed that the Sabre pilots on 7 April shot down three MiG-15s, two of which were claimed by pilots of the 51st FIW. Incidentally, the two victories claimed by Harold Fischer are not part of this total. The Americans admitted the loss of two of their F-86s on this day: in addition to Fischer's Sabre, F-86F-10 No.51-12958 from the 39th FIS was lost; most likely, it was shot down by the naval pilot Senior Lieutenant Borovinsky of the 781st IAP.

The next aerial fight took place on 11 April, but it involved only UAA pilots and pilots of the 51st FIW's 39th Squadron, which shot down three MiG-15s. A more serious clash occurred on 12 April south of the Supung hydroelectric station in the area of Pukchin, Pihyon, Sonchon, Kwakson-dong and Sinchan. The Americans launched a major raid by F-84Gs covered by Sabres of the 4th and 51st FIW. The raid began at 1000, and several groups of MiGs from all three regiments of the 32nd IAD were scrambled to repel it. Pilots of the UAA also took part in the battle.

Pilots of the 224th IAP scored first. Between 0755 and 0800, six MiGs under the command of Captain M.G. Doroshenko encountered four F-86s at an altitude of 13,000 meters in the Changseong area and attacked them. In the ensuing combat, Captain Doroshenko shot down one F-86.

One of the first to depart on a combat mission was a group from the 913th IAP, which took off at 0730. Thirty minutes later, Captain S.A. Fedorets's flight took off for the same area. Here's how he describes his part in this fight:

> On 12 April, I took off with my flight about 30 minutes after the rest of the division in order to cover the withdrawal of the main forces from the battle area and to hunt for enemy aircraft. I arrived in the combat area, where more than 100 aircraft from both sides were tangled in a giant furball. The combat was at an altitude of 14,000 meters about 50-70 kilometers south of the Supung hydroelectric station. On our side it involved all three regiments of our division. At this altitude, the entire panorama of the aerial combat was clearly laid out before me. I could see tracers from machine guns and cannons, and long trails of smoke from damaged aircraft.
>
> Suddenly over the radio I could hear the agitated voice of one of our pilots calling for rescue: "Help me, I've been hit!" Taking a look around, I saw a MiG-15 directly off to my right and about 1,500-2,000 meters below me that was flying straight and level to the north, emitting a long plume of black smoke; it was being chased by Sabres that were endlessly peppering him with machine-gun fire. Without thinking, I threw my MiG into a dive to the right and began to close on the Sabres. I gave two bursts as I closed from 300 meters down to 100 meters. After the second, the Sabre banked over to the right and went into a dive toward the earth. During

my abrupt attack, the trailing pair Aleksandrov – Shorin became separated from me and lost me, but my wingman V.A. Efremov stayed right with me. As I was closing on the F-86, I heard a warning from Efremov: "A flight of Sabres behind us." Having transitted this information, Efremov banked away to the left and I remained alone without cover. As soon as I looked up from my gun sight and took a glance around, a short burst of machine-gun fire hit my cockpit from my right and above. I immediately reacted by breaking to the right and passed underneath the Sabre, thereby coming out from under its attack. The Sabre wound up out in front of me and to my left. The American pilot turned his head and looked back at me, then popped his wing flaps and chopped his throttle, with the idea of letting me pass him so he could shoot me up at point-blank range. I realized his intention and swerved sharply to the left, giving him a quick burst as his Sabre slid past my nose. My burst struck its right wing close to the fuselage. I noticed a gaping hole up to a meter square in the Sabre's wing. The Sabre flipped over its right wing and headed downward toward the earth. This was my second victory in this combat with the enemy. Just as I was pulling out of my attack, a burst of machine-gun fire struck me from below and behind. I quickly shoved my control stick away from me and escaped the fire momentarily. My cockpit was filling with smoke and fuel fumes, and my instrument panel had been shot to pieces. Soon this same Sabre element knocked out my control over the MiG, so I leveled out my aircraft with the trim tab and decided to eject. With difficulty, I released the cockpit canopy and at an altitude of 11,000 meters, I safely ejected from my crippled MiG.

However, Captain S.A. Fedorets received credit for downing only one of the F-86s; his other claim was disallowed. On the American side, Captain Joseph McConnell, who shot down one MiG in this action, was himself shot down. He ejected over the bay, where he was pulled out of the water by a US Navy search and rescue H-19 helicopter of the 3rd Air Rescue Squadron.

The main events of the day took place between 1055 and 1120 in the Pihyon, Changseong and Taegwan-dong area, where a large brawl between Sabres and MiGs erupted, involving more than 100 aircraft from both sides. Captain M.G. Doroshenko continues the story of the given battle:

On 12 April 1953, I flew off with an eight-ship group to a point south of the hydro-electrical station, where a dogfight was already underway. When breaking off combat a bit later, a Sabre element almost accidentally collided with me; I attacked it and shot down one of them. We were then directed to the south of the coastline, and as we were approaching this town, there was a dogfight going on across the river. Here, I came under an attack from a different Sabre element at which I fired, but they headed out to sea to the south, though one of them was smoking. At first they gave me credit for downing two Sabres, but then they disallowed the second one, because it made its way to the sea.

This occurred at 1055 in the Changseong area, when Captain Doroshenko six-Mig formation engaged eight F-86s at an altitude of 13,000 meters, and in this action he knocked down one of the targeted Sabres.

The pilots of the 224th IAP under the command of D.V. Ermakov took on a group of F-86s and downed two of the Sabres while damaging one more. At 1055 six MiGs led by Senior Lieutenant A.P. Anisimov encountered six F-86s at an altitude of 12,500 meters in the vicinity of Taegwan-dong and engaged them in combat. In this dogfight Captain V.N. Lazarev shot down one of the Sabres from a range of 600 meters. However, the regiment's Senior Lieutenant Vladimir Sergeevich Markov was killed in this fight; it was he who'd been calling for help over the radio.

At 1105, a flight of MiGs from the 535th IAP under the command of regiment navigator Major V.V. Isakov spotted a pair of F-86s at an altitude of 11,000 meters in the Kusong area, and Captain V.A. Utkin attacked them from a range of 350 meters and downed one of them. The pilots of the 224th IAP had another clash with Sabres at 1115 in the vicinity of the Andong base complex, when Senior Lieutenant G.N. Berelidze's element intercepted an F-86 element at an altitude of 9,000 meters, and with an attack from above damaged the wingman's Sabre.

The deputy commander of the 224th IAP Major V.S. Starovoitov scored another victory in this swirling battle: in a head-on attack he shot down one Sabre. Starovoitov didn't see the results of his firing because he hauled his MiG into a zoom climb to avoid a collision. His wingman saw the Sabre explode.

Then, finally, that afternoon the 913th IAP was sent to repel a raid by fighter-bombers, but only eight MiGs of the regiment's 3rd Squadron led by Major V.F. Semenov at 1604, directed by ground control, broke through the forward fighter screen and reached the Pihyon area, where the F-84s were attacking ground targets. However, alerted to the approach of the MiGs, the column of fighter-bombers began to withdraw to the bay. Squadron commander Major Semenov pulled in behind a pair of the fleeing F-84G Thunderjets at an altitude of just 200 meters and shot down one of them from close range; it fell just short of the coastline. The remaining Thunderjets escaped unpunished to Korea Bay.

Chinese historians here too found a "Chinese imprint" on the battle, asserting that a Chinese pilot shot down the famous American ace Captain Joseph McConnell. The Chinese historians' version of events on this day goes as follows:

> The Americans sent 76 fighters, primarily F-86s, in 13 groups and 36 fighter-bombers in eight groups. They were spotted at 0709, and at 0735 12 MiG-15bis took off to intercept them. At an altitude of 10,000 meters, they were informed that the Americans were flying in the direction of the Yalu River and the city of Chianchen. In the air one of the Chinese pilots spotted the contrails of eight F-86s. The group commander ordered the auxiliary tanks to be dropped and to prepare for battle. At this moment a pair of pilots (leader Song Yichung and wingman Jiang Daoping) spotted one enemy aircraft to the right at an altitude of 7,000 meters. Two more F-86s attempted to close with their group from the left and to attack the leader. Jiang Daoping informed Song Yichung that he himself would attack and requested his cover, and then went after the low Sabre. He opened fire from close range (not more than 100 meters), but missed his target. Then Song radioed Jiang that the two Americans were trying to get on his tail. The pilot evaded the attack with a maneuver and fired a warning burst. In the disorganized dogfight he found himself alone, and realizing this, decided to remain at altitude and to find

the group and to link-up with it. Over Guichen he spotted four American fighters below him and attacked them. He opened fire on the leader from a range of around 600 meters; in fact, it was McConnell's F-86. The fighter erupted in flames and the pilot bailed out over the sea.

As in the cases with George Davis, Harold Fischer and other leading aces of the USAF, who were shot down in Korea, Chinese historians assert that it was in fact UAA pilots who shot down these famous aces, which is at variance with the facts. The only true statement is that UAA pilots were involved in all the aerial fights in which these famous aces were shot down, but they were all downed by the more experienced and better organized Soviet pilots of the 64th IAK. These assertions by the Chinese historians are based on reports that circulated in the mass media of the war period, when with the approval of Soviet representatives, these stories were released to the PRC and NKPR press, which announced the ringing victories of the Chinese and North Korean air forces' pilots, since the Soviet fighter regiments' participation in the war was kept concealed and it was categorically forbidden to report the victories of Soviet pilots of the 64th IAK anywhere. Thus the UAA's pilots with their mythic victories assumed the leading roles. Now, many years later, it is possible to identify the true heroes of these numerous victories in the skies of North Korea!

The results of the large aerial battle on 12 April were as follows: five enemy aircraft were destroyed and two damaged, in return for the loss of two MiGs and one pilot of the 64th IAK. According to the information of pilots of the 913th IAP, in this action two Chinese MiGs were also shot down. The Americans claimed that on 12 April the Sabre pilots destroyed seven MiGs, of which four went to the scores of the 51st FIW's pilots. The Americans place their own losses in the fighting at five aircraft and one pilot that was killed. The 4th FIW lost three of its Sabres in this battle: the 335th Squadron's F-86A No.49-1297, the pilot of which Lieutenant Norman E. Green ejected over the sea and was later rescued (he was presumably shot down by the 224th IAP's Captain M.G. Doroshenko) and F-86F No.51-2942, though the identity and fate of its pilot is not known (he was presumably shot down by the 535th IAP's Captain V.A. Utkin or the 224th IAP's Captain V.N. Lazarev); and the 334th Squadron's F-86F No.51-2891, the wounded pilot of which 1st Lieutenant Robert Frank Niemann managed to bail out, but later went missing-in-action after being seen in custody in a North Korean hospital by Soviet pilots and interrogators – most likely he was shot down by Captain Semen Fedorets, who then damaged Captain Joe McConnell's Sabre of the 51st Wing's 39th FIS. Finally, Major V.F. Semenov shot down an F-84E-25 (No.51-4854) from the 49th FBW, in the cockpit of which 1st Lieutenant James W. Wills, Jr. was killed.

After 12 April, our pilots had practically no encounters with the enemy until 18 April, and indeed if there were indeed rare meetings, they ended with no damage done to either side. The American pilots on 13, 16 and 17 April had several dogfights with UAA pilots, in which according to their claims, they shot down nine MiG-15s. The aerial fight on 17 April was the most successful one for the Americans, when the Sabre pilots shot down five MiGs, four of them going to pilots of the 51st FIW. The Americans in the combats on 16 and 17 April lost only one F-86 each day – one was from the 8th FBW, while the other was from the 4th FIW's 335th FIS; both pilots bailed out and were picked up by search and rescue teams.

Not until 18 April did the 64th IAK's pilots score their next victory in the skies of Korea. However, the story of this Sabre's downing has a little secret, which was revealed only 38 years later by a participant in this dogfight, a former pilot in the 224th IAP's 1st Squadron Askol'd Andreevich German:

> When flying on a patrol consisting of six MiGs of the regiment's headquarters group, the leader of which was the deputy regiment commander Captain V.S. Starovoistov, we were suddenly jumped by a pair of Sabres. Someone of our guys shouted, "They're attacking from the left and above!" – and I saw an F-86 element that was diving on Captain Starovoistov's lead element from the left. There was no time to reflect; every second counted. I hauled my MiG into a climb toward the attackers, though I didn't have the right to abandon my element leader Captain F.D. Reutsky; however, because the Sabres were already closing within firing range, I was compelled to do it. Noticing my maneuver, the Sabre leader pulled out of his banked approach, apparently doubting in the success of his attack and ability to escape unpunished. When I began to approach him on a transverse heading, he quickly began to turn in my direction so that we would pass each other at a high angle, which would be much more advantageous for him in the given situation and prevent me from getting a good shot at him. So we passed each other several times on intersecting courses at a full deflection angle. Realizing that this Sabre pilot kept repeating the same maneuver and was getting away from me, the next time I pulled the nose of my aircraft and my gun sight a bit earlier through his likely flight trajectory, and when he went into his maneuver, I then only had to adjust my aim a bit, so that the Sabre would pass through the central pip and I would fire with the proper lead, since the target aspect angle was almost 4/4, meaning we were nearly perpendicular to each other. My tracers flew toward the likely impact area and I watched as he passed through my tracers; his Sabre was blanketed with the flashes of shell explosions and departed underneath me, while I climbed. When I checked the surrounding airspace, I didn't see any of our own or any enemy airplanes. After landing back at base, my leader told me that the group leader V.S. Starovoistov had also fired at the wingman's Sabre, but after checking the gun camera films, there was nothing visible on Starovoistov's film, while a Sabre at relatively close range and a large target aspect angle was clearly visible on mine. A little bit later a search team found the wreckage of this Sabre, but after a meeting of the regiment's command, it was decided to give Captain Starovoistov credit for the victory over this Sabre, while they credited me with only damaging an enemy aircraft.

Archival records on this matter note: "On 18.04.1953 Captain V.S. Starovoistov shot down one F-86, while Senior Lieutenant A.A. German damaged one F-86." In reality, in this dogfight only one Sabre was brought down and A.A. German was the victorious Soviet pilot. Back then, sometimes there were cases where victories by several junior officers were awarded instead to senior commanders, which, of course, didn't enhance their authority in the eyes of their subordinates. The Sabre in question was F-86F No.52-4331 from the SAAF 2 "Flying Cheetahs" Squadron, which was damaged and had to make a forced landing. Its pilot 2nd Lieutenant P.J. Visser crash landed on the K-55 base near Osan. The pilot was uninjured.

On 21 and 22 April, 64th IAK pilots again took off to repel raids by enemy fighter-bombers in MiG Alley and wound up downing several Thunderjets. Thus, on 21 April one F-84G was bagged by the commander of the 878th IAP Lieutenant Colonel S.D. Dronov, while on the next day pilots of the Pacific Ocean Fleet's 781st IAP did well, shooting down one F-84 and damaging another. The Americans recognize the loss on 21 April of one of their carrier-based F9F-5 Panthers from VF-153, which crashed in the Wonsan area. It was fatally damaged perhaps by Lieutenant Colonel Dronov, who mistakenly identified it as an F-84. Yet Senior Lieutenant V.G. Kamenshchikov of the 781st IAP did in fact shoot down one F-84G (No.51-865) from the 49th FBW's 8th Squadron, the pilot of which 2nd Lieutenant Joseph P. Zeigler bailed out. He was observed alive on the ground, but went missing-in-action. However, on 22 April the 64th IAK did have casualties. The deputy political commander of the 224th IAP's 3rd Squadron Captain Vasilii Nikolaevich Lazarev was killed in a dogfight. A former flight commander in the 3rd Squadron, Konstantin Vasil'evich Portnov saw what happened:

> On this day we sortied in an eight-ship formation, which was led by deputy squadron commander A.P. Anisimov, who was also leading the formation's first flight. Captain V.N Lazarev, whose wingman that mission was Senior Lieutenant Levchatov, was leading the second flight, while I was flying as its second element with my wingman Senior Lieutenant A.M. Shumikhin. Early on the mission the squadron's formation fell apart and it was Lazarev's fault; he sped ahead so quickly that we couldn't catch up with him, since he was flying the hottest MiG in the regiment. He surged ahead of the rest of the formation by 1.5 to 2 kilometers and even his wingman Levchatov fell behind his leader. Lazarev, paying no attention, continued to recede in the distance out in front of us. I was now trailing behind him by at least 2.5 kilometers and there was no way I could catch him. That's when he was jumped by a pair of Sabres, though I shouted a warning over the radio and even fired my cannons, trying to get Lazarev's attention. However, at the last possible moment he saw the danger and broke sharply to the right, but in the turn he decelerated and the Sabres simply shot his MiG to pieces. There was nothing I could do to help him. That's when my wingman, who'd become separated from me in the chase, came up, and we headed back to base, en route driving away a pair of Sabres off Lazarev's wingman Senior Lieutenant Levchatov, who'd also become isolated and was under attack from an F-86 element. Here, true, we were in time; the Sabres, spotting us, dove away.

Thus, the fine pilot Captain Vasilii Nikolaevich Lazarev, who had received credit for downing one F-86 and damaging another, was killed due to his own carelessness. He was shot down by 1st Lieutenant Walter Fellman of the 336th FIS, since he was the only American pilot to shoot down a MiG on this day.

On 24 April, the 64th IAK pilots had their final air battles in the month of April. Pilots of the 913th IAP were particularly busy, flying three combat missions on this day, two of which resulted in dogfights. A participant in one of them, Lev Igorevich Maleevsky, a pilot with the 913th IAP's 2nd Squadron, describes what happened:

> At 1100, a regimental sortie with the 1st and 2nd Squadrons took place – two

eight-ship formations flew to the area of the Supung hydroelectric station. However, we didn't see any enemy over the power station and had already started back to base, when 24 F-86s pounced on us. There was a brief flurry of action before we parted peacefully and the entire group headed in the direction of Andong at an altitude of 14,000 meters. Suddenly a pair of Sabres appeared a little bit above us and it began to slide in behind my wingman Senior Lieutenant I.D. Mukovnin. I issued a warning over the radio, banked to the right toward the attacking Sabres and gave the wingman's Sabre a short burst, cutting him off from his leader. The Sabre turned away, and I swung back to the left and immediately had the F-86 in my gun sight. I only had to make a slight adjustment before opening fire. The tracers passed right through the enemy aircraft, and it flipped over and began to fall. Back at the airfield, I was informed that the aircraft downed by me did in fact go down, and it was established through an intercepted radio message that the pilot had ejected.

Pilots of the naval 781st IAP also added a damaged Sabre to the day's score. The Americans claimed to have shot down one MiG-15 on this day, but the 64th IAK had no losses.

This day also marked a major change in the command staff of the 64th IAK. Major General G.A. Lobov returned to the Soviet Union. He was replaced by Hero of the Soviet Union Major General S.V. Sliusarev, the deputy commander of the 64th IAK who had arrived in that post back in September 1952. The pilots greeted the change in corps leadership without any particular enthusiasm. A former pilot of the 676th IAP Petr Aleksandrovich Kozlov expressed the opinion of a majority of the pilots in his memoirs:

Hero of the Soviet Union Major General of Aviation S.V. Sliusarev, the last commander of the 64th IAK (1947 photo).

To this point, Hero of the Soviet Union Major General Georgii Ageevich Lobov had commanded the corps, whose orders we followed unquestioningly. We sensed that a former fighter pilot was directing us from the ground, and we understood each other without words.

At the beginning of 1953 [actually, 25 April], General Sliusarev replaced him in command of the aviation corps, whose decisions quickly showed excessive caution. This had an immediate effect on our psychological posture.

The Americans had another combat on 30 April with UAA pilots, in which pilots of the 39th FIS claimed to have downed two MiGs. However, the UAA pilots in turn shot down F-86F No.51-2803 flown by the future American ace Captain Lonnie R. Moore of the 335th FIS, though the Americans call this an operational loss not due to enemy action. Captain Moore managed to eject north of Cho-do Island and he was picked up by an H-19 helicopter.

On this same day of 30 April, a tragedy occurred on the Dapu airfield: as he was lifting off the runway on a combat mission, one drop tank detached from the wing of Senior Lieutenant Nikolai Iakovlevich Kislukhin's MiG; the aircraft swerved abruptly and crashed to the ground in an explosion. This was the 64th IAK's final loss (non-combat) in the month of April.

The 64th IAK's results in April 1953 were more than modest: its pilots shot down a total of 13 US aircraft in combat (9 F-86, 3 F-84 and 1 F-94) and damaged seven more (6 F-86 and 1 F-84), excluding the disallowed victory claims by S.A. Fedorets, A.K. Popov and others. Its own combat losses over the month of April amounted to four MiGs and two pilots, while three aircraft and two pilots were lost in non-combat incidents. The 32nd IAD did particularly well in the April fighting, destroying eight enemy aircraft in aerial combat and damaging five.

The American pilots of the three wings equipped with F-86s claimed 26 MiG-15s in April. Of them, 17 went to the 51st FIW, eight were added to the score of the 4th FIW, and pilots of the 18th FBW's 67th Squadron destroyed one MiG. In April 1953 the Americans place their own losses in combat at five F-86s, plus two more that were non-combat losses. On 14 April 1953, the pilots of the 18th FBW who were equipped with the F-86F-25 Sabre fighter-bomber version were released from participating in patrols over MiG Alley and started to carry out direct bombing and strafing attacks in the depth of MiG Alley. It was on 14 April 1953 that the pilots of the 18th FBW flew their first combat mission as Sabre fighter-bombers, targeting enemy positions in the vicinity of Munsan, and after this day they switched entirely to the carrying out the functions of ground attack aircraft.

A bit earlier, namely on 8 April, a newly updated F-86F-30 appeared over Korea, which was designed to attack ground targets. Pilots of the 8th FBW's 35th FBS began flying ground attack missions on this day in their new mounts, and a bit later they were joined by the pilots of the two other squadrons in this wing, the 36th and 80th Squadrons.

In April the UAA pilots conducted 1,472 individual combat sorties, 1,256 of which were flown by Chinese pilots and 216 by North Korean pilots. They had 30 aerial battles, in which they reportedly downed 14 enemy aircraft and damaged 11 more. Their losses in April amounted to a total of 15 MiG-15s and three pilots killed-in-action. Thus the combined losses of the 64th IAK and the UAA equaled 19 MiG-15s, thus in the best case some of the American pilots' victories can only be considered as damaged.

One pilot of the 224th IAP, Senior Lieutenant V.L. Ryzhov, recalls the American pilots who shot him down on 12 April 1953 with a sense of gratitude; not one of them allowed him to be machine-gunned as he was descending in his parachute, though one element feigned an attack, obviously for the purpose of capturing proof of the victory on the gun camera film. People told him about this once he was back on the ground. Here are their names: Major William Cosby of the 339th FIS, 1st Lieutenant George Matthews of the 25th FIS, Captain Joe McConnell of the 39th FIS, Captain Lonnie Moore of the 335th FIS, Major Roy Reed of the 39th FIS, Lieutenant Colonel George Ruddell of the 39th FIS, and 2nd Lieutenant Len Russell of the 334th FIS.

12

The Soviet pilots take the back seat

MAY 1953

May began with clashes between jet fighter interceptors of both sides. The aerial fights primarily took place on the southern boundary of MiG Alley and even out over Korea Bay. The latter dogfights points to the fact that in May, pilots of the UAA assumed an active role in the air. They had more aerial combats in this month than in any previous month dating back to November 1952. The Chinese pilots were particularly active, although the North Korean pilots also occasionally flew combat missions, and they both fought bravely and selflessly.

The first daytime aerial clashes began on 8 May and went on for three days, until 10 May. In these and in other dogfights, the North Korean regiment under the command of Kim Ji Sang particularly stood out, which fought aggressively and achieved several victories in duels with Sabres. Here are only a few names of the top commanders in this regiment: Kim Si Geng, Kang Deng Dok, Kim Sheng Uk and others. Here's a description of one of the dogfights involving Kim Sheng Uk's squadron:

> The squadron received the assignment to intercept enemy aircraft, which had penetrated to the Chongchon River area. Arriving in the designated area, the squadron commander's wingman Lee Gil Bok spotted a pair of enemy aircraft and reported this to the commander. The leader Kim Sheng Uk attacked them from above and shot one of them down. But at this point they were themselves attacked from above by a flight of four F-86s. The wingman drove off this attack, and abandoning his leader, went in hot pursuit of them. He chased them down and attacked them straightaway, downing one of the Sabres, but the other three F-86s caught him in pincers and damaged his aircraft. Things would have turned out badly for the young pilot, if his squadron hadn't hurried to his assistance. Lee Gil Bok brought his damaged MiG back to base with difficulty and landed it, but because he had abandoned his leader in combat, he was grounded for a month.

Many of the pilots who participated in this war praise the Chinese and North Korean pilots (especially the Chinese ones) for their courage and pluck in battle. If they latched onto the tail of an enemy aircraft, it was a fight to the finish with no breaking off. However, this was both a plus and a minus for the UAA pilots. The point is that the Chinese and North Korean pilots often rushed at the enemy without checking their rear first, which led to heavy losses on their part. They paid no attention to whatever was

512

going on behind them, and the American pilots often took advantage of this by catching UAA pilots who were focused on a target and frequently punished them for their carelessness. Thus, there were a lot of cases like Lee Gil Bok's, and they frequently ended woefully for the UAA pilot who abandoned his position in formation.

However, there were exceptions to the rules. For example, a pilot in Shin Kang Dong's regiment Choe Chu Wa once saved his leader by driving off an attack against him in one of the dogfights, even though by doing so, Choe placed himself under an attack by three Sabres and received damage to his MiG. However, even in his crippled aircraft he managed to fight off a second attack on his leader and downed one of the attackers. True, Choe didn't return from this dogfight.

Incidentally, rotating into and out of the action in pairs, in this period of the war the UAA had the 3rd, 4th, 6th, 12th, 15th and 17th IAD, each with two regiments, and one two-regiment North Korean IAD. Thus, though the number of fighter aviation divisions is impressive, usually only two Chinese and one North Korean aviation divisions were flying combat missions at any one time, and within a month they would rotate out of the war for rest and refitting, while two or three fresh divisions would begin flying combat missions.

Prior to 13 May 1953, when the 64th IAK's pilots resumed more active operations over MiG Alley, the American F-86 pilots shot down a total of five UAA MiGs in combats. In their turn the UAA pilots also downed several enemy aircraft. For example, the American command acknowledged the loss of one of their F-84Gs from the 49th FBW and one F-86E from the 51st FIW on 10 May due to "unknown" causes. These "unknown" causes were in fact MiG-15s of the UAA!

The pilots of the 32nd IAD and 216th IAD only flew occasional combat missions until 13 May; there were rare encounters with the enemy and they all ended without results. Yet on 13 May several clashes between the 64th IAK's pilots and pilots of the 51st FIW took place in the Anju area, which unfortunately didn't go well for our pilots. Thus, Major John C. Giraudo of the 25th FIS in one dogfight shot down the deputy commander of the 224th IAP's 1st Squadron Captain N.D. Batrakov, and he was forced to bail out. Yet a pilot of the Pacific Ocean Fleet's 781st IAP Senior Lieutenant Vasilii Georgievich Kamenshchikov was less fortunate – he was killed in a dogfight with F-86s. He was shot down by the 51st FIW's top ace, Captain Joe McConnell of the 39th FIS, whom Major A.S. Fedorets had recently "dunked" into the Yellow Sea. The Americans had no losses in these actions.

On 14 May, the 64th IAK's pilots again suffered serious losses in dogfights over the Supung hydroelectric power station. There were adverse weather conditions on this day, a dense layer of low-hanging clouds. Usually flight operations were grounded in such weather, but radar posts reported a small group of enemy aircraft heading toward the Supung power plant, so the 64th IAK command was forced to send out several groups of pilots from the 32nd IAD that were qualified to fly in difficult meteorological conditions. At first Captain Portnov's four-ship flight launched into the sky. In the vicinity of Supung at an altitude of just 150 meters the two elements of the flight lost each other. K.V. Portnov's element reversed course to the right, but Captain G.N. Berelidze's element missed the turn and continued straight ahead along the river valley, where they were unexpectedly attacked from behind by six F-86s. According to Captain G.N. Berelidze's assertion and that of his wingman Senior Lieutenant L.P. Kolesnikov, they shot down

A productive duo of the 224th IAP Senior Lieutenant G.N. Berezidze (on the left) with his wingman Senior Lieutenant L.P. Kolesnikov; China, 1953.

one F-86 in this action and Kolesnikov damaged another. However, no aircraft wreckage was located in the area, so both their victory claims were rejected. In their turn the Sabre pilots continued to harry them, and in order to separate from them, Berelidze's element began to climb through the clouds; however, when emerging above the cloud layer, the Sabres flamed Senior Lieutenant Kolesnikov's MiG. He ejected from his burning airplane and returned to the regiment three days later, whereupon he resumed flying combat missions.

A bit later, six MiGs of the 535th IAP's 3rd Squadron led by its commander I.G. Danilov departed for the same area. While patrolling over the dam, Major Danilov spotted a solitary Sabre through a hole in the cloud layer and gave the order to attack. All the Soviet elements dove through this gap in the clouds, and just then a pair of Sabres jumped the formation's tail-end pair led by Captain N.A. Khristoforov from behind. His wingman Senior Lieutenant P.P. Zabolotny's MiG erupted in flames and he ejected immediately. The Sabre that had shot him down machine-gunned the pilot in his parachute and severed seven of its lines, but everything turned out OK and Zabolotny landed unharmed. He had been shot down by 2nd Lieutenant Albert N. Cox of the 335th FIS, because Zabolotny saw yellow bands on the Sabre's wings, which meant it belonged to the 4th FIW, and on this day Cox was the only one of its pilots to have a victory over a MiG. However, our pilots also damaged one Sabre in this dogfight – Captain P.N Blinov hit the F-86. However, though our pilot was only given credit for damaging, in fact it had been shot down, but a search team from an anti-aircraft battery was the first to come upon the wreckage, so the battery took the credit for downing it, which sometimes happened as the two types of troops in Korea "shared" victories. Most likely, this was F-86E No.51-2765 of the 25th FIS, the pilot of which 1st Lieutenant Donald L. Pape was taken prisoner.

On this same day, the 224th IAP lost another MiG. A group of MiGs from the 1st Squadron took off to patrol over the Supung hydroelectric station. However, it encountered no enemy aircraft. For some reason Senior Lieutenant Iu.B. Borisov's MiG was prematurely running low on fuel, so with the authorization of the group leader, he dropped out of the formation and headed back to base alone. He didn't have enough fuel to reach the base, however, and Borisov had to eject from his MiG with its now empty fuel tanks. He came down safely and soon returned to his unit and resumed flying combat missions.

Thus on 14 May the 64th IAK lost three MiG-15s, one of which was a non-combat loss, but lost none of its pilots. The two destroyed MiGs of the 224th IAP went to the credit of 51st FIW pilots 2nd Lieutenant Edwin "Buzz" Aldrin of the 16th FIS and Major John Giraudo of the 25th FIS.

On 15 and 16 May, US fighter pilots had field days against pilots of the UAA, shooting down according to their claim 14 MiG-15s, of which 11 alone were destroyed in aerial fights on 16 May. The 4th FIW's pilots claimed the lion's share of the victories by downing eight MiGs, while its rival 51st FIW pilots downed two. In addition, the commander of the 18th FBW's 67th Squadron Major Jim Hagerstrom shot down one MiG-15, his fifth victory in the skies of Korea, and thus he became the Wing's only ace of the entire war.

Soviet pilots of the 64th IAK also flew combat missions on 15 and 16 May, but only on the former day did they have a clash with the enemy. In it, the 913th IAP's pilots did well – they shot down one F-86. The Americans acknowledge the loss of F-86E No.52-2833 of the 25th FIS on this day, the pilot of which Robert N. Amason ejected near Cho-do Island and was picked up by search and rescue – Senior Lieutenant S.N. Markov of the 913th IAP shot him down. However, in a different dogfight involving eight MiG-15s of the 535th IAP's 1st Squadron, Senior Lieutenant V.P. Krivich was shot down. Our radar posts overlooked a flight of four F-86s, which approached Major K.I. Sema's eight-ship MiG formation unnoticed, and caught our pilots with their drop tanks still attached. Before they could free themselves of the drop tanks, the Sabres shot down Krivich's MiG and just as quickly departed. Krivich safely ejected and soon returned to his unit. This was the 64th IAK's only combat loss over these two days of fighting. On 16 May pilots of the 913th IAP sparred with a group of Sabres, but no damage was done to either side.

Returning from their break, on 17 May pilots of the 216th IAD's 518th IAP did well in a dogfight with a group of F-86s in the Pihyon, Changseong, Anju area. They shot down one Sabre and damaged two others, without any losses of their own. The deputy commander of the 535th IAP Lieutenant Colonel A.S. Akimov damaged another Sabre on this day. The Americans on this day took it out on UAA pilots, downing five of their MiGs according to their claims. The American command recognized the loss of two of its F-86s on this day: F-86F No.51-12962 of the 4th FIW, the pilot of which bailed out and was picked up; and F-86F No.52-4335 of the 18th FBW's 12th Squadron, the pilot of which Lieutenant Dorris (whose first name is unknown) also bailed out near Cho-do and was rescued. Most likely, the first Sabre was shot down by Major V.A. Zhuravel' of the 518th IAP, while the second was either damaged by UAA pilots, or was one of those Sabres that was damaged by our pilots which didn't manage to make it back to base.[1]

The funeral service at the Russian military cemetery in Port Arthur (Lüshun) by his combat comrades for Soviet pilot Senior Lieutenant K.A. Rybakov of the 518th IAP, who was killed in a dogfight on 18 May 1953.

On the following day the pilots of the 216th IAD's 518th IAP scored again. Covering the area of the Supung hydroelectric station, they had several aerial fights with Sabres that were attempting to bomb it. In the course of these actions, the 518th IAP's pilots shot down two Sabres, but they themselves lost two MiGs and one pilot. However, let's cover the events in sequence. Encounters with enemy aircraft occurred in the area of the hydroelectric station not far from Changseong. Two composite flights from the 518th IAP took part in them. In one of them, 3rd Squadron flight commander Captain N.I. Kas'ianov engaged a flight of Sabres in a turning fight, which was his mistake. Although in one of the spirals Kas'ianov shot down one of the Sabres, two of the others caught Kasianov's wingman Senior Lieutenant K.A. Rybakov's MiG in a pincer and shot him down. Konstantin Alekseevich Rybakov was killed.

Meanwhile, Captain M.I. Mikhin's flight took on a different Sabre flight and achieved a victory. Here is Mikhail Ivanovich Mikhin's detailed after-action report to the commander of the 518th IAP about his ninth and final victory in the skies of Korea:

I report that on 18.05.53 in an aerial combat in the area 35-40 kilometers east of Changseong, an enemy aircraft of the F-86 type was shot down by me under the following circumstances: following a heading of 300° at an altitude of 13,400 meters, I spotted a flight of F-86s which was coming toward us and about 1,000 meters below us. Performing a split-S to the right, I went to close with the enemy and attacked the leader of the second element. I opened fire from the right at a range of 1,000 meters and a target aspect angle of 2/4. The attacked aircraft evaded the attack by departing beneath the lead pair. Then I repeated the attack from the left and above, and opened fire at a range of 700-800 meters and a target aspect angle of 1/4; the enemy aircraft abruptly rolled to the left into a dive. After a shallow climb, I went on the attack against the wingman of the first element and was forced to break off the attack with a climbing turn to starboard. While firing, I observed explosions on the left wing and the fuselage. According to the observation of my wingman, the [first] enemy aircraft never pulled out of its dive. I believe that I downed this enemy aircraft of the F-86 type. According to decrypted intelligence, the aircraft was damaged.

Attached to Mikhin's report is the following statement, translated from the Korean:

Confirmation.
On 18 May between 1430 and 1500 (Pyongyang time), an aerial combat took place over the town of Singisiu. As a result of the given combat, one enemy aircraft, heading at low altitude toward the sea from the Yongbyon District, exploded in the air, which I am confirming.
27 May 1953
Singisiu Chief of Police
Senior Major Choe Chu Hak

According to archival records, in this same action the 2nd Squadron deputy commander Major V.G. Kazakov damaged one Sabre. However, a detailed analysis of this combat revealed that Mikhin and Kazakov had both fired at one and the same Sabre. However, Mikhin fired from a range of 800 meters and his gun camera footage was indistinct, while on Kazakov's footage the Sabre was clearly visible at a range of just 150 meters. However, the regiment command awarded the victory to M.I. Mikhin, so that his personal score would be more impressive, even though Mikhin didn't request this. Even without this he had several other victories that were not officially approved, but credited to him as "damaged" enemy aircraft (for example, the dogfight on 9 September 1952, in which Mikhin shot down one F-86, but only received credit for damaging it). How Vasilii Grigor'evich Kazakov achieved his fourth, though unofficially recognized victory (V.G. Kazakov had by the end of the war five damaged enemy aircraft to his credit), he himself relates:

At an altitude of 11,000 to 13,000 meters in the area of the hydro-electrical station on the Yalu River, flying from east to west, I noticed a pair of Sabres moving in our same direction that were angling to cross our course. I decided to attack them. I alerted my wingman Captain E.I. Stadnik over the radio: "Follow me!" This was our code signal that I was going on the attack, since the enemy might be listening in on our transmissions and pass along to their pilots that someone was intending to attack them. Having received my wingman's reply, I went on the attack. I shoved my throttle forward to maximum and quickly accelerated to around 1,000 km/hour, but at this moment I heard the division commander warning over the radio from his command post that enemy fighters were heading in my direction. He warned me again, "Be more vigilant!" I couldn't reply; I had another 150-200 meters to the target and I wanted to approach even closer before I opened fire. I was stuck to my gun sight, having squeezed myself into a little ball, as if someone might notice me in the airplane. At this moment I heard in my earphones some sort of loud, puzzling sound, like glass falling from a shattered window. It turned out later that a bullet had struck my wingman's radio just as he was pressing the transmission button. I simultaneously opened fire from all my cannons and the Sabre began to burn, rolled over and went into an uncontrolled fall. I pulled out in a climbing turn to starboard as a sense of relief and joy washed over me, and radioed that the adversary was burning and falling out of control. I didn't know then that when I attacked the leader, Stadnik was attacking the wingman, but his intention was to support my attack and he didn't notice as a second pair of Sabres attacked from the side at a target aspect angle of 4/4, and several bullets struck my wingman's aircraft, smashing its radio and damaging its engine, which immediately went dead. Captain Stadnik successfully ejected and we met again a couple of days later at our base, where he acknowledged his mistake.

According to an intercepted radio transmission, the Sabre shot down by Major V.G. Kazakov fell into the sea and its pilot ejected, but he received credit for only damaging the Sabre. When the day of 18 May ended, the 64th IAK's pilots had shot down two F-86s and damaged one more, while their own losses consisted of two destroyed MiGs and one pilot killed-in-action.

The Americans claimed that their Sabre pilots on this day shot down 11 MiGs, with seven going to the 51st FIW and four to the 4th FIW. Captain Joe McConnell of the 39th FIS and Lieutenant Colonel Louis A. Green of the 336th FIS both had outstanding days, downing two MiGs each (in separate dogfights). Moreover, the Americans deny the loss of any their Sabres on 18 May.

The next dogfight between MiGs and Sabres occurred on 23 May in the area of the Andong and Miaogou airfields, because on this day the Sabres again attempted to gather a "harvest" in the area of the 64th IAK's and the UAA's forward airfields in northeast China. The first of them took place in the vicinity of the Andong. After conducting a combat mission which resulted in no contact, six MiGs from the 913th IAP's 2nd Squadron under the command of Major A.B. Popov was returning back to base. What happened over the Andong base is discussed by one of the participants on this mission, Viktor Petrovich Nikishov of the 2nd Squadron:

After our combat mission, we had arrived to land at Andong. As my leader Captain V.L. Grishenchuk was just about to touch down on the runway, I was at an altitude of 50 meters making my final turn before landing. Suddenly over the radio I heard a query, followed by an order: "Who is in their final turn? Break right, a Sabre is attacking." I instantly retracted my landing gear and landing flaps and turned toward the Sabre that was attacking "someone's MiG" that was coming in for a landing. I caught the Sabre in my sights and opened fire from all my cannons. All this took place directly over the Andong airfield. After this we were directed to the Miaogou base, which was located next to ours, and the entire personnel on the Andong base claimed in one voice that a burning F-86s passed over Andong at an altitude of 10 to 20 meters and plunged into the sea, and even steam was visible on the water. However, back at the Andong base, where I arrived a bit later from Miaogou, as I was removing my gun camera film they told me that my leader Captain Grishenchuk had been shot down – which meant that there had been a second pair of Sabres. Because of the loss of my leader, I didn't receive credit for this downed Sabre, but the deputy chief of staff told me that they had credited it to the regiment, the division and the corps.

According to archival records, the 2nd Squadron commander Major A.B. Popov received credit for this Sabre. Flight commander Captain Viktor Luk'ianovich Grishenchuk was killed by fire from Major Vermont Garrison of the 335th FIS, who achieved his fourth victory of the war on this day.

Another combat took place a little later in the vicinity of the Miaogou airfield. Its participant Vasilii Nikolaevich Aleksandrov of the 913th IAP recalls:

> The skies were overcast on the morning of 23 May. The meteorologist informed the pilots at briefing that the same weather would persist all day. On this day, we flew two combat missions as a squadron. I was leading the squadron; there was a total of eight aircraft in two flights, flying at an altitude of 7,300-7,500 meters. At the order from the command post, we jettisoned our drop tanks and one or two minutes later we spotted first six Sabres, and then another flight of F-86s. I heard over the radio that two more squadrons were being scrambled. There was a flurry of action and we broke off combat without any results. We began descending through the clouds, and we heard over the radio, "The airbase is blockaded, head to the neighboring Miaogou." I arrived just to the west of Miaogou at a speed of 800-900 km/hour, and going into the third turn, I saw this solitary Sabre that was planted firmly on the tail of a MiG and lashing it with bursts. I slid in behind this Sabre so well that he didn't even notice me, and with a long burst I shot it in two. Our pilot landed straightaway; I didn't even have time to see him, since they quickly refueled my MiG and I made the hop over to Andong.

According to archival records in these two combats V.N. Aleksandrov twice fired his cannons and in each action damaged one enemy aircraft. One can only guess at why he didn't receive victory credit for the enemy Sabre that he split in two in the Miaogou area: perhaps the fragments were so widely scattered that the search teams were able to find any material evidence, for which reason credit for a victory was frequently denied.

On this day Captain V.N Aleksandrov bailed out a pilot of the 535th IAP over the Miaogou airfield. However, a bit earlier a different Sabre managed to shoot down Senior Lieutenant Titenko's MiG as it was landing; the pilot safely ejected from his damaged MiG. He was shot down by 1st Lieutenant Samuel Johnson of the 51st Wing's 16th FIS. As a result, the score was relatively even when 23 May came to a close: two F-86s had been destroyed and one damaged, while the 64th IAK's losses amounted to two MiGs and one pilot. The Americans claimed two victories on this day, but in return confirmed the loss of only one F-86E No.51-12947 of the 335th FIS. Its pilot, Phillip A. Redpath, reached friendly lines in his stricken Sabre, but it crashed when he made a forced landing – the pilot survived, but wound up in a hospital with injuries.

The final two air battles in this month occurred on 26 and 29 May. On 26 May, primarily it was the UAA pilots that dueled with the Sabres. The Americans claimed 12 victories over the MiGs, of which 11 were added to the combat scores of pilots of the 4th FIW. Major Jack Mays of the 335th FIS and Major James Jabara of the 334th FIS, each bagging two MiGs in one action, enjoyed particularly outstanding days.

In a reversal of the normal practice, on this day the 64th IAK's pilots targeted the fighter-bombers, while the UAA pilots took on the forward screen of Sabres. In the

Lieutenant Colonel James Jabara, one of
the USAF's leading aces of the Korean
War. (USAF Museum)

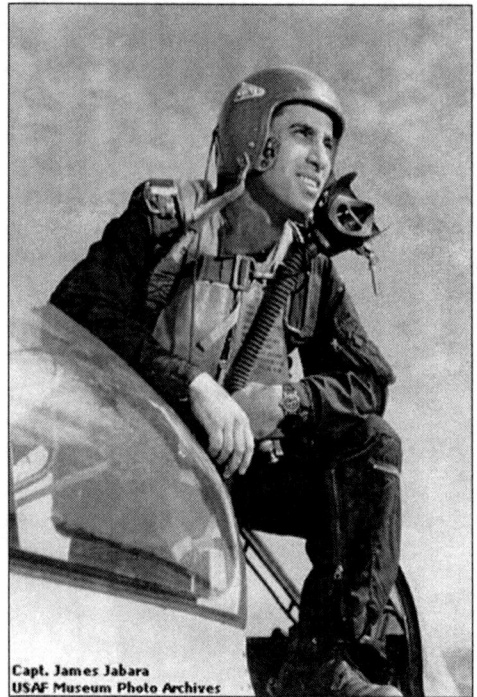

Capt. James Jabara
USAF Museum Photo Archives

Changseong – Kusong area, the pilots of the 224th IAP intercepted one of the Thunderjet groups and shot down one of them, F-84G No.51-715 of the 58th FBW's 310th FBS, which was credited to the deputy regiment commander Major V.E. Starovoistov; its pilot 1st Lieutenant James A. Van Veen was killed-in-action. The Americans, however, attribute his loss to ground fire. Senior Lieutenant M.F. Antontsev of the 878th IAP also shot down one Sabre, F-86E No.50-0631 of the 16th FIS, the pilot of which Captain Frank E. Miller, Jr. was also killed. Another F-86E of the 16th Squadron was lost on this day, the pilot of which bailed out and was rescued, but most likely this Sabre was the prize of a UAA pilot. The 64th IAK had no losses on 26 May.

In the middle of May, the 133rd IAD's 415th IAP had restaged from Mukden to the Andong airbase. Prior to this the pilots of the 415th IAP had been flying to cover the forward airfields, and between January 1953 and 29 May 1953 they had achieved only two victories without any losses. True, in one of the air battles before moving to Andong, the deputy political commander of its 1st Squadron Captain E.I. Polivaiko's MiG had been damaged in combat. His cockpit canopy had been shattered, and having fallen into a spin, he dropped to an altitude of 3,000 meters before pulling his MiG out of the spin and bringing it back to Mukden. Because of the pressure drop, Polivaiko was bleeding from the mouth and they transported him to a hospital.

The 415th IAP's pilots achieved their next victories on 29 May, though again not without suffering their own losses. On this day Senior Lieutenant Ivan Vasil'evich Pronin was killed when he was shot down by Colonel George Ruddell of the 39th FIS. Senior Lieutenant N.G. Kuprin's MiG of the same 415th IAP was also shot down, but he bailed out successfully. 2nd Lieutenant Robert Erdman of the 16th FIS was the American pilot responsible for downing Kuprin. However, the pilots of the 415th IAP also shot down one Sabre; Senior Lieutenant Pronin landed the fatal hits on it before he himself was killed. Senior Lieutenant N.M. Sokurenko of the regiment's 3rd Squadron damaged another Sabre in this action.

On this same day, pilots of the 216th IAD's 518th IAP and 676th IAP also had a dogfight with Sabres in the Anju area. One of its participants, Mikhail Petrovich Zhbanov, relates:

> While on a mission on 29 May, flying as the leader of the second flight in an eight-ship formation, I saw four F-86s emerging on the tail of Major N.F. Gnezdilov's first flight. I banked toward this hostile foursome to close on them and attacked the Sabres at a shallow deflection angle, which responded by going into a descending spiral. I opened fire and one Sabre fell out of control.

Pilots of the 518th IAP, who had hurried to join the action, shot down another F-86 without any losses. As a result, the day's totals were three F-86s destroyed and another damaged, in return for two MiGs and one pilot lost by the 64th IAK. The Americans announced two victories, which in a rare event matches the Soviet records. All three of the downed Sabres were F-86F-30s, all from the 18th FBW. 1st Lieutenant Marion K. Smotherman was killed in his F-86F No.52-4362, as was Captain Walter C. Beneke, the brother of the famous Big Band singer Tex Beneke, in his F-86F No.52-4544, though American records indicate that these were both non-combat operational losses. Relatively luckier was the pilot Joe D. Barbee, who was able to return to his base in his F-86F No.52-4354, but crashed when attempting to land it – the Sabre was destroyed, but the pilot was uninjured. The Americans wrote off all three of these Sabres three days later, on 31 May, when there was no combat at all in the skies of Korea.

Altogether in the month of May 1953, the 64th IAK's pilots downed 12 aircraft (nine F-86s, two F-84s and one F-94) and damaged 10 (eight F-86s, two F3Ds and one B-29). Two of these aircraft were destroyed and two damaged in night actions. In addition, Captains A.I. Khoitsev and I.G. Danilov of the 32nd IAD had unconfirmed victories that were not added to these totals. The Soviet losses in May amounted to 13 aircraft (of which one was a non-combat loss) and five pilots that were killed. The pilots of the 216th IAD did particularly well in the May fighting, downing six US aircraft and damaging three more.

In the month of May the UAA's pilots flew 1,254 individual combat sorties, 1,158 by its Chinese pilots and only 96 by its North Korean pilots. Together they had 35 aerial battles, in which they claimed 19 US aircraft destroyed and seven more enemy aircraft damaged. However, the losses suffered by the UAA's regiments in May were greater – 27 MiG-15s were shot down and 10 of their pilots were killed-in-action.

Thus, the combined victories and losses of the 64th IAK and the UAA in May 1953 were 31 enemy aircraft downed and 17 more aircraft damaged, while losing 39 aircraft and 15 pilots in return. The Fifth Air Force command announced that its pilots of the 4th, 51st and 67th Wings shot down a total of 56 enemy aircraft in May, which overstates the losses of the opposing side by 25 percent. The Americans place their own combat losses at just one F-86, which of course doesn't correspond with the facts. True, the Americans reported 10 non-combat losses of Sabres that month (primarily due to "fuel exhaustion").

In May 1953, the 64th IAK received a large batch of replacement pilots: approximately 80 young pilots were distributed among the 32nd IAD, 133rd IAD and 216th IAD, and the better prepared replacements soon started flying combat missions paired with more experienced pilots, while the others continued preparing for combat through training flights and mock combats.

Historians from the PRC write that changes occurred in the situation in the air in April – May 1953:

> The USAF increased their number of aircraft and changed tactics. They conducted up to 20,000 sorties each month, and simultaneously with the destruction of strategic targets, they began to strike irrigation dams and reservoirs in North Korea, while also strengthening aerial reconnaissance in the Yalu River area. They blockaded airfields and attacked aircraft as they were taking off and landing. After the Chinese suffered certain losses, they reorganized and augmented their system of early warning. Very rapidly the situation changed ….

As noted previously, the month of May 1953 marked an increase in the combat activity of the UAA, especially as our sources note, the North Korean pilots, even though the UAA's number of individual sorties in May fell by more than half, primarily due to the inclement weather. However, MiG losses in May rose sharply and almost doubled in comparison with the preceding month. For example, in the air battles on 26 May, when our pilots operated primarily against the UN fighter-bombers while the UAA pilots fought with the Sabres (evidence of the Chinese pilots' growing skill), according to their information the Americans claimed 12 victories. At the end of May, however, the Chinese scored their first night victory, when on 29 May the deputy regiment commander of the 4th IAD's 10th IAP Hou Shujun claimed to have shot down an American aircraft identified as an F-94 Starfighter (American records do not show the loss of any F-94s, but do reveal that an F3D-2 Skynight was lost that night).

A HARD JUNE, OR A TEST OF RESOLVE

In June 1953, truce negotiations were on-going in Panmunjon – the war was coming to an end, perhaps precipitated by Stalin's death in March 1953 and Kim Il Jung's growing eagerness to halt the destruction of his country's infrastructure due to the punishing American air assault. However, while diplomats were pursuing their global and strategic interests, stubborn air operations and battles continued just as before. One important event contributed to the bitter conflict in the air in June 1953: according to a mutually-reached agreement in Panmunjon, the two sides (North and South Korea) had just two months to stockpile those weapons, munitions and so forth from beyond its borders that were necessary for national defense prior to the peace settlement. In the time remaining, both sides feverishly poured as much combat equipment, supplies and ammunition as possible into the two countries, with the PDRK drawing its supplies from China and South Korea from Japan. Accordingly, each side tried to prevent the other from receiving these supplies by routinely bombing the opposing side's territory. Yet if the NKPAF executed its pin prick bombing operations only at night, using light piston-engine Po-2, Yak-18 and La-9 night bombers for this purpose, the American side applied the entire might of its Fifth Air Force fighter-bombers in daytime operations, while the two B-29 bomber groups and two wings of B-26 bombers began to fly more night missions in order to pound North Korean territory.

In view of everything laid out above, bitter aerial combats raged over North Korea both day and at night, in which the 64th IAK threw in all its available strength – three fighter aviation divisions (the 32nd IAD, 133rd IAD and the 216th IAD), and two separate air regiments. The UAA command did the same, committing seven of its fighter divisions into the June fighting. These were the 3rd, 4th, 6th, 12th, 15th, 16th and 17th IAD.

As of 1 June 1953, these UAA fighter divisions had 307 combat-ready MiG-15 and MiG-15bis fighters and 23 more under repair – a total of 330 aircraft. The 64th IAK on 1 June had 712 serviceable and 23 unserviceable MiGs in its three aviation divisions and two aviation regiments at the front, plus the two aviation divisions in reserve. This means that only approximately 1,000 jet and piston-engine combat aircraft of the Communist bloc were confronting more than 2,000 combat aircraft of the USAF's Fifth Air Force, the USNAF, the Marine Air Corps and their allies in Korea. The Communist bloc had approximately 500 combat-ready aircraft in reserve. On 1 June 1953, the 64th IAK had 405 MiG-15bis fighters deployed at its forward bases in Manchuria, while the UAA contributed another 300 MiGs, for a total of a bit more of 700 combat-ready MiG-15 fighters.

The first major clash erupted already on 1 June, when the Americans undertook a large fighter-bomber raid in the Anju area. To repel it, pilots of the 32nd IAD and 216th IAD took on the Sabres of the forward screen, while the Pacific Ocean Fleet's 781st IAP, which took off early that morning from Andong, broke through to the area where enemy F-86F-25 fighter-bombers of the 8th and 18th FBW were operating. An armada of fighter-bombers covered by Sabres of the 4th FIW headed for the Anju area after crossing the coastline. They were flying at various altitudes between 12,000 and 13,000 meters. In this action, the naval pilots shot down one Sabre and damaged another. Squadron commander Captain I.F. Klochkov also damaged one fighter-bomber in this dogfight, but received no official credit for this. However, the "pilot-sailors" also suffered a bitter loss – Senior Lieutenant Vasilii Stepanovich Timoshin didn't return from the mission. Captain Lonnie Moore of the 4th FIW's 335th Squadron shot him down. The pilots of the 32nd IAD and 216th IAD had several clashes with F-86s on 1 June, but they scored no victories, as neither side reported any losses in these dogfights.

On 4 June, UAA pilots shot down the British pilot John King, who was an exchange pilot in the 25th FIS – the wreckage of his F-86 remained on Korean soil. The UAA pilots also shot down a Thunderjet on 6 June. In addition, in the interval between 1 June and 4 June, two F-86F-30 Sabres were lost, one from the 18th FBW, the other from the 15th TRS. Possibly, one of them was the victim of the 781st IAP's Senior Lieutenant Naidenov, who had one victory on 1 June. The Americans claim, however, that both of these Sabres crashed soon after taking off.

However, these events were overshadowed by an enormous dogfight in the Changseong area on 5 June, in which up to 100 MiGs of the 32nd IAD, 216th IAD and the Pacific Fleet's 781st IAP took part, together with UAA fighter divisions. Sabres of both the 4th and 51st FIW fought on the American side.

The combat on 5 June was triggered not far from the Supung hydroelectric power station, south of the Yalu River near Changseong. On one combat patrol, eight MiGs of the 224th IAP's 3rd Squadron led by Major P.S. Mironov tangled with eight F-86s, and Senior Lieutenant G.N. Berelidze shot down one of them, thereby achieving his fifth victory in the skies of Korea and becoming an ace, as well as the 224th IAP's top-scoring pilot. However, this victory was spoiled by the loss of Senior Lieutenant N.P. Krasnikov's MiG. In the course of the dogfight he became separated from his leader Major P.S. Mironov; alone, he wound up far to the northwest of Dapu. He didn't have enough fuel left to reach his base, so he decided to eject, which he did. He soon returned to his unit. This wasn't a combat loss, but it was a pity that a combat-ready MiG-15 was lost without combat. In other clashes on this day, pilots of the 676th IAP damaged one Sabre while losing one MiG in return, and pilots of the 781st IAP shot down one F-86. The 676th IAP pilot Senior Lieutenant Leonid Solov'ev was shot down, but he success-fully bailed out.

A tragedy occurred in the vicinity of the Dapu base involving the Pacific Ocean Fleet's 781st IAP. When taking off on a mission, Senior Lieutenant E.P. Kuchurenko's flight of four MiGs was attacked and decimated by eight Sabre "hunters" that swooped down on it from the direction of the bay. Senior Lieutenant Boris Vladimirovich Pushkarev's MiG took fatal hits soon after taking off and the pilot was killed. The Sabres then attacked Kuchurenko's lead element and his wingman Senior Lieutenant Vladimir Fedorovich Tsarenko was shot down at an altitude of approximately 500 meters – he ejected, but lacked sufficient altitude for his parachute to open and he was killed when he hit the ground. Kuchurenko managed to release his drop tanks and fired at one of the Sabre flights. He even managed to hit one of the Sabres, but then his own aircraft took hits from an F-86 and was set afire. He ejected at the edge of the airbase, but he had climbed to enough altitude for his parachute to deploy fully and he survived. Two of these MiGs were shot down by pilots of the 335th and 336th FIS, possibly by the pair of Lieutenant Colonel Julian Hayes and 1st Lieutenant Frank Frasier of the 336th Squadron, who each downed one MiG on this day, or by Captain Lonnie Moore and his wingman 2nd Lieutenant William Schrimsher who bagged two MiGs as a pair.

However, elsewhere the Sabres also took losses: Senior Lieutenant A.I. Kutsygin and Captain O.P. Fedotov each shot down one F-86 over the Yalu River in the Andong area, but this was small comfort for the naval pilots of the 781st IAP after losing three MiGs and two pilots so quickly after take-off.

As a result, 5 June 1953 was a day of significant losses for both sides. The Soviet pilots claimed three F-86s downed and one F-86 damaged. Their own losses amounted to four aircraft and two pilots, plus an additional non-combat loss of a MiG. The Americans claimed to have shot down nine MiG-15s on 5 June, of which seven went to the credit of pilots of the 4th FIW, while the other two were achieved by two pilots of the 51st FIW. In addition to the other 4th FIW pilots named above, in the fighting on 5 June Major Vermont Garrison of the 335th FIS distinguished himself by downing two MiGs in one dogfight. The Americans acknowledged the loss of two of their F-86s on this day. One of them was F-86E No.51-2762 of the 51st Wing's 16th FIS, which was shot down, but its pilot, an RAF exchange pilot with the squadron Flight Lieutenant James A. Ryan bailed out and was picked up by a search and rescue team. The other, F-86F-30 No.52-4421 of the 8th FBW's 35th Squadron, was also shot down and its pilot 1st Lieutenant John E. Southerland was killed.

On 7 June, dogfights took place in the Changseong – Taechon area, in which pilots of the 535th IAP shot down one Sabre and damaged another. Another F-86 was also shot down in this same combat area by pilots of the Pacific Ocean Fleet's 781st IAP, while pilots of the 133rd IAD's 726th IAP completed the scoring by damaging another Sabre. These dogfights ended without any losses on our side, but once again the 64th IAK lost two aircraft over the Dapu airbase, this time not while landing, but on takeoff. The 535th IAP was scrambled in response to an alarm and from behind the hills two F-86 elements unexpectedly appeared and attacked Senior Lieutenant S.A. Dorokhov's tail-end pair in the 2nd Squadron's formation and the six-ship formation of the 3rd Squadron from below. Dorokhov's wingman Senior Lieutenant Koriagin, when he heard the warning from the ground that Sabres were attacking, broke sharply to the left and abandoned his leader; now alone, Stepan Aleksandrovich Dorokhov's MiG was attacked by one F-86 as he was accelerating after takeoff. Dorokhov tried to maneuver, but this didn't save him – apparently one of the Sabre bursts killed him or left him badly wounded, because his MiG dropped one wing and arced smoothly into the ground beyond the hills in the vicinity of the Dapu airfield. The other Sabre element at this time caught 3rd Squadron flight commander Captain Petr Nikitivich Blinov in a pincer and flamed his MiG; he landed his burning aircraft on one wheel, because the other two wouldn't lower, and as the MiG decelerated, it fell onto one wing and broke up. Blinov, fortunately, never lost consciousness and managed to leap out of his cockpit, which almost immediately then exploded on the runway. Blinov came away from this frightening incident with only light bruises and abrasions.

The US Fifth Air Force command announced that its Sabre pilots on 7 June shot down five MiGs, four of which went to the score of the 4th FIW; Captain Ralph Parr of the 335th FIS claimed two MiGs in one dogfight. Two F-86s were also lost according to American records: a MiG seriously damaged one of them, F-86F No.51-2905 of the 39th FIS. Later this Sabre was evidently written off. Another F-86F-30 No.52-4384 of the 18th FBW's 67th Squadron officially "crashed when taking off"; its pilot Robert T. Miller fortunately survived. Captain A.G. Andreev of the 535th IAP was the one responsible for the damage to the first Sabre, while in fact the second was the kill achieved by Captain D.V. Semenov of the naval 781st IAP.

On 10 June the Americans attempted to throw a scare into the Communist pilots by launching a raid to the area of the Dapu airfield, where several dogfights occurred. On this day, the 913th IAP's 3rd Squadron under the command of Major S.A. Fedorets was on stand-by for guarding the Dapu base. A group of 20 F-86F-30 Sabre fighter-bombers approached the airfield from the direction of the bay at an altitude of 500-800 meters. At an order from the regiment command post: "Everyone scramble. The enemy is over the base", S.A. Fedorets's eight-ship formation took off, and without raising their landing gear, our pilots began to jettison their drop tanks, because the enemy was already practically above them. After taking off they made a turn at low altitude and emerged below and behind one group of F-86s. Fedorets attacked the Sabre group leader and hit the F-86 with a full volley from all his cannons at the nearly point-blank range of 200 meters, and the Sabre exploded. At the same time Fedorets's wingman Senior Lieutenant A.K. Popov fired at the wingman's Sabre and saw his shells strike his target; damaged, it soon fell into the bay while trying to escape. Having lost two Sabres in the course of a minute, the enemy group fled the area of the airfield and returned to Korea Bay, which was a no-fly area for our pilots.

Having landed their MiGs back at base, Fedorets watched as technicians surrounded his fighter and examined something with keen interest. When he climbed out of his cockpit, he saw a gash on the left side of his fuselage that stretched from its nose to below the cockpit, and a large, jagged hole in the center of the wing about 25-30 centimeters wide. It turned out that a bolt from the exploded Sabre's wing slat had slashed his fuselage, and penetrating the wing's skin, had become lodged in one of the spars. Major S.A. Fedorets had come back from this combat with this "souvenir", which was a unique confirmation of his sixth victory in the war.

However, the fighting in the air around the Dapu airbase didn't end with this action. In order to cover the division's MiGs returning from a mission and their landing at Dapu, Major M.G. Doroshenko's eight-ship squadron formation was scrambled into the air, as well as a separate element consisting of the commander of the 224th IAP Major D.V. Ermakov and a wingman. While covering UAA MiGs and those of its own division as they were coming in for a landing, the pilots of this squadron drove off several attempts by separate pairs of F-86s to attack the vulnerable MiGs. D.V.

Commander of the 224th IAP, Hero of the Soviet Union Lieutenant Colonel D.V. Ermakov (in the center) with pilots of his regiment during R&R in the city of Dal'nii (Dalian), 1953. Sitting on the left is one of the regiment's aces Senior Lieutenant B.N. Sis'kov.

Ermakov timely spotted one Sabre element overhead and thwarted their intentions with his attack. The Sabres immediately began to flee to the bay, but Ermakov in pursuit attacked one of them again and shot it down, while the second managed to reach the sanctuary of the bay.

Captain A.D. Shamraev of Major Doroshenko's 2nd Squadron also damaged one F-86 over the airfield, after which the flight controller on this day, the deputy commander of the 224th IAP Major V.S. Starovoistov gave the all-clear signal and told the squadron to make their landings. However, while circling to land, a pair of F-86s unexpectedly appeared at low altitude from behind the hills and swung in behind squadron commander Major M.G. Doroshenko's element. Doroshenko, receiving a warning from the command post about the Sabre attack, immediately retracted his landing gear and broke left into a climbing turn. However, the Sabres were still sitting on his tail, and things would have gone badly for Major Doroshenko if the deputy squadron commander Senior Lieutenant G.A. Vasil'ev hadn't arrived just in time to shoot one of the Sabres off Doroshenko's tail. The F-86 crashed to the earth not far from the base. Thus, the squadron commander had been saved from likely death by a comrade. The downed Sabre pilot turned out to be a black man.

Altogether, on this day four US aircraft (three F-86s and one F-84) were shot down by the 64th IAK's pilots and two more F-86s were damaged (though one of them still rests on the bottom of the sea). The F-84 was shot down in a night combat by pilots of the 298th NIAP. Soviet losses comprised just one MiG. Despite the vigorous defense of the airfields, Sabres still managed to shoot down Captain Vasilii Balandin's MiG of the Pacific Fleet's 781st IAP as it was landing, but he managed to eject from his aircraft. In the process, he broke a humerus and sprained his neck and as a result he wound up in a hospital. Having landed not far from the airfield, Balandin was unable to walk unaided because of his injuries. Chinese picked him up and carried him almost 20 kilometers at a run back to the airfield on a stretcher. As a reward for this, the regiment commander Lieutenant Colonel Snopkov gave them one million *yuan* from his own funds – for the Chinese this was a large amount of money!

The Americans claimed that on 10 June 1953 they shot down three MiG-15s, all by pilots of the 4th FIW and two of which were downed in one combat by Major James Jabara of the 334th FIS, while Captain V. Balandin, most likely, was shot down by Captain Ralph Parr of the 335th Squadron. In their turn the Americans recognize the loss of only two of their Sabres. The first, F-86F-30 No.52-4339 of the 18th FBW's 12th Squadron, was shot down by Major Fedorets of the 913th IAP, and its pilot Captain Robert A. Coury bailed out, but was taken prisoner. Captain Floyd W. Saltze, who was flying the F-86F No.51-2938 lost this day, was killed when his Sabre crashed when making a forced landing. Presumably, Major D.V. Ermakov of the 224th IAP was the Soviet pilot that inflicted the damage to Saltze's Sabre.

The next encounter between MiGs and Sabres took place on 13 June in the Changseong area. Pilots of the 676th IAP were the heroes of the day, who successfully engaged a group of F-86F-30 fighter-bombers from the 18th FBW's 12th FBS. Major M.D. Karatun shot down two of the fighter-bombers, while Captain A.E. Matiashev and A.P. Tabakov downed one each. True, soon after Captain Tabakov achieved his victory, he was shot down in turn by 1st Lieutenant Don Forbes, but he successfully ejected and returned to his regiment.

However, a tragic event occurred at the Andong Air Base which cast a pall over the day's satisfactory outcome. When landing, a recently arrived replacement pilot in the 913th IAP's 2nd Squadron Senior Lieutenant Vasilii Ivanovich Borisov had to make a dead-stick landing because his fuel was gone, and he crashed and was killed when he tried to set the MiG down on the runway. Thus, the day's results were two F-86F-30 fighter-bombers destroyed in exchange for two MiGs and one pilot (though one of the losses was unrelated to combat). The Americans on 13 June 1953 scored just one victory. The Americans also acknowledge the loss of only one Sabre on this day: F-86F-30 No.52-4380 of the 18th FBW's 12th Squadron didn't return from a mission, and its pilot 1st Lieutenant Chadwick B. Smith was killed.

The pilots of the 64th IAK had one of their most successful combats of the month on 14 June when repelling the next large raid by Fifth Air Force fighter-bombers in the Anju area. Swarms of MiGs from the 32nd IAD and 133rd IAD responded to it, and the pilots of the 726th IAP stood out, downing two F-86F-30 and damaging another, while pilots of the fraternal 415th IAP damaged another Sabre. There were no Soviet losses. Pilots of the 224th IAP also distinguished themselves by adding two more Sabres to the day's totals, one of which was shot down by the regiment commander Hero of the Soviet Union D.V. Ermakov. He struck the right wing of a Sabre with a 37mm shell, which blew a chunk from it, but the F-86 staggered out to the bay, where the pilot ejected. Finally, the last Sabre of the day was shot down by Captain P.N. Blinov of the 535th IAP, and here's how it happened in his own words:

> There had been a squadron sortie to cover a target, but the mission passed without encountering any enemy aircraft and we returned to base. Everyone else had already landed, but I and my wingman Sashka Kolpakov, who had recently arrived in our regiment as a replacement, decided to get in a little extra practice flying as an element in the vicinity of the base. Then just as we were making a turn, I spotted a solitary aircraft flying below us. At first I thought it was one of our MiGs, but just in case I radioed a query to the command post to check if any other of our guys were still in the air. They answered that we were the last two MiGs in the air around the airfield. I realized that this was an enemy airplane, stealthily slipped in behind it, and fired a burst of shells at it from all three cannons at close range. I saw that it had started to smoke, and it began to head back toward the bay. I thought the Sabre pilot had hit his afterburners and was fleeing. I didn't chase him, because my MiG's fuel tanks were already running low, so we returned to base and made a safe landing there. I didn't even put in a claim that I had fired at the enemy aircraft, much less shot it down, because I myself wasn't certain that I had done so. However, when all the gun camera film was developed, it was clear that there had been an enemy fighter in the sights of one MiG at a range of 700-800 meters. The regiment commander assembled us and asked, "Who fired their cannons on this mission?" I replied that I had fired. Then Karataev said, "Do you know that you shot down the enemy aircraft?" to which I replied that I did not. That's how I learned that I was being given credit for downing this Sabre; evidently they had established through intercepted radio messages that this Sabre never returned to its base.

The results of the day of combats for the 64th IAK's pilots were six F-86s destroyed and one damaged in return for the loss of one aircraft – Senior Lieutenant V.I. Pimenov's MiG of the 224th IAP's 1st Squadron had been shot down, but he managed to bail out safely. It is curious on this day that the Americans awarded no victory credit to any of their pilots. However, the Americans do report the loss of four of their Sabres on this day due to a variety of reasons. Three of them were F-86F-30 fighter-bombers, one (No.52-4323) from the 18th FBW's 12th FBS, the other (No.52-4486) from the 49th FBW's 80th FBS. Both of their pilots 1st Lieutenant James H. Allston and 2nd Lieutenant William J. Hummer were killed. Hummer is officially listed as missing-in-action though no egress was noted when his Sabre failed to pull out of a bomb run, crashed and exploded. Pilot 1st Lieutenant Edward Dillon of the 12th FBS was also shot down in his F-86F-30 No.52-4319. Although he managed to bail out, he was captured by the North Koreans. Finally, F-86F No.51-2923 of the 4th FIW's 334th Squadron was shot down, but its pilot 1st Lieutenant Richard W. Frailey bailed out and was picked up an SA-16 rescue airplane. The Americans describe his loss as operational, not due to enemy action, and note that he was possibly shot down by friendly fire.

The next air battle between the Soviet and American pilots occurred on 16 June. The Americans again were attempting to destroy the Supung power station, and dogfights went on above it. On this day pilots of the 878th IAP were fortunate. They encountered a group of F-84 Thunderjets not far from the Supung hydroelectric power station. UAA

Captain N.M. Zameskin's flight poses in front of his MiG-15bis; Miaogou 1953.
From left to right: Senior Lieutenant V.V. Kashin, Senior Lieutenant E.K. Kaloshin,
Senior Lieutenant A. Kulesh and Major N.M. Zameskin

pilots took on the covering Sabres. Having broken through to the strike aircraft, pilots of the 878th IAP's 3rd Squadron under the leadership of Hero of the Soviet Union Major V.V. Egorov scattered their formation and in pursuit of the fleeing Thunderjets, shot down four of them, two of which went to the personal score of the squadron commander Major Egorov himself. Here is how the 3rd Squadron's Nikolai Mikhailovich Zameskin, a participant in this action, describes it:

> When we descended to the area where the fighter-bombers were operating, I noticed bomb explosions and smoke on the ground. Plainly, the first enemy aircraft had already dropped their loads. Then I spotted one enemy airplane flying back toward the bay low along the river channel. I decided to pursue with my wingman. The chase was made difficult and dangerous by the fact that we were flying no higher than the surrounding hills. My all-seeing wingman Vasia Kashin timidly mentioned over the radio, "We're going to crash!" This threw some cold water on my combat ardor. Keeping the target in sight, we climbed to a safer altitude, supposing that our prey would do the same thing. We were right. The adversary apparently decided that there was no danger and calmly began to climb, for all practical purposes placing himself right under our cannons. It was an F-84 Thunderjet. We then only had time to watch the aircraft explode on the ground. We only had a little fuel left, so we headed back to base with a climb and safely made a landing just as our fuel was running out.

However, Zameskin didn't receive official credit for this victory, either because it was difficult to find the wreckage of the enemy airplane in the nearly inaccessible mountainous terrain of North Korea, or because our anti-aircraft gunners had found the wreckage first and were able to add it to their score.

One more dogfight took place on this day involving pilots of the 913th IAP: two of its squadrons sortied (the 2nd and the 3rd) with a total of 16 MiGs. They encountered a group of Sabres in the Anju region, but the F-86s refused combat and departed for the sea. Our group was then re-directed and given the order to head to the area of the Supung hydroelectric station, where they were jumped by F-86s and a brawl erupted. In the course of it, flight commander Pert Semenovich Potapov was cut off from the 2nd Squadron's formation. He shouted over the radio, "I've been hit; they're shooting at me!" No one had time to help him. He was shot down and ejected at low altitude; however, he didn't have time to adopt a proper position in his seat before being catapulted, and the enormous G-forces of the ejection broke his back. He was dead before he hit the ground. In this dogfight the 913th IAP pilots paid back the enemy with interest by downing three F-86s, two of which went to pilots of the 3rd Squadron and one that was downed by the commander of the 2nd Squadron, Major A.B. Popov. True, in this dogfight the MiG of Senior Lieutenant V.P. Nikishov, Major's Popov's wingman, took combat damage, and he made a landing in his riddled fighter at Anshan, where he left his damaged aircraft, and having received a new MiG, he immediately flew back to Andong.

As a result, on 16 June the 64th IAK's pilots downed seven enemy aircraft (four F-84s and three F-86s); in addition, there was the one F-84 that was downed by Captain N.M. Zameskin, who received no official credit for it. Their own losses amounted to one MiG-15 and one pilot. The Americans assert that their Sabre pilots on 16 June shot down five MiGs, with pilots of the 51st FIW, who fought with UAA MiGs, claiming four of the MiGs, while Major Stephen L. Bettinger of the 336th FIS, who later became the USAF's final ace in Korea, claimed a victory over one MiG, which evidently must have been Captain P.S. Popov's fighter. The Americans themselves acknowledged the loss of four Sabres. One of them, F-86F-30 No.52-4582, flown by 1st Lieutenant Don R. Forbes of the 18th FBW's 12th Squadron, made a forced landing back in South Korean territory, in the process of which it crashed and had to be written off, but the pilot survived. Yet the 51st FIW's Lieutenant Colonel John Giraudo of the 25th FIS was supposedly hit by enemy ground fire while flying his F-86E No.51-2832, and he himself was taken prisoner. More likely, he was shot down by our pilots, though the Americans preferred to report that their Sabres weren't downed in air-to-air combat, but by ground fire, especially when it regards such an important "bird" as the commander of the 25th FIS, who already had two victories over MiGs in the skies of Korea to his credit. Two F-86F-30s were also lost on this day, No.52-4452 and No.52-4388. The first belonged to the 8th FBW's 36th FBS, and its pilot 1st Lieutenant Donald McKaig[2] was rescued, while the second crashed when landing back at its base and was damaged beyond repair. The identity of its pilot and his fate are presently unknown. Since our pilots claimed only three victories over Sabres on this day, then likely one of these four Sabres was shot down by a UAA pilot or it was one of the pilots whose Sabre had been damaged by our pilots on 14 June, but it wasn't written off by the Americans until 16 June. Finally, the Americans recognize the loss of two of their F-84G Thunderjets (No.50-1190 and No.51-10443) on this day. The first belonged to the 49th FBW's 7th FBS and its pilot Lieutenant Peter B. Richardson was killed, though American records list him as missing-in-action. The second Thunderjet was from the 58th FBW's 311th FBS, and its pilot 1st Lieutenant Vincent F. Lombardo was also killed on this mission. Thus the Americans suffered serious losses in this day both in aircraft and pilots.

On 18 June, several more dogfights between MiGs and Sabres developed over the area of the Supung hydroelectric station. One of them took place over the dam and involved eight MiGs of the 913th IAP's 1st Squadron under the command of Major S.A. Fedorets. Soon a group of 20 F-86F-30 Sabre fighter-bombers appeared on the scene at an altitude of 6,000 to 7,000 meters. The MiGs scattered their formation with an attack, forcing the Sabres to release their drop tanks and to jettison their bombs, which fell distant from the target. Then the Sabres joined battle, and in it the young pilot Lieutenant Ivan Petrovich Kriklivets, who had recently arrived as a replacement and was flying just his eighth combat mission, was shot down. He was downed by Colonel Robert P. Baldwin, commander of the 51st FIG, or by Lieutenant Dickenson, an RAF pilot on temporary assignment with the Group's 25th FIS, since only the pilots of this squadron of the 51st FIW frequently flew missions as fighter-bombers.

Lieutenant Kriklivets ejected directly over the reservoir and came down in his parachute in the water right next to the spillway; no one had time to rescue him and he drowned. A bit later in this same area, pilots of the 216th IAD's 518th IAP and 676th IAP had a joint dogfight, in which two F-86F-30s were shot down by pilots of the 518th IAP, but Sabres of the 4th FIW which had hurriedly arrived on the scene shot down Lieutenant Boris Vasil'evich Korshunov of the 518th IAP, who was also a recent replacement in the regiment. He was shot down in a lightning attack from above; the pilot made no attempt to escape his burning MiG and apparently had been killed in his cockpit.

Pilots of the 518th IAP a week before the ceasefire (from left to right): Captain I.A. Vit'ko, Captain N.Z. Brazhenko, Hero of the Soviet Union Captain M.I. Mikhin, Captain M.S. Bannov, Captain V.A. Smirnov, Senior Lieutenant M.P. Kalitov and Senior Lieutenant M.S. Didenko – China, 21 July 1953.

The 676th IAP's Senior Lieutenant Pletnev's MiG also received combat damage in the dogfight, and when landing at Andong it crashed. The pilot escaped with a few injuries, none of which was life-threatening.

As a result, over the day the 64th IAK's pilots shot down two F-86s while losing three MiGs and two inexperienced pilots in return. The Americans claimed that their pilots downed five MiGs on 18 June 1953, three of which went to the score of the 4th FIW, with two of these being claimed in one action by Captain Ralph S. Parr of the 335th FIS. In their turn the pilots of the 518th IAP shot down one F-86F-30 No.52-4325 belonging to the 18th FBW, the pilot of which James M. Bellows, Jr. was killed. They downed another F-86F-30 No.52-4367 of the 8th FBW's 36th FBS and its pilot 2nd Lieutenant Jimmy L. Escalle went missing-in-action. They were shot down by Captain M.P. Kalitov and Senior Lieutenant E.K. Iakushev. Hence the losses on both sides this day were painful.

On 19 June the Americans launched another fighter-bomber raid, and in the area of Taegwan-dong, a dogfight took place involving pilots of the 216th IAD and Sabres of the 8th FBW, as well as Sabre interceptors belonging to the 4th and 51st FIW. At an altitude of 8,000 meters, eight MiGs of the 878th IAP's 3rd Squadron under the command of Major V.V. Egorov engaged a dozen F-86s in combat. In the course of it, one F-86 element attacked Captain I.G. Semenov's element and shot down his wingman, Senior Lieutenant V.V. Kashin, who safely bailed out. But then Captain E.K. Koloshin's element quickly came to the rescue and shot down both of the Sabres. Captain Koloshin shot down the lead Sabre, while his wingman, the recently arrived replacement Senior Lieutenant A. Kulesh downed the wingman. To be honest, later he was only given credit for damaging this Sabre. Both sides continually fed fresh forces into the air battle and in subsequent actions, pilots of the 216th IAD claimed two more Sabres as destroyed, while losing another MiG. This was the MiG of Senior Lieutenant M. Aver'ianov of the 878th IAP, but he successfully bailed out.

The day's victory totals amounted to three F-86s and one damaged by the 64th IAK (or more precisely, the 216th IAD). Its own losses were three aircraft and one pilot – on this day while on a training flight, the young pilot Senior Lieutenant Vil' Pavlovich Kulaev, who had recently arrived as a replacement in the 224th IAP, went into a spin from which he never recovered, and he died in the cockpit of his MiG. This was the 64th IAK's third death of a pilot in 24 hours, but this loss was non-combat.

The Americans claimed that on 19 June their Sabre pilots shot down six MiG-15s, with three each going to the pilots of the 4th FIW and the 51st FIW. However, the American losses on this day were also high: they acknowledged that four F-86s and one F-84 failed to return from combat missions. Three of the 8th FBW's F-86F-30s were shot down. Albert V. Hodges, a 1st Lieutenant in the 36th FBS was shot down in his F-86F No.52-4455, and although he managed to bail out, he was taken prisoner. The 35th FBS pilot Captain Charles W. Gunther went down in his F-86F No.52-4531 and he was killed. Another 35th Squadron F-86F (No.52-4244) was fatally damaged, but its pilot Sumner managed to bail out and was picked up by a rescue helicopter. To these it must be added that F-86E No.52-2855 belonging to the 51st Wing's 39th FIS was shot down and its pilot 2nd Lieutenant Allan K. Rudolph was also killed when his Sabre crashed 4 kilometers northeast of Namsi. The downed F-84F most likely went to the score of the UAA's pilots.

The adversaries didn't meet again until 22 June, when a large dogfight erupted over MiG Alley, which involved pilots of the 32nd IAD, 216th IAD and of the Pacific Fleet's 781st IAP. Captain B.N. Sis'kov, who downed one Sabre (his fourth victory in the skies of Korea) and a flight commander in the 781st IAP Senior Lieutenant A.I. Kutsygin, who downed one Sabre and damaged another, both had luck this day. However, the pilot of the 676th IAP's 1st Squadron Senior Lieutenant Matvei Grigor'evich Sapegin particularly distinguished himself this day, when he shot down two F-86s in one dogfight. As he relates:

> Returning from a combat mission together with my leader Captain Iu.A. Varkov to our Miaogou airfield, I spotted a pair of Sabres below us, which were stealthily approaching the base in order to find some easy pickings among our pilots that were coming in for a landing. I notified the leader over the radio, "Sabres below!" He transmitted in response, "Attack, and I'll cover." I immediately went into an attacking run, and having closed with the totally unsuspecting Sabres, from close range I shot down the wingman's Sabre first. The leader went into a circle, but I stayed latched onto his tail. Even though the Sabre was more maneuverable in the horizontal, I hauled my MiG around in such a tight turn that I nearly blacked out, and with unbelievable strain I managed to knock it down as well with the fire from my cannons. For this action over the Miaogou airbase, I was awarded the Order of Lenin.

However, the 676th IAP also lost one MiG on this day: Senior Lieutenant Pustovar's MiG was damaged in the dogfight and it crashed when he attempted to land it back at base. The MiG had to be written off and the pilot received injuries.

Another crash took place on this day at a Mukden airfield. Eight MiGs of the 913th IAP's 3rd Squadron were scrambled in response to an alarm, and when the order "Cast iron" (jettison the drop tanks) was given, Captain I.I. Karpov's left wing tank failed to release. At his leader's command, he turned back toward base and decided to land at the nearest airfield. But when landing on a wet runway after a recent rain shower, Karpov's MiG couldn't stop in time and it ran off the end of the runway, where it flipped over. As a result the MiG was damaged beyond repair, but the pilot remained alive and unharmed.

On this day, another pilot of the 913th IAP was shot down. There was a sortie by eight MiGs of the 1st Squadron, and in a dogfight with a group of F-86s Captain N.A. Khristoforov drove off an attack by an F-86 element on his leader Captain E.G. Aseev, but he himself came under an attack by a different Sabre element and was shot down. Khristoforov safely ejected and soon returned to his squadron.

According to 64th IAK records, on 22 June its pilots shot down four F-86s and damaged one more, while losing three MiGs in return (one of which was a non-combat loss). Fortunately, there were no fatalities or serious injuries among the affected Soviet pilots. The American Fifth Air Force command claimed that the pilots of the 4th and 51st FIW shot down seven MiGs, six of them going to the score of the 51st Fighter Wing's pilots. In its turn, the American command acknowledged the loss of one F-86F No.51-2929 belonging to the 334th FIS; its pilot Waymond C. Nutt managed to reach his base in it, but it crashed when coming in for a landing – the pilot survived, but the Sabre had to be written off.[3] Another Sabre, F-86E No.50-0645, flown by Samuel S. Jackson of the 335th FIS, was written off two days later as a non-combat loss, supposedly due to a take-off accident resulting in a belly landing, which is not very credible.

Two days later on 24 June, 64th IAK pilots, namely the 133rd IAD's 415th IAP, had just one dogfight with Sabres. The deputy political commander of the 1st Squadron Captain Evgenii Ivanovich Polivaiko, who took part in this mission, describes what happened:

> There was a group sortie to cover the Supung hydroelectrical station. Unexpectedly four Sabres dropped out of the clouds and immediately went after the aircraft of the leader, regiment commander Hero of the Soviet Union P.F. Shevelev. The regiment commander's wingman Captain Arkadii Georgievich Alikin, seeing that he had no chance to drive off the Sabres' attack, interposed his MiG between the attackers and the regiment commander's aircraft, thereby saving his life. However, Alikin himself came under fire from the lead Sabre's six heavy-caliber machine guns and was shot up at point blank range. Two bullets struck our pilot in the back, but despite this, he managed to eject, but he was already dead when he landed; he was buried with full military honors at the Russian cemetery in the city of Port Arthur (Lushunku).

Colonel P.F. Shevelev immediately took revenge for the death of his wingman by immediately counterattacking one of the F-86 elements and shooting down one of the

Sabres. Thus, the action ended in a draw. The Americans, true, claimed that they shot down eight MiGs on this day, but plainly they were also dogfighting with UAA pilots, because the 64th IAK lost only one MiG that day. Six of the eight MiGs claimed on 24 June were shot down by pilots of the 4th FIW. Major Foster L. Smith of the 335th FIS, who downed two MiGs in two separate actions, had a day to remember. American records show that only one Sabre, F-86F-30 No.52-4447 of the 18th FBW's 67th FBS, was lost on this day after its engine flamed out; it crashed at the end of the runway and its pilot 1st Lieutenant Maxwell J. Shipp was killed. However, again it is more likely that this Sabre's engine had been damaged by MiG cannon fire.

Two more air battles took place on 27 June over the Supung hydroelectric station. They both involved pilots of the 32nd IAD. A participant in one of them, a former pilot of the 224th IAP's 1st Squadron Iulii Borisovich Borisov, describes it this way in his memoirs:

> There was a four-ship sortie to cover the power station. The regiment commander Hero of the Soviet Union D.V. Ermakov himself was leading the flight. I and N.K. Odintsov were flying together as the second element. Already toward the end of the patrol while returning to base, we saw four Sabres dive on the regiment commander's pair. Odintsov and I attacked the second element, which had overshot us as it followed its lead element. Odintsov shouted to me: "Boria, take the one on the right." I heard him and attacked the wingman's Sabre, and from a range of 200 meters fired at it with a volley from all three cannons. I watched the shells strike home. Shell explosions were visible on the F-86's wing, and then fragments began to fly away from it, followed by smoke. However, I overshot it and in a climbing turn to starboard I saw the flash of an explosion on the ground. Odintsov also shot down the lead Sabre, and without any losses we returned to base, where we were fervently congratulated for saving regiment commander Ermakov and for downing the enemy aircraft.

A little later in the same area the pilots of the 913th IAP's 1st Squadron also had a successful dogfight. Captain A.K. Popov and Senior Lieutenant V.N. Aleksandrov each claimed a Sabre, without any losses on the Soviet side. However, the Sabres tarnished the 913th IAP's victorious day, by shooting down the regiment commander Major V.A. Marchenko's MiG as it was taking off from Andong. He didn't even have time to jettison his drop tanks before he was jumped and shot down. Marchenko was able to eject safely.

So on 27 June the 64th IAK destroyed four F-86s while losing just one MiG in return. The Americans assert that on this day pilots of the 51st FIW's 25th Squadron shot down two MiG-15s. It is possible that over the Andong airfield they shot down another MiG belonging to the UAA. The Americans admit to the loss of just one Sabre on this day: F-86F-30 No.52-4334 of the 18th FBW, the pilot of which bailed out and was rescued. Two days later, the Americans acknowledged the loss of another F-86F-30 No.52-4312 from the same 18th FBW, the pilot of which Major Flamm D. Harper bailed out and was picked up by an H-19 rescue helicopter. Could it be possible that in actual fact this Sabre was shot down on 27 June, but wasn't written off until 29 June as a non-combat loss?

One of the final air battles in the month took place on 29 June, and it ended with a tragic incident of this war, about which I want to speak in more detail. On this day, eight MiG-15s of the 676th IAP's 1st Squadron under the command of Hero of the Soviet Union and deputy regiment commander Lieutenant Colonel I.M. Gorbunov took off into the sky. Here's how a participant on this mission, Mikhail Petrovich Zhbanov, remembers it:

> On this day, eight MiGs under the command of Hero of the Soviet Union Ivan Mikhailovich Gorbunov took off on a combat mission. I had already taken the 1st Squadron under my command and on this mission I was leading the second flight. Upon taking off we were immediately directed to head to the Andong area. At an altitude of 2,000 meters we were attacked by eight F-86s while we were still carrying our drop tanks and our airspeed was low. The attack targeted my flight. Gorbunov only had time to say over the radio, "They are attacking from the left and above." I responded that I could see them, and shouted that I was striking them at their altitude and I took my flight into a climbing turn to port. At this moment a second group of four Sabres attacked Gorbunov's flight, as a result of which Ivan Mikhailovich was shot down, and he ejected over the area of Wulongbei. As he was descending in his parachute he was shot by the Sabres, since the Americans viewed gun camera footage of a parachutist as proof of an aerial victory. The American pilots "forgot" to switch off their machine guns while filming the parachutist.

In this same action, Senior Lieutenant M.G. Sapegin of the 1st Squadron also shot down one Sabre. However, this victory was not at all comparable to the grief that settled over the pilots of the 676th IAP. Hero of the Soviet Union Ivan Mikhailovich Gorbunov was much loved in the regiment and respected for his combat accomplishments and his concern for the well-being of others. Having learned of this cruel excess by the American pilots, the pilots of the entire 64th IAK were greatly enraged, since there were unwritten rules about treating a defeated foe with respect. Soviet pilots over the entire period of the war never once perpetrated a similar cruelty to downed American pilots, while the Americans sinned in this way more than once. There were previous cases of shooting at our pilots as they were descending in parachutes after ejecting from their fatally damaged aircraft, though it is true that none of these incidents ended in the death of the pilots, but in the case of I.M. Gorbunov this gunnery "practice" ended in a tragedy. This dastardly act lies on the conscience of those 51st FIW's pilots who each claimed to have downed a MiG on this day, which does not bestow honor to them as either pilots or as people.

On this day, the following American pilots claimed victories:

1. Henry Buttelmann (1st Lieutenant, 25th FIS)
2. Ronald B. Howell, Jr. (1st Lieutenant, 16th FIS)
3. John H. Granville-White (Lieutenant, 39th FIS, on exchange from the RAF)
4. George W. Jensen (1st Lieutenant, 16th FIS)
5. Thomas E. Nott (1st Lieutenant, 16th FIS)
6. Kenneth L. Palmer (1st Lieutenant, 16th FIS)

All of these pilots were with the 51st FIW. The Americans on this day lost F-86F No.52-4457 from the 8th FBW's 80th FBS, the pilot of which 2nd Lieutenant Joseph M. Quagley was killed.

On 30 June the final air battle of the month took place, in which the Americans were primarily dogfighting with UAA pilots. The 64th IAK's pilots had just one aerial combat, which didn't result in any victories for our pilots, but one aircraft was lost. Senior Lieutenant Levchatov's MiG of the 224th IAP was shot down, but the pilot safely bailed out. This was the IAK's final loss in the June fighting.

However, an earnest clash took place between UAA pilots and pilots of the 4th and 51st FIW. The Americans claimed that on 30 June 1953, the pilots of these two fighter wings in their F-86s shot down a total of 16 (!) MiGs. Of these, 12 fell to the pilots of the 4th FIW, of which number Major James Jabara of the 334th FIS and Captain Ralph Parr of the 335th FIS each claimed two.

According to records of the 64th IAK, the overall results of the June battles were as follows: 41 enemy aircraft were shot down by the IAK's pilots in aerial combat, which included 36 F-86s and four F-84s, and another 12 enemy aircraft were damaged (9 F-86s, two B-29s and one B-26). Of this total, only one aircraft was destroyed and three damaged in night actions. Losses amounted to 26 MiG-15s and 11 pilots, of which four aircraft and one pilot were not combat losses.

In their turn the UAA pilots flew 1,026 individual combat sorties in June and had 26 aerial combats, in which they downed 15 US aircraft and damaged four more. The UAA's losses over the month were 11 downed MiG-15s and seven pilots killed-in-action. Thus, the total combat losses between these allies amounted to 33 aircraft and 17 pilots, while four more aircraft were lost due to non-combat reasons.

The American command claimed that in the month of June, the pilots of the 18th FBW and of the 4th and 51st FIW downed 77 (!) MiG-15 jet fighters in aerial combat. Even if you include MiGs that were only damaged in the dogfights, this figure overstates the real number of losses on our side by more than twice over. To be sure, the Americans own losses in the month of June 1952 were heavy: according to records of the Fifth Air Force command, 23 F-86 fighters were lost, of which 14 were destroyed in combat, while the remaining nine Sabres were not considered losses due to combat.

However, the 64th IAK's losses would have been smaller, had the training given to the young pilots who arrived as replacements in May 1953 been more professional, and had they had more flight time in the cockpit of the MiG-15 before being sent into action. Four of the 11 pilots killed in the month of June were young pilots who had arrived in the 64th IAK as replacements.

In addition, June 1953 was marked by the fact that at the beginning of the month two fresh aviation divisions arrived in the 64th IAK, which entered the IAK reserve and were based on the Mukden and Anshan bases while they prepared for combat in the skies of Korea. The first to arrive at rear airfields of the 64th IAK from the Liaodong Peninsula was Colonel A.I. Khalutin's 37th IAD, consisting of three regiments (the 236th IAP commanded by Major D.V. Golovanov, the 282nd IAP commanded by Hero of the Soviet Union A.A. Barsht, and the 940th IAP, commanded by Lieutenant Colonel Titov). All of these regiments were equipped with MiG-15bis fighters. A bit later the 100th IAD arrived from Iaroslavl' under the command of Colonel A.F. Dvornik. This division included the 9th GIAP commanded by Colonel Sergeev, the 731st IAP under the command of Lieutenant Colonel Zhakhov, and the 735th IAP. All of these three regiments were equipped with the MiG-15bis and were based in Mukden and Anshan.

JULY 1953: THE GUNS OF WAR FALL SILENT

In July the weather deteriorated even further, and for all practical purposes an extended pause in the air war ensued until 11 July. At an assembly of the PLAAF's Party Committee it was observed that although the war had been going on for more than two years, it should be continued while further studying the combat experience of its partner and that of the opposing side. For their part, the American aircraft repeatedly but unsuccessfully attempted to destroy the hydroelectric power station in Lagushao and the bridge across the Yalu River, while avoiding zones of MiG activity.

Groups of F-84G and F-86F-30 fighter-bombers from the 8th, 18th, 49th, 58th and 474th FBW in these days sustained active operations, but did not enter the operational zone of the 64th IAK. If they spotted groups of MiGs approaching, the fighter-bombers would withdraw to safe zones like the Yellow Sea and behind the front lines. The pilots of the Sabre fighter interceptors of the 4th and 51st FIW acted in a similar fashion, shunning active combats with the MiGs and avoiding encounters.

Occasionally only small groups of MiGs from the UAA would fly down to the Anju area or further to the border of the 38th Parallel, but the 64th IAK's pilots focused on their primary missions – covering their bases Dapu, Miaogou, and Andong, guarding the bridge across the Yalu connecting Andong and Sinuiju, and protecting the Supung power station. Simultaneously they introduced the pilots of the 64th IAK's newly arrived IAD to the combat situation: the pilots of the 32nd IAD worked to bring the pilots of Colonel A.I. Khalutin's 37th IAD up to speed, while the 216th IAD's pilots worked similarly with Colonel A.F. Dvornik's division. Frequently the pilots of these two newly arrived divisions conducted joint patrol flights together, beginning in the middle of July to the Anju area. But when the enemy made an appearance, only the veterans of the 32nd IAD and 216th IAD would engage in battle, since there was a strict order for the pilots of the 37th IAD and 100th IAD not to join in – the command was protecting the inexperienced pilots. At the same time these new divisions were necessary to provide fresh reserves, since the pilots of the 32nd IAD and 216th IAD were already worn out by their tour of duty, and it was unknown what the opposing side might do in the final days of the war.

In addition, the regiments of the 32nd IAD and 216th IAD continued to work to improve the combat skills of the batch of replacements they had received back in May. Some of them participated in the first aerial combat of the month, which took place on 1 July. Here's what one of the participants in this fight, a pilot of the 535th IAP's 3rd Squadron Fedor Il'ich Masleev has to say about it:

> On 1 July we were flying a combat mission at a low altitude of 500-800 meters to cover the Supung dam. That evening the Americans, who had been unable to destroy the dam with high-altitude bombing were making an effort to breach the dam from low altitude, using for this purpose F-84G and F-86F-30 fighter-bombers. Thus, we were also flying at low altitude. I was part of Captain P.N. Blinov's flight of four MiGs, leading the second element, and my wingman was a young pilot who had recently arrived as a replacement. Soon we encountered a group of Sabres (it seems that there were four) and we engaged it in combat. Suddenly I heard Blinov's voice, "They're attacking me!" Indeed, I saw a Sabre on his tail. I immediately attacked it and opened fire on it from behind at a range of

not more than 400 meters. The Sabre, trailing smoke, fell into a descending left turn and disappeared below. I couldn't keep an eye on it, since neither the combat situation nor the altitude permitted this. I radioed Blinov that everything was OK and in essence the action ended with this, as the Sabres broke off combat; we safely returned to our base at Dapu. This mission lasted for just 20 minutes, and the fight itself for just 2 or 3 minutes. After examining my gun camera film, they credited me with damaging this enemy aircraft, and this was only shortly before the regiment departed back to the Soviet Union.

A similar combat mission occurred on 4 July as well; once again Captain P.N Blinov led a flight of four MiGs to the area of the hydroelectric station, but they encountered no enemy, so while returning to the Dapu airfield, they decided to have a mock dogfight for the benefit of the two young pilots in the flight. They didn't release their drop tanks in order to save time for turning the aircraft around on the ground for another sortie. In this friendly sparring session, during one maneuver a drop tank on Lieutenant Aleksandr Nikolaevich Kolpakov's MiG broke free; striking the rudder, it disabled the aircraft and it fell into a spin from which it never recovered. Kolpakov never ejected and crashed together with his MiG. This was the 64th IAK's first loss in the month of July, and it was a non-combat loss at that.

On subsequent days there were more aerial clashes in the area of Andong and the Supung hydroelectric station, but these were infrequent and only involved small groups from each side. They were all fleeting encounters between flights of four to six aircraft which ended with no results for either side.

On 11 July, however, again the Sabre pilots were able to take advantage of MiGs as they were coming in for a landing. Major John Bolt, an exchange pilot from the Marine Corps with the 51st FIW's 39th FIS, shot down two MiGs. One of them was that of Senior Lieutenant M.L. Abidin of the 518th IAP, who managed to eject safely.

The 64th IAK's pilots didn't score their first victory in the final month of the war until 12 July. On this day there were aerial battles in the vicinity of the Andong and Dapu airfields, where Sabre "hunters" were again trying to ambush someone among the 64th IAK's or UAA's pilots. Unfortunately, they were successful once again. Thus, in the area of the Andong airfield complex, where the naval 781st IAP was based, the Sabres caught a group of its MiGs as it was landing and shot down Captain Viktor Mikhailovich Belov from an altitude of just 150 meters. His MiG crashed to the ground and disintegrated together with its pilot. This was the final pilot of the Pacific Ocean Fleet's 781st IAP to die in action, and his remains lie in the Russian cemetery in Port Arthur. A participant in this mission Vadim Petrovich Sazhim, described this unhappy incident in more detail:

There was this airfield at Dapu, which was located among the mountains. Radar couldn't see anything. Usually it was blockaded when our group was taking off or landing. We were coming in for a landing without fuel, but the airfield was firmly blockaded. I had almost nothing but fumes in my fuel tanks. My leader Ikonopistsev escorted me around to the final turn and gave me the order to land. Once I had separated from him, that's when I spotted a pair of Sabres behind me that was turning in my direction. I abruptly lowered my nose and dropped to an altitude of 10 to 15 meters and arrived at the runway at this altitude between the hills. I barely had time to lower my landing gear. Then Ikonopistsev shouted over the radio, "They're firing at you!" but I was already down on the runway. Glancing back, I saw an aircraft burning on the ground – it was Captain Belov's MiG. At this same moment I saw a MiG rolling toward me – we quickly turned right to avoid a collision. That's how it happened! They shot Belov down at an altitude of 150-200 meters. He was coming in for a landing behind me. We knew that the Sabre's gun sight radar at low altitudes wasn't suited for firing from a higher altitude. Why Belov didn't descend like I did is incomprehensible!

On this mission, the six MiGs of the 781st IAP under the command of Lieutenant Colonel N.D. Snopkov had been directed toward a group of approximately 30 F-86F-30s. Vadim Petrovich Sazhin relates what happened next:

Not for from the border between China and the PDRK, near the shoreline of Korea Bay (15-20 kilometers distant from it) there was a grenade factory. Enemy F-86-30 fighter-bombers often struck it with bombs. They would come in from the direction of the bay, dive on the factory, release their bombs, and then become typical Sabres ready to engage MiGs in combat. That's why we had to oppose them at altitudes of 600-1,000 meters. It happened that we weren't the only ones operating there; groups from other regiments would simultaneously arrive together with us. They [the F-86F Sabres] would be in a hurry to release their bombs, striving to free themselves of their loads as quickly as possible.

So, on this particular mission we ran into a large group of their fighter-bombers. There was a lot of firing; in general it was a complete hornet's nest. Our task in this six-ship formation was, of course, to protect the regiment commander. We had to divert part of the Sabres onto us in order to give the commander the possibility of escaping into the clouds. It was in this particular dogfight that we in fact observed a collision between two F-86s – they collided when pulling out of their dives. I wasn't the only one to witness this; other pilots of our group did as well.

The Americans acknowledge the loss of two of their F-86s with the Bureau Numbers 51-2836 and 51-12972 from the 4th FIW's 335th FIS, the pilots of which 1st Lieutenant Eugene G. Aldridge and 1st Lieutenant Albert Cox went missing-in-action. It was the collision of these two Sabres that Sazhin witnessed. They were officially credited to the scores of Captain D.V. Semenov and Senior Lieutenant A.I. Kutsygin as "damaged".

On this day pilots of the 32nd IAD flew three combat missions, all of which led to dogfights. On the morning combat mission, in the Andong – Gisiu area six MiGs of the 224th IAP's 2nd Squadron tangled with a group of F-86s and V.A. Zhitnev shot down one Sabre. F-86s in turn flamed Aleksandr Ivanovich Galin's MiG, and he ejected from his burning aircraft. Thus this dogfight ended in a draw, but when ejecting, the young pilot Galin, who was one of the regiment's recent replacements, was killed. Galin had assumed an incorrect posture when ejecting, and having suffered a broken spinal column, he was already dead when he reached the ground.

After lunch the pilots of the 224th IAP flew another combat sortie to the Andong area, but Captain B.I. Sis'kov's six-MiG formation didn't encounter any enemy and returned to their base. Sabres were waiting for them to go into their landing pattern. A pilot of the

224th IAP Iulii Borisovich Borisov, one of the men on this particular mission, recalls what happened:

> We were returning from a combat mission; I was the wingman to the group leader Captain B.N. Sis'kov, and when coming in for a landing at our Dapu airfield, my "alarmist" (an instrument that gave warning of an enemy aircraft to your rear) went off. I informed Sis'kov about this and requested that he check the airspace behind me. My leader saw two black specks, but he was certain that these were our aircraft returning from a combat mission. Yet instead it was a Sabre element that closed quickly and peppered us with .50-caliber bullets. I immediately shouted, "Sabres attacking!" I broke sharply to starboard, but the Sabres continued to shoot up my aircraft before streaking past our element and pulling out of their attack in a climb. However, here Boris Sis'kov attacked them, having lined up on their tails, and he shot down one of them. My engine started to run roughly, and something that was not quite smoke and not quite steam appeared in my cockpit and I immediately went in for a landing. However, my landing gear refused to lower; I overshot the beginning of the runway and came down hard somewhere in the middle of it, and then bounded off to one side of it onto a dirt road that ran next to it. With this my aircraft broke apart: the tail flew off, and then both wings; only my cockpit remained intact. When touching down, my head slammed forward against the gunsight and cracked my head, and having bent the sight's supporting bracket and its reflector, I wound up with my head almost touching the bullet-proof glass, but in general everything turned out OK. I scrambled out of the cockpit with a bloodied face and ran off to one side. A column of vehicles of a refueling unit was moving along the road, which gathered me up and took me to the aid station, where they bandaged my head.

The F-86 downed by Sis'kov went to his score as only "damaged" – apparently, it reached the bay where the pilot abandoned it; in this case and others like it, the 64th IAK didn't credit the pilot with a victory, but at best credited him with damaging the aircraft.

However, the action in the vicinity of the Dapu airfield didn't end with this: in order to sweep the airspace clear above the base, four MiGs of the 224th IAP's 1st Squadron arrived from a neighboring base, but they themselves came under attack from elements of Sabre "hunters", which shot down Senior Lieutenant A.A. German's MiG. He successfully ejected and landed safely in his parachute.

On this day the 913th IAP lost one more aircraft. Six MiGs of the 913th IAP's 2nd Squadron sparred with a group of Sabres in the Gisiu area, with no results. When returning to base, two F-86s attacked Senior Lieutenant L.I. Maleevsky's MiG that was bringing up the rear of the group's formation and attempted to shoot it down. Maleevsky spotted them in time and pulled up into a climb, and at an altitude of 15,000 meters the Sabres gave up the chase and headed back to the bay. Their gunnery hadn't been accurate; only one bullet struck the wing. Maleevsky started to return to base by himself, but the division command post ordered the entire group to land at Mukden, because Sabres were prowling in the vicinity of their own airfield. However, still 40-50 kilometers short of Mukden, Maleevsky ran out of fuel and the engine stopped. He received an order to eject, which he did safely.

At the end of the day, the 64th IAK reported its pilots had destroyed one F-86 and damaged another three Sabres. Its own losses were large: five MiGs and the death of two pilots. The Americans in their turn claimed seven victories over MiGs on this day, five of them going to pilots of the 4th FIW. The 335th Squadron's Captain Lonnie Moore had a great day, downing two MiGs in separate actions. In addition to the two F-86s lost as a result of the collision, the Americans acknowledged the loss of one more F-86F-30 No.52-4491 from the 8th FBW, the pilot of which bailed out and was rescued. Apparently Senior Lieutenant Zhitnev of the 224th IAP shot this Sabre fighter-bomber down. Incidentally, the Americans wrote off all three of these Sabres on 11 July, but our records indicate they were all lost on 12 July.

On 15 July yet another of the recently arrived replacements, a young pilot with the 535th IAP's 3rd Squadron Senior Lieutenant Gagarinov, was attacked in the vicinity of his airfield and his MiG took damage. He came in for a landing, but overshot the mark for setting down the aircraft; it jumped beyond the end of the runway and crashed, but the pilot was OK. He'd been attacked by the USAF's No. 2 ace in this war, Major James Jabara of the 334th FIS. This was his 15th and final victory in the skies of Korea. Captain Clyde Curtin of the 335th FIS claimed another MiG on this day. The 64th IAK did not go empty handed – the deputy squadron commander of the 535th IAP, while flying a mission with the regiment's 3rd Squadron, shot down one F-86.

The following day, 16 July, pilots of the 2nd Squadron of the 133rd IAD's 726th IAP had a successful dogfight with Sabres of the 4th FIW, in which the squadron commander Major V.Ia. Fedorets shot down one F-86. Captain V. Panteleev and Major N.I. Ivanov each damaged a Sabre. True, the 726th IAP did lose one MiG – Senior Lieutenant G.P. Shishkin was shot down, but he safely ejected from his crippled aircraft. Nikolai Ivanovich Ivanov talks about his final victory in this war:

We were on one of the last missions of the war. We already knew that there would soon be a truce; the Americans knew this as well, and [at this point] no one wanted to die. On this day the entire regiment sortied; I was leading a squadron and my primary focus was to preserve the formation and not to lose anyone. Thus when I spotted Sabres far in the distance, I didn't immediately launch an attack.

They were crossing our front at a somewhat higher altitude. I thought then that the Americans screwed up. They had an altitude advantage, but when I began to turn in their direction, they didn't do anything in response to my attack. Coming out of the turn and closing on them I opened fire, but they didn't perform any sort of defensive maneuver, even having seen my tracers. I began to fire at long range, at 800 meters or even more, and while I was closing I continued to fire, giving three bursts. Suddenly a Sabre – hey-ho! – began to smoke and headed downward. That's how my final mission in Korea ended.

On this day six MiGs of the 913th IAP's 2nd Squadron engaged a group of Sabres in a dogfight in the vicinity of the Supung power station, in which Senior Lieutenant L.F. Kaz'min shot down one Sabre, but we also had one of the recent replacement pilots Senior Lieutenant Pavlov shot down. He ejected from his riddled MiG and soon returned to the regiment.

UAA pilots also clashed with Sabres on this day and achieved several victories. Pilots of a North Korean regiment under the command of Major Kim Ji Sang were particularly successful in the months of June and July. For this reason on 17 July 1953 he was awarded with the high title Hero of the PDRK. By this time Major Kim Ji Sang had personally destroyed four enemy aircraft in aerial combat and damaged one more. From May to 17 July, the pilots of Kim Ji Sang's regiment shot down 25 enemy aircraft in air battles and damaged an additional five.

The final results of 16 July were two F-86s downed by 64th IAK pilots and another two damaged, while losing two MiG-15s in return. The Americans claimed four victories over MiGs on this day, two each falling to the 4th and 51st FIW.

Pilots of the 133rd IAD achieved their final victories in the skies of Korea on 17 July. Pilots of the 726th IAP's 3rd Squadron were the lucky ones – Captain V. Panteleev shot down one Sabre in a dogfight and Captain P.G. Kolotov damaged another. In this their last dogfight in Korea, the 726th IAP pilots lost no MiGs, though it is true that Senior Lieutenant S.V. Kauchuk's MiG took combat damage and he had to land it on the new Chinese base at Dagushan (north of Dapu), while the rest of the squadron returned to Anshan.

On 18 July the 64th IAK's pilots had several dogfights in the Andong – Gisiu area. In one of them with a group of F-86s, another of the recent replacement pilots was shot down. Senior Lieutenant V.I. Potibenko of the 535th IAP's 1st Squadron took hits to his MiG. He safely ejected, but when landing fell on a rocky slope, which resulted in a broken arm and an injured spine. He was taken to a hospital, and after treatment he received a medical discharge. Most likely, he'd been shot down by Captain Lonnie Moore of the 335th FIS, but possibly this was done instead by Major Foster Smith from the same squadron; both of these pilots of the 4th FIW, according to American claims, achieved victories on 18 July. The Americans deny the loss of any of their Sabres in the course of the fighting between 13 and 19 July, while reporting the loss of three of their F-84G Thunderjets. It is possible that one or two of them were downed by our pilots, who confused them with Sabres, and perhaps one or two by pilots of the UAA, though the Americans attribute all of these lost Thunderjets to ground fire.

The most intense and bitter combats in the skies of Korea in the final month of the war took place on 19 and 20 July. On 19 July the Soviet pilots had two aerial combats, in which they shot down one F-86 and lost their final two MiGs and the last pilot who was killed-in-action in this war. A participant in one of these dogfights, the former squadron commander Semen Alekseevich Fedorets of the 913th IAP, talks about his experience in it:

> On this day our squadron was scrambled in response to an alarm in order to repel a raid by Sabres that were heading toward the Supung hydroelectric station. The enemy group wasn't large – up to 12 aircraft. The IAK command post failed to detect the approaching enemy group and was very late in scrambling us. We were flying in a six-ship formation at low altitude. Visibility was poor; the cloud cover was 7/10 or 8/10 at an altitude of 600 to 1,500 meters. When approaching the hydroelectric station from the west, a flight of Sabres from the forward screen dove on us. I went into a spiral to the left and we shook out the formation into a column of elements, and then we engaged the Sabres in combat. One of the Sabres attacked Senior Lieutenant Gerasimchuk's MiG and gave it a burst. He responded

by hauling the control stick back into his belly and going into a climb, but he had to have made it a steeper climbing turn at maximum G's. While climbing at an angle of 60°, he was given another well-aimed burst from straight behind and his aircraft erupted in flames. Gerasimchuk ejected.

Driving off an attack against his wingman, Senior Lieutenant E.G. Aseev gave one Sabre a long burst and exhausted his ammunition. The Sabre buzzed off and turned around to the left in a dive to take a course back to its base. Meanwhile, I was continuing to spiral and I saw the entire scene of this dogfight. I intercepted one Sabre that was on a crossing course from my right, closed with it, and gave it a burst at a target aspect angle of 1/4. The Sabre headed straight down and plummeted into the ground in a dive. When he had ejected at high speed, Gerasimchuk's parachute had become tangled and it failed to open fully. Thus, a recent replacement combat pilot in my squadron, Lieutenant Nikolai Petrovich Gerasimchuk was killed on his twelfth combat mission.

Gerasimchuk was the final Soviet pilot to be killed-in-action in this war. In turn, Major Fedorets's victory was the last one for the 913th IAP in the war, and his seventh and final victory in the skies of Korea. With his seven official victories (he failed to receive credit for one more), Major Semen Alekseevich Fedorets became the 32nd IAD's top-scoring ace and the highest scoring pilot in the entire 64th IAK in 1953. In the seven months of fighting in 1953, none of the other pilots of the 64th IAK had so many victories!

In a different action on this day Sabres shot down one of the 781st IAP's MiGs. A pair of Sabres had slipped in from the direction of the bay unnoticed and attacked a group of MiGs from the naval 781st IAP out of the sun. Senior Lieutenant E.I. Lugovtsev's MiG was hit and he ejected at an altitude of 11,000 meters. They attempted to attack him again, but Senior Lieutenant Ikonopistsev and his wingman Senior Lieutenant Sazhin cut off this attempt, and Lugovtsev safely landed on North Korean territory. The story of regiment navigator Lugovtsev continued and almost ended tragically for him. As is known, all of our pilots wore Chinese uniforms, but over this uniform our pilots usually wore leather flight jackets, and on the ground it was difficult to distinguish between an American pilot and a Soviet pilot. Usually the Chinese and North Korean soldiers and civilians identified our pilots by the reddish leather boots they wore. Yet on this mission Lugovtsev took off wearing simple high shoes, and this almost played a cruel joke on him. Coming to earth not far from Andong, Chinese seized him, tied him up, and began to drag him by rope to their Special Department. Lugovtsev was saved by the fact that one of our mobile anti-aircraft batteries rolled past him. The soldiers overheard his Russian expletives, stopped, and took him from the Chinese. They then delivered him to the hospital in Andong – he had also injured his spine when ejecting, and for a long time he walked around wrapped in a plaster cast. This was the last MiG lost by the 64th IAK in this war.

However, on this day, as well as on 20 July, bitter fighting went on in the depth of MiG Alley, in which primarily North Korean pilots took part, including Major Kim Ji Sang's regiment. Over these two days of fierce dogfights, the pilots of his regiment claimed 11 F-86s destroyed and another three damaged, of which two of the Sabres were shot down by regiment commander Hero of the PDRK Major Kim Ji Sang himself, thereby raising his personal score to six victories. True, his regiment also suffered heavy losses, since according to the claim of the American side they shot down 13 MiGs in the dogfights on 19 and 20 July, 10 on the first day and three on the second. Of these 13 MiG-15s lost over the two days of fighting, only two belonged to the 64th IAK, while the rest belonged to the UAA. Pilots of the 4th FIW claimed 10 of these 13 victories. Captain Clyde Curtin of the 335th FIS had a particularly memorable day on 19 July 1953, when he downed two MiGs simultaneously in one dogfight. Major Thomas Sellers, a US Navy exchange pilot with the 335th FIS, achieved twin victories in a dogfight on 20 July. In the fighting on 19 July, two aces of the 4th FIW achieved their final victories in the war: Captain Lonnie Moore of the 335th FIS and Lieutenant Colonel Vermont Garrison. Both pilots raised their personal score to 10 MiGs and thereby became double aces. The American side acknowledged the loss of only three of their F-84Gs from the 58th and 474th FBW on 19 July, the pilots of which all were killed in the cockpits of their fighter-bombers. As always, the Americans maintain that they were all knocked down by enemy ground fire, but it is more likely that they were shot down by UAA pilots. Meanwhile the Americans confirm Major S.A. Fedorets's victory, but place it on the following day: most likely, the victim of our ace was F-86F-30 No.52-4469 from the 8th FBW's 35th Squadron, the pilot of which 1st Lieutenant John F. Thees was killed.

On 20 July pilots of the 64th IAK achieved their final victories in this war, while dueling with American pilots in one of the final dogfights in the skies of Korea. On this day the IAK's pilots primarily flew missions to the area of the Supung hydroelec-tric station and Andong to cover important strategic targets. Pilots of the naval 781st IAP, who took off in an eight-ship formation under the command of deputy regi-ment commander Major P.P. Bakaras' to cover the railroad bridge across the Yalu in the Andong area, distinguished themselves. Already at take-off, a large group of F-86s attacked them. Releasing their drop tanks, the regiment's pilots took on the Sabres at a nap-of-the-earth altitude. They opened fire at the enemy from ranges of 500 to 800 meters. As a result, the naval pilots, who had been caught in a tactically unfavorable situ-ation, with great courage, pluck and resolve downed two F-86s and damaged another, thanks to the timely warning from the regiment command post and the superb coop-eration between their elements and flights that they showed. Major A.N. Chirkov and Senior Lieutenant Z.M. Sherstnev received credit for the victories, while Captain I.F. Klochkov was the one who damaged one of the Sabres. It is gratifying as well that in this action our pilots had no losses.

It is possible that it was pilots of the 32nd IAD's 224th IAP who achieved the final Soviet victories in the skies of Korea, which went to the credit of the deputy commander of the 1st Squadron Captain B.N. Sis'kov and Senior Lieutenant V.I. Klimov. Vladimir Ivanovich Klimov shares more details with us about how it happened:

> The weather on this day was bad – low clouds, visibility of 4 kilometers. At the time I was now an element leader, but my wingman, who had recently arrived as a replace-ment, wasn't ready to fly in such difficult meteorological conditions, so they didn't take Senior Lieutenant Morozov on this mission. I was assigned to fly wingman to Captain Boris Sis'kov. We were scrambled from the Andong airfield in six MiGs, which were being led by the deputy regiment commander Lieutenant Colonel V.S. Starovoistov; Senior Lieutenant N.K. Odintsov was leading the second element, while Captain Sis'kov led the third. We had already assembled in the air before

exiting the first turn, and then we were given our combat assignment – to cover the Supung hydroelectric station at an altitude of 300-400 meters. The cloud layer was somewhat higher over the reservoir. We passed over the dam several times as we patrolled back and forth. We were warned that there were no enemy below the clouds, but at a high altitude above the clouds, several enemy flights were overhead. We jettisoned our drop tanks, and ten minutes later the command arrived: "Wrap it up and proceed to the Dapu airfield." We stayed in our formation of a wedge of elements and headed towards Dapu.

Before reaching the airfield the leader shifted us into a right-echeloned formation, and we began to go into our landings from an altitude of 100-150 meters. We received a warning from the command post: "Be alert, Sabres are after you." But we were covered by clouds, and Starovoistov disbanded our [combat] formation. I wound up on the outside and began to throttle back for the landing. That's when I heard the sound of the "alarmist" and Sis'kov's voice over the radio: "Take a look back!" I glanced back and saw a pair of Sabres on our tail below and behind us. I shoved the throttle forward and abruptly went into a climbing turn to port, so far as the clouds would allow.

The Sabres were too late to fire a burst, and one of them passed behind the tail of my aircraft. Then the Sabres themselves overshot us, I slightly banked my aircraft, caught one of them directly in my sights, and gave it a burst of six shells from my 37mm cannon and 20 shells from my smaller cannons. Both Sabres then disappeared into the clouds. My leader Captain Sis'kov had also fired at the lead Sabre, but we didn't observe any results, since the clouds swallowed up both of the F-86s. We were the last to make a landing, and there wasn't a single bullet hole in either of our MiGs. Boris and I were both lucky on this day, because they found both of our Sabres 40 kilometers away from the airfield on the coast of the bay; the search team leader Captain Belukha brought us the details. He informed us that one of the pilots of the F-86s that we had downed had ejected over the coastline, while the other was killed in the cockpit of his Sabre. That evening Boris Sis'kov and I celebrated our victory with a drink and then began to prepare for a new combat day.

Both of these downed Sabres belonged to the 4th FIW. According to American records, Sabre No.52-2863 experienced an engine flameout on its approach to the K-14 Base at Suwon, and its pilot 2nd Lieutenant Kenneth O. Polenske of the 336th FIS later died in a hospital. The other pilot from the same squadron was Thomas Sellers, the Marine exchange pilot from VMF-115 who was flying F-86E No.51-12973, but failed to return from this mission – he was likely killed when his Sabre came down.

These were also the final combat fatalities of the American Fifth Air Force in this war. On this day, Major Stephen L. Bettinger of the 336th FIS achieved his fifth victory, but he himself was shot down in his F-86E No.51-2836 and became a prisoner-of-war.[4]

In addition to these three F-86s lost on this day, three more F-86s failed to return safely to base. One, another Sabre from the 336th FIS, was being flown by Richard T. Gibson. It was damaged, and although Gibson managed to reach his base at Suwon, there he abandoned the crippled F-86E No.51-4469 rather than attempt to land it. The 51st FIW also lost one Sabre (No.51-2756); its pilot 2nd Lieutenant Gerald W. Knott was providing air cover for the rescue of a pilot and "crashed for unknown reasons". Knott was killed. Finally, an F-86F-30 fighter-bomber with the Bureau Number 52-4469 being flown by John W. Thees of the 8th Fighter-bomber Wing's 35th Squadron was hit by anti-aircraft fire over the target and crashed; no egress was noted, but Thees is listed as missing-in-action. Thus, 20 July 1953 was one of the more successful days for the pilots of the 64th IAK, who achieved such a large victory without any losses.

The last aerial combat of this war, in which any enemy aircraft were shot down, was on 22 July. It involved pilots of the US 25th FIS and pilots of the UAA. According to their claims, the American pilots downed three MiGs. The American ace 1st Lieutenant Henry Buttelman scored his seventh and final victory of the war. The US Navy pilot and future astronaut Major John Glenn (an exchange pilot with the 25th FIS) shot down another MiG. The 25th Squadron's 2nd Lieutenant Sam Young, in a dogfight with four MiGs, shot down the last MiG-15 of the air war in the skies of Korea – this was the young pilot's first victory and the last one for the 51st FIW in this war.

The Soviet pilots of the 64th IAK possibly scored their final victory of the war in a night action on 21 July. The deputy commander of the 298th NIAP's 3rd Squadron Captain N.M Valivov fired on an enemy night bomber and damaged it, and if it didn't manage to reach its base in Japan, then this was in fact the last victory of the Soviet pilots in the Korean air war. Our pilots continued to carry out their combat duties and flew combat patrols up until 27 July, the final day of the war. They had a few encounters with enemy aircraft, but they were fleeting and without any real intensity, and ended with no results for either side.

The Americans, according to their claim, achieved their final victory of the war on its last day, 27 July, but in essence this was more a crime than a victory. In the middle of the day on 27 July, a Soviet Air Force Il-12 transport aircraft took off on a scheduled flight from Port Arthur, carrying a total of 21 flight officers and personnel, as well as medical officers of the Pacific Ocean Fleet's air force together with the crew. It was headed for Vladivostok. The Il-12, bypassing North Korea, was flying over PRC territory. However in the area of the Chinese city of Hirin, which lies 300 kilometers from the border between China and North Korea, four USAF F-86F fighters from the 4th FIW's 335th FIS pounced on this unarmed, solitary transport aircraft bearing Soviet recognition markings. Captain Ralph Parr was leading this Sabre flight, and at 1230 he spotted this Il-12 and moved to close with it. Approaching to within very close range, Parr clearly saw the Soviet recognition markings, but he attacked and shot down the defenseless aircraft. Indeed his wingman 1st Lieutenant Edwin Scaffee confirmed this. Everyone aboard the aircraft perished. According to available information, the American pilots knew beforehand what sort of airplane it would be and where they were supposed to intercept it, since Sabre pilots had never before flown so deeply into Chinese territory. However, the Americans to this day claim that they shot down this Il-12 over the border area of Manchuria and had mistakenly identified it as a Chinese transport plane. But even if that is the case, downing a defenseless Chinese aircraft over territory belonging to the People's Republic of China is still considered an act of terror.

According to a different version of the story, the Americans were especially hunting for this transport aircraft, and from intelligence information knew the day and time of its departure, and Captain Parr's flight was specifically scrambled to intercept it. The Americans believed that on this day the Il-12 would be carrying Soviet naval command staff from the Liaodong Peninsula back to the Soviet Union. Indeed, on this day a Party conference was being held at the naval base in Port Arthur. The entire political command staff of the Pacific Ocean Fleet was attending it. After the conference ended, they were supposed to fly to Vladivostok aboard this Il-12. However, the Party conference ran longer than scheduled, and the transport plane had been given a restricted time for its scheduled flight, so instead of the command staff, members of the Fleet's medical commission boarded the plane. The Americans apparently knew about the scheduled departure of our commanders, but didn't know that at the last moment there was a change in the passengers on this scheduled flight. However it happened, this dastardly act by the American pilots and command brings them no honor and remains a black spot on the entire Fifth Air Force in Korea. With the destruction of this Il-12, Captain Parr achieved his 10th "victory" and became a double ace in the 4th Fighter Wing. However, the death of totally innocent people will always be on the conscience of this pilot.

One can judge how the war ended for us from the story of Vadim Petrovich Sazhin, a former pilot in the Pacific Ocean Fleet's 781st IAP:

> The war ended in Korea at midnight on 27 July 1953; we learned about this the day before. The day of 27 July was an interesting one: we flew no sorties before mid-day because of a compact layer of low clouds, but later the clouds became patchy. We were sitting in conversation circles, smoking and talking about what our lives would be like after the war. At this moment, I spotted two F-86s in a gap in the clouds. I hollered "Air raid!" However, at first everyone thought I was joking, but this pair of Sabres swooped down low over the airfield and fired several bursts from their machine guns. The smoking circles quickly broke up as everyone scrambled for whatever cover they could find. Later we laughed at each other over the way people jumped. No one was hurt, nor did the parked MiGs take any damage. The Sabres apparently were only giving us a "festive" salute in honor of the war's ending, and in this fashion congratulated us on its conclusion!
>
> On this day there were sorties, but without any action; both sides preferred not to risk anything on the last day of the war. That evening there was a corresponding celebratory dinner. That's how the war ended for us.

According to official reports from both sides, the results of this, the last month of the war, were as follows. The pilots of the 64th IAK in the aerial battles of July 1953 shot down 10 enemy aircraft (all of them F-86s) and damaged another eight – seven F-86s and one B-29. Their own losses over the period amounted to 13 MiGs and four pilots, of which two aircraft and one pilot were non-combat losses. In July, pilots of the 32nd IAD and 133rd IAD showed the greatest activity. The pilots of the former achieved six victories and damaged another enemy aircraft, while the pilots of the 133rd IAD had two victories and damaged three enemy aircraft. The increasing experience of the 781st IAP's pilots also led to better results for them, as they downed two US aircraft and damaged three more.

The Chinese had their final air battles on 16 and 19 July; on these days 54 MiG-15s of the 4th IAD, 6th IAD and 17th IAD took on large groups of Americans and downed four aircraft and damaged two. According to our records, UAA pilots (probably North Koreans) also encountered Sabres of the 25th FIS on 22 July, in which as already noted the Americans claimed three victories by Buttelman, Glenn and Young.

The UAA pilots flew 606 individual combat sorties in the month of July, 380 by the Chinese pilots and 226 by the North Korean pilots. The pilots had 16 group aerial combats, in which they claim to have downed 17 US aircraft and damaged six enemy aircraft. Their own losses over the period amounted to 17 MiG-15s, and nine UAA pilots were killed-in-action. From these data it turns out that the 64th IAK and the UAA combined lost 30 aircraft and 13 pilots. The American records this time closely coincide with ours, since according to the American command, the pilots of the 4th and 51st FIW destroyed 34 enemy aircraft in July, 33 MiG-15s and the one ill-fated Il-12. The squadrons equipped with F-86 Sabres lost 10 of them over the month, but according to the Americans only four due to combat. These numbers do not include the victories and losses of the US Navy Air Force and the Marine Corps, which distinguished themselves in night combats. For example, Lieutenant Guy Bordelon of VS-3 Squadron in his F4U-5M Corsair fighter in the month of July in the Seoul area shot down five North Korean Po-2, Yak-18 and La-9 light night bombers in night actions. To this it should be added that in the middle of the month the Americans staged their final night missions with B-29 bombers, focusing on the network of North Korean airfields, where over the final months of the war feverish work was going on to lay down concrete runways and to expand each airfield's entire infrastructure. The main target was the major North Korean airbase at Sinuiju. The first nighttime B-29 strike against this base took place back on 20 June 1953, but on 10 July 1953, they again bombed the railroad bridge located nearby with the force of 16 B-29 bombers from the 98th BG. After 20 July, North Korean airfields at Uiju, Siniuju, Namsi, Taechon, Pyong-ni, Pyongyang and Saamchan were all subjected to night attacks. B-29s hit them with 500-kilogram bombs and napalm. For example, on 21 July at 0100, 15 B-29s from Okinawa again bombed the airfield at Sinuiju (on this mission, pilots of the 298th NIAP damaged one B-29), while the next morning, nine B-29s launched a follow-up raid against this base.

On the morning of 24 July, Fifth Air Force fighter-bombers launched a new attack against Sinuiju, which was followed that night by yet another B-29 raid against the airfield. The final airstrike against the Sinuiju airfield took place on 27 July shortly before 2200, when the truce was set to begin. These attacks were not coincidental, because aircraft arriving from the Soviet Union through China were accumulating on the Sinuiju airbase. A pilot of the 224th IAP Askol'd Andreevich German, being in the hospital in Andong across the river from Sinuiju after ejecting, was a witness as several dozen shipping containers holding MiG-15s arrived at the Sinuiju airfield; they were a gift by Stalin to Mao Zedong and Kim Il Sung. However, the next night, having received information from agents through intelligence channels that a large number of aircraft had arrived at the airfield in Sinuiju, a large group of B-29s heavily bombed the airfield with large bombs and napalm, and burned up a large portion of the shipped MiGs while still in their containers. Thus, the American air raids against the North Korean airfield network were not a coincidence nor were they unsuccessful.

The airfield at Taechon was another major North Korean airbase. On the night of 23 July 1953, 11 B-29s heavily bombed it, and a follow-up raid against Taechon came on the night of 26 July by four B-29s. Also in July 1953, US Navy carrier aircraft and Marine aircraft increased their strikes against North Korean airfields in the eastern part of the country, including the complex of airfields in the Wonsan area as well as at

Yonpo, Kilchu, Hamhung, Chongjin, Hoeryong and elsewhere. Other non-hard surface airfields across the entire country were subjected to attacks.

However, arguably no matter how hard the Americans tried, the bombing didn't genuinely affect the course of the war. On 27 July at 2200 (1200 local time), the truce went into effect. One of the bloodiest wars after the Second World War, which took the lives of 4,000,000 people, came to an end.

The results of the 64th IAK's pilots for the year 1953 were as follows: between 1 January and 27 July 1953, they destroyed 109 enemy aircraft (98 F-86s and 11 F-84s) in daytime aerial combat and damaged 57 more (53 F-86s and four F-84s). In addition, in night actions pilots of the 351st and 298th NIAP shot down 13 enemy aircraft (seven B-29s, three F-94s, two F-84s and one B-26) and damaged six others (four B-29s, one B-26 and one F3D). Their own losses over the half-year of combat were 86 aircraft and 31 pilots, of which 18 aircraft and five pilots were non-combat losses. Thus the combat losses in 1953 amounted to 68 MiG-15s and 26 pilots.

Already after the end of combat operations, according to revised data from the 64th IAK headquarters, in 1953 its pilots in 508 group daytime aerial battles downed 126 enemy aircraft (114 F-86s and 11 F-84s). To this should be added the 13 enemy aircraft downed in 1953 in 59 night combats, so the total number of victories achieved by the pilots of the 64th IAK for the year 1953 was 139. Plainly, material evidence had been located to confirm a number of questionable victory claims by its pilots, which had previously only been credited to them as "damaged". As a result, the number of damaged enemy aircraft fell by 16 F-86s and one F-84, thereby dropping this number to 40.

In addition, in 1953 the UAA's pilots had 209 group daytime aerial combats, in which they downed 89 enemy aircraft and damaged 32 more. In several nighttime interceptions Chinese pilots shot down another F-94, so their total number of destroyed enemy aircraft was 90. Their own losses over the period amounted to 85 MiG-15s and 34 pilots, plus another 21 MiG-15s that were damaged in combat. This figure does not include those light bombers of the Po-2, Yak-18, LaGG-9 and Tu-2 types that were lost in night raids.

After the conclusion of combat operations, in August the 216th IAD left the roster of the 64th IAK and returned to the Soviet Union (to the Baku Military District), as did the 32nd IAD (to the Maritime District) and the 133rd IAD (to Iaroslavl'). The naval 781st IAP also returned to Vladivostok to re-join its parent 165th IAD of the Pacific Ocean Fleet. Each of these units had made an important contribution to the 64th IAK's combat work.

The pilots of the 133rd IAD during their time in combat operations as part of the 64th IAK in the skies of Korea shot down 85 enemy aircraft in air battles and damaged another 30. Their own losses were 30 MiG-15bis and 16 pilots. The division's top-scoring pilots in each regiment were: in the 147th GIAP, Captain Iu.N. Dobrovichan of the 147th GIAP, who scored three victories in night actions and damaged one more enemy aircraft, and the regiment's Majors N.I. Shkodin and F.G. Afanas'ev, who achieved three victories each in daytime combats; in the 415th IAP, Captain V.P. Lepikov who became an ace with five victories in the skies of Korea; and in the 726th IAP, Captain N.I. Ivanov, who achieved three victories and damaged another enemy aircraft, and Major K.N. Degtiarov, who also had three victories.

The pilots of the 216th IAD over their time of service in the 64th IAK shot down 108 enemy aircraft and damaged 49 more. Their own losses amounted to 57 MiGs and 16 pilots. This IAD produced several aces, including its top-scoring pilot, the 518th IAP's Captain M.I. Mikhin, who achieved nine victories in the skies of Korea and received credit for damaging three more enemy aircraft. In the 676th IAP, Captain M.F. Iudin, who achieved five victories, became an ace, while Captain Iu.A. Varkov and Senior Lieutenant M.G. Sapegin nearly reached this title by downing four US aircraft each, plus credit for one enemy aircraft damaged each. The 878th IAP's ace was Major N.M. Zameskin, who according to the revised data had seven individual victories and two shared victories. The 216th IAD's Captain Mikhail Ivanovich Mikhin was awarded the high title Hero of the Soviet Union on 14 July 1953.

The 32nd IAD's pilots during their time of participating in combat operations in the skies of Korea downed 79 enemy aircraft in aerial combat and damaged 34. Their own losses equaled 66 aircraft and 17 pilots. Its 224th IAP produced two aces, Captains G.N. Berelidze and B.N. Sis'kov, who each downed five enemy aircraft and damaged another. The top-scoring pilot in the 535th IAP was Captain V.A. Utkin, who downed four US aircraft in the war and damaged another four. Then, finally, Major S.A. Fedorets of the 913th IAP became an ace and ended the war with seven victories in Korea.

In night actions pilots of the 351st NIAP destroyed 16 enemy aircraft and damaged seven more. Their own losses were four aircraft (two La-11 and two MiG-15s) and one pilot. The regiment's top-scoring pilot was Major Anatolii Mikhailovich Karelin, who became an ace by downing six US aircraft in the night skies of Korea and damaging two more. He became a Hero of the Soviet Union by a 14 July 1953 decree. The pilots of the 298th NIAP downed four US aircraft in night combats and damaged six. Their own losses amounted to two aircraft and one pilot.

The pilots of the Pacific Ocean Fleet's 578th IAP shot down four US aircraft and damaged two. Their own losses consisted of 11 MiG-15s and two pilots. Major V.D. Andriushenko led the scoring in this regiment with one enemy aircraft destroyed to his credit, plus one more damaged. The pilots of the Fleet's 781st IAP did much better, shooting down 12 US aircraft and damaging seven while part of the 64th IAK. Its own losses were still relatively heavy – nine MiGs and five pilots.

After the departure of these fighter aviation division formations, the 64th IAK remained in northeast China until the end of 1954, after which, having transferred all of its remaining fighters to the PLAAF, the corps was dissolved and Colonel A.I. Khalutin's and Colonel A.F. Dvornik's two fighter aviation divisions departed for the Soviet Union, together with the 298th IAP. Thus, the Soviet 64th Special IAK, which was created in 1950 in order to execute combat assignments in the PRC and the PDRK, ceased its existence.

The 64th IAK carried out all the duties placed upon it successfully and fully, reliably guarding all the important targets in its zone of responsibility against raids by the UN air forces. Over the entire period of combat operations in the skies of the PRC and North Korea between 1 November 1950 and 27 July 1953, according to Soviet official records, the pilots of the 64th IAK engaged in 1,872 aerial combats, in the course of which they destroyed 1,106 enemy aircraft, of which 650 were F-86s. Their own losses amounted to a total of 335 aircraft and more than 120 pilots.

The Chinese eventually committed 10 fighter aviation divisions (21 regiments, 672 pilots) and 28 bombers crews in the three flying groups from two bomber aviation divisions to the fighting. By the end of the war the UAA had seven divisions numbering almost 900 combat aircraft, including 635 MiG-15 and MiG-15bis jet fighters. In addition, 59,733 soldiers of the PLAAF's ground forces (excluding aviation and administrative units that took no direct part in the fighting -- the rear personnel and leaders and pilot cadres of the aviation schools) also participated in combat operations. Altogether according to Chinese data, 26,491 individual combat sorties were flown by Chinese pilots, and 2,467 groups took off on combat missions. They had 366 group aerial combats, which involved a total of 4,872 PLAAF aircraft.

Chinese data on the number of victories and losses of the PLAAF remained unchanged for several decades after the war: already back in 1960, the top Chinese ace Wang Hai, who by this time had risen to the rank of lieutenant general and was serving as the PLAAF's Chief of the Political Administration, claimed that the Chinese pilots over the entire war shot down or damaged 425 enemy aircraft. Recent PRC publications state that the Chinese pilots of the 12 PLAAF divisions that served in Korea shot down 330 enemy aircraft and damaged 95. However, according to the data of our General Staff in the Russian Federation Ministry of Defense's Central Archives, altogether the UAA pilots (both Chinese and North Korean) shot down 271 enemy aircraft. Their own losses, according to Chinese sources, were 231 destroyed and 151 damaged aircraft, in which 116 pilots (according to our sources, 126 pilots) were killed. In the opinion of Hero of the Soviet Union S.M. Kramarenko, the UAA pilots, by downing 271 enemy aircraft and losing 231 of their own, achieved "a good result".

Statistics show that the UAA pilots shot down the following number and types of UN aircraft: 181 F-86s (of which five were F-86F-30 fighter-bombers), 27 F-84s, 30 F-80s, one F-94, 12 F-51, one F-82, 15 F4U-5s, two Gloster Meteors and one B-26. Strangely, the data do not include any downed B-29s. The anti-aircraft gunners of the PDRK's and PRC's ground forces through their combined efforts claim to have destroyed another 1,284 enemy aircraft.

According to the Russian Federation Ministry of Defense's Central Archive records, over the war the UAA pilots flew more than 22,000 individual combat sorties (excluding piston-engine aircraft), including 11,028 between November 1952 and July 1953, and engaged in 250 aerial combats, in which 598 pilots fired at enemy targets. They downed 139 enemy aircraft and damaged 45 in aerial fights. The UAA's own losses over the period, again according to Soviet records, amounted to 155 MiG-15s and 45 pilots.

The PLAAF 3rd IAD was the top-scoring Chinese fighter division; it destroyed or damaged 114 enemy aircraft. Its own losses were 43 MiG-15s destroyed with 18 damaged, and 18 pilots of this division were killed-in-action. A number of sources especially note the 12th IAD, as well as an additional fighter aviation division commanded by Zheng Changhua, who had previously commanded the 12th IAD's 34th IAP. It isn't identified, but reportedly had 47 downed enemy aircraft to its credit, including two by Zheng personally.

Among the other authors of the "collective victories", the record-setter was the 1st Flying Group of the 3rd IAD's 9th IAP, which destroyed or damaged 29 enemy aircraft; it was commanded by Wang Hai, who later rose to become the Commander-in-Chief of the PLAAF. Later it was asserted that they achieved this result in 80 aerial combats, but judging from everything, this figure of enemy aircraft destroyed includes the subsequent personal victories achieved by the squadron's pilots after their transfer to different squadrons and regiments. Wang Hai himself had four downed and five damaged enemy aircraft to his personal credit (with these nine victories, he shares first and second place with Zhao Baotong's 7+2 victories). Wang Hai and Sun Shenlu (posthumously), who scored seven victories in the war before being killed in action on 3 December 1952, both became Combat Heroes, 1st Class. Jiao Jingwen with four victories to his personal credit was awarded the title Combat Hero, 2nd Class. Other pilots of the squadron, Liu Delin (3) Zhou Fengxing (2), Ma Baotang, Zhan Tse, Ma Liangiu and Yang Tsiunio (each with one personal victory) all became Honored People's Military Activists of various classes. All of the squadron's pilots also received North Korean honors and decorations. Subsequently the squadron received a unit award of the 1st Class, and it was given the honorific title of "Wang Hai".

In the PRC, other heroic unit's achievements are especially noted: the 3rd Flying Group of the 4th IAD's 10th IAP shot down or damaged 20 enemy aircraft; and the 2nd Flying Group of the 3rd IAD's 9th IAP, which shot down or damaged 12 enemy aircraft. Zhao Baotong's squadron shot down or damaged 17 enemy aircraft, and received the honorific title "Heroic Squadron" in the Chinese North East Military District's air force.

Among the Chinese flights, the 3rd Flying Group's 7th Flight of the 3rd IAD's 7th IAP had the best result – 16 victories, just ahead of the 1st Flying Group's 2nd Flight of the 15th IAD's 45th IAP, which scored 14 victories. The 3rd Flying Group's 9th Flight of the 3rd IAD's 9th IAP stands out – eight victories with no losses, and which it is noted "operated courageously".

According to American sources, the US in Korea had 40 aces who downed at least five enemy aircraft. Despite the fact that the American pilots and commanders considered the Chinese PLAAF to be "tyros", nevertheless the PLAAF had no less than 12 pilots who became aces by downing five or more aircraft, as well as another 27 who downed or damaged four aircraft.

As a result, 68 men of the PLAAF received military decorations of the 1st Degree, among which 21 were awarded the title "Combat Hero". A complete list of the Chinese aces has not yet been found, but the Chinese themselves first of all note Zhao Baotong, who received a personal expression of gratitude from Mao Zedong, and Wang Hai (each with nine victories). Behind these two pilots are Liu Wudi (eight victories, with supposedly four in one action, which is dubious) and Sun Shenlu (seven). The Chinese call Lu Min (five victories) the "Sabre-killing Master", and Zhang Jihui (four victories) is honored for his victory over the American ace George Davis. They all received the title Combat Hero, 1st Class and awards for their "special achievements".

Among their remaining aces, the Chinese particularly noted Han Decai with five victories, including one over the "double ace" Harold Fischer; Li Han, who was credited with downing the first American aircraft; Wang Tianbao, who shot down a Sabre while piloting a piston-engine La-11; and the "Chinese Gostello" Bi Wubin, who during the bombing of Cho-do Island directed his burning bomber together with its crew into a target.[5]

According to Soviet records, Soviet fighter pilots between November 1950 and July 1953 shot down 1,106 enemy aircraft in 1,872 separate air battles. The 64th IAK's anti-aircraft artillery between June 1951 and 27 July 1953 destroyed 153 enemy aircraft, so altogether the 64th IAK's forces destroyed 1,259 enemy aircraft of various types (see Tables 12.1 and 12.2).

Table 12.1 The number of aircraft (by types) downed by the 64th IAK in the period
between 1 November 1950 and 27 July 1953

Type	Number	Type	Number
F-86	650	Gloster Meteor	28
F-86F-30	1	F-80	121
F-51	30	F-84	178
F4U-5	2	B-26	8
F-47	2	B-29	69
F-94	13	B-45	2
		Other	2

Table 12.2 Aircraft losses of the UN due to Soviet anti-aircraft artillery fire between
June 1951 and 27 July 1953

Type	Number	Type	Number
F-86	35	F-51	5
F-86F-30	6	B-26	17
F-80	47	B-29	7
F-84	25	Other	12

Taken together, the Soviet, Chinese and North Korean fighter pilots in the period between November 1950 and 27 July 1953 downed 1,307 aircraft. Of this number, 75 percent of all the enemy aircraft destroyed in Korea were the responsibility of the Soviet pilots, which once again confirms their decisive contribution to the damaged inflicted on the enemy. If we include the claims of the anti-aircraft artillery and "anti-aircraft riflemen" of the NKPA and the CPV, then a total of 2,814 American aircraft and those of its allied countries were destroyed.

The total losses of the contingent of Soviet forces in Korea amounted to 299 men, of which 138 were officers and 161 were sergeants and soldiers. The Soviet aviation divisions that took part in repelling raids by the US air forces lost 120 pilots. The losses in personnel among the anti-aircraft artillery units were 68 killed-in-action and 165 wounded. The losses in aircraft in the aerial battles conducted by pilots of the contingent of Soviet forces amounted to 335 MiG-15 and MiG-15bis fighter jets.

The following pilots were awarded the title Hero of the Soviet Union for rendering international assistance to the Korean people in their "Patriotic Liberation War" of 1950-1953:

1. Bakhaev, Stepan Antonovich – Major, deputy squadron commander in the 523rd IAP. He flew 166 combat missions, participated in 72 aerial battles, and personally shot down 11 enemy aircraft. Decree dated 13 November 1951.

2. Boitsov, Arkadii Sergeevich – Captain, deputy squadron commander for political affairs in the 16th IAP. He completed approximately 108 combat missions, took part in more than 50 aerial combats, and personally downed seven enemy aircraft. Decree dated 14 July 1953.

3. Dokashenko, Nikolai Grigor'evich – Captain, flight commander in the 17th IAP. He flew approximately 120 combat missions, participated in 45 aerial combats, and personally downed nine enemy aircraft. Decree dated 22 October 1951.

4. Ges', Grigorii Ivanovich – Captain, squadron commander in the 176th GIAP. He flew approximately 120 combat missions, took part in more than 50 aerial fights, and personally downed eight enemy aircraft. Decree dated 10 October 1951.

5. Karelin, Anatolii Mikhailovich – Major, deputy commander of the 351st NIAP. Flew more than 50 combat missions, engaged in more than 10 night combats, and personally downed six enemy aircraft. Decree dated 14 July 1953.

6. Kramarenko, Sergei Makarovich – Captain, deputy squadron commander in the 176th GIAP. Completed 149 combat missions, took part in 60 aerial combats, and personally downed 14 enemy aircraft. Decree dated 10 October 1951.

7. Lobov, Georgii Ageevich – Major General of Aviation, commander of the 64th IAK. Flew 25 combat missions and engaged in 10 aerial combats, in which he personally downed four enemy aircraft. Decree dated 10 October 1951.

8. Mikhin, Mikhail Ivanovich – Captain, deputy squadron commander in the 518th IAP. Flew 140 combat missions, engaged in 67 aerial fights, and personally downed nine enemy aircraft while damaging three more. Decree dated 14 July 1953

9. Naumenko, Stepan Ivanovich – Major, deputy squadron commander in the 29th GIAP. Completed approximately 70 combat missions, took part in more than 20 aerial combats, and personally downed four enemy aircraft. Decree dated 12 May 1951.

10. Obraztsov, Boris Aleksandrovich (posthumously) – Senior Lieutenant, pilot in the 176th GIAP. Flew approximately 90 combat missions, took part in approximately 30 aerial fights, and personally downed four enemy aircraft. Decree dated 10 October 1951.

11. Os'kin, Dmitrii Pavlovich – Major, commander of the 523rd IAP. Flew approximately 150 combat missions, engaged in 62 aerial combats, and personally downed 15 enemy aircraft. Decree dated 13 November 1951.

12. Okhai, Grigorii Ull'ianovich – Captain, assistant commander of the 523rd IAP. Completed 122 combat missions, took part in 68 aerial combats and personally downed 11 enemy aircraft. Decree dated 13 November 1951.

13. Pepeliaev, Evgenii Georgievich – Colonel, commander of the 196th IAP. Flew 108 combat missions, took part in 38 aerial combats, and personally downed 20 enemy aircraft. Decree dated 22 April 1952.

14. Ponomarev, Mikhail Sergeevich – Captain, squadron commander in the 17th IAP. Flew 175 combat missions, engaged in 96 aerial combats, and personally downed 10 enemy aircraft. Decree dated 13 November 1951.

15. Pulov, Grigorii Ivanovich – Lieutenant Colonel, commander of the 17th IAP. Completed 120 combat missions, took part in more than 50 air fights, and personally downed eight enemy aircraft. Decree dated 22 April 1952.

16. Samoilov, Dmitrii Aleksandrovich – Senior Lieutenant, senior pilot in the 523rd IAP. Flew 161 combat missions, engaged in 50 aerial combats, and personally downed 11 enemy aircraft. Decree dated 13 November 1951.

17. Shchukin, Lev Kirillovich – Captain, squadron commander in the 18th GIAP. Flew 121 combat missions, took part in 37 aerial combats, and personally downed 15 enemy aircraft. Decree dated 13 November 1951.
18. Shebanov, Fedor Akimovich – Senior Lieutenant, pilot in the 196th IAP. Completed approximately 100 combat missions, participated in 45 aerial fights, and personally downed six enemy aircraft. Decree dated 10 October 1951.
19. Smorchkov, Aleksandr Pavlovich – Lieutenant Colonel, deputy commander of the 18th GIAP. Flew 142 combat missions, took part in 52 aerial combats, and personally downed 13 enemy aircraft and shared one group victory. Decree from 13 November 1951.
20. Stel'makh, Evgenii Mikhailovich (posthumously) – Senior Lieutenant, pilot in the 18th GIAP. Flew 15 combat missions, participated in five aerial combats, and personally downed two enemy aircraft. Decree dated 10 October 1951.
21. Subbotin, Serafim Pavlovich – Captain, regiment navigator of the 176th GIAP. Flew more than 100 combat missions, engaged in more than 50 aerial combats, and personally downed nine enemy aircraft. Decree dated 10 October 1951.
22. Sutiagin, Nikolai Vasil'evich – Captain, deputy squadron commander in the 17th IAP. Flew 149 combat missions, took part in 66 aerial combats, and personally downed 22 enemy aircraft. Top-scoring Soviet ace in the Korean War. Decree dated 10 October 1951.

ENDNOTES

1   According to the KORWALD loss incident summary for Sabre F-86F 52-4335, this was an operational loss not due to enemy action.
2   Some sources give the pilot as 1st Lieutenant Paul Gushwa.
3   Michael T. Stowe's website http://www.accident-report.com, which investigates US military aviation incidents around the world, asserts that F-86F No.51-2929 went down in an accident 2 miles north of the Tsuiki Air Base in Japan, which clearly suggests that this was a non-combat loss.
4   American loss records for this day, 20 July 1953, are contradictory regarding the particular Sabre each pilot was flying. For example, in the case of Major Bettinger, the KORWALD Loss Incident Summary states that rather than F-86F No.51-2824 "Little Mike/Ohio Mike", he was instead flying F-8E No.51-2836. Seidov's account represents a "best effort" to clear up the muddle and is not definitive.
5   Nikolai Frantsevich Gostello, Captain (1908-1941) was a Russian bomber pilot who earned the USSR's highest honor, Hero of the Soviet Union, on 26 June 1941 when he directed his crippled and burning bomber into an enemy troop concentration. This act of self-sacrifice was highly publicized and quickly became known throughout the Red Army and the Soviet public.

13

Outcomes of the air war

Conflict along the 38th Parallel, which cost approximately 4,000,000 lives, continued for 38 months. Combat operations on the ground went with alternating success until 10 July 1951, when the front lines stabilized in the area of the 38th Parallel. After this, fighting took on a local, positional character, which didn't bring success to either of the warring sides. On the sea, combat operations were totally of a unilateral nature, as only one side – the UN forces – deployed a powerful fleet, since the PDRK didn't have its own navy.

Yet combat operations in the air continued with greater or lesser intensity for the entire three years of the war. Both sides committed a large number of combat aircraft to the war and used their respective air forces actively.

The air war in the skies of Korea that has been described in this book can be divided into five stages, based on the operations of the aviation of the Communist bloc, which consisted of three allied countries – the USSR, the PRC and the PDRK. The military air forces of the socialist camp actively participated in this war and opposed the powerful air forces of the UN countries and especially the United States, since almost 98% of the UN air force consisted of squadrons of the USAF, USNAF and the Marine Air Corps.

The first stage lasted from 25 June to 1 November 1950. In this period, the fledgling and tiny North Korean air force attempted to conduct combat operations against a powerful armada of 1,340 combat aircraft of US Fifth Air Force in the Far East and South Korea's own tiny air force (a total of 20 aircraft that saw action). We'll note that the North Korean KPAAF consisted of 239 aircraft of various types, all of Soviet manufacture from the Second World War. Meanwhile almost half of the air units of the 5th Air Force in the Far East were already equipped with jet aircraft. Moreover, the combat training and experience of the American pilots far surpassed the training and combat skills of the young North Korean pilots.

To this it should be added that the United Nations constantly increased the size of their air force in Korea. For example, on 29 June 1950, the RAAF's 77 Squadron began combat operations in their F-51 Mustangs, followed in July by the RAAF's 30 and 36 Transport Squadrons with their C-47 Skytrains. Also in July, the South Korean Air Force's 1st Squadron was created and equipped with F-51 Mustangs, and a bit later (in November and December 1950), the SAAF's 2 Squadron joined the UN air force with their F-51D fighter-bombers, while Greece contributed its C-47 Skytrain-equipped 13th Transport Squadron.

In addition, in July 1950 five aircraft carriers of the British Royal Navy and the Royal Australian Navy began operating off the coast of Korea with their 11 squadrons of carrier-based aircraft, as well as three separate reconnaissance squadrons equipped with

558   RED DEVILS OVER THE 38TH PARALLEL

the Short Sunderland Mark V flying boat patrol bomber. Pilots of the Royal Canadian Air Force also participated in the war – Canada contributed one squadron of DS-4M North Star transport airplanes to the war effort, and in addition, 20 Canadian exchange pilots served in the USAF.

Of course, the inexperienced and small North Korean air force could hardly stand up against such a force arrayed against it. It was simply destroyed on its airfields and in a few aerial combats.

The second stage of the air war began on 1 November 1950, when Soviet pilots of just one reduced-strength fighter aviation division equipped with approximately 100 aircraft joined the fighting. However, this Soviet fighter division, General I.V. Belov's 151st GIAD, flew the Soviet Union's most modern and advanced fighter of that period, the MiG-15. This division fought for only two weeks in 1950, but in that short time it brought about a fundamental turning point in the course of the air war in Korea. The UN air force began to suffer substantial losses and was more frequently unable to carry out its combat missions. Gradually, the number of MiG-15 jet fighters based on the Chinese airfields situated close to the border with North Korea increased. Two more Soviet reduced-strength fighter aviation divisions arrived to assist the 151st GIAD, and by the end of 1950 the number of Soviet MiGs in Manchuria had grown to 200. One event that influenced the course of the war was the creation of the 64th Special IAK PVO at the end of 1950 on the basis of these divisions.

Up until April 1951, these three Soviet fighter aviation divisions, rotating in and out of action, gave reliable protection to all the important strategic sites entrusted to them. Gradually, they expanded their area of operations to as far south as Anju in North Korea by April 1951.

The third period began with a change in the roster of the 64th IAK, which was completed by June 1951. Two new Soviet fighter divisions, the 303rd IAD and 324th IAD, entered the fighting. These were both elite Soviet air units, staffed with pilots who had a great deal of combat experience and many hours of flight time in jet aircraft. With the entry of these two Soviet fighter divisions into the war, control over the area, which soon became known as MiG Alley, became firmer, and the enemy became much less confident and much more cautious whenever entering this area. The Americans noted that in this phase of the war, the MiGs were more aggressive, and the pilots sitting in their cockpits were tough and dangerous adversaries.

This was when the 64th IAK was at its strongest over the entire period of the war, since it was precisely the pilots with the 64th IAK at this time who neutralized American superiority in the air in MiG Alley, destroyed several of the Fifth Air Force's squadrons, and it was precisely their "work" that forced the Fifth Air Force command to withdraw its piston-engine fighter-bombers from the area where the MiGs operated – those units equipped with the F-51 Mustang, as well as the piston-engine carrier aircraft, since they were suffering heavy losses due to the MiG-15. In the spring and autumn of 1951, the bomber groups equipped with the B-29 medium bomber also suffered serious setbacks and losses from MiG cannon fire, and the Strategic Air Command was forced to shift these bombers to night operations in order to reduce their losses.

It was in this period that the Soviet pilots of the 64th IAK achieved their highest number of victories against the US and UN pilots, downing approximately 550 enemy aircraft in aerial combats. For their successful combat actions in the skies of Korea, 18 of the pilots and both commanders of the 303rd and 324th IAD were awarded the high title Hero of the Soviet Union.

However, for the sake of objectivity, it is necessary to note that at least a third of the victories credited to the pilots of these divisions are only presumed. Frequently, an enemy airplane was only damaged, but wasn't shot down. The point is that in this period, pilot claims for victories were confirmed by the 64th IAK only on the basis of gun camera footage and pilot de-briefings. The 64th IAK still didn't have search teams, and only occasionally did confirmation of fallen enemy aircraft arrive from ground units.

When examining the frames from the gun camera film that purport to show the victories by the 303rd IAD and 324th IAD pilots, one comes to the opinion that a portion of these "victories" are questionable, since the fire was conducted from great ranges (800-1,000 meters); although the enemy aircraft is visible in the gun sight, there is no confidence at all that it was actually shot down. In addition, there is no material evidence in the form of items from the wreckage of downed aircraft for the majority of the victories awarded in this period. Thus in reality, these two fighter aviation divisions' victory totals are likely overstated. However, in no way does this diminish the achievements of the pilots of the 303rd IAD and 324th IAD or cast doubt upon the decorations and honors these pilots received – their honors were deserved, and it is not their fault if the 64th IAK command didn't apply exacting work to the confirmation of all the pilots' victories, or if in some cases the victories of certain pilots were inflated.

In addition, today it is known for certain that the Americans also have a large number of questionable "victories" that were awarded even though our MiG-15s returned to base; however, it is quite unlikely that they will go through an objective revision, and the victory totals of their pilots will not be restated. Indeed, it is honest to recognize that this isn't done anywhere in the world. After each war, one side asserts its data on its victories and losses, while the other side puts forward its own data; the respective numbers always differ greatly. The victories of the Soviet pilots will also not be revised – the 303rd IAD was officially credited with more than 300 victories, and thus this number of victories will remained fixed throughout history. The opposing side can dispute the number of victories and losses – the Americans in fact have been doing this ever since the Korean War ended, but that's their business!

After this period, the leadership shifted to the other extreme – it didn't give credit for as many victories as it should have, and began to manipulate the process, assigning credit for a kill to someone other than the one responsible, thereby lowering the scores of some pilots and inflating that of others. Victories by rank-and-file pilots were taken from them and awarded instead to their commanders in an effort to enhance their prestige. Veterans of the war talk about this to the present day.

The fourth period of the air war in the skies of Korea was the least successful, and it began in January 1952 with the third turnover in the 64th IAK's roster: two new fighter aviation divisions from the USSR's PVO organization, the 97th IAD and 190th IAD, arrived to replace the veteran but worn down 303rd and 324th IAD. In the period of their combat operations (which ran from the end of January until the middle of August 1952), Soviet influence over MiG Alley was weakened – the enemy began to feel more at ease, and it is no coincidence that it was in this period that the Fifth Air Force command was able to stage a number of successful combat operations. In this period we not only began to lose our control of the airspace in MiG Alley, we also couldn't even protect our own bases. Almost 50% of the losses of these two fighter aviation divisions occurred in the area of our own airfields as the MiGs were taking off or landing. The number of victories fell sharply, while the number of losses showed a marked increase. Thus, only one pilot in either of these two divisions was awarded the title Hero of the Soviet Union for what was a rather modest number of victories (six downed enemy aircraft). However, the majority of criticism should not be addressed to the pilots of the 64th IAK, but to its command, as well as to the high command back in Moscow. It was their fault alone that pilots of the Red Army's PVO, who'd been trained only to intercept small groups of enemy bombers and solitary enemy aircraft within the framework of the conception of the anticipated nuclear war that was circulating at that time. They were thrown into the slaughterhouse of this war virtually unprepared for the given conditions of the air war. They weren't ready to conduct high-speed, turning dogfights with the enemy's maneuverable fighter and fighter-bomber aircraft, in this case, with those of the US Fifth Air Force in Korea. To this it should be added that the pilots of these fighter divisions were young and lacked a lot of combat experience or flight time in jet aircraft, and they were inserted into the fighting hastily, without adequate preparation. This explains the high combat losses and the yielding of the initiative in this period of the war.

True, there were also other objective factors behind the reduction in victories and the increasing losses in this period of the war; in 1952 the US Fifth Air Force turned almost entirely to using jet fighters and fighter-bombers, the number of which by this time had doubled. The enemy's aircraft had also improved in quality – updated F-86E Sabres and F-84D Thunderjets were now flying missions, and the F-86E in particular now appeared in large numbers, and this also affected the tide of the aerial war, which now shifted to the advantage of the opposing side.

In view of the deteriorating situation in the skies of Korea, the Soviet Air Force high command made the decision to implement another rotation in the 64th IAK's complement of fighter aviation divisions and to withdraw the 97th IAD and 190th IAD back to the Soviet Union. Already in June 1952, two fresh PVO aviation divisions arrived from the Soviet Union, the 133rd IAD and 216th IAD. Thus the final and lengthiest fifth period of the air war in Korea began, which lasted from July 1952 until nearly August 1953. There had been yet another rotation in the 64th IAK's units, but a turning point in the air war didn't result. The fighting took on a local, protracted character and went with alternating success.

Although the 133rd IAD and 216th IAD were more experienced, all the same, they had previously been carrying out the functions of the PVO air force – defending strategic sites against smalls groups of enemy bombers. There were no longer such large-scale air operations across the length and breadth of MiG Alley, as there had been in 1951. Back then the Red Army's pilots had themselves been actively prowling for enemy groups and operating to force enemy aircraft out of one area of MiG Alley or another, but in 1952 and 1953, this was almost never done – the fighter aviation divisions of the 64th IAK purely carried out the functions of the PVO, providing point defense to some important sites or other in North Korea. True, it must be said that the PVO pilots, having studied the tactics of their new adversary, still provided reliable defense to the North Korean sites entrusted to them against enemy air raids.

For the sake of objectivity, it also must be said that the enemy was constantly improving the quality of its complement of aircraft: the F-86E fighters were replaced by the more powerful and maneuverable F-86F of various modifications (F1, F-25, F-30). Moreover the US Fifth Air Force in 1953 replaced almost half of its fighter-bombers; new F-86F-30 fighter-bombers arrived to replace the outdated F-80 Shooting Stars in those fighter-bomber wings equipped with them, while those fighter-bomber wings flying the F-84D and F-84E Thunderjets received the latest modification, the F-84G. Thus in 1953 our pilots fought in the skies of Korea only against the latest versions of the Sabre and Thunderjet.

In contrast, the same version of our best fighter of that period, the MiG-15bis, equipped the units of the 64th IAK throughout the war; however, by 1953 it had lost its previous advantages. In essence, the Sabre and the MiG were comparable across a number of indicators, and the man sitting in the cockpit made the difference in combat. Was he a young, inexperienced pilot, or an experienced professional, possessing extensive combat experience and high skill? The PVO commander-in-chief Marshal A.Ia. Savitsky's decision to send young and inexperienced PVO pilots, who averaged only 30-50 hours of flight in jet aircraft, as replacements to the 64th IAK was wrong and only contributed to the fact that they became easy prey for the experienced pilots of the USAF's 4th and 51st FIW. The Soviet Union did have a lot of Red Army Air Force units, which had accumulated enormous combat experience in the Second World War, and the pilots of which were highly-skilled and had a lot of time in jet aircraft. If they had been sent to the 64th IAK instead of the PVO units, then probably the course of combat operations in the skies of Korea would have changed fundamentally to our advantage, but this wasn't done.

Another mistake by the Soviet Air Force high command and the 64th IAK was its chosen system of rotating entire units in and out of the aviation corps. The introduction of the new fighter divisions was done hurriedly, not gradually, and without adequate study of the theater of combat operations and of the enemy and his tactics, and this always led to unjustifiably large losses. The system used by the Americans, rotating individual pilots in and out of the theater, was more sensible. They fluidly replaced pilots within the Fifth Air Force's squadrons and groups, while keeping those units in constant action.

Typically, pilots returned to the United States after completing 100 combat missions or a disabling wound; thus the younger, less experienced pilots, which were introduced into the fighting gradually and carefully, were always flying with experienced veterans. A young, newly arrived pilot made their first combat sorties only after passing through a program of mock dogfights with the experienced pilots of the 4th and 51st Fighter Wings, which passed along to them the valuable lessons learned in combatting the MiG. After this, the young pilot would fly combat missions as the wingman to a more experienced pilot, and in the first few sorties they wouldn't get involved in combat, but would observe it from the side, studying the enemy's tactics under the leader's supervision. Only then would the new guy be allowed to participate in dogfights.

Nothing like this was done in the 64th IAK. Pilots were quickly thrown into combat, and only in the course of one or two months of hard combat experiences would they become familiar with the enemy's unique characteristics and tactics, while at the same time suffering unnecessary losses in equipment and, more importantly, in men.

The last thing I would like to bring to the reader's attention is the unequal conditions the two side's pilots faced when flying and fighting in the skies of Korea, which are rarely mentioned in publications and works by Western authors and historians. I'm referring to the fact that the Soviet pilots were forbidden by their command to converse in Russian in the air, to cross the coastline of the Yellow Sea, or to approach any nearer than 50-60 kilometers to the front lines to avoid become prisoners, because the participation of the Soviet pilots in the air war was an official secret. Of all these restrictions, only the first was already lifted in the very first actions, because it had stupid consequences and led to needless pilot losses. The other two restrictions remained in effect until the end of combat operations in Korea. Because of these no-fly restrictions, our pilots could only encounter the enemy when they were already near or over their targets, because the strike groups usually came in from the direction of the sea, nor could they pursue the withdrawing enemy. Often the Soviet pilots had an advantageous position for an attack, but they couldn't use it, because the enemy was over the sea. A great number of damaged US aircraft, taking advantage of this circumstance, escaped MiG pursuit by crossing the coastline out to sea, and if this restriction hadn't been in place, then I'm sure the American combat losses would have increased sharply.

The Americans were fully aware of these restrictions on the Soviet MiG pilots and constantly exploited them, reducing their time to target when they were vulnerable to MiGs by flying most of the mission over the sea, and then escaping MiG pursuit by withdrawing to the sea. It should be added that the American pilots were also officially forbidden to cross the Yalu River and attack the airfields in northeast China. However, the Fifth Air Force command either didn't know the extent to which this ban was being breached by the pilots of the 4th and 51st FIW, or it closed its eyes to these violations, which led to the nearly continuous blockading of the front-line airfields in Manchuria close to the North Korean border, and hence to the 64th IAK's large losses during landings and take-offs at these bases.

There were also cases when Sabre pilots fired on MiGs that were parked on the ground; true, there were no casualties, but the MiGs sometimes took damage from the Sabre fire. If the Soviet air forces had operated openly in this war, and if there had been none of these restrictions, then over the sea and in the area of their South Korean air bases, the American pilots would have felt far less comfortable in the theater of combat operations.

A few words now about our coalition's allies in this war: the PDRK's air force primarily fought actively only in the first two months of the war, before it was completely wiped out. Soviet advisers and instructors rebuilt it within the PRC in 1951, and with their assistance, new units of the KPAAF were created, equipped with MiG fighters. Up until the middle of 1952, primarily only one night fighter unit under the command of Pak Deng Sik flew combat missions. In the middle of 1952, Kan Zhen Deng's (or Kan Chon Dok's) fighter aviation regiment began to fly combat missions with its MiG-15s. A full North Korean IAD didn't enter the fighting as part of the UAA until November 1952. The most active period for the North Korean pilots came toward the end of the war, more precisely in February 1953, when two North Korean fighter divisions equipped with MiG-15s and the same Pak Deng Sik's night fighter unit joined the UAA.

According to North Korean data, published in the journal *Novaia Koreia* [*New Korea*] in 1955, the North Korean Air Force destroyed 164 enemy aircraft over the course of the war, including 44 F-86s, 11 B-26s, 11 B-29s and 98 other types. The North Koreans reported destroying another 287 enemy aircraft on the ground, including 12 B-29, 10 B-26 and 265 other types. The top-scoring fighter regiment was PDRK Hero Kim Di

San's 56th GIAP. This fighter regiment destroyed a total of 102 enemy aircraft in aerial combat and on the enemy's airfields, 11 of which were B-29s. The North Koreans claim that this regiment destroyed approximately 60 enemy aircraft in 1950 in the first months of the war, and another 36 F-86s between April and 27 July 1953. Many pilots of this regiment became Heroes of the PDRK, including the first North Korean heroes of this war Kim Ki Ok, Lee Don-gyu, Lee Mun-sun and others. Another top regiment in the KPAAF was the one commanded by Kim Tal-won, which scored its first victory on 5 November 1950. Over the years of the war, the pilots of this regiment shot down more than 40 US aircraft in aerial combat. Pilots of this regiment also received the exalted title Hero of the PDRK, two of them posthumously. An Shen-zun shot down two US aircraft and sank one enemy destroyer, while Pek Gi-rak shot down four US aircraft in aerial battles. Hero of the PDRK Ree Su-an took command of this regiment following Kim Tal-won.

The Chinese People's Volunteers entered the air war in January 1951; their air force was represented initially by only the 10th IAP. However, the Unified Air Army was created in April 1951, primarily on the basis of PLAAF units – the first two aviation divisions to begin fighting under the UAA were the PLAAF's 3rd IAD and 4th IAD. They were equipped with MiG-15s and consisted of two fighter aviation regiments each. By the end of the war, the UAA now had six or seven PLAAF fighter divisions equipped with MiG-15 and MiG-15bis jet fighters.

In 1960 Lieutenant General Wang Hai, at the time the chief of the PLAAF's political directorate reported to the press that the Chinese People's Volunteer air units shot down or damaged 425 enemy aircraft in the war in Korea between 1950 and 1953. Many pilots of the UAA were awarded the title Hero of the PRC of different classes. General Wang Hai himself as a participant in this war commanded first a flight, then a flying group and a regiment before ending the war as the deputy commander of an IAD, and personally shot down nine US aircraft.

The UAA's 3rd and 12th IAD were the top-scoring divisions in Korea. It is known that one of the UAA's IAD, commanded by Zhen Zhan Hua downed 47 US aircraft during its time of participating in this war, two of which were downed by Zhen Zhan Hua personally.

However, according to recent data found in the Russian Ministry of Defense's Central Archive, the statistics of the UAA's combat operations in Korea are as follows: from November 1952 until the end of July 1953 the UAA pilots flew 11,028 individual combat sorties and had 250 aerial combats in which 598 UAA pilots fired their cannons. They downed 139 enemy aircraft in air-to-air combat and damaged 44 more. Their own losses over this period comprised 155 MiG-15s and 45 pilots who were killed-in-action. These figures do not include the operations of the North Korean Air Force's piston-engine aircraft.

The UAA's complete record in the war looks like this: the Chinese PLAAF entered the war in December 1950 (the 10th IAP arrived in Andong then, but didn't begin flying combat sorties until January 1951). The UAA was organized in April 1951 and the Chinese 3rd IAD and 4th IAD entered the fighting. In March 1952, three more Chinese fighter aviation divisions, the 2nd IAD, 6th IAD and 15th IAD, became operational, and two more Chinese IAD joined the UAA in May 1952. The North Korean Air Force was re-introduced into the fighting at the beginning of 1952 in the strength of just one aviation division. By the end of 1952, their number had been brought up to three aviation divisions, two of which (both IAD) served in the UAA, while the third was a night unit that operated independently. Altogether, the Chinese and North Korean pilots flew a total of 22,000 individual combat sorties during the war and engaged in 366 aerial combats, in which they downed 271 enemy aircraft, including 176 F-86, 5 F-86F-30, 27 F-84s, 30 F-80s, 12 F-51s, 15 F4U-5s, 1 B-26, 2 Gloster Meteors, 1 F-82 and 2 aircraft of other types. Their own losses amounted to 231 MiG-15s and 126 pilots. These data do not include the North Korean Air Force's and PLAAF's piston-engine aircraft operations. If they were included, the UAA's victories and losses would have been higher. Another 1,284 enemy aircraft were destroyed by the CPV and NKPA anti-aircraft artillery and small arms fire.

During the time of their combat operations in the skies of Korea between 1950 and 1953, the pilots of the 64th IAK flew approximately 64,000 individual combat sorties with an aggregate flight time of around 50,000 hours, engaged in 1,872 air-to-air combats, and shot down 1,097 enemy aircraft, including 642 F-86, 178 F-84, 121 F-80, 13 F-94, two F4U-5, 28 Gloster Meteors, 2 AD-1, 69 B-29, 30 F-51, 8 B-26, and two B-45 aircraft. The other losses consisted of other types. Their own losses amounted to 319 MiG-15 and La-11 fighters, and more than 120 pilots were killed-in-action. For the list of those names of the 64th IAK's pilots who died in non-combat incidents or who were killed-in-action, see Appendix 1.

In addition, the 64th IAK's four anti-aircraft artillery divisions that were nominally part of the corps (the 28th, 35th, 87th and 92nd Divisions) claimed a total 153 enemy aircraft destroyed, including 35 F-86, 5 F-86F-30, 25 F-84, 47 F-80, 5 F-51, 17 B-26, 7 B-29 and 12 aircraft of other types. The anti-aircraft artillery divisions lost a total of 64 dead and 65 wounded; six anti-aircraft guns and one searchlight were destroyed.

Thus, altogether the air force of the coalition of the three Communist nations destroyed 1,368 enemy aircraft (by MiG-15s alone) over the course of the war, though as I have stated above, this figure is undoubtedly inflated. Its own losses in aerial combats amounted to 550 MiG-15s, and 246 pilots were killed-in-action. The total number of enemy aircraft destroyed in the skies of Korea when including those downed by the three countries' anti-aircraft artillery rises to 2,805 aircraft. If we also add those victories achieved in aerial combats and those aircraft destroyed on the ground by the KPAAF's and the PLAAF's piston-engine aircraft, then the total number of enemy aircraft destroyed in the war reaches 2,900.

If we take the loss statistics of the USAF and those of the US Navy and Marine Corps air forces as reported by the American side, the USAF acknowledges losing 1,466 aircraft in combat, of which 147 (!) were lost in aerial combat and 78 were lost due to unknown causes. The US Naval Air Force and the Marine Air Corps lost another 1,248 aircraft in Korea. The other countries of the UN coalition, which contributed air units and pilots to the war effort (Great Britain, Australia and South Africa, primarily), lost another 152 aircraft in the skies of Korea.

Thus, the total aircraft losses of the UN coalition in this war, according to Western sources, amounted to 2,866 airplanes. The US air forces had 1,144 pilots killed in this war, another 306 were wounded, 214 were taken prisoner-of-war with eventual repatriation, and another 40 went missing in action.

Epilogue

And so, the 38th Parallel. Very many different opinions exist on this subject, the Berlin Wall, the "wall" along the 17th Parallel in Vietnam, and others. President of the United States of America Bill Clinton, who attended the unveiling of a memorial to the American troops who died in the 1950-1953 Korean War (in memory of the 54,000 American lives it took), was asked, "Why has it taken so long to create this memorial; really, was our war such a secret as it has been for the Soviets?" replied in his own very individual fashion, "Since the 38th Parallel exists, that means we didn't win this war."

The history of mankind can be defined as the history of wars in the process of replacing social-political orders. Thus doesn't the logical conclusion ask itself, that with his answer President Bill Clinton preordained the victor in this war – the commonwealth of the countries of the socialist camp?

One can judge the level of skill of pilots by the number of kills that they achieve. The "MiG Killers" (those 40 aces of the United States air forces) shot down almost as many aircraft as did our 22 Heroes of the Soviet Union, who earned this title in this war. The American search and rescue of pilots during the war (almost 1,000 men) should be noted, and those men still missing-in-action should be remembered. This war cost the United States of America approximately 4 billion dollars. Approximately 3 million lives were lost as the result of air strikes. The air war didn't spare anyone who sat in an aircraft cockpit – aces or Heroes of the Soviet Union. The fate of the pilots is various and accordingly speaks for itself: Thyng, Mahurin, Davis, Fischer, McConnell, Shchukin, Stel'makh, Obraztsov, Shebanov, Novoselov. Once, when recently captured B-29 crew members complained about their detention in one of the temporary holding pens, screening officials asked if they would like to be turned over to the Korean personnel that they'd just been targeting. The complainants categorically rejected the opportunity for such a meeting.

There were incidents where American pilots showed an inhumane attitude toward people: firing at pilots descending in parachutes and machine-gunning peasants laboring in the rice fields. Well, the response was more than adequate. Once, personnel of the 64th IAK witnessed a cart that was taking children somewhere, to which an American pilot had been harnessed, and a Korean woman was lashing him onward with a whip (kid-glove treatment in the East, actually). Fellow writers and certain contemporary social and governmental officials have taken the role upon themselves as judges in the evaluation of Soviet military forces beyond the border of the Soviet Union. This assessment is invariably negative. The war in Korea is no exception. Who gave these "chicken hawks", who didn't earn their stars on the battlefield, and who've never left their bureaucrat's office, to rewrite history to promote their own personal ambitions? These are legal actions of the "new type" to the benefit of their overlords; meanwhile, life goes on, and new troops are going to Yugoslavia, Zaire, the Congo, Chechnia, Karabakh, Abkhazia ...

Time and history will judge who won in Korea, since both sides, both governments are striving for the reunification of the Korean nation, which was artificially divided. We wish them success in this, but only by following the path of peace.

A committee of veterans from the Ukraine was not given the opportunity to lay wreathes on the graves of their fallen brothers-in-arms in the Russian cemetery in Lushunku (Port Arthur) in honor of those fellow soldier-internationalists of the war in Korea; despite the fact that a delegation from the Ukraine spent time in China in 1995, the veterans were simply denied entry. Veterans of the Korean War from Russia also still cannot visit the graves of their wartime comrades who were buried in the Russian cemetery in present-day Lushunku. Only a few Heroes of the Soviet Union were able to do this, being perfunctory members of government delegations. However, in 1997 American pilots of the Flying Tigers' veterans group, which included Harold Fischer, laid wreathes to commemorate the Soviet pilots who were killed in the Korean War.

For the sake of justice, the internationalist deeds of the men of the 64th IAK in the Korean War should be remembered. They deserve the honor and kind remembrance of every generation!

Appendix I

Non-combat pilot losses of the 64th IAK

Date	Rank	Name	Unit	Cause
27 August 1950	Senior Lieutenant	Kuznetsov, I.M.	72nd GIAP	Encephalitis
12 March 1951	Senior Lieutenant	Sokov, V.P.	28th GIAP	Collision
12 March 1951	Senior Lieutenant	Bushmelev, V.F.	28th GIAP	Collision
25 April 1951	Senior Lieutenant	Kukhmakov, B.D.	17th GIAP	
11 May 1951	Senior Lieutenant	Kotov, N.K.	17th GIAP	
8 August 1951	Senior Lieutenant	Gurilov, N.V.	351st IAP	
30 January 1952	Senior Lieutenant	Iakovlev, I.I.	523rd IAP	
24 February 1952	Senior Lieutenant	Vasil'ev, A.N.	821st IAP	Collision
15 September 1952	Senior Lieutenant	Chumachenko, M.I.	878th IAP	
6 October 1952	Lieutenant	V'iunik, G.K.	16th IAP	
24 October 1952	Lieutenant	Korzh, V.F.	878th IAP	Collision
5 April 1953	Senior Lieutenant	Shkurko, N.	298th IAP	
30 April 1953	Senior Lieutenant	Kislukhin, N.Ia.	676th IAP	
13 June 1953	Senior Lieutenant	Borisov, V.I.	913th IAP	
19 June 1953	Senior Lieutenant	Kulaev, V.P.	224th IAP	
4 July 1953	Lieutenant	Kolpakov, A.N.	535th IAP	

Appendix II

Pilots of the 64th IAK killed in action

Date	Rank	Name	Unit	Status
9 November 1950	Captain	Grachev, M.F.	139th GIAP	
11 November 1950	Captain	Nasonov, M.P.	28th GIAP	
18 November 1950	Captain	Tarshinov, A.I.	139th GIAP	
4 December 1950	Senior Lieutenant	Rumiantsev, K.V.	29th GIAP	Remains not recovered
6 December 1950	Senior Lieutenant	Serikov, N.N.	29th GIAP	Remains not recovered
7 December 1950	Senior Lieutenant	Pavlenko, P.A.	29th GIAP	
22 December 1950	Senior Lieutenant	Barsegian, S.A.	177th IAP	
23 January 1951	Senior Lieutenant	Grebenkin, G.M.	29th GIAP	
17 March 1951	Captain	Dubrovin, V.M.	72nd GIAP	
24 March 1951	Senior Lieutenant	Savinov, Iu.P.	72nd GIAP	
3 April 1951	Senior Lieutenant	Nikitichenko, P.D.	176th GIAP	
9 April 1951	Senior Lieutenant	Slabkin, F.V.	176th GIAP	
1 June 1951	Senior Lieutenant	Stel'makh, E.M.	18th GIAP	
23 June 1951	Senior Lieutenant	Negodiaev, V.F.	176th GIAP	
25 June 1951	Senior Lieutenant	Ageev, N.A.	18th GIAP	
26 June 1951	Senior Lieutenant	Arganovich, E.N.	17th IAP	
8 July 1951	Senior Lieutenant	Obukhov, B.A.	523rd IAP	
11 July 1951	Senior Lieutenant	Larionov, I.	196th IAP	Remains not recovered
11 July 1951	Senior Lieutenant	Obraztsov, B.A.	176th GIAP	
24 August 1951	Lieutenant	Svistun, G.K.	523rd IAP	
2 September 1951	Senior Lieutenant	Kolpikov, S.T.	18th GIAP	
2 September 1951	Senior Lieutenant	Akatov, V.S.	18th GIAP	
2 October 1951	Captain	Morozov, I.N.	17th IAP	
23 October 1951	Senior Lieutenant	Khurtin, V.N.	523rd IAP	
26 October 1951	Senior Lieutenant	Shebanov, F.D.	196th IAP	
2 November 1951	Senior Lieutenant	Shuliat'ev, A.I.	18th GIAP	
4 November 1951	Senior Lieutenant	Filimonov, V.P.	523rd IAP	Remains not recovered

Date	Rank	Name	Unit	Status
8 November 1951	Senior Lieutenant	Travin, A.F.	196th IAP	
28 November 1951	Captain	Shatalov, G.T.	523rd IAP	
5 December 1951	Senior Lieutenant	Ryzhkov, A.D.	196th IAP	
5 December 1951	Senior Lieutenant	Baturov, A.I.	18th GIAP	
6 January 1952	Senior Lieutenant	Stepanov, V.G.	18th GIAP	
16 January 1952	Senior Lieutenant	Sapozhnikov, B.P.	18th GIAP	
17 January 1952	Senior Lieutenant	Filippov, A.V.	176th GIAP	
9 February 1952	Senior Lieutenant	Troitsky, I.I.	16th IAP	
21 February 1952	Senior Lieutenant	Kozhevnikov, A.P.	16th IAP	
21 February 1952	Senior Lieutenant	Shershakov, V.N.	16th IAP	
22 February 1952	Senior Lieutenant	Savinov, E.P.	16th IAP	
27 February 1952	Senior Lieutenant	Derevianko, L.P.	256th IAP	
11 March 1952	Senior Lieutenant	Ivanov, A.P.	16th IAP	
11 March 1952	Senior Lieutenant	Zenakov, N.I.	494th IAP	
24 March 1952	Senior Lieutenant	Filippov, E.V.	148th GIAP	
24 March 1952	Captain	Liubovinkin, P.S.	148th GIAP	
1 April 1952	Senior Lieutenant	Chernikov, N.I.	821st IAP	
2 April 1952	Senior Lieutenant	Voronov, A. Ia.	494th IAP	
13 April 1952	Senior Lieutenant	Shebenko, V.M.	494th IAP	
21 April 1952	Captain	Naumov, N.I.	16th IAP	
21 April 1952	Senior Lieutenant	Selivanov, D.S.	256th IAP	
21 April 1952	Senior Lieutenant	Tolmatsky, S.A.	256th IAP	
3 May 1952	Senior Lieutenant	Efremov, M.I.	494th IAP	
20 May 1952	Captain	Kalmanson, V.E.	256th IAP	
25 May 1952	Senior Lieutenant	Krasulin, F.S.	256th IAP	
27 May 1952	Senior Lieutenant	Akhmov	282nd IAP	
31 May 1952	Captain	Denisov, I.F.	821st IAP	
22 June 1952	Senior Lieutenant	Pozhidaev, V.A.	147th GIAP	
4 July 1952	Senior Lieutenant	Shmagunov, V.V.	821st IAP	
1 August 1952	Captain	Gorobchenko, V.S.	726th IAP	
1 August 1952	Captain	Kostin, A.A.	726th IAP	
1 August 1952	Senior Lieutenant	Tsvetkov, L.M.	726th IAP	
4 August 1952	Senior Lieutenant	Krutskikh, V.P.	494th IAP	
5 August 1952	Senior Lieutenant	Iazev, S.S.	16th IAP	
6 August 1952	Senior Lieutenant	Kochetov, M.I.	878th IAP	
20 August 1952	Major	Shekhovtsov, A.A.	726th IAP	
24 August 1952	Captain	Poltavets, G.M.	147th GIAP	
31 August 1952	Captain	Eremchenko, F.S.	518th IAP	
4 September 1952	Senior Lieutenant	Titov, A.A.	415th IAP	
4 September 1952	Senior Lieutenant	Zatolokin, M.I.	415th IAP	
7 September 1952	Senior Lieutenant	Shikunov, I.M.	535th IAP	
9 September 1952	Captain	Pronin, K.P.	147th GIAP	

Date	Rank	Name	Unit	Status
9 September 1952	Major	Sova, I.K.	726th IAP	
9 September 1952	Senior Lieutenant	Kapunov, I.I.	726th IAP	
14 September 1952	Captain	Chernavin, V.	518th IAP	
15 September 1952	Senior Lieutenant	Efimov, I.V.	676th IAP	
21 September 1952	Senior Lieutenant	Shinaev, I.I.	147th GIAP	
21 September 1952	Captain	Bodnia, F.A.	676th IAP	
26 September 1952	Senior Lieutenant	Orlov, A.G.	878th IAP	
29 September 1952	Senior Lieutenant	Meshcheriakov, I.V.	578th IAP	
3 October 1952	Lieutenant	Fedorov, B.V.	535th IAP	
9 October 1952	Senior Lieutenant	Svechkar', A.P.	878th IAP	
11 October 1952	Lieutenant	Postnikov, I.I.	578th IAP	
18 November 1952	Senior Lieutenant	Beliakov, N.M.	781st IAP	
18 November 1952	Senior Lieutenant	Pakhomkin, V.I.	781st IAP	
18 November 1952	Senior Lieutenant	Vandaev, A.I.	781st IAP	
21 November 1952	Major	Bogdanov, I.I.	415th IAP	
14 January 1953	Senior Lieutenant	Sokolov, N.P.	224th IAP	
15 January 1953	Senior Lieutenant	Mishchenko, V.M.	726th IAP	
19 February 1953	Senior Lieutenant	Sokolov, I.K.	535th IAP	
8 March 1953	Senior Lieutenant	Chepusov, D.I.	878th IAP	
9 March 1953	Senior Lieutenant	Rochikashvili, V.I.	224th IAP	
9 March 1953	Senior Lieutenant	Kuan, V.N.	224th IAP	
14 March 1953	Senior Lieutenant	Sedashev, V.N.	518th IAP	
12 April 1953	Senior Lieutenant	Markov, V.S.	224th IAP	
22 April 1953	Captain	Lazarev, V.N.	224th IAP	
13 May 1953	Lieutenant	Kamenshchikov, V.G.	781st IAP	
18 May 1953	Senior Lieutenant	Rybakov, K.A.	518th IAP	
23 May 1953	Captain	Grishenchuk, V.L.	913th IAP	
29 May 1953	Captain	Pronin, I.V.	415th IAP	
1 June 1953	Senior Lieutenant	Timoshin, V.S.	781st IAP	
5 June 1953	Senior Lieutenant	Tsarenko, V.F.	781st IAP	
5 June 1953	Senior Lieutenant	Pushkarev, B.V.	781st IAP	
7 June 1953	Senior Lieutenant	Dorokhov, S. L.	535th IAP	
16 June 1953	Captain	Potapov, P.S.	913th IAP	
18 June 1953	Captain	Kriklivets, I.P.	913th IAP	
18 June 1953	Lieutenant	Korshunov, B.V.	518th IAP	
24 June 1953	Captain	Alikin, A.G.	415th IAP	
29 June 1953	Lieutenant Colonel	Gorbunov, I.V.	676th IAP	
12 July 1953	Lieutenant	Galin, A.I.	224th IAP	
12 July 1953	Captain	Belov, V.M.	781st IAP	
19 July 1953	Lieutenant	Gerasimchuk, N.P.	224th IAP	

Several more pilots died in hospitals as a result of diseases or wounds. Deceased senior command staff members were transported back to the Soviet Union in zinc coffins for burial in Voroshilov-Ussuriisk.

Index

INDEX OF MILITARY UNITS

INDEX OF PEOPLE

INDEX OF PLACES

INDEX OF AIRCRAFT TYPES

Related titles published by Helion & Company

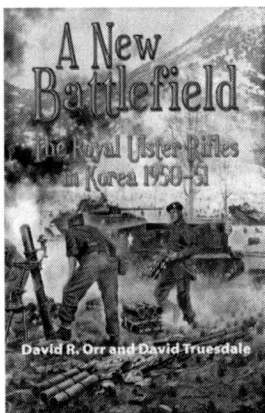

A New Battlefield. The Royal Ulster Rifles
in Korea 1950-51
David R. Orr & David Truesdale
ISBN 978-1-908916-92-1 (paperback)
ISBN 978-1-908916-29-7 (eBook)

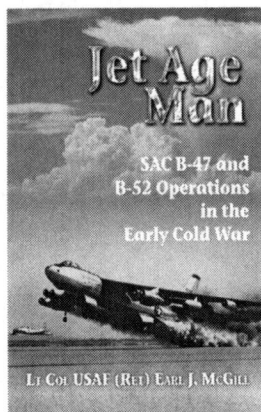

Jet Age Man. SAC B-47 and B-52
Operations in the Early Cold War
Lt Col USAF Earl J. McGill (Ret.)
ISBN 978-1-909384-94-1 (paperback)
ISBN 978-1-909384-31-6 (eBook)

Black Tuesday over Namsi. B-29s vs MIGs –
The Forgotten Air Battle of the Korean War,
23 October 1951
Lt Col USAF Earl J. McGill (Ret.)
ISBN 978-1-909384-38-5 (paperback)
ISBN 978-1-908916-08-2 (eBook)

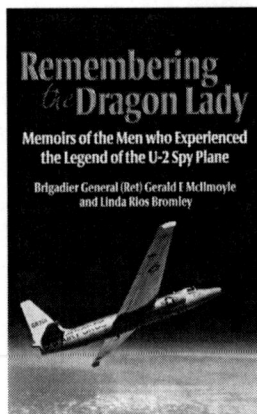

Remembering the Dragon Lady. Memoirs
of the men who experienced the legend of
the U-2 spy plane
Brig Gen (Ret.) Gerald E. McIlmoyle
& Linda Rios Bromley
ISBN 978-1-908916-93-8 (paperback)
ISBN 978-1-907677-85-4 (eBook)

CPSIA information can be obtained at www.ICGtesting.com
Printed in the USA
BVOW05s0853050514

352478BV00004B/19/P

9 781909 384415